BY ELLERY SEDGWICK

THE HAPPY PROFESSION

ATLANTIC HARVEST
Memoirs of the *Atlantic*

ATLANTIC HARVEST

Memoirs of the *Atlantic*

Atlantic Harvest

MEMOIRS OF THE *ATLANTIC*

Wherein are to be found stories, anecdotes, and opinions, controversial and otherwise; together with a variety of matter, relevant and irrelevant, accompanied by certain obdurate convictions

Compiled by ELLERY SEDGWICK

For thirty years Editor of the *Atlantic Monthly*

AN ATLANTIC MONTHLY PRESS BOOK

LITTLE, BROWN AND COMPANY · BOSTON

1947

FIRST EDITION

Published September 1947

ATLANTIC–LITTLE, BROWN BOOKS
ARE PUBLISHED BY
LITTLE, BROWN AND COMPANY
IN ASSOCIATION WITH
THE ATLANTIC MONTHLY PRESS

PRINTED IN THE UNITED STATES OF AMERICA

TO THE DAUGHTERS OF MY HOUSE AND HEART

"Is not old wine wholesomest?
Old pippins, toothsomest?"

— *Westward Hoe*

JOHN WEBSTER and
THOMAS DEKKER 1604

To the Reader, Gentle and Ungentle

THIS is a book of three generations. Changing tastes, aspirations, and interests run through it. We live in an age cumbered with itself: perspectives are few and short but very useful. Of the events of the last fourscore years we know almost too much; of the inner transformation which gives them their significance much too little. With two world wars behind us, we are astonished to see ourselves a different people.

What has made us so? Perhaps it is disillusion. The emotion of the war to preserve the Union surged over Americans in a great wave of optimism. It rolled on for forty years. I remember the crest of the wave, coming at the turn of the century. The conquest of the Philippines seemed to bring us to the summit of territorial greatness. Then of a sudden we were afraid of our destiny and of ourselves. A note of cynicism crept into the national chorus. The cock-a-doodle-doo of the Fourth of July oration lost its clarion self-confidence. Human perfectibility, the creed of the Nineteenth Century, seemed a debatable question. We were a different people.

God and the Devil are twin parts of one idea, and the truth is the Devil was dying. He had been a strong support to the faltering, prodding them from behind while God beckoned them before. We became less sure of convictions long unquestioned. The oasis ahead might be a mirage. Certainties had become doubts. Doubts were crystallizing into skepticism. When I was a boy at school with a white collar and a whiter soul I used to sing with conviction: —

> So vile I am, how dare I hope to stand
> In the pure whiteness of that holy land?

and believed it. Ten years later I doubted the vileness as I doubted the pure whiteness ahead. I began to perceive the alteration in men's minds. My grandfather was positive that Heaven would open for him. My father hoped for the miracle of eternity. I neither hope nor fear; and as for my children, they do not consider the subject sufficiently important for discussion.

Other changes there are of course, a profusion of them. The adult grows from the stripling. Civilization is at work. Surfaces are polished. Manners perk up. Our present business is with writing and writing has become steadily more professional, although few conjectured it might support so large a segment of the population. Indeed, looking back over fifty years of publishing, nothing is more surprising than the increase in the material rewards of writing. The manna which once on the chosen few fluttered down from Heaven now rains upon a mighty company. Writing is no longer an avocation. It takes its place with law and medicine as a profession calculated to support the hungriest family. A generation ago writing men wrote for butter, not for bread. Take the case of one of the most eminent among them. William Dean Howells gained great and enduring praise for *Silas Lapham,* and many another understanding novel of American character, yet writing provided him with but meager sustenance. Through an important part of his life Mr. Howells was employed in our Foreign Service. Later in his career as sub-editor of the *Atlantic* he enjoyed a salary of twenty-six hundred dollars a year, assuming, to balance the munificence of his employers, the express obligation of contributing essays to "The Contributors' Club," a department of the magazine. It was only after thorough seasoning that he became editor of the *Atlantic*. Writers and editors are divergent classifications of the *genus homo*. Looking back upon the days when he guided the modest movement of the magazine he remarked to me that in turning from the writing of novels to the editing of monthlies, ten years had been filched from his life. The writing years before and after had simply been telescoped together, and to his career, his interest and his education, the interval had meant nothing.

To show what an author suffers by adopting an alien profession I will relate an experience of this gentlest and most delightful of men. At one point in his career, the seduction of a large salary induced him to become editor of the *Cosmopolitan Magazine*. The proprietor was one John Brisben Walker, famous in those days for the ruthless energy with which he pushed his enterprise to success. Mr. Howells's novels were the antithesis of the strident fiction characteristic of popular taste. His selection as editor of a monthly like the *Cosmopolitan* was little short of preposterous, but nonetheless his was a name which looked well in large print, and Mr. Walker proposed to take full advantage of it. He announced the advent of Mr. Howells's editorship in the spirit of Phineas Barnum heralding the arrival of his White Elephant or of Jo-Jo, the Dog-Faced Boy, spreading full-page advertisements through the papers. Then he waited for results. Mr. Howells consulted his own taste and purchased a number of contributions full of gentle humor and quiet effectiveness. He had been at his desk but a few weeks when his employer, like the diligent man of business he was, took an account of stock. He entered Mr. Howells's office with a bundle of accepted manuscripts under his arm and a look full of suppressed fury.

"Mr. Howells," he said, "be so good as to return these to your contributors."

Mr. Howells thought a moment and then replied: "Mr. Walker, I will prepare the bill of fare for your dinner but I will not wash the dishes." The end was not far off.

In the old days contributions to a magazine in large measure wrote themselves. Intense experience cried aloud for expression. But as time went on and urbanity slipped into the place of conviction, men wrote because they had the will to write or else had adopted the worldly wisdom of Dr. Johnson's: "Sir, a man's a blockhead to write except for money." If it be true that literature holds up the glass to life, some understanding of the changes we have inherited will break upon the reader and even upon the judicious skipper among these pages.

ANTHOLOGIES, say the Greeks, are flowers garlanded to keep forever fresh, blossoms which otherwise might wither on their separate stalks. Nowadays we prefer our literary nosegays in varied colors. Often the colors are in violent opposition. This matters not to the contemporary taste, provided that each is of its own true shade. Much of the effect comes from contrast, but here as always it is individual excellence that counts.

For an Anglo-Saxon anthology perhaps a more satisfying analogy may be drawn from a dinner table amply spread. A good cook reckons on a dozen shades of appetite. American taste runs to the solid, yet salads are often tempting. But more than amplitude is needed. Even roast beef may pall, and choice must be wide. This morning I came on a passage in Evelyn's *Journal* which gives point to these remarks. In his diary for 1680 Sir John gives his critique of a dinner full of misspent pains.

> The entertainment was exceedingly civil, but besides a good olio, the dishes were trifling, hashed and condited after their way, not at all fit for an English stomach which is for solid meat. There were yet good fowls but roasted to coal, nor were the sweetmeats good.

This advice is all the sounder for its indirection, and I have taken thought of its bearing upon a sister art. The dishes set forth in this volume are neither hashed nor trifling. A good olio is not wanting. There is solid meat for the stomach, American or English, and in the choice of sweetmeats, pains have been taken.

To the cook his dinner. To the editor his book. They have parallel responsibilities. Good viands are not enough for the cook. Neither is an excellent medley sufficient for the editor. Individuality must be stirred into the cook's sauces, personality into an editor's choices. Over an anthology, as over the magazines whence it came, the editor's shadow must pass.

Long, long ago, when Germans were a decent people, one of them wrote a story familiar to my childhood. The Devil was abroad as usual, and as usual he took up with a man sorely in need of his help. I forget whether it was fame, fortune, or a pretty girl that he so urgently desired. At any rate, the man whispered his secret and the Devil was wholly accommodating. He would give all his friend asked. His return? Nothing but an unsubstantial trifle. With that the Devil stooped, as Devils do with special grace, and plucking one corner of the man's shadow, made a neat roll of its whole length and walked jauntily away with the package beneath his arm. If the hero of this tale was an editor, when he lost his shadow he lost everything. For if one thing is more essential than the rest, it is that the editor's shadow should rest squarely on his magazine. The magazine should reflect not always his opinions but invariably things he cares about.

Now a shadow is a very different thing from a reflection. It is its antithesis. All but the outline is gone, the intangible essence remains. It is characteristic as a man's accent or the first crinkle of his smile. To a friend it means more than a photograph. Preserve it and you have all of him not subject to mortality.

When I was a boy I spent many holidays at an island camp. In the evenings a familiar amusement was to take a sheet of prepared paper, white on one side, black on the other. Each of the company was placed in turn beneath a powerful lamp so that the profile fell sharply upon the white side of a sheet fixed firmly upon a screen. Then someone skilled with the pencil traced the outline with meticulous care. Next the shadow picture was cut out, reversed, and hung upon the line. If the work is well done, no portrait can convey a more accurate impression of personality. Everything is blacked out but the thing itself. If there is "character," here is a graph of it. If not, you feel the absence in your marrowbones. To young men and women about to marry I suggest this pastime.

Coming back again to magazines, the editor's shadow, essential as it is, must not be allowed to blacken the page. It need be but dimly in the background of the reader's mind, but there it must be. Without it a magazine is but a hodgepodge packaged for commercial conveniences and that, as you and I well know, is just what most of them are.

So the first rule for editing is "Let your shadow fall full upon the page."

And the second rule for editing a monthly magazine is never to forget that its life lasts just thirty days. In that brief span all its vitality must be compressed. Time carefully. Don't print for eternity. Print for *now*.

There is no Rule Three.

How happy a man might be to ship his manuscript off to the printer and have his heart whisper, "There goes a good book." He may hope, but to know takes intuition. Picking up the best book in the language, I note how modest is the confidence of the writer. "It is not my intention," he says, "to deter the reader by expatiating on the variety or importance of the subject which I have undertaken to treat, since the merit of the choice would seem to render the expatiation still more apparent, still less excusable." Such a warning should make authors and editors shun the hawking of their wares in or out of a preface. I make no claim then for the excellence of my content beside the comforting assurance that but a tiny fraction of it has been written by myself, and that the selection of the material has been not the task of a season, but the continuing labor of an editorship which extended over thirty years of the *Atlantic*'s history.

It is an American boast that native illiteracy has shrunk to less than five per cent. That is at the bottom of the pyramid, but of the top, can it be said that five per cent know how to read? Exclude prodigies who, with the gross voracity of a Macaulay, swallow chapters whole, engraving them for life on a photo-plasmic mind. Theodore Roosevelt took exuberant satisfaction in draining as it were the pages of his Pigskin Library, letting his eye slide down the center and dragging head and tail of each line after it. The strenuous life is all right if it agrees with your digestion, but reading should not be strenuous exercise. To me the art lies not so much in giving the mind to the book, as in grafting the book upon the mind, confirming, rejecting, criticizing one's own thoughts and opinions in the light of new knowledge. If you give yourself to a book, the price you pay is one thin slice after another of your individuality, but if you make the book your own, exercising the royal power to annex, dismember, or destroy, then you have new money in the bank.

A practical illustration of this thesis occurs to me which, had I known it fifty years ago, might have made me an educated man. My friend of many years, Newton Baker, spent his happiest hours in the spacious library of his house on Shaker Heights near Cleveland. As I used to wander along his shelves picking out a book here and there, I would notice that on the flyleaf of each was written not only a brief précis of the book, but a sentence or two of comment showing what the gist of it had meant to Mr. Baker. He told me that the moment the last page was turned, he made it his invariable practice to jot down just what he thought of a book, just how far it fitted into his education. I have good reason to know the uselessness of excellent resolves to keep a commonplace book, jotting therein the inner kernel of an evening's reading. This is so cumbersome a practice that it needs a stronger character than mine to follow it. But had I only caught myself young, I might have taught myself to follow Mr. Baker's convenient and profitable habit.

I cannot put pen to paper discussing an editor's task without thanking my lucky stars for the happiness it has given me through long decades. A gipsy once told me that the bright star, Aldebaran, was in the ascendant when I was born. That was the star, you will remember, which brought life and liberty to Quentin Durward's outlandish friend Hayraddin Maugrabin. Certainly it brought luck to me. Think of being paid for fishing in the morning's mail: a letter from a missionary's wife in the Solomon Islands stranded among cannibal neighbors, while in a distant pasture her husband pursued an errant sheep no blacker than the rest but dearer perhaps to God and him; another from the Woman Homesteader in the bleak Northwest whose courage was tonic to the soul; still another giving a shrewd report of political breezes in Kansas where the Cagliostro of the hour was preaching the transplantation of goat glands as the sovereign remedy for physical infirmity, gaining thereby a fortune, immense and ardent support at the polls, and, incidentally, confirming the editor in his belief that the more furiously democratic education moves forward, the more resolutely it sticks in the same place.

A happy conglomerate for a working day!

WHAT is excellent," wrote Emerson, "as God lives is permanent." That is profoundly true, but what is there in a book that defies time? A magazine editor has but one idea in his head — interest here and now. If interest is at white heat and the magazine hot off the press, the editor thinks as much about the future as the promoter, pocketing a profit on his deal, thinks about eternity. But the editor of an anthology has a longer responsibility. To permanence he can hardly aspire, but a degree of semipermanence is a practicable ideal, and that is his target. Interest fades with time. The bright new curtains you hang in your show window lose their color in the sun of a second spring. For literature there is one fast dye, one only, and that is style.

Of course an event can be permanently interesting, or an adventure, or an unfamiliar truth, suddenly driven home. But events recur, adventures have their parallel, new truths are apt to be the truths your grandfather got from his grandfather in a slightly different form. Style, on the other hand, is forever unique. It is personal as the nose on your face and cannot be duplicated. In truth it is the distillation of the writer's mind, and if writing is precious, it is style that makes it so.

How little do the dictionaries know of this! I quote from the pachydermous Webster: Style is "the quality which gives distinctive excellence to artistic expression, consisting especially in the appropriateness and choiceness of relation between subject, medium, and form, and individualized by the temperamental characteristics of the artist."

There you have it. Ye Gods and little fishes what a paradox! Webster's "style" is the negation of style. You might as well define the iridescence of a moth's wing by enumerating the chemical compounds of the capillary filaments that go to make it so. Style is the man, his aspiration and his limitation all in one. If he is a memorable man, his style will tell you of him through the ages.

Style varies with every temperament. Sometimes it is torrential, sometimes combative. Occasionally it is achieved through a certain parsimony in words. In a satirical passage understatement always tells. I chance on an excellent example in the opening sentence of a story by that intermittent and malformed genius, Ambrose Bierce.

> Early one June morning in 1872, I murdered my father — an act which made a deep impression on me at the time.

Style varies with the man who makes it. The test is: will it make the author's message stick like a burr in your memory? I quote an example that gives a gay twist to a solemn occasion. It must be twenty years ago that I read in a Missouri newspaper this lively account of an execution. I still have it letter-perfect.

> At half-past five the trap was sprung and Thomas J. Mulloy, dressed in a neat-fitting blue suit, a turn-down collar and a black cravat, was ushered into the presence of his God.

Can you not see the man who wrote that; his felt clapped on one side of his head, a cigarette drooping from his lips, his sharp little intelligence squeezing the last drop of drama out of his opportunity? He put all newspaperdom into a single sentence. His may not have been the best style, but style he had and fit to be remembered.

Sensibly or insensibly, style interests every man who has a seeing eye for the printed page. It was a great event in my education when one day during my boyhood Matthew Arnold, master of the art, called on my mother. I remember to this day his introduction of his wife. "Mrs. Sedgwick," he said, "let me present Mrs. Arnold, *free from the taint of philanthropy*." The talk that followed bore much on style. Mr. Arnold remarked that Americans had a strain of poetry in their discourse. What Englishmen call the "sea" Americans call "ocean," and for us "fall" is apt to be "autumn"; both poetic words. But what lies deepest in my recollection is the horror Mr. Arnold expressed at the style of American newspapers. I must say he made his point. The *Cincinnati Enquirer,* a copy of which had fallen into his hands, had, and I believe still has, a curious custom of concentrating attention on its topmost headline by permitting a single word in enormous letters to fill the column. A tragedy similar to the one described by my Missouri friend had just been enacted, and the *Enquirer* headlined it thus:—

JERKED

TO JESUS

In Mr. Arnold's opinion, it was the reporter, rather than the criminal, who deserved the noose, and doubtless in a more civilized America, his opinion would prevail.

IT IS no use pretending that all the forty-seven contributions which make up this volume are protected by style from the ravages of Time. They are selected not as copybook examples but by the editor's test of interest applied quite without regard to the date of composition. Some of them after fifty years hold the attention quite as readily as they did on the day of their birth. Others have varied and insistent claims, but a few owe their very lives to style. Take, for example, one very simple story, the few pages of "Buttercup-Night" by John Galsworthy. How free those pages are from the sense of time, how full of everlastingness, of human sympathy, and the beauty of stillness in a lovely world. For an instant all nature, bird and beast, the flowers, the pilgrim of the story, and the sky above them all, are one. You feel the emotion of it — if a sense of being is emotion — and the reader's mind holds the illusion as in a glass case, to be dwelt on again in some stillest hour. What is here? A field of buttercups, an old man nursing a sick mare, the stars overhead, and the sense of the oneness of Creation. Only that and style.

Or take another — a noble instance — Lord Moulton's "Law and Manners." There is more here than the elevation of the thought, the constant admonition that it is natural laws which most require natural obedience. Something immutable comes over the argument and develops it, a sense of its eternal rightness, and that is style.

Style, I think, is inseparable from personality. The measure of its serenity or its animation, its power, its clarity, its charm goes deeper than the writer's discipline. They are elements in his character.

The works of Shakespeare are, of course, the supreme instance. Facts regarding his life, incredible as has been the industry in ferreting them out, are few enough. But the plays are there and the sonnets are there, the sympathies and prejudices, the loves and hates are there. However obscure the circumstance, the manner of man who wrote them could not be clearer had Titian drawn his portrait.

Let me take a more modest and casual instance. As I write these words, a paragraph from a book I am reading furnishes an example. Its author, one Reginald Farrer, an adventurous botanist, has been scaling the mountains of Tibet in search of rare and beautiful plants. That was about all I knew of him until I came to consider this paragraph, written while the horror of the first universal war rolled across half the world to his lonely mountain camp.

The stormy year now closes with comparative peace over exhausted China, and the blackest storm over Europe. It is something to have flower-fields and beauties to remember amid the enveloping universal darkness of the world. For the utmost griefs of beings, races, and continents come and pass, but the beauty of a poppy-petal on an alpine fell, the child of a day at the mercy of wind or hail, that has its hour and passes also, continues immortally recurring through the ages, outliving the crash of kingdoms and civilisations and their evanescent agonies. More and more deeply do flowers give consolation in the wreckage of life, and the heart of the gardener can never be wholly sad so long as the impregnable beauty of life goes on being born of the earth to which we all return. The sprouting little Crocus in spring is more King of eternity than the Kaisers; and the faith of a flower moves the mountains of the world.

There is beauty here, but beyond the beauty much may be told. Beneath the botanist is the man passionately in love with flowers and with the Nature that brings them into being, but it is love from within rather than admiration for what is without. The writer's whole personality is merged with what he describes; his life an infinitesimal fraction of one infinite whole. The indivisible river of existence flows through him and all things else. There is no surprise when I look into another volume written by an associate of his and find that long before he wrote this passage Reginald Farrer accepted the Buddhist faith and the Buddhist philosophy.

I find comfort in remembering that death came to Farrer on one of his most distant expeditions. A man whose mind has ranged so far must have been envious of a lonely grave. Let his epitaph be written in lines, most beautiful perhaps among the works of women:—

The earth that wakes one human heart to feeling
Can center both the worlds of Heaven and Hell.

An admired friend of mine, Mr. Herbert Read, is much given to the discussion of style and kindred subjects. His are profitable words, and although the passage I read yesterday deals with the long novel rather than with short passages either of fact or of fiction, I will quote it.

The good health of an art which undertakes so immediately to reproduce life must demand that it be perfectly free. The only obligation to which we may hold a novel without incurring accusation of being arbitrary is that it be interesting. The general responsibility lies upon it, but it is the only one I can think of. The ways in which it is exhibited to accomplish the result of interesting us strike me as innumerable and such as can only suffer from being marked out or fenced in by prescription. They are various as the temperament of men and they are successful in proportion as they reveal a particular mind, different from others. A novel is in its broadest definition, a personal, a direct impression of life: that to begin with constitutes its value which is greater or less according to the intensity of the impression.

These canons have been in the editor's mind long before Mr. Read wrote them on the Tables of the Law, and to their principle he has been obedient in making his selections for this book.

THE test of genius lies I suppose in the fresh ground it breaks. And that means it must create the taste for which it seeks approval. I speak of genius, for six of my contributors — and six in forty-six or so makes a rich amalgam — can lay fair claim to it, although it would be unfair to hold the examples which represent them here as expressive of their highest moments. My readers must be content with something less overwhelming, but possibly quite as agreeable to their taste. Of originality which is a constituent of genius there is, I think, an abundance scattered through this volume; but what endears these contributors to the editor is their attitude toward their own work. They have not the irritating consciousness that their reputations are at stake. They write for the love of writing. Moreover they write to be read and meet the reader on what might be grounds of his own choosing. I speak of the bulk of them — they court the reader's companionship. To the devil with pulpits! Ivory towers be damned! There is too much prosing in ivory towers and atmosphere can be too thin for common lungs to breathe.

I have a friend condemned by his university to lecturing for life. By way of mental adjustment to his sentence he has invented a pastime which he plays with his five-year-old son. The game is called "Lowell Lecturing." First the son is audience; the father stands impressively by the desk. "Ladies and gentlemen," he begins, "Umm-umm-umm-umm-buzz-buzz-buzz-buzz." The audience wags his head drowsily from side to side, then lets it fall gradually to rest, drooping against his chest — and snores. That marks the boy's turn. He takes the rostrum. The father slumps in the chair. "Gen'lmen and ladies," begins the child, "Umm-umm-umm-umm-buzz-buzz-buzz-buzz." The father's head sways from side to side. For a moment he supports it with his hand. Then down it sinks upon his breast. A single snore and the game is over.

How admirable an exercise for the sermonizing temperament! It is a deathblow to pontification: an invitation to the humanities. From pride of intellect, from uncharitableness to one's readers, from tongue in cheek, from nose in air, from superiority to common earth, good Lord deliver us!

Some day a clever editor will invent a thermometer for taking the temperament of authors. This is an instrument much needed. Neither Fahrenheit nor centigrade has degrees enough in the scale to measure it. From below zero to boiling it goes and far, far beyond. The editor, his hand on the author's pulse, must have a pretty definite idea of the degree of generated heat. He must comprehend his author's temperament and gauge his blood pressure.

The natural simile for editing is angling, not in a lake where fish feel the lassitude of smooth water, but in the brawlingest of brooks. Then the lightness of the cast, the colors of the fly, make all the difference. A "Coachman" may be the taste of some sedative trout, a "Jock Scot" may do the business for others, but the big fellow hugging the waterfall may not bat an eye until the flash of a "Scarlet Ibis" breaks down his reserve. So it is with the editor's lures. If the magazine is big enough and rich enough, the method most in vogue is to dangle a check at the end of the line. That is fishing with a piece of pork! There are authors enough who would be ashamed to say what they would not do for a thousand dollars! Unfortunately that pleasant way is barred to the *Atlantic,* and in tempting an author, particularly if he is an unknown quantity and not a writer by profession, the editor has to rely upon the sheer attraction of the suggestion he makes and the form in which he makes it. If he has read a writer's books and has an idea of the cast of his mind, he shapes his invitation accordingly, and in the case of public men proposes some subject which the politician regards as important to the next step in his career.

To take an interesting example. When, in 1927, it looked as if Governor Smith would be the candidate of the Democratic Party for President, the high hurdle in his path was his affiliation with the Catholic Church. There is no social poison comparable to the venom of religious prejudice, and a whispering campaign had already begun, suggesting that the selection of Smith would be an invitation to the Pope to govern America. The question was dynamite, and I well knew that to write the candidate for an article on that subject would draw a blank. I took a more devious route. There lived in New York a certain highly qualified lawyer, one Charles Marshall, an expert on ecclesiastical polity. This gentleman, being a High Church Anglican, loved Rome as the Devil loves Holy Water. It is odd but it is true that the closer a Churchman comes doctrinally to the Catholic and Apostolic Church the more intense is his horror of the machinations of Roman policies; and this astute legalist was in deadly and daily terror of the influence of The Woman of Babylon. Anything that he would write would be wholly beyond the interest, even beyond the comprehension, of many *Atlantic* readers, but realizing that such an article by such an authority would place the debate on a high intellectual level, I invited Mr. Marshall to discuss the danger of dual allegiance, enjoining upon him to invest the article with all the pomp of legal logic, of precedent, and of ecclesiastical theory.

Mr. Marshall complied, and his unreadably intelligent paper was set instantly in galley proof. One set of these galleys I sent to Franklin Roosevelt, whom I had known since Groton days and who was on the threshold of his wonderful career, and asked him to persuade Governor Smith to answer it. My argument was that the insistent question would inevitably be threshed out and that Smith had simply the choice of a dirty rough-and-tumble in the streets, or of elevating the discussion to a level worthy of the candidate for the presidency of the United States. Mr. Roosevelt's reply was categorical. Governor Smith, he said, would never fight a political battle by involving himself in a religious controversy. That would be contrary to American principles. I expected the refusal, and took another path. A second set of galleys I dispatched to Mrs. Moskowitz, the remarkable woman who was the heart and soul of the Governor's campaign. A few days later she called me on the telephone. My proposal, she said, had been submitted to the "General Staff." It had been rigorously analyzed. It had been approved. The candidate could speak out with dignity and effect. It was the honest way, the Smith way, but — and here she became intensely serious — such pronouncement as I asked might make or break his candidacy and she could not proceed until she was absolutely certain of my integrity. If she put this heavy responsibility into my hands it must be with absolute assurance that I would follow instructions with meticulous care. It was a matter of life and death.

I told Mrs. Moskowitz to take three days to consider. I gave her the names of a number of my friends who were friends of hers. Assurance she could get from them; but, come Hell or high water, she would find me worthy of trust. On the following Friday she telephoned me she was satisfied and that the *Atlantic* should have a reply to Mr. Marshall.

The week that followed was in his contemplative years a source of much merriment to Al Smith. What had he to do with ecclesiastical polity? He was American to the last drop of his blood. He was Catholic heart and soul. He loved his country and he worshiped God. When these simplicities became involved in ecclesiastico-political argument, it was all beyond him. His action at the time was to summon his Board of Strategy — priests and professors — men learned in law and history, politicians who had been born the day before yesterday and never in all the years taken their eyes from the political football. They wrote the article, rewrote it, scrutinized every sentence with a magnifying glass, and then Governor Smith studied it just as he used, when a boy at the parochial school, to study the ultimate intricacies of Aquinas and Jerome brought down to school level. With a touch here and there he put Al Smith into all of it and made it his very own.

The riot of excitement that article caused! Hardly a daily paper in the United States but reprinted it. It led to theft and injunctions and a complicated lawsuit (which it gave the editor huge satisfaction to win), and it sent off Governor Smith's campaign to a flying start.

Every editor, of course, has his own method. I have heard it sworn to in New York in the old days, that Frank Munsey cabled the Pope direct, setting forth the influence of *Munsey's Magazine* and inviting the Holy Father to contribute a paper on "Home Life in the Vatican," and to put snap in it. Of that story I have my suspicion, but what an editor like Frank Munsey will not do to attract attention in the world, a quiet man shrinks from recording.

When correspondence with an author has been long continued and a certain specious friendship rests upon it, an editor gets to know the oddities and the quiddities which protect writers from the commonplace and give to each his place in the world. King Charles's head is always to be kept in mind, and if the editor does not learn his lesson here below I sometimes think that when the time comes for his transfer to a higher sphere, he may find himself a semicelestial impresario with a galaxy of heavenly prima donnas to keep in hand. That should complete his training! As a contributor grows in importance and success, the editor's touch must be lighter and more delicate. Discipline is relaxed and whims are indulged. But standards are standards, and I do not believe an editor should come to heel at any author's whistle. I recall small but characteristic altercations with Mrs. Wharton. She lived in Paris and wrote by Jamesian standards. Her spelling and punctuation followed the English tradition. The *Atlantic* usage was its own but it followed the main currents of American practice. So it was that when the "u's" were taken out of Mrs. Wharton's "parlours" and "colours" and semicolons were substituted for her dashes, she altered to the original form every correction made in her galley proofs. It was very obvious that the *Atlantic* reader, noticing variant spelling and punctuation in the magazine, would ascribe the deviations simply to careless proofreading; and careless proofreading the editor abhorred. The issue was joined. *Atlantic* habits must be respected, but Mrs. Wharton was an artist and the work of artists must not be retouched. I pondered the question, printed the article precisely as the author demanded, and simply subjoined this footnote: —

In this story certain divergencies in spelling and punctuation from the established practice of the *Atlantic* are made at the request of the author.

Mrs. Wharton was irritated, but after all, she had had her woman's way and the editor his professional satisfaction.

Speaking of this remarkable lady, I cannot resist setting down an incident showing her fidelity to her master.

Years after she had written her masterpiece, I chanced to reread *Ethan Frome*. Of the stories of two decades, not one it seemed to me traveled lighter toward posterity, with less superfluous baggage. None seemed surer of permanence. Yet I had grown up in the New England where Ethan Frome dwelt and marveled where she had found the material for his stark and terrible history. Yankees on the remote farms are a dour race, consenting under duress to a Calvinistic Providence, and gritting their teeth to withstand it. But the Yankees I knew were in their spiritual inheritance Scotch, and Ethan Frome was an Aeschylean.

I wrote to Mrs. Wharton making inquiry and she bade me turn to Henry James. Somewhere in *America Revisited,* I think, runs the passage: "Trim New England farm houses with their green blinds and Cenci-like interiors." I quote from distant memory, but the phrase pointed plainly to the origin of a story that bites like acid into memory.

I knew it was true, for as I read her letter a forgotten picture started up before my mind. Wandering one day among the outbuildings of a ramshackle farm, I was startled by a piercing shriek coming from a woodshed. I flung open the door and there chained to an upright joist, with a chair to sit on, bread and water by her side, was a hag with streaming hair, horribly insane.

THE ATLANTIC HARVEST that is garnered here contains contributions from some forty-six authors. In its essence I think of the book as a record of friendship, but as I turn the pages great gaps appear crowded with faces still living in my thoughts. Friends once made my life, but when I seek to make an ampler choice among them for this book the Four Horsemen of an editor's Apocalypse, Press, Paper, Price, and Publisher, stand firmly in my way. The book they tell me has grown big enough. No doubt it has, yet of a very few of those I miss most keenly I must say at least a word.

During the '90s when I chanced to be on the scene, the glory of Harvard was her Department of Philosophy, and the glory of the Department of Philosophy was the hearty divergence between the creeds of one professor and the next. There seemed no focal point at which any philosophy touched any other. The planets wheeled each in its eccentric orbit with no sun to restrain them. One remembers the truth-telling snapshot of William James and Josiah Royce perched together atop a stone wall while tearing the universe apart. "Papa," begged Peggy James, camera in hand, "don't let him be so sober. Make him laugh." James raised a monitory forefinger. "Damn the absolute!" he said just as the button was pressed, and now two laughing faces tell their philosophic story.

Two other memorable figures were members of the department: Santayana, the sceptical ironist who accepts the Catholic Church "except for its dogma" (which seems to me strikingly like accepting Heaven except for God), and Palmer, the classicist, child of the Puritans, whom at that time I thought of as a sort of Wesleyan minister, but after I had grown up, knew to be beloved among men.

Small-boned and fragile, with the gentlest of scholar's faces, George Herbert Palmer walked about the yard the symbol of benignity, but in the classroom his countenance would take on a quizzical expression as he sprang his trap and caught his student in the neatest of inconsistencies. His talk was full of fun with little sharp unexpected turns. Boys are sent to Harvard to grow up. Would that I had grown up and then been sent to Harvard! It was long after I was earning a living, even after that living ceased to be wholly precarious, that I really came to know Professor Palmer. He had made a translation of the *Odyssey* and a million copies of it had been sold. He had written the biography of his wife, Alice Freeman Palmer, President of Wellesley, with whom, being a professor at Harvard himself, he had lived a separate and loving life, and made of it a story unparalleled among domestic biographies. His books I read and delighted in, but not until I used to stay with him at Boxford did I understand the source of that delight.

Professor Palmer lived in his ancestral home, an epitome of New England. The chimney, he told me, was forty-four feet in girth and from its many facets an open fireplace warmed every room. Everything was in the strait tradition, simple and seemly. We strolled, my wife and I, over his wood lot where he took his exercise, chopping firewood just as he had chopped it when a boy. The conversation ranged through Homer, leapt the chasm to Milton and Marvell, and then exfoliated among the metaphysical poets, always coming to rest in the serenities of George Herbert, the saint whose name he bore and whose faith he practised. In the evening he would take down a volume of Herbert and read aloud to us in his delicate and precise enunciation. Then before bed called us he would talk of the Puritans from whom he came. The Puritans! The very name has become a byword, yet even in its extreme dilution, where is the stock that gives a tougher element of strength and courage to the American conglomerate?

FRIENDSHIP is a kaleidoscope and I think next of a man made in a very different pattern, William Beebe.

Certain critics maintain of Will Beebe that, while he calls it science, he makes it literature. I say, "Thank God for that!" Till he came down the jungle trail, hoatzins and iguanas, ithomiids, and Scarlet-thighed Leaf-walkers lived amongst us in a desert of arid prose. Here is an artist who has given them the prismatic colors of poetry; and who can say they are less alive for that! One thinks of Brooklyn as safely prosaic, but Will was born there. Jules Verne was his fairy godfather and, with an injudicious mixture of G. A. Henty, presided over his youth. You can see their busy spirits at work in him to this day.

How much better is one passion than two! Will owes a single allegiance to the Creature Kingdom and looks on mankind as the least desirable species thereof. From his aeroplane in the First World War he caught a bird's-eye view of men, found it unsuited to his tastes, and after an honorable discharge sought peace in the teeming jungle of Guiana. The pleasant somnolence of rest is anathema to him. Between expeditions he classifies, reflects, records, but his personal contentment is in direct relation to his proximity to the forest clearing or the ocean floor.

I am forever interested in what people regard as the summit of life's satisfactions. The highest pinnacle of Beebe's heaven is to lie in the spiky grass of a Sarawak jungle in an agonizing posture, prone on his belly, watching the behavior of pheasants in the mating season, while an army of ants devour him alive and a band of head-hunting Dyaks hover about, near enough to give a shimmer of danger to the atmosphere. Hardly second in his scale of felicities is to be lowered in his "bathysphere" at Nonsuch, Bermuda, three thousand and twenty-eight feet below the surface, and on ocean's bottom to affront obscene creatures of the sea on ground of their own choosing. Beebe's mightiest work has been his *Monographs of the Pheasants* in four volumes of sumptuous folio. Of these birds, the most exquisite work of Nature, there are in this round world nineteen groups: and nineteen of them the explorer caught by camera or gun and imprisoned in his book, closing forever one fascinating path of pioneer research. That journey took him seventeen months, during which he followed an iridescent trail from Java to the Vale of Kashmir. Of these magnificent books, ornithology is not the only reward. If it is beauty you seek, there are excelling photographs; there are exquisitely colored plates; and not infrequently the brilliant text will give you an idea of what the ultimate can be.

Three score and ten is near at hand for Will Beebe, but as I write, he is hurrying his departure on a new journey. Here's happy hunting to him, a safe return, and another journey, and another, and still another before the last and longest!

In the days when Boston was pleasantest, there lived here Lorin and Margaret Deland. The Good Book requires of married people that they twain shall be one flesh, and the union of Lorin and Margaret Deland was the perfect exemplification of that command. Divergent in talent, their friends thought of them as a single personality. She was a novelist who combined distinction with success, and he might best be called, perhaps, a broker in ideas. His was a most ingenious mind, not consecutive but extraordinarily illuminating. A cocktail of a mind it was. He would shake you up ideas for an advertising slogan, or devise an intricate and revolutionary maneuver for the Harvard football team, just as readily as he would map a campaign for Phillips Brooks and Trinity Church, plan a novel political reform, or reconstitute a charity. Lorin Deland never grew old following the beaten path, but he was no laggard. Witness his lively chronicle of his engagement to Margaret Campbell, as Mrs. Deland once was. She has left the record of it:—

At 5.00 P.M.—He arrived. She saw him from an upper window, getting out of the stage.

At 6.00 P.M.—Somebody introduced them, on the staircase.

At 6.30 P.M. — With the length of the supper table between them, they looked at each other occasionally.

At 7.30 P.M. — They met in the hotel parlor.

At 8.15 P.M. — He asked her to dance the Lancers.

At 9.00 P.M. — They sat on an ancient horsehair sofa, and talked of the weather.

At 9.30 P.M. — They fell in Love.

His life, all of it, was a good deal like that.

As young married people with a consolidated income of one hundred and twenty-five dollars a month, the husband laid down these three rules: —

1st: Don't want what you can't afford.
2nd: Go without if you must — *but never go in debt.*
3rd: When you can't have necessities and luxuries at the same time — give up two or three necessities and take a luxury.

As I transcribe this sagacious code I think of the wisest advice given to me as a young man just engaged and enjoying a salary not fifty cents too large for two: "Never keep accounts. They destroy your peace of mind. Never forget it is for happiness you are marrying." In the teeth of the economists I pass on to others this salutary maxim.

The right career for Lorin Deland, at least so one friend thinks, would have been as a professional adviser in family perplexities. Industry has adopted the idea: why should not families enjoy it? In a riper world there would be room for such a career. But Lorin Deland was obliged to earn his dollars as the straightener-out of business perplexities. His imagination would play about commercial problems, always using as its fulcrum his understanding of that cohesive bundle of contrarieties which we call human nature. Lorin Deland made that his lifelong study. Wherever he went he carried with him an invisible willow wand, his *dowser,* which would bend double over the hidden springs of men's desire.

Space fails me but not memory. I think of two men who between them perhaps have written more of the *Atlantic* than any half dozen others. Gamaliel Bradford, last of an austere and famous line, with a face sensitive and delicate as his "psychographs" of distinguished men, made no less than twenty-six contributions to the *Atlantic*. In style and temper wholly opposite, the other most constant visitor to the *Atlantic* was Dallas Lore Sharp.

Sharp was an evangelist, a lifelong preacher of the Gospel according to John Burroughs. For although his quenchless enthusiasm stemmed from Agassiz, it was from Oom John's friendship that his inspiration came, from that and from a more exalted source, for he read his Bible with the zeal of a Covenanter. Every morning while oatmeal and pancakes grew visibly colder, the Patriarch (Sharp began his patriarchy about the age of twenty-one), Mrs. Sharp, and multitudinous young Sharps would read a chapter of Scripture, each taking an alternate verse. From Genesis to Revelations they would go and round the course again, permitting, as Sharp used to tell me, no verse however embarrassing to give them pause. The Sharp farm was on Mullein Hill, well within Boston's radius of intellect. He reigned there, like Alexander Selkirk, observant monarch of all he surveyed, following with intensest interest the habits of God's creatures. Not the wink of a rabbit's eye escaped him nor the unfolding of a bud of the lesser celandine.

The breed of the New England naturalist, long may it survive! Torrey is gone, Bowles is gone, John Phillips is gone, Sharp is gone, but their spirit lives abroad in the land. Increasing year by year, Public Reservations praise them, bird sanctuaries acknowledge them, field, wood, and river consecrate their remembrance, and lovers of the open road, leaving behind the golf course scarring the face of Nature, make for the unfenced country, praising their name.

Yet in common gratitude I must speak of one friend more. Before my coming there presided over the *Atlantic* the Yankee embodiment of the humanities. It is muted praise that is most grateful to Professor Bliss Perry and I rise to greet him simply as Fisherman and Scholar. Which the obverse and which the reverse of the medal I can hardly say. Not that the wily trout actually whisks between him and his Emerson. Each has its season, and the debt of scholarship to angling has been too often and too eloquently proved for us to dispute it.

To be a Perry, father, son, or grandson — or a daughter of the Perry name for that matter — is to teach. As statesmanship in the Cecils, morality in the Adamses, swollen lips in the Hapsburgs, or politics with the Roosevelts, so teaching will run in the Perry family to the remotest generation. It is rumored, to be sure, there is a Perry in business, but that legendary exception proves the rule. Teaching is the Perry business. Chiron the centaur herding his young heroes, Mark Hopkins straddling his log, such is every Perry in the classroom; and in this day of crime committed in the name of education, thank God for that! I think with gratitude of Father Perry at Williams College teaching to all and sundry that morality and Free Trade are one and indivisible, and I can see his smiling face in Heaven.

To Bliss Perry I owe a personal and unpaid debt. For ten years he guided the *Atlantic* in the apostolic succession just before I came along, and if the tradition of convictions upheld with urbanity still survives in the magazine, the credit is all his.

I HEAR the low voice of women readers murmuring that in this collection there are thirty-one masculine names, while only fifteen are feminine. How about the wisdom of this, to say nothing of the propriety? Is it because the editor is a man to begin with — with a full store of man's prejudice? There may be sundry grains of truth in the accusation, but in his defense the editor may say that though the judge wears trousers, a clear majority of the jury is dressed in frocks. Most readers, discursive readers that is, are women — and even a male editor would hardly be so foolish as to let an innate prejudice stand in the way of his reading public. Something beyond prejudice is behind this editor's choice. Admitting that he is one of those who hold the judgment of Portia supremely biased, when by a charming casuistry she chouses Shylock out of his legitimate profit, and that Vox Populi and Vox Dei speak divergent things in utterly different voices, he has a parcel of remarks to make in his defense.

Were I a good Catholic, I would take my stand on the consistent judgments of the Fathers for a dozen centuries. St. Chrysostom sums them up with moderation: "Woman is a *desirable* calamity." But it is not fair for a heretic to hide behind alien fortifications. I appeal to history. In no field of competition has woman won a blue — except in the very territory that concerns us — writing. Even here half and more than half that field has been pre-empted by men. This is a singular and indicative fact. Sequestered through the centuries from other intellectual pursuits, the opportunity for writing has been wide open to woman. Through the unobstructed gateway of Arts and Letters she has trooped singly and in regiments. It is absurd to think of her as a newcomer. If the domains of science and of philosophy have restricted her entrance, wide provinces have for two centuries been freely open for her to invade. History, poetry, painting, and fiction have been at the beck of her choice. In history her record speaks for itself. Here I am reminded of a real disappointment of my own. As part of a legacy of books, I was once permitted to make my choice from a large cabinet. Five volumes in polished calf attracted me. "Macaulay's History of England," was printed on the gilded backstraps. Happening to own no copy of that Whiggish masterpiece in good print, I rejoiced, but when I opened the parcel I was hardly reassured by the title page. "The History of England in Five Volumes," it read, by Catherine Macaulay. Miss Macaulay was an industrious and a talented lady, but with all the chivalry in the world I felt that she had been superseded by a more illustrious expositor of the name.

In painting, to what women should we give the prize? To Madame Lebrun, a ribbon, but it must be red, not blue; to Rosa Bonheur, possibly an honorable mention for her virility, to Miss Cassatt only a red, though hers, I clearly admit, must be dyed a most brilliant vermilion.

Turn to poetry. Sappho, you say brightly, whether you have read her few hundred scattered lines or not. Then you pause, pause for some twenty-four centuries and you mutter, Christina Rossetti and Emily Brontë, both precious names and Emily's, by virtue of two poems, immortal. Here I, too, pause in some amusement. Palgrave's first *Golden Treasury,* thanks to the perfect pitch of the ear of Tennyson, who sat always at Palgrave's elbow, is within its compass of an unrivaled excellence. It contains the names of seventy-nine men contributors and of five women: Anne Lindsay, Lady Nairn, Mary Lamb, Jane Elliott, and — Phoebus Apollo! — Mrs. Barbauld. These and not Emily Brontë! But even if you come to later years and pick up Mrs. Browning, if you do pick her up, and our own elfin Emily Dickinson, the scales are heavy against you. Women do have emotions and can modern bias — indeed moderns are chivalrously disinclined to respect their convictions regarding women. It goes back to a remote past not only in the Western but in the Eastern world. Only yesterday I picked up a little figure of a Japanese god dating from the Twelfth Century. It was the familiar figure of Anzu Myro, a sort of Briareus with half a dozen arms whose special care is the emotional relation of the sexes. In his uppermost right hand Anzu clasps the thunderbolts of passion. In the left is a bell. The thunderbolt represents the indestructible unchangeable masculine, the bell the feminine, eternally mutable, unchangingly changing. So it has been in men's minds and so it will remain.

All generalizations are wrong and this, in part, among them. But there remains a residue of truth and this brings me to the query I put at the outset of this digression. In compiling this Anthology, I have in general apportioned the recital of facts to men and to men I have generally entrusted the more speculative matters, but to women much of the personal philosophy, much of the fiction. If the occasional reader delves more deeply into this vague and misty subject and calls for a bill of particulars, I recommend reading in succession the comparable stories here included of Thomas Bailey Aldrich's and Mrs. Wharton's, for God and nature meant one story to be written by man, the other by woman. And what man could have composed "Twenty Minutes of Reality"? — or take Miss Anne Douglas Sedgwick's exquisite "Daffodils." You will not find its counterpart in the fruit of man's labors.

Male and female, created He them.

How many people, I wonder, realize the extent to which reading is an integral part of life? "Si jeunesse savoit; si vieillesse pouvoit," is an age-old cry of distress, but would it not be wise and reasonable to include in the education of boys and girls some notion of the importance of budgeting time? Such a system would compound the length of days at a usurer's rates. Taking my hint from a chance suggestion of Sidney Smith, I look back as I should have looked forward, upon the seventy-two years of my life that I best remember. An hour a day is three years. This means twenty-four years gone for sleep, twenty-four to express them. One would suppose the lyric certain to give them th ripest opportunity, but there the record stands.

Fiction remains, and in the domain of fiction woman makes h bid. All her resources of intelligence and enthusiasm, her patience, h delicate understanding of human nature, sluiced from closed regic of high endeavor, pour torrentially into the great reservoir of ficti When women entered politics, Mr. Choate's toast to the sex rose to occasion. "Women, once our superiors, now our equals!" In polit the compliment, if compliment it was, was scarcely justified, for addition of women to our voting lists has doubled the costs a complexities of our elections without changes in their fundamental c come. We have multiplied our problems, but we have not multipl the intelligence with which to solve them. In our immediate busin the writing of fiction, women, once our equals, are in a fair way become our superiors. It is true they may lack the masterful ha with which great novelists like Conrad and Hardy create a hun world shadowed by overarching Fate. They may not have the br social sweep of a Lewis or even of a Hemingway, but in the nicety their observation of life, in their ingenuity, in the fidelity of their p trayal of human nature, they do not seem to me to take a second pl Indeed centuries before woman sat in the driver's seat of the family her ancient servitude served her in good stead. When women, al with their chattels, were merely the property of men, they had to be servant, they had to understand their masters and themselves, t had to be subtle, devious, and ingenious, they had to understand ultimate springs of conduct. Such knowledge was their salvat physical and mental, and now the training of their long indent makes itself felt in their novels and their stories. They may not h full vibrant intellectual energy, except in rare instances, but t instinct has a prehensile quality, attaching itself to its object and a lambent flame heartening it into life. The higher intellectual train oftentimes I think, develops the brain at the expense of the insti and instinct is the primal source of woman's power.

Mutabile Semper Femina! How axiomatic to men it seems, h prejudiced to women! But the whole philosophy of sex is based on variableness of woman. She may not be the light quivering aspen the poet, but to men she remains unpredictable. And this is nc balance it for work. Eight years (intolerable waste yet woman would double it!) to dressing, eight to eating, four years for play, and four, I fear, for idleness. That makes up the sum, and where does reading come in? Evidently that most precious time of all has been filched piecemeal from the incessant business of life, and yet, looking at my balance in the bank, I see it has paid infinitely the highest dividends. Had I been the intelligent child of superintelligent parents, reading, twelve years of it at the least, one hour in six, would have been the first item in the budget, and the rest of the business of life would have been squeezed to decent proportions.

If life is liberty and reading can give it Andes and Himalayas or keep it flat as prairie grass, it follows that reading should be concentrated. In theory reading should embrace the newspaper and the classics — these alone are essential — and stop there; but theories like budgets have a way of bulging this way and that. Let us compromise and follow the rule of reason. Our reading time, surely, is too precious to waste. Let each of us set a standard for himself and cling to it. Such a standard I have sought in this volume.

Reading time is sowing time and the harvest is certain. Chip and chisel then, from every other occupation; browbeat every other taskmaster. Be miserly about this whole business of reading and learn from the miser too that what you hoard is worth hoarding. This is no counsel of perfection. It is commonsensical as Poor Richard, and it deals with something of more consequence than his penny saving a pound. The plain truth is there is no happiness like literate happiness. I am not talking of the scholar's rewards but of the contentment of the very ordinary man who, when he grows old, finds it uncomfortable to have a brain so empty that only his miseries rattle round inside. What you put into permanent storage must have the clink of gold in it.

In making this collection these considerations press upon me. I have included nothing which it has not diverted me to read, nothing which, having read before, I do not remember with pleasure. The book is not dedicated to Literature with the big L or a small. My target is interest and amusement, for it is interest that makes life livable and amusement that makes us equal to the enduring of it.

Contents

ATLANTIC HARVEST

Memoirs of the *Atlantic*

JAMES NORMAN HALL
1887–

James Norman Hall began in 1887; behind his cradle, the backdrop of an Iowa farm. The silver spoon in his mouth was a shining talent for writing. Other gifts of his fairy godmother were strong affection for a few, friendliness for many, and a queasy distaste for the crowd. One thing he has ever abhorred; personal advertisement. He lets his work stand for itself. To write this brief preface is a ticklish business even for a friend of thirty-five years.

For it must have been about 1912 that I first knew Hall. After graduation at his Iowa College of Grinnell, he had come to Boston and, characteristically enough, was working for the Society for the Prevention of Cruelty to Children. His cast of mind has never altered. But it was a little holiday he took in 1914 which fixed the pattern of his life. He had sailed to England and pedaled through the lovely countryside, enjoying the impersonal society of the pubs while eschewing newspapers as prime invaders of a man's privacy. On August third of that terrific year he turned up at his little room in London. It was not the London he had left. The rumbling old city had become a bedlam. Shouting crowds surged through the streets. There were platforms in Trafalgar Square. The First Hundred Thousand were signing up.

Hall's compass points true north. With him it was not a matter of debate. He joined the endless queue, and that night he went to bed, an American recruit in the Ninth Battalion Royal Fusiliers. His account of Kitchener's Mob, published in the Atlantic Monthly, began a life intimacy with the magazine. But the news of his enlistment brought no joy to Iowa. The intercession of Ambassador Page was sought by the family, but it was not until Hall had served his machine gun in the Battle of Loos and learned what war means through a bitter campaign, that our Embassy succeeded in setting him free. As Ambassador Page told me at the time, his release was a fussy business, for the son was no quitter, but the senior Hall rejoiced. Then Norman consulted his pocket compass. Within a week, I think it was, he had signed up with the Lafayette Escadrille and was off again for France.

Evidently Hall was meant for something. He was constantly in combat. He shot down his five planes, became an ace, and was twice shot down himself. On the first occasion he drifted to safety in a French trench, but the second time, no such luck. The Germans got him and kept him. No news came and tragic rumor took its place. He was badly wounded, done for, dead. I wrote in all directions. Eventually reports convinced me that the last chapter was closed and, when other friends of his suggested that I write his Memoir, I began to sort the letters. Suddenly that posthumous fame of his was wrecked. A letter turned up penciled in his familiar hand. He had escaped from prison or, as he would prefer to phrase it, sauntered to freedom in the confusion that engulfed all Germany at the end of 1918.

It was while he was an aviation cadet in France that Hall first met Charles Nordhoff. The two young men were wandering about the camp, each with an Atlantic Monthly in his hand. The old yellow cover was their introduction, and their joint story began.

Having lived one overflowing life, Hall began another. Since his emigration, Tahiti has been the center of his material existence. Everywhere but there, nostalgia attacks him. There it was he met his delightful wife, one Sarah Winchester, daughter of a Scotch sea captain and a Tahitian lady. There have been born his children, Conrad Lafcadio Hall, names that pay tribute to his twin masters, and an engaging daughter. There is his library with shelf on shelf of his closest companions. There are his flowers, his fruit trees, and his ocean. There is society where none intrude, and there the lonely clatter of his typewriter breaks the silence of the Southern Seas.

His works, or most of them, everybody knows. One cannot picture Captain Bligh without Hall at his elbow; and other books of the firm of Hall and Nordhoff, such as Men Against the Sea and No More Gas, have diverted the literate in print and the illiterate on the screen — not to speak of Hall's personal creation, Doctor Dogbody, who is entitled to a one-legged immortality quite his own. But the contemplative among us like his essays — almost — best. Hall has the reflective sense. The world focuses in his pocket mirror. He is a child of Lamb with less sweetness of thought and more subterranean fire. His hates have grown subconscious with the years, but below they burn *bright. Politics he loathes and, as he admits himself, he is at heart an anarchist — an anarchist heading a party of one.*

In American letters the partnership of Hall and Nordhoff[1] *is unique. They do not collaborate; they fuse. Their scheme is, after the closest give-and-take in the construction of a story, to write alternate chapters. Then the chapters coalesce. Even sentences bear the stamp of a common genius. Corn and beans make succotash but in the fruity puddings of Hall and Nordhoff there are no disparate elements. Their novels are of one substance, one flavor, and one enormous zest.*

The strange thing is that these are two men of strong and individual personalities. When either writes a book of his own, it is as if some powerful chemical reagent had dissolved the indissoluble. The nostalgic beauty of Lost Island, *for instance, is unadulterated Hall.*

Sing

A Song of Sixpence

JAMES NORMAN HALL

SEVERAL years ago while living at Papeete, the capital of Tahiti in French Oceania, I found myself so low in funds that it seemed the part of wisdom to retire for a time to one of the remote country-districts until I could repair my fortunes. On the windward side of the island, thirty-five miles from the town, I found an attractive place about an acre in extent, with a one-room house on it precisely suited to my needs. My verandah overlooked the sea, and a clear mountain-stream flowed through my small domain, so that I had both fresh- and salt-water bathing; but a more important feature than either of these was the cheapness of the rental — $3.00 per month.

The land thereabout was so fertile that I decided to make a vegetable garden. In the tropics gardening would be a delightful occupation, and it might easily prove so profitable that I should never again need to resume my old trade of journalism. So I set to work, hopefully enough, glad of the necessity which had brought me to this decision.

The experience was disillusioning. Millions of tiny red ants carried

[1] As I correct these proofs, a telegram comes. His reading lamp still lighted, Charles Nordhoff has closed his book forever. E. S.

away most of my seed, and, if any happened to be overlooked by the ants, the moment they sent forth green shoots these were sheared off by land crabs. After three months of patient effort all that I had to show for my toil was two ears of sweet corn (or, better, corncobs, for the rats had eaten off the kernels), three small tomatoes, and one squash. Having estimated my time as worth, at a modest figure, twenty cents an hour, and adding expenditures for seed, garden tools, and so forth, I found that these vegetables cost me $15.50 each.

Nevertheless I resolved to try once more, and ordered from America a fresh supply of seed — a small quantity this time, for my funds were getting low; and furthermore, because of my innumerable enemies I meant to garden on a reduced front. But when I had cleared away the weeds — how marvelously they had flourished meanwhile, without care! — and saw the hosts of ants drawn up in waiting battalions, and the ground perforated like a sieve with the holes of land crabs, and a crab at the entrance of each hole, waving his keen-edged nippers in the air, I lost heart. "It is useless," I thought. "I'd better go back to journalism. Although not a lucrative profession, it is more profitable than gardening, and if I practise it faithfully I should be able to earn at least twenty cents an hour." Therefore I put away my tools and left Nature to plant whatever she would in my garden plot. She chose, as before, lantana and false tobacco.

That afternoon I was oiling and cleaning my typewriter, which had long been rusting in disuse, when a Chinaman named Hop Sing drove past my door in his dilapidated spring-wagon. He lived a quarter of a mile down the lagoon beach from my place, in a house which he himself had built from the boards of old packing-cases and roofed over with flattened-out biscuit-tins. I knew that he had a vegetable garden, — although he raised only sweet potatoes, watermelons, and a very tough variety of field corn, — so I hailed him, thinking he might find use for my dollar's worth of seed. He stopped, willingly enough, and I brought out to him a small packet each of beans, sweet corn (Golden Bantam), squash, pumpkin, lettuce, and tomato seed, all of the best varieties. Hop grunted expressions of mild interest while I explained what the various packets contained, and, when I had finished, asked: "How much?" "Oh, nothing at all," I replied. "A little present for you." He grasped the back of the seat to steady himself, perhaps, from the shock of receiving a present in that heathen land, and his black eyes glittered a trifle more brightly; but these were the only evidences of emotion — if it may be called emotion — that he displayed.

I forgot Hop Sing forthwith; there were other things to think of, chiefly the precarious state of my finances. Having counted on my garden to furnish food, I had spent my little capital all too freely. Luckily my rent was paid several months in advance, but I had left only 128 francs — a little more than $5.00 American, at the current rate of exchange — and not a penny coming in until I had written something, story, sketch, or what not. The manuscript would have to be sent to America, and even though it should be accepted at once — a remote possibility — I could not hope to receive a cheque for at least three months. How was I to live in the meantime? There were bananas on my place and about fifty coconut palms; but my landlord, a native, reserved the right to both the nuts and the fruit, which was no more than fair, considering the modest rental he asked for house and grounds. The nuts were gathered as they fell and the bananas picked green to send to the Papeete market. I thought of fishing, but, remembering past experiences, I knew it would be foolish to count on that. I had no better luck at fishing than at gardening. No, I should have to live, somehow, on my 128 francs. That, of course, was impossible, so I resolved not even to try. I kept 28 francs for incidental expenses, spent 25 francs for native tobacco, — if I was to write I should have to smoke, — and the remainder for sweet potatoes and tinned beef. When the food was gone — well, I should worry about that when the time came.

Three days later I was on page two of a sketch which I planned to call "Settling Down in Polynesia," a story of some experiences I had had the year before. It was Sunday, but necessity knows no holy days and I was doing my utmost to work. The mere fact of having to work seemed to make accomplishment impossible. I had written and rewritten the two pages of my story, vainly trying with each new draft to blacken page three. I was aroused from a mood of profound dejection by a knock at the back door. It was Hop Sing, and with him were his wife, their three small children, and a wizened little man with a scant beard and shaped like an interrogation point. Hop was dressed in a clean cotton undershirt and a pair of dungaree trousers. His wife wore a pyjama-suit of black silk, and her hair was elaborately dressed. She carried one child on her arm, led another by the hand, and had a third, the baby, in a sling at her back. The children were beautifully dressed, and each of them had on a little skullcap of blue silk with flowers and butterflies embroidered on it in gold thread. The ancient wore a coat like a dressing-gown. He was very feeble and got down from the wagon with difficulty. It was pathetic to see the effort it cost him to walk. He would advance his staff a few inches and, grasping it with both hands, make a shuffling hop up to it. Then he would rest for a moment while gathering strength for a new effort. We helped him up the steps and at length all were seated on the verandah, Mrs. Sing sitting sidewise on her chair because of the baby in the sling. My unwashed breakfast-dishes were on the kitchen table, and several slices of fried sweet potato on a greasy plate looked anything but appetizing. I was ashamed of the disorder of the place, the more so because this was the first visit I had ever had from the Sing family. Both Hop and his wife looked about in appraising fashion, but whether they approved or disapproved it was impossible to judge from their faces.

"My fadda-law," said Sing, indicating the old man.

I smiled and nodded.

A rather long silence followed. I felt embarrassed and could think of nothing to say.

"What name you?" he then asked.

I told him. Another interval of silence. I gave my forefinger to the baby on Mrs. Sing's lap. It clasped it gravely and held on. Mrs. Sing smiled. Her father, too, smiled; at least his face wrinkled suddenly, like a pool into which a pebble has been thrown. The small baby in the sling was asleep, its chubby arms sticking straight out. It looked like a doll rather than a real baby. The oldest child, a boy of six or seven, had the curious mature look and the air of profound wisdom common to many Chinese children.

Sing took from his pocket one of the packets of seeds I had given him.

"What name this?" he asked.

"That? Corn, sweet corn — Golden Bantam. Very good. Tahiti corn no good — too tough. This corn fine."

"Where you get?"

"From America," I replied.

He brought forth the other packets.

"All this Melican seed?"

I told him that it was, and the best that could be bought.

He was silent for a moment. Then he said: "Make fine garden now. No have good seed before. Make plenty big tomato now, plenty squash, plenty corn. Bimeby you see."

Thinking of my three tomatoes, about the size of marbles, I was not sanguine about Sing's being plenty big. However, I expressed the hope that they might be. I brought out my seed catalogue and showed him pictures of the various vegetables. He was much interested and exchanged remarks in Chinese with his father-in-law. Meanwhile one of those heavy local showers common at Tahiti in the rainy season broke with violence. The thunder of water on my tin roof was deafening. Soon the cloud melted into pure sunlight, the last of it descending in a fine mist shot through with rainbow lights. Sing then went to his wagon and returned with three huge watermelons. He made a second excursion, bringing this time a live fowl, a bottle of Dubonnet (vin apéritif), and a basket containing seventeen eggs. All of these articles he placed on my kitchen table.

"Littly plesent, you," he said with a deprecatory gesture. Mrs. Sing and her father then rose, and all three shook my hand, bidding me good-bye with smiles and nods. A moment later they drove off, leaving me astonished at this expression of Chinese friendliness.

It would be difficult to exaggerate the value to me of their generous gift. Tinned beef is a nourishing food, but I had lost all relish for it during the Great War. As for sweet potatoes, I had eaten so many while knocking about the Pacific on trading schooners that I could hardly endure the sight of them. How welcome, then, was this more palatable food! I planned to have a chicken dinner at once, but on second thought decided not to kill my fowl. Perhaps she would lay, and if I could somehow procure a rooster I might, from that small beginning, raise enough chickens to provide for all my needs. So I staked the hen out in the dooryard, with a string tied to her leg; and, having found several coconuts partly eaten by rats, I broke these open and gave her a good meal. Then, having dined on a six-egg omelet with half a watermelon for dessert, I resumed my work with interest and enthusiasm. All the afternoon the bell of my typewriter rang with the steady persistence of an alarm gong at a railroad crossing, and pages of manuscript fell from my hands like autumn leaves after a heavy frost. By six o'clock that evening I had reached the end of my "Settling Down" story.

I had no time to lose if I were to get it in the north-bound mail. The monthly steamer from New Zealand to San Francisco was due at Papeete on Monday. I decided to go into town to post the manuscript, not being willing to trust the native mail-carrier with so precious a document. A motor-bus ran daily between Papeete and Taravao, a village just beyond my place, but the fare for the round-trip was twenty-four francs. I should need at least ten francs for stamps and expenses in town, so I decided to walk in to Papeete and, if I had enough money left, to ride back. Therefore, having fortified myself with a small glass of Dubonnet and another six-egg omelet, I set out.

It was a beautiful night, dewy and still and fresh, with a full moon rising above the palm trees on the Taravao isthmus. The road wound this way and that around the shoulders of the hills, now skirting the sea, now crossing the mouths of broad valleys where the *hupé*—the night breeze from the interior—blew cool and refreshing. I had glimpses through the trees of lofty precipices festooned with the silvery smoke of waterfalls and, on the left hand, of the lagoon bordered by the barrier reef where great combers, rising to break on the coral, caught the moonlight in lines of white fire. From native houses along the road came snatches of song, a strange mixture of airs, part French, part Tahitian, to the accompaniment of guitars, accordions, and mouth-organs. On verandahs here and there women were busy with their ironing, sitting cross-legged on the floor with a lamp beside them, and far out on the lagoon the lights of the fishermen were already beginning to appear.

I walked briskly along the moonlit road, feeling at peace with the world and with myself. How pleasant it would be, I thought, really to settle down in this remote tropical paradise, to remain here for the rest of my life. Where could I find kindlier people, or a life more suited to one of my indolent habits? If it were true that a man's wealth may be estimated in terms of the things he can do without, then in that sense I might hope soon to achieve affluence. Material possessions added little to the sum of one's happiness, and I could always earn enough at writing to provide for the simple necessities of life. Whenever the mild-eyed melancholy tropical wolves came sniffing apologetically at my door I could knock off a story of one sort or another; then I could live on the proceeds of the sale of it until it became necessary to write another.

So I mused, proceeding on my way; but at length, toward midnight, when I had covered about half the distance to Papeete, I found myself again thinking of food. The nourishment stored in my second six-egg omelet had already been absorbed and its energy expended. I had a drink of water from a mountain stream and tightened my belt a notch or two.

"I'll have a good breakfast when I get to town," I thought. For three francs I could buy a large portion of chop suey at one of the Chinese restaurants; that would have to suffice until I returned to the country, which I meant to do at once, as soon as I had posted my manuscript.

At a place where the road followed a lonely strip of beach I came to a thatched hut, and sitting near it, by a fire of driftwood, were an old native man and woman. I stopped for a moment to enjoy the beauty of the scene. The stems of the palm trees were black against the firelight, which flickered over the faces of the old couple and cast huge shadows behind them. They saw me, and the old man called out, "*Haere mai ta maa!* (Come and eat!)" This is merely a friendly greeting, and I replied in the usual way, "*Paia vau* (I'm not hungry)"; but if my empty stomach could have spoken it would have made indignant denial of that statement. But evidently they really meant that I should partake of their midnight supper. They were roasting in the coals what appeared to be shellfish and some sort of native vegetable, and an appetizing fragrance filled the air. "Come!" said the old woman in the native tongue. "Try this, it is very good"—and putting several generous portions in a coconut shell she held it up to me.

Good? I should think it was! The meat of the shellfish was as delicately flavored as that of the finest lobster, and the vegetable had a mealy, nutlike taste. My hosts seemed delighted at my appetite and urged more food upon me. "Eat! Eat!" said the old man. "We have plenty—enough for a dozen," and he pointed to several buckets filled with uncooked food; so I ate with a will.

"What kind of shellfish are these?" I asked. "Did you get them on the reef?"

"Shellfish! These are not shellfish; they're *tupas*."

"What!" I exclaimed. *Tupas* are land crabs, and those I was eating with such relish were members of the pestiferous family, countless in number, which had assisted the ants in ruining my garden. I didn't know they were edible, but the old man told me that Tahitians thought them a great delicacy, which they are, in truth. As for the vegetable, it was not a vegetable at all, but a nut, the fruit of the *mapé,* the Pacific chestnut-tree. These trees flourish at Tahiti. They are found along the banks of streams and in moist or swampy places. There was a grove of them on my place, and the ground beneath was littered with nuts that I had never bothered to examine, not knowing that they were of value. I was appalled at thought of the time and effort I had wasted trying to make a garden, when all the while there was an inexhaustible food-supply at hand, to be enjoyed without labor, to be had for the mere taking. But no; the taking of land crabs could not be such a simple matter. I remembered the wariness of those which infested my garden plot. They did all their damage in my absence. The moment they saw me coming they scurried to their holes and, if I made so much as a move in their direction, dodged down to safety. I had once caught one by digging him out, but that cost me two hours of hard work.

I asked the old man how he caught them and he showed me a method so simple and reasonable that I wondered I had not thought of it. He had a fishpole and line, but instead of a hook at the end of the line he tied there a bunch of green leaves from the hibiscus tree. These leaves and the blossoms of the hibiscus are the principal food of land crabs. We went a little way from the hut to a spot in full moonlight where there were many crab-holes. "Now stand very still," he said. In a moment the crabs, which had scurried away at our approach, came warily up again. He then cast his bait very much as one does in fly-fishing. Immediately several crabs came sidling toward it. They fastened their nippers in the leaves, each of them trying to drag the bundle to his hole. The old man then gave a deft jerk to the line, and the crabs, not being able to disengage their nippers quickly enough, were dragged to his feet. He pounced upon them and threw them into the bucket with the others. I then tried my hand, with such success that I was tempted to forgo my journey to town. I wanted to go home at once and begin fishing in my garden, but more prudent counsels prevailed. One's appetite for food so plentiful and so easily procured might become jaded in time; furthermore, I should need a certain amount of money for clothing, shaving materials, tobacco, and so forth. Therefore, having bade farewell to my kindly hosts, I proceeded on my way and reached Papeete at dawn, just as the steamer that was to carry my manuscript to America was entering the harbor. Stamps for the precious parcel cost three francs. I then breathed over it a silent prayer and slipped it into the letter-chute.

Papeete is a colorful town, particularly in the early morning when the inhabitants are going to and from the market. Everyone is in the streets then, and the French and Chinese restaurants are filled with people exchanging gossip over their morning coffee. I had an excellent breakfast at a cost of four francs, and then strolled here and there doubly enjoying the gayety of the scene after my long sojourn in the country. I was walking along the Quai de Commerce looking at the shipping when someone touched my shoulder. It was a bald fat little

Chinaman who had evidently been running after me, for he was out of breath and could not speak for a moment. Then he began talking in Chinese-Tahitian, a sort of *bêche-de-mer* that I don't understand. I shook my head. He renewed his efforts, speaking very earnestly and rapidly, and presently I caught the name "Hop Sing."

"Hop Sing?" I said.

"*É! É!* (Yes! Yes!)" he replied, and of a sudden he found some English words.

"You know Hop Sing? Hop Sing flen, you?"

"Yes," I said. "I know him. Hop Sing live close me, Papeari."

Papeari is the name of the district where I was living.

The Chinaman's face glowed with pleasure.

"*Maitai! Maitai!* (Good! Good!) Hop Sing send me letta. I know name, you. You give seed; put in gloun, make garden. *Maitai! Maitai!* Hop Sing glad. Me glad. Hop Sing brudda-law me."

"What name you?" I asked.

"Lee Fat. Keep store over there," and he pointed down the street. "When you go back Papeari?"

"Go this morning on motor-bus."

"Goo-bye," the Chinaman said, and rushed away as though he had not a moment to lose. I was surprised at the abrupt leave-taking and stood looking after him, hardly knowing what to make of the encounter, touched at thought of this odd little man chasing me down the street to thank me for the trifling favor I had done his brother-in-law.

I sat on a bench near the post office to wait for the motor-bus. "The Beachcombers' Bench" it was called, for it was usually occupied on steamer day by waifs and strays from all parts of the world, men who sat there waiting for the distribution of the monthly mail, always expecting letters containing money and nearly always disappointed. "I'm in the same boat now," I thought. "Three months hence I'll be sitting here nursing the same forlorn hope." It was possible, of course, that my manuscript would sell at once, but, remembering past experiences, I knew it would be foolish to count on it. Well, I still had twenty-one francs, and I should have nine left after paying my bus fare. Certainly I should not starve, with land crabs and mapé nuts to eat, and meanwhile I should work at the journalistic trade as never before, sending manuscripts north by every steamer as long as I had money for postage. Having made this resolve, I put my worries aside.

It was nearly midday when I arrived at Papeari. While I was paying my fare to the driver, the boy who attended to the distribution of parcels put a box down beside me.

"You've made a mistake," I said. "That isn't mine."

"Yes it is," he replied.

"No, no. I didn't have a box and I've ordered nothing from town."

He insisted, however, that it was mine. A Chinaman had brought it just before the bus left the market, he said, and had paid for its carriage to my place. I still thought there was some mistake, but upon prying off the lid I found a card with "Lee Fat, No. 118" printed on it. (Every Chinaman at Tahiti has a number. This is for some governmental purpose; to keep track of them, perhaps.) Under the name was written, in pencil, "Mr. Hall, for you." The parcel contained the following articles: one two-pound box of New Zealand chocolates, a large paper bag of lichi nuts, one quart of champagne (Louis Roederer), and a beautiful lacquered box with a gold dragon on the lid. In this box were two silk handkerchiefs and a silk pyjama-suit.

I was tempted to open the champagne at once, that I might drink long life and abundant health to Hop Sing and his brother-in-law, Lee Fat, No. 118; but I had no ice, and I knew that I could not drink, alone, a quart of champagne without having a headache the following day. So I tied a string to the bottle and lowered it into the cistern to keep cool. Then I went out to attend to my chicken.

She was gone. The string was still tied to the stake, but she had worked her leg out of the noose and vanished. After a long search I found her under the back steps. I reached in, very cautiously, to grasp her. She pecked at my hand and, as I drew her forth, gave utterance to the indignant squawks common to hens when they are sitting. Surely enough, she had laid an egg and was sitting on it; evidently she had been ready to sit when Hop Sing brought her to me. The egg under her was unfertilized, of course, so I took that out. Then I made her a nest of excelsior out of Lee Fat's box, and placed in it the five eggs remaining of Hop Sing's gift. The hen settled down on them with contented cluckings and, when comfortable, closed her eyes as much as to say, "Now then, all I ask is to be fed from time to time; and twenty-one days hence we shall see what we shall see."

It seems to me now that the definite upward trend in the graph of my fortunes began that afternoon when I started land-crab fishing. The results not only flattered my vanity — sadly in need of flattery — but gave me renewed confidence. "At last," I thought, "I am a success at something." I could not eat a tenth of the crabs I had caught, so I made a pen of stakes set closely together and deeply into the ground, and turned the surplus loose inside it. They immediately dug new holes for themselves, but this did not disturb me, for I knew I could easily catch them again. I fished all over my two-acre estate with such success that I had to enlarge the pen several times, and even then, and despite the fact that some of the crabs dug their way out, there were so many inside that the ground was honeycombed with their burrows. It occurred to me that by feeding them regularly on hibiscus leaves and blossoms I might add to their size and increase the delicacy of their flavor. The experiment was highly successful. The crabs thrived upon the regular and abundant food and I thrived upon them. At the time of Hop Sing's visit, what through worry and an uncongenial diet, I was very thin, but within six weeks I had gained fourteen pounds.

Meanwhile, upon the appointed day, my hen stepped out of her nest, followed by five bits of animated fluff. I was quite as proud of them as she was, and doubtless took more credit to myself on that occasion than the facts warranted. I fed both the hen and her brood on a mixture of roasted land-crabs and mapé nuts, and never have I seen chickens grow so rapidly.

It may seem incredible that my bottle of champagne should have remained unbroached during this time, but such is the case. In my interest in crab and chicken farming I had quite forgotten it; but one day, when my landlord was gathering coconuts in a near-by grove, I asked him to share it with me. He was more than willing, and at the first glass his habitually reserved attitude toward me altered at once. I then learned the reason for this attitude. He told me that his last tenant, an Australian, had not only eaten bananas and coconuts to which he had no right, but had gone away without paying his rent. We drank confusion to this scurvy tenant wherever he might be. Several of my landlord's children had accompanied him to the house, and I shared with them the box of New Zealand chocolates. It was a merry little party, and after much pleasant talk my landlord left me with repeated expressions of good will. The following morning I found on my back verandah a large bunch of bananas and a gunny sack filled with oranges and mangoes, and thereafter I was never without these delicious fruits, gifts from my landlord and his family. Not infrequently Mata, his wife, would send me, by one of the children, baked fish, breadfruit, and mountain plantain wrapped in green leaves, fresh from her native oven. I was overwhelmed with benefits and remembered with deep gratitude that I owed them all to Hop Sing.

His garden was flourishing; all of the seeds I had given him had sprouted and gave promise of a rich harvest under his patient, ceaseless care. He was always at work, and so too was Mrs. Sing, despite the demands on her time made by three small children. Sometimes of a late afternoon I walked down to their place, and usually found Mrs. Sing in a shed back of the house, where she sorted and cleaned bunches of lettuce and string beans for the market. All of her members were busy at once. She rocked the smallest baby, which hung in a little cradle from a rafter, by means of a cord attached to her foot. Every now and then she would pull another cord which hung just above her head, and this one ran, by a system of pulleys, to the garden, where there was a sort of jumping-jack scarecrow to frighten away the mynah birds; and meanwhile the fresh vegetables got themselves cleaned and deftly packed in little baskets. Sing was a baker as well as a gardener, and four times per week, after his long day's toil, he made the rounds of the district selling crisp loaves and pineapple tarts to the native population. Invariably, during these excursions, he left something at my gate, either a tart or a loaf of bread or a basket of vegetables, and to my great relief nothing I could do or say served to dry up his fountain of gratitude for my wretched little gift of seed.

Under these circumstances the weeks passed so pleasantly and quickly that steamer day — the third since the posting of my manuscript — was at hand before I realized it. I walked into town once more and waited on the familiar bench for the distribution of the mail. I waited all through the afternoon until everyone in Papeete and its environs had called for their letters. I waited until the sun was sinking behind the mountains of Moorea and the post office was about to close. Then, summoning all my resolution, I mounted the steps and walked toward the delivery window, saying inwardly, "It's useless to ask; I'm quite certain to be disappointed." The girl who presided there went hastily through a small heap of letters.

"No, there's nothing for you," she said, smiling pleasantly.

I made a ghastly attempt to smile in return and was going toward the door when she called, "Oh! Just a moment! What name did you say?"

I repeated it, enunciating the words with the utmost care.

"Yes, there's one letter," she said. "Fifty centimes postage due."

Having paid this, I had left only a twenty-five-centime piece, the smallest coin in use in French Oceania. But little that mattered. The letter contained a gracious note accepting my manuscript, and a cheque for five hundred dollars!

To those living luxurious lives in the high latitudes five hundred dollars may seem a trifling sum, but to me it was a fortune. With the half of it I could pay the rental for my house and grounds for a period of nearly seven years, and, provided I lived as modestly in the future as I had in the immediate past, the two hundred and fifty remaining would suffice for other expenses for a much longer time. But now, with bright vistas of ease and plenty and peace of mind opening out before me, I found myself perversely considering the possibility of leaving Tahiti. The north-bound steamer to San Francisco was expected in three days' time, and I fell to considering the varied experience I might now have by virtue of movement and my five hundred dollars. Remembering my past fortunes as a journalist, I knew that it was the part of wisdom to stay here where living was, for the first time, within my means; and yet, if I did not go now, I might never again have enough money for a steamship ticket. I walked the streets long after everyone else was in bed, in an agony of indecision, and at last, as the clock in the cathedral was striking two, the decision was made.

Hop Sing was in town on the day of my departure. He had driven to market with garden produce, and both he and Lee Fat came to see me off. Fat insisted on my accepting a pair of Russian-leather bedroom-slippers and a Chinese fan of blue silk embroidered with gold butterflies. Sing's parting gift was a basket of tomatoes as large as oranges, and a dozen ears of sweet corn, Golden Bantam — the first fruits from the seeds I had given him. They smiled good-byes as the steamer backed away from the wharf; then I went at once to my cabin, in order that departure from that most beautiful of islands might be a little less poignant. While I was unpacking my bag the cabin steward looked in.

"You've been assigned to the doctor's table, sir," he said. "It's a table for four, but this trip there's only one other gentleman there besides the doctor."

"All right," I replied. "And by the way, will you please have this corn prepared and served at luncheon? Take a couple of ears for yourself if you care to."

"Thank you, sir. I guess the other gentleman at your table will be glad to see this. He ain't half complained about the food, and to tell you the truth, it's not what it might be."

The doctor did not come down for luncheon. I had just seated myself when the other passenger at his table came in. He was a tall, spare man with a drooping white moustache and a bilious complexion. He was dressed in a baggy linen coat, knickerbockers, and low white shoes. He sat down without even a nod in my direction and, adjusting a pair of nose-glasses, picked up the menu card, puffing out his cheeks as he examined it, letting the air escape slowly through his lips. He struck me as being a man hard to please in the matter of food, no matter how good it might be. He was partaking of a fish course of creamed tinned salmon when the steward brought in a platter with ten splendid ears of Golden Bantam corn steaming on it. He gazed at it in astonishment.

"Take this away," he said to the steward, pushing the dish of salmon to one side, "and bring me a plate."

Never have I seen a man give himself up to the enjoyment of food with such purely physical abandon. One would have thought he had not eaten for days. When he had finished his third ear he said, "Steward, where does this corn come from? It's not on the card."

"No, sir, it's not on the regular bill. It's a gift to the table from the gentleman sitting opposite you."

He gave me a quick glance as though he had just then become aware of my presence.

"Consider yourself thanked, sir," he said brusquely.

I nodded.

"Is this corn of your own growing?"

"Well, yes, in a sense," I replied.

He ploughed a hasty furrow along his fourth ear before speaking again. Then he said, "What do you mean by 'in a sense'? You either raised it or you didn't, I should think."

He had a waspish, peppery way of speaking, as though he had been long accustomed to asking whomever whatever he liked with the certainty of a deferential reply. In view of the fact that he was eating my — or rather Hop Sing's — corn, I felt that he might have made an effort at least to be gracious. Therefore I merely said, as coldly as possible, "Oh, you'd have to live at Tahiti to understand that." Having finished my luncheon, I rose, bowed slightly, and left him there, still eating corn.

Half an hour later I was standing at the rail, aft, watching the peak of Orofena, the highest mountain at Tahiti, disappearing below the horizon. A hand was laid on my arm, and turning I found my luncheon companion.

"Well, young man," he said, "one would say you were thinking of jumping overboard."

"I *have* been thinking of it," I replied, "but it's too far to swim back now."

"You like Tahiti as much as that? Well, I don't wonder. An island where they grow such delicious corn must be a good place to live. I ate six of those ears — finished the lot, in fact."

"I'm glad you enjoyed it," I replied.

"See here! You mustn't mind my manner. I've got dyspepsia, and a wayward liver and an enlarged spleen — Lord knows what all else the matter with me. Gives me a sort of jaundiced outlook on life. But I want you to know that I'm grateful. Sweet corn is one of the few things I can eat without suffering afterward. Now then, tell me something about your island. I didn't go ashore. Useless trying to see a place in six hours. It's only an aggravation."

I scarcely know how it came about, but within a few minutes I was talking as freely as to an old friend. I told him of the beauty of the islands, of the changing life, of the mingling races, of the strange outcroppings of savagery through the shale of what in those parts is called civilization. Presently I cut off short, thinking he might be bored.

"Not at all," he said. "Well, you've had an interesting time, evidently, and you seem to have made good use of your eyes and ears. Too bad you're not a journalist. I don't suppose you've ever tried your hand at writing?"

"Yes, occasionally," I replied. "In fact, journalism is my trade, if I may be said to have a trade."

"Got any of your stuff with you?"

"A few sketches."

"Do you mind letting me see them?"

"Not at all," I said; and so, at his suggestion, I brought him a small sheaf of things, six slight papers on various subjects, each of them about two thousand words in length. He settled himself in his deck-chair and adjusted his glasses.

"Come back in an hour's time," he said, "and I'll tell you what I think of them."

He thought two of them worthless, and curiously enough they were the ones I thought best.

"But these four are not bad. What do you want for them?"

"Do you mean you would like to buy them?"

"Yes, of course. But I forgot to tell you — I'm manager of a newspaper syndicate in America. We can use these sketches. Tropical-island stuff is always popular. It's all bosh about the waning of interest in the South Seas. It never wanes and never will as long as life is what it is in America. Well, what do you want for them?"

"Oh, I don't know," I said. I was about to add, "Would one hundred dollars be too much?" — meaning one hundred for the four — when he interrupted me.

"Give you a hundred and fifty each for them. Is that satisfactory?"

I admitted that it was — quite satisfactory.

Adam — "Our General Ancestor," as Milton calls him — was undoubtedly the first husbandman, and a highly successful one during the early part of his career. But, even under the exceptionally favorable conditions prevailing in the Garden of Eden before The Fall, I doubt whether he ever reaped a richer or more varied harvest than I did in my garden at Tahiti. And it all came from a dollar's worth of seed.

December 1925

ALFRED EDWARD NEWTON

1863–1940

He did not know, so he said, a kilowatt from an ampere, but he knew how to hire them that did and made a fortune in electrical circuits. But he was not a money-maker for nothing. He had grown up in a Yankee household dedicated to thrift. In that little cottage there was but one thing of value, a shelf of books, and on that shelf three dog-eared volumes of Boswell's Johnson. These volumes were Edward Newton's education. He knew them forwards; he knew them backwards. They opened a bay window into the Eighteenth Century and he jumped through it.

Our first acquaintance grew out of a letter he sent the Atlantic, *introducing the point at issue with so neat a quotation that I was enchanted with the incongruity of a literary epistle typed on the stationery of a candy manufacturer (for it seemed that that very month Newton was taking a flier in sugar-plums). He had written much but never for publication, and as our correspondence grew,* The Amenities of Book Collecting *came into being. No bacillus of such powerful potentiality has ever made its appearance since the virus of collecting first entered the American blood stream. The mustiness of old bookstores took on a luminous haze. First editions were chalked up to heights undreamed, and the princes of the trade, Rosenbach, Gabriel Wells, and George D. Smith became emperors in their own right.*

Newton was an intensely personal man, and it was the personal side of books he most enjoyed. Biography was his supreme delight, biography and the last catalogue from Sotheby's illustrating the next great sale. He loved to talk with Eighteenth Century men, with Chauncey Tinker, E. V. Lucas, Frederick Pottle, or R. B. Adam of Buffalo, Master of the Department Store, Master of the Age of Johnson, and the rest of the fraternity, gowned professors or lay brothers alike: but I am not sure whether he did not love best of all firing the hearts of youthful pilgrims who trooped to "Oak Knoll." They were for the most part graduates of his fan mail, who had or hoped to earn a hundred dollars to begin their collections by picking up first editions "uncut" of some neglected author. It was these disciples of his who set prices aflame, rummaging secondhand bookstores; young Aladdins trading new books for old ones and making glad the rusty hearts of booksellers, who, erasing the penciled "$1.50 remainder" on the flyleaf, could now make the book a bargain at "$15.00. Rare."

Blessed be prejudice! How it sharpens the outline of a man. If Newton loved, Newton hated. He hated cant, he loathed dullness, he execrated politics. Knowing nothing of America, he was convinced that west of Philadelphia lay sterile and unbroken desert. Light came only from the east, and every year to London he would go and for a month follow the footsteps of Doctor Johnson from Gough Square to Lichfield and back. Once again in London he would select each spring in Savile Row a shepherd's plaid that ticked a little louder than its predecessor, choose a dozen stiff round collars of the Yorkshire breed for his bureau drawer, catch Birkbeck Hill or John Burns for dinner, enjoy half a dozen evenings at the Old Vic, or with Gilbert and Sullivan; endow the house where Doctor Johnson lived in marvelous strange company; and then home to his electric circuit.

What joy he brought his friends: the plump checkerboard figure, the merry blue eye, the eruptive talk about books (the only things worth talking about); the contentious word about the President, always followed by a sputter; the parenthetic intimation that politics be damned; a choice story choicely told; an aphorism or two after the manner of the Great Cham; sparks flying everywhere and high above the buzz of conversation, the Newtonian pennant of victory snapping in the breeze.

When Newton died, mine was a sadder world. His passions it is true were never mine. First editions, uncut pages, foxed sheets, original wrappers; they are leather and prunella to me. Give me large print, good paper, wide margins, a volume light to the hand: these are my personal ultimates. But when it comes to an Association book, though I do not covet it as I covet a Persian miniature or a page of Caxton's Bible, or something beautiful like that, little tremors do shoot up and down my spine. How I should like to handle that copy of the Lyrical Ballads which the impudent Trelawney saw Wordsworth cutting with a buttery knife; and an affectionate inscription from James Boswell on the sacred flyleaf of The Life is delightful to me to behold. It was for such marginalia I used to look, browsing in Newton's Hesperidean library. These things are part and parcel of the "Caliph" as I see him standing under the portrait of Doctor Johnson overhanging his mantel, and my thoughts travel on to the scene of his Memorial Service.

Years before, while Newton was in his prime, I chanced to send him a transcription of a famous passage in a personal will and testament of another bookman, Edmond de Goncourt. Doubtless a dozen friends had likewise spoken of it, but I recall our letters about it and I have no doubt it became the inspiration of that Memorial Service, the most appropriate I have ever known, the most instinct with the personality which friends are called together to remember. No chapel was the scene of it, but an auction room where the possessions which enriched Newton's life on earth were distributed, not among the heirs of his body but among his spiritual inheritors who cultivated his delights and expanded with his emotions.

Here is the passage in Edmond de Goncourt's will: —

> My desire is that my drawings, my prints, my ornaments and my books, in a word the works of art which have made the happiness of my life, shall not endure the frigid Tomb of a museum and the lethargic glance of the indifferent passer-by; and I stipulate that they shall all be dispersed under the hammer of the auctioneer and that the beatitude which the acquisition of every item once gave me shall be again invoked for the delight of every inheritor of my tastes.

Never was Newton's presence more palpably felt than in the New York auction room on Fifty-seventh Street on that evening. The bookmen of the English-speaking world were there, the magnificoes of the trade interspersed with simple lovers of the language, librarians, troops of friends. The stage was set as if for a Greek tragedy: the altar of immolation in the center and the auctioneer standing beside it as the High Priest holding the hammer of Fate. Most of us were unaccustomed to the ritual of the auction room and little shivers of excitement ran through the rows when the bidding grew furious and some volume of peculiar glory was laid upon the block.

"Number 214!" cried the resonant voice of the auctioneer. There was a hush like that which precedes the reading of Scripture. "Number 214," an edition of The Life which bears this inscription: "To James Boswell, Esquire, Junior, from his affectionate father, the Authour."

The bids went up by thousands, then by hundreds. Minutes seemed hours and then came sudden silence as when a bell tolls the final notes. Going — Going — Gone.

Hardly had the audience recovered its equilibrium than Number 217 was announced.

"217, Boswell, James. A letter to the people of Scotland on the alarming Attempt to injure the Articles of the Union and Introducing a Most Pernicious Innovation by Diminishing the Number of Lords in Session. 8 vo., Full polished calf, gilt-edged, three or four leaves very slightly foxed."

"First edition, a most desirable Association Volume, being a presentation copy from James Boswell to Edmund Burke, inscribed on the verso of the half-title: 'To the Right Honourable Edmund Burke from the Authour.' "

Again the drama, the mounting thrill, the climax. The spindling volume hardly more than pamphlet size seemed pathetically slender in the midst of so mighty a fuss, but as it changed masters I felt a profound emotion. It was borne in on my soul that Eddie Newton was dead.

"What Might Have Been"

An Episode in the Life of Charles Lamb

A. EDWARD NEWTON

I

On a cold, raw day in December, 1882, there was laid to rest in Brompton Cemetery, in London, an old lady, — an actress, — whose name, Frances Maria Kelly, meant little to the generation of theatre-goers, then busy with the rising reputation of Henry Irving and Ellen Terry. She was a very old lady when she died — ninety-two, to be exact; she had outlived her fame and her friends, and few followed her to her grave.

I have said that the day was cold and raw. I do not know certainly that it was so; I was not there; but for my sins I have passed many Decembers in London, and take the right, in Charles Lamb's phrase, to damn the weather at a venture.

Fanny Kelly, as she was called by the generations that knew her, came of a theatrical family, and most of her long life had been passed on the stage. She was only seven when she made her first appearance at Drury Lane, at which theatre she acted for some thirty-six years, when she retired; subsequently she established a school of dramatic art and gave from time to time what she termed "Entertainments," in which she sometimes took as many as fourteen different parts in a single evening. With her death the last link connecting us with the age of Johnson was broken. She had acted with John Philip Kemble and with Mrs. Siddons. By her sprightliness and grace she had charmed Fox and Sheridan and the generations which followed, down to Charles Dickens, who had acted with her in private theatricals at her own private theatre in Dean Street, — now the Royalty, — taking the part of Captain Bobadil in *Every Man in his Humor*.

Nothing is more evanescent than the reputation of an actor. Every age lingers lovingly over the greatness of the actors of its own youth; thus it was that the theatre-goer of the eighteen-eighties only yawned when told of the grace of Miss Kelly's Ophelia, of the charm of her Lydia Languish, or of her bewitchingness in "breeches parts." To some she was the old actress for whom the government was being solicited to do something; a few thought of her as the old maiden lady who was obsessed with the idea that Charles Lamb had once made her an offer of marriage.

It was well known that, half a century before, Lamb had been one of her greatest admirers. Every reader of his dramatic criticisms and his letters knew that; they knew, too, that in one of his daintiest essays, perhaps the most exquisite essay in the language, "Dream Children, A Reverie," Lamb, speaking apparently more autobiographically than usual even for him, says, —

> Then I told how, for seven long years, in hope sometimes, sometimes in despair, yet persisting ever, I courted the fair Alice W——n; and, as much as children could understand, I explained to them what coyness, and difficulty, and denial meant to maidens — when suddenly, turning to Alice, the soul of the first Alice looked out at her eyes with such a reality of representment, that I became in doubt which of them stood there before me, or whose that bright hair was; and while I stood gazing, both the children gradually grew fainter to my view, receding and still receding, till nothing at last but two mournful features were seen in the uttermost distance, which, without speech, strangely impressed upon me the effects of speech: "We are not of Alice, nor of thee, nor are we children at all. The children of Alice call Bartrum father. We are nothing; less than nothing, and dreams. We are only what might have been."

I am quoting, not from the printed text, but from the original manuscript, which is my most cherished literary possession; and this lovely peroration, if such it may be called, is the only part of the essay which has been much interlineated or recast. It appears to have occasioned Lamb considerable difficulty; there was obviously some searching for the right word; a part of it, indeed, was entirely rewritten.

The coyness, the difficulty, and the denial of Alice: was it not immortally written into the record by Lamb himself? Miss Kelly's rejection of an offer of marriage from him must be a figment of the imagination of an old lady, who, as her years approached a century, had her dream-children, too — children who called Lamb father.

There the matter rested. Fanny Kelly was by way of being forgotten: all the facts of Lamb's life were known, apparently, and he had lain in a curiously neglected grave in Edmonton Churchyard for seventy years. Innumerable sketches and lives and memorials of him, "final" and otherwise, had been written and read. His letters — not complete, perhaps, but volumes of them — had been published and read by the constantly increasing number of his admirers, and no one suspected that Lamb had had a serious love-affair — the world accepting without reserve the statement of one of his biographers that "Lamb at the bidding of duty remained single, wedding himself to the sad fortunes of his sister."

Then, quite unexpectedly, in 1903, John Hollingshead, the former manager of the Gaiety Theatre, discovered and published two letters of Charles Lamb written on the same day, July 20, 1819. One, a long letter in Lamb's most serious vein, in which he formally offers his hand, and in a way his sister's, to Miss Kelly, and the other a whimsical, elfish letter, in which he tries to disguise the fact that in her refusal of him he has received a hard blow.

By reason of this important discovery, every line that Lamb had written in regard to Fanny Kelly was read with new interest, and an admirable biography of him by his latest and most sympathetic critic, Edward Verrall Lucas, appearing shortly afterwards, was carefully studied to see what, if any, further light could be thrown upon this interesting subject. But it appears that the whole story has been told in the letters, and students of Lamb were thrown back upon the already published references.

In the Works of Lamb, published in 1818, Lamb had addressed to Miss Kelly a sonnet:—

You are not, Kelly, of the common strain,
That stoop their pride and female honor down
To please that many-headed beast, the town,
And vend their lavish smiles and tricks for gain;
By fortune thrown amid the actor's train,
You keep your native dignity of thought;
The plaudits that attend you come unsought,
As tributes due unto your natural vein.
Your tears have passion in them, and a grace
Of genuine freshness, which our hearts avow;
Your smiles are winds whose ways we cannot trace,
That vanish and return we know not how—
And please the better from a pensive face,
And thoughtful eye, and a reflecting brow.

And early in the following year he had printed in a provincial journal an appreciation of her acting, comparing her, not unfavorably, with Mrs. Jordan, who, in her day, then over, is said to have had no rival in comedy parts.

Lamb's earliest reference to Miss Kelly, however, appears to be in a letter to the Wordsworths, in which he says that he can keep the accounts of his office, comparing sum with sum, writing "Paid" against one and "Unpaid" against t'other (this was long before the days of scientific bookkeeping and much-vaunted efficiency), and still reserve a corner of his mind for the memory of some passage from a book, or "the gleam of Fanny Kelly's divine plain face." This is an always quoted reference and seems correctly to describe the lady, who is spoken of by others as an unaffected, sensible, clear-headed, warm-hearted woman, plain but engaging, with none of the vanities or arrogance of the actress about her. It will be recalled that Lamb had no love for blue-stocking women, and speaking of one, said, "If she belonged to me I would lock her up and feed her on bread and water till she left off writing poetry. A female poet, or female author of any kind, ranks below an actress, I think." This shortest way with minor poets has, perhaps, much to recommend it.

It was Lamb's whim in his essays to be frequently misleading, setting his signals at full speed ahead when they should have been set at danger, or, at least, at caution. Thus in his charming essay "Barbara S——" (how unconsciously one invariably uses this adjective in speaking of anything Lamb wrote), after telling the story of a poor little stage waif, receiving by mistake a whole sovereign instead of the half a one justly due for a week's pay, and how she was tempted to keep it, but did not, he adds, "I had the anecdote from the mouth of the late Mrs. Crawford." Here seemed to be plain sailing, and grave editors pointed out who Mrs. Crawford was: they told her maiden name, and for good measure threw in the names of her several husbands. But Lamb, in a letter to Bernard Barton in 1825, speaking of these essays, said, "Tell me how you like 'Barbara S——.' I never saw Mrs. Crawford in my life, nevertheless 'tis all true of somebody." And some years later, not long before he died, to another correspondent he wrote, "As Miss Kelly is just now in notoriety,"—she was then giving an entertainment called "Dramatic Recollections" at the Strand Theatre,—"it may amuse you to know that 'Barbara S——' is all of it true of her, being all communicated to me from her own mouth. Can we not contrive to make up a party to see her?"

There is another reference to Miss Kelly, which, in the light of our subsequent knowledge, is as dainty a suggestion of marriage with her as can be found in the annals of courtship. It appeared in *The Examiner* just a fortnight before Lamb's proposal, which was shortly to follow. In a criticism of her acting as Rachel in *The Jovial Crew,* now forgotten, Lamb was, he says, interrupted in the enjoyment of the play by a stranger who sat beside him remarking of Miss Kelly, "What a lass that were to go a gypsying through the world with!" Knowing how frequently Lamb addressed Elia, his other self, and Elia, Lamb, may we not suppose that on this occasion the voice of the stranger was the voice of Elia? Was it unlikely that Miss Kelly, who would see the criticism, would hear the voice and recognize it as Lamb's? I love to linger over these delicate incidents of Lamb's courtship, which was all too brief.

II

But what of Mary? I think she cannot but have contemplated the likelihood of her brother's marriage and determined upon the line she would take in that event. Years before she had written, "You will smile when I tell you I think myself the only woman in the world who could live with a brother's wife, and make a real friend of her, partly from early observations of the unhappy example I have just given you, and partly from a knack I know I have of looking into people's real character, and never expecting them to act out of it—never expecting another to do as I would in the same case."

Mary Lamb was an exceptional woman; and even though her brother might have thought he kept the secret of his love to himself, she would know and, I fancy, approve. Was it not agreed between them that she was to die first? and when she was gone, who would be left to care for Charles?

Before I come to the little drama—tragedy one could hardly call it—of Lamb's love-affair as told in his own way by his letters, I may be permitted to refer to two letters of his to Miss Kelly, one of them relatively unimportant, the other a few lines only, both unpublished, which form a part of my own Lamb collection. These letters, before they fell from high estate, formed a part of the "Sentimental Library" of Harry B. Smith, to whom I am indebted for much information concerning them. It will be seen that both these letters work themselves into the story of Lamb's love-affair, which I am trying to tell. So far as is known, four letters are all that he ever addressed to the lady: the two above referred to, and the proposal and its sequel, in the collection of Mr. Huntington of New York, where I saw them not long ago. I have held valuable letters in my hand before, but this letter of Lamb! I confess to an emotional feeling with which the mere book-collector is rarely credited. The earlier and briefer letter is pasted into a copy of the first edition of the *Works of Charles Lamb,* 1818, "in boards, shaken," which occupies a place of honor on my shelves. It reads: "Mr. Lamb, having taken the liberty of addressing a slight compliment to Miss Kelly in his first volume, respectfully requests her acceptance of the collection, 7 June, 1818." The compliment, of course, is the sonnet already quoted.

The second letter was written just ten days before Lamb asked Miss Kelly to marry him. The bones playfully referred to were small ivory discs, about the size of a two-shilling piece, which were allotted to leading performers for the use of their friends, giving admission to the pit. On one side was the name of the theatre; on the other the name of the actor or actress to whom they were allotted. The letter reads: —

Dear Miss Kelly, —

If your bones are not engaged on Monday night, will you favor us with the use of them? I know, if you can oblige us, you will make no bones about it; if you cannot, it shall break none betwixt us. We might ask somebody else; but we do not like the bones of any strange animal. We should be welcome to dear Miss Linton's, but then she is so plump there is no getting at them. I should prefer Miss Iver's — they must be ivory, I take it for granted — but she is married to Mr. ——, and become bone of his bone; consequently can have none of her own to dispose of. Well, it all comes to this: if you can let us have them, you will, I dare say; if you cannot, God rest your bones. I am at an end of my bon-mots.

C. Lamb.

9th *July,* 1819.

This characteristic note in Lamb's best punning manner ("I fancy I succeed best in epistles of mere fun; puns and that nonsense") may be regarded as a prologue to the drama played ten days later, the whole occupying but the space of a single day.

And now the curtain is lifted on the play in which Lamb and Miss Kelly are the chief actors. Lamb is in his lodgings in Great Russell Street, Covent Garden, the individual spot he likes best in all London. Bow Street Police Court can be seen through the window, and Mary Lamb seated thereby, knitting, glances into the busy street as she sees a crowd of people follow in the wake of a constable, conducting a thief to his examination. Lamb is seated at a table, writing. We, unseen, may glance over his shoulder and see the letter which he has just finished.

Dear Miss Kelly, — We had the pleasure, *pain,* I might better call it, of seeing you last night in the new Play. It was a most consummate piece of acting, but what a task for you to undergo! at a time when your heart is sore from real sorrow! It has given rise to a train of thinking, which I cannot suppress.

Would to God you were released from this way of life; that you could bring your mind to consent to take your lot with us, and throw off forever the whole burden of your Profession. I neither expect nor wish you to take notice of this which I am writing, in your present over-occupied & hurried state.—But to think of it at your pleasure. I have quite income enough, if that were to justify me for making such a proposal, with what I may call even a handsome provision for my survivor. What you possess of your own would naturally be appropriated to those for whose sakes chiefly you have made so many hard sacrifices. I am not so foolish as not to know that I am a most unworthy match for such a one as you, but you have for years been a principal object in my mind. In many a sweet assumed character I have learned to love you, but simply as F. M. Kelly I love you better than them all. Can you quit these shadows of existence, & come & be a reality to us? Can you leave off harassing yourself to please a thankless multitude, who know nothing of you, & begin at last to live to yourself & your friends?

As plainly & frankly as I have seen you give or refuse assent in some feigned scene, so frankly do me the justice to answer me. It is impossible I should feel injured or aggrieved by your telling me at once, that the proposal does not suit you. It is impossible that I should ever think of molesting you with idle importunity and persecution after your mind [is] once firmly spoken—but happier, far happier, could I have leave to hope a time might come when our friends might be your friends; our interests yours; our book-knowledge, if in that inconsiderable particular we have any little advantage, might impart something to you, which you would every day have it in your power ten thousand fold to repay by the added cheerfulness and joy which you could not fail to bring as a dowry into whatever family should have the honor and happiness of receiving *you,* the most welcome accession that could be made to it.

In haste, but with entire respect & deepest affection, I subscribe myself

C. Lamb.

20 *July,* 1819.

No punning or nonsense here. It is the most serious letter Lamb ever wrote—a letter so fine, so manly, so honorable in the man who wrote it, so honoring to the woman to whom it was addressed, that, knowing Lamb as we do, it can hardly be read without a lump in the throat and eyes suffused with tears. The letter is folded and sealed and sent by a serving-maid to the lady, who lives hard by in Henrietta Street, just the other side of Covent Garden—and the curtain falls.

Before the next act we are at liberty to wonder how Lamb passed the time while Miss Kelly was writing her reply. Did he go off to the "dull drudgery of the desk's dead wood" at East India House, and there busy himself with the prices of silks or tea or indigo, or did he wander about the streets of his beloved London? I fancy the latter. In any event the curtain rises a few hours later, and Lamb and his sister are seen as before. She has laid aside her knitting. It is late afternoon. Lamb is seated at the table endeavoring to read, when a maid enters and hands him a letter; he breaks the seal eagerly. Again we look over his shoulder and read: —

HENRIETTA STREET, *July* 20th, 1819.

An early & deeply rooted attachment has fixed my heart on one from whom no worldly prospect can well induce me to withdraw it, but while I thus frankly & decidedly decline your proposal, believe me, I am not insensible to the high honour which the preference of such a mind as yours confers upon me — let me, however, hope that all thought upon this subject will end with this letter, & that you henceforth encourage no other sentiment towards me than esteem in my private character and a continuance of that approbation of my humble talents which you have already expressed so much and so often to my advantage and gratification.

Believe me I feel proud to acknowledge myself

Your obliged friend

F. M. KELLY.

Lamb rises from his chair and attempts to walk over to where Mary is sitting; but his feelings overcome him, and he sinks back in his chair again as the curtain falls. It moves quickly, the action of this little drama. The curtain is down but a moment, suggesting the passage of a single hour. When it is raised, Lamb is alone; he is but forty-five, but looks an old man. The curtains are drawn, lighted candles are on the table. We hear the rain against the windows. Lamb is writing, and for the last time we intrude upon his privacy.

Now poor Charles Lamb, now dear Charles Lamb, "Saint Charles," if you will! Our hearts go out to him; we would comfort him if we could. But read slowly one of the finest letters in all literature: a letter in which he accepts defeat instantly, but with a smile on his face; tears there may have been in his eyes, but she was not to see them. See Lamb in his supreme rôle — *of a man.* How often had he urged his friends to play that difficult part — which no one could play better than he. The letter reads: —

DEAR MISS KELLY, — *Your injunctions shall be obeyed to a tittle.* I feel myself in a lackadaisical no-how-ish kind of a humor. I believe it is the rain, or something. I had thought to have written seriously, but I fancy I succeed best in epistles of mere fun; puns & that nonsense. You will be good friends with us, will you not? Let what has past "break no bones" between us. You will not refuse us them next time we send for them?

Yours very truly,
C. L.

P. S. Do you observe the delicacy of not signing my full name?
N. B. Do not paste that last letter of mine into your book.

We sometimes say the English are not good losers. To think of Charles Lamb may help us to correct that opinion. All good plays of the period have an epilogue. By all means this should have one; and ten days later Lamb himself provided it. It appeared in *The Examiner,* where, speaking of Fanny Kelly's acting in "The Hypocrite," he said, —

She is in truth not framed to tease or torment even in jest, but to utter a hearty Yes or No; to yield or refuse assent with a noble sincerity. We have not the pleasure of being acquainted with her, but we have been told that she carries the same cordial manners into private life.

The curtain falls! The play is at an end.

May 1918

THOMAS BAILEY ALDRICH

1836–1907

Thomas Bailey Aldrich was not genuine Boston as he liked to say, but Boston-plated. Bred in the ancestral mansion at Portsmouth, New Hampshire, celebrated in his Story of a Bad Boy *(one of the happiest chronicles in the whole history of mischief), he wandered about the country in company with his restless father. Turned loose in New York at sixteen, he cultivated for decades the vicissitudes of periodical journalism. Lady Luck was coy. One fragile magazine after another sank with him on board, but Aldrich himself was quite unsinkable. His epitaph on one such demise is admirable. "This paper," he wrote, "is discontinued for lack of funds which is, by a coincidence, precisely the reason for which it was started." But, sink or swim, Aldrich kept his pen sharp and acquired a delicate mastery of the trade of writing both prose and verse, abhorring in his soul the slop and slither of journalism. His delicate ear detected the faintest dissonance in verse or frailty in prose. When, in 1881, he succeeded Mr. Howells in the* Atlantic *chair, he brought with him the hopeless gospel of perfection. Breadth and range he lacked but never taste.*

In his pleasant biography Ferris Greenslet has this to say of the fourth Editor of the Atlantic: —

> *He chose for his purpose a little back room at No. 4 Park Street, reached by a spiral stairway much resembling the pictures of Dante's Purgatorio with the terrestrial Paradise at its summit. Its windows overlooked that haunt of ancient peace, the Old Granary Burying-Ground, where, as he liked to say, lay those who would never submit any more manuscript. But any melancholy that might have arisen from the scenery was mitigated by an open fire of cannel coal, by a pipe, — an engine which had not hitherto been in favor in that office, but which was expressly nominated in the bond between the editor and his publisher, — and by the constant attendance of his setter "Trip." Once when Trip ate a sonnet, Aldrich asked, "How did he know it was doggerel?"*

If you disbelieve all this read "Two Bites at a Cherry."

Two Bites at a Cherry

THOMAS BAILEY ALDRICH

I

As they both were Americans, and typical Americans, it ought to have happened in their own country. But destiny has no nationality, and consequently no patriotism; so it happened in Naples.

When Marcus Whitelaw strolled out of his hotel that May morning, and let himself drift with the crowd along the Strada del Duomo until he reached the portals of the ancient cathedral, nothing was more remote from his meditation than Mrs. Rose Mason. He had not seen her for fifteen years, and he had not thought of her, except in an intermittent fashion, for seven or eight. There had, however, been a period, covering possibly four years, when he had thought of little else. During that heavy interim he had gone about with a pang in his bosom, — a pang that had been very keen at the beginning, and then had gradually lost its edge. Later on, that unmaterialized hand which obliterates even the deep-carved grief on headstones effectually smoothed out the dent in Whitelaw's heart.

Rose Jenness at nineteen had been singularly adapted to making dents in certain kinds of hearts. Her candor and unselfishness, her disdain of insincerity in others, and her unconsciousness of the spells she cast had proved more fatal to Whitelaw than the most studied coquetry would have done. In the deepest stress of his trouble he was denied the consolation of being able to reproach her with duplicity. He had built up his leaning tower of hopes without any aid from her. She had been nothing but frank and unmisleading from first to last. Her beauty she could not help. She came of a line of stately men and handsome women. Sir Peter Lely painted them in Charles the Second's time, and Copley found them ready for his canvas in the colonial period. Through some remote cross of Saxon and Latin blood the women of this family had always been fair and the men dark. In Rose Jenness the two characteristics flowered. When New England produces a blonde with the eyes of a brunette, the world cannot easily match her, especially if she have that rounded slenderness of figure which is one of our very best Americanisms.

Without this blended beauty, which came to perfection in her suddenly, like the blossoms on a fruit-tree, Whitelaw would have loved

Rose all the same. Indeed, her physical loveliness had counted for little in his passion, though it had afterwards haunted him almost maliciously. That she was fair of person who had so many gracious traits of mind and disposition was a matter of course. He had been slower than others in detecting the charm that wrapt her as she slipped into womanhood. They had grown up together as children, and had known no separation, except during the three years Whitelaw was with the Army of the Potomac, — an absence broken by several returns to the North on recruiting service, and one long sojourn after a dangerous hurt received at Antietam. He never knew when he began to love Rose, and he never knew the exact moment when he ceased to love her. But between these two indefinable points he had experienced an unhappiness that was anything but indefinite. It had been something tangible and measurable; and it had changed the course of his career.

Next to time, there is no surer medicine than hard work for the kind of disappointment we have indicated. Unfortunately for Whitelaw, he was moderately rich by inheritance, and when he discovered that Rose's candid affection was not love, he could afford to indulge his wretchedness. He had been anxious for distinction, for her sake; but now his ambition was gone. Of what value to him were worldly prizes, if she refused to share them? He presently withdrew from the legal profession, in which he had given promise of becoming a brilliant pleader, who had pleaded so unsuccessfully for himself, and went abroad. This was of course after the war.[1]

It was not her fault that all communication between them ceased then and there. He would have it so. The affair had not been without its bitterness for Rose. Whitelaw was linked in some way with every agreeable reminiscence of her life; she could not remember the time when she was not fond of him. There had been a poignancy in the regret with which Rose had seen the friend who was dear to her transforming himself into a lover for whom she did not care in the least. It had pained her to give him pain, and she had done it with tears in her eyes.

Eighteen months later Rose was Mrs. Mason, tears and all. Richard Mason was a Pacific Railroad king *en herbe,* with a palace in San Francisco, whither he immediately transported his bride. The news reached Whitelaw in Seville, and gave him a twinge. His love, according to his own diagnosis, was already dead; it was presumably, then, a mus-

[1] What a comment on the placid eighties! Americans had but one war to refer to. E. S.

cular contraction that caused it to turn a little in its coffin. The following year some question of investment brought him back to the United States, where he traveled extensively, carefully avoiding California. He visited Salt Lake City, however, and took cynical satisfaction in observing what a large amount of connubial misery there was to the square foot. Yet when a rumor came to him, some time subsequently, that Rose herself was not very happy in her marriage, he had the grace to be sincerely sorry. "The poor transplanted Rose!" he murmured. "She was too good for him; she was too good for anybody."

This was four years after she had refused to be his wife; time had brought the philosophic mind, and he could look back upon the episode with tender calmness, and the desire to do justice to every one. Meanwhile, Rose had had a boy. Whitelaw's feelings in respect to him were complicated.

Seven or eight years went by, the greater part of which Whitelaw passed in England. There he heard nothing of Mrs. Mason, and when in America he heard very little. The marriage had not been fortunate, the Masons were enormously wealthy, and she was a beauty still. The Delaneys had met her, one winter, at Santa Barbara. Her letters home had grown more and more infrequent, and finally ceased. Her father had died, and the family was broken up and scattered. People whom nobody knew occupied the old mansion on the slope of Beacon Hill. One of the last spells of the past was lifted for Whitelaw when he saw strange faces looking out of those sun-purpled window-panes.

If Whitelaw thought of Mrs. Mason at intervals, it was with less distinctness on each occasion; the old love-passage, when he recalled it of an evening over his cigar, or in the course of some solitary walk, had a sort of phantasmal quality about it. The sharp grief that was to have lasted forever had resolved itself into a painless memory. He was now on that chilly side of forty where one begins to take ceremonious leave of one's illusions, and prefers Burgundy to Champagne.

When the announcement of Richard Mason's death was telegraphed East, Whitelaw read the telegram in his morning paper with scarcely more emotion than was shown by the man who sat opposite him reading the stock quotations. This was in a carriage on the Sixth Avenue elevated railway; for Whitelaw chanced to be in New York at the moment, making preparations for an extended tour in Russia and its dependencies. The Russian journey proved richer in novelty than he had anticipated, and he remained nearly three years in the land of the Tsars. On returning to western Europe he was seized with the humor to revisit certain of the Italian cities,—Ravenna, Rome, Venice, and Naples. It was in Naples that he found himself on that particular May morning to which reference has been made.

Whitelaw had never before happened to be in the city during the *festa* of San Gennaro. There are three of these festivals annually,—in May, September, and December. He had fallen upon the most picturesque of the series. The miracle of the Liquefaction of the Blood of St. Januarius was to take place at nine o'clock that forenoon in the cathedral, and it was a spectacle which Whitelaw had often desired to witness.

So it was that he followed the crowd along the sunny *strada,* and shouldered his way into the church, where the great candles were already lighted. The cool atmosphere of the interior, pleasantly touched with that snuffy, musky odor which haunts Italian churches, was refreshing after the incandescent heat outside. He did not mind being ten or twelve minutes too early.

Whitelaw had managed to secure a position not far from the altar-rail, and was settling himself comfortably to enjoy the ceremony, with his back braced against a marble column, when his eyes fell upon the profile of a lady who was standing about five yards in advance of him in an oblique line.

II

For an instant that face seemed to Whitelaw a part of the theatric unreality which always impresses one in Roman Catholic churches abroad. The sudden transition from the white glare of the street into the semi-twilight of the spacious nave; the soft bloom of the stained windows; the carving and gilding of choir and reredos; the draperies and frescoes; and the ghostly forms of incense slowly stretching upward, like some of Blake's weird shapes, to blend themselves with the shadows among the Gothic arches,—all these instantly conspire to lift one from the commonplace level of life. With such accessories, and in certain moods, the mind pliantly lends itself to the incredible.

During possibly thirty seconds Whitelaw might have been mistaken for the mate of one of those half-length figures in alto-relievo set against the neighboring pilasters, so grotesque and wooden was his expression. Then he gave a perceptible start. That gold hair, in waves of its own on the low brows, the sombre eyelashes,—he could not see her eyes from where he stood,—the poise of the head, the modeling of the throat,—whom could that be but Rose Jenness? He had involuntarily eliminated the Mason element, for the sight of her had taken him straight back to the days when there were no Pacific Railroad despots.

Fifteen years (good heavens! was it fifteen years?) had not touched a curve of the tall, slight figure. He was struck by that, as she stood there, with her satin basque buttoned up to the lace neckerchief knotted under her chin, for an insidious chill lurked in the air. The garment fitted closely, accentuating every line of the slender waist and flower-like full bust. At the left of the corsage was a bunch of violets, held by a small silver clasp, — the self-same violets, he was tempted to believe, that she had worn the evening he parted with her tragically in the back drawing-room of the house on Beacon Hill. Neither she nor they had faded. All the details of that parting flashed upon him with strange vividness: the figure-piece by Hunt above the funereal fireplace; the crimson India shawl hurriedly thrown over the back of a chair and trailing on the floor; Rose standing in the middle of the dimly-lighted room and holding out to him an appealing hand, which he refused to take. He remembered noticing, as he went home, dazed, through the moonlight, that the crisp crocuses were in bloom in the little front yards of the houses on Mount Vernon Street. It was May then, and it was May now, and there stood Rose. As he gazed at her a queer sense of old comradeship — the old friendship that had gone to sleep when love awakened — began softly to stir in his bosom.

Rose in Italy! Then he recollected one of the past rumors that had floated to him touching her desire for foreign travel, and Mason's sordid absorption in his railway schemes. Now that she was untrammeled, she had come abroad. She had probably left home with her son soon after Mason's death, and had been flitting from one Continental city to another ever since, in the tiresome American fashion. That might well have befallen without Whitelaw hearing of it in Russia. The lists of new arrivals were the things he avoided in reading *Galignani,* just as he habitually avoided the newly arrived themselves.

There was no hesitation in his mind as to the course he should pursue. The moment he could move he would go to Rose, and greet her without embarrassment or any *arrière pensée.* It was impracticable to move at present, for the people were packed about him as solidly as dates in a crate. Meanwhile, he had the freedom of his eyes. He amused himself with recognizing and classifying one by one certain evidences of individuality in Rose's taste in the matter of dress. The hat, so subdued in color and sparing of ornament as to make it a mystery where the rich effect came from, — there was a great deal of her in that. He would have identified it at once as Rose's hat if he had picked it up in the Desert of Sahara. Noting this, and the long mouse-colored gloves which reached to the elbow, and would have reached to the shoulder if they had been drawn out smooth, Whitelaw murmured to himself, "Rue de la Paix!" He had a sensation of contiguity to a pair of high-heeled kid boots with rosettes at the instep, such as are worn in all weathers by aristocratic shepherdesses in Watteau's pink landscapes. That, however, was an unprovoked incursion into the territory of conjecture, for Whitelaw could see only the upper portion of Rose.

He was glad, since accident had thrown them together, that accident had not done it in the first twelvemonth of Rose's widowhood. Any mortuary display on her part would, he felt, have jarred the wrong note in him, and spoiled the pleasure of meeting her. But she was out of mourning now; the man was dead, had been dead three years, and ought to have lived and died in the pterodactyl period, to which he properly belonged. Here Whitelaw paused in his musing, and smiled at his own heat, with a transient humorous perception of it. Let the man go; what was the use of thinking about him?

Dismissing the late Richard Mason, who really had not been a prehistoric monster, and had left Mrs. Mason a large fortune to do what she liked with, Whitelaw fell to thinking about Rose's son. He must be quite thirteen years old, our friend reflected. What an absurdly young-looking woman Rose was to be the mother of a thirteen-year-old boy! — doubtless a sad scapegrace, answering to the definition which Whitelaw remembered that one of his strong-minded countrywomen had given of the typical bad boy, — a boy who looks like his mother and behaves like his father. Did Rose's son look like his mother?

Just then Rose slightly turned her head, and Whitelaw fancied that he detected an inquiring, vaguely anxious expression in her features, as if she were searching for some one in the assemblage. "She is looking for young Mason," he soliloquized; which was precisely the fact. She glanced over the church, stared for an instant straight past Whitelaw, and then resumed her former position. He had prepared himself to meet her gaze; but she had not seen him. And now a tall Englishman, with an eyeglass that gleamed like a head-light, came and planted himself, as if with malice prepense, between the two Americans.

"The idiot!" muttered Whitelaw, between his teeth.

Up to the present point he had paid no attention whatever to St.

Januarius. The apparition of his early love, in what might be called the bloom of youth, was as much miracle as he could take in at once. Moreover, the whole of her was here, and only a fragment of the saint. Whitelaw was now made aware, by an expectant surging of the crowd in front and the craning of innumerable necks behind him, that something important was on the tapis.

A priest, in ordinary non-sacramental costume, had placed on the altar, from which all but the permanent decorations had been removed, a life-size bust of St. Januarius in gold and silver, inclosing the remains of the martyr's skull. Having performed this act, the priest, who for the occasion represented the archbishop, took his stand at the left of the dais. Immediately afterwards a procession of holy fathers, headed by acolytes bearing lighted candelabra, issued from behind the high altar, where the saints' relics are kept in a tabernacle on off days and nights. An imposing personage half-way down the file carried a tall brass monstrance, in which was suspended by a ring an oblong flat crystal flask, or case, set in an antique reliquary of silver, with handles at each end. This contained the phenomenal blood.

Having deposited the monstrance on the altar, the custodian reverently detached the relic, and faced the audience. As he held up the flask by the handles and slowly turned it round, those nearest could distinguish through the blurred surface a dark yellowish opaque substance, occupying about two thirds of the vessel. It was apparently a solid mass, which in a liquid form might have filled a couple of sherry glasses. The legend runs that the thoughtful Roman lady who gathered the blood from the ground with a sponge inadvertently let drop a bit of straw into the original phial. This identical straw, which appears when the lump is in a state of solution, is considered a strong piece of circumstantial evidence. It is a remarkable fact, and one that by itself establishes the authenticity of San Gennaro, that several of his female descendants always assist at the liquefaction, — a row of very aged and very untidy Neapolitan ladies, to whom places of honor are given on these occasions.

Shut out from Rose, — for the obnoxious Englishman completely blockaded her, — Whitelaw lent himself with faintly stimulated interest to the ceremony, which was now well under way. He was doubtful of many things, and especially skeptical as to matters supernatural. Accepting the miracle at its own valuation, — at par value, as he put it, — what conceivable profit could accrue to mankind from the smelting of that poor old gentleman's coagulated blood? How had all this mediæval mummery survived the darkness in which it was born!

With half-listless eye, Whitelaw watched the priest as he stood at the rail, facing the spectators and solemnly reversing the reliquary. From time to time he paused, and held a lighted candle behind the flask in order to ascertain if any change had taken place, and then resumed operations amid the breathless silence. An atmosphere charged with suspense seemed to have settled upon the vast throng.

Six — eight — ten minutes passed. The priest had several times repeated his investigation; but the burnt-sienna-like mass held to its consistency. In life St. Januarius must have been a person of considerable firmness, a quality which his blood appeared still to retain, even after the lapse of more than fourteen centuries.

A thrill of disappointment and dismay ran through the multitude. The miracle was not working; in fact, had refused to work! The attendants behind the chancel rail wore perturbed faces. Two of the brothers turned to the altar and began saying the Athanasian Creed, while here and there a half-inarticulate prayer or a deep muttering of protest took flight from the congregation; for the Neapolitans insist on a certain degree of punctuality in St. Januarius. Any unreasonable delay on his part is portentous of dire calamity to the city, — earthquake or pestilence. The least that can be predicted is an eruption of Mount Vesuvius. Even so late as the eighteenth century a failure of the miracle usually led to panic and violence. To-day such a result is hardly possible, though in the rare instances when the martyr procrastinates a little the populace fall to upbraiding their patron saint with a vehemence that is quite as illogical in its way.

Whitelaw himself was nearly ripe to join in some such demonstration. Transfixed to the marble column, — like a second St. Sebastian, — and pierced with innumerable elbows, he had grown very impatient of the whole business. There was Rose within twenty feet of him, and he could neither approach her nor see her! He heartily wished that when Proconsul Dracontius threw St. Januarius to the lions, in the amphitheatre of Pozzuoli, the lions had not left a shred of him, instead of tamely lapping his hand. Then Dracontius would not have been obliged to behead the man; then that Roman lady would not have come along with her sponge; then he, Marcus Whitelaw, a free-born American citizen, would not have been kept standing there a lifetime, waiting for an opportunity to say a word to his old love!

He felt that he had much to say to Rose. The barrier which had separated him from her all these years had been swept away. The whole situation was changed. If she were willing to accept the friendship which she once stipulated as the only tie possible between them, he was ready to extend it to her now. If she had not altered, if she remained her old candid, cordial self, what a pleasure it would be to him to act as her cicerone in Naples!—for Naples was probably *terra incognita* to Rose. There were delightful drives along the Riviere di Chiaia; excursions to Pompeii, Baiæ, and Solfatara; trips by steamer to Capri, Sorrento, and Amalfi. He pictured the two of them drifting in a boat into the sapphirine enchantment of the Blue Grotto at Capri,—the three of them, rather; for "By Jove!" he reflected, "we should have to take the boy with us." This reflection somewhat dashed his spirits. The juvenile Mason would be a little bore; and if he didn't look like his mother, and *did* look like his father, the youth would be a great bore. Now as Whitelaw had never seen the late Mr. Mason, or even a counterfeit presentment of him, any resemblance that might chance to exist between the father and the son was not likely to prove aggressive. This reflection also occurred to Whitelaw, and caused him to smile. He had a touch of that national gift of humorous self-introspection which enables Americans, almost alone among human bipeds, to smile at their own expense.

While these matters were passing through his mind, and he had given up all hope of extricating himself from his predicament until the end of the ceremony, a sudden eddy swirled round the column, the crowd wavered and broke, and Whitelaw was free. The disintegration of the living mass was only momentary, but before it could close together again he had contrived to get three yards away from the site of his martyrdom. Further advance then became difficult. By dint of pushing and diplomatic elbowing he presently gained another yard. The goal was almost won.

A moment later he stood at Rose's side.

III

Rose had her head turned three quarters to the right, and was unaware that any one had supplanted the tall English gentleman recently looming on her left. Whitelaw drew a long breath, and did not speak at once, but stood biting his under lip with an air of comic irresolution. He was painfully conscious that it was comic. He had, in fact, fallen into an absurd perplexity. How should he address her? He did not quite dare to call her "Rose," and every fibre of his being revolted against calling her "Mrs. Mason." Yet he must address her in some fashion, and instantly. There was one alternative, — not to address her. He bent down a little, and touched her lightly on the shoulder.

The lady wheeled sharply, with a movement that must have been characteristic of her, and faced him. There was no hesitation or reservation in voice or manner as she exclaimed, "Marc!" and gave one of the mouse-colored gloves into his keeping for twenty seconds or so. She had spoken rather loud, forgetting circumstance and place in her surprise, and several of the masculine bystanders smiled sympathetically on *la bella Americana.* There was the old ring to her voice, and it vibrated musically on Whitelaw's ear.

"Rose," he said, in an undertone, "I can't tell you how glad I am of this. I begin to believe that things are planned for me better than I can plan them."

"This was planned charmingly, — but it was odd to make us meet in Naples, when we have so much room at home to meet in."

"The odd feature of it to me is that it doesn't appear odd. I don't see how anything else could have happened without breaking all the laws of probability."

"It seems much too good to be true," said Rose gayly.

She was unaffectedly happy over the encounter, and the manner of it. She had caused Whitelaw a deep mortification in days passed, and though it had been the consequence of no fault of her own — had, indeed, been entirely Whitelaw's — she had always wanted the assurance of his forgiveness. That he had withheld through long years; and now he forgave her. She read the pardon in his voice and eyes. Rose scanned him a little curiously, though with no overt act of curiosity. He had grown stouter, but the added fullness was not unbecoming: he used to be too spare for his stature. His sharp New England face belonged to a type that seldom loses its angles. The scar, in the shape of a cross, on his left cheek was decorative. The handsomely moulded upper lip was better without the mustache. There were silvery glints here and there where the chestnut hair was brushed back from the temples. These first few scattering snowflakes of time went well with his bronzed complexion; for he was as brown as an Indian, from travel. On the whole, fifteen years had decidedly adorned him.

"How long have you been here? — in Naples, I mean," questioned Whitelaw, again under his breath.

"A week; and you?"

"Since yesterday. I came chiefly for this *festa.*"

"I didn't dream you were so devout."

"The conversion is recent; but henceforth I swear by St. Januarius through thick and thin, though as a general thing I prefer him thin,—when it doesn't take too long."

"If any one should hear you!" whispered Rose, glancing round furtively.

"Why, the Church itself doesn't cling very strongly to the miracle nowadays, and would gladly be rid of it; but the simple folk of the Santa Lucia quarter and the outlying volcanoes insist on having their St. Januarius. I imagine it would cost a revolution to banish him. Rose, when did you leave home?"

"Last March. Hush!" she added, laying a finger to her lip. "Something is happening in the chancel."

The martyr's blood had finally given signs of taking the proper sanguine hue, to the intense relief of the populace, from which arose a dull multitudinous murmur, like that of a distant swarm of bees. The priest, with a gleam of beatific triumph in his cavernous eyes, was holding the reliquary high aloft. The vast congregation swayed to and fro, and some tumult was created by devotees in the background endeavoring to obtain coignes of vantage nearer the altar.

"Surely, you have not trusted yourself alone in this place," said Whitelaw.

"No, I'm with you," Rose answered, smiling.

"But you didn't come unattended?"

"Richard came with me: we got separated immediately on entering the cathedral, and lost each other."

"Richard,—that's the name of your son," remarked Whitelaw, after a pause. The father's name!

"Yes, and I want you to see him. He's a fine fellow."

"I should like to see him," said Whitelaw, perfunctorily.

"He is very clever,—not like me."

"I hope he's as unaware of his cleverness as you are of yours, Rose."

"I'm quite aware of mine. I only said that his was different. That spoils your compliment. He's to remain over here at school,—in Germany,—if I can make up my mind in the autumn to leave him. When do you return to America, Marc?"

"In the autumn," said Whitelaw, promptly, a little to his own surprise, for until then he really had had no plan.

"Perhaps we can arrange to go back on the same steamer," suggested Rose. "We crossed in the *Cuba,* and liked her. She's advertised to sail on the 17th of September: how would that suit you, for example?"

The suggestion smiled upon Whitelaw, and he was about to reply, when a peal from the great organ, announcing the consummation of the miracle, reverberated through the church and cut him short. As the thunders died away, the voices of chanting priests ascended from the chancel, where some choir-boys were strewing rose leaves over the marble steps leading to the altar. At the same moment the boom of a heavy gun, fired from the ramparts of the Castel dell' Ovo, shook the windows. The city ordnance was saluting St. Januarius, — a custom that has since fallen into desuetude.

"Look!" exclaimed Rose, laying her hand impulsively on Whitelaw's arm. "See the birds! That's an exquisite fancy!"

A flock of sparrows had been let loose, and were beating the misty air with uncertain wings, darting hither and thither through the nave and under the arches, in search of resting-places on frieze and cornice and jutting stonework. Meanwhile the priest had stepped down from the dais, and was passing among the people, who crowded round him to press their lips and foreheads to the flask inclosed in the reliquary. The less devotional, and those who had already performed the rite, were slowly wending their way to the various outlets on the strada.

"I am glad it's over," declared Whitelaw.

"To think," observed Rose, reflectively, "that he has got to go all through it again to-morrow!"

"Who?"

"That poor dear saint."

"Oh," laughed Whitelaw, "I thought you meant me. He doesn't mind it; it's his profession. There are objects more deserving of your pity: I, for instance, who have no sort of talent for martyrdom. You should have seen me, — pinned to that column, like an entomological specimen, for forty mortal minutes! I wouldn't go through it again for a great deal."

"Not for the sake of meeting an old friend?"

"It was the old friend that made it particularly intolerable. To be so near her, and not able to speak to her; and part of the time not to have even the consolation of seeing the sweep of the ring-dove's wing on the left side of her new Paris hat!"

Rose looked up into his face, and smiled in a half-absent way. She was far from averse to having a detail of her toilet noticed by those she liked. In former days Whitelaw had had a quick eye in such trifles, and his remark seemed to her a veritable little piece of the pleasant past, with an odd, suggestive flavor about it. She had slipped her hand through his arm, and the pair were moving leisurely with the stream towards one of the leather-screened doors opening upon the vestibule. The manner in which Rose lent herself to his step, and a certain subtile something he recognized in the light pressure of her weight, carried him, in his turn, very far back into the olden time. The fifteen years, like the two and thirty years in Tennyson's lyric, were as a mist that rolls away. It appeared to Whitelaw as if they had never been separated, or had parted only yesterday. How naturally and sweetly she had picked up the dropped thread of the old friendship! The novelty of her presence had evaporated at the first words she had spoken; only the pleasure of it remained. To him there was nothing strange or unexpected in their wholly unexpected and entirely strange meeting. As he had told her, he did not see how anything else could have happened. Already he had acquired the habit of being with her!

"Good heavens!" he said to himself, "it can't be that I am falling in love with Rose over again!"

The idea brought a flickering smile to Whitelaw's lips, — the idea of falling in love at first sight, after a decade and a half!

"What are you smiling at?" she demanded, looking up alertly.

"I didn't know I was smiling."

"But you were; and an unexplained smile, when two persons are alone together, with two thousand others, is as inadmissible as whispering in company."

Whitelaw glanced at her with an amused, partly embarrassed expression, and made no response. They were passing at the instant through a narrow strip of daylight slanted from one of the great blazoned windows, and he was enabled to see Rose's face with more distinctness than he hitherto had done. If it had lost something of its springtide bloom and outline, — and he saw that that was so, — it had gained a beauty of a rarer and richer sort. There was a deeper lustre to the dark-fringed eyes, as if they had learned to think, and a greater tenderness in the curves of the mouth, as if it had learned to be less imperious. How handsome she was, — handsomer than she had been at nineteen!

In his rapid survey Whitelaw's eye had lighted on the small clasp holding the violets to her corsage, — and rested there. The faint flush that came to his cheek gradually deepened.

"Is that the clasp I gave you when you were a girl?" he finally asked.

"You recognize it? — yes."

"And you've kept the trifle all these centuries!"

"That's not polite,—when I was a girl! I kept it because it was a birthday gift, because it *was* a trifle; then from habit, and now the centuries have turned it into a bit of priceless bric-à-brac."

Somehow Rose's explanation did not seem to him quite so exquisite as the fact itself.

Whitelaw was now conscious of a very perceptible acceleration in the flow of the current that was bearing them towards the cathedral entrance. It was not his purpose that they should reach it just yet. Their brief dialogue, carried on in undertone, and the early part of it with ecclesiastical interruptions, had been desultory and unsatisfying. He should of course see much of Rose during her stay in Naples, for he had no intention of leaving it while she remained; but the opportunity of having her to himself might not re-occur, and he had certain things to say to her which could not be said under any other condition. So many opportunities of various kinds had escaped him in the course of life that he resolved not to let this one slip. On the right of the eastern transept, he remembered, was a heavenly little chapel,—the chapel of the Seripandis,—where they might converse without restraint, if once they could get there.

Watching his chance, Whitelaw began a skillful oblique movement, and in a few minutes the two found themselves free of the crowd and in front of a gilded iron fencing, the gate of which stood open.

"But this isn't the way out!" exclaimed Rose.

"I'm aware of it," said Whitelaw. "You've never visited the church before, have you?"

"No."

"Then you ought to see some of the chapels. They contain things by Spagnoletto, Domenichino, and others. In this one, for instance, is an Assumption by Perugino. It would be a pity to miss that, now you are on the spot."

"I'm afraid I haven't time for sightseeing, Marc," she answered, drawing out a diminutive watch and pressing a spring in the stem. "I've an engagement at ten"—

"Well, that leaves you more than half an hour," he interrupted, glancing over Rose's shoulder at the timepiece.

"But meanwhile, Richard will be searching for me everywhere."

"Then he can't fail to find you here," said Whitelaw adroitly. "He has probably given you up, however, and gone back to the hotel."

"Perhaps he has," assented Rose, irresolutely.

"In which case, I'll take you home, or wherever you wish to be taken, when it's necessary for you to go."

"Oh, I'll not trouble you. The carriage was ordered to wait at the corner just below the church,—the driver wasn't able to get nearer. That was to be our point of rendezvous. I don't know—perhaps I ought to go now."

Rose stood a second or two in an attitude of pretty hesitation, with her hand resting on one of the spear-heads of the gate; then she stepped into the chapel.

IV

"It isn't Perugino at his best," said Whitelaw, after a silence; "it has been restored in places, and not well done. I like some of his smaller canvases; but I don't greatly care for Perugino."

"Then why on earth have you dragged me in here to see it?" cried Rose.

"Because I care for you," he answered, smiling at the justice of her sudden wrath. As he turned away from the painting his countenance became grave.

"You've an original way of showing it. If I cared for any one, I wouldn't pick out objects of no interest for her to look at."

"Frankly, Rose, I wasn't willing to let you go so soon. I wanted a quiet half hour's talk with you. I had two or three serious things to say,—things that have long been on my mind,—and a chapel seemed the only fitting place to say them in."

This rather solemn exordium caused Rose to lift her eyelashes curiously.

"I want to speak of the past," said Whitelaw.

"No, don't let us speak of that," she protested hurriedly.

"After all this time, Rose, I think I have a kind of right"—

"No, Marc, you have no right whatever"—

—"to ask your forgiveness."

"My forgiveness—for what?"

"For my long silence, and sullenness, and brutality generally. It wasn't a crime in you not to love me in the old days, and I acted as if I regarded it as one. I was without any justification in going away from you in the mood I did that night."

"I was very, very sorry," said Rose gently.

"I should at once have accepted the situation, and remained your friend. That was a man's part, and I failed to play it. After a while, when I had recovered my reason, it was too late. It appears to be one of the conditions, if not the sole condition, of my existence that I should be too late. The occasion always slips away from me. When your — when I heard of Mr. Mason's death, if I had been another man, I'd have written to you, — sent you some sort of kindly message, for the old time's sake. The impulse to do so came to me three months afterwards. I sat down one day and began to write; then the futility and untimeliness of the whole thing struck me, and I tore up the letter."

"I wish you had not," said Rose. "A word from you then, or before Mr. Mason's death, would have been welcome to me. I was never willing to lose your friendship. After your first return from Europe, and you were seeing something of your own country, as every American ought to do, I hoped that you would visit San Francisco. I greatly desired that you should come and tell me, of your free will, that I was not to blame. If I had been, perhaps I wouldn't have cared."

"You were blameless from beginning to end. I don't believe you ever said or did an insincere thing in your life, Rose. I simply misunderstood. The whole story lies in that. You were magnanimous to waste any thought whatever upon me. When I reflect on my own ungenerous attitude I am ashamed to beg your pardon."

"I've not anything to forgive," Rose replied; and then she added, looking at him with a half-rueful smile, "I suppose it was unavoidable, under the circumstances, that we should touch on this matter. Perhaps it was the only way to exorcise the ghost of the past. At all events, I am glad that you've said what you have; and now let it go. Tell me about yourself, Marc."

"I wish I could. There's no more biography to me than if I were Shakespeare."

"What have you done all this while?"

"Nothing."

"Where have you been?"

"Everywhere."

"No pursuit, no study, no profession?"

"Oh, yes; I'm a professional nomad, — an alien wherever I go. I'm an Englishman in America, and an American in England. They don't let up on me in either country."

"Isn't there a kind of vanity in self-disparagement, Marc? Seriously, if you are not doing your own case injustice, hasn't this been a rather empty career? A colonel at twenty-four, and nothing ever after!"

"Precisely,—just as if I had been killed at Antietam." He wanted to say, "on Beacon Hill."

"With your equipment, every path was open to you. Most men have to earn their daily bread with one hand, while they are working for higher things with the other. You had only the honors to struggle for. To give up one's native land, and spend years in aimless wandering from place to place,—it seems positively wicked."

"I've had some conscience in the matter," pleaded Whitelaw: "I might have written books of travel, and made a stock-company of my *ennui*."

"You ought to have married, Marc," said Rose sententiously.

"I?" Whitelaw stared at her. How could Rose say a thing like that!

"Every man ought to marry," she supplemented.

"I admit the general proposition," he returned, slowly, "but I object to the personal application. To the mass of mankind,—meaning also womankind,—marriage may be the only possible thing; but to the individual, it may be the one thing impossible. I would put the formula this way: Every one ought to wish to marry; some ought to be allowed to marry; and others ought to marry twice,—to make the average good."

"That sounds Shakespearean,—like your biography; but I don't think I've quite caught the idea."

"I'm positive that *I* haven't," said Whitelaw, with a short laugh. "It was my purpose to pay a handsome tribute to matrimony, and to beg to be excused."

Rose remained silent a moment, with one finger pressed against her cheek, making a little round white dent in it, and her eyes fixed upon the kneeling figure of Cardinal Carafa at the left of Perugino's picture. Then she turned, and fixed her eyes upon Whitelaw's figure.

"Have you never," she asked,—"have you never, in all your journeyings, met a woman whom you liked?"

"I cannot answer you," he responded gravely, "without treading on forbidden ground. May I do that? When I first came abroad, I fancy I rather hated women,—that was one of the mild manifestations of my general insanity. Later, my hatred changed to morbid fastidiousness. My early education had spoiled me. I have, of course, met many admirable women, and admired them—at a safe distance."

"And thrown away your opportunities."

"But if I loved no one?"

"Admiration would have served."

"I don't agree with you, Rose."

"A man may do worse than make what the world calls a not wholly happy marriage."

Whitelaw glanced at her out of the corner of his eye. Was that an allusion to the late Richard Mason? The directness was characteristic of Rose; but the remark was a trifle too direct for *convenance*. If there were any esoteric intent in the words, her face did not betray it. But women can look less conscious than men.

"It seems to me," she went on, "that even an unromantic, commonplace union would have been better than the lonely, irresponsible life you have led, accepting your own statement of it, — which I don't wholly. A man should have duties outside of himself; without them he is a mere balloon, inflated with thin egotism, and drifting nowhere."

"I don't accept the balloon," protested Whitelaw, not taking kindly to Rose's metaphor. "That presupposes a certain internal specific buoyancy which I haven't, if I ever had it. My type in the inanimate kingdom would be a diving-machine continually going down into wrecks in which there isn't anything to bring up. I would have it ultimately find the one precious ingot in the world."

"Oh, Marc," cried Rose, earnestly, with just a diverting little touch of maternal solicitude in the gesture she made, — "oh, Marc, I hope some day to see you happily married."

"You don't think it too late, then?"

"Too late? Why, you are only forty-three; and what if you were seventy-three? *On a l'âge de son cœur.*"

"Mine throws no light on the subject," said Whitelaw, with a thrill which he instantly repressed. "I suspect that my heart must be largely feminine, for it refuses to tell me its real age. At any rate, I don't trust it. Just now it is trying to pass itself off for twenty-five or thirty."

From time to time, in the course of this conversation, a shadow, not attributable to any of the overhanging sculpture of the little Gothic chapel, had rested on Whitelaw's countenance. He had been assailed by strange surprises and conflicting doubts. Five or ten minutes before, the idea of again falling in love with Rose had made him smile. But was he not doing it, had he not done it, or, rather, had he not always loved her, more or less unconsciously? And Rose? Her very candor perplexed and baffled him, as of old. She had always been a stout little Puritan, with her sense of duty; but that did not adequately explain the warmth with which she had reproved him for his aimless way of life. Why should his way of life so deeply concern her, unless . . . unless . . . In certain things she had said there had been a significance that seemed perfectly clear to him, though it had not lain upon the surface of the spoken words. Why had she questioned him so inquisitorially? Why had she desired to know if he had formed any new lines of attachment? That indirect reference to her own unfortunate marriage? And then—though she explained it lightly—had she not worn his boyish gift on her bosom through all those years? The suggestion that they should return home on the same steamer contained in itself a whole little drama. What if destiny had brought him and Rose together at last! He did not dare think of it; he did not dare acknowledge to himself that he wished it.

Whitelaw was now standing in the centre of the contracted apartment, a few feet from his companion, and regarding her meditatively. The cloud was gone from his brow, and a soft light had come into the clear gray eyes. Her phrase curled itself cunningly about his heart,—*on a l'âge de son cœur!* He was afraid to speak again, lest an uncontrollable impulse should hurry him into speaking of his love; and that, he felt, would indeed be precipitate. But the silence which had followed his last remark was growing awkwardly long. He must break it with some platitude, if he could summon one.

"Now that my anatomization is ended," he said, tentatively, "isn't it your turn, Rose? I have made a poor showing, as I warned you I should."

"My life has been fuller than yours," she returned, bending her eyes upon him seriously, "and richer. I have had such duties and pleasures as fall to most women, and such sorrow as falls to many. . . . I have lost a child."

The pathos of the simple words smote Whitelaw to the heart. "I—I had not heard," he faltered; and a feeling of infinite tenderness for her came over him. If he had dared, he would have gone to Rose and put his arm around her; but he did not dare. He stood riveted to the marble floor, gazing at her mutely.

"I did not mean to refer to that," she said, looking up, with a lingering dimness in the purple lashes. "No, don't let us talk any more of the past. Speak to me of something else, please."

"The future," said Whitelaw: "that can give us no pain—until it comes, and is gone. What are your plans for the summer?"

"We shall travel. I want Richard to see as much as he can before he's tied down to his studies, poor fellow!"

"Where do you intend to leave him at school?" inquired Whitelaw, with a quite recent interest in Richard.

"At Heidelberg or Leipsic: it is not decided."

"And meanwhile what's to be your route of travel?"

"We shall go to Sweden and Norway, and perhaps to Russia. I don't know why, but it has been one of the dreams of my life to see the great fair at Nijni-Novgorod."

"It is worth seeing," said Whitelaw.

"It will be at its height in August,—a convenient time for us. We could scarcely expect to reach St. Petersburg before August."

"I have just returned from Russia," he said, "after three years of it."

"Then you can give me some suggestions."

"Traveling there has numerous drawbacks, unless one knows the language. French, which serves everywhere in western Europe, is nearly useless in the majority of places. All educated Russians, of course, speak French or German; but railway-guards and drosky-drivers, and the persons with whom the mere tourist is brought most in contact, know only Russian."

"But we've an excellent courier," rejoined Rose, "who speaks all the tongues of Babel. His English is something superb."

"When do you start northward?" asked Whitelaw, turning on her quickly, with a sudden subtile prescience of defeated plans.

"To-morrow."

"To-morrow!" he echoed, in consternation. "Then I am to see nothing of you!"

"If you've no engagement for to-night, come to the hotel. I should be very glad to"—

"Where are you staying?"

"At the United States, on the Chiatamone, like true patriots."

"I've no engagement," said Whitelaw, bewilderedly.

Rose to leave Naples to-morrow! That killed all his projects,—the excursions in the environs, and all! She was slipping through his fingers . . . he was losing her forever! There was no time for temporizing or hesitation. He must never speak, or speak now. Perhaps it would not seem abrupt or even strange to her. If so, Rose should remember that his position as a lover was exceptional,—he had done his wooing fifteen years before! He confessed to himself—and he had often confessed it to that same severe critic of manners—that possibly his wooing had been somewhat lacking in dash and persistence then. But to-day he would win her, as he might perhaps have won her years ago, if he had not been infirm of purpose, or pigeon-livered, or too proud,—which was it? He had let a single word repulse him, when the chances were he might have carried her by storm, or taken her by siege. How young he must have seemed, even in her young eyes! Now he had experience and knowledge of the world, and would not be denied. The doubts and misgivings that had clouded his mind for the last quarter of an hour were blown away like meadow-mists at sunrise. At last he saw clearly. He loved Rose; he had never really loved her until this moment! For other men there were other methods; there was but one course for him. No; he would not go to the hotel that night—as a suitor. His fate should be sealed then and there, in the chapel of the Seripandis.

Whitelaw straightened himself, wavering for an instant, like a jib-sheet when it loses the wind; then he crossed the narrow strip of tessellated pavement that lay between him and Rose, and stood directly in front of her.

"Rose," he said, and there was a strange pallor creeping into his cheeks, "there have been two miracles wrought in this church to-day. It is not only St. Januarius who has, in a manner, come to life again. I, too, have come to life. I've returned once more to the world of living men and women. Do not send me back! Let *me* take you and your boy to Russia, Rose!"

Rose gave a start, and cast a swift, horrified look at Whitelaw's face. "Marc!" she cried, convulsively grasping the wrist of the hand which he had held out to her, "is it possible you haven't heard—has no one told you—don't you *know* that I have married again"—

She stopped abruptly, and released his wrist.

A man in a frayed, well-brushed coat, with a courier's satchel depending from a strap over his shoulder, was standing outside the iron grille which separated the chapel from the main church.

"Madama," said the courier, as he respectfully approached through the gate, "it is ten o'clock. The Signor Schuyler and Master Richard are waiting with the carriage at the corner of the Strada dell' Anticgolia. They bade me inform Madama."

January 1886

HENRY VILLARD

1835–1900

Henry Villard was no ordinary journalist. Both before and after his experiences with Lincoln he lived a life of intensity and vast variety. Scion of a distinguished Bavarian family, his republican outlook early clashed with his father's conservatism and, when the time for his military service approached, the young adventurer decamped to America and followed the immigrant's path from job to job. Learning English as he went, he became a reporter for the German-American press, ran a country newspaper, and graduated into the larger sphere of the great New York dailies. After Lincoln's much debated speech at Columbus Villard wrote to the New York Herald that the President-elect was "a man of immense force and power, tremendously rough and tremendously honest," and, in spite of his sour antipathy to Lincoln, the owner of the paper, James Gordon Bennett, let the phrase stand.

The Lincoln of this story is not the more than mortal of Sandburg's saga. The mists of legend had not closed about him. Villard draws him in his habit as he lived — shrewd, loutish, powerful, wrestling with his angel.

It must be remembered that Villard wrote his recollections some forty years after the event. But he had his dispatches to guide him and probably his notes, so that the vivid picture of Lincoln here set down holds much of its primal freshness.

Villard's subsequent career often lent itself to cynical interpretation, especially as regards the collapse of the Northern Pacific Railroad under his management, but his record as a master builder of American transportation still stands.

As a historical document this story contains two minute errors and, as every Lincolnian student works with a microscope at his elbow, I chronicle them. When his train took the President-elect to Washington, there was certainly a larger crowd than "about a hundred people" crowding the platform, and Mrs. Lincoln did not join her husband until the train reached Indianapolis. These are minutiae. In its large outline this is a unique portrait of Lincoln, written by a dispassionate observer of sound, quick, and penetrating mind. Nothing perhaps is more remarkable about it than that the reporter was a young man of twenty-five, still a German citizen, and with an acquaintance with the English language that had not been in existence seven full years.

Recollections of Lincoln

HENRY VILLARD

I

THE first joint debate between Douglas and Lincoln which I attended (the second in the series of seven) took place on the afternoon of August 27, 1858, at Freeport, Illinois. It was the great event of the day, and attracted an immense concourse of people from all parts of the state. Douglas spoke first for an hour, followed by Lincoln for an hour and a half; upon which the former closed in another half hour. The Democratic spokesman commanded a strong, sonorous voice, a rapid, vigorous utterance, a telling play of countenance, impressive gestures, and all the other arts of the practiced speaker. As far as all external conditions were concerned, there was nothing in favor of Lincoln. He had a lean, lank, indescribably gawky figure, an odd-featured, wrinkled, inexpressive, and altogether uncomely face. He used singularly awkward, almost absurd, up-and-down and sidewise movements of his body to give emphasis to his arguments. His voice was naturally good, but he frequently raised it to an unnatural pitch. Yet the unprejudiced mind felt at once that, while there was on the one side a skillful dialectician and debater arguing a wrong and weak cause, there was on the other a thoroughly earnest and truthful man, inspired by sound convictions in consonance with the true spirit of American institutions. There was nothing in all Douglas's powerful effort that appealed to the higher instincts of human nature, while Lincoln always touched sympathetic chords. Lincoln's speech excited and sustained the enthusiasm of his audience to the end. When he had finished, two stalwart young farmers rushed on the platform, and, in spite of his remonstrances, seized and put him on their shoulders and carried him in that uncomfortable posture for a considerable distance. It was really a ludicrous sight to see the grotesque figure holding frantically to the heads of his supporters, with his legs dangling from their shoulders, and his pantaloons pulled up so as to expose his underwear almost to his knees. Douglas made dexterous use of this incident in his next speech, expressing sincere regret that, against his wish, he had used up his old friend Lincoln so completely that he had to be carried off the stage. Lincoln retaliated by saying at the first opportunity that he had known Judge Douglas long and well, but there was nevertheless one thing he could not say of him, and that was that the Judge always told the truth.

I was introduced to Lincoln at Freeport, and met him frequently afterwards in the course of the campaign. I must say frankly that, although I found him most approachable, good-natured, and full of wit and humor, I could not take a real personal liking to the man, owing to an inborn weakness for which he was even then notorious and so remained during his great public career. He was inordinately fond of jokes, anecdotes, and stories. He loved to hear them, and still more to tell them himself out of the inexhaustible supply provided by his good memory and his fertile fancy. There would have been no harm in this but for the fact that, the coarser the joke, the lower the anecdote, and the more risky the story, the more he enjoyed them, especially when they were of his own invention. He possessed, moreover, a singular ingenuity in bringing about occasions in conversation for indulgences of this kind. I have to confess, too, that, aside from the prejudice against him which I felt on this account, I shared the belief of a good many independent thinkers at the time, including prominent leaders of the Republican party, that, with regard to separating more effectively the anti-slavery Northern from the pro-slavery Southern wing of the Democracy, it would have been better if the reëlection of Douglas had not been opposed.

The party warfare was hotly continued in all parts of the state from early summer till election day in November. Besides the seven joint debates, both Douglas and Lincoln spoke scores of times separately, and numerous other speakers from Illinois and other states contributed incessantly to the agitation. The two leaders visited almost every county in the state. I heard four of the joint debates, and six other speeches by Lincoln and eight by his competitor. Of course, the later efforts became substantial repetitions of the preceding ones, and to listen to them grew more and more tiresome to me. As I had seen something of political campaigns before, this one did not exercise the full charm of novelty upon me. Still, even if I had been a far more callous observer, I could not have helped being struck with the efficient party organizations, the skillful tactics of the managers, the remarkable feats of popular oratory, and the earnestness and enthusiasm of the audiences I witnessed. It was a most instructive object-lesson in practical party politics, and filled me with admiration for the Anglo-American method of working out popular destiny.

In other respects, my experiences were not altogether agreeable. It was a very hot summer, and I was obliged to travel almost continuously. Illinois had then only about a million and a half of inhabitants, poorly constructed railroads, and bad country roads, over which latter I had to journey quite as much as over the former. The taverns in town and country, as a rule, were wretched; and, as I moved about with the candidates and their followers and encountered crowds everywhere, I fared miserably in many places. Especially in the southern part of the state, then known as "Egypt" and mostly inhabited by settlers from the Southern states, food and lodging were nearly always simply abominable. I still vividly remember the day of semi-starvation, and the night with half-a-dozen room-mates, I passed at Jonesboro', where the third joint debate took place.

I firmly believe that, if Stephen A. Douglas had lived, he would have had a brilliant national career. Freed by the Southern rebellion from all identification with pro-slavery interests, the road would have been open to the highest fame and position for which his unusual talents qualified him. As I took final leave of him and Lincoln, doubtless neither of them had any idea that within two years they would be rivals again in the Presidential race. I had it from Lincoln's own lips that the United States Senatorship was the greatest political height he at the time expected to climb. He was full of doubt, too, of his ability to secure the majority of the Legislature against Douglas. These confidences he imparted to me on a special occasion which I must not omit to mention in detail before leaving this subject.

He and I met accidentally, about nine o'clock on a hot, sultry evening, at a flag railroad station about twenty miles west of Springfield, on my return from a great meeting at Petersburg in Menard County. He had been driven to the station in a buggy and left there alone. I was already there. The train that we intended to take for Springfield was about due. After vainly waiting for half an hour for its arrival, a thunderstorm compelled us to take refuge in an empty freight car standing on a side track, there being no buildings of any sort at the station. We squatted down on the floor of the car and fell to talking on all sorts of subjects. It was then and there he told me that, when he was clerking in a country store, his highest political ambition was to be a member of the state Legislature. "Since then, of course," he said laughingly, "I have grown some, but my friends got me into *this* business [meaning the canvass]. I did not consider myself qualified for the United States Senate, and it took me a long time to persuade myself that I was. Now, to be sure," he continued, with another of his peculiar laughs, "I am convinced that I am good enough for it; but, in spite of it all, I am saying to myself every day: 'It is too big a thing for you; you will never get it.' Mary [his wife] insists, however, that I am going to be Senator and President of the United States, too." These last words he followed with a roar of laughter, with his arms around his knees, and shaking all over with mirth at his wife's ambition. "Just think," he exclaimed, "of such a sucker as me as President!"

He then fell to asking questions regarding my antecedents, and expressed some surprise at my fluent use of English after so short a residence in the United States. Next he wanted to know whether it was true that most of the educated people in Germany were "infidels." I answered that they were not openly professed infidels, but such a conclusion might be drawn from the fact that most of them were not church-goers. "I do not wonder at that," he rejoined; "my own inclination is that way." I ventured to give expression to my own disbelief in the doctrine of the Christian Church relative to the existence of God, the divinity of Christ, and immortality. This led him to put other questions to me to draw me out. He did not commit himself, but I received the impression that he was of my own way of thinking. It was no surprise to me, therefore, to find in the writings of his biographers Ward Hill Lamon and W. H. Herndon that I had correctly understood him. Our talk continued till half-past ten, when the belated train arrived. I cherish this accidental rencontre as one of my most precious recollections, since my companion of that night has become one of the greatest figures in history.

I went from Jonesboro' to Chicago, and remained there till after the election. I considered the outcome so uncertain that I did not venture any predictions in my correspondence. Douglas himself, I knew, was much in doubt; Lincoln and his friends were very confident, and therefore bitterly disappointed by the result.

LINCOLN AND THE BUFFALO ROBE

[In 1859 Mr. Villard went as correspondent of the *Cincinnati Commercial* to Colorado to report upon the newly discovered gold regions. On his return journey over the plains, which was made in a two-horse wagon, there occurred the meeting described by him as follows: —]

About thirty miles from St. Joseph an extraordinary incident occurred. A buggy with two occupants was coming toward us over the open prairie. As it approached, I thought I recognized one of them, and, sure enough, it turned out to be no less a person than Abraham Lincoln! I stopped the wagon, called him by name, and jumped off to shake hands. He did not recognize me with my full beard and pioneer's costume. When I said, "Don't you know me?" and gave my name, he looked at me, most amazed, and then burst out laughing. "Why, good gracious! you look like a real Pike's Peaker." His surprise at this unexpected meeting was as great as mine. He was on a lecturing tour through Kansas. It was a cold morning, and the wind blew cuttingly from the northwest. He was shivering in the open buggy, without even a roof over it, in a short overcoat, and without any covering for his legs. I offered him one of my buffalo robes, which he gratefully accepted. He undertook, of course, to return it to me, but I never saw it again. After ten minutes' chat, we separated. The next time I saw him he was the Republican candidate for the Presidency.

II

[In the last days of November, 1860, the Associated Press sent Mr. Villard to Springfield, Illinois, to report current events at that place by telegraph, until the departure of Mr. Lincoln for Washington. This duty brought Mr. Villard into daily relations with the President-elect, who gave him a most friendly welcome and bade him ask for information at any time he wished it.]

Mr. Lincoln soon found, after his election, that his modest two-story frame dwelling was altogether inadequate for the throng of local callers and of visitors from a distance, and, accordingly, he gladly availed himself of the offer of the use of the governor's room in the Capitol building. On my arrival, he had already commenced spending a good part of each day in it. He appeared daily, except Sundays, between nine and ten o'clock, and held a reception till noon, to which all comers were admitted, without even the formality of first sending in cards. Whoever chose to call received the same hearty greeting. At noon, he went home to dinner and reappeared at about two. Then his correspondence was given proper attention, and visitors of distinction were seen by special appointment at either the State House or the hotel. Occasionally, but very rarely, he passed some time in his law office. In the evening, old friends called at his home for the exchange of news and political views. At times, when important news was expected, he would go to the telegraph or newspaper offices after supper, and stay there till late. Altogether, probably no other president-elect was so approachable to everybody, at least during the first weeks of my stay. But he found in the end, as was to be expected, that this popular practice involved a good deal of fatigue, and that he needed more time for himself; and the hours he gave up to the public were gradually restricted.

I was present almost daily for more or less time during his morning receptions. I generally remained a silent listener, as I could get at him at other hours when I was in need of information. It was a most interesting study to watch the manner of his intercourse with callers. As a rule, he showed remarkable tact in dealing with each of them, whether they were rough-looking Sangamon County farmers still addressing him familiarly as "Abe," sleek and pert commercial travelers, staid merchants, sharp politicians, or preachers, lawyers, or other professional men. He showed a very quick and shrewd perception of and adaptation to individual characteristics and peculiarities. He never evaded a proper question, or failed to give a fit answer. He was ever ready for an argument, which always had an original flavor, and, as a rule, he got the better in the discussion. There was, however, one limitation to the freedom of his talks with his visitors. A great many of them naturally tried to draw him out as to his future policy as President regarding the secession movement in the South, but he would not commit himself. The most remarkable and attractive feature of those daily "levees," however, was his constant indulgence of his story-telling propensity. Of course, all the visitors had heard of it and were eager for the privilege of listening to a practical illustration of his preëminence in that line. He knew this, and took special delight in meeting their wishes. He never was at a loss for a story or an anecdote to explain a meaning or enforce a point, the aptness of which was always perfect. His supply was apparently inexhaustible, and the stories sounded so real that it was hard to determine whether he repeated what he had heard from others, or had invented himself.

None of his hearers enjoyed the wit — and wit was an unfailing ingredient — of his stories half as much as he did himself. It was a joy indeed to see the effect upon him. A high-pitched laughter lighted up his otherwise melancholy countenance with thorough merriment. His body shook all over with gleeful emotion, and when he felt particularly good over his performance, he followed his habit of drawing his knees, with his arms around them, up to his very face, as I had seen him do in 1858. I am sorry to state that he often allowed himself altogether too much license in the concoction of the stories. He seemed to be bent upon making his hit by fair means or foul. In other words, he never hesitated to tell a coarse or even outright nasty story, if it served his purpose. All his personal friends could bear testimony on this point. It was a notorious fact that this fondness for low talk clung to him even in the White House. More than once I heard him "with malice aforethought" get off purposely some repulsive fiction in order to rid himself of an uncomfortable caller. Again and again I felt disgust and humiliation that such a person should have been called upon to direct the destinies of a great nation in the direst period of its history. Yet his achievements during the next few years proved him to be one of the great leaders of mankind in adversity, in whom low leanings only set off more strikingly his better qualities. At the time of which I speak, I could not have persuaded myself that the man might possibly possess true greatness of mind and nobility of heart. I do not wish to convey the idea, however, that he was mainly given to trivialities and vulgarities in his conversation; for, in spite of his frequent outbreaks of low humor, his was really a very sober and serious nature, and even inclined to gloominess to such an extent that all his biographers have attributed a strongly melancholic disposition to him.

I often availed myself of his authorization to come to him at any time for information. There were two questions in which the public, of course, felt the deepest interest, and upon which I was expected to supply light, namely, the composition of his Cabinet, and his views upon the secession movement that was daily growing in extent and strength. As to the former, he gave me to understand early, by indirection, that, as everybody expected, William H. Seward and S. P. Chase, his competitors for the presidential nomination, would be among his constitutional advisers. It was hardly possible for him not to recognize them, and he steadily turned a deaf ear to the remonstrances that were made against them as "extreme men" by leading politicians from the Border States, particularly from Kentucky and Missouri. As to the remaining members of his Cabinet, they were definitely selected much later, and after a protracted and wearisome tussle with the delegations of various states that came to Springfield to urge the claims of their "favorite sons." I shall refer again to this subject.

No one who heard him talk upon the other question could fail to discover his "other side," and to be impressed with his deep earnestness, his anxious contemplation of public affairs, and his thorough sense of the extraordinary responsibilities that were coming upon him. He never refused to talk with me about secession, but generally evaded answers to specific interrogatories, and confined himself to generalizations. I was present at a number of conversations which he had with leading public men upon the same subject, when he showed the same reserve. He did not hesitate to say that the Union ought to, and in his opinion would, be preserved, and to go into long arguments in support of the proposition, based upon the history of the republic, the homogeneity of the population, the natural features of the country, such as the common coast, the rivers and mountains, that compelled political and commercial unity. But he could not be got to say what he would do in the face of Southern secession, except that as President he should be sworn to maintain the Constitution of the United States, and that he was therefore bound to fulfill that duty. He met in the same general way the frequent questions whether he should consider it his duty to resort to coercion by force of arms against the states engaged in attempts to secede. In connection therewith I understood him, however, several times to express doubts as to the practicability of holding the slave states in the Union by main force, if they were all determined to break it up. He was often embarrassed by efforts of radical anti-slavery men to get something out of him in encouragement of their hopes that the crisis would result in the abolition of slavery. He did not respond as they wished, and made it clear that he did not desire to be considered an "abolitionist," and that he still held the opinion that property in slaves was entitled to protection under the Constitution, and that its owners could not be deprived of it without due compensation. Consciously or unconsciously, he, like everybody else, must have been influenced in his views by current events. As political passion in the South rose higher and higher, and actual defiance of Federal authority by deeds of violence occurred almost daily after his election, culminating in the formal secession of seven states and the establishment of the Southern Confederacy under Jefferson Davis at Montgomery, Alabama, the belief, which he doubtless had originally, that by a conciliatory course as President he could pacify the rebellious states, must have become shaken. Still, I think I interpret his views up to the time of his departure for Washington correctly in saying that he had not lost faith in the preservation of peace between the North and the South, and he certainly did not dream that his principal duty would be to raise great armies and fleets, and the means to maintain them, for the suppression of the most determined and sanguinary rebellion, in defense of slavery, that our planet ever witnessed.

The Jacksonian "doctrine" that "to the victors belong the spoils" was still so universally the creed of all politicians, that it was taken for granted there would be a change not only in all the principal, but also in all the minor, Federal offices. It was also expected that the other time-honored party practice of a division of executive patronage among the several states would be carried out. Accordingly there appeared deputations from all the Northern and Border States at Springfield to put in their respective claims for recognition. Some of them came not only once, but several times. From a number of states several delegations turned up, representing rival factions in the Republican ranks, each pretending to be the rightful claimant. Almost every state presented candidates for the Cabinet and for the principal diplomatic and departmental offices. The hotel was the principal haunt of the place-hunters. The tricks, the intrigues, and the manœuvres that were practiced by them in pursuit of their aims came nearly all within the range of my observation, as it was my duty to furnish the earliest possible news of their success or failure. As a rule, the various sets of spoilsmen were very willing to take me into their confidence, but it was not always easy to distinguish what was true in their communications from what they wished me to say to the press purely in furtherance of their interests. Among the political visitors the most prominent I met were: Simon Cameron, S. P. Chase, Thurlow Weed, Lyman Trumbull, N. B. Judd, Richard J. Oglesby, Francis P. Blair, Sr. and Jr., B. Gratz Brown, William Dennison, D. C. Carter of Ohio, Henry J. Winter, and Oliver P. Morton. Thurlow Weed was by far the most interesting figure and the most astute operator among them all.

From what I have said, it will be understood that the President-elect had a hard time of it with the office-seekers. But as he himself was a thorough believer in the doctrine of rotation in office, he felt it his duty to submit to this tribulation. The Cabinet appointments, other than those already named, were especially troublesome to him. There was an intense struggle between Indiana and Illinois, most embarrassing inasmuch as there were several candidates from his own state, all intimate personal friends. Then came the bitter contest between the Border States of Kentucky, Missouri, and Maryland, and the Pennsylvania cabals pro and contra Simon Cameron. Amidst all his perplexities, Lincoln displayed a good deal of patience and shrewdness in dealing with these personal problems. His never-failing stories helped many times to heal wounded feelings and mitigate disappointments. But he gradually showed the wear and tear of these continuous visitations, and finally looked so careworn as to excite one's compassion.

THE JOURNEY TO WASHINGTON

During the month of January, 1861, there appeared in Springfield one W. S. Wood, a former hotel manager and organizer of pleasure excursions, I believe, from the interior of New York state, who, on the recommendation of Thurlow Weed, was to take charge of all the arrangements for the journey of the President-elect to Washington. He was a man of comely appearance, greatly impressed with the importance of his mission, and inclined to assume airs of consequence and condescension. As he showed a disposition to ignore me, I made a direct appeal to Mr. Lincoln, who instructed him that I was to be one of the presidential party. In fact, I was the only member of the press forming part of it as far as Cincinnati, although Messrs. Nicolay and Hay, for some unexplained reason, fail to mention me in naming the members of the party.

The start on the memorable journey was made shortly after eight o'clock on the morning of Monday, February 11. It was a clear, crisp winter day. Only about one hundred people, mostly personal friends, were assembled at the station to shake hands for the last time with their distinguished townsman. It was not strange that he yielded to the sad feelings which must have moved him at the thought of what lay behind and what was before him, and gave them utterance in a pathetic formal farewell to the gathering crowd, as follows:—

"My Friends,—No one not in my position can appreciate the sadness I feel at this parting. To this people I owe all that I am. Here I have lived more than a quarter of a century; here my children were born, and here one of them lies buried. I know not how soon I shall see you again. A duty devolves upon me which is, perhaps, greater than that which has devolved upon any other man since the days of Washington. He never would have succeeded except for the aid of Divine Providence, upon which he at all times relied. I feel that I cannot succeed without the same Divine aid which sustained him, and in the same Almighty Being I place my reliance for support; and I hope you, my friends, will all pray that I may receive that Divine assistance, without which I cannot succeed, but with which success is certain. Again I bid you all an affectionate farewell."

I reproduce this here, as but for me it would not have been preserved in the exact form in which it was delivered. It was entirely extemporized, and, knowing this, I prevailed on Mr. Lincoln, immediately after starting, to write it out for me on a "pad." I sent it over the wires from the first telegraph station. I kept the pencil manuscript for some time, but, unfortunately, lost it in my wanderings in the course of the civil war.

Our traveling companions at the start were (besides Mr. and Mrs. Lincoln and their three sons) W. S. Wood; J. G. Nicolay and John Hay; two old personal friends of Mr. Lincoln, Judge David Davis of Bloomington, afterwards Associate Justice of the United States Supreme Court, and N. B. Judd of Chicago, who had the promise of the Secretaryship of the Interior; Dr. W. S. Wallace, a brother-in-law; Lockwood Todd, a relative of Mrs. Lincoln, who was employed on several important political missions during the next few months; and Ward Hill Lamon, a lawyer of Bloomington, who afterwards became United States Marshal for the District of Columbia, and as such a sort of major-domo at the White House, and finally the author of a biography of Abraham Lincoln. For describing him in this as an infidel Lamon was much and unjustly attacked. He brought a banjo along, and amused us with negro songs. There was also a military escort, consisting of Colonel Edwin Vose Sumner, the white-haired commander of a cavalry regiment of the regular army, and of Major David Hunter, Captain John Pope, and Captain Hazard of the same service. Colonel Sumner, Major Hunter, and Captain Pope became well-known commanding generals during the war. Another "military" character, a sort of pet of Mr. Lincoln, was Colonel E. E. Ellsworth, who, though a mere youth, of small but broad figure, curly black head, and handsome features, had achieved considerable local notoriety as a captain of a crack "Zouave" militia company in Chicago. He was one of the first victims of the civil war, being shot by a rebel while raising the United States flag at Alexandria, Virginia.

The party had a special train, composed at first only of an ordinary passenger car, — there were no parlor or drawing-room or sleeping cars in those days, — a baggage-car, and engine. The first day's journey took us from the capital of Illinois to that of Indiana. Until we reached the boundary of the latter state, the demonstrations along the route were insignificant, except at Decatur, where a great crowd, headed by Richard J. Oglesby, then a hotel-keeper, but subsequently a general in the war, Governor, and United States Senator, greeted the future Chief Magistrate, who delivered another farewell speech. At the boundary, the train was boarded by a large delegation of leading Indianians, including Schuyler Colfax, Henry S. Lane, Caleb B. Smith, and Thomas H. Nelson. At Lafayette, a great crowd awaited our coming, and the President-elect had to appear and speak to them. At Indianapolis, where the first day's journey ended, he was formally welcomed by Governor Oliver P. Morton, and replied to him at length. His speech was remarkable for the first public intimation that he should consider it his duty as President to retake the properties of the United States, including the forts unlawfully seized by the rebellious states, and otherwise reëstablish the authority of the Federal Government.

The next stage of the journey was from Indianapolis to Cincinnati; the third, from Cincinnati to Columbus; the fourth, from Columbus to Pittsburg; the fifth, from Pittsburg to Cleveland; the sixth, from Cleveland to Buffalo, where a rest was taken over Sunday. The eighth day the journey was continued as far as Albany, and on the following day we reached New York. Everywhere there were formal welcomes by the state or municipal authorities and by great crowds of people, with brass bands, and public and private receptions. In different localities pleasant variations were offered in the way of serenades, torchlight processions, and gala theatrical performances. Altogether, the President had every reason to feel flattered and encouraged by the demonstrations in his honor. But the journey was a very great strain upon his physical and mental strength, and he was well-nigh worn out when he reached Buffalo. He must have spoken at least fifty times during the week. In the kindness of his heart — not from any love of adulation, for he really felt very awkward about it — he never refused to respond to a call for his appearance wherever the train stopped. While he thus satisfied the public curiosity, he disappointed, by his appearance, most of those who saw him for the first time. I could see that impression clearly written on the faces of his rustic audiences. Nor was this surprising, for they certainly saw the most unprepossessing features, the gawkiest figure, and the most awkward manners. Lincoln always had an embarrassed air, too, like a country clodhopper appearing in fashionable society, and was nearly always stiff and unhappy in his off-hand remarks. The least creditable performance en route was his attempt to say something on the question of tariff legislation in his Pittsburg speech. What he said was really nothing but crude, ignorant twaddle, without point or meaning. It proved him to be the veriest novice in economic matters, and strengthened my doubts as to his capacity for the high office he was to fill. So poor was his talk that most of the Republican papers, while they printed it, abstained from comment.

After ten days of the wearisome sameness of the "performances" at the several halting-places, I was very sick of the "traveling show," and I therefore asked to be relieved from my duties on reaching New York. My request was granted, and I remained behind. It turned out that I lost only the reception in Independence Hall in Philadelphia, as the journey was cut short by the incognito night run of the President from Harrisburg to Washington. This sudden move on his part created at the time considerable disappointment, even among his warmest political followers, being regarded as an evidence of unwarranted fear. But subsequent events and developments proved his course to have been a wise one.

February 1904

"MARK TWAIN"

SAMUEL LANGHORNE CLEMENS

1835–1910

It is from the deepest springs that laughter bubbles most buoyantly. Your familiar jester is a flippant fellow, the true humorist is a paradox. He will not cry, so laugh he must; and the louder the laughter, the more intolerable the melancholy that forces it. A long, lank figure, a saturnine face, white flannels, and an eternal cigar have become the living symbol of benevolent American humor, yet Samuel Clemens was a bitter, sad, sardonic man. He loved his friends, he joked through life, but of mankind he thought in terms of well-nigh universal contempt, and held their virtues unworthy to be compared with a dog's devotion. It is treason and worse for me to utter it, but he himself said so and triply underscored the words. I call especially to witness that most philosophic of all his books: The Mysterious Stranger. *And in these half-forgotten stories of his which he sent to the* Atlantic *so long ago, under all the jocularity lie seriousness and melancholy. His mask is on to be sure. He has an audience to win which cries aloud for laughter, but completely as Candide in Voltaire's last chapter, he has learned what life has taught him and enfranchised himself from the cheerful theory of Leibnitz that this is the best possible of worlds.*

A True Story, Repeated Word for Word as I Heard It

MARK TWAIN

It was summer time, and twilight. We were sitting on the porch of the farm-house, on the summit of the hill, and "Aunt Rachel" was sitting respectfully below our level, on the steps,—for she was our servant, and colored. She was of mighty frame and stature; she was sixty years old, but her eye was undimmed and her strength unabated. She was a cheerful, hearty soul, and it was no more trouble for her to laugh than it is for a bird to sing. She was under fire, now, as usual when the day was done. That is to say, she was being chaffed without mercy, and was enjoying it. She would let off peal after peal of laughter, and then sit with her face in her hands and shake with throes of enjoyment which she could no longer get breath enough to express. At such a moment as this a thought occurred to me, and I said:—

"Aunt Rachel, how is it that you've lived sixty years and never had any trouble?"

She stopped quaking. She paused, and there was a moment of silence. She turned her face over her shoulder toward me, and said, without even a smile in her voice:—

"Misto C——, is you in 'arnest?"

It surprised me a good deal; and it sobered my manner and my speech, too. I said:—

"Why, I thought—that is, I meant—why, you *can't* have had any trouble. I've never heard you sigh, and never seen your eye when there wasn't a laugh in it."

She faced fairly around, now, and was full of earnestness.

"Has I had any trouble? Misto C——, I's gwyne to tell you, den I leave it to you. I was bawn down 'mongst de slaves; I knows all 'bout slavery, 'ca'se I ben one of 'em my own se'f. Well, sah, my ole man—dat's my husban'—he was lovin' an' kind to me, jist as kind as you is to yo' own wife. An' we had chil'en—seven chil'en—an' we loved dem chil'en jist de same as you loves yo' chil'en. Dey was black, but de Lord can't make no chil'en so black but what dey mother loves 'em an' wouldn't give 'em up, no, not for anything dat's in dis whole world.

"Well, sah, I was raised in ole Fo'ginny, but my mother she was raised in Maryland; an' my *souls!* she was turrible when she'd git started! My *lan'!* but she'd make de fur fly! When she'd git into dem tantrums, she always had one word dat she said. She'd straighten herse'f up an' put her fists in her hips an' say, 'I want you to understan' dat I wa'n't bawn in de mash to be fool' by trash! I's one o' de ole Blue Hen's Chickens, *I* is!' 'Ca'se, you see, dat's what folks dat's bawn in Maryland calls deyselves, an' dey's proud of it. Well, dat was her word. I don't ever forgit it, beca'se she said it so much, an' beca'se she said it one day when my little Henry tore his wris' awful, an' most busted his head, right up at de top of his forehead, an' de niggers didn't fly aroun' fas' enough to 'tend to him. An' when dey talk' back at her, she up an' she says, 'Look-a-heah!' she says, 'I want you niggers to understan' dat I wa'n't bawn in de mash to be fool' by trash! I's one o' de ole Blue Hen's Chickens, *I* is!' an' den she clar' dat kitchen an' bandage' up de chile herse'f. So I says dat word, too, when I's riled.

"Well, bymeby my ole mistis say she's broke, an' she got to sell all de niggers on de place. An' when I heah dat dey gwyne to sell us all off at oction in Richmon', oh de good gracious! I know what dat mean!"

Aunt Rachel had gradually risen, while she warmed to her subject, and now she towered above us, black against the stars.

"Dey put chains on us an' put us on a stan' as high as dis po'ch,— twenty foot high,—an' all de people stood aroun', crowds an' crowds. An' dey'd come up dah an' look at us all roun', an' squeeze our arm, an' make us git up an' walk, an' den say, 'Dis one too ole,' or 'Dis one lame,' or 'Dis one don't 'mount to much.' An' dey sole my ole man, an' took him away, an' dey begin to sell my chil'en an' take *dem* away, an' I begin to cry; an' de man say, 'Shet up yo' dam blubberin',' an' hit me on de mouf wid his han'. An' when de las' one was gone but my little Henry, I grab' *him* clost up to my breas' so, an' I ris up an' says, 'You shan't take him away,' I says; 'I'll kill de man dat tetches him!' I says. But my little Henry whisper an' say, 'I gwyne to run away, an' den I work an' buy yo' freedom.' Oh, bless de chile, he always so good! But dey got him—dey got him, de men did; but I took and tear de clo'es mos' off of 'em, an' beat 'em over de head wid my chain; an' *dey* give it to *me,* too, but I didn't mine dat.

"Well, dah was my ole man gone, an' all my chil'en, all my seven chil'en—an' six of 'em I hain't set eyes on ag'in to dis day, an' dat's twenty-two year ago las' Easter. De man dat bought me b'long' in Newbern, an' he took me dah. Well, bymeby de years roll on an' de waw come. My marster he was a Confedrit colonel, an' I was his family's cook. So when de Unions took dat town, dey all run away an' lef' me all by myse'f wid de other niggers in dat mons'us big house. So de big Union officers move in dah, an' dey ask me would I cook for *dem*. 'Lord bless you,' says I, 'dat's what I's *for*.'

"Dey wa'n't no small-fry officers, mine you, dey was de biggest dey *is;* an' de way dey made dem sojers mosey roun'! De Gen'l he tole me to boss dat kitchen; an' he say, 'If anybody come meddlin' wid you, you jist make 'em walk chalk; don't you be afeard,' he say; 'you's 'mong frens, now.'

"Well, I thinks to myse'f, if my little Henry ever got a chance to run away, he'd make to de Norf, o' course. So one day I comes in dah whah de big officers was, in de parlor, an' I drops a kurtchy, so, an' I up an' tole 'em 'bout my Henry, dey a-listenin' to my troubles jist de same as if I was white folks; an' I says, 'What I come for is beca'se if he got away and got up Norf whah you gemmen comes from, you might 'a' seen him, maybe, an' could tell me so as I could fine him ag'in; he was very little, an' he had a sk-yar on his lef' wris', an' at de top of his forehead.' Den dey look mournful, an' de Gen'l say, 'How long sence you los' him?' an' I say, 'Thirteen year.' Den de Gen'l say, 'He wouldn't be little no mo', now—he's a man!'

"I never thought o' dat befo'! He was only dat little feller to *me,* yit. I never thought 'bout him growin' up an' bein' big. But I see it den. None o' de gemmen had run acrost him, so dey couldn't do nothin' for me. But all dat time, do' *I* didn't know it, my Henry *was* run off to de Norf, years an' years, an' he was a barber, too, an' worked for hisse'f. An' bymeby, when de waw come, he ups an' he says, 'I's done barberin',' he says; 'I's gwyne to fine my old mammy, less'n she's dead.' So he sole out an' went to whah dey was recruitin', an' hired hisse'f out to de colonel for his servant; an' den he went all froo de battles everywhah, huntin' for his ole mammy; yes indeedy, he'd hire to fust one officer an' den another, tell he'd ransacked de whole Souf; but you see *I* didn't know nuffin 'bout *dis*. How was *I* gwyne to know it?

"Well, one night we had a big sojer ball; de sojers dah at Newbern was always havin' balls an' carryin' on. Dey had 'em in my kitchen, heaps o' times, 'ca'se it was so big. Mine you, I was *down* on sich doin's; beca'se my place was wid de officers, an' it rasp' me to have dem common sojers cavortin' roun' my kitchen like dat. But I alway' stood aroun' an' kep' things straight, I did; an' sometimes dey'd git my dander up, an' den I'd make 'em clar dat kitchen, mine I *tell* you!

"Well, one night — it was a Friday night — dey comes a whole plattoon f'm a *nigger* ridgment dat was on guard at de house, — de house was head-quarters, you know, — an' den I was jist a-*bilin'!* Mad? I was jist a-*boomin'!* I swelled aroun', an' swelled aroun'; I jist was a-itchin' for 'em to do somefin for to start me. *An'* dey was a-waltzin' an a-dancin'! *my!* but dey was havin' a time! an' I jist a-swellin' an' a-swellin' up! Pooty soon, 'long comes *sich* a spruce young nigger a-sailin' down de room wid a yaller wench roun' de wais'; an' roun' an' roun' an' roun' dey went, enough to make a body drunk to look at 'em; an' when dey got abreas' o' me, dey went to kin' o' balancin' aroun', fust on one leg an' den on t'other, an' smilin' at my big red turban, an' makin' fun, an' I ups an' says, '*Git* along wid you! — rubbage!' De young man's face kin' o' changed, all of a sudden, for 'bout a second, but den he went to smilin' ag'in, same as he was befo'. Well, 'bout dis time, in comes some niggers dat played music an' b'long' to de ban', an' dey *never* could git along widout puttin' on airs. An' de very fust air dey put on dat night, I lit into 'em! Dey laughed, an' dat made me wuss. De res' o' de niggers got to laughin', an' den my soul *alive* but I was hot! My eye was jist a-blazin'! I jist straightened myself up, so, — jist as I is now, plum to de ceilin', mos', — an' I digs my fists into my hips, an' I says, 'Look-a-heah!' I says, 'I want you niggers to understan' dat I wa'n't bawn in de mash to be fool' by trash! I's one o' de ole Blue Hen's Chickens, *I* is!' an' den I see dat young man stan' a-starin' an' stiff, lookin' kin' o' up at de ceilin' like he fo'got somefin, an' couldn't 'member it no mo'. Well, I jist march' on dem niggers, — so, lookin' like a gen'l, — an' dey jist cave' away befo' me an' out at de do'. An' as dis young man was a-goin' out, I heah him say to another nigger, 'Jim,' he says, 'you go 'long an' tell de cap'n I be on han' 'bout eight o'clock in de mawnin'; dey's somefin on my mine,' he says; 'I don't sleep no mo' dis night. You go 'long,' he says, 'an' leave me by my own se'f.'

"Dis was 'bout one o'clock in de mawnin'. Well, 'bout seven, I was up an' on han', gittin' de officers' breakfast. I was a-stoopin' down by de stove, — jist so, same as if yo' foot was de stove, — an' I'd opened de stove do' wid my right han', — so, pushin' it back, jist as I pushes yo' foot, — an' I'd jist got de pan o' hot biscuits in my han' an' was 'bout to raise up, when I see a black face come aroun' under mine, an' de eyes a-lookin' up into mine, jist as I's a-lookin' up clost under yo' face now; an' I jist stopped *right dah,* an' never budged! jist gazed, an' gazed, so; an' de pan begin to tremble, an' all of a sudden I *knowed!* De pan drop' on de flo' an' I grab his lef' han' an' shove back his sleeve,

— jist so, as I's doin' to you, — an' den I goes for his forehead an' push de hair back, so, an' 'Boy!' I says, 'if you an't my Henry, what is you doin' wid dis welt on yo' wris' an' dat sk-yar on yo' forehead? De Lord God ob heaven be praise', I got my own ag'in!'

"Oh, no, Misto C——, *I* hain't had no trouble. An' no *joy!*"

November 1874

Edward Mills and George Benton

A Tale

MARK TWAIN

THESE two were distantly related to each other, — seventh cousins, or something of that sort. While still babies they became orphans, and were adopted by the Brants, a childless couple, who quickly grew very fond of them. The Brants were always saying, "Be pure, honest, sober, industrious, and considerate of others, and success in life is assured." The children heard this repeated some thousands of times before they understood it; they could repeat it themselves long before they could say the Lord's Prayer; it was painted over the nursery door, and was about the first thing they learned to read. It was destined to become the unswerving rule of Edward Mills's life. Sometimes the Brants changed the wording a little, and said, "Be pure, honest, sober, industrious, considerate, and you will never lack friends."

Baby Mills was a comfort to everybody about him. When he wanted candy and could not have it, he listened to reason, and contented himself without it. When Baby Benton wanted candy, he cried for it until he got it. Baby Mills took care of his toys; Baby Benton always destroyed his in a very brief time, and then made himself so insistently disagreeable that, in order to have peace in the house, little Edward was persuaded to yield up his playthings to him.

When the children were a little older, Georgie became a heavy expense in one respect: he took no care of his clothes; consequently, he shone frequently in new ones, which was not the case with Eddie. The boys grew apace. Eddie was an increasing comfort, Georgie an increasing solicitude. It was always sufficient to say, in answer to Eddie's petitions, "I would rather you would not do it,"—meaning swimming, skating, picnicking, berrying, circusing, and all sorts of things which boys delight in. But *no* answer was sufficient for Georgie; he had to be humored in his desires, or he would carry them with a high hand. Naturally, no boy got more swimming, skating, berrying, and so forth than he; no boy ever had a better time. The good Brants did not allow the boys to play out after nine in summer evenings; they were sent to bed at that hour; Eddie honorably remained, but Georgie usually slipped out of the window toward ten, and enjoyed himself till midnight. It seemed impossible to break Georgie of this bad habit, but the Brants managed it at last by hiring him, with apples and marbles, to stay in. The good Brants gave all their time and attention to vain endeavors to regulate Georgie; they said, with grateful tears in their eyes, that Eddie needed no efforts of theirs, he was so good, so considerate, and in all ways so perfect.

By and by the boys were big enough to work, so they were apprenticed to a trade: Edward went voluntarily; George was coaxed and bribed. Edward worked hard and faithfully, and ceased to be an expense to the good Brants; they praised him, so did his master; but George ran away, and it cost Mr. Brant both money and trouble to hunt him up and get him back. By and by he ran away again,—more money and more trouble. He ran away a third time,—and stole a few little things to carry with him. Trouble and expense for Mr. Brant once more; and, besides, it was with the greatest difficulty that he succeeded in persuading the master to let the youth go unprosecuted for the theft.

Edward worked steadily along, and in time became a full partner in his master's business. George did not improve; he kept the loving hearts of his aged benefactors full of trouble, and their hands full of inventive activities to protect him from ruin. Edward, as a boy, had interested himself in Sunday-schools, debating societies, penny missionary affairs, anti-tobacco organizations, anti-profanity associations, and all such things; as a man, he was a quiet but steady and reliable helper in the church, the temperance societies, and in all movements looking to the aiding and uplifting of men. This excited no remark, attracted no attention,—for it was his "natural bent."

Finally, the old people died. The will testified their loving pride in Edward, and left their little property to George,—because he "needed it"; whereas, "owing to a bountiful Providence," such was not the case with Edward. The property was left to George conditionally: he must buy out Edward's partner with it; else it must go to a benevolent organization called the Prisoner's Friend Society. The old people left a letter, in which they begged their dear son Edward to take their place and watch over George, and help and shield him as they had done.

Edward dutifully acquiesced, and George became his partner in the business. He was not a valuable partner: he had been meddling with drink before; he soon developed into a constant tippler, now, and his flesh and eyes showed the fact unpleasantly. Edward had been courting a sweet and kindly spirited girl for some time. They loved each other dearly, and — But about this period George began to haunt her tearfully and imploringly, and at last she went crying to Edward, and said her high and holy duty was plain before her, — she must not let her own selfish desires interfere with it: she must marry "poor George" and "reform him." It would break her heart, she knew it would, and so on; but duty was duty. So she married George, and Edward's heart came very near breaking, as well as her own. However, Edward recovered, and married another girl, — a very excellent one she was, too.

Children came, to both families. Mary did her honest best to reform her husband, but the contract was too large. George went on drinking, and by and by he fell to misusing her and the little ones sadly. A great many good people strove with George, — they were always at it, in fact, — but he calmly took such efforts as his due and their duty, and did not mend his ways. He added a vice, presently, — that of secret gambling. He got deeply in debt; he borrowed money on the firm's credit, as quietly as he could, and carried this system so far and so successfully that one morning the sheriff took possession of the establishment, and the two cousins found themselves penniless.

Times were hard, now, and they grew worse. Edward moved his family into a garret, and walked the streets day and night, seeking work. He begged for it, but it was really not to be had. He was astonished to see how soon his face became unwelcome; he was astonished and hurt to see how quickly the ancient interest which people had had in him faded out and disappeared. Still, he *must* get work; so he swallowed his chagrin, and toiled on in search of it. At last he got a job of carrying bricks up a ladder in a hod, and was a grateful man in consequence; but after that *nobody* knew him or cared anything about him. He was not able to keep up his dues in the various moral organizations to which he belonged, and had to endure the sharp pain of seeing himself brought under the disgrace of suspension.

But the faster Edward died out of public knowledge and interest, the faster George rose in them. He was found lying, ragged and drunk, in the gutter, one morning. A member of the Ladies' Temperance Refuge fished him out, took him in hand, got up a subscription for him, kept him sober a whole week, then got a situation for him. An account of it was published.

General attention was thus drawn to the poor fellow, and a great many people came forward, and helped him toward reform with their countenance and encouragement. He did not drink a drop for two months, and meantime was the pet of the good. Then he fell, — in the gutter; and there was general sorrow and lamentation. But the noble sisterhood rescued him again. They cleaned him up, they fed him, they listened to the mournful music of his repentances, they got him his situation again. An account of this, also, was published, and the town was drowned in happy tears over the re-restoration of the poor beset and struggling victim of the fatal bowl. A grand temperance revival was got up, and after some rousing speeches had been made the chairman said, impressively, "We are now about to call for signers; and I think there is a spectacle in store for you which not many in this house will be able to view with dry eyes." There was an eloquent pause, and then George Benton, escorted by a red-sashed detachment of the Ladies of the Refuge, stepped forward upon the platform and signed the pledge. The air was rent with applause, and everybody cried for joy. Everybody wrung the hand of the new convert when the meeting was over; his salary was enlarged next day; he was the talk of the town, and its hero. An account of it was published.

George Benton fell, regularly, every three months, but was faithfully rescued and wrought with, every time, and good situations were found for him. Finally, he was taken around the country lecturing, as a reformed drunkard, and he had great houses and did an immense amount of good.

He was so popular at home, and so trusted, — during his sober intervals, — that he was enabled to use the name of a principal citizen, and get a large sum of money at the bank. A mighty pressure was brought to bear to save him from the consequences of his forgery, and it was partially successful, — he was "sent up" for only two years. When, at the end of a year, the tireless efforts of the benevolent were crowned with success, and he emerged from the penitentiary with a pardon in his pocket, the Prisoner's Friend Society met him at the door with a situation and a comfortable salary, and all the other benevolent people came forward and gave him advice, encouragement, and help. Edward

Mills had once applied to the Prisoner's Friend Society for a situation, when in dire need, but the question, "Have you been a prisoner?" made brief work of his case.

While all these things were going on, Edward Mills had been quietly making head against adversity. He was still poor, but was in receipt of a steady and sufficient salary, as the respected and trusted cashier of a bank. George Benton never came near him, and was never heard to inquire about him. George got to indulging in long absences from the town; there were ill reports about him, but nothing definite.

One winter's night some masked burglars forced their way into the bank, and found Edward Mills there alone. They commanded him to reveal the "combination," so that they could get into the safe. He refused. They threatened his life. He said his employers trusted him, and he could not be traitor to that trust. He could die, if he must, but while he lived he would be faithful; he would not yield up the "combination." The burglars killed him.

The detectives hunted down the criminals; the chief one proved to be George Benton. A wide sympathy was felt for the widow and orphans of the dead man, and all the newspapers in the land begged that all the banks in the land would testify their appreciation of the fidelity and heroism of the murdered cashier by coming forward with a generous contribution of money in aid of his family, now bereft of support. The result was a mass of solid cash amounting to upwards of five hundred dollars,—an average of nearly three eighths of a cent for each bank in the Union. The cashier's own bank testified its gratitude by endeavoring to show (but humiliatingly failed in it) that the peerless servant's accounts were not square, and that he himself had knocked his brains out with a bludgeon to escape detection and punishment.

George Benton was arraigned for trial. Then everybody seemed to forget the widow and orphans in their solicitude for poor George. Everything that money and influence could do was done to save him, but it all failed; he was sentenced to death. Straightway the governor was besieged with petitions for commutation or pardon: they were brought by tearful young girls; by sorrowful old maids; by deputations of pathetic widows; by shoals of impressive orphans. But no, the governor—for once—would not yield.

Now George Benton experienced religion. The glad news flew all around. From that time forth his cell was always full of girls and women and fresh flowers; all the day long there was prayer, and hymn-singing, and thanksgivings, and homilies, and tears, with never an interruption, except an occasional five-minute intermission for refreshments.

This sort of thing continued up to the very gallows, and George Benton went proudly home, in the black cap, before a wailing audience of the sweetest and best that the region could produce. His grave had fresh flowers on it every day, for a while, and the head-stone bore these words, under a hand pointing aloft: "He has fought the good fight."

The brave cashier's head-stone has this inscription: "Be pure, honest, sober, industrious, considerate, and you will never—"

Nobody knows who gave the order to leave it that way, but it was so given.

The cashier's family are in stringent circumstances, now, it is said; but no matter; a lot of appreciative people, who were not willing that an act so brave and true as his should go unrewarded, have collected forty-two thousand dollars—and built a Memorial Church with it.

August 1880

JOHN BUCHAN

1875–1940

All the talents were John Buchan's birthright. Scholar, storyteller, publisher, Lord High Commissioner standing in the King's place before the General Assembly of The Kirk of Scotland, historian, Governor-General: he was all of them together and by turns. I knew him first as a young disciple of Sir Alfred Milner who, in the pacification of South Africa, sowed the seeds of the British Commonwealth. I well remember one long, rewarding week end — it must have been in 1918. We tramped over the hills of Oxford, Buchan and I, talking poetry and history, John pointing out the spot where Clough had sat and whither Arnold returned to write in "Thyrsis" a tribute such as friend has seldom paid to friend. One long morning we browsed among his books at Elsfield, the Manor House of which he was proud to be master. Built directly on the highway, it demonstrated thereby its Twelfth Century pedigree, and in its sunny garden the Great Cham once drank sixteen cups of tea, and as Bozzy and Buchan after him took pains to record, walked all of six miles from Oxford for the privilege. Our talk turned serious, and we spoke of the choice spirits of our generation sacrificed on the altar of what was then "The Great War." Buchan called the roll of lost friends; brightest and best among them Raymond Asquith, lately dead on the fields of the Somme. Often in history Prime Ministers' sons have shone at Oxford, but none more brilliantly than he, master in college debate and beloved exceedingly. His father kept summoning him to enter the serious fray of law and politics, but he was loath to leave a life where accomplishment was never cumbered with detraction and envy was a jest. When Buchan had spoken to him of inevitable duties ahead, Raymond had laughingly replied: —

If I had my way with affairs of state
I'd wrap them up in Livy,
I'd throw the Great Seal in the grate
And the Privy Seal in the privy!

How these old scraps of memory return when one has loved and lost a friend!

Many times after that visit our paths crossed, Buchan's and mine, the last when, as Governor-General of Canada, he came to receive a degree from Harvard. I caught sight of his tall gray topper shining like Navarre's panache amongst the multitude of American beavers, and complimented him on the perfection of his little speech. He had spoken that day on the essentials of education which to him were Humility, Humanity, and Humor, and had closed by quoting the beautiful leave-taking of Queen Elizabeth: "Farewell, dear Oxford, God bless thee and increase thy sons in number, in holiness, and in virtue." He seemed pleased but surprised too by my enthusiasm.

A year later, when amid all the cares of the high office of Governor-General of the Commonwealth of Canada, when a greater war was on, he toiled through the long Northern evenings writing a classical biography of Augustus Caesar based on original sources, I wrote marveling at the complexity of his scholarship and at his finding energy and time. We were both growing old then and I closed my letter by asking how he was planning to spend Life Everlasting. For me, I said, few arguments for the satisfactions of immortality appealed to the imagination, and that when my time came I should be all for declining, except for an intense desire to see and talk with a very few of the mighty dead. "While you, John," I said, "will be in closest attendance on the Court of Augustus, bringing all your diplomatic talents into celestial play, you may notice the furtive figure of a friend Heaven-bent on searching out his two primal favorites among the immortals, P. Vergilius Maro and Sir Walter Scott." Straightway his answer returned. Buchan warned me against duping myself with false hopes. Among ten thousand times ten thousand, those were the two Shining Ones whom he himself loved best. To them he would straightway hie, blocking the way of any interloper. What chance could there be for me!

It was but a little while after, that for him the curtain was drawn aside. John Buchan had his wish, and now after these years of satisfaction, he may still give me my chance.

The Watcher by the Threshold

JOHN BUCHAN

I

A CHILL evening in the early October of the year 189– found me driving in a dogcart through the belts of antique woodland which form the lowland limits of the hilly parish of More. The Highland express, which brought me from the north, took me no farther than Perth. Thence it had been a slow journey in a disjointed local train, till I emerged on the platform at Morefoot, with a bleak prospect of pot stalks, coal heaps, certain sour corn lands, and far to the west a line of moor where the sun was setting. A neat groom and a respectable trap took the edge off my discomfort, and soon I had forgotten my sacrifice and found eyes for the darkening landscape. We were driving through a land of thick woods, cut at rare intervals by old long-frequented highways. The More, which at Morefoot is an open sewer, became a sullen woodland stream, where the brown leaves of the season drifted. At times we would pass an ancient lodge, and through a gap in the trees would come a glimpse of chipped crowstep gable. The names of such houses, as told me by my companion, were all famous. This one had been the home of a drunken Jacobite laird, and a kind of north country Medmenham. Unholy revels had waked the old halls, and the devil had been toasted at many a hell-fire dinner. The next was the property of a great Scots law family, and there the old Lord of Session, who built the place, in his frouzy wig and carpet slippers, had laid down the canons of Taste for his day and society. The whole country had the air of faded and bygone gentility. The mossy roadside walls had stood for two hundred years; the few wayside houses were toll bars or defunct hostelries. The names, too, were great: Scots baronial with a smack of France,—Chatelray and Riverslaw, Black Holm and Fountainblue. The place had a cunning charm, mystery dwelt in every cranny, and yet it did not please me. The earth smelt heavy and raw; the roads were red underfoot; all was old, sorrowful, and uncanny. Compared with the fresh Highland glen I had left, where wind and sun and flying showers were never absent, all was chilly and dull and dead. Even when the sun sent a shiver of crimson over the crests of certain firs, I felt no delight in the prospect. I admitted shamefacedly to myself that I was in a very bad temper.

I had been staying at Glenaicill with the Clanroydens, and for a week had found the proper pleasure in life. You know the house with its old rooms and gardens, and the miles of heather which defend it from the world. The shooting had been extraordinary for a wild place late in the season; for there are few partridges, and the woodcock are notoriously late. I had done respectably in my stalking, more than respectably on the river, and creditably on the moors. Moreover, there were pleasant people in the house,—and there were the Clanroydens. I had had a hard year's work, sustained to the last moment of term, and a fortnight in Norway had been disastrous. It was therefore with real comfort that I had settled myself down for another ten days in Glenaicill, when all my plans were shattered by Sibyl's letter. Sibyl is my cousin and my very good friend, and in old days when I was briefless I had fallen in love with her many times. But she very sensibly chose otherwise, and married a man Ladlaw,—Robert John Ladlaw, who had been at school with me. He was a cheery, good-humored fellow, a great sportsman, a justice of the peace, and deputy lieutenant for his county, and something of an antiquary in a mild way. He had a box in Leicestershire to which he went in the hunting season, but from February till October he lived in his moorland home. The place was called the House of More, and I had shot at it once or twice in recent years. I remembered its loneliness and its comfort, the charming diffident Sibyl, and Ladlaw's genial welcome. And my recollections set me puzzling again over the letter which that morning had broken into my comfort. "You promised us a visit this autumn," Sibyl had written, "and I wish you would come as soon as you can." So far common politeness. But she had gone on to reveal the fact that Ladlaw was ill; she did not know how, exactly, but something, she thought, about his heart. Then she had signed herself my affectionate cousin, and then had come a short, violent postscript, in which, as it were, the fences of convention had been laid low. "For Heaven's sake, come and see us," she scrawled below. "Bob is terribly ill, and I am crazy. Come at once." To cap it she finished with an afterthought: "Don't bother about bringing doctors. It is not their business."

She had assumed that I would come, and dutifully I set out. I could not regret my decision, but I took leave to upbraid my luck. The thought of Glenaicill, with the woodcock beginning to arrive and the Clanroydens imploring me to stay, saddened my journey in the morning, and the murky, coaly, midland country of the afternoon completed my depression. The drive through the woodlands of More failed to raise my spirits. I was anxious about Sibyl and Ladlaw, and this accursed country had always given me a certain eeriness on my first approaching it. You may call it silly, but I have no nerves and am little susceptible to vague sentiment. It was sheer physical dislike of the rich deep soil, the woody and antique smells, the melancholy roads and trees, and the flavor of old mystery. I am aggressively healthy and wholly Philistine. I love clear outlines and strong colors, and More with its half tints and hazy distances depressed me miserably. Even when the road crept uphill and the trees ended, I found nothing to hearten me in the moorland which succeeded. It was genuine moorland, close on eight hundred feet above the sea, and through it ran this old grass-grown coach road. Low hills rose to the left, and to the right, after some miles of peat, flared the chimneys of pits and oil works. Straight in front the moor ran out into the horizon, and there in the centre was the last dying spark of the sun. The place was as still as the grave save for the crunch of our wheels on the grassy road, but the flaring lights to the north seemed to endow it with life. I have rarely had so keenly the feeling of movement in the inanimate world. It was an unquiet place, and I shivered nervously. Little gleams of loch came from the hollows, the burns were brown with peat, and every now and then there rose in the moor jags of sickening red stone. I remembered that Ladlaw had talked about the place as the old Manann, the holy land of the ancient races. I had paid little attention at the time, but now it struck me that the old peoples had been wise in their choice. There was something uncanny in this soil and air. Framed in dank mysterious woods and a country of coal and ironstone, at no great distance from the capital city, it was a sullen relic of a lost barbarism. Over the low hills lay a green pastoral country with bright streams and valleys, but here, in this peaty desert, there were few sheep and little cultivation. The House of More was the only dwelling, and, save for the ragged village, the wilderness was given over to the wild things of the hills. The shooting was good, but the best shooting on earth would not persuade me to make my abode in such a place. Ladlaw was ill; well, I did not wonder. You can have uplands without air, moors that are not health-giving, and a country life which is more arduous than a townsman's. I shivered again, for I seemed to have passed in a few hours from the open noon to a kind of dank twilight.

We passed the village and entered the lodge gates. Here there were trees again,—little innocent new-planted firs, which flourished ill. Some large plane trees grew near the house, and there were thickets upon thickets of the ugly elderberry. Even in the half darkness I could see that the lawns were trim and the flower beds respectable for the season; doubtless Sibyl looked after the gardeners. The oblong whitewashed house, more like a barrack than ever, opened suddenly on my sight, and I experienced my first sense of comfort since I left Glenaicill. Here I should find warmth and company; and sure enough, the hall door was wide open, and in the great flood of light which poured from it Sibyl stood to welcome me.

She ran down the steps as I dismounted, and, with a word to the groom, caught my arm and drew me into the shadow. "Oh, Henry, it was so good of you to come. You mustn't let Bob think that you know he is ill. We don't talk about it. I'll tell you afterwards. I want you to cheer him up. Now we must go in, for he is in the hall expecting you."

While I stood blinking in the light, Ladlaw came forward with outstretched hand and his usual cheery greeting. I looked at him and saw nothing unusual in his appearance; a little drawn at the lips, perhaps, and heavy below the eyes, but still fresh-colored and healthy. It was Sibyl who showed change. She was very pale, her pretty eyes were deplorably mournful, and in place of her delightful shyness there were the self-confidence and composure of pain. I was honestly shocked, and as I dressed my heart was full of hard thoughts about Ladlaw. What could his illness mean? He seemed well and cheerful, while Sibyl was pale; and yet it was Sibyl who had written the postscript. As I warmed myself by the fire, I resolved that this particular family difficulty was my proper business.

II

The Ladlaws were waiting for me in the drawing-room. I noticed something new and strange in Sibyl's demeanor. She looked at her husband with a motherly, protective air, while Ladlaw, who had been the extreme of masculine independence, seemed to cling to his wife with a curious appealing fidelity. In conversation he did little more than echo her words. Till dinner was announced he spoke of the weather, the shooting, and Mabel Clanroyden. Then he did a queer thing; for when I was about to offer my arm to Sibyl he forestalled me, and clutching her right arm with his left hand led the way to the dining room, leaving me to follow in some bewilderment.

I have rarely taken part in a more dismal meal. The House of More has a pretty Georgian paneling through most of the rooms, but in the dining room the walls are level and painted a dull stone color. Abraham offered up Isaac in a ghastly picture in front of me. Some photographs of the Quorn hung over the mantelpiece, and five or six drab ancestors filled up the remaining space. But one thing was new and startling. A great marble bust, a genuine antique, frowned on me from a pedestal. The head was in the late Roman style, clearly of some emperor, and in its commonplace environment the great brows, the massive neck, and the mysterious solemn lips had a surprising effect. I nodded toward the thing, and asked what it represented.

Ladlaw grunted something which I took for "Justinian," but he never raised his eyes from his plate. By accident I caught Sibyl's glance. She looked toward the bust, and laid a finger on her lips.

The meal grew more doleful as it advanced. Sibyl scarcely touched a dish, but her husband ate ravenously of everything. He was a strong, thickset man, with a square kindly face burned brown by the sun. Now he seemed to have suddenly coarsened. He gobbled with undignified haste, and his eye was extraordinarily vacant. A question made him start, and he would turn on me a face so strange and inert that I repented the interruption.

I asked him about the autumn's sport. He collected his wits with difficulty. He thought it had been good, on the whole, but he had shot badly. He had not been quite so fit as usual. No, he had had nobody staying with him. Sibyl had wanted to be alone. He was afraid the moor might have been undershot, but he would make a big day with keepers and farmers before the winter.

"Bob has done pretty well," Sibyl said. "He hasn't been out often, for the weather has been very bad here. You can have no idea, Henry, how horrible this moorland place of ours can be when it tries. It is one great sponge sometimes, with ugly red burns and mud to the ankles."

"I don't think it's healthy," said I.

Ladlaw lifted his face. "Nor do I. I think it's intolerable, but I am so busy I can't get away."

Once again I caught Sibyl's warning eye as I was about to question him on his business.

Clearly the man's brain had received a shock, and he was beginning to suffer from hallucinations. This could be the only explanation, for he had always led a temperate life. The distrait, wandering manner was the only sign of his malady, for otherwise he seemed normal and mediocre as ever. My heart grieved for Sibyl, alone with him in this wilderness.

Then he broke the silence. He lifted his head and looked nervously around till his eye fell on the Roman bust.

"Do you know that this countryside is the old Manann?" he said.

It was an odd turn to the conversation, but I was glad of a sign of intelligence. I answered that I had heard so.

"It's a queer name," he said oracularly, "but the thing it stood for was queerer. Manann, Manaw," he repeated, rolling the words on his tongue. As he spoke, he glanced sharply, and, as it seemed to me, fearfully, at his left side.

The movement of his body made his napkin slip from his left knee and fall on the floor. It leaned against his leg, and he started from its touch as if he had been bitten by a snake. I have never seen a more sheer and transparent terror on a man's face. He got to his feet, his strong frame shaking like a rush. Sibyl ran round to his side, picked up the napkin and flung it on a sideboard. Then she stroked his hair as one would stroke a frightened horse. She called him by his old boy's name of Robin, and at her touch and voice he became quiet. But the particular course then in progress was removed, untasted.

In a few minutes he seemed to have forgotten his behavior, for he took up the former conversation. For a time he spoke well and briskly. "You lawyers," he said, "understand only the dry framework of the past. You cannot conceive the rapture, which only the antiquary can feel, of constructing in every detail an old culture. Take this Manann. If I could explore the secret of these moors, I would write the world's greatest book. I would write of that prehistoric life when man was knit close to nature. I would describe the people who were brothers of the red earth and the red rock and the red streams of the hills. Oh, it would be horrible, but superb, tremendous! It would be more than a piece of history; it would be a new gospel, a new theory of life. It would kill materialism once and for all. Why, man, all the poets who have deified and personified nature would not do an eighth part of my work. I would show you the unknown, the hideous, shrieking mystery at the back of this simple nature. Men would see the profundity of the old crude faiths which they affect to despise. I would make a picture of our shaggy, sombre-eyed forefather, who heard strange things in the hill silences. I would show him brutal and terror-stricken, but wise, wise, God alone knows how wise! The Romans knew it, and they learned what they could from him, though he did not tell them much. But we have some of his blood in us, and we may go deeper. Manann! A queer land nowadays! I sometimes love it and sometimes hate it, but I always fear it. It is like that statue, inscrutable."

I would have told him that he was talking mystical nonsense, but I had looked toward the bust, and my rudeness was checked on my lips.

The moor might be a common piece of ugly waste land, but the statue was inscrutable, — of that there was no doubt. I hate your cruel heavy-mouthed Roman busts; to me they have none of the beauty of life, and little of the interest of art. But my eyes were fastened on this as they had never before looked on marble. The oppression of the heavy woodlands, the mystery of the silent moor, seemed to be caught and held in this face. It was the intangible mystery of culture on the verge of savagery, — a cruel, lustful wisdom, and yet a kind of bitter austerity which laughed at the game of life and stood aloof. There was no weakness in the heavy-veined brow and slumbrous eyelids. It was the face of one who had conquered the world, and found it dust and ashes; one who had eaten of the tree of the knowledge of good and evil, and scorned human wisdom. And at the same time, it was the face of one who knew uncanny things, a man who was the intimate of the half-world and the dim background of life. Why on earth I should connect the Roman grandee[1] with the moorland parish of More I cannot say, but the fact remains that there was that in the face which I knew had haunted me through the woodlands and bogs of the place, — a sleepless, dismal, incoherent melancholy.

"I bought that at Colenzo's," Ladlaw said, "because it took my fancy. It matches well with this place?"

I thought it matched very ill with his drab walls and Quorn photographs, but I held my peace.

"Do you know who it is?" he asked. "It is the head of the greatest man the world has ever seen. You are a lawyer and know your Justinian."

The Pandects are scarcely part of the daily work of a common-law barrister. I had not looked into them since I left college.

"I know that he married an actress," I said, "and was a sort of all-round genius. He made law, and fought battles, and had rows with the Church. A curious man! And wasn't there some story about his selling his soul to the devil, and getting law in exchange? Rather a poor bargain!"

I chattered away, sillily enough, to dispel the gloom of that dinner table. The result of my words was unhappy. Ladlaw gasped and caught

[1] I have identified the bust, which, when seen under other circumstances, had little power to affect me. It was a copy of the head of Justinian in the Tesci Museum at Venice, and several duplicates exist, dating apparently from the seventh century, and showing traces of Byzantine decadence in the scroll work on the hair. It is engraved in M. Delacroix's Byzantium and, I think, in Windscheid's Pandektenlehrbuch. Author.

at his left side, as if in pain. Sibyl, with tragic eyes, had been making signs to me to hold my peace. Now she ran round to her husband's side and comforted him like a child. As she passed me, she managed to whisper in my ear to talk to her only, and let her husband alone.

For the rest of dinner I obeyed my orders to the letter. Ladlaw ate his food in gloomy silence, while I spoke to Sibyl of our relatives and friends, of London, Glenaicill, and any random subject. The poor girl was dismally forgetful, and her eye would wander to her husband with wifely anxiety. I remember being suddenly overcome by the comic aspect of it all. Here were we three fools alone in the dank upland: one of us sick and nervous, talking out-of-the-way nonsense about Manann and Justinian, gobbling his food and getting scared at his napkin; another gravely anxious; and myself at my wits' end for a solution. It was a Mad Tea-Party with a vengeance: Sibyl the melancholy little Dormouse, and Ladlaw the incomprehensible Hatter. I laughed aloud, but checked myself when I caught my cousin's eye. It was really no case for finding humor. Ladlaw was very ill, and Sibyl's face was getting deplorably thin.

I welcomed the end of that meal with unmannerly joy, for I wanted to speak seriously with my host. Sibyl told the butler to have the lamps lighted in the library. Then she leaned over toward me and spoke low and rapidly: "I want you to talk with Bob. I'm sure you can do him good. You'll have to be very patient with him, and very gentle. Oh, please try to find out what is wrong with him. He won't tell me, and I can only guess."

The butler returned with word that the library was ready to receive us, and Sibyl rose to go. Ladlaw half rose, protesting, making the most curious feeble clutches at his side. His wife quieted him. "Henry will look after you, dear," she said. "You are going into the library to smoke." Then she slipped from the room, and we were left alone.

He caught my arm fiercely with his left hand, and his grip nearly made me cry out. As we walked down the hall, I could feel his arm twitching from the elbow to the shoulder. Clearly he was in pain, and I set it down to some form of cardiac affection, which might possibly issue in paralysis.

I settled him in the biggest armchair, and took one of his cigars. The library is the pleasantest room in the house, and at night, when a peat fire burned on the old hearth and the great red curtains were drawn, it used to be the place for comfort and good talk. Now I noticed changes. Ladlaw's bookshelves had been filled with the Proceedings of antiquarian societies and many light-hearted works on sport. But now the Badminton library had been cleared out of a shelf where it stood most convenient to the hand, and its place taken by an old Leyden reprint of Justinian. There were books on Byzantine subjects of which I never dreamed he had heard the names; there were volumes of history and speculation, all of a slightly bizarre kind; and to crown everything, there were several bulky medical works with gaudily colored plates. The old atmosphere of sport and travel had gone from the room with the medley of rods, whips, and gun cases which used to cumber the tables. Now the place was moderately tidy and somewhat learned, and I did not like it.

Ladlaw refused to smoke, and sat for a little while in silence. Then of his own accord he broke the tension.

"It was devilish good of you to come, Harry. This is a lonely place for a man who is a bit seedy."

"I thought you might be alone," I said, "so I looked you up on my way down from Glenaicill. I'm sorry to find you feeling ill."

"Do you notice it?" he asked sharply.

"It's tolerably patent," I said. "Have you seen a doctor?"

He said something uncomplimentary about doctors, and kept looking at me with his curious dull eyes.

I remarked the strange posture in which he sat, his head screwed round to his right shoulder, and his whole body a protest against something at his left hand.

"It looks like a heart," I said. "You seem to have pains in your left side."

Again a spasm of fear. I went over to him, and stood at the back of his chair.

"Now for goodness' sake, my dear fellow, tell me what is wrong. You're scaring Sibyl to death. It's lonely work for the poor girl, and I wish you would let me help you."

He was lying back in his chair now, with his eyes half shut, and shivering like a frightened colt. The extraordinary change in one who had been the strongest of the strong kept me from realizing its gravity. I put a hand on his shoulder, but he flung it off.

"For God's sake, sit down!" he said hoarsely. "I'm going to tell you, but I'll never make you understand."

I sat down promptly opposite him.

"It's the devil," he said very solemnly.

I am afraid that I was rude enough to laugh. He took no notice, but sat, with the same tense, miserable air, staring over my head.

"Right," said I. "Then it is the devil. It's a new complaint, so it's as well I did not bring a doctor. How does it affect you?"

He made the old impotent clutch at the air with his left hand. I had the sense to become grave at once. Clearly this was some serious mental affection, some hallucination born of physical pain.

Then he began to talk in a low voice, very rapidly, with his head bent forward like a hunted animal's. I am not going to set down what he told me in his own words, for they were incoherent often, and there was much repetition. But I am going to write the gist of the odd story which took my sleep away on that autumn night, with such explanations and additions as I think needful. The fire died down, the wind arose, the hour grew late, and still he went on in his mumbling recitative. I forgot to smoke, forgot my comfort, — everything but the odd figure of my friend and his inconceivable romance. And the night before I had been in cheerful Glenaicill!

. . . .

He had returned to the House of More, he said, in the latter part of May, and shortly after he fell ill. It was a trifling sickness, — influenza or something, — but he had never quite recovered. The rainy weather of June depressed him, and the extreme heat of July made him listless and weary. A kind of insistent sleepiness hung over him, and he suffered much from nightmare. Toward the end of July his former health returned, but he was haunted with a curious oppression. He seemed to himself to have lost the art of being alone. There was a perpetual sound in his left ear, a kind of moving and rustling at his left side, which never left him by night or day. In addition, he had become the prey of nerves and an insensate dread of the unknown.

Ladlaw, as I have explained, was a commonplace man, with fair talents, a mediocre culture, honest instincts, and the beliefs and incredulities of his class. On abstract grounds, I should have declared him an unlikely man to be the victim of an hallucination. He had a kind of dull bourgeois rationalism, which used to find reasons for all things in heaven and earth. At first he controlled his dread with proverbs. He told himself it was the sequel of his illness or the lightheadedness of summer heat on the moors. But it soon outgrew his comfort. It became a living second presence, an *alter ego* which dogged his footsteps. He grew acutely afraid of it. He dared not be alone for a moment, and clung to Sibyl's company despairingly. She went off for a week's visit in the beginning of August, and he endured for seven days the tortures of the lost. The malady advanced upon him with swift steps. The presence became more real daily. In the early dawning, in the twilight, and in the first hour of the morning it seemed at times to take a visible bodily form. A kind of amorphous featureless shadow would run from his side into the darkness, and he would sit palsied with terror. Sometimes, in lonely places, his footsteps sounded double, and something would brush elbows with him. Human society alone exorcised it. With Sibyl at his side he was happy; but as soon as she left him, the thing came slinking back from the unknown to watch by him. Company might have saved him, but joined to his affliction was a crazy dread of his fellows. He would not leave his moorland home, but must bear his burden alone among the wild streams and mosses of that dismal place.

The 12th came, and he shot wretchedly, for his nerve had gone to pieces. He stood exhaustion badly, and became a dweller about the doors. But with this bodily inertness came an extraordinary intellectual revival. He read widely in a blundering way, and he speculated unceasingly. It was characteristic of the man that as soon as he left the paths of the prosaic he should seek his supernatural in a very concrete form. He assumed that he was haunted by the devil,—the visible personal devil in whom our fathers believed. He waited hourly for the shape at his side to speak, but no words came. The Accuser of the Brethren in all but tangible form was his ever present companion. He felt, he declared, the spirit of old evil entering subtly into his blood. He had sold his soul many times over, and yet there was no possibility of resistance. It was a Visitation more undeserved than Job's, and a thousandfold more awful.

For a week or more he was tortured with a kind of religious mania. When a man of a healthy secular mind finds himself adrift on the terrible ocean of religious troubles he is peculiarly helpless, for he has not the most rudimentary knowledge of the winds and tides. It was useless to call up his old carelessness; he had suddenly dropped into a new world where old proverbs did not apply. And all the while, mind you, there was the shrinking terror of it,—an intellect all alive to the torture and the most unceasing physical fear. For a little he was on the far edge of idiocy.

Then by accident it took a new form. While sitting with Sibyl one day in the library, he began listlessly to turn over the leaves of an old book. He read a few pages, and found the hint of a story like his own. It was some French Life of Justinian, one of the unscholarly productions of last century, made up of stories from Procopius and tags of Roman law. Here was his own case written down in black and white; and the man had been a king of kings. This was a new comfort, and for a little — strange though it may seem — he took a sort of pride in his affliction. He worshiped the great Emperor, and read every scrap he could find on him, not excepting the Pandects and the Digest. He sent for the bust in the dining room, paying a fabulous price. Then he settled himself to study his imperial prototype, and the study became an idolatry. As I have said, Ladlaw was a man of ordinary talents, and certainly of meagre imaginative power. And yet from the lies of the Secret History and the crudities of German legalists he had constructed a marvelous portrait of a man. Sitting there in the half-lighted room, he drew the picture: the quiet cold man with his inheritance of Dacian mysticism, holding the great world in fee, giving it law and religion, fighting its wars, building its churches, and yet all the while intent upon his own private work of making his peace with his soul, — the churchman and warrior whom all the world worshiped, and yet one going through life with his lip quivering. He Watched by the Threshold ever at the left side. Sometimes at night, in the great Brazen Palace, warders heard the Emperor walking in the dark corridors, alone, and yet not alone; for once, when a servant entered with a lamp, he saw his master with a face as of another world, and something beside him which had no face or shape, but which he knew to be that hoary Evil which is older than the stars.

Crazy nonsense! I had to rub my eyes to assure myself that I was not sleeping. No! There was my friend with his suffering face, and it was the library of More.

And then he spoke of Theodora, — actress, harlot, *dévote,* empress. For him the lady was but another part of the uttermost horror, a form of the shapeless thing at his side. I felt myself falling under the fascination. I have no nerves and little imagination, but in a flash I seemed to realize something of that awful featureless face, crouching ever at a man's hand, till darkness and loneliness come, and it rises to its mastery. I shivered as I looked at the man in the chair before me. These dull eyes of his were looking upon things I could not see, and I saw their terror. I realized that it was grim earnest for him. Nonsense or no, some devilish fancy had usurped the place of his sanity, and he was being slowly broken upon the wheel. And then, when his left hand twitched,

I almost cried out. I had thought it comic before; now it seemed the last proof of tragedy.

He stopped, and I got up with loose knees and went to the window. Better the black night than the intangible horror within. I flung up the sash and looked out across the moor. There was no light; nothing but an inky darkness and the uncanny rustle of elder bushes. The sound chilled me, and I closed the window.

"The land is the old Manann," Ladlaw was saying. "We are beyond the pale here. Do you hear the wind?"

I forced myself back into sanity and looked at my watch. It was nearly one o'clock.

"What ghastly idiots we are!" I said. "I am off to bed."

Ladlaw looked at me helplessly. "For God's sake, don't leave me alone!" he moaned. "Get Sibyl."

We went together back to the hall, while he kept the same feverish grasp on my arm. Some one was sleeping in a chair by the hall fire, and to my distress I recognized my hostess. The poor child must have been sadly wearied. She came forward with her anxious face.

"I'm afraid Bob has kept you very late, Henry," she said. "I hope you will sleep well. Breakfast at nine, you know." And then I left them.

III

Over my bed there was a little picture, a reproduction of some Italian work, of Christ and the Demoniac. Some impulse made me hold my candle up to it. The madman's face was torn with passion and suffering, and his eye had the pained furtive expression which I had come to know. And by his left side there was a dim shape crouching.

I got into bed hastily, but not to sleep. I felt that my reason must be going. I had been pitchforked from our clear and cheerful modern life into the mists of old superstition. Old tragic stories of my Calvinist upbringing returned to haunt me. The man dwelt in by a devil was no new fancy, but I believed that science had docketed and analyzed and explained the devil out of the world. I remembered my dabblings in the occult before I settled down to law,—the story of Donisarius, the monk of Padua, the unholy legend of the Face of Proserpine, the tales of *succubi* and *incubi,* the Leannain Sith and the Hidden Presence. But here was something stranger still. I had stumbled upon that very possession which fifteen hundred years ago had made the monks of New Rome tremble and cross themselves. Some devilish occult force, lingering through the ages, had come to life after a long sleep. God knows what earthly connection there was between the splendid Emperor of the World and my prosaic friend, or between the glittering shores of the Bosporus and this moorland parish! But the land was the old Manann! The spirit may have lingered in the earth and air, a deadly legacy from Pict and Roman. I had felt the uncanniness of the place; I had augured ill of it from the first. And then in sheer disgust I rose and splashed my face with cold water.

I lay down again, laughing miserably at my credulity. That I, the sober and rational, should believe in this crazy fable was too palpably absurd. I would steel my mind resolutely against such harebrained theories. It was a mere bodily ailment, — liver out of order, weak heart, bad circulation, or something of that sort. At the worst it might be some affection of the brain, to be treated by a specialist. I vowed to myself that next morning the best doctor in Edinburgh should be brought to More.

The worst of it was that my duty compelled me to stand my ground. I foresaw the few remaining weeks of my holiday blighted. I should be tied to this moorland prison, a sort of keeper and nurse in one, tormented by silly fancies. It was a charming prospect, and the thought of Glenaicill and the woodcock made me bitter against Ladlaw. But there was no way out of it. I might do Ladlaw good, and I could not have Sibyl worn to death by his vagaries.

My ill nature comforted me, and I forgot the horror of the thing in its vexation. After that I think I fell asleep and dozed uneasily till morning. When I woke I was in a better frame of mind. The early sun had worked wonders with the moorland. The low hills stood out fresh-colored and clear against a pale October sky; the elders sparkled with frost; the raw film of morn was rising from the little loch in tiny clouds. It was a cold, rousing day, and I dressed in good spirits and went down to breakfast.

I found Ladlaw looking ruddy and well; very different from the broken man I remembered of the night before. We were alone, for Sibyl was breakfasting in bed. I remarked on his ravenous appetite, and he smiled cheerily. He made two jokes during the meal; he laughed often, and I began to forget the events of the previous day. It seemed to me that I might still flee from More with a clear conscience. He had forgotten about his illness. When I touched distantly upon the matter he showed a blank face.

It might be that the affection had passed; on the other hand, it might return to him at the darkening. I had no means to decide. His manner was still a trifle distrait and peculiar, and I did not like the dullness in his eye. At any rate, I should spend the day in his company, and the evening would decide the question.

I proposed shooting, which he promptly vetoed. He was no good at walking, he said, and the birds were wild. This seriously limited the possible occupations. Fishing there was none, and hill-climbing was out of the question. He proposed a game at billiards, and I pointed to the glory of the morning. It would have been sacrilege to waste such sunshine in knocking balls about. Finally we agreed to drive somewhere and have lunch, and he ordered the dogcart.

In spite of all forebodings I enjoyed the day. We drove in the opposite direction from the woodland parts, right away across the moor to the coal country beyond. We lunched at the little mining town of Borrowmuir, in a small and noisy public house. The roads made bad going, the country was far from pretty, and yet the drive did not bore me. Ladlaw talked incessantly,—talked as I had never heard man talk before. There was something indescribable in all he said, a different point of view, a lost groove of thought, a kind of innocence and archaic shrewdness in one. I can only give you a hint of it by saying that it was like the mind of an early ancestor placed suddenly among modern surroundings. It was wise with a remote wisdom, and silly (now and then) with a quite antique and distant silliness.

I will give instances of both. He provided me with a theory of certain early fortifications, which must be true, which commends itself to the mind with overwhelming conviction, and yet which is so out of the way of common speculation that no man could have guessed it. I do not propose to set down the details, for I am working at it on my own account. Again, he told me the story of an old marriage custom, which till recently survived in this district,—told it with full circumstantial detail and constant allusions to other customs which he could not possibly have known of. Now for the other side. He explained why well water is in winter warmer than a running stream, and this was his explanation: at the antipodes our winter is summer; consequently, the water of a well which comes through from the other side of the earth must be warm in winter and cold in summer, since in our summer it is winter there. You perceive what this is. It is no mere silliness, but a genuine effort of an early mind, which had just grasped the fact of the antipodes, to use it in explanation.

Gradually I was forced to the belief that it was not Ladlaw who was talking to me, but something speaking through him, something at once wiser and simpler. My old fear of the devil began to depart. This spirit, the exhalation, whatever it was, was ingenuous in its way, at least in its daylight aspect. For a moment I had an idea that it was a real reflex of Byzantine thought, and that by cross-examining I might make marvelous discoveries. The ardor of the scholar began to rise in me, and I asked a question about that much-debated point, the legal status of the *apocrisiarii*. To my vexation he gave no response. Clearly the intelligence of this familiar had its limits.

It was about three in the afternoon, and we had gone half of our homeward journey, when signs of the old terror began to appear. I was driving, and Ladlaw sat on my left. I noticed him growing nervous and silent, shivering at the flick of the whip, and turning halfway round toward me. Then he asked me to change places, and I had the unpleasant work of driving from the wrong side. After that I do not think he spoke once till we arrived at More, but sat huddled together, with the driving rug almost up to his chin,—an eccentric figure of a man.

I foresaw another such night as the last, and I confess my heart sank. I had no stomach for more mysteries, and somehow with the approach of twilight the confidence of the day departed. The thing appeared in darker colors, and I found it in my mind to turn coward. Sibyl alone deterred me. I could not bear to think of her alone with this demented being. I remembered her shy timidity, her innocence. It was monstrous that the poor thing should be called on thus to fight alone with phantoms.

When we came to the House it was almost sunset. Ladlaw goc out very carefully on the right side, and for a second stood by the horse. The sun was making our shadows long, and as I stood beyond him it seemed for a moment that his shadow was double. It may have been mere fancy, for I had not time to look twice. He was standing, as I have said, with his left side next the horse. Suddenly the harmless elderly cob fell into a very panic of fright, reared upright, and all but succeeded in killing its master. I was in time to pluck Ladlaw from under its feet, but the beast had become perfectly unmanageable, and we left a groom struggling to quiet it.

In the hall the butler gave me a telegram. It was from my clerk, summoning me back at once to an important consultation.

IV

Here was a prompt removal of my scruples. There could be no question of my remaining, for the case was one of the first importance, which I had feared might break off my holiday. The consultation fell in vacation time to meet the convenience of certain people who were going abroad, and there was the most instant demand for my presence. I must go, and at once; and, as I hunted in the time-table, I found that in three hours' time a night train for the south would pass Borrowmuir which might be stopped by special wire.

But I had no pleasure in my freedom. I was in despair about Sibyl, and I hated myself for my cowardly relief. The dreary dining room, the sinister bust, and Ladlaw crouching and quivering, — the recollection, now that escape was before me, came back on my mind with the terror of a nightmare. My first thought was to persuade the Ladlaws to come away with me. I found them both in the drawing-room, — Sibyl very fragile and pale, and her husband sitting as usual like a frightened child in the shadow of her skirts. A sight of him was enough to dispel my hope. The man was fatally ill, mentally, bodily; and who was I to attempt to minister to a mind diseased?

But Sibyl, — she might be saved from the martyrdom. The servants would take care of him, and, if need be, a doctor might be got from Edinburgh to live in the house. So while he sat with vacant eyes staring into the twilight, I tried to persuade Sibyl to think of herself. I am frankly a sun worshiper. I have no taste for arduous duty, and the quixotic is my abhorrence. I labored to bring my cousin to this frame of mind. I told her that her first duty was to herself, and that this vigil of hers was beyond human endurance. But she had no ears for my arguments.

"While Bob is ill I must stay with him," she said always in answer, and then she thanked me for my visit, till I felt a brute and a coward. I strove to quiet my conscience, but it told me always that I was fleeing from my duty; and then, when I was on the brink of a nobler resolution, a sudden overmastering terror would take hold of me, and I would listen hysterically for the sound of the dogcart on the gravel.

At last it came, and in a sort of fever I tried to say the conventional farewells. I shook hands with Ladlaw, and when I dropped his hand it fell numbly on his knee. Then I took my leave, muttering hoarse nonsense about having had a "charming visit," and "hoping soon to see them both in town." As I backed to the door, I knocked over a lamp on a small table. It crashed on the floor and went out, and at the sound Ladlaw gave a curious childish cry. I turned like a coward, and ran across the hall to the front door, and scrambled into the dogcart.

The groom would have driven me sedately through the park, but I must have speed or go mad. I took the reins from him and put the horse into a canter. We swung through the gates and out into the moor road, for I could have no peace till the ghoulish elder world was exchanged for the homely ugliness of civilization. Once only I looked back, and there against the sky line, with a solitary lit window, the House of More stood lonely in the red desert.

December 1900

WILLIAM JAMES

1842–1910

It was a great occasion when these words were first spoken. Booker Washington was to make an oration and Bliss Perry a speech. From William James much was expected. Modestest of mortals, James slipped into the banqueting room and, taking Perry's arm, led him into a remote corner.

"But Professor James," said Perry, "of course you will be at the Head table."

James gave him a look of dumb despair. Then he said, "Yesterday I repeated my piece over to my wife twelve several times without one hitch — and now I can't remember the first paragraph."

Perry comforted him. "But Mr. James, it is not oratory that people want of you, it is thought and wisdom. Booker Washington will delight them, but what you say will be remembered. Why go through this agony? Let your paper lie open before you. That will give you confidence. Simply look up from time to time. Whatever the applause today, tomorrow's newspapers will tell the real story and that story will go on."

James glanced at him like a reprieved prisoner.

In another instant both were called to the Head table, and James gave to the world the first outline of his famous argument on "The Moral Equivalent of War."

Perry followed James, and when he sat down after a speech delivered in his easy graceful manner, James twitched his elbow. "Professor Perry," he whispered, "what an orator you are!"

Perry's speech and Washington's lie buried beneath the snows of yesteryear, but James's lives on in the world of tomorrow.

Remarks at the Peace Banquet[1]

WILLIAM JAMES

I AM only a philosopher, and there is only one thing that a philosopher can be relied on to do. You know that the function of statistics has been ingeniously described as being the refutation of other statistics. Well, a philosopher can always contradict other philosophers. In ancient times philosophers defined man as the rational animal; and philosophers since then have always found much more to say about the rational than about the animal part of the definition. But looked at candidly, reason bears about the same proportion to the rest of human nature that we in this hall bear to the rest of America, Europe, Asia, Africa, and Polynesia. Reason is one of the very feeblest of Nature's forces, if you take it at any one spot and moment. It is only in the very long run that its effects become perceptible. Reason assumes to settle things by weighing them against one another without prejudice, partiality, or excitement; but what affairs in the concrete are settled by is and always will be just prejudices, partialities, cupidities, and excitements. Appealing to reason as we do, we are in a sort of a forlorn hope situation, like a small sand-bank in the midst of a hungry sea ready to wash it out of existence. But sand-banks grow when the conditions favor; and weak as reason is, it has the unique advantage over its antagonists that its activity never lets up and that it presses always in one direction, while men's prejudices vary, their passions ebb and flow, and their excitements are intermittent. Our sand-bank, I absolutely believe, is bound to grow,—bit by bit it will get dyked and break-watered. But sitting as we do in this warm room, with music and lights and the flowing bowl and smiling faces, it is easy to get too sanguine about our task, and since I am called to speak, I feel as if it might not be out of place to say a word about the strength of our enemy.

Our permanent enemy is the noted bellicosity of human nature. Man, biologically considered, and whatever else he may be in the bargain, is simply the most formidable of all beasts of prey, and, indeed, the only one that preys systematically on its own species. We are once for all adapted to the military *status*. A millennium of peace would not breed the fighting disposition out of our bone and marrow, and a function so

[1] This banquet was given in Boston on the closing day of the World's Peace Congress, October 7, 1904.

ingrained and vital will never consent to die without resistance, and will always find impassioned apologists and idealizers.

Not only men born to be soldiers, but non-combatants by trade and nature, historians in their studies, and clergymen in their pulpits, have been war's idealizers. They have talked of war as of God's court of justice. And, indeed, if we think how many things beside the frontiers of states the wars of history have decided, we must feel some respectful awe, in spite of all the horrors. Our actual civilization, good and bad alike, has had past wars for its determining condition. Great-mindedness among the tribes of men has always meant the will to prevail, and all the more so if prevailing included slaughtering and being slaughtered. Rome, Paris, England, Brandenburg, Piedmont, — soon, let us hope, Japan, — along with their arms have made their traits of character and habits of thought prevail among their conquered neighbors. The blessings we actually enjoy, such as they are, have grown up in the shadow of the wars of antiquity. The various ideals were backed by fighting wills, and where neither would give way, the God of battles had to be the arbiter. A shallow view, this, truly; for who can say what might have prevailed if man had ever been a reasoning and not a fighting animal? Like dead men, dead causes tell no tales, and the ideals that went under in the past, along with all the tribes that represented them, find to-day no recorder, no explainer, no defender.

But apart from theoretic defenders, and apart from every soldierly individual straining at the leash, and clamoring for opportunity, war has an omnipotent support in the form of our imagination. Man lives *by* habits, indeed, but what he lives *for* is thrills and excitements. The only relief from Habit's tediousness is periodical excitement. From time immemorial wars have been, especially for non-combatants, the supremely thrilling excitement. Heavy and dragging at its end, at its outset every war means an explosion of imaginative energy. The dams of routine burst, and boundless prospects open. The remotest spectators share the fascination. With that awful struggle now in progress on the confines of the world, there is not a man in this room, I suppose, who doesn't buy both an evening and a morning paper, and first of all pounce on the war column.

A deadly listlessness would come over most men's imagination of the future if they could seriously be brought to believe that never again *in saecula saeculorum* would a war trouble human history. In such a stagnant summer afternoon of a world, where would be the zest or interest?

This is the constitution of human nature which we have to work against. The plain truth is that people *want* war. They want it anyhow; for itself; and apart from each and every possible consequence. It is the final bouquet of life's fireworks. The born soldiers want it hot and actual. The non-combatants want it in the background, and always as an open possibility, to feed imagination on and keep excitement going. Its clerical and historical defenders fool themselves when they talk as they do about it. What moves them is not the blessings it has won for us, but a vague religious exaltation. War, they feel, is human nature at its uttermost. We are here to do our uttermost. It is a sacrament. Society would rot, they think, without the mystical blood-payment.

We do ill, I fancy, to talk much of universal peace or of a general disarmament. We must go in for preventive medicine, not for radical cure. We must cheat our foe, politically circumvent his action, not try to change his nature. In one respect war is like love, though in no other. Both leave us intervals of rest; and in the intervals life goes on perfectly well without them, though the imagination still dallies with their possibility. Equally insane when once aroused and under headway, whether they shall be aroused or not depends on accidental circumstances. How are old maids and old bachelors made? Not by deliberate vows of celibacy, but by sliding on from year to year with no sufficient matrimonial provocation. So of the nations with their wars. Let the general possibility of war be left open, in Heaven's name, for the imagination to dally with. Let the soldiers dream of killing, as the old maids dream of marrying. But organize in every conceivable way the practical machinery for making each successive chance of war abortive. Put peace-men in power; educate the editors and statesmen to responsibility; — how beautifully did their trained responsibility in England make the Venezuela incident abortive! Seize every pretext, however small, for arbitration methods, and multiply the precedents; foster rival excitements and invent new outlets for heroic energy; and from one generation to another, the chances are that irritations will grow less acute and states of strain less dangerous among the nations. Armies and navies will continue, of course, and will fire the minds of populations with their potentialities of greatness. But their officers will find that somehow or other, with no deliberate intention on any one's part, each successive "incident" has managed to evaporate and to lead nowhere, and that the thought of what might have been remains their only consolation.

The last weak runnings of the war spirit will be "punitive expeditions." A country that turns its arms only against uncivilized foes is, I think, wrongly taunted as degenerate. Of course it has ceased to be heroic in the old grand style. But I verily believe that this is because it now sees something better. It has a conscience. It knows that between civilized countries a war is a crime against civilization. It will still perpetrate peccadillos, to be sure. But it is afraid, afraid in the good sense of the word, to engage in absolute crimes against civilization.

December 1904

GEOFFREY HOUSEHOLD

1903–

I had never heard of him when his first story arrived, but when I cabled accepting it with joy, I added that his name was worth a hundred thousand readers. At the time, of course, I held that "Household" was a word assumed for the good of the trade, but when I discovered that this substantial asset had been transmitted to him by a thoughtful parent, it seemed the happiest of omens. Geoffrey went to Oxford and, in accordance with his mission in life, brought home a First Class in English literature, but when after graduation he became confidential secretary to the management of the Bank of Rumania at Bucharest, friends suspected his career had gone off the rails. It was some time before he got a new start. He drifted about the Balkans, came to know them like the palm of his hand, and then found in Spain his other country, learning to think in Castilian and to speak in proverbs.

Household's first visit to the United States was timed with indiscretion. He and the Great Depression arrived simultaneously. Once, you remember, it was pointed out by Samuel Butler that Hypothetics — behavior predicated upon circumstance and infinitely the most important course for life — is not taught in the universities, but somewhere Household had acquired the rudiments of the art. When he was hungry he tossed off historical playlets for Columbia to broadcast, and soon immersed himself in an extraordinary enterprise, no less than the compilation of an Encyclopedia for Children. To the callousness of foisting such erudition on boys and girls he gave no thought. All knowledge was his oyster and he devoured it with voracity. From AARON to AZTEC he went, from BAALBEK to BYZANTIUM, plugging alphabetically through all the scholarship in the world until an "N" stared him in the face. At this point a sharp contraction in his employer's expenditures occurred and Household was thrown upon the world, knowing, as he would philosophically observe, precisely half of universal knowledge — the top half — everything describable through the first thirteen letters of the alphabet. Fortunately that included Hell and Heaven. The other half Household has still to learn, but he is hard at it.

"Patience, and shuffle the cards."

The Salvation of Pisco Gabar

GEOFFREY HOUSEHOLD

THE *Santa Juana* glided towards the equator with the overpowering coast of Peru five miles to port. The setting sun rested neatly on the tangent of the horizon as if an almighty sextant were about to shoot it. To the east the vast yellow foothills of the Andes turned green and purple where the level rays dug into scattered deposits of copper and gold. From his deck chair on the after verandah Manuel Gabar watched the metallic immensities of the coast. His pleasure was calm and reflective, for he was used to having beauty spread for him on enormous canvases.

His origin was unknown and of no great interest to himself or to his friends. His passport declared him Ecuadorian; but that he knew was untrue, since he himself had bought the document from a friendly official in Guayaquil. His native language was Spanish. His name was one of his earliest recollections, and he was sure it was his; but it gave no definite clue to his ancestry. Nor did his appearance. He was a shortish, powerful man with slightly bandy legs and a snub nose. High cheekbones and wide mouth were evidence of some Indian blood on the mother's side. Gray eyes, thick dark hair on head, hands, and chest, suggested a Central European immigrant as father. A charity school had picked him off the streets of Buenos Aires, taught him to read, and given him to the sea. The sea taught him self-reliance and socialism and cast him up again in South America. Since then he had been a good citizen of the five Andean republics, courteous to all men, breaking only such laws as were meant to be broken, and employing his rough energy and his capital (when he had any) in developing odds and ends of trade that nobody else had thought of.

Gabar had an inquiring mind and was well able to divert himself by elementary speculations on man, his surroundings, and the reasons for both. At the moment it was geology that interested him. He wondered whether the Andes were still pushing westwards into the Pacific. They gave so definite an impression of an advancing wave topped by all the mineral débris of a continent. He also wondered if schools of mining could teach one to spot an exploitable quantity of precious metal by its appearance under the horizontal rays of the setting sun. He had an exaggerated respect for secular schools of all sorts, never realizing that they could but analyze and express the accumulated experience of such adventurers in life as he himself.

His reverie was broken by a pleasant but too determined voice.

"If the señor permits, I will join him for a moment."

Gabar looked round. The setting sun was blotted out by a tall pyramid of black cassock. Almost startled by the silence of the priest's approach and the blackness of him at close quarters, he followed the pyramid to its apex and met the commanding eyes of Don Jesús.

Manuel Gabar welcomed companionship; he was entirely without prejudice against human beings of any color or class, of any degree of virtue or criminality. But he could not abide priests. To him they were enemies of the intellect, moneygrubbers, hypocrites, and buffoons in the fancy dress of piety. Being naturally courteous, he was even more resentful of the intrusion than a ruder man would have been. But he said nothing. There was nothing to say. It was obvious that Don Jesús intended to sit down with or without his permission. He was a magnificent blue-jowled Basque in the flower of middle age. He joined in the deck games and would certainly become a bishop.

"The señor will pardon my interruption," said Don Jesús, "but am I right in supposing that he lands tomorrow morning at Mollendo?"

"You are."

"I have a great favor to ask you, if you would be so kind."

"At your complete service," replied Gabar with conventional politeness, adding, with detestation of himself and the title, "reverend padre."

After all, he argued, what did it matter? One said "friend" to cutthroats, "chief" to naked savages, "caballero" to gringo oil drillers — why not "reverend" to a priest?

"My friend, Don José-Maria, also lands at Mollendo," the priest said. "He is an old man and before this journey he had never left the plateau. Might I ask you to see him through customs and as far as Arequipa by the train?"

"Yes, but — "

"You yourself, I suppose, are going to Arequipa?"

"I am," said Gabar.

He would have dearly loved to say he was not. But all the trains from Mollendo passed through Arequipa. It was also certain that he and this José-Maria would leave Mollendo together by the first train after the arrival of the *Santa Juana*. Nobody ever left Mollendo by any but the first train.

"In that case you and he will be traveling companions. I commend him to your courtesy."

"Very well," said Gabar. "Very well. I shall be delighted. But I am not a wet nurse, you understand. I won't take any responsibility for him. You had better know that I am not fond of the Church."

"You will like Don José-Maria. He is only a child. So pious, so simple, an angel among Indians! He understands them very well — too well, perhaps. But there! He is left to himself and we cannot blame him if he takes his own line."

"I blame nobody," said Gabar. "We are animals. Will you have a pisco?"

For the first time in his life he had invited a priest to have a drink. It was not that he liked Don Jesús. He detested him. But it was Gabar's fixed habit to drink while talking. His friends had nicknamed him Pisco Gabar — not that he drank more than was reasonable, but he considered the delectable Peruvian grape spirit a necessary prelude to conversation. Even in the Montaña, — the network of valleys that ran down from the Andes to become the Amazon, — where he traveled with only such essentials as could be carried on his back, he was never without a tepid half litre of pisco to celebrate the improbable meeting of another white man.

Don Jesús was flattered when laymen invited him to have a drink. He seldom refused, but never took more than one. Gabar ordered two pisco-sours. They drank them while Don Jesús talked with worldly and accomplished ease. Gabar answered him chiefly with scowls. He was slightly, and inconsistently, shocked by the priest. At last he made an effort at politeness.

"Have you come from Europe, reverend padre?"

"No, no, my dear sir! From Buenos Aires, from the Eucharistic Congress. A stupendous spectacle! A hundred thousand of the faithful of all nations attending open-air Mass! A supreme affirmation of the faith of America!"

"The opium of the people," grumbled Pisco Gabar.

"Pardon?"

"I said religion was the opium of the people," repeated Gabar, with the determination of a martyr before his judge.

"I have heard," said Don Jesús, unruffled, "that opium is very comforting. Are you a communist, señor?"

"I think for myself and I do not believe all I am told. I am a human being, a worker!"

Pisco Gabar was eager for battle, and rapidly mustering his antireligious munitions, which included Marx, Paine, Ingersoll, some Mexican pronunciamentos, and the invincible materialism of his own spirit. But Don Jesús had no difficulty in perceiving his intention, and avoided engagement. He would willingly have tackled a heretic, but with an atheist there was no common ground for discussion.

"A worker?" asked Don Jesús. "A miner, I believe?"

"I am against the whole rotten system," began Gabar excitedly. "Now take the Mexican Church, for example—"

"Gold!" Don Jesús interrupted dreamily. "Gold! A fascinating subject! You should ask Don José-Maria about gold. Of course his parish is a little difficult to reach."

"Where gold is, it is always difficult to reach," said Gabar. "But it can be done."

"The spirit of the *conquistadores!* You should have been born four hundred years ago!"

"In my way I follow their tradition," said Gabar, flattered. "In my way!"

It was true. For several years Pisco Gabar had been engaged in a trade of his own invention as profitable and uncomfortable as any in Latin America. The streams of the Montaña were full of alluvial gold. They paid to wash, but did not pay to work intensively. The cost of transporting machinery was prohibitive. Some of the valleys were earthly paradises, but only a mule could reach them. Others were drenched in summer by the steady purposeful rains of the Amazon, and in winter by the steady purposeful rains of the Pacific. Even the English went mad after 365 continual days and nights of rain. The Indians worked intermittently at panning the inaccessible streams, but the gold dust had small value to them. A day spent in hunting or cultivation was more productive. Sometimes a trusted fellow tribesman would set off with the communal bag of gold to Cuzco or the nearest mine and return, if he were neither robbed nor tempted to drink, with such goods as he could carry on his back. It was hardly worth while carrying the gold to a market.

Pisco Gabar hit on the idea of carrying a market to the gold. He established small depots of cotton and leather goods, nails, tools, beads, and whatever was light to carry and considered by primitive minds to be either useful or decorative. At these depots he loaded his back and that of a mule and vanished into the tumbled forests. Weeks later he appeared at the edge of civilization alone and on foot, having given his goods, his animal, and sometimes his coat and shirt in exchange for the ounces of gold dust at his belt. The profit, Gabar explained to Don Jesús, was considerable, but so was the benefit to the Indians. He was, he admitted, a parasite, although a useful one. He compared his function in the Montaña to that of a waste-paper merchant (a profession which he had also followed) in a town. He called as regularly as he could, took away an unwanted commodity, and gave unexpected value in return.

II

At seven the following morning the *Santa Juana* lay two miles off Mollendo. A string of barges, loaded with copper and alpaca, undulated towards her over the long Pacific swell. The tender heaved up and down alongside, her gunwale at one moment below the foot of the gangway and, at the next, ten steps up. The brown boatmen fended her off skillfully while with lazy patience they watched Don José-Maria saying his farewells. Gabar, already seated in the tender, began to look at his watch. He was not in a hurry, nor indeed did he ever allow hurry to afflict him, but he objected to being kept waiting by a priest.

José-Maria insisted on saying good-bye to all the passengers who were up, and was only with difficulty restrained from waiting to say good-bye to those who were still in their bunks. He was seven-eighths pure Indian, yellow and fat and given to simple ecstasies. Since Buenos Aires he had lived in a pious daze. The Congress and the journeying by rail and water had opened the gates of the world to him. He who had never been off the highlands of Peru in his life had dwelt in a modern city, had heard the Holy Father speak over the radio, had realized the true meaning of distance and seas and lands beyond them, had found to his amazement that there were actually Christians who spoke neither Spanish nor Quechua; it was difficult to understand how they could say their prayers. He believed that death would be something like his voyage to Buenos Aires — a stupendous experience shattering all preconceived ideas and startling him with the truth of angels, as had the truth of automobiles.

In his sadness at the end of this adventure he lost count and bade farewell to captain, officers, and passengers over and over again. This done, he lingered at the gangway making a third interminable speech of thanks to Don Jesús. Gabar cut it short by pressing the button of the tender's siren. The sudden and commanding growl brought Don José-Maria hastily down the gangway.

The boatman, settling his straw hat firmly on his head, extended his hand and told the priest to jump. José-Maria bent his knees, prepared, but hesitated. The boat sunk far below him. He regarded the rise and fall of the swell in benevolent surprise. With his almond eyes and yellow beaming countenance he resembled a rotund Chinese statuette. The boat rose again and he grasped the outstretched wrist, but still he did not jump. Nor did he let go. The tender sunk from under the boatman, who squirmed and kicked in mid-air like a hooked fish. Don José-Maria, having hung on at first from terror and now hanging on lest the boatman should drop, tried to get both hands to the job and overbalanced.

Gabar hurled himself forward to break their fall. José-Maria landed safely cushioned on him and the unfortunate boatman. While they extricated themselves indignantly, he remained in an unwieldy black ball, his eyes shut and his lips moving in prayer. As no one was hurt, the tender chugged off towards Mollendo.

"I have more luck than I merit," murmured José-Maria. "I am always in peril by land and sea, yet mercifully delivered."

"You try your pet saint too far," said Gabar coldly.

"Impossible; especially when he works through such kindly instruments as yourself, Don Manuel. I am very grateful to you."

"No reason to be! I'd have done the same for anyone," Gabar answered ungraciously. "Are you all right?"

"Yes, yes, Don Manuel! A little bruised, a little shaken, but I only need a glass of spirits."

"I can offer you some pisco."

"Thank you. Thank you. You are very kind."

Gabar drew out a half litre of pisco, conveniently placed among his pyjamas at the top of his bag, and offered it to José-Maria. The priest put it to his lips and drank three quarters of the contents.

"Thank you. You are very kind," he repeated. "I was in great need. Don Jesús did not wish me to drink on board. He is a stern man. Very stern."

"He certainly gets his own way," said Gabar resentfully.

"So clear! So knowledgeable in this world! He told me there were four things I was not to do. Let me see! Four things. I was not to drink — that was one. And second — he said I was not to let you leave me till we got to Arequipa."

"The hell he did!"

"And there were two more. I was not to forget — let me see! My glasses? No, I have them. My trunk? No, it was not that. It contains all I possess, Don Manuel, for I thought I might be years on the road. And then there is a present in it for one much greater than I. No, I could never forget my trunk. Let me see! What was it I must not forget? . . . Ah, my passport!"

Don José-Maria began to search through his pockets. He looked at Gabar with the simplicity of a child.

"I have forgotten it," he said.

Gabar with unconcealed disgust told the boatman to put back to the ship. He silently consigned Don Jesús to the deepest pit of hell and Don José-Maria to a lunatic asylum, with the added hope that each of them would meet his destiny before there was time for him to deliver the old fool at Arequipa.

"I will go and get it," said José-Maria, jumping up energetically as soon as they lay alongside the *Santa Juana.*

Gabar hastily got between the priest and the gangway. He did not dread the difficulty of reëmbarking the old gentleman so much as the lengthy good-byes which he was certain to say all over again. He hailed Don Jesús, asking him to search José-Maria's cabin for the passport.

"It would be so much better if I went myself," suggested José-Maria appealingly.

In a few minutes Don Jesús returned with the passport. He handed it to a steward, waved good-bye curtly, and turned away with a certain air of annoyance as the man brought it down to the tender.

"He is angry with me," José-Maria sighed.

"It doesn't matter if he is."

"Oh, not about the passport. No! But he must have seen the empty bottles."

"The empty bottles?"

"Yes, Don Manuel. You see, I felt seasick, and as Don Jesús did not like me to drink and as I needed a little cheer for my stomach's sake . . ."

Pisco Gabar began to choke with laughter. José-Maria's besetting sin was obvious. Hypocrites! What hypocrites! He did his best to feel indignant, but was overcome by amusement. He began to like José-Maria, chiefly because the old man had annoyed Don Jesús. And then it was really impossible to dislike anyone so simple.

"What was the fourth thing Don Jesús told you to remember?" he asked.

"I forget," answered José-Maria humbly. "*Ay!* It is hard to remember so many things. I am no traveler, Don Manuel. Once a week I go from Huanca del Niño to Chiquibamba — twenty kilometres, Don Manuel — and that is all the traveling I have done since I left the seminary at Cuzco."

"Huanca del Niño? I have seen a track that leads there. It starts from the valley of the Inambari."

"Our only road, Don Manuel. A devil of a road! But it matters little, since it is seldom trodden."

"Isn't there a fort or temple up at Huanca?"

"There are great walls, and within them was once a temple. But it is now a church, Don Manuel — my church."

Gabar, whose memory was crisscrossed by the lines of obscure pathways, knew the lower end of the track that wound up to Huanca del Niño from the valley of the Inambari. His Indian friends had told him that it was one of the ancient roads from the Montaña to the altiplano, and that up on the bare hillsides, where vegetable growth was slow to cover, it was still paved. This he doubted. Huanca he knew only by name as one of the towering bluffs thrown out by the Andes towards the Amazon, and by a solitary glimpse of it from ten thousand feet below. On the distant sky line had been a straight line of somewhat paler yellow than the yellow flanks of the mountain, which suggested that the summit was crowned by prehistoric masonry.

III

The tender drew alongside the jetty and Don José-Maria hastily followed his black tin trunk ashore and into the customs shed. Gabar went in search of the inspector, for he never paid customs duties on his own west coast. He would have indignantly denied that he bribed, but he took great satisfaction in being on friendly — genuinely friendly — terms with all those in authority. He especially liked to give christening presents to their children. As he seldom entered any port more than once in nine months, he was sure to find that the inspector's señora was either expecting or recovering.

The inspector, with tears in his eyes and gestures of arms and shoulders which violently suggested the upward movement of a corkscrew, was explaining to Gabar the latest obstetrical problem when a customs officer saluted and interrupted them.

"There's a priest," he said. "A mad priest! He put a curse on me in Quechua. Not, of course, that I believe in such nonsense, being an educated man and a servant of the republic. Still, it is an insult to the uniform and one is not comfortable— "

"One is not," said Gabar, instantly making a friend for life. "And so I will remove the curse."

He pronounced an impressive blessing in the Indian language.

"You all know that I am no friend of the Church," Gabar went on. "It does not fit into our system. But this old fool is in my charge."

"In that case, friend Pisco, it is different," said the inspector cordially.

They found José-Maria sitting broodily on his tin trunk and glaring, so far as it was possible for his eyes to glare, at an interested crowd of idlers.

"He shall not touch it, Don Manuel! He asked me to open it and I opened it, but he shall not put his hands inside. It is sacrilege. I cannot allow it!"

"You see, Señor Pisco, he is mad! I said so!" exclaimed the customs officer triumphantly. "My hands are clean—look at them! And I am always ready to use discretion. I would never embarrass a traveler by exposing to the public what he would rather they did not see!"

"I am sure of it," said Gabar solemnly. "But the reverend padre is very obstinate, and we do not want discussions."

The inspector, for the sake of the onlookers, sternly ordered José-Maria's trunk to be carried to his office, and from there sent it through the gates with Pisco's baggage, which naturally was not examined. On the way to the station the priest overwhelmed Pisco with thanks, which he waved aside with the remark that, had he known Don José-Maria did not wish to expose the contents of his trunk, it could have been arranged without so much fuss.

"What have you got there?" he asked. "More empty bottles?"

"Don Manuel," replied José-Maria, "if I had not received so many favors from you, I should not forgive that question. I am a sinner, but not so wretched that I would pack the signs of my folly next to a sacred garment."

Gabar was so surprised by this answer that he apologized. The old man had suddenly and unexpectedly put on the full authority of the Church. José-Maria retreated into a dignified silence, while Gabar let himself go in mental abuse of priests in general and this particular nuisance that had been inflicted on him. It occurred to him, however, that he only really liked José-Maria when he *was* a nuisance. His theory was promptly proved right at the station, for there the priest discovered that he had forgotten the fourth essential which Don Jesús had told him not to forget. It was his return ticket. As José-Maria had only a few centavos in his pocket, Gabar paid his fare to Arequipa. Don José-Maria, who had no idea of how to get money from Arequipa to Mollendo and had had gloomy indefinite visions of sleeping on the streets and growing his own maize on the rubbish heaps, was correspondingly grateful.

Gabar's gold peddling had not yet been discussed. José-Maria had heard of it from Don Jesús and wished to invite the trader to bring a stock of goods to Huanca del Niño. He hesitated to do so because he did not consider a few ounces of gold worth weeks of traveling, and, feeling very dependent on Gabar's kindliness, did not wish to abuse it. Pisco, on his part, had given little thought to Don Jesús' advice to ask José-Maria about gold, believing it on later reflection to be a jesuitical lie.

Now that the train was climbing fussily up into the desert foothills and no further difficulties immediately threatened, José-Maria asked Gabar what route he would take on his next journey.

"To Cuzco and north," answered Gabar, "unless anything offers at this end of the country."

José-Maria was silent for a minute or two while he considered whether or not he should accept, without further polite preliminaries, this invitation to talk.

"It's very hot in the train," Gabar said, taking down from the rack a fresh bottle of pisco which he had bought on the way to the station and handing it to José-Maria. The priest said a short grace and applied his lips to the bottle. He decided that he might take courage.

"How much gold would you expect, Don Manuel, to make it worth your while, if you were to take a long, a very difficult journey to a very distant pueblo?"

"As much as a man can carry and still carry his food," Gabar replied.

"Not more?"

"*Hombre!* I've seldom got so much!"

"I think if you came to Huanca and Chiquibamba," said José-Maria timidly, "we could trade you all you could carry. That is — if you stayed a little while."

Gabar took a pull at the bottle.

"Where do your people get their gold?" he asked. "Have you found an Inca treasure or do you pan streams?"

"Neither one nor the other, Don Manuel. There is a bank of pebbles, and when we have enough water in the stream we wash them down a trough and a little gold remains behind at the bottom."

"Good God! But with pumps and hoses you could get millions out of those gravel beds!"

"It may be so, Don Manuel. I know nothing of that. But there is hardly enough water for ourselves, and none for the troughs except in the two months of rain."

"In that case it looks like my usual business," said Gabar calmly—he was used to having his dreams of instant wealth swiftly shattered. "How do I get to Huanca? Isn't there a road from the altiplano without going down to the Inambari?"

"*Ay!* If only there were! There was such a road in colonial days. But many years ago, before my time, perhaps two hundred years ago, the western side of the hill was washed away. And now a man must go down from Cuzco to the Montaña and up again to Huanca. But you will travel with me, Don Manuel, and a guide will show us the way."

"Another pisco?" suggested Gabar, avoiding the invitation.

"Thank you, Don Manuel. It is indeed hot in the train."

"I know the way to the foot of your mountain," Gabar said. "But what happens then?"

"You follow the track up, always up, till you come to a steep gully which cuts a line of cliffs. Here one must turn right or left along the foot of the cliffs. The right path leads to Huanca and the left to Chiquibamba. There is a patch of bog below the fork."

"What would you like me to bring your people?"

"Some tools and rough steel for working, Don Manuel, and a few pretty things for the women. I like to see them look well at Mass. And some images. Saint Joseph, I advise."

"I will not encourage superstition," declared Gabar firmly. "No saints!"

"What a pity you do not believe! It is a shame that so good a man should be a heathen! But do not be angry with me if I ask you to bring some little Saint Josephs. Quite little ones, Don Manuel. The Child and His Blessed Mother can never feel neglected by us, but my parishioners have so little to put them in mind of poor Saint Joseph. And they will pay you well, Don Manuel. Gold for little Saint Josephs that only cost you a sol apiece at Cuzco!"

"It's against my principles," said Gabar. "I can't be bought. And I will not be a party to perpetuating the present system!"

"I do not understand," said Don José-Maria unhappily. "How is it possible that you can hate what is so simple and good? I will pray for you, Don Manuel."

"If it gives you any pleasure," remarked Gabar, shrugging his shoulders, "you can add the other hundred million workers who don't believe fairy tales."

IV

At Arequipa, Gabar handed over Don José-Maria to a bevy of local churchmen who were at the station to meet him. The priest intended to stay there for a week or two while he made arrangements for a guide and transport to take him home. Gabar, although he had developed a toleration for José-Maria, had no intention of being his companion on a journey which would certainly last ten days and possibly more. When he saw the old man again, he pleaded urgent business in the north and roundly declared that if he were to go to Huanca at all it must be immediately. He made a selection of the goods he had in store at Arequipa and took them by rail to Cuzco, where he bought two llamas and a mule. Within a week he was on his way to the upper Inambari.

It needed a fine eye for country to cross half a dozen of the great herring-bones of ravines and ridges lying with their heads up against the main range and their tails in the Brazilian forest. Pisco Gabar traveled partly by instinct and partly by inquiry from occasional Indians. A compass was useless, since most of the time he was traveling in the only direction allowed by the ribs of the herring, which was never at any given moment the direction in which he wanted to go. The going for man and animals was appallingly hard. A day's march was a scramble up from a gorge; a laborious working in zigzags through semitropical forest, where the mincing steps and high-carried heads of the llamas well expressed their distaste for such vulgar luxuriance; rough trampling over the scrub above the tree line; and a rush over the barren hilltop in order to get out of the wind and down into shelter for the night's camp — twenty miles across country from the previous camp, but not more than three by the straight line of an imaginary tunnel.

There were, however, few serious discomforts, for that part of the

Montaña was a paradise of trees, flowers, and running water. Even the insects were more spectacular than bloodthirsty. Pisco was accustomed to the utter loneliness of the Montaña, and loved it. His religious emotions — he himself would never have called them such — were satisfied by the worship of nature. He delighted to muse by his campfire on the curious habits of orchids, pumas, caverns, and storms, and to find explanations. But he was unaware that his own appreciation of them also demanded an explanation.

On the evening of the eighth day he camped on the upper Inambari at the foot of the track which led to Huanca del Niño. He was up before dawn, and two hours later on top of the ridge that bordered the river. A close-set group of conical mountains faced him, their peaks rising to an average height of 16,000 feet. This was the eastern rampart of the main range. The high points which appeared to be peaks were not really such, but bluffs rising comparatively little from the altiplano beyond. On one of them he saw again the straight yellowish-white line of a pre-Inca wall, flattening the top of the escarpment and marking the site of Huanca del Niño.

The track dived off the ridge into a last valley and then began to climb the irregular ravine that separated the height of Huanca from its neighbor, which was, he supposed, Chiquibamba. The llamas quickened their pace towards the undecorated horizon of their desires.

Pisco, plodding ahead of his animals, was fascinated by the track. What the Indians had told him about it was true. It had a purposefulness lacking in the familiar paths of the Montaña. The latter scuttered from cover to cover like the savages who had made them. They had been widened and deepened by *arrieros* and their pack animals, but they preserved their inconsequential lines. The track which he now followed was narrow and rough, but it struck out boldly along the contour lines and had a certain air of triumph in surmounting rather than circumventing the minor obstacles in its path. Pisco was aware of pride in it. It was not the absurd self-satisfaction with which an American arrogates to himself, merely by virtue of living on the same continent, the achievements of a people without the remotest relationship to him in blood or culture, but a pride of closer parentage. Pisco was unconscious of his Indian blood when he was dealing with white civilization or forest savages, yet he felt a community of thought and interest, which did not at all fit his habitual conception of himself, with the builders of this road.

The trees had given place to low scrub when he came to the little patch of bog which José-Maria had described. He was right up against the main escarpment. The ravine rose sharply ahead of him in a tumble of rocks. A natural platform which the hand of man had certainly aided by leveling and facing overhung the bog, and two paths led off it at right angles to the track up which he had come.

The right-hand path, leading to Huanca, looked a hair-raising piece of mountaineering. It followed the foot of the cliff, while the slope beneath it grew steeper and steeper until the path was a mere ledge on a sheer face of rock. Pisco decided to tackle it in the morning and camped on the platform.

With the rising sun throwing its angle into stronger relief, the path clung more firmly to the mountain side. It was definitely, though primitively, engineered, paved here and there with massive stones, and cut a little back into the cliffs where the natural slopes and ledges were not wide enough for easy passage. After leading him up for some two thousand feet, the track turned on to the northern shoulder of the mountain. At the bend was a niche in the rock, marked, so that no traveler should miss it, with a black cross. A three-foot cow's horn hung from a hook within the niche. Pisco Gabar had seen a similar horn in the Argentine Andes and knew its use. It invited the passer-by to give warning of his approach, since the path was about to become so narrow that two mules could not pass abreast. He put it to his lips and blew a doleful blast that might have proceeded from the cow itself. Then he waited twenty minutes, in case an arriero should be already on the path, meanwhile tightening the girths of his three animals.

Gabar found the track spectacular rather than alarming, for he had as good a head for heights as his own llamas. It was about three feet wide, with a slope on the inner side which, while not quite perpendicular, was quite unclimbable, and a sheer drop on the outer side. The path, varying little in width, clung to the edge of this precipice for a full mile. Then it opened out, passed another horn for the use of descending travelers, and wound up a wind-swept slope of scanty turf and gravel which continued as far as the wall of Huanca del Niño.

V

There were no pure whites in Huanca, though half the population of the pueblo had a little white blood. They preferred to speak Quechua, but, if Spanish were required, they spoke it with a perfect accent, an archaic diction, and a very limited vocabulary. Gabar was welcomed with grave, unquestioning hospitality, and then, when he said he had come by invitation of Don José-Maria, with frank curiosity and good-fellowship.

There was a drink-shop which called itself an inn and was used as one when an occasional trader or arriero visited Huanca. Gabar was given the room of honor which had been prepared for the diocesan inspector a year earlier with furniture lent by the whole pueblo. Since they were not a little proud of the room and it was easier to leave the furniture where it was than to take it back, the place had remained a permanent exhibition of their treasures. It would have been pretty clean had not the chickens adopted two Tarragona chamber pots as nesting places.

Every evening the patio of the inn became a shop where all the inhabitants congregated whether or not they had gold to sell. Business was accompanied by leisurely drinking and interminable stories. There was plenty of gold. Tiny quantities of dust were even used as an internal currency, as small change to adjust the equitable exchange of commodities. After a week Gabar had traded goods worth about £40 in Arequipa, including one of his llamas, for over a pound and a half of gold dust—which meant that he had more than trebled his outlay. Finding that he had then exhausted the market, he decided to try his luck at Chiquibamba. He left Huanca in the early afternoon, intending to camp at the natural platform above the bog.

Pisco Gabar swung down the path in an excellent humor. Huanca del Niño could make him a nice little fortune, especially if he visited it after the rainy season, when the inhabitants would work their gravel bank intensively and hold the proceeds for his coming. At the same time he was treated by the pueblo as a benefactor and even as an easy mark for keen traders, for he haggled no more than was necessary to gain their respect. He had not a care in the world. All of three senses were thoroughly satisfied. The smell of the animals, of leather, and mountain air tickled his nostrils. His belly regurgitated a pleasing flavor of rice, roast kid, and alcohol. His fingers toyed with the wash-leather bags in his belt, squeezing the soft, heavy dust. The mule and the llama tripped confidently after him. At this moment, rounding a bend in the path, he came face to face with Don José-Maria.

"*Padre de mi alma!* How are you?"

José-Maria looked at him with mingled fear and pleasure.

"Don Manuel! I am glad to see you! That goes without saying. But what are we going to do? How was I to know you were on the way down?"

Gabar awoke to his surroundings.

"*Condenado* that I am! I forgot to blow the horn!"

He strung together some blazing jewels of oaths which ended before completing their rhythmical pattern, partly from respect for Don José-Maria and partly because Gabar suddenly looked down past his left knee and became aware of the emptiness beyond.

"And you, padre! You did not blow the horn either!"

"I blew it, my son. But it was not very loud. I have been so long in the lowlands that my breath does not come as easily as it did. Yet you would have heard had you waited and listened."

"The fault is mine," admitted Gabar. "And now, how are we going to pass?"

They stood facing one another like a metope carved on the face of the rock. The two men formed the high and central point of the design. Behind José-Maria were a mule, carrying his tin trunk, and a donkey for riding; behind Gabar, his pack-mule and the remaining llama.

"We cannot pass," answered José-Maria.

"Let us sit down," Gabar said. "There is nothing impossible."

The two sat down on the path with their backs against the rock and their heels overhanging two hundred feet of sheer cliff. Ten thousand feet below, the Montaña spread out its tumble of hills mapped into orderliness by the occasional gleaming threads of water. In the far distance the green of the forest faded away into the blue of tropical haze. It was utterly silent except for the tinkle of bridles and bits and the occasional snatches of wind that sung and stabbed like giant insects.

"A cigarette?" suggested Gabar.

"Thank you, my son."

"And a pisco, perhaps?"

"With pleasure. I have not eaten nor drunk since morning."

Gabar stood up to fetch a bottle from the mule's pack. The full realization of their position came to him when he found that he could not get at the straps. The inner pack was jammed against the rock, and the mule refused to be forced any closer to the edge. The outer pack could be reached by pushing the mule's head to the rock and standing alongside its neck. But it was by no means a healthy position. One's life depended on the uncertain patience of the mule.

"It seems we must go thirsty, padre."

Gabar pulled his heavy poncho over his head and wrapped himself in its folds before sitting down again. He looked perfectly prepared to spend the night where he was, and thus in the master position for any bargaining there might be. Both knew that the only solution was for one of them to sacrifice his mule. But neither was yet ready to admit it. There was no hurry.

"How is it you are alone, padre?"

"I hired my guide only as far as the Inambari, Don Manuel. He was a Montaña man and did not wish to climb to the altiplano."

"And the animals are yours?"

"They belong to the Church, Don Manuel, and were lent to me in Cuzco. I have become very fond of them. This one,"—he reached up and stroked the mule's muzzle,—"is almost a Christian."

"This one," said Gabar, waving a hand at his mule, "has a soul like mine. He eats when there is food and fasts when there is none."

Don José-Maria also drew on his poncho and made no reply. For half an hour they sat side by side without a word. Finally the priest said reproachfully:—

"You did not blow the horn, Don Manuel."

"I did not blow the horn," Gabar agreed, stating it as a matter of fact without a shade of guilt or regret in his voice. "Shall I roll you another cigarette?"

"Thank you, Don Manuel. You are very courteous."

José-Maria preserved silence till he had smoked it. Then he murmured:—

"It is a shame you are not a Christian."

"Why?"

"Because,"—José-Maria hesitated, feeling that he had been forced on to dangerous ground,—"because you would give way to a priest."

"Equally I might cut his throat," said Gabar, "and give him a little push and a little push to each of his animals. There are plenty of Christians who would do so."

"But you would not," answered José-Maria calmly.

"You are right. Instead of that, I shall offer to buy your mule."

"It is not mine to sell. It belongs to the Church."

"Then give the money to the Church."

"I have no authority, Don Manuel. And I love this mule like a son. You must give way to me, for you did not blow the horn. Kill your own mule."

"I will not. I should lose half my goods with him. You saw for yourself that I could not get the pack off. Sell me your mule and name your price."

"No, my son. God will decide between us."

The pack animals pawed and fussed impatiently. The sun had passed westwards over the brow of the mountain and it was turning cold. Gabar got up and endeavored to force his mule back along the path, though he knew it was a hopeless task. The mule backed three yards willingly, two resentfully, put down a hind leg in space, kicked, and refused to budge. Gabar sat down again, rolling more cigarettes.

"Reverend padre," he said, "when I was at school the priests taught me that Christians should sacrifice themselves."

Don José-Maria groaned.

"So I have said to myself for two hours past. But I find that I am not a saint."

"I will pay well for your mule. To you or to the Church, as you wish."

"Well, perhaps I will let you buy him. But, Don Manuel, all I possess is in that trunk. All I have ever possessed. You must get it off first."

"I doubt if I can."

"Then — nothing!"

"I will see," said Gabar.

He edged past José-Maria and seized the mule by the bridle. He had to brace one leg firmly against the rock in order to send mule and trunk over the precipice, and the movement was enough to show José-Maria his intention. The priest with astonishing swiftness snatched his other leg from under him, leaving him hanging to the mule's neck for support.

"Do not fear! I have you fast, Don Manuel," he said quickly. "But you must not throw my trunk over!"

"Let me go!" yelled Gabar. "I swear I will not!"

"It is well," said the priest, allowing him to recover his balance. "And now stand aside and let me unrope the trunk!"

"You can't, priest of the devil!" exclaimed Gabar. "It's suicide."

"At least I will try," José-Maria answered. "I am in my own country now, Don Manuel. I shall do what I like!"

He stood on the foot of ground between the mule's neck and empty air, holding the bridle with his right hand and casting off the lashings with his left. The trunk slipped downwards and outwards, supported only by the prominence of José-Maria's stomach. Gabar caught his bridle hand and hung on.

"Everything is lost," said José-Maria mildly, resigning himself to the inevitable. "If I move, it will fall. *Bueno!* Then we shall be content to save what is not mine. Hold me fast, Don Manuel!"

Gabar, amazed at his obstinacy, tautened his grip on the priest's right hand. With his left, José-Maria felt for the catch, opened the trunk, and extracted a flat cardboard box marked with the name of a Buenos Aires department store. As soon as he stepped back, the trunk slid off the mule's back, hit the edge of the path with one corner, and vanished into space. José-Maria sadly leaned over the cliff to watch the funeral of all his transportable possessions.

"After all, you are a saint, padre," said Gabar consolingly.

"I do not want flattery, my son — especially from you who would not know a saint if he stood before you in the very robes of Heaven. We will now speak of the price of my mule. How much is it worth in Cuzco?"

Gabar opened the animal's mouth and felt its forelegs.

"It's a very poor mule," he said. "For ten libras one could buy two such in Cuzco. But I will give you eight."

"It will cost you sixteen," said José-Maria.

Gabar from sheer habit had offered rather more than half the real value of the mule. José-Maria knew this, and Gabar, aware that he knew, suddenly felt ashamed of himself.

"I will pay you sixteen," he said apologetically. "Will you have it in goods or gold?"

"Neither. You will pay it to the Archdeacon of Cuzco when you next go there."

"How do you know I will pay?"

"You are honest."

"Many thanks! Then it's a deal?"

"Not yet. I have sold you the mule at a fair price, but now I want the price of my trunk. It held things I have treasured since childhood, Don Manuel."

"You will say, padre."

"To-morrow is the fiesta of our Child, the Niño of Huanca. You will attend the Mass, and you will help to carry the image. He is a very ancient Niño and he will be more beautiful to-morrow than he has ever been. This" — Don José-Maria held up the cardboard box as if it were the Host — "is for him."

"Nothing more?"

"Nothing more."

Gabar considered the condition. He did not like it. He was enraged by the superstitions of the average pueblo, and nauseated at the thought of his own pious assistance at the midsummer festival of Christmas Day.

"I offer you another sixteen libras," he said.

"I am not interested, Don Manuel."

"I won't accept," said Gabar furiously.

"Then we will stay here."

"But I don't believe in your miserable Niño! I should be out of place. It would be an indecency!"

Don José-Maria said nothing.

"It's a joke!" shouted Gabar. "Think of me carrying an image!"

José-Maria still said nothing. He drew his poncho round him, carefully keeping between Gabar and the mule.

"Very well!" said Gabar, beaten. "Then I accept! I go to Mass and I carry the image. But that is all."

"That is all I ask of you, my son."

José-Maria turned on his heel, inserted his bulk between the mule's neck and the rock, and heaved forwards. The beast reared up and then set forth on its last and swiftest journey to the Inambari. The priest unconcernedly walked through the space it had occupied and patted the shivering donkey. He persuaded it, not without difficulty, to turn round, and the little procession marched downwards towards the widening of the path. Gabar, his mule, and the donkey were shaken and ill at ease. Don José-Maria and the llama, since they had lived their lives in closer touch with the law of gravity, were less disturbed by its pitiless violence. At the niche where hung the lower horn there was room to turn. They re-formed the caravan and retraced their steps.

VI

José-Maria had a triumphal entry into Huanca del Niño. As soon as his people saw him toiling up the last slope, the town, perched on its isolated promontory, awoke like a colony of sea gulls. Strident voices of women called to their children. The church bell clanged with the irregular speed of a fire alarm. Men shouted their welcome. The feet of excited animals clattered on hard stone. The inhabitants crowded round their priest, kissing his hand and asking innumerable questions. Gabar's unexpected return was accepted without comment. Except for a swift and kindly greeting here and there, he was ignored. Stabling his two animals at the inn, he climbed to the top of the wall and sat down to watch the hubbub in the plaza at his feet.

The wall was an integral part of the town rather than a fortification. The outer face, crowning and continuing the escarpment, was well preserved. The irregular polygons of the Cyclopean masonry fitted one another as precisely as the cells of a honeycomb. Since he contemptuously dismissed all legends, Pisco Gabar did not believe the Indian tradition that the builders had known how to liquefy stones and pour them together, but he had no alternative explanation to offer. On the inner side the masonry merged into the existing town, forming the foundations for houses and lanes. The plaza itself was a stone terrace within the prehistoric building. One side of the square was occupied by the sixteenth-century church. The colonial architects had evidently added nothing but a tower, a roof, and some upper courses of masonry to a temple already in existence. The church lamps were lit as he watched, and the dusky plaza began to wink with candles and torches. José-Maria was being escorted to his church. It was clear that the priest was the temporal and spiritual ruler of his people with an absolutism that his Indian ancestors, however powerful, might have envied.

The spontaneous show of affection for and pride in the priest filled Pisco with disgust. If only these Peruvian Indians could see what had been accomplished by their cousins in Mexico! If only they would unite against priests and landlords, and organize a state which should preserve the best of the ancient culture and reject the alien influence of the Church! Pisco Gabar identified himself with the Indians and mestizos, since they were the true proletariat; and his reverence for their great civilizations, first felt on the way up from the Inambari, had increased during his stay at Huanca.

He saw José-Maria cross the plaza between ranks of frankly worshiping men. Pisco swore aloud. One could have understood it had they been women; but that these men, faced day and night with the barren realities of their cruel plateau, should believe in infantile superstitions — *santísima virgen!* In what was this folly any better than the old religions? José-Maria might have been a feather-crowned priest of the sun, going to the same temple from the same house with the same adoring crowds believing in the same fairy tales! Pisco Gabar got up angrily from his perch, aware that somewhere in his line of thought there was a contradiction. It made him uneasy, for his wonted thoughts on religion were simple enough to be crystal clear.

He returned to the inn. It was completely deserted. His room was exactly as he had left it that morning, except that the hens had returned to their favorite nesting place. He boiled three new-laid eggs on his spirit lamp, ate them, and lay down on the unmade bed. He was awakened about three hours later by José-Maria and a party of his parishioners.

"Where were you, Don Manuel? We looked for you. My friends want to thank you for all you did for me. I told them how you saved me in the boat and how you would not let me be left behind at Mollendo. Get up and join us! You must eat and drink before midnight. To-morrow, remember, you have to fast till after Mass!"

Gabar was touched by the welcome extended to him by Don José-Maria and his boon companions. It had seemed to him that he had been cordially received before, but there was now an extra warmth in their hospitality which made him feel as if he himself were a son of the pueblo. He had expected a lessening of his popularity owing to the inconvenience he had caused their beloved priest on the road. But this episode had run widely and humorously from mouth to mouth until Gabar appeared in it as a comic hero rather than the villain.

"Would you all believe," roared José-Maria, "that this man, this friend, is a heathen?"

"Let us take him to see the Niño!" exclaimed one of the men. "Then he must believe. Our Niño is so pretty — so divine a child!"

"It is good," said José-Maria. "Let us drink a last *copa* and all go to see the Niño."

Gabar's protests were overruled. They treated him as a curiosity, as a fellow whose education had been oddly neglected, and they were all sure that the fault could be quickly remedied. He joined good-humoredly in the procession to the church.

As far as the door it was a carousal which then instantly changed into a pilgrimage. The men entered silently and reverently and knelt before the famous Niño.

The head of the image was a splendid piece of portrait pottery, brought up from the coast by the Incas or their conquerors. It was the head of a gentle child, the sensitive lips caught at the beginning of a laugh. Two emeralds had been set deep in the painted eyes, giving a curious effect of unworldly life, and changing expression with the moving lights. The fine hawk nose and high cheekbones were hardly formed, but promised the later beauty of a true Child of the Sun. It was robust and living portraiture — the face of a child compelling obedience because so happy and so sure that its innocent desires would be granted.

The body was hidden under a stiffly embroidered surplice of linen.

Round its neck and pinned to its smock were the offerings of the faithful; a pearl necklace, some silver spurs, earrings of all sorts, and many little crudely moulded shapes of pure gold. In this it was not different from the average image in any poor Peruvian church. But the head was an astonishing and accidental conception of an Indian Christ.

"Isn't he pretty?" asked Don José-Maria proudly.

"He is very original," Gabar admitted.

This remark was taken as high praise, for had not Don Manuel traveled all over the world and seen many much more splendid images? The men nodded their heads wisely, implying that they had known all along that their Niño would compel this heathen's admiration.

"Since we are here," said José-Maria, "I will show you what I have brought him for to-morrow's fiesta."

He disappeared into the sacristy and came back with the cardboard box which he had saved from his falling trunk.

"When I was in Buenos Aires," he explained, "I saw so many rich. There must be more rich people there than in all the rest of the world. And so well dressed! I would never have believed it! So I thought I would buy a new garment for our Niño. I went to a shop — such a shop, as big as a town and with all the goods in it brought from Europe, they say! There was a shopman — most courteous, altogether a caballero — who asked me what I wanted. I told him there was a child in my pueblo whom I loved, and I wished to buy for him a very rich, very simple dress. I asked him to give me what the Buenos Aires children would wear on a Sunday, the wealthiest, noblest children! This" — he reverently opened the box — "is what he sold me."

It was a white sailor suit — blouse, trousers, blue collar, black scarf, and a jaunty little cap with *H.M.S. Triumph* embroidered in gold across the ribbon.

Don José-Maria's parishioners gasped with delight. It was so white, so little, so beautiful. And was that really what rich children wore? *Vaya! Vaya!* How proud they would be of the Niño! Gabar hastily sat down behind a pillar, exploding with laughter. Incredible José-Maria! Amazing superstition! He looked at the image and his laughter changed to indignation. It was such an exquisite head. It ought to be in the Lima Museum. And they were going to put a carnival hat on it and double their prayers! The men, chattering excitedly, began to disperse. Gabar composed his face, slipped away unnoticed, and made his way back to the inn.

The following morning the lanes of Huanca del Niño were packed.

Many of the inhabitants of Chiquibamba had come in for the day, and there were some solemn semi-Christian Indians from the Montaña. Pisco Gabar attended Mass in accordance with his promise and, when it was over, took his place in the procession with the three other bearers who were to carry the Niño. The image was mounted on a solid stage carried by four poles projecting from the corners. The beauty of the face was actually set off by the cap across the terra-cotta forehead. The Niño looked like a small boy laughing in joy at his new suit. The crowd was charmed by this realism. The image had not and had never had any legs, — a fact that had escaped notice under the surplice, — but José-Maria had got over the difficulty by stuffing the white sailor trousers with straw. Nobody but Gabar seemed to see anything odd in that. If God had no legs it was obviously their duty to supply them.

The procession left the churchyard and started slowly round the plaza. It was led by riders, shouting, letting off firearms, and mounted insecurely on the only horses the two pueblos possessed. Then followed Don José-Maria and his acolytes; then the Niño on the shoulders of the four bearers; then the faithful, carrying candles in their hands — some of them with a candle between each pair of fingers, thereby obliging friends and relatives who had vowed to bear a candle in the procession but had been prevented from attending.

Pisco soon realized that Don José-Maria had not only wished him to perform a religious penance, but had deliberately chosen him as a porter because of his strength and steadiness. All the people thronged around the image, praying, kneeling, dancing, offering drink to the thirsty bearers. His three colleagues were soon none too steady on their feet and yielding to the small excitable sea of human beings which washed against them. He found himself in command of the party and entirely responsible, by quick anticipation of their erratic movements, for keeping the Niño in a fairly perpendicular position.

Every few minutes the procession stopped at a house or corner, a patch of cultivation or a water channel, which José-Maria blessed in Latin, afterwards freely and fervently translating the blessing into Quechua. He used the correct words of power, and thus delivered his hearers from any temptation they might have to employ occasional pagan rites of their own. Pisco's shoulder, though protected by a leather pad, ached abominably from the continual raising up and setting down of the image. He was still fasting and very thirsty. He began to accept some of the cups of maize spirit proffered to him on all sides.

Up to the wall went the procession, with José-Maria almost dancing ahead. The crowd chanted whatever came into their heads, and sudden tenor voices threw their impromptu poems into the thin mountain air. Pisco cursed his companions, adjuring them for their pride in the Niño to stop trying to dance. He was completely absorbed by his job, a little affected by the prevailing hysteria, and gathering an obscure and obstinate affection for the Niño, which any man is bound to feel for an object he is struggling to save from destruction.

At last the procession returned to the church. The faithful dispersed to their houses and to food. The other three bearers and a few of his favorite parishioners went into the sacristy with José-Maria. Pisco was momentarily left alone in the church. He sat down on the altar steps and rubbed his shoulder.

"You," he said to the Niño, "should be very grateful to me."

The exquisite little face laughed at him. The sailor cap was awry, and the Niño looked as if he had been enjoying the fun.

"You ought to be ashamed of that suit," said Pisco solemnly. "You are of the people. You have nothing to do with the present system. You understand us."

The Niño continued to smile. His face was nobly unconscious of the suit. He seemed to Pisco to be returning a diviner pity for his human one. Pisco felt very weary and very much alone.

"You," he said, "have nothing to do with the Church. They put things into your mouth that you never thought. I've seen the same thing myself. The priests and politicians and philosophers make us all say what we don't really think."

The tears came up into his eyes. On a sudden impulse he rolled over on to his knees before the image, and whispered:—

"O Son of God, help us to make the earth as you would have it be."

January 1936

SARAH ORNE JEWETT

1849–1909

In her perceptive essay on the genius of Miss Jewett, Miss Cather[1] *quotes from a letter of her friend and teacher: "The thing," Miss Jewett wrote, "that teases the mind over and over for years and at last gets itself put down rightly on paper, whether little or great, belongs to Literature." Miss Cather goes on to say that of American books there are but three which she feels have within them the certain possibility of long, long life,* The Scarlet Letter, Huckleberry Finn, *and* The Country of the Pointed Firs. *This is doubtless too rigorous a compression, but certain it is that, if the reader's criterion be unattainable perfection, Miss Jewett's contribution toward the goal is permanent. Of Maine her simple folk are denizens as ineradicable as the herons nesting among the pointed firs and the pungent bayberries along the rock-fringed creeks.*

Miss Jewett was born to complete understanding of her race. The first Jewett in colonial history ran away to sea and never a Jewett since has breathed inland air. The family captained their own schooners to some purpose and Miss Jewett's grandfather, who traded with the East, built the spacious old homestead where she was born and lived and died. Twice only I saw her, but her delicate profile still lingers in my memory. With me her manners were reserved. She was not without, I think, some consciousness of self; and I, of course, had not been born in the State o' Maine and so earned a native right to her confidence. Her wide and generous culture came from her father, but her passion for the perfect was her own, and the maxims of Flaubert were ever in her active consciousness.

[1] *The second friend to die while I correct these proofs. Miss Cather went this morning: April 24, 1947. E. S.*

The Queen's Twin

SARAH ORNE JEWETT

I

The coast of Maine was in former years brought so near to foreign shores by its busy fleet of ships that among the older men and women one still finds a surprising proportion of travelers. Each seaward stretching headland with its high-set houses, each island of a single farm, has sent its spies to view many a land of Eshcol. One may see plain, contented old faces at the windows, whose eyes have looked at far-away ports, and known the splendors of the Eastern world. They shame the easy voyager of the North Atlantic and the Mediterranean: they have rounded the Cape of Good Hope and braved the angry seas of Cape Horn in small wooden ships; they have brought up their hardy boys and girls on narrow decks; they were among the last of the Northmen's children to go adventuring to unknown shores. More than this one cannot give to a young state for its enlightenment. The sea captains and the captains' wives of Maine knew something of the wide world, and never mistook their native parishes for the whole instead of a part thereof; they knew not only Thomaston and Castine and Portland, but London and Bristol and Bordeaux, and the strange-mannered harbors of the China Sea.

One September day, when I was nearly at the end of a summer spent in a village called Dunnet Landing, on the Maine coast, my friend Mrs. Todd, in whose house I lived, came home from a long, solitary stroll in the wild pastures, with an eager look, as if she were just starting on a hopeful quest instead of returning. She brought a little basket with blackberries enough for supper, and held it toward me so that I could see that there were also some late and surprising raspberries sprinkled on top, but she made no comment upon her wayfaring. I could tell plainly that she had something very important to say.

"You haven't brought home a leaf of anything?" I ventured to this practiced herb-gatherer. "You were saying yesterday that the witch-hazel might be in bloom."

"I dare say, dear," she answered in a lofty manner. "I ain't goin' to say it wasn't; I ain't much concerned either way 'bout the facts o' witch-hazel. Truth is, I've been off visitin'; there's an old Indian footpath leadin' over towards the Back Shore, through the great heron swamp, that anybody can't travel over all summer. You have to seize your time some day just now, while the low ground's summer-dried as it is to-day, and before the fall rains set in. I never thought of it till I was out o' sight o' home, and I says to myself, 'To-day's the day certain!' and stepped along smart as I could. Yes; I've been visitin'. I did get into one spot that was wet underfoot before I noticed; you wait till I get me a pair o' dry woolen stockin's, in case of cold, and I'll come an' tell ye."

Mrs. Todd disappeared, — I could see that something had deeply interested her. She might have fallen in with either the sea serpent or the lost tribes of Israel, such was her air of mystery and satisfaction. She had been away since just before mid-morning, and as I sat waiting by my window I saw the last red glow of autumn sunshine flare along the gray rocks of the shore and leave them cold again, and touch the far sails of some coastwise schooners so that they stood like golden houses on the sea.

I was left to wonder longer than I liked. Mrs. Todd was making an evening fire and putting things in train for supper; presently she returned, still looking warm and cheerful after her long walk.

"There's a beautiful view from a hill over where I've been," she told me; "yes, there's a beautiful prospect of land and sea. You wouldn't discern the hill from any distance, but 'tis the pretty situation of it that counts. I sat there a long spell, and I did wish for you. No, I didn't know a word about goin' when I set out this mornin'." (As if I had openly reproached her!) "I only felt one o' them travelin' fits comin' on, an' I ketched up my little basket; I didn't know but I might turn and come back, time for dinner. I thought it wise to set out your luncheon for you in case I didn't. Hope you had all you wanted; yes, I hope you had enough?"

"Oh yes, indeed!" said I. My landlady was always peculiarly bountiful in her supplies when she left me to fare for myself, as if she made a sort of peace-offering or affectionate apology.

"You know that hill with the old house right on top, over beyond the heron swamp. You'll excuse me for explainin'," Mrs. Todd began, "but you ain't so apt to strike inland as you be to go right alongshore. You know that hill; there's a path leadin' right over to it that you have to look sharp to find nowadays. It belonged to the up-country Indians when they had to make a carry to the Landing here, to get to the out' islands. I've heard the old folks say that there used to be a place across a ledge where they'd worn a deep track with their moccasin feet, but I never could find it. 'Tis so overgrown in some places that you keep losin' the path in the bushes, and findin' it as you can, but it runs pretty straight considerin' the lay o' the land, and I keep my eye on the sun and the moss that grows one side o' the tree trunks. Some brook's been choked up, and the swamp's bigger than it used to be. Yes; I did get in deep enough, one place!"

I showed the solicitude that I felt. Mrs. Todd was no longer young, and, in spite of her strong great frame and spirited behavior, I knew that certain ills were apt to seize upon her, and would some day end by leaving her lame and ailing.

"Don't you go to worryin' about me," she insisted. "Settin' still's the only way the Evil One'll ever get the upper hand o' me. Keep me movin' enough, an' I'm twenty year old summer an' winter both. I don't know why 'tis, but I've never happened to mention the one I've been to see. I don't know why I never happened to speak the name of Abby Martin, for I often give her a thought; but 'tis a dreadful out-o'-the-way place where she lives, and I haven't seen her myself for three or four years. She's a real good, interesting woman, and we're well acquainted; she's nigher mother's age than mine, but she's very young-feeling. She made me a nice cup o' tea, and I don't know but I should have stopped all night if I could have got word to you not to worry."

Then there was a serious silence before Mrs. Todd spoke again to make a formal announcement.

"She is the Queen's Twin," and Mrs. Todd looked steadily to see how I might bear the great surprise.

"The Queen's Twin?" I repeated.

"Yes; she's come to feel a real interest in the Queen, and anybody can see how natural 'tis. They were born the very same day, and you would be astonished to see what a number o' other things have corresponded. She was speaking o' some o' the facts to me today, an' you'd think she'd never done nothing but read history. I see how earnest she was about it as I never did before. I've often and often heard her allude to the facts; but now she's got to be old, and the hurry's all over with her work, she's come to live a good deal in her thoughts, as folks often do, and I tell you 'tis a sight o' company for her. If you want to hear about Queen Victoria, why, Mis' Abby Martin'll tell you everything. And the prospect from that hill I spoke of is as beautiful as anything in this world; 'tis worth while your goin' over to see her, just for that."

"When can you go again?" I demanded eagerly.

"I should say to-morrow," answered Mrs. Todd, — "yes, I should say to-morrow; but I expect 'twould be better to take one day to rest, in between. I considered that question as I was comin' home, but I hurried so that there wa'n't much time to think. It's a dreadful long way to go with a horse. You have to go 'most as far as the old Bowden place, an' turn off to the left, a master long, rough road; an' then you have to turn right round as soon as you get there, if you mean to get home before nine o'clock at night. But to strike across country from here, there's plenty o' time in the shortest day, and you can have a good hour or two's visit besides. 'Tain't but a very few miles, and it's pretty all the way along. There used to be a few good families over there, but they've died and scattered, so now she's far from neighbors. There, she really cried, she was so glad to see anybody comin'. You'll be amused to hear her talk about the Queen, but I thought twice or three times, as I set there, 'twas about all the company she'd got."

"Could we go day after to-morrow?" I asked.

"'Twould suit me exactly," said Mrs. Todd.

II

One can never be so certain of good New England weather as in the days when a long easterly storm has blown away the warm late-summer mists, and cooled the air so that however bright the sunshine is by day, the nights come nearer and nearer to frostiness. There was a cold freshness in the morning air when Mrs. Todd and I locked the house door behind us; we took the key of the fields into our own hands that day, and put out across country as one puts out to sea. When we reached the top of the ridge behind the town, it seemed as if we had anxiously passed the harbor bar, and were comfortably in open sea at last.

"There, now!" proclaimed Mrs. Todd, taking a long breath. "Now I do feel safe. It's just the weather that's liable to bring somebody to spend the day. I've had a feeling of Mis' Elder Caplin from North Point bein' close upon me ever since I waked up this mornin', an' I didn't want to be hampered with our present plans. She's a great hand to visit; she'll be spendin' the day somewhere from now till Thanksgivin'; but there's plenty o' places at the Landin' where she goes, an' if I ain't there she'll just select another. I thought mother might be in, too, 'tis so pleasant; but I run up the road to look off this mornin' before you was awake, and there was no sign o' the boat. If they hadn't started by that time, they wouldn't start just as the tide is now; besides, I see a lot o' mackerelmen headin' Green Island way, and they'll detain William. No, we're safe now; an' if mother should be comin' in to-morrow, we'll have all this to tell her. She an' Mis' Abby Martin's very old friends."

We were walking down the long pasture slopes, toward the dark woods and thickets of the low ground. They stretched away northward like an unbroken wilderness; the early mists still dulled much of the color, and made the uplands beyond look like a very far-off country.

"It ain't so far as it looks from here," said my companion reassuringly; "but we've got no time to spare, either," and she hurried on, leading the way with a fine sort of spirit in her step. Presently we struck into the old Indian footpath, which could be plainly seen across the long-unploughed turf of the pastures, and followed it among the thick, low-growing spruces. There the ground was smooth and brown underfoot, and the thin-stemmed trees held a dark and shadowy roof overhead. We walked a long way without speaking; sometimes we had to push aside the branches, and sometimes we walked in a broad aisle where the trees were larger. It was a solitary wood, birdless and beastless; there was not even a rabbit to be seen, or a crow high in air to break the silence.

"I don't believe the Queen ever saw such a lonesome trail as this," said Mrs. Todd, as if she followed the thoughts that were in my mind. Our visit to Mrs. Abby Martin seemed in some strange way to concern the high affairs of royalty. I had just been thinking of English landscapes, and of the solemn hills of Scotland with their lonely cottages and stone-walled sheepfolds, and the wandering flocks on high cloudy pastures. I had often been struck by the quick interest and familiar allusion to certain members of the royal house which one found in distant neighborhoods of New England. Whether some old instincts of personal loyalty have survived all changes of time and national vicissitudes, or whether it is only that the Queen's own character and disposition have won friends for her so far away, it is impossible to tell. But to hear of a twin sister was the most surprising proof of intimacy of all, and I must confess that there was something remarkably exciting to the imagination in my morning walk. To think of being presented at Court in the usual way was, for the moment, quite commonplace.

III

Mrs. Todd was swinging her basket to and fro like a schoolgirl as she walked, and at this moment it slipped from her hand and rolled lightly along the ground. I picked it up and gave it to her, whereupon she lifted the cover and looked in with anxiety.

"'Tis only a few little things, but I don't want to lose 'em," she explained humbly. "'Twas lucky you took the other basket if I was goin' to roll it round. Mis' Abby Martin complained o' lacking some pretty pink silk to finish one o' her little frames, an' I thought I'd carry her some, and I had a bunch o' gold thread that had been in a box o' mine this twenty year. I never was one to do much fancywork, but we're all liable to be swept away by fashion. And then there's a small packet o' very choice herbs that I gave a good deal of attention to; they'll smarten her up, and give her the best of appetites, come spring. She was tellin' me that spring weather is very wiltin' an' tryin' to her, and she was beginnin' to dread it already. Mother's just the same way. If I could prevail on mother to take some o' these remedies in good season, 'twould make a world o' difference; but she gets all downhill before I have a chance to hear of it, and then William comes in to tell me, sighin' and bewailin' how feeble mother is. 'Why can't you remember 'bout them good herbs that I never let her be without?' I say to him,—he does provoke me so; and then off he goes, sulky enough, down to his boat. Next thing I know, she comes in to go to meetin', wantin' to speak to everybody and feelin' like a girl. Mis' Martin's case is very much the same, but she's nobody to watch her. William's kind o' slow-moulded, but there, any William's better than none when you get to be Mis' Martin's age."

"Hadn't she any children?" I asked.

"Quite a number," replied Mrs. Todd grandly; "but some are gone, and the rest are married and settled. She never was a great hand to go about visitin'. I don't know but Mis' Martin might be called a little peculiar. Even her own folks has to make company of her: she never slips in and lives right along with the rest as if 'twas at home, even in her own children's houses. I heard one o' her sons' wives say once she'd much rather have the Queen to spend the day, if she could choose between the two; but I never thought Abby was so difficult as that. I used to love to have her come. She may have been sort o' ceremonious, but very pleasant and sprightly if you had sense enough to treat her her own way. I always think she'd know just how to live with great folks, and feel easier 'long of them an' their ways. Her son's wife's a great driver with farm work, boards a great tableful o' men in hayin'-time, an' feels right in her element. I don't say but she's a good woman an' smart, but sort o' rough. Anybody that's gentle-mannered an' precise like Mis' Martin would be a sort o' restraint.

"There's all sorts o' folks in the country, same's there is in the city," concluded Mrs. Todd gravely, and I as gravely agreed. The thick woods were behind us now, and the sun was shining clear overhead; the morning mists were gone, and a faint blue haze softened the distance; as we climbed the hill where we were to see the view it seemed like a summer day. There was an old house on the height, facing southward; a mere forsaken shell of an old house with empty windows that looked like blind eyes. The frost-bitten grass grew close about it like brown fur, and there was a single crooked bough of lilac holding its green leaves close by the door.

"We'll just have a good piece of bread an' butter now," said the commander of the expedition, "and then we'll hang up the basket on some peg inside the house, out o' the way o' the sheep, and have a han'some entertainment as we're comin' back. She'll be all through her little dinner when we get there, Mis' Martin will; but she'll want to make us some tea, an' we must have our visit, an' be startin' back pretty soon after two. I don't want to cross all that low ground again after it's begun to grow chilly. An' it looks to me as if the clouds might begin to gather late in the afternoon."

Before us lay a splendid world of sea and shore. The autumn colors brightened the landscape already; here and there at the edge of a dark tract of pointed firs stood a row of bright swamp maples like scarlet flowers. The blue sea and the great tide inlets were untroubled by the lightest winds.

"Poor land, this is," sighed Mrs. Todd, as we sat down to rest on the worn doorstep. "I've known three good hard-workin' families that come here full o' hope an' pride, and tried to make somethin' o' this farm, but it beat 'em all. There's one small field that's excellent for potatoes if you let half of it rest every year, but the land's always hungry. Now you see them little peakèd-topped spruces an' fir balsams comin' up over the hill all green an' hearty; they've got it all their own way! Seems sometimes as if wild natur' got jealous over a certain spot, and wanted to do just as she'd a mind to. You'll see here; she'll do her own ploughin' an' harrowin' with frost an' wet, an' plant just what she wants, and wait for her own crops. Man can't do nothin' with it, try as he may. I tell you, those little trees means business!"

I looked down the slope, and felt as if we ourselves were likely to be surrounded and overcome if we lingered too long. There was a vigor of growth, a persistence and savagery about the sturdy little trees, that put weak human nature at complete defiance. One felt a sudden pity for the men and women who had been worsted after a long fight in that lonely place; one felt a sudden fear of the unconquerable immediate forces of nature, as acute as the irresistible moment of a thunderstorm.

"I can recollect the time when folks were shy o' those woods we just come through," said Mrs. Todd seriously. "The men folks themselves never'd venture into 'em alone; if their cattle got strayed, they'd collect whoever they could get and start off all together. They said a person was liable to get bewildered in there alone, and in old times folks had been lost. I expect there was considerable fear left over from the old Indian times and the poor days o' witchcraft; anyway, I've seen bold men act kind o' timid. Some women o' the Asa Bowden family went out one afternoon berryin', when I was a girl, and got lost, and was out all night; they found 'em middle o' the mornin' next day, not half a mile from home, scared 'most to death, an' sayin' they'd heard wolves and other beasts sufficient for a caravan. Poor creatur's, they'd strayed at last into a kind of low place amongst some alders, an' one of 'em was so overset she never got over it, an' went off in a sort o' slow decline. 'Twas like them victims that drowns in a foot o' water, but their minds did suffer dreadful. Some folks is born afraid of the woods and all wild places, but I must say they've always been like home to me."

I glanced at the resolute, confident face of my companion. Life was very strong in her, as if some force of nature were personified in this simple-hearted woman, and gave her cousinship to the ancient deities. She might have walked the primeval fields of Sicily; her strong gingham skirts might at that very moment bend the slender stalks of asphodel, and be fragrant with trodden thyme, instead of the brown wind-brushed grass of New England and frost-bitten goldenrod. She was a great soul, was Mrs. Todd, and I her humble follower, as we went our way to visit the Queen's Twin, leaving the bright view of the sea behind us, and descending to a lower countryside through the dry pastures and fields.

The farms all wore a look of gathering age, though the settlement was, after all, so young. The fences were already fragile, and it seemed as if the first impulse of agriculture had soon spent itself without hope of renewal. The better houses were always those that had some hold upon the riches of the sea; a house that could not harbor a fishing boat in some neighboring inlet was far from being sure of every-day comforts. The land alone was not enough to live upon in that stony region; it belonged by right to the forest, and to the forest it fast returned. From the top of the hill where we had been sitting we had seen prosperity in the dim distance, where the land was good and the sun shone upon fat barns, and where warm-looking houses with three or four chimneys apiece stood high on their solid ridge above the bay.

As we drew nearer to Mrs. Martin's, it was sad to see what poor bushy fields, what thin and empty dwelling-places, had been left by those who had chosen this disappointing part of the northern country for their home. We crossed the last field and came into a narrow rain-washed road, and Mrs. Todd looked eager and expectant, and said that we were almost at our journey's end.

"I do hope Mis' Martin'll ask you into her best room, where she keeps all the Queen's pictures. Yes, I think likely she will ask you; but 'tain't everybody she deems worthy to visit 'em, I can tell you!" said Mrs. Todd warningly. "She's been collectin' 'em an' cuttin' 'em out o' newspapers an' magazines time out o' mind; and if she heard of anybody sailin' for an English port, she'd contrive to get a little money to 'em and ask to have the last likeness there was. She's 'most covered her best-room wall now: she keeps that room shut up sacred as a meetin'-house! 'I won't say but I have my favorites amongst 'em,' she told me t'other day, 'but they're all beautiful to me as they can be.' And she's made some kind o' pretty little frames for 'em all. You know there's always a new fashion o' frames comin' round: first 'twas shell-work, and then 'twas pine cones, and beadwork's had its day, and now she's much concerned with perforated cardboard worked with silk. I tell you, that best room's a sight to see! But you mustn't look for anything elegant," continued Mrs. Todd, after a moment's reflection. "Mis' Martin's always been in very poor, strugglin' circumstances. She had ambition for her children, though they took right after their father an' had little for themselves; she wa'n't over an' above well married, however kind she may see fit to speak. She's been patient an' hard-workin' all her life, and always high above makin' mean complaints of other folks. I expect all this business about the Queen has buoyed her over many a shoal place in life. Yes, you might say that Abby'd been a slave, but there ain't any slave but has some freedom."

IV

Presently I saw a low gray house standing on a grassy bank close to the road. The door was at the side, facing us, and a tangle of snowberry bushes and cinnamon roses grew to the level of the window sills. On the doorstep stood a bent-shouldered little old woman. There was an air of welcome and of unmistakable dignity about her.

"She sees us coming!" exclaimed Mrs. Todd in an excited whisper.

"There, I told her I might be over this way again, if the weather held good, and if I came I'd bring you. She said right off she'd take great pleasure in havin' a visit from you. I was surprised; she's usually so retirin'."

Even this reassurance did not quell a faint apprehension on our part; there was something distinctly formal in the occasion, and one felt that consciousness of inadequacy which is never easy for the humblest pride to bear. On the way I had torn my dress in an unexpected encounter with a little thorn bush; I could now imagine how it felt to be going to Court and forgetting one's feathers or Court train.

The Queen's Twin was oblivious of such trifles; she stood waiting with a calm look until we came near enough to take her kind hand. She was a beautiful old woman, with clear eyes and a lovely quietness and genuineness of manner; there was not a trace of anything pretentious about her, or high-flown, as Mrs. Todd would say comprehensively. Beauty in age is rare enough in women who have spent their lives in the hard work of a farmhouse; but autumn-like and withered as this woman may have looked, her features had kept, or rather gained, a great refinement. She led us into her old kitchen, and gave us seats, and took one of the little straight-backed chairs herself, and sat a short distance away, as if she were giving audience to an ambassador. It seemed as if we should all be standing; one could not help feeling that the habits of her life were more ceremonious, but that for the moment she assumed the simplicities of the occasion.

Mrs. Todd was always Mrs. Todd,—too great and self-possessed a soul for any occasion to ruffle. I admired her calmness, and presently the slow current of neighborhood talk carried us easily along; we spoke of the weather and the small adventures of the way, and then, as if I were after all not a stranger, our hostess turned almost affectionately to speak to me.

"The weather will be growing dark in London now. I expect that you've been in London, dear?" she said.

"Oh yes," I answered. "Only last year."

"It is a great many years since I was there; along in the forties," said Mrs. Martin. "'Twas the only voyage I ever made. Most of my neighbors have been great travelers. My brother was master of a vessel, and his wife usually sailed with him; but that year she had a young child more frail than the others, and she dreaded the care of it at sea. It happened that my brother got a chance for my husband to go as supercargo, being a good accountant, and came one day to urge him to take it. He was very ill disposed to the sea, but he had met with losses, and I saw my own opportunity and persuaded them both to let me go too. In those days they didn't object to a woman's being aboard to wash and mend; the voyages were sometimes very long. And that was the way I come to see the Queen."

Mrs. Martin was looking straight in my eyes, to see if I showed any genuine interest in the most interesting person in the world.

"Oh, I am glad you saw the Queen," I hastened to say. "Mrs. Todd has told me that you and she were born the very same day."

"We were indeed, dear," said Mrs. Martin, and she leaned back comfortably and smiled as she had not smiled before. Mrs. Todd gave a satisfied nod and glance, as if to say that things were going on as well as possible in this anxious moment.

"Yes," Mrs. Martin resumed, as she drew her chair a little nearer, " 'twas a very remarkable thing: we were born the same day, and at exactly the same hour, after you allowed for all the difference in time. My father figured it out sea-fashion. Her Royal Majesty and I opened our eyes upon this world together: say what you may, 'tis a bond between us."

Mrs. Todd assented with an air of triumph, and untied her hat strings and threw them back over her shoulders with a gallant air.

"And I married a man by the name of Albert, just the same as she did; and all by chance, for I didn't get the news that she had an Albert, too, till a fortnight afterward; news was slower coming then than it is now. My first baby was a girl, and I called her Victoria after my mate; but the next one was a boy, and my husband wanted the right to name him, and took his own name and his brother Edward's; and pretty soon I saw in the paper that the little Prince o' Wales had been christened just the same. After that I made excuse to wait till I knew what she'd named her children. I didn't want to break the chain, so I had an Alfred and my darling Alice that I lost long before she lost hers, and there I stopped. If I'd only had a dear daughter to stay at home with me, same's her youngest one, I should have been so thankful! But if only one of us could have a little Beatrice, I'm glad 'twas the Queen; we've both seen trouble, but she's had the most care."

I asked Mrs. Martin if she lived alone all the year, and was told that she did except for a visit now and then from one of her grandchildren, "the only one that really likes to come an' stay quiet 'long o' grandma. She always says, quick as she's through her schoolin' she's goin' to live with me all the time. But she's very pretty an' has taking ways," said

Mrs. Martin, looking both proud and wistful, "so I can tell nothing at all about it. Yes, I've been alone most o' the time since my Albert was taken away, and that's a great many years; he had a long time o' failing and sickness first." (Mrs. Todd's foot gave an impatient scuff on the floor.) "An' I've always lived right here. I ain't like the Queen's Majesty, for this is the only palace I've got," said the dear old thing, smiling again. "I'm glad of it, too. I don't like changing about, an' our stations in life are set very different. I don't require what the Queen does, but sometimes I've thought 'twas left to me to do the plain things she don't have time for. I expect she's a beautiful housekeeper; nobody couldn't have done better in her high place, and she's been as good a mother as she's been a queen."

"I guess she has, Abby," agreed Mrs. Todd instantly. "How was it you happened to get such a good look at her? I meant to ask you again when I was here t'other day."

"Our ship was layin' in the Thames, right there above Wapping. We was dischargin' cargo, and under orders to clear as quick as we could for Bordeaux to take on an excellent freight o' French goods," explained Mrs. Martin eagerly. "I heard that the Queen was goin' to a great review of her army, and would drive out o' her Buckin'ham Palace about ten o'clock in the mornin'; and I run aft to Albert, my husband, and brother Horace where they was standin' together by the hatchway, and told 'em they must one of 'em take me. They laughed, I was in such a hurry, and said they couldn't go; and I found they meant it and got sort of impatient when I begun to talk, and I was 'most broken-hearted; 'twas 'most all the reason I had for makin' that hard voyage. Albert couldn't help often reproachin' me, for he did so resent the sea, an' I'd known how 'twould be before we sailed; but I'd minded nothin' all the way till then, and I just crep' back to my cabin an' begun to cry. They was disappointed about their ship's cook, an' I'd cooked for fo'c's'le an' cabin myself all the way over; 'twas dreadful hard work, 'specially in rough weather; we'd had head winds an' a six weeks' voyage. They'd acted sort of ashamed o' me when I pled so to go ashore, an' that hurt my feelin's most of all. But Albert come below pretty soon. I'd never given way so in my life, an' he begun to act frightened, and treated me gentle, just as he did when we was goin' to be married; an' when I got over sobbin' he went on deck an' saw Horace an' talked it over what they could do; they really had their duty to the vessel, and couldn't be spared that day. Horace was real good when he understood everything, an' he come an' told me I'd more than worked my passage, an' was goin' to do just as I liked now we was in port. He'd engaged a cook, too, that was comin' aboard that mornin', and he was goin' to send the ship's carpenter with me, a nice fellow from up Thomaston way; he'd gone to put on his shore clothes as quick 's he could. So then I got ready, and we started off in the small boat and rowed up river. I was afraid we were too late, but the tide was setting up very strong, and we landed an' left the boat to a keeper, and I run all the way up those great streets and across a park. 'Twas a great day, with sights o' folks everywhere, but 'twas just as if they was nothin' but wax images to me. I kep' askin' my way, an' runnin' on, with the carpenter comin' after as best he could; and just as I worked to the front o' the crowd by the palace the gates was flung open and out she came, — all prancin' horses and shinin' gold, — and in a beautiful carriage there she sat: 'twas a moment o' heaven to me. I saw her plain, and she looked right at me so pleasant and happy, just as if she knew there was somethin' different between us from other folks."

There was a moment when the Queen's Twin could not go on, and neither of her listeners could ask a question.

"Prince Albert was sitting right beside her in the carriage," she continued. "Oh, he was a beautiful man. Yes, dear, I saw 'em both together, just as I see you now; and then she was gone out o' sight in another minute, and the common crowd was all spread over the place, pushin' an' cheerin'. 'Twas some kind o' holiday, an' the carpenter and I got separated, an' then I found him again after I didn't think I should, an' he was all for makin' a day of it and goin' to show me all the sights, — he'd been in London before; but I didn't want nothin' else, an' we went back through the streets down to the waterside an' took the boat. I remember I mended an old coat o' my Albert's as good as I could, sittin' in the sun on the quarter deck all that afternoon, and 'twas all as if I was livin' in a lovely dream. I don't know how to explain it, but there hasn't been no friend I've felt so near to me ever since."

One could not say much, only listen. Mrs. Todd put in a discerning question now and then, and Mrs. Martin's eyes shone brighter and brighter as she talked. What a lovely gift of imagination and true affection was in this fond old heart! I looked about the plain New England kitchen, with its wood-smoked walls, its homely braided rugs on the worn floor, and all its simple furnishings. The loud-ticking clock seemed to encourage us to speak. At the other side of the room was an early newspaper portrait of Her Majesty the Queen of Great Britain and Ireland. On a shelf below were some flowers in a little glass dish, as if they were put before a shrine.

"If I could have had more to read, I should have known 'most everything about her," said Mrs. Martin wistfully. "I've made the most of what I did have, and thought it over and over till it came clear. I sometimes seem to have her all my own, as if we'd lived right together. I've often walked out into the woods alone and told her what my troubles was, and it always seemed as if she told me 'twas all right, an' we must have patience. I've got her beautiful book about the Highlands,—'twas dear Mis' Todd here that found out about her printing it, and got a copy for me; and it's been a treasure to my heart, just as if 'twas written right to me. I always read it Sundays now for my Sunday treat. Before that I used to have to imagine a good deal; but when I come to read her book, I knew what I expected was all true. We do think alike about so many things," said the Queen's Twin, with affectionate certainty. "You see, there is something between us, being born just at the same time: 'tis what they call a birthright. She's had great tasks put upon her, being the Queen, an' mine has been the humble lot; but she's done the best she could, nobody can say to the contrary, and there's something between us; she's been the great lesson I've had to live by. She's been everything to me. An' when she had her Jubilee, oh, how my heart was with her!"

"There, 'twouldn't play the part in her life it has in mine," said Mrs. Martin generously, in answer to something one of her listeners had said. "Sometimes I think, now she's older, she might like to know about us. When I think how few old friends anybody has left at our age, I suppose it may be just the same with her as it is with me; perhaps she would like to know how we came into life together. But I've had a great advantage in seeing her, an' I can always fancy her goin' on while she don't know nothin' yet about me,—except she may feel my love stayin' her heart sometimes, an' not know just where it comes from. An' I dream about our being together out in some pretty fields, young as ever we was, and holdin' hands as we walk along. I'd like to know if she ever has that dream, too. I used to have days when I made believe she did know, an' was comin' to see me," confessed the speaker shyly, with a little flush on her cheeks, "and I'd plan what I could have nice for supper; and I wasn't goin' to let anybody know she was here havin' a good rest, except I'd wish you, Almira Todd, or dear Mis' Blackett would happen in, for you'd know just how to talk with her.

You see, she likes to be up in Scotland, right out in the wild country, better than she does anywhere else."

"I'd really love to take her out to see mother at Green Island," said Mrs. Todd, with a sudden impulse.

"Oh yes, I should love to have you," answered Mrs. Martin, and then she began to speak in a lower tone. "One day I got thinkin' so about my dear Queen," she said, "an' livin' so in my thoughts, that I went to work an' got all ready for her, just as if she was really comin'. I never told this to a livin' soul before, but I feel you'll understand. I put my best fine sheets and blankets I spun an' wove myself, on her bed, and I picked some pretty flowers and put 'em all round the house; an' I worked as hard an' happy as I could all day, and had as nice a supper ready as I could get, sort of tellin' myself a story all the time. She was comin', an' I was goin' to see her again, an' I kep' it up until nightfall; an' when I see the dark an' it come to me I was all alone, the dream left me, an' I sat down on the doorstep an' felt all foolish an' tired. An' if you'll believe it, I heard steps comin', an' an old cousin o' mine come wanderin' along, one I was apt to be shy of. She wasn't all there, as folks used to say, but harmless enough, and a kind of poor old talking body. An' I went right to meet her when I first heard her call, 'stead o' hidin', as I sometimes did, an' she come in dreadful willin', an' we set down to supper together; 'twas a supper I should have had no heart to eat alone."

"I don't believe she ever had such a splendid time in her life as she did then. I heard her tell all about it afterward!" exclaimed Mrs. Todd compassionately. "There, now I hear all this, it seems just as if the Queen might have known, and couldn't come herself, so she sent that poor old creatur' that was always in need!"

Mrs. Martin looked timidly at Mrs. Todd, and then at me. " 'Twas childish o' me to go an' get supper," she confessed.

"I guess you wa'n't the first one to do that," said Mrs. Todd. "No, I guess you wa'n't the first one who's got supper that way, Abby" — and then for a moment she could say no more.

Mrs. Todd and Mrs. Martin had moved their chairs a little, so that they faced each other, and I, at one side, could see them both.

"No, you never told me o' that before, Abby," said Mrs. Todd gently. "Don't it show that, for folks that have any fancy in 'em, such beautiful dreams is the real part o' life? But to most folks the common things that happens outside 'em is all in all."

Mrs. Martin did not appear to understand at first, strange to say, when the secret of her heart was put into words; then a glow of pleasure and comprehension shone upon her face. "Why, I believe you're right, Almira!" she said, and turned to me.

"Wouldn't you like to look at my pictures of the Queen?" she asked, and we rose and went into the best room.

V

The midday visit seemed very short. September hours are brief to match the shortening days. The great subject was dismissed for a while after our visit to the Queen's pictures, and my companions spoke much of lesser persons until we drank the cup of tea which Mrs. Todd had foreseen. I happily remembered that the Queen herself is said to like a proper cup of tea, and this at once seemed to make her Majesty kindly join so remote and reverent a company.

Mrs. Martin's thin cheeks took on a pretty color like a girl's. "Somehow, I always have thought of her when I made it extra good," she said. "I've got a real china cup that belonged to my grandmother, and I believe I shall call it hers now."

"Why don't you?" responded Mrs. Todd warmly, with a delightful smile.

Later they spoke of a promised visit which was to be made in the Indian summer to the Landing and Green Island; but I observed that Mrs. Todd presented the little parcel of dried herbs, with full directions, for a cure-all in the spring, as if there were no real chance of their meeting again first. As we looked back from the turn of the road the Queen's Twin was still standing on the doorstep watching us away, and Mrs. Todd stopped and stood still for a moment before she waved her hand again.

"There's one thing certain, dear," she said to me, with great discernment: "it ain't as if we left her all alone!"

Then we set out upon our long way home, over the hill where we lingered in the afternoon sunshine, and through the dark woods across the heron swamp.

February 1899

PATRICIO LAFCADIO TESSIMA CARLOS HEARN

1850–1904

"Carpets, pianos, windows, curtains, brass-bands, churches, how I hate them! Would I had been a savage: the curse of civilized cities is upon me."

Those were true words, spoken less in heat than in conviction. Lafcadio Hearn hated western civilization with his whole heart. In a sense he was civilized far beyond it, half of him, the other half was pure savage. His body liked to lose itself in the Negro jungles of New Orleans and the West Indies. His mind was an aeolian harp played upon by high rare notes such as human ear can seldom catch.

As he hated the world, so the world hated him. His mother, a beautiful Greek, was notoriously unchaste, and his father, Major Hearn of the British Army, a brute beast. Born beside that Leucadian promontory where Sappho leaps everlastingly into the sea, he died in Japan amid a people not unakin to his mother's legendary race. Deserted by that mother, he spent his miserable youth a victim of his father's family. Stunted, hideously defaced by the loss of an eye, wracked by disease, he suffered everything the Devil could invent. The single gift of fortune that befell his youth was a brief sojourn in a Jesuit school in France, from which, perversely enough, he ran away: that and the genius that burned within him.

Pitchforked first into England, then at nineteen into America, wherever he went he led an outcast's life, finding his only respite from contumely in joining successive colonies of Negroes where no man was better than his mate. The morbidities were his daily food, and curiously enough it was from them he plucked his first success. The details of a notorious and gruesome murder fascinated him. His account of it, published in a Cincinnati newspaper, was a masterpiece of the macabre. In the recesses of their hearts succulent morsels of this sort are what Americans most enjoy, and the story was a huge success. Hearn was placed on a newspaper pay roll at a salary of not less than twenty-five dollars a week, and then when it came to light that he was living with a Negress, off the pay roll he went again, never to know even a modest competence till time and chance took him to Japan and made a university professor of him.

The Japan that Hearn knew, seemed to unlock his soul. He loved the silken delicacy of manners. He loved the esoteric ways of thought. He loved the intimate detail of the landscape. The experience was the antithesis of everything he had known before and the immense relief of it seemed to open every pore of his body and mind to the sweet influences about him. The tidal wave of cruelty and greed which has since overwhelmed Japan was far in the future. Hearn became not only a citizen of Japan but a Japanese. He had found his native country and interpreted her in a long series of books which, to those who understand them, are a unique glory of literature.

On the palm of his hand Lafcadio Hearn bore from birth the carmine print of a thumb such as is said to be the hallmark of Romany descent. It may have been his gipsy ancestors who passed on to him that waywardness of disposition which frustrated almost every attempt to do him kindness. But certainly his precious years in France, his intimacy with the vast body of French literature, and his minute study of the art of Gautier and Baudelaire fed the flame of his peculiar genius. His prose, strong, clear, and exquisitely flexible owed more to French than to English models. But it has no real precedent and belongs to its maker alone.

Of American literature his books are no part. In the days of his littleness England lost, America disowned him. Now in the lasting days of his greatness we can at least be thankful that whereas once we were blind, now we see.

A Living God

LAFCADIO HEARN

I

Of whatever dimension, the temples or shrines of pure Shintō are all built in the same archaic style. The typical shrine is a windowless oblong building of unpainted timber, with a very steep overhanging roof; the front is the gable-end; and the upper part of the perpetually closed doors is wooden lattice-work, — usually a grating of bars closely set and crossing each other at right angles. In most cases the structure is raised slightly above the ground on wooden pillars; and the queer peaked façade with its visor-like apertures, and the fantastic projections of beam-work above its gable-angle, might remind the European traveler of certain old Gothic forms of dormer. There is no artificial color. The plain wood soon turns, under the action of rain and sun, to a natural gray, varying according to surface exposure from the silvery tone of birch-bark to the sombre gray of basalt. So shaped and so tinted, the isolated country *yashiro* may seem less like a work of joinery than a feature of the scenery, — a rural form related to nature as closely as rocks and trees, — a something that came into existence only as a manifestation of Oho-tsuchi-no-Kami, the Earth-god, the primeval Soul of the land.

Why certain architectural forms produce in the beholder a feeling of weirdness is a question about which I should like to theorize some day; at present I shall venture only to say that Shintō shrines evoke such a feeling. It grows with familiarity instead of weakening; and a knowledge of popular beliefs is apt to intensify it. We have no English words by which these queer shapes can be sufficiently described, much less any language able to communicate the peculiar impression which they make. Those Shintō terms which we loosely render by the words "temple" and "shrine" are really untranslatable; I mean that the Japanese ideas attaching to them cannot be conveyed by translation. The so-called "august house" of the Kami is not so much a temple, in the classic meaning of the term, as it is a haunted room, a spirit-chamber, a ghost-house; many of the lesser divinities being veritably ghosts, — ghosts of great warriors and heroes and rulers and teachers, who lived and loved and died hundreds or thousands of years ago. I fancy that to the Western mind the word "ghost-house" will convey, better than such terms as "shrine" and "temple," some vague notion of the strange character of the Shintō *miya* or *yashiro,* — containing in its perpetual dusk nothing more substantial than symbols or tokens, the latter probably of paper. Now the emptiness behind the visored front is more suggestive than anything material could possibly be; and when you remember that millions of people during thousands of years have worshiped their great dead before such *yashiro,* that a whole race still believes those buildings tenanted by viewless conscious personalities, you are apt also to reflect how difficult it would be to prove the faith absurd. Nay! in spite of Occidental reluctances, in spite of whatever you may think it expedient to say or not to say at a later time about the experience, you may very likely find yourself for a moment forced into the attitude of respect toward possibilities. Mere cold reasoning will not help you far in the opposite direction. The evidence of the senses counts for little: you know there are ever so many realities which can neither be seen nor heard nor felt, but which exist as forces, — tremendous forces. Then again you cannot mock the conviction of forty millions of people while that conviction thrills all about you like the air, — while conscious that it is pressing upon your psychical being just as the atmosphere presses upon your physical being. As for myself, whenever I am alone in the presence of a Shintō shrine, I have the sensation of being haunted; and I cannot help thinking about the possible apperceptions of the haunter. And this tempts me to fancy how I should feel if I myself were a god, — dwelling in some old gray shrine on the summit of a hill, guarded by stone lions and shadowed by a holy grove.

Elfishly small my habitation might be, but never too small, because I should have neither size nor form. I should be only a vibration, — a motion invisible as of ether or of magnetism; though able sometimes to shape me a shadow-body, in the likeness of my former visible self, when I should wish to make apparition.

As air to the bird, as water to the fish, so would all substance be permeable to the essence of me. I should pass at will through the walls of my dwelling to swim in the long gold bath of a sunbeam, to thrill in the heart of a flower, to ride on the neck of a dragon-fly.

Power above life and power over death would be mine, and the power of self-extension, and the power of self-multiplication, and the power of being in all places at one and the same moment. Simultaneously in a hundred homes I should hear myself worshiped, I should inhale the vapor of a hundred offerings; each evening, from my place within a hundred household shrines, I should see the holy lights lighted for me in lamplets of red clay, in lamplets of brass,—the lights of the Kami, kindled with purest fire and fed with purest oil.

But in my yashiro upon the hill I should have greatest honor: there betimes I should gather the multitude of my selves together; there should I unify my powers to answer supplication.

From the dusk of my ghost-house I should look for the coming of sandaled feet, and watch brown supple fingers weaving to my bars the knotted papers which are records of vows, and watch the motion of the lips of my worshipers making prayer:—

—"*Harai tamai kiyomé tamai to Kami imi tami!* . . . We have beaten drums, we have lighted fires, yet the land thirsts and the rice fails. Deign out of thy divine pity to give us rain, O Daimyōjin!"

—"*Harai tamai kiyomé tamai to Kami imi tami!* . . . I am dark, too dark, because I have toiled in the field, because the sun hath looked upon me. Deign thou augustly to make me white, very white,—white like the women of the city, O Daimyōjin!"

—"*Harai tamai kiyomé tamai to Kami imi tami!* . . . For Tsukamoto Motokichi our son, a soldier of twenty-nine: that he may conquer and come back quickly to us,—soon, very soon,—we humbly supplicate, O Daimyōjin!"

Sometimes a girl would whisper all her heart to me: "Maiden of eighteen years, I am loved by a youth of twenty. He is good; he is true; but poverty is with us, and the path of our love is dark. Aid us with thy great divine pity!—help us that we may become united, O Daimyōjin!" Then to the bars of my shrine she would hang a thick soft tress of hair,—her own hair, glossy and black as the wing of the crow, and bound with a cord of mulberry-paper. And in the fragrance of that offering,—the simple fragrance of her peasant youth,—I, the ghost and god, should find again the feelings of the years when I was man and lover.

Mothers would bring their children to my threshold, and teach them to revere me, saying, "Bow down before the great bright God; make homage to the Daimyōjin." Then I should hear the fresh soft clapping of little hands, and remember that I, the ghost and god, had been a father.

Daily I should hear the plash of pure cool water poured out for me, and the tinkle of thrown coin, and the pattering of dry rice into my wooden box, like a pattering of rain; and I should be refreshed by the spirit of the water, and strengthened by the spirit of the rice.

Festivals would be held to honor me. Priests, black-coiffed and linen-vestured, would bring me offerings of fruits and fish and seaweed and rice-cakes and rice-wine, — masking their faces with sheets of white paper, so as not to breathe upon my food. And the *miko* their daughters, fair girls in crimson *hakama* and robes of snowy white, would come to dance with tinkling of little bells, with waving of silken fans, that I might be gladdened by the bloom of their youth, that I might delight in the charm of their grace. And there would be music of many thousand years ago, — weird music of drums and flutes, and songs in a tongue no longer spoken, while the miko, the darlings of the gods, would poise and pose before me: —

. . . "*Whose virgins are these, — the virgins who stand like flowers before the Deity? They are the virgins of the august Deity.*

"*The august music, the dancing of the virgins, the Deity will be pleased to hear, the Deity will rejoice to see.*

"*Before the great bright God the virgins dance, — the virgins all like flowers newly opened.*" . . .

Votive gifts of many kinds I should be given: painted paper lanterns bearing my sacred name, and towels of divers colors printed with the number of the years of the giver, and pictures commemorating the fulfillment of prayers for the healing of sickness, the saving of ships, the quenching of fire, the birth of sons.

Also my Karashishi, my guardian lions, would be honored. I should see my pilgrims tying sandals of straw to their necks and to their paws, with prayer to the Karashishi-Sama for strength of foot.

I should see fine moss, like emerald fur, growing slowly, slowly, upon the backs of those lions; I should see the sprouting of lichens upon their flanks and upon their shoulders, in specklings of dead-silver, in patches of dead-gold; I should watch, through years of generations, the gradual sideward sinking of their pedestals undermined by frost and rain, until at last my lions would lose their balance, and fall, and break their mossy heads off. After which the people would give me new lions of another form, — lions of granite or of bronze, with gilded teeth and gilded eyes, and tails like a torment of fire.

Between the trunks of the cedars and pines, between the jointed columns of the bamboos, I should observe, season after season, the changes of the colors of the valley: the falling of the snow of winter and the falling of the snow of cherry-flowers; the lilac spread of the *gengebana;* the blazing yellow of the *natané;* the sky-blue mirrored in flooded levels, — levels dotted with the moon-shaped hats of the toiling people who would love me; and at last the pure and tender green of the growing rice.

The *moku*-birds and the *uguisu* would fill the shadows of my grove with ripplings and purlings of melody; the bell-insects, the crickets, and the seven marvelous cicadæ of summer would make all the wood of my ghost-house thrill to their musical storms. Betimes I should enter, like an ecstasy, into the tiny lives of them, to quicken the joy of their clamor, to magnify the sonority of their song.

But I never can become a god, — for this is the nineteenth century; and nobody can be really aware of the nature of the sensations of a god — unless there be gods in the flesh. Are there? Perhaps — in very remote districts — one or two. There used to be living gods.

Anciently any man who did something extraordinarily great or good or wise or brave might be declared a god after his death, no matter how humble his condition in life. Also good people who had suffered great cruelty and injustice might be apotheosized; and there still survives the popular inclination to pay posthumous honor and to make prayer to the spirits of those who die voluntary deaths under particular circumstances, — to souls of unhappy lovers, for example. (Probably the old customs which made this tendency had their origin only in the wish to appease the vexed spirit, although to-day the experience of great suffering seems to be thought of as qualifying its possessor for divine conditions of being; and there would be no foolishness whatever in such a thought.) But there were even more remarkable deifications. Certain persons, while still alive, were honored by having temples built for their spirits, and were treated as gods; not, indeed, as national gods, but as lesser divinities, — tutelar deities, perhaps, or village-gods. There was, for instance, Hamaguchi Gohei, a farmer of the district of Arita in the province of Kishu, who was made a god before he died. And I think he deserved it.

II

Before telling the story of Hamaguchi Gohei, I must say a few words about certain laws — or, more correctly speaking, customs having all the force of laws — by which many village communities were ruled in pre-Meiji times. These customs were based upon the social experience of ages; and though they differed in minor details according to province or district, their main signification was everywhere about the same. Some were ethical, some industrial, some religious; and all matters were regulated by them, even individual behavior. They preserved peace, and they compelled mutual help and mutual kindness. Sometimes there might be serious fighting between different villages, — little peasant wars about questions of water-supply or boundaries; but quarreling between men of the same community could not be tolerated in an age of vendetta, and the whole village would resent any needless disturbance of the internal peace. To some degree this state of things still exists in the more old-fashioned provinces: the people know how to live without quarreling, not to say fighting. Anywhere, as a general rule, Japanese fight only to kill; and when a sober man goes so far as to strike a blow, he virtually rejects communal protection, and takes his life into his own hands with every probability of losing it.

The private conduct of the other sex was regulated by some remarkable obligations entirely outside of written codes. A peasant girl, before marriage, enjoyed far more liberty than was permitted to city girls. She might be known to have a lover; and unless her parents objected very strongly, no blame would be given to her: it was regarded as an honest union, — honest, at least, as to intention. But having once made a choice, the girl was held bound by that choice. If it were discovered that she met another admirer secretly, the people would strip her naked, allowing her only a *shuro*-leaf for apron, and drive her in mockery through every street and alley of the village. During this public disgrace of their daughter, the parents of the girl dared not show their faces abroad; they were expected to share her shame, and they had to remain in their house, with all the shutters fastened up. Afterward the girl was sentenced to banishment for five years. But at the end of that period she was considered to have expiated her fault, and she could return home with the certainty of being spared further reproaches.

The obligation of mutual help in time of calamity or danger was the most imperative of all communal obligations. In case of fire, especially, everybody was required to give immediate aid to the best of his or her ability. Even children were not exempted from this duty. In towns and cities, of course, things were differently ordered; but in any little country village the universal duty was very plain and simple, and its neglect would have been considered unpardonable.

A curious fact is that this obligation of mutual help extended to religious matters: everybody was expected to invoke the help of the gods for the sick or the unfortunate, whenever asked to do so. For example, the entire village might be ordered to make a *sendo-mairi*[1] on behalf of some one seriously ill. On such occasions the Kumi-cho (each Kumi-cho was responsible for the conduct of five or more families) would run from house to house, crying, "Such and such a one is very sick: kindly hasten all to make a sendo-mairi!" Thereupon, however occupied for the moment, every soul in the settlement was expected to hurry to the temple,—taking care not to trip or stumble on the way, as a single misstep during the performance of a sendo-mairi was believed to mean misfortune for the sick. . . .

III

Now concerning Hamaguchi.

From immemorial time the shores of Japan have been swept, at irregular intervals of centuries, by enormous tidal waves,—tidal waves caused by earthquakes or by submarine volcanic action. These awful sudden risings of the sea are called by the Japanese *tsunami.* The last one occurred on the evening of June 17, 1896, when a wave nearly two hundred miles long struck the northeastern provinces of Miyagi, Iwaté, and Aomori: wrecking scores of towns and villages, ruining whole districts, and destroying nearly thirty thousand human lives. . . . The story of Hamaguchi Gohei is the story of a like calamity which happened long before the era of Meiji, on another part of the Japanese coast.

He was an old man at the time of the occurrence that made him famous. He was the most influential resident of the village to which he belonged: he had been for many years its *muraosa,* or headman; and he was not less liked than respected. The people usually called him *Ojiisan,* which means Grandfather; but, being the richest member of the community, he was sometimes officially referred to as the Chōja.

[1] To perform a *sendo-mairi* means to make one thousand visits to a temple, and to repeat one thousand invocations to the deity. But it is considered necessary only to go from the gate, or the torii of the temple-court, to the place of prayer, and back, one thousand times, repeating the invocation each time; and the task may be divided among any number of persons,—ten visits by one hundred persons, for instance, being quite as efficacious as a thousand visits by a single person.

He used to advise the smaller farmers about their interests, to arbitrate their disputes, to advance them money at need, and to dispose of their rice for them on the best terms possible.

Hamaguchi's big thatched farmhouse stood at the verge of a small plateau, overlooking a bay. The plateau, mostly devoted to rice culture, was hemmed in on three sides by thickly wooded summits. From its outer verge the land sloped down in a huge green concavity, as if scooped out, to the edge of the water; and the whole of this slope, some three quarters of a mile long, was so terraced as to look, when viewed from the open sea, like an enormous flight of green steps, divided in the centre by a narrow white zigzag, a streak of mountain road. Ninety thatched dwellings and a Shintō temple, composing the village proper, stood along the curve of the bay; and other houses climbed straggling up the slope for some distance on either side of the narrow road leading to the Chōja's home.

One autumn evening Hamaguchi Gohei was looking down from the balcony of his house at some preparations for a merry-making in the village below. There had been a very fine rice-crop, and the peasants were going to celebrate their harvest by a dance in the court of the *ujigami*.[2] The old man could see the festival banners (*nobori*) fluttering above the roofs of the solitary street, the strings of paper lanterns festooned between bamboo poles, the decorations of the shrine, and the brightly colored gathering of the young people. He had nobody with him that evening but his little grandson, a lad of ten; the rest of the household having gone early to the village. He would have accompanied them had he not been feeling less strong than usual.

The day had been oppressive; and in spite of a rising breeze, there was still in the air that sort of heavy heat which, according to the experience of the Japanese peasant, at certain seasons precedes an earthquake. And presently an earthquake came. It was not strong enough to frighten anybody; but Hamaguchi, who had felt hundreds of shocks in his time, thought it was queer,—a long, slow, spongy motion. Probably it was but the after-tremor of some immense seismic action very far away. The house crackled and rocked gently several times; then all became still again.

As the quaking ceased Hamaguchi's keen old eyes were anxiously turned toward the village. It often happens that the attention of a person gazing fixedly at a particular spot or object is suddenly diverted by the

[2] Shintō parish temple.

sense of something not knowingly seen at all,—by a mere vague feeling of the unfamiliar in that dim outer circle of unconscious perception which lies beyond the field of clear vision. Thus it chanced that Hamaguchi became aware of something unusual in the offing. He rose to his feet, and looked at the sea. It had darkened quite suddenly, and it was acting strangely. It seemed to be moving against the wind. *It was running away from the land.*

Within a very little time the whole village had noticed the phenomenon. Apparently no one had felt the previous motion of the ground, but all were evidently astounded by the movement of the water. They were running to the beach, and even beyond the beach, to watch it. No such ebb had been witnessed on that coast within the memory of living man. Things never seen before were making apparition; unfamiliar spaces of ribbed sand and reaches of weed-hung rock were left bare even as Hamaguchi gazed. And none of the people below appeared to guess what that monstrous ebb signified.

Hamaguchi Gohei himself had never seen such a thing before; but he remembered things told him in his childhood by his father's father, and he knew all the traditions of the coast. He understood what the sea was going to do. Perhaps he thought of the time needed to send a message to the village, or to get the priests of the Buddhist temple on the hill to sound their big bell. . . . But it would take very much longer to tell what he might have thought than it took him to think. He simply called to his grandson:—

"Tada!—quick,—very quick! . . . Light me a torch."

Taimatsu, or pine-torches, are kept in many coast dwellings for use on stormy nights, and also for use at certain Shintō festivals. The child kindled a torch at once; and the old man hurried with it to the fields, where hundreds of rice-stacks, representing most of his invested capital, stood awaiting transportation. Approaching those nearest the verge of the slope, he began to apply the torch to them,—hurrying from one to another as quickly as his aged limbs could carry him. The sun-dried stalks caught like tinder; the strengthening sea-breeze blew the blaze landward; and presently, rank behind rank, the stacks burst into flame, sending skyward columns of smoke that met and mingled into one enormous cloudy whirl. Tada, astonished and terrified, ran after his grandfather, crying,

"Ojiisan! why? Ojiisan! why?—why?"

But Hamaguchi did not answer: he had no time to explain; he was thinking only of the four hundred lives in peril. For a while the child stared wildly at the blazing rice; then burst into tears, and ran back to the house, feeling sure that his grandfather had gone mad. Hamaguchi went on firing stack after stack, till he had reached the limit of his field; then he threw down his torch, and waited. The acolyte of the hill-temple, observing the blaze, set the big bell booming; and the people responded to the double appeal. Hamaguchi watched them hurrying in from the sands and over the beach and up from the village, like a swarming of ants, and, to his anxious eyes, scarcely faster; for the moments seemed terribly long to him. The sun was going down; the wrinkled bed of the bay, and a vast sallow speckled expanse beyond it, lay naked to the last orange glow; and still the sea was fleeing toward the horizon.

Really, however, Hamaguchi did not have very long to wait before the first party of succor arrived,—a score of agile young peasants, who wanted to attack the fire at once. But the Chōja, holding out both arms, stopped them.

"Let it burn, lads!" he commanded,—"let it be! I want the whole *mura* here. There is a great danger,—*taihen desŭ!*"

The whole village was coming; and Hamaguchi counted. All the young men and boys were soon on the spot, and not a few of the more active women and girls; then most of the older folk, and mothers with babies at their backs, and even children,—for children could help to pass water; and the elders too feeble to keep up with the first rush could be seen well on their way up the steep ascent. The growing multitude, still knowing nothing, looked alternately, in sorrowful wonder, at the flaming fields and at the impassive face of their Chōja. And the sun went down.

"Grandfather is mad,—I am afraid of him!" sobbed Tada, in answer to a number of questions. "He is mad. He set fire to the rice on purpose: I saw him do it!"

"As for the rice," cried Hamaguchi, "the child tells the truth. I set fire to the rice. . . . Are all the people here?"

The Kumicho and the heads of families looked about them, and down the hill, and made reply: "All are here, or very soon will be. . . . We cannot understand this thing."

"*Aré!*" shouted the old man at the top of his voice, pointing to the open. "Say now if I be mad!"

Through the twilight eastward all looked, and saw at the edge of the dusky horizon a long, lean dim line like the shadowing of a coast where no coast ever was,—a line that thickened as they gazed, that broadened as a coast-line broadens to the eyes of one approaching it, yet incomparably more quickly. For that long darkness was the returning sea, towering like a cliff, and coursing more swiftly than the kite flies.

"*Tsunami!*" shrieked the people; and then all shrieks and all sounds and all power to hear sounds were annihilated by a nameless shock heavier than any thunder, as the colossal swell smote the shore with a weight that sent a shudder through all the hills, and a foam-burst like a blaze of sheet-lightning. Then for an instant nothing was visible but a storm of spray rushing up the slope like a cloud; and the people scattered back in panic from the mere menace of it. When they looked again, they saw a mad torment of tossing water over the place of their homes. It drew back roaring, and tearing out the bowels of the land as it went. Twice, thrice, five times the sea struck and ebbed, but each time with lesser surges; then it returned to its ancient bed and stayed,—still raging, as after a typhoon.

On the plateau for a time there was no word spoken. All stared speechlessly at the desolation beneath,—the horror of hurled rock and naked riven cliff, the bewilderment of scooped-up deep-sea wrack and shingle shot over the empty site of dwelling and temple. The village was not; the greater part of the fields were not; even the terraces had ceased to exist; and of all the homes that had been about the bay there remained nothing recognizable except two straw roofs tossing madly far out at sea. The after-terror of the death escaped and the stupefaction of the general loss kept all lips dumb, until the voice of Hamaguchi was heard again, observing gently, "That was why I set fire to the rice."

He, their Chōja, now stood among them almost as poor as the poorest; for his wealth was gone—but he had saved four hundred lives by the sacrifice. Little Tada ran to him, and caught his hand, and asked forgiveness for having said naughty things. Whereupon the people woke up to the knowledge of why they were alive, and began to wonder at the simple, unselfish foresight that had saved them; and the headmen prostrated themselves in the dust before Hamaguchi Gohei, and the people after them.

Then the old man wept a little, partly because he was happy, and partly because he was aged and weak and had been sorely tried.

"My house remains," he said, as soon as he could find words, automatically caressing Tada's brown cheeks; "and there is room for many. Also the temple on the hill stands; and there is shelter there for the others."

Then he led the way to his house; and the people cried and shouted.

The period of distress was long, because in those days there were no means of quick communication between district and district, and the help needed had to be sent from far away. But when better times came, the people did not forget their debt to Hamaguchi Gohei. They could not make him rich; nor would he have suffered them to do so, even had it been possible. Moreover, gifts would never have sufficed as an expression of their reverential feeling towards him; for they believed that the ghost within him was divine. So they declared him a god, and thereafter called him Hamaguchi Daimyōjin, knowing they could give him no greater honor; and truly no greater honor in any country could be given to mortal man. And when they rebuilt the village, they built a temple to the spirit of him, and fixed above the front of it a tablet bearing his name in Chinese text of gold; and they worshiped him there, with prayer and with offerings. How he felt about it I cannot say; I know only that he continued to live in his old thatched home upon the hill, with his children and his children's children, just as humanly and simply as before, while his soul was being worshiped in the shrine below. A hundred years and more he has been dead; but his temple, they tell me, still stands, and the people still pray to the ghost of the good old farmer to help them in time of fear or trouble.

. . . . .

I asked a Japanese philosopher and friend to explain to me how the peasants could rationally imagine the spirit of Hamaguchi in one place while his living body was in another. Also I inquired whether it was only one of his souls which they had worshiped during his life, and whether they imagined that one soul to have detached itself from the rest merely to receive homage.

"The peasants," my friend answered, "think of the mind or spirit of a person as something which, even during life, can be in many places at the same instant. . . . Such an idea is, of course, quite different from any Western ideas about the soul."

"Any more rational?" I mischievously asked.

"Well," he responded, with a Buddhist smile, "if we accept the doctrine of the unity of all mind, the idea of the Japanese peasant would appear to contain at least some adumbration of truth. I could not say so much for your Western notions about the soul."

December 1896

JOHN MUIR

1838–1914

Among the glories of the Lord's handiwork I put trees first. Their biographers are rare and for the most part inadequate, but there is a noble line of them stretching from Sir John Evelyn to Charles Sprague Sargent, and for infectious enthusiasm no name in the list stands above John Muir's. What do the redwoods of California not owe to him! As grand a talker as an inspired Scot can be, an hour with him meant a lifetime of remembrance. For many happy years he went camping with "Oom John" Burroughs, the philosopher of Slabsides, and Francis Browne, editor of the Chicago Dial, *the only fragment of Emersonianism that ever stuck to Chicago. But Muir's defect was egoism, and eventually the friends parted. Later the enlightened magnate, E. H. Harriman, took him on "The Harriman Expedition," and the Muir Glacier is a memorial of their voyage of discovery. The present story describes an episode of Muir's early life, when first he escaped patriarchal authority and gave rein to his own ingenious mind.*

With Muir the child was father of the man, as a thousand incidents of his juvenile precocity could testify. From the age of fifteen he was up with the dawn studying to some purpose grammar and mathematics, always with Milton and the Bible at his elbow to help him shape his permanent and noble style. While he was a student at the University of Wisconsin (where his auspicious entrance is described in the article that follows), early rising became more difficult owing to the lateness of the hour at which he blew out his lamp. It was an emergency, so John met it. Each night on lying down he would connect his toe with an alarm clock, set to go off at daybreak and fitted with an ingenious contraption which, like a vision of Duty, brought next morning before his sleepy eyes a succession of textbooks in precisely the sequence he had arranged the night before.

To Muir the whole miracle of nature was epitomized in the redwoods he loved and served. But behind plant life lay geology, and the more tremendous the obstacle Nature presented to humankind, the more passionate was his desire to pass the barrier. Glaciers and mountaintops exercised over him an irresistible fascination.

If the present story lures the reader to Muir's books, it will have served its purpose. The company of the judicious who prefer books to men, and earth and sky to human history, is eternally in need of recruits.

Out of the Wilderness

JOHN MUIR

I LEARNED arithmetic in Scotland without understanding any of it, although I had the rules by heart. But when I was about fifteen or sixteen years of age I began to grow hungry for real knowledge, and persuaded father, who was willing enough to have me study provided my farm work was kept up, to buy me a higher arithmetic. Beginning at the beginning, in one summer I easily finished it, without assistance, in the short intervals between the end of dinner and the afternoon start for the harvest and hay-fields, accomplishing more without a teacher in a few scraps of time, than in years in school before my mind was ready for such work. Then in succession I took up algebra, geometry, and trigonometry, and made some little progress in each, and reviewed grammar. I was fond of reading, but father brought only a few religious books from Scotland.

Fortunately, several of our neighbors brought a dozen or two of all sorts of books, which I borrowed and read, keeping all of them except the religious ones carefully hidden from father's eye. Among these were Scott's novels, which, like all other novels, were strictly forbidden, but devoured with glorious pleasure in secret. Father was easily persuaded to buy Josephus's *Wars of the Jews,* and D'Aubigné's *History of the Reformation,* and I tried hard to get him to buy Plutarch's *Lives,* which, as I told him, everybody, even religious people, praised as a grand good book; but he would have nothing to do with the old pagan until the graham bread and anti-flesh doctrines came suddenly into our backwoods neighborhood, making a stir something like phrenology and spirit-rappings, which were mysterious in their attacks as influenza. He then thought it possible that Plutarch might be turned to account on the food question by revealing what those old Greeks and Romans ate to make them strong; so at last we gained our glorious Plutarch.

Dick's *Christian Philosophy,* which I borrowed from a neighbor, I thought I might venture to read in the open, trusting that the word "Christian" would be proof against its cautious condemnation. But father balked at the word "Philosophy," and quoted from the Bible a verse which spoke of "philosophy falsely so-called." I then ventured to speak in defense of the book, arguing that we could not do without at least a little of the most useful kinds of philosophy.

"Yes, we can," he said, with enthusiasm, "the Bible is the only book human beings can possibly require throughout all the journey from earth to heaven."

"But how," I contended, "can we find the way to heaven without the Bible, and how after we grow old can we read the Bible without a little helpful science? Just think, father, you cannot read your Bible without spectacles, and millions of others are in the same fix; and spectacles cannot be made without some knowledge of the science of optics."

"Oh," he replied, perceiving the drift of the argument, "there will always be plenty of worldly people to make spectacles."

To this I stubbornly replied with a quotation from the Bible with reference to the time coming when "all shall know the Lord from the least even to the greatest," and then who will make the spectacles? But he still objected to my reading that book, called me a contumacious quibbler too fond of disputation, and ordered me to return it to the accommodating owner. I managed, however, to read it later.

On the food question father insisted that those who argued for a vegetable diet were in the right, because our teeth showed plainly that they were made with reference to fruit and grain, and not for flesh like those of dogs and wolves and tigers. He therefore promptly adopted a vegetable diet, and requested mother to make the bread from graham flour instead of bolted flour. Mother put both kinds on the table, and meat also, to let all the family take their choice; and while father was insisting on the foolishness of eating flesh, I came to her help by calling his attention to the passage in the Bible which told the story of Elijah the Prophet, who, when he was pursued by enemies who wanted to take his life, was hidden by the Lord by the brook Cherith, and fed by ravens; and surely the Lord knew what was good to eat, whether bread or meat. And on what, I asked, did the Lord feed Elijah? On vegetables or graham bread? No, he directed the ravens to feed his prophet on flesh. The Bible being the sole rule, father at once acknowledged that he was mistaken. The Lord never would have sent flesh to Elijah by the ravens if graham bread were better.

I remember as a great and sudden discovery that the poetry of the Bible, Shakespeare, and Milton was a source of inspiring, exhilarating, uplifting pleasure and I became anxious to know all the poets, and saved up small sums to buy as many of their books as possible. Within three or four years I was the proud possessor of parts of Shakespeare's, Milton's, Cowper's, Henry Kirk White's, Campbell's, and Akenside's works, and quite a number of others seldom read nowadays. I think it was in my fifteenth year that I began to relish good literature with enthusiasm, and smack my lips over favorite lines; but there was desperately little time for reading, even in the winter evenings — only a few stolen minutes now and then.

Father's strict rule was, straight to bed immediately after family worship, which in winter was usually over by eight o'clock. I was in the habit of lingering in the kitchen with a book and candle after the rest of the family had retired, and considered myself fortunate if I got five minutes' reading before father noticed the light and ordered me to bed; an order that, of course, I immediately obeyed. But night after night I tried to steal minutes in the same lingering way; and how keenly precious those minutes were, few nowadays can know. Father failed, perhaps, two or three times in a whole winter to notice my light for nearly ten minutes, magnificent golden blocks of time, long to be remembered like holidays or geological periods. One evening when I was reading Church History father was particularly irritable and called out with hope-killing emphasis, "*John, go to bed!* Must I give you a separate order every night to get you to go to bed? Now, I will have no irregularity in the family; you *must* go when the rest go, and without my having to tell you." Then, as an after-thought, as if judging that his words and tone of voice were too severe for so pardonable an offense, he unwarily added, "If you *will* read, get up in the morning and read. You may get up in the morning as early as you like."

That night I went to bed wishing with all my heart and soul that somebody or something might call me out of sleep to avail myself of this wonderful indulgence; and next morning, to my joyful surprise, I awoke before father called me. A boy sleeps soundly after working all day in the snowy woods, but that frosty morning I sprang out of bed as if called by a trumpet blast, rushed downstairs scarce feeling my chilblains, enormously eager to see how much time I had won; and, when I held up my candle to a little clock that stood on a bracket in the kitchen, I found that it was only one o'clock. I had gained five hours, almost half a day! "Five hours to myself!" I said, "five huge, solid hours!" I can hardly think of any other event in my life, any discovery I ever made that gave birth to joy so transportingly glorious as the possession of these five frosty hours.

In the glad tumultuous excitement of so much suddenly acquired time-wealth I hardly knew what to do with it. I first thought of going on with my reading, but the zero weather would make a fire necessary, and it occurred to me that father might object to the cost of firewood that took time to chop. Therefore I prudently decided to go down cellar, where I at least would find a tolerable temperature very little below the freezing point, for the walls were banked up in the fall to keep the potatoes from freezing. There were a few tools in a corner of the cellar, a vise, a few files, a hammer, and so forth, that father had brought from Scotland, but no saw excepting a coarse, crooked one that was unfit for sawing dry hickory or oak. So I made a fine-tooth saw suitable for my work out of a strip of steel that had formed part of an old-fashioned corset, that cut the hardest wood smoothly. I also made my own brad-awls and punches, a pair of compasses, and so forth, out of wire and old files, and went to work on a model of a self-setting sawmill I had invented.

Next morning I managed joyfully to get up at the same gloriously early hour. My cellar workshop was immediately under father's bed and the filing and tapping in making cog-wheels, journals, cams, and so forth, must no doubt have annoyed him; but with the permission he had granted, in his mind, and doubtless hoping that I would soon tire of getting up at one o'clock, he impatiently waited about two weeks before saying a word. I did not vary more than five minutes from one o'clock all winter, nor did I feel any bad effects whatever, nor did I think at all about the subject as to whether so little sleep might be in any way injurious; it was a grand triumph of will power over cold and common comfort and work-weariness in abruptly cutting down my ten hours' allowance of sleep to five. I simply felt that I was rich beyond anything I could have dreamed of or hoped for. I was far more than happy. Like Tam-o'-Shanter, I was "glorious, O'er a' the ills of life victorious."

Father, as was customary in Scotland, gave thanks and asked a blessing before meals, not merely as a matter of form and decent

Christian manners, for he regarded food as a gift derived directly from the hands of the Father in heaven. Therefore every meal was to him a sacrament requiring conduct and attitude of mind not unlike that befitting the Lord's supper. No idle word was allowed to be spoken at our table, much less any laughing or fun or story-telling. When we were at the breakfast-table, about two weeks after the great golden time-discovery, father cleared his throat, preliminary, as we all knew, to saying something considered important. I feared that it was to be on the subject of my early rising, and dreaded the withdrawal of the permission he had granted on account of the noise I made, but still hoping that, as he had given his word that I might get up as early as I wished, he would as a Scotchman stand to it, even though it was given in an unguarded moment and taken in a sense unreasonably far-reaching. The solemn sacramental silence was broken by the dreaded question, —

"John, what time is it when you get up in the morning?"

"About one o'clock," I replied in a low, meek, guilty tone of voice.

"And what kind of a time is that, getting up in the middle of the night and disturbing the whole family?"

I simply reminded him of the permission he had freely granted me to get up as early as I wished.

"I *know* it," he said, in an almost agonizing tone of voice; "I *know* I gave you that miserable permission, but I never imagined that you would get up in the middle of the night."

To this I cautiously made no reply, but continued to listen for the heavenly one-o'clock call, and it never failed.

After completing my self-setting sawmill I dammed one of the streams in the meadow and put the mill in operation. This invention was speedily followed by a lot of others, — water-wheels, curious door-locks and latches, thermometers, hygrometers, pyrometers, clocks, a barometer, an automatic contrivance for feeding the horses at any required hour, a lamp-lighter and fire-lighter, an early-or-late-rising machine, and so forth.

After the sawmill was proved and discharged from my mind, I happened to think it would be a fine thing to make a timekeeper which would tell the day of the week and the day of the month, as well as strike like a common clock and point out the hours; also to have an attachment whereby it could be connected with a bedstead to set me on my feet at any hour in the morning; also to start fires, light lamps, and so forth. I had learned the time laws of the pendulum from a book, but with this exception I knew nothing of time-keepers, for I had never seen the inside of any sort of clock or watch. After long brooding, the novel clock was at length completed in my mind, and was tried and found to be durable, and to work well and look well, before I had begun to build it in wood. I carried small parts of it in my pocket to whittle at when I was out at work on the farm, using every spare or stolen moment within reach without father's knowing anything about it.

In the middle of summer, when harvesting was in progress, the novel time-machine was nearly completed. It was hidden upstairs in a spare bedroom where some tools were kept. I did the making and mending on the farm; but one day at noon, when I happened to be away, father went upstairs for a hammer or something and discovered the mysterious machine back of the bedstead. My sister Margaret saw him on his knees examining it, and at the first opportunity whispered in my ear, "John, fayther saw that thing you're making upstairs." None of the family knew what I was doing, but they knew very well that all such work was frowned on by father, and kindly warned me of any danger that threatened my plans. The fine invention seemed doomed to destruction before its time-ticking commenced, although I had carried it so long in my mind that I thought it handsome, and like the nest of Burns's wee mousie it had cost me mony a weary whittling nibble. When we were at dinner several days after the sad discovery, father began to clear his throat, and I feared the doom of martyrdom was about to be pronounced on my grand clock.

"John," he inquired, "what is that thing you are making upstairs?"

I replied in desperation that I didn't know what to call it.

"What! You mean to say you don't know what you are trying to do?"

"Oh, yes," I said, "I know very well what I am doing."

"What then is the thing for?"

"It's for a lot of things," I replied, "but getting people up early in the morning is one of the main things it is intended for; therefore, it might perhaps be called an early-rising machine."

After getting up so extravagantly early, to make a machine for getting up perhaps still earlier seemed so ridiculous that he very nearly laughed. But after controlling himself, and getting command of a sufficiently solemn face and voice, he said severely, "Do you not think it is very wrong to waste your time on such nonsense?"

"No," I said meekly, "I don't think I'm doing any wrong."

"Well," he replied, "I assure you I do; and if you were only half as zealous in the study of religion as you are in contriving and whittling these useless, nonsensical things, it would be infinitely better for you. I want you to be like Paul, who said that he desired to know nothing among men but Christ and Him crucified."

To this I made no reply, gloomily believing my fine machine was to be burned, but still taking what comfort I could in realizing that anyhow I had enjoyed inventing and making it.

After a few days, finding that nothing more was to be said, and that father, after all, had not had the heart to destroy it, all necessity for secrecy being ended, I finished it in the half-hours that we had at noon, and set it in the parlor between two chairs, hung moraine boulders, that had come from the direction of Lake Superior, on it for weights, and set it running. We were then hauling grain into the barn. Father at this period devoted himself entirely to the Bible and did no farm work whatever. The clock had a good loud tick and when he heard it strike, one of my sisters told me that he left his study, went to the parlor, got down on his knees, and carefully examined the machinery, which was all in plain sight, not being inclosed in a case. This he did repeatedly, and evidently seemed a little proud of my ability to invent and whittle such a thing, though careful to give no encouragement for anything more of the kind in future.

But somehow it seemed impossible to stop. Inventing and whittling faster than ever, I made another hickory clock, shaped like a scythe to symbolize the scythe of Father Time. The pendulum is a bunch of arrows symbolizing the flight of time. It hangs on a leafless mossy oak snag showing the effect of time, and on the snath is written, "All flesh is grass." This, especially the inscription, rather pleased father, and of course mother and all my sisters and brothers admired it. Like the first, it indicates the days of the week and month, starts fires and beds at any given hour and minute, and though made more than fifty years ago, is still a good timekeeper.

My mind still running on clocks, I invented a big one like a town clock, with four dials, with the time figures so large they could be read by all our immediate neighbors as well as ourselves when at work in the fields, and on the side next the house the days of the week and month were indicated. It was to be placed on the peak of the barn roof. But just as it was all but finished father stopped me, saying that it would bring too many people around the barn. I then asked permission to put it on the top of a black oak tree near the house. Studying the larger main branches I thought I could secure a sufficiently rigid foundation for it, while the trimmed sprays and leaves would conceal the angles of the cabin required to shelter the works from the weather, and the two-second pendulum, fourteen feet long, could be snugly incased on the side of the trunk. Nothing about the grand, useful time-keeper, I argued, would disfigure the tree, for it would look something like a big hawk's nest. "But that," he objected, "would draw still bigger, bothersome trampling crowds about the place, for who ever heard of anything so queer as a big clock on the top of a tree." So I had to lay aside its big wheels and cams and rest content with the pleasure of inventing it, and looking at it in my mind and listening to the deep, solemn throbbing of its long two-second pendulum, with its two old axes back to back for the bob.

One of my inventions was a large thermometer made of an iron rod, about three feet long and five-eighths of an inch in diameter, that had formed part of a wagon-box. The expansion and contraction of this rod was multiplied by a series of levers made of strips of hoop-iron. The pressure of the rod against the levers was kept constant by a small counterweight, so that the slightest change in the length of the rod was instantly shown on a dial about three feet wide, multiplied about thirty-two thousand times. The zero point was gained by packing the rod in wet snow. The scale was so large that the big black hand on the white painted dial could be seen distinctly, and the temperature read, while we were ploughing in the field below the house. The extremes of heat and cold caused the hand to make several revolutions. The number of these revolutions was indicated on a small dial marked on the larger one. This thermometer was fastened on the side of the house, and was so sensitive that when any one approached it within four or five feet the heat radiated from the observer's body caused the hand of the dial to move so fast that the motion was plainly visible, and when he stepped back, the hand moved slowly back to its normal position. It was regarded as a great wonder by the neighbors, and even by my own all-Bible father.

Talking over plans with me one day, a friendly neighbor said, "Now, John, if you wish to get into a machine-shop, just take some of your inventions to the state fair, and you may be sure that as soon as they are seen they will open the door of any shop in the country for you. You will be welcomed everywhere." And when I doubtingly asked if people would care to look at things made of wood, he said, "Made of wood! Made of wood! What does it matter what they're made of when they are so out-and-out original. There's nothing else like them in the world. That is what will attract attention, and besides they're mighty handsome things anyway to come from the backwoods." So I was encouraged to leave home and go at his direction to the state fair when it was being held in Madison.

When I told father that I was about to leave home, and inquired whether, if I should happen to be in need of money, he would send me a little, he said, "No. Depend entirely on yourself." Good advice, I suppose, but surely needlessly severe for a bashful home-loving boy who had worked so hard. I had the gold sovereign that my grandfather had given me when I left Scotland, and a few dollars, perhaps ten, that I had made by raising a few bushels of grain on a little patch of sandy, abandoned ground. So when I left home to try the world I had only fifteen dollars in my pocket.

Strange to say, father carefully taught us to consider ourselves very poor worms of the dust, conceived in sin, and so forth, and devoutly believed that quenching every spark of pride and self-confidence was a sacred duty, without realizing that in so doing he might, at the same time, be quenching everything else. Praise he considered most venomous, and tried to assure me that when I was fairly out in the wicked world, making my own way, I would soon learn that, although I might have thought him a hard taskmaster at times, strangers were far harder. On the contrary, I found no lack of kindness and sympathy. All the baggage I carried was a package made up of the two clocks and a small thermometer made of a piece of old washboard, all three tied together, with no covering or case of any sort, the whole looking like one very complicated machine.

The aching parting from mother and my sisters was of course hard to bear. Father let David drive me down to Pardeeville, a place I had never before seen, though it is only nine miles south of the Hickory Hill farm. When we arrived at the village tavern it seemed deserted. Not a single person was in sight. I set my clock baggage on the rickety platform. David said good-bye and started for home, leaving me alone in the world. The grinding noise made by the wagon in turning short brought out the landlord, and the first thing that caught his eye was my strange bundle. Then he looked at me and said, "Hello, young man, what's this?"

"Machines," I said, "for keeping time and getting up in the morning, and so forth."

"Well! Well! That's a mighty queer get-up. You must be a Down-East Yankee. Where did you get the pattern for such a thing?"

"In my head," I said.

Some one down the street happened to notice the landlord looking intently at something and came up to see what it was. Three or four people in that little village formed an attractive crowd, and in fifteen or twenty minutes the greater part of the population of Pardeeville stood gazing in a circle around my strange hickory belongings. I kept outside of the circle to avoid being seen, and had the advantage of hearing the remarks without being embarrassed.

I stayed overnight at this little tavern, waiting for a train. In the morning I went to the station, and set my bundle on the platform. Along came the thundering train, a glorious sight; the first train I had ever waited for. When the conductor saw my queer baggage, he cried, "Hello! What have we here?"

"Inventions for keeping time, early rising, and so forth. May I take them into the car with me?"

"You can take them where you like," he replied, "but you had better give them to the baggage-master. If you take them into the car they will draw a crowd and might get broken."

So I gave them to the baggage-master, and made haste to ask the conductor whether I might ride on the engine. He good-naturedly said, "Yes, it's the right place for you. Run ahead, and tell the engineer what I say." But the engineer bluntly refused to let me on, saying, "It don't matter what the conductor told you. *I* say you can't ride on my engine."

By this time the conductor, standing ready to start his train, was watching to see what luck I had, and when he saw me returning came ahead to meet me.

"The engineer won't let me on," I reported.

"Won't he?" said the kind conductor. "Oh, I guess he will. You come down with me." And so he actually took the time and patience to walk the length of that long train to get me on to the engine.

"Charlie," said he, addressing the engineer, "don't you ever take a passenger?"

"Very seldom," he replied.

"Anyhow, I wish you would take this young man on. He has the strangest machines in the baggage car I ever saw in my life. I believe he could make a locomotive. He wants to see the engine running. Let him on." Then, in a low whisper, he told me to jump on, which I did gladly, the engineer offering neither encouragement nor objection.

As soon as the train was started the engineer asked what the "strange thing" the conductor spoke of really was.

"Only inventions for keeping time, getting folks up in the morning, and so forth," I hastily replied; and before he could ask any more questions I asked permission to go outside of the cab to see the machinery. This he kindly granted, adding, "Be careful not to fall off, and when you hear me whistling for a station you come back, because if it is reported against me to the superintendent that I allow boys to run all over my engine, I might lose my job."

Assuring him that I would come back promptly, I went out and walked along the footboard on the side of the boiler, watching the magnificent machine rushing through the landscape as if glorying in its strength like a living creature. While seated on the cow-catcher platform I seemed to be fairly flying, and the wonderful display of power and motion was enchanting. This was the first time I had ever been on a train, much less a locomotive, since I had left Scotland. When I got to Madison I thanked the kind conductor and engineer for my glorious ride, inquired the way to the fair, shouldered my inventions, and walked to the fair-ground.

When I applied for an admission ticket at a window by the gate I told the agent that I had something to exhibit.

"What is it?" he inquired.

"Well, here it is. Look at it."

When he craned his neck through the window and got a glimpse of my bundle he cried excitedly, "Oh! *you* don't need a ticket — come right in."

When I inquired of the agent where such things as mine should be exhibited, he said, "You see that building up on the hill with a big flag on it? That's the Fine Arts Hall and it's just the place for your wonderful invention."

So I went up to the Fine Arts Hall and looked in, wondering if they would allow wooden things in so fine a place.

I was met at the door by a dignified gentleman who greeted me kindly and said, "Young man, what have we got here?"

"Two clocks and a thermometer," I replied.

"Did you make these? They look wonderfully beautiful and novel and must I think prove the most interesting feature of the fair."

"Where shall I place them?" I inquired.

"Just look around, young man, and choose the place you like best, whether it is occupied or not. You can have your pick of all the building, and a carpenter to make the necessary shelving and assist you in every way possible!"

So I quickly had a shelf made large enough for all of them, went out on the hill and picked up some glacial boulders of the right size for weights, and in fifteen or twenty minutes the clocks were running. They seemed to attract more attention than anything else in the hall. I got lots of praise from the crowd and the newspaper reporters. The local press reports were copied into the Eastern papers. It was considered wonderful that a boy on a farm had been able to invent and make such things, and almost every spectator foretold good fortune. But I had been so lectured by my father to avoid praise, above all things, that I was afraid to read those kind newspaper notices, and never clipped out or preserved any of them, just glanced at them, and turned away my eyes from beholding vanity, and so forth. They gave me a prize of ten or fifteen dollars, and a diploma for wonderful things not down in the list of exhibits.

I was looking around in the meantime to find out where I should go to seek my fortune. An inventor at the fair, by the name of Wiard, was exhibiting an ice-boat he had invented to run on the upper Mississippi from Prairie du Chien to St. Paul during the winter months, explaining how useful it would be thus to make a highway of the river while it was closed to ordinary navigation by ice. After he saw my inventions, he offered me a place in his foundry and machine-shop in Prairie du Chien, and promised to assist me all he could. So I made up my mind to accept his offer and rode with him to Prairie du Chien in his ice-boat, which was mounted on a flat car. I soon found, however, that he was seldom at home, and that I was not likely to learn much at his small shop. I found a place where I could work for my board and devote my spare hours to mechanical drawing, geometry, and physics. Making but little headway, however, although the Pelton family for whom I worked were very kind, I made up my mind after a few months' stay in Prairie du Chien to return to Madison, hoping that in some way I might be able to gain an education.

At Madison I raised a few dollars by making and selling a few of those bedsteads that set the sleepers on their feet in the morning—inserting in the footboard the works of an ordinary clock that could be bought for a dollar. I also made a few dollars addressing circulars in an insurance office, while at the same time I was paying my board by taking care of a pair of horses and going errands. This is of no great interest except that I was thus earning my bread while hoping that something might turn up that would enable me to make money enough to enter the state university. This was my ambition, and it never wavered, no matter what I was doing. No university it seemed to me could be more admirably situated, and as I sauntered about it, charmed with its fine lawns and trees and beautiful lakes, and saw the students going and coming with their books, and occasionally practicing with a theodolite in measuring distances, I thought that if I could only join them it would be the greatest joy of life. I was desperately hungry and thirsty for knowledge and willing to endure anything to get it.

One day I chanced to meet a student who had noticed my inventions at the fair and now recognized me. And when I said, "You are fortunate fellows to be allowed to study in this beautiful place; I wish I could join you,"—"Well, why don't you?" he asked. "I haven't money enough," I said. "Oh, as to money," he reassuringly explained, "very little is required. I presume you're able to enter the Freshman class, and you can board yourself, as quite a number of us do, at a cost of about a dollar a week. The baker and milkman come every day. You can live on bread and milk." "Well," I thought, "maybe I have money enough for at least one beginning term." Anyhow I couldn't help trying.

With fear and trembling, overladen with ignorance, I called on Professor Stirling, the dean of the faculty, who was then acting president, presented my case, told him how far I had got on with my studies at home, and that I hadn't been to school since leaving Scotland at the age of eleven years (excepting one short term of a couple of months at a district school), because I could not be spared from the farm work. After hearing my story the kind professor welcomed me to the glorious university—next, it seemed to me, to the Kingdom of Heaven. After a few weeks in the preparatory department, I entered the Freshman class. In Latin I found that one of the books in use I had already studied in Scotland. So after an interruption of a dozen years I began my Latin over again where I had left off; and strange to say, most of it came back to me, especially the grammar which I had committed to memory at the Dunbar Grammar School.

During the four years that I was in the university I earned enough in the harvest-fields during the long summer vacations to carry me through the balance of each year, working very hard, cutting with a cradle four acres of wheat a day, and helping to put it in the shock. But having to buy books and paying I think thirty-two dollars a year for instruction, and occasionally buying acids and retorts, glass tubing, bell-glasses, flasks, and so forth, I had to cut down expenses for board now and then to half a dollar a week.

One winter I taught school ten miles north of Madison, earning much-needed money at the rate of twenty dollars a month, "boarding round," and keeping up my university work by studying at night. As I was not then well enough off to own a watch, I used one of my hickory clocks, not only for keeping time, but for starting the school-fire in the cold mornings, and regulating class times. I carried it out on my shoulder to the old log schoolhouse, and set it to work on a little shelf nailed to one of the knotty, bulging logs. The winter was very cold, and I had to go to the schoolhouse and start the fire about eight o'clock, to warm it before the arrival of the scholars. This was a rather trying job, and one that my clock might easily be made to do. Therefore, after supper one evening, I told the head of the family with whom I was boarding that if he would give me a candle I would go back to the schoolhouse and make arrangements for lighting the fire at eight o'clock, without my having to be present until time to open the school at nine. He said, "Oh, young man, you have some curious things in the school-room, but I don't think you can do that." I said, "Oh, yes! It's easy"; and in hardly more than an hour the simple job was completed.

I had only to place a teaspoonful of powdered chlorate of potash and sugar on the stove hearth near a few shavings and kindlings, and at the required time make the clock, through a simple arrangement, touch the inflammable mixture with a drop of sulphuric acid. Every evening after school was dismissed I shoveled out what was left of the fire into the snow, put in a little kindling, filled up the big box-stove with heavy oak wood, placed the lighting arrangement on the hearth, and set the clock to drop the acid at the hour of eight; all this requiring only a few minutes.

The first morning after I had made this simple arrangement I invited the doubting farmer to watch the old squat schoolhouse from a window that overlooked it, to see if a good smoke did not rise from the stove-pipe. Sure enough, on the minute, he saw a tall column curling gracefully up through the frosty air; but, instead of congratulating me on my success, he solemnly shook his head and said in a hollow, lugubrious voice, "Young man, you will be setting fire to the schoolhouse." All winter long that faithful clock-fire never failed, and by the time I got to the schoolhouse the stove was usually red-hot.

At the beginning of the long summer vacations I returned to the Hickory Hill farm to earn the means in the harvest-fields to continue my university course, walking all the way to save railroad fares. And although I cradled four acres of wheat a day, I made the long hard sweaty day's work still longer and harder by keeping up my study of plants. At the noon hour I collected a large handful, put them in water to keep them fresh, and after supper got to work on them, and sat up till after midnight, analyzing and classifying, thus leaving only four hours for sleep; and by the end of the first year after taking up botany I knew the principal flowering plants of the region.

I received my first lesson in botany from a student by the name of Griswold who is now county judge of the county of Waukesha, Wisconsin. In the university he was often laughed at on account of his anxiety to instruct others, and his frequently saying with fine emphasis, "Imparting instruction is my greatest enjoyment."

Nevertheless I still indulged my love of mechanical inventions. I invented a desk in which the books I had to study were arranged in order at the beginning of each term. I also made a bed which set me on my feet every morning at the hour determined on, and in dark winter mornings just as the bed set me on the floor it lighted a lamp. Then, after the minutes allowed for dressing had elapsed, a click was heard and the first book to be studied was pushed up from a rack below the top of the desk, thrown open, and allowed to remain there the number of minutes required. Then the machinery closed the book and allowed it to drop back into its stall; then moved the rack forward and threw up the next in order, and so on, all the day being divided according to the times of recitation, and the time required and allotted to each study. Besides this, I thought it would be a fine thing in the summer-time when the sun rose early, to dispense with the clock-controlled bed-machinery, and make use of sunbeams instead. This I did simply by taking a lens out of my small spy-glass, fixing it on a frame on the sill of my bedroom window, and pointing it to the sunrise; the sunbeams focused on a thread burned it through, allowing the bed-machinery to put me on my feet. When I wished to get up at any given time after sunrise I had only to turn the pivoted frame that held the lens the requisite number of degrees or minutes. Thus I took Emerson's advice and hitched my dumping-wagon bed to a star.

Although I was four years at the university, I did not take the regular course of studies, but instead picked out what I thought would be most useful to me, particularly chemistry, which opened a new world, and mathematics and physics, a little Greek and Latin, botany and geology. I was far from satisfied with what I had learned, and should have stayed longer. Anyhow I wandered away on a glorious botanical and geological excursion, which has lasted nearly fifty years and is not yet completed, always happy and free, poor and rich, without thought of a diploma or of making a name, urged on and on through endless inspiring Godful beauty.

From the top of a hill on the north side of Lake Mendota I gained a last wistful lingering view of the beautiful university grounds and buildings where I had spent so many hungry and happy and hopeful days. There with streaming eyes I bade my blessed Alma Mater farewell. But I was only leaving one university for another, the Wisconsin University for the University of the Wilderness.

February 1913

MRS. ASQUITH [*Lady Oxford*]
1864–1945

Those who loved her, loved her well, and the brilliancy of her wayward chatter was for her generation the favorite talk of London. Margot Tennant was the daughter of a rich ironmaster. Among that exalted coterie of friends known as Souls, she was pre-eminent, and the name of one or another of the bachelors of that famous group was often linked with hers. We all remember the classical reply of Mr. Balfour when congratulations on his "engagement" to Margot Tennant were pressed upon him. "Why I was thinking of having a career of my own!" It was a widower, Mr. Asquith, whom she married, and never has 10 Downing Street had so exuberant a mistress, dividing the world into her slaves, her excoriators, and Mr. Kipling, whose ungallant apostrophe to "The Woman with the Serpent's Tongue" exceeded the facts almost as far as it outstripped the proprieties. Lady Oxford, as she became, might have the tongue of an asp but her heart was the heart of a St. Bernard dog.

One day I had been lunching at her table, and as I slipped on my overcoat she followed me into the hall for a personal word. "Have you been keeping any pleasant society?" she asked. I told her that the day before I had had a wonderful evening dining with Lord Milner. It was 1918; Milner was one of the five members of the War Cabinet and perhaps the wisest man in the Empire. "Poor Milner," she said, "he must be desperately dejected." "Why," I exclaimed, "the whole evening long he was buoyancy itself." "Ah," she replied, "but his life was ruined when I declined to marry him."

Such frankness is certainly engaging, and the story that follows is full of it.

A Double Event

MRS. ASQUITH

I OPENED my eyes at 8 o'clock on a bright morning in June, and found them fixed on my ball-dress. I looked at the clock; I saw I had exactly one hour in which to bathe, dress, breakfast, and get to Paddington.

Out of bed in an instant, I shouted for my maid. She had not been eight years with me for nothing. My habit, long coat, buff waistcoat, hat, boots, gloves, were all put out. I munched toast while she brushed my hair.

I always find that the double tie is the toilette trap in dressing for riding. Pulling up the centre under the chin, pinning down the sides, while keeping a straight line at the top of the turnover, is touch and go. It was June, however,—a month in which no one hunts but young ladies in fiction; and I need hardly say my tie was perfect. I pushed my arms into a covert coat, and, rushing downstairs, jumped into a hansom.

Hansoms are now as extinct as dueling or garrotting. No one can deny that they had every fault: you caught your dress getting in, you fell on your head getting out; if it rained, you were soaked, or if the window was down and the horse slipped, your head went through the glass. But it was a highly becoming conveyance, and generally went along quickly; unfortunately for me, this hansom went painfully slowly. I delayed it by poking my whip up through the trap-door and shouting, "Hurry up! I will give you five shillings more!" I gave this up as the lash of the eager driver tingled over my face (another danger to which a hansom exposed you), and full of grim determination,—as the Ulstermen said in 1914,—I made up my mind that I would have to race for the train.

I was going to a famous horse-dealer in Swindon, to try hunters for myself, Ribblesdale, and other members of the family. Elaborate arrangements had been made for me to join my sister, Mrs. Graham Smith, later on in the afternoon, and to miss this train would not only have put the family about, but have cheated me of riding strange horses over strange fences—an amusement which made my spirits rise.

I ran into the station; my train was moving slowly out. A porter was standing in an open doorway of one of the compartments. I jumped onto the step, caught hold of his coat, shouted, "Don't shut the door," and as he stepped off, I stepped in. My gratitude knew no bounds. I threw the man ten shillings — if he had shut the door, or shown any fear, I should have been done. Trains move off with great dignity, and if travelers would move on — instead of crawling like rolling-stock — fewer trains would be lost.

Out of breath, but full of gladness, I looked at my top-boots and wondered how many of my friends wore loose boots with thick soles to them. Everyone has a different sort of vanity; mine went to my head, not to my feet: two pairs of stockings and loose boots were essential to my comfort out hunting.

Apropos of this, I must digress a little. The present Duke of Beaufort's father once scolded me for wearing tight boots, — we were riding back to Badminton with the hounds on a cold evening, — and I assured him that they were so loose that if one of the hunt servants would pick up my boot, I could kick it into the road. He challenged me. I kicked my boot off with the greatest ease.

It was not my boots but my hats from Mr. Lock in St. James's Street that I fancied. From the hoop to the hobble is not a more violent change than from the riding hats of 1893 to the riding hats of 1917. I see young ladies riding in the Row with very wide flat brims and no crowns to their hats. Rotten Row has always had a good many loose horses with riders on them, so perhaps it is not fair to judge from this. I dare say if I went back to Melton I would see men and women with crowns to their hats. But I must return to my train.

After arranging a pillow at my back and tucking a rug round me, I looked at my fellow travelers. A beautiful old man in a roomy blue overcoat sat reading near the window, with his hat off. He had a beard of black and silver, and curling black and silver hair, a fine studio head with onyx eyes, and a thin large aquiline nose. An unworldly-looking youth sat next to him, arranging papers and letters in elastic bands. The seat next to the young man was piled high with letters, documents, and papers of every description.

I watched with interest the awe with which the old gentleman inspired the young man. Every time there was a flaw in the packets the young man's chin retreated further and his attitude became more servile.

For the first time I noticed labels on the windows at each side of the carriage. I said to myself, "Hullo! I am not in my right place. I must apologize for having thrust myself into this reserved carriage." How had I best begin? In my youth I called men "Sir"; this was peculiar to myself and by no means a fashion (I was born at a later period than *The Fairchild Family*).

I fidgeted about, with an occasional glance at the old man. Suddenly I caught his lively eye fixed on me.

"I am sorry, sir, that I hurled myself into this carriage. I see it has been reserved for you; but missing this train would have been a serious matter to me."

The Old Gentleman.—You need not apologize. I do not mind at all. I was afraid you might hurt yourself—what you did was very dangerous—you must never do it again. Why would it have been serious for you to have missed this train? [He said this in a grave tone, and added threateningly] What are you going to do?

She.—I am going to try horses for myself and my brother-in-law. What are you going to do?

He [very deliberately].—I am going to save souls.

She.—You are sanguine!

He.—Don't you believe in saving souls?

I confess I thought it a poignant pretension; but he was so bold and good-looking that I did not want to appear unsympathetic.

She.—Yes, I know what you mean. Can't say I have ever seen the process, though I have often heard of conversion. There is something morally vulgar to me in trying to get rapidly familiar with men's souls.

He [indignantly].—When you are dealing with the drunken and the depraved, you must not be morally aristocratic. You know nothing of real life—I have only to look at you to see that you are not only very young but extremely inexperienced. Look at me, young lady, and tell me truly. When have *you* seen souls flickering out for want of a little light? What do *you* know of the depravity that devastates whole districts? The world you know is not the real world at all! What sort of a world is yours? I do not suppose you have ever seen a pauper! Have you ever been to a workhouse? I don't suppose you have ever seen a lunatic. Have you ever been to an asylum? I don't suppose you have ever seen a convict. Have you ever been in a prison? Have you ever been into a public-house and seen men—yes, and women too—grappling and fighting in the sight of God before the eyes of man, stiff with drink?

He paused and after a reproachful look at me continued, "What do *you* know about drink? You have probably never seen drunkenness in your life."

She.—Oh! haven't I just! I am Scotch.

He [not listening].—Fighting, not with their fists, young woman, but with their souls. The morally aristocratic won't help us much here! What is wanted are workmen and workwomen. I am thinking of the next world—you are thinking of this. I can see you are fond of this world and its amusements—perhaps you are fashionable?

She.—Oh, dear, no!

He.—Who is your brother-in-law?

She.—Ribblesdale.

He.—What is your name?

She.—It won't convey anything to you. I am quite uninteresting!

He.—On the contrary, you interest me.—Do you believe in Hell?

She [decidedly].—No, nor do you.

Much surprised at this remark, he took off his coat and as he leaned forward, I saw "Salvation Army" embroidered on his blue jersey. So this was General Booth! I had heard much of him and Mrs. Booth, I had had close personal experience of their work in my districts (Whitechapel and Wapping), but I did not want our conversation to be interrupted by any autobiography, so I went on rapidly,—

"You *think* you do, but you *don't*. Holding Hell over the heads of the drunken and depraved is playing down to the lowest side, even of these poor people. This is the weak part of your teaching: you excite fear, and a sort of spiritual fever."

He.—If you were not a rich, idle, self-indulgent young lady, you would see that what you call spiritual fever *I* call spiritual hunger. This does not belong to the lowest side of humanity, but the highest. Spiritual torpor *is* Hell.

She.—If that is the kind of Hell you mean, I *do* believe in it. I have always thought Hell is within us—just as I think Heaven is, and as certainly as I think God is above us.

He.—There is a deal of nonsense in that kind of talk. Good is good, evil is evil, and God is God. Heaven is Heaven and Hell is Hell. Don't be equivocal and ecclesiastical, but be frank with your faith. Don't be sly, like the High Churchmen. I believe in Hell and I believe in Heaven. You say Heaven lies within us; does it only lie within us? Is there no destination—only the route?

She.—I did not mean that! You may as well say a corridor and Calvary are the same. Of course no one would go on walking or fighting if there was no goal, unless they were fools or saints; but fear of Hell is not a good incentive. Threats would have no effect upon me! I would much rather feel that my nature responded to love than to fear.

Why worry about Hell? Heaven is the light to hold before your flickering souls. I can't argue on theology. I feel like the child who was flying its kite high on a misty day. When they said, "Do you enjoy flying your kite when you can't see it?" the child said, "Oh! yes, I always feel it tugging at me."

The old man liked this story. He said, "I was not talking of theology, I was only defending myself when you were saying my army does not appeal to the highest in human beings. I say it does. If you had what I call spiritual hunger and you call spiritual fever, you would not be wasting your time trying horses for your brother-in-law."

Relieved at this departure from theology, and noticing a slight twinkling of his eye I said,—

"I see no great harm in trying horses for my brother-in-law."

He.—What sort of man is Lord Ribblesdale?

She.—He's a fine rider and a great judge of a horse.

He.—Is he a *good* man?

She.—One of the best! Now, general, what you want to know is how much field for conversion you can find in me and my family, and how to start about it. In practice conversion is extremely risky: it is like a practical joke. You can never know if the end is satisfactory; in conversation it is vain—making—It is not a good topic. It is ultimately dull, as it means different things to different men. Don't let us talk about conversion—I want to know about your wife and your society.

He.—My wife was the most wonderful woman God ever made. This society was entirely her idea; it was her creation, not mine.

He spoke of her with deep feeling—of her amazing oratory and true goodness. I could only say what I had heard about her, and how much I admired him, his family, and his work. He was not very forthcoming, which disappointed me. I longed to know much more about himself and how the idea of the Salvation Army started, but he never pursued any subject for long; he was a restless listener. I asked him if his wife believed in Hell.

He [guardedly].—I think she would have agreed with you about Hell. What is the name of your father?

She.—My father is called Charles Tennant; he makes chemicals in Glasgow and gold in the Mysore mines in India.

He.—You are Margot Tennant. I know all about you. (I felt inclined to say, "Oh! do you?") Your father refused to give our army any money.

She.—I don't think my father ever refused to give money to any one in his life. He knows the value of money too well not to give; he is a very happy man and suffers none of the apprehension, suspicion, and low temperature of the rich. My father would never understand your army and he hates noise.

He.—Noise!!

She.—Yes, you know your lassies thrum tea-trays for hours in the streets, and shout even on grass slopes where people play golf. The seventeenth hole at St. Andrews—on the road where your people parade—is a very ticklish hole; my father is irritable and highly strung—

He.—Are you?

She.—*Very;* noise is physical pain to me. It does not take much to put you out when you are putting.

He [not listening, but watching me closely].—Do you say your prayers?

She.—Always.

He.—Would you like to pray now in this carriage?

She [gravely].—Certainly, if you would like to.

General Booth was unprepared for this answer. He had made up his mind that I was a fearless, frivolous female. He had been baulked in his scheme of conversion by a conversational digression and was anxious to return to the charge. For a moment neither of us spoke; then with a courteous movement of his hand to me he said, "Let us kneel and pray."

The young lieutenant, the general, and I knelt down in a row, with our elbows on the opposite seats of the carriage. He opened by exhortation: Would God "bless and be near this our sister"? He was not censorious, but I noticed that he emphasized the word "quietness" in quoting St. Paul: "In quietness and confidence lies our strength."

He prayed erect upon his knees, with an upright head, throwing his long hair back. I shall never forget that prayer: I found myself not merely conforming, but acquiescing and praying. He was perfectly unself-conscious; humble, without being self-centred; grateful, without being complacent; original and uneccentric; full of ideas, without being jumpy; reverent, imaginative, and, to me, deeply moving.

He finished and we all got up. I took his hand, pressed it with both of mine, and thanked him. I told him how much I had liked his prayer. We sat down in silence. He asked me what I had got in my writing-case. I took out books and a few photographs and trifles, and showed them to him. None of these interested him at all.

I always travel with a little leather commonplace book in which I have copied from the writings of many authors quotations concerning death and prayer. He took up the book and asked me to lend it to him. I did not want to do this, as I have never had much success in lending books to friends. There were a few empty pages, and I said, "You write something in my book for me; I cannot lend it to you; I have never shown this to any one."

He did not give me back the book, but held it in his hand.

He.—I suppose when you get home you will make a good story of our talk and journey to-day.

She.—If you regret it I will tell no one, but otherwise I shall certainly tell my sister.

He [smiling].—And the brother-in-law?

She.—Yes, all of them—but I don't know what you mean by "good story." If you mean that *I* think it funny to pray, you are completely out in your calculations.

He.—You haven't often knelt in a train before, and prayed, have you?

She.—No, never. I generally say my prayers to myself, but I have often prayed out loud with my factory-girls, and never observed any of them take it amiss.

He.—Shall I ever see you again? Will you ride down Rotten Row in one of my Salvation bonnets?

She.—No. I think they are hideous. I can see that your converts have been very conventional people; you take it for granted that I am vain and worldly, and you want to startle me into loving God. I have always believed in the Salvation Army, and given money to it, but I don't see that riding in your bonnet would bring in more souls or more subscriptions.

He.—It would be an advertisement.

She.—It would cover you, me, and your soldiers with ridicule.

He.—Christ did not mind being ridiculed.

She.—He would not have liked being advertised—Just write in my book, will you? I will give you my address so that you won't forget me.

He wrote in silence. We were nearing Swindon station. I felt very sorry to part with my dear old new friend.

He gave me back the book. I read what he had written:—

"What is life for but to walk in harmony with God, to secure that disposition and character which will fit us for the enjoyments and employments and companionships of Heaven—and to spend and be spent for the temporal and eternal weal of this suffering world? — WILLIAM BOOTH."

I shut my little book and put it in my bag.

He. — I am very glad to have met you: we will pray for each other, and meet soon.

He took my hand in both of his.

I told him I had loved his prayer and would never forget him; that he must come and see me, or if he wanted me, I would go and see him. We said good-bye, and remained friends till he died.

I was met at Swindon by the horse-dealer in a buggy — a little man of mild eye, gentle voice, and full-blooded brogue. He talked of the horses he had got for me to see. I did not listen much; I wished I had been with the general, for our journey had been too short. I wanted to read again what he had written, but my bag was under a horse-cloth at my feet, and we went at such a pace that I felt that I could not open the bag without upsetting all the things; so I engaged in the following conversation:

"Havoc is the one for you — a little short in the rib but a foine shoulther, and *great* stroide. I took him with the duke's hounds over some rails in the corner, and not *warn*" ["one," which he pronounced as if it rhymed with *tarn*] "followed. There's a bit of a gray mare you shall see in the ring; she goes a little quick at her fences, but — "

She [rather snappily]. — I loathe a rusher!

The Dealer. — *That she is not!* [with great emphasis]. She has great courage. If you gave her the office she would jump into a conservatory — this is what you'll be wanting for the Leicestershire bottoms — there'll be no gates there.

She. — You're wrong; it's the best-gated country in the world.

He. — And is that so? But it only takes one fall to kill you down there, and here no one is the worse for a roll or two.

She. — That is true. What else have you got for me to try? In your letter you recommend Dandelion.

He [with a melting eye]. — Sure and I did. He's a beautiful horse — something to conjure with! — thoroughbred — all but in the book — full of proide and vanity! He is difficult to ride in the small enclosures; it's the shires he is wanting. If he puts you down I'll give him to you. I thought of entering him for the Grand National, but Lord Lonsdale said to me, "Racing will be the ruin of him."

We were tearing down the road when he pulled up suddenly at a brick house set in laurels and surrounded by sheds and stables; I saw through the trees a large paddock with a tan ring and fancy fences.

He [throwing the reins to an ostler and taking his watch out of his pocket].—Five miles in ten minutes, and only gave ten pound for you!

"Liar!" I said to myself, collecting my things.

We went into the loose boxes to look at the hunters. Bustling stablemen stripped one animal after the other in monotonous succession. I am always at a loss what to say on these occasions, so begged him to get his man as soon as possible to ride whatever was ready over the fences for me.

He.—It's yourself shall choose; which shall it be?

She.—What about Dandelion?

He.—Oh! you shall ride him yourself with me later on, down the road.

She.—Down the road? You mean over the fences!

He.—Not just at first—you must feel him under you! Jim! bring the gray mare to the paddock—we'll walk on.

We walked down to the gate and into the field, Jim following on the gray. I could see that Jim was a fine rider—long stirrups, a loose easy seat, and brimless hat. The gray, so far from being a little mare, struck me as big, angular, and gawky. The moment her large feet touched the ring she shot off! Jim handled her well, but as she approached the first fence, which was small and bushy, she rushed at it like a bull at a flag, took off from her stomach, and, hardly rising at all, landed twenty feet the other side. The fence closed up behind her, and one might have supposed she had never touched it—in Leicestershire I knew the fence would either have been taken up by the roots or I would have been taken home on a hurdle. It was the same with every fence in the ring. Had it not been for Jim, who with gigantic strength and iron nerve forced her to rise from her quarters at the only two obstacles of any merit, they must have parted company.

"Good Heavens!" I said; "if she's not a rusher I've never seen one! I hope you give Jim high wages!"

He.—Bless your soul, I wouldn't give a curse for a horse who, with the one fence leapt, hadn't the next one challenged!

Although I was rather amused, I was by no means mollified by this; I felt it had been an unlucky show. The dealer quickly perceived what was in my mind. His voice was very tender, almost caressing, as he said,—

"It's summer, and the divils don't get half enough exercise; I sell them off too quick! It's meself that should look after them."

She. — Really, it's useless to show me this kind of animal! Let us see Comedy, the Havoc horse, or Dandelion. What about the great Dandelion?

He did not respond to this, but went on wondering how he could remove the evil impression that the gray had made on me.

"Ah! if the mare had been fit you'd have had a foine ride this morning!"

"Not I! My only chance would be if she was tired, and then she'd lay me out for dead."

"Is it the gray mare you mean? *She would not.* I'd gladly be in prison for the stealing of her! Jim's not a rider like yourself; I wouldn't take two hundred for her. Now I'll tell you what I'll do — I'll get her fit and give you a mount with the duke, and you can break her neck and I'll say never a word!"

"She'll break mine, and then neither of us will be in a position to argue. Let us see Dandelion."

He bustled off to bring out the favorite. I stood on the stone block and saw two men bringing out Dandelion — one leading him, and the other walking by his side with a towel over his arm.

Dandelion was, I must say, a most fascinating horse — to look at; dark chestnut, his coat shining like the back of a violin; a short back, loose elbows, and not a blemish anywhere. Something in his appearance reminded me of a Disraeli novel — the quivering nostril of his little nose, the rather vindictive roving eye. He looked like a brilliant adventurer. If this horse was all that he said, both my fortune and the dealer's were made.

I watched him coming toward me; his walk was resolute and elastic. Something moved in the laurels, and he stopped at once. I could see that he was terribly observant; the second ostler instantly clutched the other rein close to the bit, Dandelion pointed his toes and danced up to the block at an impossible angle for me to mount.

The Dealer. — Begorra! Bad luck to it! he is fresh too. Now, boys, steady! steady with the cloth!

This mysterious, almost clerical expression mystified me for a moment; a third stable-boy came out, and, winking rapidly at one of his companions, assisted with great energy in holding a towel round Dandelion's restless head, covering his eyes. The horse, quivering all over, was gently pushed to the block. My heart sank. Why did the ostler wink? Why had I come at all? Why get out at Swindon when I might have gone on to Wales with General Booth? My old friend was right. I was a rich, self-indulgent young lady—I was doing exactly what I liked. (*Was* I?) This would never do; it was high time to show some spirit.

She.—What is all this paraphernalia about, pray?

He [persuasively].—You never liked a quiet one now, did you? Dandelion is high-strung—he is over-bred and never could endure the block.

She.—But you said I was to mount off the block. Very well, I don't mind; take the towel off his eyes and put me up from the ground.

He.—Bless your soul, you're on him but for the putting of your foot out.

I stood perfectly still on the block.

Ostler [soothingly].—It's all right, lady! You needn't be frightened.

She [indignantly].—I am not frightened, but Dandelion is!

He [with forced animation].—Bless your soul! Is it Dandelion that would be frightened? It would take a new Heaven and a new Hell to scare him.

With great boldness he stroked the only part of the horse's neck that was uncovered, saying soothingly,—

"There, there! Come, come! You're a g-r-a-t-e horse, aren't you!"

I put my foot into the stirrup. Suddenly changing from coozle to caution, the dealer shouted,—

"Steady! Steady, boys! Let go."

I was up; the three men burst away like squibs as Dandelion flung the towel to the earth with an ugly upward jerk of the head. After that we did not seem to get into position: I could not feel his mouth; Dandelion's head was reposing on my chest like a camel's. Great Heavens! He had a swivel neck! Why had I never noticed this? I felt a mixture of irascibility and apprehension creeping into my blood, as the dealer and I rode off side by side down the road in perfect silence.

Dandelion dropped his head. Feeling happier, I said with the courage of a hard funker, "No one can try a horse on the road; let us gallop round the fences in the paddock."

"There is foine grass by the side of the road further on. Let us start steady—it's very hot."

I kept my eye on him. He was watching Dandelion with a look of intense anxiety; his face was shining like the blest with perspiration, but he said nothing. We walked on side by side at a studied pace, when suddenly I felt Dandelion's quarters rise and his forelegs hit the ground with uncalled-for violence. The reins hung in festoons; he rolled his head toward my chin, and after hearing a great cry as of one in pain a long, long way off, followed by the roar of a donkey engine in my brain, I knew no more —

When I "came to," figures and furniture seemed to nod and throb around me. A thunderstorm was going on with the windows shut — a perpetual wail of "Holy Virgin! say you're not dead!" was mixed up with a good deal of blurr and bustle.

When I regained complete consciousness, I found myself in the dealer's parlor with hot-water bottles all round me, the dealer, the doctor, and the district nurse talking to each other, and the stable boys peeping in at the windows.

The Doctor. — Megrims, you call it?

The Dealer [very subdued]. — Sure, that is right, sir.

We never quite knew who was the hero of the good story.

August 1917

JOHN GALSWORTHY

1867–1933

There was a singular charm about him. Always shy at the outset, his serious handsome face would light suddenly with inner laughter when some comic quirk of human nature came under discussion. But the wrongs of the world were never long absent from his thoughts. Injustice to man he hated fiercely and cruelty to beasts still more. I have been told that his was a fortunate youth and that at Oxford his familiarity with Euclid and Thucydides was eclipsed by a profound comprehension of the race track. At any rate, jockeys, sports with their checkered waistcoats, touts and trainers lingered lovingly in his mind as you can see for yourself in that delightful story of his, "Had a Horse."

It was not until after his graduation that, wandering about Montmartre, he turned into the slums of Paris and opened his eyes on a world of degradation he had not supposed existed.

Galsworthy was often in America and, if his hopes are not liars, he is in Tucson at this moment, for some of the aeons of his immortality he always meant to spend there loping the hills over in an Arizona saddle. More than one visit he paid to me in Boston. Once when I asked him what he wanted most to see, he replied that he had heard much of the solid taste of the successful middle class over here, and might he see a really typical example? So, unbeknownst to him, I telephoned to Mrs. Jack Gardner asking whether I might not bring him to tea at her Palace. When we emerged from the cab before the semi-Venetian façade, Galsworthy screwed in his monocle and looked with approval. "Ampler than I had expected," he remarked, "but what restrained and excellent taste!" Then we passed through the grille. The garden was all glorious with bloom, the fountain was playing, and birds fluttered about against the pink background of the courtyard wall on which, says tradition, Mrs. Gardner herself had laid the first color, perched on a ladder with pail and brush. It was a garden of Paradise, and as Galsworthy gazed at it his monocle fell from his eye and with a burst of silent laughter he muttered, "Oh, this American middle class!"

On another visit I placed him at dinner between two wonderful old ladies, Mrs. Bell, "Child of genius," as Mrs. James T. Fields often called her, and Mrs. Gardner herself, her three legendary rows of pearls falling to her waist and pendant from them her ruby, a miracle of light that long ago men must have murdered for. As we walked out from dinner Galsworthy whispered, "Tell me about them." And I replied, "The run of the American middle class."

One talk with him I shall always remember. I was staying with the Galsworthys at Peterborough on the edge of the South Downs. Somehow I could not sleep and was sitting ruminating on the side of my bed when my host knocked. He was in his pajamas. "Not sleeping?" he said. "I can't either." We fell into sober talk of man's inhumanity to man and all that sort of thing. And then I said, "What of the individual? Is there further hope or fear? The personal is all we really care for and can there be a personal survival?" He sat silent for a time and then he spoke slowly: "You and I are drops in a boundless ocean. The wind ruffles its calm and myriads of tiny wavelets flash from the surface, changing from blue to rippling sapphire and silver. As the sun catches them in turn, each takes on its own individual form. For some small fraction of a second each is a thing of prismatic and ultimate beauty — infinite are the shades of color and of form. Each has its breath of time, its air, its sun. Then each falls back becoming one with all things. That is the picture I have of our existence."

Another night at dinner I asked how he enjoyed his fan mail, and Mrs. Galsworthy took up the theme. He adores it, she said, and that very week a letter had come which of all his compliments he had liked best. Then she told the story; but since in a recent preface she has given the letter verbatim, I quote it too.

Dear Mr. Galsworthy,

Thinking you may be somewhat interested, I am writing about a happening in London. Late one bright afternoon I walked down the Haymarket. Just as I turned into Cockspur Street I came face to face with a man whom I instantly recognized as some one I *knew, but whose name for the moment had escaped me. It was apparent he did not recall me, and passed on. Trying to recall where and when I had met this man, I suddenly realized that I did know him well. It was Soames Forsyte.*

Buttercup-Night

JOHN GALSWORTHY

WHY is it that in some places there is such a feeling of life being all one; not merely a long picture-show for human eyes, but a single breathing, glowing, growing thing, of which we are no more important a part than the swallows and magpies, the foals and sheep in the meadows, the sycamores and ash trees and flowers in the fields, the rocks and little bright streams, or even than the long fleecy clouds and their soft-shouting drivers, the winds?

True, we register these parts of being, and they — so far as we know — do not register us; yet it is impossible to feel, in such places as I speak of, the busy, dry, complacent sense of being all that matters, which in general we humans have so strongly.

In these rare spots, that are always in the remote country, untouched by the advantages of civilization, one is conscious of an enwrapping web or mist of spirit, the glamorous and wistful wraith of all the vanished shapes that once dwelt there in such close comradeship.

It was Sunday of an early June when I first came on one such, far down in the West country. I had walked with my knapsack twenty miles; and, there being no room at the tiny inn of the very little village, they directed me to a wicket gate, through which by a path leading down a field I would come to a farmhouse where I might find lodging. The moment I got into that field I felt within me a peculiar contentment, and sat down on a rock to let the feeling grow. In an old holly tree rooted to the bank about fifty yards away, two magpies evidently had a nest, for they were coming and going, avoiding my view as much as possible, yet with a certain stealthy confidence which made one feel that they had long prescriptive right to that dwelling-place.

Around, as far as one could see, there was hardly a yard of level ground; all was hill and hollow, that long ago had been reclaimed from the moor; and against the distant folds of the hills the farmhouse and its thatched barns were just visible, embowered amongst beeches and some dark trees, with a soft bright crown of sunlight over the whole. A gentle wind brought a faint rustling up from those beeches, and from a large lime tree that stood by itself; on this wind some little snowy clouds, very high and fugitive in that blue heaven, were always moving over. But what struck me most were the buttercups. Never was field so lighted up by those tiny lamps, those little bright pieces of flower china out of the Great Pottery. They covered the whole ground, as if the sunlight had fallen bodily from the sky, in tens of millions of gold patines; and the fields below as well, down to what was evidently a stream, were just as thick with the extraordinary warmth and glory of them.

Leaving the rock at last, I went toward the house. It was long and low and rather sad, standing in a garden all mossy grass and buttercups, with a few rhododendrons and flowery shrubs, below a row of fine old Irish yews. On the stone verandah a gray sheep-dog and a very small golden-haired child were sitting close together, absorbed in each other. A pleasant woman came in answer to my knock, and told me, in a soft, slurring voice, that I might stay the night; and dropping my knapsack, I went out again.

Through an old gate under a stone arch I came on the farmyard, quite deserted save for a couple of ducks moving slowly down a gutter in the sunlight; and noticing the upper half of a stable-door open, I went across, in search of something living. There, in a rough loose-box, on thick straw, lay a black long-tailed mare with the skin and head of a thoroughbred. She was swathed in blankets, and her face, all cut about the cheeks and over the eyes, rested on an ordinary human's pillow, held by a bearded man in shirt-sleeves; while, leaning against the white-washed walls, sat fully a dozen other men, perfectly silent, very gravely and intently gazing. The mare's eyes were half closed, and what could be seen of them dull and blueish, as though she had been through a long time of pain. Save for her rapid breathing, she lay quite still, but her neck and ears were streaked with sweat, and every now and then her hind-legs quivered spasmodically. Seeing me at the door, she raised her head, uttering a queer half-human noise, but the bearded man at once put his hand on her forehead, and with a "Woa, my dear — woa, my pretty!" pressed it down again, while with the other hand he plumped up the pillow for her cheek. And, as the mare obediently let fall her head, one of the men said in a low voice, "I never see anything so like a Christian!" and the others echoed, in chorus, "Like a Christian — like a Christian!"

It went to one's heart to watch her, and I moved off down the farm lane into an old orchard, where the apple trees were still in bloom, with bees — very small ones — busy on the blossoms, whose petals were dropping on the dock leaves and buttercups in the long grass. Climbing over the bank at the far end, I found myself in a meadow the like of which — so wild and yet so lush — I think I have never seen. Along one hedge of its meandering length was a mass of pink may-flower; and between two little running streams grew quantities of yellow water-iris — "daggers," as they call them; the "print-frock" orchid too was everywhere in the grass, and always the buttercups. Great stones coated with yellowish moss were strewn among the ash trees and dark hollies; and through a grove of beeches on the far side, such as Corot might have painted, a girl was running, with a youth after her, who jumped down over the bank and vanished. Thrushes, blackbirds, yaffles, cuckoos, and one other very monotonous little bird were in full song; and this, with the sound of the streams and the wind, and the shapes of the rocks and trees, the colors of the flowers, and the warmth of the sun, gave one a feeling of being lost in a very wilderness of nature. Some ponies came slowly from the far end, — tangled, gypsy-headed little creatures, — stared, and went off again at speed. It was just one of those places where any day the Spirit of all Nature might start up in one of those white gaps that separate the trees and rocks. But though I sat a long time waiting — hoping — She did not come.

They were all gone from the stable when I went back up to the farm, except the bearded nurse and one tall fellow, who might have been the "Dying Gaul" as he crouched there in the straw; and the mare was sleeping — her head between her nurse's knees.

That night I woke at two o'clock to find it almost as bright as day, with moonlight coming in through the flimsy curtains. And, smitten with the feeling that comes to us creatures of routine so rarely — of what beauty and strangeness we let slip by without ever stretching out hand to grasp it — I got up, dressed, stole downstairs, and out.

Never was such a night of frozen beauty, never such dream-tranquillity. The wind had dropped, and the silence was such that one hardly liked to tread even on the grass. From the lawn and fields there seemed to be a mist rising — in truth, the moonlight caught on the dewy buttercups; and across this ghostly radiance the shadows of the yew trees fell in dense black bars. Suddenly I bethought me of the mare. How was she faring, this marvelous night? Very softly opening the door into the yard, I tiptoed across. A light was burning in her box.

And I could hear her making the same half-human noise she had made in the afternoon, as if wondering at her feelings; and instantly the voice of the bearded man talking to her as one might talk to a child: "Oover, my darlin'; yu've a-been long enough o' that side. Wa-ay, my swate — yu let old Jack turn yu, then!" Then came a scuffling in the straw, a thud, that half-human sigh, and his voice again: "Putt your 'ead to piller, that's my dandy gel. Old Jack wouldn' 'urt yu; no more'n if yu was the Queen!" Then only her quick breathing could be heard, and his cough and mutter, as he settled down once more to his long vigil.

I crept very softly up to the window, but she heard me at once; and at the movement of her head the old fellow sat up, blinking his eyes out of the bush of his grizzled hair and beard. Opening the door, I said, —

"May I come in?"

"Oo ay! Come in, zurr, if yu'm a mind tu."

I sat down beside him on a sack. And for some time we did not speak, taking each other in. One of his legs was lame, so that he had to keep it stretched out all the time; and awfully tired he looked, gray-tired.

"You're a great nurse!" I said at last. "It must be tiring work, watching out here all night."

His eyes twinkled; they were of that bright gray kind through which the soul looks out.

"Aw, no!" he said. "Ah don't grudge it vur a dumb animal. Poor things — they can't 'elp theirzelves. Many's the naight ah've zat up with 'orses and beasts tu. 'Tes en me — can't bear to zee dumb creatures zuffer!" And laying his hand on the mare's ears, "They zay 'orses aven't no souls. 'Tes my belief they've souls zame as us. Many's the Christian ah've seen ain't got the soul of an 'orse. Same with the beasts; 'tes only they'm can't spake their minds."

"And where," I said, "do you think they go to when they die?"

He looked at me a little queerly, fancying perhaps that I was leading him into some trap; making sure, too, that I was a real stranger, without power over his body or soul — for humble folk must be careful in the country; then, reassured, and nodding in his beard, he answered knowingly, —

"Ah don't think they goes so very far!"

"Why? Do you ever see their spirits?"

"Naw, naw; I never zeen none; but, for all they zay, ah don't think none of us goes such a brave way off. There's room for all, dead or alive. An' there's Christians ah've zeen — well, ef they'm not dead for gude, then neither aren't dumb animals, for sure."

"And rabbits, squirrels, birds, even insects? How about them?"

He was silent, as if I had carried him a little beyond the confines of his philosophy, then shook his head: —

"'Tes all a bit dimsy. But yu watch dumb animals, even the laste littlest one, an' yu'll zee they knows a lot more'n what we du; an' they du's things tu that putts shame on a man's often as not. They've a got that in them as passes show." Not noticing my stare at that unconscious plagiarism, he went on, "Ah'd zooner zet up of a naight with an 'orse than with an 'uman — they've more zense, and patience." And stroking the mare's forehead, he added, "Now, my dear, time for yu t' 'ave yure bottle."

I waited to see her take her draft, and lay her head down once more on the pillow. Then, hoping he would get a sleep, I rose to go.

"Aw, 'tes nothin' much," he said, "this time o' year; not like in winter. 'Twill come day before yu know, these buttercup-nights."

And twinkling up at me out of his kindly bearded face, he settled himself again into the straw.

I stole a look back at his rough figure propped against the sack, with the mare's head down beside his knee, at her swathed black body, and the gold of the straw, the white walls, and dusky nooks and shadows of that old stable illumined by the "dimsy" light of the old lantern. And with the sense of having seen something holy, I crept away up into the field where I had lingered the day before, and sat down on the same halfway rock.

Close on dawn it was, the moon still sailing wide over the moor, and the flowers of this "buttercup-night" fast closed, not taken in at all by her cold glory! Most silent hour of all the twenty-four — when the soul slips half out of sheath, and hovers in the cool; when the spirit is most in tune with what, soon or late, happens to all spirits; hour when a man cares least whether or no he be alive, as we understand the word.

"None of us goes such a brave way off — there's room for all, dead or alive." Though it was almost unbearably colorless, and quiet, there was warmth in thinking of those words of his; in the thought, too, of the millions of living things snugly asleep all round; warmth in realizing that unanimity of sleep. Insects and flowers, birds, men, beasts, the very leaves on the trees — away in slumberland.

Waiting for the first bird to chirrup, one had perhaps even a stronger feeling than in daytime of the unity and communion of all life, of the subtle brotherhood of living things that fall all together into oblivion, and, all together, wake. When dawn comes, while moonlight is still powdering the world's face, quite a long time passes before one realizes how the quality of the light has changed; so it was day before I knew it. Then the sun came up above the hills; dew began to sparkle, and color to stain the sky. That first praise of the sun from every bird and leaf and blade of grass, the tremulous flush and chime of dawn! One has strayed so far from the heart of things, that it comes as something strange and wonderful! Indeed, I noticed that the beasts and birds gazed at me as if I simply could not be there, at this hour that so belonged to them. And to me, too, they seemed strange and new — with that in them "as passes show," and as of a world where man did not exist, or existed only as just another form of life, another sort of beast. It was one of those revealing moments when we see our proper place in the scheme; go past our truly irreligious thought: "Man, hub of the Universe!" that has founded most religions. One of those moments when our supreme importance will not wash either in the bath of purest spiritual ecstasy, or in the clear fluid of scientific knowledge; and one sees clear, with the eyes of true religion, man playing his little, not unworthy, part in the great game of Perfection.

But just then began the crowning glory of that dawn — the opening and lighting of the buttercups. Not one did I actually see unclose, yet, all of a sudden, they were awake, the fields once more a blaze of gold.

January 1914

MARGARET PRESCOTT MONTAGUE

1878–

Margaret Montague was always deaf, she was always nearly blind. In her circle of vision when she grew to maturity, merely a thin segment of light was left. The doctor, after examining her eyes and looking up the family record, told her she had perhaps a year left to look out on her tiny share of the world, and it was a question whether to employ the precious twelvemonth in learning to use a typewriter for the blind or in finishing a novel of which the returns might be important to the family exchequer. We had met at dinner a year or two before, and had formed a friendship which has lasted until this day. Who would not be a friend of Margaret Montague; of her serenity, her laughter, and her certainty of the Lord's goodness, proof against the arrows of evil?

One day as I sat in my office, Miss Montague was announced. Might she have ten minutes with me absolutely alone? With the resolute step of the blind who will not part with their own control of life, she took a chair just across my desk and, holding out both hands, said in her pleasant, even voice: "I have but a few minutes. You are my friend. There is one question I must ask you. Are you certain of personal immortality?"

I was far from certain. Indeed even the desirability of another life was a much debated matter in my mind. One life I had found very interesting, very desirable, but, like beauty and love, impermanence lent it a peculiar charm. Life was important because it was uncertain. I could not but be utterly frank, yet I could say that faith was the single key to truth vouchsafed to us and that she possessed it although I had it not. Credo quia impossibile is the Sesame to open the Locked Door.

For a quarter of an hour we talked with complete honesty, perfect understanding. Then she put her wrist watch close to her eyes. "My time is up," she said. I led her to the elevator and went down with her to her cab drawn up at the curb. "What shall I tell the driver?"

"Go straight to the Massachusetts General Hospital," she replied, and then I knew what I had guessed. The surgeon was waiting for her and life was in the balance.

The next morning I telephoned to a doctor friend. "She is all right," he said. "The tumor was benign."

Weeks later, just after her recovery, she came again to my office, her face glowing with happiness. She told me her experience and I asked her very earnestly to make a record of it before the colors faded. "I will," she said, "but it can never be published. It belongs too absolutely to me myself."

But, twenty-four months later, the record was published, and over eight hundred letters testified to the response of readers to whom "What is Reality?" is an abiding question. When it appeared the contribution bore no name, and it was several years before Miss Montague consented to the disclosure of her identity.

Twenty Minutes of Reality

MARGARET P. MONTAGUE

As a child I was afraid of world without end, of life everlasting. The thought of it used to clutch me at times with a crushing sense of the inevitable, and make me long to run away. But where could one run? If never-ending life were true, then I was already caught fast in it, and it would never end. Perhaps it had never had a beginning. Life everlasting, eternity, forever and ever: these are tremendous words for even a grown person to face; and for a child — if he grasp their significance at all — they may be hardly short of appalling. The picture that Heaven presented to my mind was of myself, a desperate little atom, dancing in a streak of light around and around and around forever and ever. I do not know what could have suggested such an idea; I only know that I could not think of myself caught there in eternity like a chip in a whirlpool, or say "round again, and round again, and round again" for more than a minute, without hypnotizing myself into a state of sheer terror. Of course, as I grew older I threw off this truly awful conception; yet shorn of its crudeness and looked at with grown-up eyes, there were moments when, much as I believed in, and desired, eternal life, that old feeling of "round again, and round again" would swoop back upon me with all its unutterable weariness, and no state of bliss that I could imagine seemed to me proof forever against boredom. Nevertheless, I still had faith to believe that eternity and enjoyment of life could in some way be squared, though I did not see how it was to be done. I am glad that I had, for I came at last to a time when faith was justified by sight, and it is of that time that I wish to write here.

If this paper ever chances to be printed, it will be read, I think, by two sets of persons. There will be those who will wonder if I speak of something that is really there, or who will be quite sure that I do not — that I either imagined or made up the whole thing, or else that it was entirely due to the physical condition of convalescence. Others there will be, who will believe that I am speaking of the truth that is there, because they, too, have seen it. These last will think that it was not because I was returning to health that I imagined all life as beautiful, but that with the cleared vision that sometimes attends convalescence I "saw into reality," and felt the ecstasy which is always there, but which we are enabled to perceive only on very rare and fleeting occasions.

It is these last for whom I wish to write. If this clearing of the vision is an occasional occurrence of convalescence, then what I saw is of far more value than it would be had my experience been unique.

I do not really know how long the insight lasted. I have said, at a rough guess, twenty minutes. It may have been a little shorter time, it may have been a little longer. But at best it was very transitory.

It happened to me about two years ago, on the day when my bed was first pushed out of doors to the open gallery of the hospital. I was recovering from a surgical operation. I had undergone a certain amount of physical pain, and had suffered for a short time the most acute mental depression which it has ever been my misfortune to encounter. I suppose that this depression was due to physical causes, but at the time it seemed to me that somewhere down there under the anæsthetic, in the black abyss of unconsciousness, I had discovered a terrible secret, and the secret was that there was no God; or if there was one, He was indifferent to all human suffering.

Though I had hardly reëstablished my normal state of faith, still the first acuteness of that depression had faded, and only a scar of fear was left when, several days later, my bed was first wheeled out to the porch. There other patients took their airing and received their visitors; busy internes and nurses came and went, and one could get a glimpse of the sky, with bare gray branches against it, and of the ground, with here and there a patch of melting snow.

It was an ordinary cloudy March day. I am glad to think that it was. I am glad to remember that there was nothing extraordinary about the weather, nor any unusualness of setting — no flush of spring or beauty of scenery — to induce what I saw. It was, on the contrary, almost a dingy day. The branches were bare and colorless, and the occasional half-melted piles of snow were a forlorn gray rather than white. Colorless little city sparrows flew and chirped in the trees, while human beings, in no way remarkable, passed along the porch.

There was, however, a wind blowing, and if any outside thing intensified the experience, it was the blowing of that wind. In every other respect it was an ordinary commonplace day. Yet here, in this everyday setting, and entirely unexpectedly (for I had never dreamed of such a thing), my eyes were opened, and for the first time in all my life I caught a glimpse of the ecstatic beauty of reality.

I cannot now recall whether the revelation came suddenly or gradually; I only remember finding myself in the very midst of those wonderful moments, beholding life for the first time in all its young intoxication of loveliness, in its unspeakable joy, beauty, and importance. I cannot say exactly what the mysterious change was. I saw no new thing, but I saw all the usual things in a miraculous new light — in what I believe is their true light. I saw for the first time how wildly beautiful and joyous, beyond any words of mine to describe, is the whole of life. Every human being moving across that porch, every sparrow that flew, every branch tossing in the wind, was caught in and was a part of the whole mad ecstasy of loveliness, of joy, of importance, of intoxication of life.

It was not that for a few keyed-up moments I *imagined* all existence as beautiful, but that my inner vision was cleared to the truth so that I *saw* the actual loveliness which is always there, but which we so rarely perceive; and I knew that every man, woman, bird, and tree, every living thing before me, was extravagantly beautiful, and extravagantly important. And as I beheld, my heart melted out of me in a rapture of love and delight. A nurse was walking past; the wind caught a strand of her hair and blew it out in a momentary gleam of sunshine, and never in my life before had I seen how beautiful beyond all belief is a woman's hair. Nor had I ever guessed how marvelous it is for a human being to walk. As for the internes in their white suits, I had never realized before the whiteness of white linen; but much more than that, I had never so much as dreamed of the mad beauty of young manhood. A little sparrow chirped and flew to a nearby branch, and I honestly believe that only "the morning stars singing together, and the sons of God shouting for joy" can in the least express the ecstasy of a bird's flight. I cannot express it, but I have seen it.

Once out of all the gray days of my life I have looked into the heart of reality; I have witnessed the truth; I have seen life as it really is—ravishingly, ecstatically, madly beautiful, and filled to overflowing with a wild joy, and a value unspeakable. For those glorified moments I was in love with every living thing before me—the trees in the wind, the little birds flying, the nurses, the internes, the people who came and went. There was nothing that was alive that was not a miracle. Just to be alive was in itself a miracle. My very soul flowed out of me in a great joy.

No one can be as happy as I was and not have it show in some way. A stranger passing paused by my bed and said, "What are you lying here all alone looking so happy about?" I made some inadequate response as to the pleasure of being out-of-doors and of getting well. How could I explain all the beauty that I was seeing? How could I say that the gray curtain of unreality had swirled away and that I was seeing into the heart of life? It was not an experience for words. It was an emotion, a rapture of the heart.

Besides all the joy and beauty and that curious sense of importance, there was a wonderful feeling of rhythm as well, only it was somehow just beyond the grasp of my mind. I heard no music, yet there was an exquisite sense of time, as though all life went by to a vast, unseen melody. Everything that moved wove out a little thread of rhythm in this tremendous whole. When a bird flew, it did so because somewhere a note had been struck for it to fly on; or else its flying struck the note; or else again the great Will that is Melody willed that it should fly. When people walked, somewhere they beat out a bit of rhythm that was in harmony with the whole great theme.

Then, the extraordinary importance of everything! Every living creature was intensely alive and intensely beautiful, but it was as well of a marvelous value. Whether this value was in itself or a part of the whole, I could not see; but it seemed as though before my very eyes I actually beheld the truth of Christ's saying that not even a sparrow falls to the ground without the knowledge of the Father in Heaven. Yet *what* the importance was, I did not grasp. If my heart could have seen just a little further I should have understood. Even now the tips of my thoughts are forever on the verge of grasping it, forever just missing it. I have a curious half-feeling that somewhere, deep inside of myself, I know very well what this importance is, and have always known; but I cannot get it from the depth of myself into my mind, and thence into words. But whatever it is, the importance seemed to be nearer to beauty and joy than to an anxious morality. I had a feeling that it was in some way different from the importance I had usually attached to life.

It was perhaps as though that great value in every living thing was not so much here and now in ourselves as somewhere else. There is a great significance in every created thing, but the significance is beyond our present grasp. I do not know what it is; I only know that it is there, and that all life is far more valuable than we ever dream of its being. Perhaps the following quotation from Milton may be what I was conscious of: —

> What if earth
> Be but the shadow of Heaven, and things therein
> Each to each other like, more than on earth is thought.

What if here we are only symbols of ourselves, and our real being is somewhere else, — perhaps in the heart of God? Certainly that unspeakable importance had to do with our relationship to the great Whole; but what the relationship was, I could not tell. Was it a relationship of love toward us, or only the delight in creation? But it is hardly likely that a glimpse of a cold Creator could have filled me with such an extravagant joy, or so melted the heart within me. For those fleeting, lovely moments I did indeed, and in truth, love my neighbor as myself. Nay, more: of myself I was hardly conscious, while with my neighbor in every form, from wind-tossed branches and little sparrows flying, up to human beings, I was madly in love. Is it likely that I could have experienced such love if there were not some such emotion at the heart of Reality? If I did not actually see it, it was not that it was not there, but that I did not see quite far enough.

Perhaps this was because I was still somewhat in the grip of that black doubt which I had experienced, and of which I have spoken. I think it was owing to this doubt also that afterwards I had a certain feeling of distrust. I was afraid that all that beauty might be an uncaring joy. As if, though we were indeed intensely important in some unguessed way to the great Reality, our own small individual sorrows were perhaps not of much moment. I am not sure that I actually had this feeling, as it is very difficult, after the lapse of almost two years, to recapture in memory all the emotions of so fleeting and so unusual an experience. If I did, however, I comfort myself, as I have said, with the thought of the intense joy that I experienced. The vision of an uncaring Reality would hardly have melted me to such happiness. That the Creator is a loving Creator I believe with all my heart; but this is belief, not sight. What I saw that day was an unspeakable joy and loveliness, and a value to all life beyond anything that we have knowledge of; while in myself I knew a wilder happiness than I have ever before or since experienced.

Moreover, though there was nothing exactly religious in what I saw, the accounts given by people who have passed through religious conversion or illumination come nearer to describing my emotions than anything else that I have come across.

These testimonies I read almost a year after my hospital episode. I came upon them by chance and was astonished to find that they were describing very much what I had passed through. I think if I had had nothing to match them in my own experience I should almost certainly have felt sure that these people, because of the emotional excitement within themselves, imagined all the beauties that they described. Now I believe that they are describing what is actually there. Nor are poets making up — as the average mind believes, and as I think I always believed — the extravagant beauty of which they sing. They are telling us of the truth that is there, and that they are occasionally enabled to see.

Here are some of the testimonies offered by people who have experienced illumination in one form or another.

"Natural objects were glorified," one person affirms. "My spiritual vision was so clarified that I saw beauty in every natural object in the universe." Another says, "When I went into the field to work, the glory of God appeared in all his visible creation. I well remember we reaped oats, and how every straw and beard of the oats seemed, as it were, arrayed in a kind of rainbow glory, or to glow, if I may so express it, in the glory of God." The father of Rabindranath Tagore thus describes his illumination: "I felt a serenity and joy which I had never experienced before . . . the joy I felt . . . that day overflowed my soul. . . . I could not sleep that night. The reason of my sleeplessness was the ecstasy of soul; as if moonlight had spread itself over my mind for the whole of that night." And when Tagore speaks of his own illumination he says, "It was morning; I was watching the sunrise in Free School Street. A veil was suddenly drawn and everything I saw became luminous. The whole scene was one perfect music; one marvelous rhythm." (Note his sense of rhythm, of which I also was conscious.)

"The houses in the street, the children playing, all seemed part of one luminous whole — inexpressibly glorified." (Perhaps the significance of that tremendous importance which I felt, but failed to grasp, was that we are all parts of a wonderful whole.) "I was full of gladness, full of love for every tiniest thing."

And this was what — in a smaller degree — I, too, saw for those fleeting moments out there upon the hospital porch. Mine was, I think, a sort of accidental clearing of the vision by the rebirth of returning health. I believe that a good many people have experienced the same thing during convalescence. Perhaps this is the way in which we should all view life if we were born into it grown up. As it is, when we first arrive we are so engaged in the tremendous business of cutting teeth, saying words, and taking steps, that we have no time for, and little consciousness of, outside wonders; and by the time we have the leisure for admiration life has lost for us its first freshness. Convalescence is a sort of grown-up rebirth, enabling us to see life with a fresh eye.

Doubtless almost any intense emotion may open our "inward eye" to the beauty of reality. Falling in love appears to do it for some people. The beauties of nature or the exhilaration of artistic creation does it for others. Probably any high experience may momentarily stretch our souls up on tip-toe, so that we catch a glimpse of that marvelous beauty which is always there, but which we are not often tall enough to perceive.

Emerson says, "We are immersed in beauty, but our eyes have no clear vision." I believe that religious conversion more often clears the eyes to this beauty of truth than any other experience; and it is possible that had I not still been somewhat under that black cloud of doubt, I should have seen further than I did. Yet what I did see was very good indeed.

The following quotation from Canon Inge may not be entirely out of place in this connection: "Incidentally I may say that the peculiar happiness which accompanies every glimpse of insight into truth and reality, whether in the scientific, æsthetic, or emotional sphere, seems to me to have a greater apologetic value than has been generally recognized. It is the clearest possible indication that the truth is for us the good, and forms the ground of a reasonable faith that all things, if we could see them as they are, would be found to work together for good to those who love God."

In what I saw there was nothing seemingly of an ethical nature. There were no new rules of conduct revealed by those twenty minutes.

Indeed, it seemed as though beauty and joy were more at the heart of Reality than an over-anxious morality. It was a little as though (to transpose the quotation),

> I had slept and dreamed that life was duty,
> But waked to find that life was beauty.

Perhaps at such times of illumination there is no need to worry over sin, for one is so transported by the beauty of humanity, and so poured out in love toward every human being, that sin becomes almost impossible.

Perhaps duty may merely point the way. When one arrives at one's destination it would be absurd to go back and reconsult the guide-post. Blindness of heart may be the real sin, and if we could only purify our hearts to behold the beauty that is all about us, sin would vanish away. When Christ says, "Seek ye the Kingdom of God; and all these things shall be added unto you," He may mean by "all these things" spiritual virtues even more than things temporal, such as what we shall eat, and wherewithal we shall be clothed. It may be that He stood forever conscious of a transcendent beauty, and joy, and love, and that what grieved Him most was mankind's inability to behold what was there before their very eyes.

Perhaps, too, this may be the great difference between the saints and the Puritans. Both are agreed that goodness is the means to the end, but the saints have passed on to the end and entered into the realization, and are happy. (One of the most endearing attributes of saints of a certain type was — or rather is, for one refuses to believe that saints are all of the past — their childlike gayety, which can proceed only from a happy and trustful heart.) The Puritan, on the other hand, has stuck fast in the means — is still worrying over the guide-posts, and is distrustful and over-anxious.

It is like walking and dancing. One could never dance unless he had first learned to walk, or continue to dance unless walking were always possible; yet if one is too intent upon the fact of walking, dancing becomes impossible. The Puritan walks in a worried morality; the saint dances in the vision of God's love; and doubtless both are right dear in the sight of the Lord, but the saint is the happiest.

Father Tyrrell says, "For Jesus the moral is not the highest life, but its condition."

Some may object that I preach a dangerous doctrine; others, that I am trying to whip a mad moment of Pagan beauty into line with Christian thought. Possibly I am; yet I am trying not to do the one or the other. I am merely wondering, and endeavoring to get at the truth of something that I saw.

And all the beauty is forever there before us, forever piping to us, and we are forever failing to dance. We could not help but dance if we could see things as they really are. Then we should kiss both hands to Fate and fling our bodies, hearts, minds, and souls into life with a glorious abandonment, an extravagant, delighted loyalty, knowing that our wildest enthusiasm cannot more than brush the hem of the real beauty and joy and wonder that is always there.

This is how, for me, all fear of eternity has been wiped away. I have had a little taste of bliss, and if Heaven can offer this, no eternity will be too long to enjoy the miracle of existence. But that was not the greatest thing that those twenty minutes revealed, and that did most to end all dread of life everlasting. The great thing was the realization that weariness, and boredom, and questions as to the use of it all, belong entirely to unreality. When once we wake to Reality — whether we do so here or have to wait for the next life for it, — we shall never be bored, for in Reality there is no such thing.

Chesterton has pointed out the power for endless enjoyment of the same thing which most children possess, and suggested that this is a God-like capacity; that perhaps to God his creation always presents itself with a freshness of delight; that perhaps the rising of the sun this morning was for Him the same ecstatic event that it was upon the first day of its creation. I think it was the truth of this suggestion that I perceived in those twenty minutes of cleared vision, and realized that in the youth of eternity we shall recapture that God-like and child-like attribute which the old age and unreality of Time have temporarily snatched from us.

No; I shall have no more fear of eternity. And even if there were no other life, this life here and now, if we could but open our dull eyes to see it in its truth, is lovely enough to require no far-off Heaven for its justification. Heaven, in all its spring-tide of beauty, is here and now, before our very eyes, surging up to our very feet, lapping against our hearts; but we, alas, know not how to let it in!

Once again, when I was almost recovered, I had another fleeting visitation of this extreme beauty. A friend came into my room dressed for the opera. I had seen her thus a great number of times before, but for a moment I saw her clothed in all that wild beauty of Reality, and, as before, my heart melted with joy at the sight. But this second occasion was even more transitory than the first, and since then I have had no return. Tagore's illumination, he says, lasted for seven or eight days, and Jacob Boehme knew a "Sabbath calm of the soul that lasted for seven days," during which he was, as it were, inwardly surrounded by a divine light. "The triumph that was then in my soul," he says, "I can neither tell nor describe; I can only liken it to a resurrection from the dead."

And this miraculous time was with him for a whole week, while I have only tasted it for those few short minutes! But he was a saint, and had really ascended to the holy hill of the Lord through clean hands and a pure heart, while I was swept there momentarily, and, as it were, by accident, through the rebirth of returning health. But when the inspired ones testify to a great joy and a great beauty I too can cry, "Yes, I have seen it also! Yes, O beauty, O Reality, O Mad Joy! I too have seen you face to face!" And though I have never again touched the fullness of that ecstatic vision, I know all created things to be of a beauty and value unspeakable, and I shall not fail to pay homage to all the loveliness with which existence overflows. Nor shall I fear to accord to all of life's experiences, whether sad or gay, as high, as extravagant, and as undismayed a tribute of enthusiasm as I am capable of.

Perhaps some day I shall meet it face to face again. Again the gray veil of unreality will be swirled aside; once more I shall see into Reality. Sometimes still, when the wind is blowing through trees, or flowers, I have an eery sense that I am almost in touch with it. The veil was very thin in my garden one day last summer. The wind was blowing there, and I knew that all that beauty and wild young ecstasy at the heart of life was rioting with it through the tossing larkspurs and rose-pink canterbury bells, and bowing with the foxgloves; only I just could not see it. But it is there — it is always there — and some day I shall meet it again. The vision will clear, the inner eye open, and again all that mad joy will be upon me. Some day — not yet perhaps — but some day!

May 1916

EDITH WHARTON

1862–1937

It was with old New York in the days of its "innocence," when the First Families ruled by divine right, that Mrs. Wharton was most naturally preoccupied. The fine old foursquare houses of Washington Square and University Place formed a background where she felt perfectly at home. Yet the influences which shaped her art were utterly alien to all of this. Henry James, whom she deemed first among novelists, and Paul Bourget, apostle of culture and of style, lighted her on her brilliant way. But although Mrs. Wharton was an international figure, she was dependent upon American audiences and always listened to the wise counsel of Mr. Burlingame, editor of Scribner's Magazine, *and of his accomplished confrère, Mr. William Crary Brownell.*

By another contradiction of genius the most perfect of her books, which with the least baggage has set out on the longest journey, seemed to make a complete break both with her predilections and with her teachers. When she sat down to write the elemental story of Ethan Frome *her alien experience could not help her and counsel was of no avail. She fell back upon a remarkable intuition.*

The inspiration first came to her in Lenox. "I had an uneasy sense," she wrote, "that the New England of fiction bore little resemblance to the harsh and beautiful land as I had seen it. Even the abundant enumeration of sweet-fern, asters and mountain-laurel, and the conscientious reproduction of the vernacular, left me with the feeling that the outcropping granite had been overlooked."

The outcropping granite! Not in Hawthorne, not in any novelist whose fame has made him a part of New England forever, is there such understanding of the race that granite breeds as you can find on almost any page of Ethan Frome. *The writing of it was "the moment" in Mrs. Wharton's career. She recognized it and her introduction to the story is I think the only instance in her books of a deliberate dissection of the problem she faced.*

That problem was the determination of method. How could she give the story complete reality? If she watched her characters as authors do from a providential seat on high, who would believe her? If she pretended to pick up her information from some gossip, who that knows New England would hold it conceivable that an inarticulate native could have recorded the story, much less understood its tragic significance? In a flash she saw the answer. She would respect the deep-rooted reticence of the people she sought to draw by allowing "each of her characters to contribute to the narrative just so much as he or she is capable of understanding what is to them a complicated and mysterious case." Her solution is a high achievement in the art of storytelling.

To those who would study a novelist's mind, I recommend the reading of Mrs. Wharton's short preface. Here I will merely quote another of her intuitive canons. "It appears to me," she wrote, "that, while an air of artificiality is lent to a tale of complex and sophisticated people which the novelist causes to be guessed at and interpreted by any mere looker-on, there need be no such drawback if the looker-on is sophisticated, and the people he interprets are simple."

In the story included in this volume the people to be interpreted are as sophisticated as the artist who interprets them. How delicately Mrs. Wharton adapts her method to the new problem!

As I have intimated, it was Henry James whose influence with her was at once most persuasive and convincing. With him their long intimacy was rather gingerly begun. It was in 1902 that her sister-in-law sent an early collection of her stories to the Master and this was his reply: "I take to her very kindly as regards her diabolical little cleverness, the quantity of intention and intelligence in her style, and her sharp eye for an interesting kind of subject. They (the stories) have made me want to get hold of the little lady and pump the pure essence of my wisdom and experience into her."

The tale from the Atlantic which follows, though written early in her career, is an admirable illustration of one of Mrs. Wharton's cosmopolitan moods.

The House of the Dead Hand

EDITH WHARTON

I

"Above all," the letter ended, "don't leave Siena without seeing Doctor Lombard's Leonardo. Lombard is a queer old Englishman, a mystic or a madman (if the two are not synonymous), and a devout student of the Italian Renaissance. He has lived for years in Italy, exploring its remotest corners, and has lately picked up an undoubted Leonardo, which came to light in a farmhouse near Bergamo. It is believed to be one of the missing pictures mentioned by Vasari, and is at any rate, according to the most competent authorities, a genuine and almost untouched example of the best period.

"Lombard is a queer stick, and jealous of showing his treasures; but we struck up a friendship when I was working on the Sodomas in Siena three years ago, and if you will give him the enclosed line you may get a peep at the Leonardo. Probably not more than a peep, though, for I hear he refuses to have it reproduced. I want badly to use it in my monograph on the Windsor drawings, so please see what you can do for me, and if you can't persuade him to let you take a photograph or make a sketch, at least jot down a detailed description of the picture and get from him all the facts you can. I hear that the French and Italian governments have offered him a large advance on his purchase, but that he refuses to sell at any price, though he certainly can't afford such luxuries; in fact, I don't see where he got enough money to buy the picture. He lives in the Via Papa Giulio."

Wyant sat at the table d'hôte of his hotel, re-reading his friend's letter over a late luncheon. He had been five days in Siena without having found time to call on Doctor Lombard; not from any indifference to the opportunity presented, but because it was his first visit to the strange red city and he was still under the spell of its more conspicuous wonders — the brick palaces flinging out their wrought-iron torch-holders with a gesture of arrogant suzerainty; the great council-chamber emblazoned with civic allegories; the pageant of Pope Julius on the Library walls; the Sodomas smiling balefully through the dusk of mouldering chapels — and it was only when his first hunger was appeased that he remembered that one course in the banquet was still untasted.

He put the letter in his pocket and turned to leave the room, with a nod to its only other occupant, an olive-skinned young man with lustrous eyes and a low collar, who sat on the other side of the table, perusing the *Fanfulla di Domenica.* This gentleman, his daily vis-à-vis, returned the nod with a Latin eloquence of gesture, and Wyant passed on to the ante-chamber, where he paused to light a cigarette. He was just restoring the case to his pocket when he heard a hurried step behind him, and the lustrous-eyed young man advanced through the glass doors of the dining-room.

"Pardon me, sir," he said in measured English, and with an intonation of exquisite politeness; "you have let this letter fall."

Wyant, recognizing his friend's note of introduction to Doctor Lombard, took it with a word of thanks, and was about to turn away when he perceived that the eyes of his fellow diner remained fixed on him with a gaze of melancholy interrogation.

"Again pardon me," the young man at length ventured, "but are you by chance the friend of the illustrious Doctor Lombard?"

"No," returned Wyant, with the instinctive Anglo-Saxon distrust of foreign advances. Then, fearing to appear rude, he said with a guarded politeness: "Perhaps, by the way, you can tell me the number of his house. I see it is not given here."

The young man brightened perceptibly. "The number of the house is thirteen; but any one can indicate it to you — it is well known in Siena. It is called," he continued after a moment, "the House of the Dead Hand."

Wyant stared. "What a queer name!" he said.

"The name comes from an antique hand of marble which for many hundred years has been above the door."

Wyant was turning away with a gesture of thanks, when the other added: "If you would have the kindness to ring twice."

"To ring twice?"

"At the doctor's." The young man smiled. "It is the custom."

It was a dazzling March afternoon, with a shower of sun from the mid-blue, and a marshalling of slaty clouds behind the umber-colored hills. For nearly an hour Wyant loitered on the Lizza, watching the shadows race across the naked landscape and the thunder blacken in the west; then he decided to set out for the House of the Dead Hand. The map in his guidebook showed him that the Via Papa Giulio was one of the streets which radiate from the Piazza, and thither he bent his course, pausing at every other step to fill his eye with some fresh image of weather-beaten beauty. The clouds had rolled upward, obscuring the sunshine and hanging like a funereal baldachin above the projecting cornices of Doctor Lombard's street, and Wyant walked for some distance in the shade of the beetling palace fronts before his eye fell on a doorway surmounted by a sallow marble hand. He stood for a moment staring up at the strange emblem. The hand was a woman's — a dead drooping hand, which hung there convulsed and helpless, as though it had been thrust forth in denunciation of some evil mystery within the house, and had sunk struggling into death.

A girl who was drawing water from the well in the court said that the English doctor lived on the first floor, and Wyant, passing through a glazed door, mounted the damp degrees of a vaulted stairway with a plaster Æsculapius mouldering in a niche on the landing. Facing the Æsculapius was another door, and as Wyant put his hand on the bell-rope he remembered his unknown friend's injunction, and rang twice.

His ring was answered by a peasant woman with a low forehead and small close-set eyes, who, after a prolonged scrutiny of himself, his card, and his letter of introduction, left him standing in a high, cold ante-chamber floored with brick. He heard her wooden pattens click down an interminable corridor, and after some delay she returned and told him to follow her.

They passed through a long saloon, bare as the ante-chamber, but loftily vaulted, and frescoed with a seventeenth-century Triumph of Scipio or Alexander — martial figures following Wyant with the filmed melancholy gaze of shades in limbo. At the end of this apartment he was admitted to a smaller room, with the same atmosphere of mortal cold, but showing more obvious signs of occupancy. The walls were covered with tapestry which had faded to the gray-brown tints of decaying vegetation, so that the young man felt as though he were entering a sunless autumn wood. Against these hangings stood a few tall cabinets on heavy gilt feet, and at a table in the window three persons were seated: an elderly lady who was warming her hands over a brazier, a girl bent above a strip of needle-work, and an old man.

As the latter advanced toward Wyant, the young man was conscious of staring with unseemly intentness at his small round-backed figure, dressed with shabby disorder and surmounted by a wonderful head, lean, vulpine, eagle-beaked as that of some art-loving despot of the Renaissance: a head combining the venerable hair and large prominent eyes of the humanist with the greedy profile of the adventurer. Wyant, in musing on the Italian portrait-medals of the fifteenth century, had often fancied that only in that period of fierce individualism could types so paradoxical have been produced; yet the subtle craftsmen who committed them to the bronze had never drawn a face more strangely stamped with contradictory passions than that of Doctor Lombard.

"I am glad to see you," he said to Wyant, extending a hand which seemed a mere framework held together by knotted veins. "We lead a quiet life here and receive few visitors, but any friend of Professor Clyde's is welcome." Then, with a gesture which included the two women, he added dryly: "My wife and daughter often talk of Professor Clyde."

"Oh yes — he used to make me such nice toast; they don't understand toast in Italy," said Mrs. Lombard in a high plaintive voice.

It would have been difficult, from Doctor Lombard's manner and appearance, to guess his nationality; but his wife was so inconsciently and ineradicably English that even the silhouette of her cap seemed a protest against Continental laxities. She was a stout fair woman, with pale cheeks netted with red lines. A brooch with a miniature portrait sustained a bogwood watch-chain upon her bosom, and at her elbow lay a heap of knitting and an old copy of *The Queen*.

The young girl, who had remained standing, was a slim replica of her mother, with an apple-cheeked face and opaque blue eyes. Her small head was prodigally laden with braids of dull fair hair, and she might have had a kind of transient prettiness but for the sullen droop of her round mouth. It was hard to say whether her expression implied ill-temper or apathy; but Wyant was struck by the contrast between the fierce vitality of the doctor's age and the inanimateness of his daughter's youth.

Seating himself in the chair which his host advanced, the young man tried to open the conversation by addressing to Mrs. Lombard some random remark on the beauties of Siena. The lady murmured a resigned assent, and Doctor Lombard interposed with a smile: "My dear sir, my wife considers Siena a most salubrious spot, and is favorably impressed by the cheapness of the marketing; but she deplores the total absence of muffins and cannel coal, and cannot resign herself to the Italian method of dusting furniture."

"But they don't, you know — they don't dust it!" Mrs. Lombard protested, without showing any resentment of her husband's manner.

"Precisely — they don't dust it. Since we have lived in Siena we have not once seen the cobwebs removed from the battlements of the Mangia. Can you conceive of such housekeeping? My wife has never yet dared to write it home to her aunts at Bonchurch."

Mrs. Lombard accepted in silence this remarkable statement of her views, and her husband, with a malicious smile at Wyant's embarrassment, planted himself suddenly before the young man.

"And now," said he, "do you want to see my Leonardo?"

"*Do* I?" cried Wyant, on his feet in a flash.

The doctor chuckled. "Ah," he said, with a kind of crooning deliberation, "that's the way they all behave — that's what they all come for." He turned to his daughter with another variation of mockery in his smile. "Don't fancy it's for your *beaux yeux,* my dear; or for the mature charms of Mrs. Lombard," he added, glaring suddenly at his wife, who had taken up her knitting and was softly murmuring over the number of her stitches.

Neither lady appeared to notice his pleasantries, and he continued, addressing himself to Wyant: "They all come — they all come; but many are called and few are chosen." His voice sank to solemnity. "While I live," he said, "no unworthy eye shall desecrate that picture. But I will not do my friend Clyde the injustice to suppose that he would send an unworthy representative. He tells me he wishes a description of the picture for his book; and you shall describe it to him — if you can."

Wyant hesitated, not knowing whether it was a propitious moment to put in his appeal for a photograph.

"Well, sir," he said, "you know Clyde wants me to take away all I can of it."

Doctor Lombard eyed him sardonically. "You're welcome to take away all you can carry," he replied; adding, as he turned to his daughter: "That is, if he has your permission, Sybilla."

The girl rose without a word, and laying aside her work, took a key from a secret drawer in one of the cabinets, while the doctor continued in the same note of grim jocularity: "For you must know that the picture is not mine — it is my daughter's."

He followed with evident amusement the surprised glance which Wyant turned on the young girl's impassive figure.

"Sybilla," he pursued, "is a votary of the arts; she has inherited her fond father's passion for the unattainable. Luckily, however, she also recently inherited a tidy legacy from her grandmother; and having seen the Leonardo, on which its discoverer had placed a price far beyond my reach, she took a step which deserves to go down to history: she invested her whole inheritance in the purchase of the picture, thus enabling me to spend my closing years in communion with one of the world's masterpieces. My dear sir, could Antigone do more?"

The object of this strange eulogy had meanwhile drawn aside one of the tapestry hangings, and fitted her key into a concealed door.

"Come," said Doctor Lombard, "let us go before the light fails us."

Wyant glanced at Mrs. Lombard, who continued to knit impassively.

"No, no," said his host, "my wife will not come with us. You might not suspect it from her conversation, but my wife has no feeling for art — Italian art, that is; for no one is fonder of our early Victorian school."

"Frith's *Railway Station,* you know," said Mrs. Lombard, smiling. "I like an animated picture."

Miss Lombard, who had unlocked the door, held back the tapestry to let her father and Wyant pass out; then she followed them down a narrow stone passage with another door at its end. This door was iron-barred, and Wyant noticed that it had a complicated patent lock. The girl fitted another key into the lock, and Doctor Lombard led the way into a small room. The dark panelling of this apartment was irradiated by streams of yellow light slanting through the disbanded thunder clouds, and in the central brightness hung a picture concealed by a curtain of faded velvet.

"A little too bright, Sybilla," said Doctor Lombard. His face had grown solemn, and his mouth twitched nervously as his daughter drew a linen drapery across the upper part of the window.

"That will do — that will do." He turned impressively to Wyant. "Do you see the pomegranate bud in this rug? Place yourself there — keep your left foot on it, please. And now, Sybilla, draw the cord."

Miss Lombard advanced and placed her hand on a cord hidden behind the velvet curtain.

"Ah," said the doctor, "one moment: I should like you, while looking at the picture, to have in mind a few lines of verse. Sybilla — "

Without the slightest change of countenance, and with a promptness which proved her to be prepared for the request, Miss Lombard began to recite, in a full round voice like her mother's, St. Bernard's invocation to the Virgin, in the thirty-third canto of the *Paradise.*

"Thank you, my dear," said her father, drawing a deep breath as she ended. "That unapproachable combination of vowel sounds prepares one better than anything I know for the contemplation of the picture."

As he spoke the folds of velvet slowly parted, and the Leonardo appeared in its frame of tarnished gold.

From the nature of Miss Lombard's recitation Wyant had expected a sacred subject, and his surprise was therefore great as the composition was gradually revealed by the widening division of the curtain.

In the background a steel-colored river wound through a pale calcareous landscape; while to the left, on a lonely peak, a crucified Christ hung livid against indigo clouds. The central figure of the foreground, however, was that of a woman seated in an antique chair of marble with bas-reliefs of dancing mænads. Her feet rested on a meadow sprinkled with minute wild-flowers, and her attitude of smiling majesty recalled that of Dosso Dossi's Circe. She wore a red robe, flowing in closely fluted lines from under a fancifully embroidered cloak. Above her high forehead the crinkled golden hair flowed sideways beneath a veil; one hand drooped on the arm of her chair; the other held up an inverted human skull, into which a young Dionysus, smooth, brown and sidelong as the St. John of the Louvre, poured a stream of wine from a high-poised flagon. At the lady's feet lay the symbols of art and luxury: a flute and a roll of music, a platter heaped with grapes and roses, the torso of a Greek statuette, and a bowl overflowing with coins and jewels; behind her, on the chalky hilltop, hung the crucified Christ. A scroll in a corner of the foreground bore the legend: *Lux Mundi.*

Wyant, emerging from the first plunge of wonder, turned inquiringly toward his companions. Neither had moved. Miss Lombard stood with her hand on the cord, her lids lowered, her mouth drooping; the doctor, his strange Thoth-like profile turned toward his guest, was still lost in rapt contemplation of his treasure.

Wyant addressed the young girl.

"You are fortunate," he said, "to be the possessor of anything so perfect."

"It is considered very beautiful," she said coldly.

"Beautiful — *beautiful!*" the doctor burst out. "Ah, the poor, worn out, overworked word! There are no adjectives in the language fresh enough to describe such pristine brilliancy: all their brightness has been worn off by misuse. Think of the things that have been called beautiful, and then look at *that!*"

"It is worthy of a new vocabulary," Wyant agreed.

"Yes," Doctor Lombard continued, "my daughter is indeed fortunate. She has chosen what Catholics call the higher life — the counsel of perfection. What other private person enjoys the same opportunity of understanding the master? Who else lives under the same roof with an untouched masterpiece of Leonardo's? Think of the happiness of being always under the influence of such a creation; of living *into* it; of partaking of it in daily and hourly communion! This room is a chapel; the sight of that picture is a sacrament. What an atmosphere for a young life to unfold itself in! My daughter is singularly blessed. Sybilla, point out some of the details to Mr. Wyant: I see that he will appreciate them."

The girl turned her dense blue eyes toward Wyant; then, glancing away from him, she pointed to the canvas.

"Notice the modelling of the left hand," she began in a monotonous voice; "it recalls the hand of the Mona Lisa. The head of the naked genius will remind you of that of the St. John of the Louvre, but it is more purely pagan and is turned a little less to the right. The embroidery on the cloak is symbolic: you will see that the roots of this plant have burst through the vase. This recalls the famous definition of Hamlet's character in *Wilhelm Meister*. Here are the mystic rose, the flame, and the serpent, emblem of eternity. Some of the other symbols we have not yet been able to decipher."

Wyant watched her curiously: she seemed to be reciting a lesson.

"And the picture itself?" he said. "How do you explain that? *Lux Mundi*—what a curious device to connect with such a subject! What can it mean?"

Miss Lombard dropped her eyes: the answer was evidently not included in her lesson.

"What, indeed?" the doctor interposed. "What does life mean? As one may define it in a hundred different ways, so one may find a hundred different meanings in this picture. Its symbolism is as many-faceted as a well-cut diamond. Who, for instance, is that divine lady? Is it she who is the true *Lux Mundi*—the light reflected from jewels and young eyes, from polished marble and clear waters and statues of bronze? Or is that the Light of the World, extinguished on yonder stormy hill, and is this lady the Pride of Life, feasting blindly on the wine of iniquity, with her back turned to the light which has shone for her in vain? Something of both these meanings may be traced in the picture; but to me it symbolizes rather the central truth of existence: that all that is raised in incorruption is sown in corruption; art, beauty, love, religion; that all our wine is drunk out of skulls, and poured for us by the mysterious genius of a remote and cruel past."

The doctor's face blazed: his bent figure seemed to straighten itself and become taller.

"Ah," he cried, growing more dithyrambic, "how lightly you ask what it means! How confidently you expect an answer! Yet here am I who have given my life to the study of the Renaissance; who have violated its tomb, laid open its dead body, and traced the course of every muscle, bone and artery; who have sucked its very soul from the pages of poets and humanists; who have wept and believed with Joachim of Flora, smiled and doubted with Æneas Sylvius Piccolomini; who have patiently followed to its source the least inspiration of the masters, and groped in neolithic caverns and Babylonian ruins for the first unfolding tendrils of the arabesques of Mantegna and Crivelli; and I tell you that I stand abashed and ignorant before the mystery of this picture. It means nothing — it means all things. It may represent the period which saw its creation; it may represent all ages past and to come. There are volumes of meaning in the tiniest emblem on the lady's cloak; the blossoms of its border are rooted in the deepest soil of myth and tradition. Don't ask what it means, young man, but bow your head in thankfulness for having seen it!"

Miss Lombard laid her hand on his arm.

"Don't excite yourself, father," she said in the detached tone of a professional nurse.

He answered with a despairing gesture. "Ah, it's easy for you to talk. You have years and years to spend with it; I am an old man, and every moment counts!"

"It's bad for you," she repeated with gentle obstinacy.

The doctor's sacred fury had in fact burnt itself out. He dropped into a seat with dull eyes and slackening lips, and his daughter drew the curtain across the picture.

Wyant turned away reluctantly. He felt that his opportunity was slipping from him, yet he dared not refer to Clyde's wish for a photograph. He now understood the meaning of the laugh with which Doctor Lombard had given him leave to carry away all the details he could remember. The picture was so dazzling, so unexpected, so crossed with elusive and contradictory suggestions, that the most alert observer, when placed suddenly before it, must lose his coördinating faculty in a sense of confused wonder. Yet how valuable to Clyde the record of such a work would be! In some ways it seemed to be the summing up of the master's thought, the key to his enigmatic philosophy.

The doctor had risen and was walking slowly toward the door. His daughter unlocked it, and Wyant followed them back in silence to the room in which they had left Mrs. Lombard. That lady was no longer there, and he could think of no excuse for lingering.

He thanked the doctor, and turned to Miss Lombard, who stood in the middle of the room as though awaiting further orders.

"It is very good of you," he said, "to allow one even a glimpse of such a treasure."

She looked at him with her odd directness. "You will come again?" she said quickly; and turning to her father she added: "You know what Professor Clyde asked. This gentleman cannot give him any account of the picture without seeing it again."

Doctor Lombard glanced at her vaguely; he was still like a person in a trance.

"Eh?" he said, rousing himself with an effort.

"I said, father, that Mr. Wyant must see the picture again if he is to tell Professor Clyde about it," Miss Lombard repeated with extraordinary precision of tone.

Wyant was silent. He had the puzzled sense that his wishes were being divined and gratified for reasons with which he was in no way connected.

"Well, well," the doctor muttered, "I don't say no — I don't say no. I know what Clyde wants — I don't refuse to help him." He turned to Wyant. "You may come again — you may make notes," he added with a sudden effort. "Jot down what occurs to you. I'm willing to concede that."

Wyant again caught the girl's eye, but its emphatic message perplexed him.

"You're very good," he said tentatively, "but the fact is the picture is so mysterious — so full of complicated detail — that I'm afraid no notes I could make would serve Clyde's purpose as well as — as a photograph, say. If you would allow me — "

Miss Lombard's brow darkened, and her father raised his head furiously.

"A photograph? A photograph, did you say? Good God, man, not ten people have been allowed to set foot in that room! A *photograph?*"

Wyant saw his mistake, but saw also that he had gone too far to retreat.

"I know, sir, from what Clyde has told me, that you object to having any reproduction of the picture published; but he hoped you might let me take a photograph for his personal use — not to be reproduced in his book, but simply to give him something to work by. I should take the photograph myself, and the negative would of course be yours. If you wished it, only one impression would be struck off, and that one Clyde could return to you when he had done with it."

Doctor Lombard interrupted him with a snarl. "When he had done with it? Just so: I thank thee for that word! When it had been rephotographed, drawn, traced, autotyped, passed about from hand to hand, defiled by every ignorant eye in England, vulgarized by the blundering praise of every art-scribbler in Europe! Pah! I'd as soon give you the picture itself: why don't you ask for that?"

"Well, sir," said Wyant calmly, "if you will trust me with it, I'll engage to take it safely to England and back, and to let no eye but Clyde's see it while it is out of your keeping."

The doctor received this remarkable proposal in silence; then he burst into a laugh.

"Upon my soul!" he said with sardonic good humor.

It was Miss Lombard's turn to look perplexedly at Wyant. His last words and her father's unexpected reply had evidently carried her beyond her depth.

"Well, sir, am I to take the picture?" Wyant smilingly pursued.

"No, young man; nor a photograph of it. Nor a sketch, either; mind that, — nothing that can be reproduced. Sybilla," he cried with sudden passion, "swear to me that the picture shall never be reproduced! No photograph, no sketch — now or afterward. Do you hear me?"

"Yes, father," said the girl quietly.

"The vandals," he muttered, "the desecrators of beauty; if I thought it would ever get into their hands I'd burn it first, by God!" He turned to Wyant, speaking more quietly. "I said you might come back — I never retract what I say. But you must give me your word that no one but Clyde shall see the notes you make."

Wyant was growing warm.

"If you won't trust me with a photograph I wonder you trust me not to show my notes!" he exclaimed.

The doctor looked at him with a malicious smile.

"Humph!" he said; "would they be of much use to anybody?"

Wyant saw that he was losing ground and controlled his impatience.

"To Clyde, I hope, at any rate," he answered, holding out his hand. The doctor shook it without a trace of resentment, and Wyant added: "When shall I come, sir?"

"To-morrow — to-morrow morning," cried Miss Lombard, speaking suddenly.

She looked fixedly at her father, and he shrugged his shoulders.

"The picture is hers," he said to Wyant.

In the ante-chamber the young man was met by the woman who had admitted him. She handed him his hat and stick, and turned to unbar the door. As the bolt slipped back he felt a touch on his arm.

"You have a letter?" she said in a low tone.

"A letter?" He stared. "What letter?"

She shrugged her shoulders, and drew back to let him pass.

II

As Wyant emerged from the house he paused once more to glance up at its scarred brick façade. The marble hand drooped tragically above the entrance: in the waning light it seemed to have relaxed into the passiveness of despair, and Wyant stood musing on its hidden meaning. But the Dead Hand was not the only mysterious thing about Doctor Lombard's house. What were the relations between Miss Lombard and her father? Above all, between Miss Lombard and her picture? She did not look like a person capable of a disinterested passion for the arts; and there had been moments when it struck Wyant that she hated the picture.

The sky at the end of the street was flooded with turbulent yellow light, and the young man turned his steps toward the church of San Domenico, in the hope of catching the lingering brightness on Sodoma's St. Catherine.

The great bare aisles were almost dark when he entered, and he had to grope his way to the chapel steps. Under the momentary evocation of the sunset, the saint's figure emerged pale and swooning from the dusk, and the warm light gave a sensual tinge to her ecstasy. The flesh seemed to glow and heave, the eyelids to tremble; Wyant stood fascinated by the accidental collaboration of light and color.

Suddenly he noticed that something white had fluttered to the ground at his feet. He stooped and picked up a small thin sheet of note-paper, folded and sealed like an old-fashioned letter, and bearing the superscription: —

To the Count Ottaviano Celsi.

Wyant stared at this mysterious document. Where had it come from? He was distinctly conscious of having seen it fall through the air, close to his feet. He glanced up at the dark ceiling of the chapel; then he turned and looked about the church. There was only one figure in it, that of a man who knelt near the high altar.

Suddenly Wyant recalled the question of Doctor Lombard's maid-servant. Was this the letter she had asked for? Had he been unconsciously carrying it about with him all the afternoon? Who was Count Ottaviano Celsi, and how came Wyant to have been chosen to act as that nobleman's ambulant letter-box?

Wyant laid his hat and stick on the chapel steps and began to explore his pockets, in the irrational hope of finding there some clue to the mystery; but they held nothing which he had not himself put there, and he was reduced to wondering how the letter, supposing some unknown hand to have bestowed it on him, had happened to fall out while he stood motionless before the picture.

At this point he was disturbed by a step on the floor of the aisle, and turning, he saw his lustrous-eyed neighbor of the table d'hôte.

The young man bowed and waved an apologetic hand.

"I do not intrude?" he inquired suavely.

Without waiting for a reply, he mounted the steps of the chapel, glancing about him with the affable air of an afternoon caller.

"I see," he remarked with a smile, "that you know the hour at which our saint should be visited."

Wyant agreed that the hour was indeed felicitous.

The stranger stood beamingly before the picture.

"What grace! What poetry!" he murmured, apostrophizing the St. Catherine, but letting his glance slip rapidly about the chapel as he spoke.

Wyant, detecting the manœuvre, murmured a brief assent.

"But it is cold here — mortally cold; you do not find it so?" The intruder put on his hat. "It is permitted at this hour — when the church is empty. And you, my dear sir — do you not feel the dampness? You are an artist, are you not? And to artists it is permitted to cover the head when they are engaged in the study of the paintings."

He darted suddenly toward the steps and bent over Wyant's hat.

"Permit me — cover yourself!" he said a moment later, holding out the hat with an ingratiating gesture.

A light flashed on Wyant.

"Perhaps," he said, looking straight at the young man, "you will tell me your name. My own is Wyant."

The stranger, surprised, but not disconcerted, drew forth a coroneted card, which he offered with a low bow. On the card was engraved: —

Il Conte Ottaviano Celsi.

"I am much obliged to you," said Wyant; "and I may as well tell you that the letter which you apparently expected to find in the lining of my hat is not there, but in my pocket."

He drew it out and handed it to its owner, who had grown very pale.

"And now," Wyant continued, "you will perhaps be good enough to tell me what all this means."

There was no mistaking the effect produced on Count Ottaviano by this request. His lips moved, but he achieved only an ineffectual smile.

"I suppose you know," Wyant went on, his anger rising at the sight of the other's discomfiture, "that you have taken an unwarrantable liberty. I don't yet understand what part I have been made to play, but it's evident that you have made use of me to serve some purpose of your own, and I propose to know the reason why."

Count Ottaviano advanced with an imploring gesture.

"Sir," he pleaded, "you permit me to speak?"

"I expect you to," cried Wyant. "But not here," he added, hearing the clank of the verger's keys. "It is growing dark, and we shall be turned out in a few minutes."

He walked across the church, and Count Ottaviano followed him out into the deserted square.

"Now," said Wyant, pausing on the steps.

The Count, who had regained some measure of self-possession, began to speak in a high key, with an accompaniment of conciliatory gesture.

"My dear sir — my dear Mr. Wyant — you find me in an abominable position — that, as a man of honor, I immediately confess. I have taken advantage of you — yes! I have counted on your amiability, your chivalry — too far, perhaps? I confess it! But what could I do? It was to oblige a lady" — he laid a hand on his heart — "a lady whom I would die to serve!" He went on with increasing volubility, his deliberate English swept away by a torrent of Italian, through which Wyant, with some difficulty, struggled to a comprehension of the case.

Count Ottaviano, according to his own statement, had come to Siena some months previously, on business connected with his mother's property; the paternal estate being near Orvieto, of which ancient city his father was syndic. Soon after his arrival in Siena the young Count had met the incomparable daughter of Doctor Lombard, and falling deeply in love with her, had prevailed on his parents to ask her hand in marriage. Doctor Lombard had not opposed his suit, but when the question of settlements arose it became known that Miss Lombard, who was possessed of a small property in her own right, had a short time before invested the whole amount in the purchase of the Bergamo Leonardo. Thereupon Count Ottaviano's parents had politely suggested that she should sell the picture and thus recover her independence; and this proposal being met by a curt refusal from Doctor Lombard, they had withdrawn their consent to their son's marriage. The young lady's attitude had hitherto been one of passive submission; she was horribly afraid of her father, and would never venture openly to oppose him; but she had made known to Ottaviano her intention of not giving him up, of waiting patiently till events should take a more favorable turn. She seemed hardly aware, the Count said with a sigh, that the means of escape lay in her own hands; that she was of age, and had a right to sell the picture, and to marry without asking her father's consent. Meanwhile her suitor spared no pains to keep himself before her, to remind her that he, too, was waiting and would never give her up.

Doctor Lombard, who suspected the young man of trying to persuade Sybilla to sell the picture, had forbidden the lovers to meet or to correspond; they were thus driven to clandestine communication, and had several times, the Count ingenuously avowed, made use of the doctor's visitors as a means of exchanging letters.

"And you told the visitors to ring twice?" Wyant interposed.

The young man extended his hands in a deprecating gesture. Could Mr. Wyant blame him? He was young, he was ardent, he was enamored! The young lady had done him the supreme honor of avowing her attachment, of pledging her unalterable fidelity; should he suffer his devotion to be outdone? But his purpose in writing to her, he admitted, was not merely to reiterate his fidelity; he was trying by every means in his power to induce her to sell the picture. He had organized a plan of action; every detail was complete; if she would but have the courage to carry out his instructions he would answer for the result. His idea was that she should secretly retire to a convent of which his aunt was the Mother Superior, and from that stronghold should transact the sale of the Leonardo. He had a purchaser ready, who was willing to pay a large sum; a sum, Count Ottaviano whispered, considerably in excess of the young lady's original inheritance; once the picture sold, it could, if necessary, be removed by force from Doctor Lombard's house, and his daughter, being safely in the convent, would be spared the painful scenes incidental to the removal. Finally, if Doctor Lombard were vindictive enough to refuse his consent to her marriage, she had only to make a *sommation respectueuse,* and at the end of the prescribed delay no power on earth could prevent her becoming the wife of Count Ottaviano.

Wyant's anger had fallen at the recital of this simple romance. It was absurd to be angry with a young man who confided his secrets to the first stranger he met in the streets, and placed his hand on his heart whenever he mentioned the name of his betrothed. The easiest way out of the business was to take it as a joke. Wyant had played the wall to this new Pyramus and Thisbe, and was philosophic enough to laugh at the part he had unwittingly performed.

He held out his hand with a smile to Count Ottaviano.

"I won't deprive you any longer," he said, "of the pleasure of reading your letter."

"Oh, sir, a thousand thanks! And when you return to the casa Lombard, you will take a message from me—the letter she expected this afternoon?"

"The letter she expected?" Wyant paused. "No, thank you. I thought you understood that where I come from we don't do that kind of thing—knowingly."

"But, sir, to serve a young lady!"

"I'm sorry for the young lady, if what you tell me is true"—the Count's expressive hands resented the doubt—"but remember that if I am under obligations to any one in this matter, it is to her father, who has admitted me to his house and has allowed me to see his picture."

"*His* picture? Hers!"

"Well, the house is his, at all events."

"Unhappily—since to her it is a dungeon!"

"Why doesn't she leave it, then?" exclaimed Wyant impatiently.

The Count clasped his hands. "Ah, how you say that—with what force, with what virility! If you would but say it to *her* in that tone—you, her countryman! She has no one to advise her; the mother is an idiot; the father is terrible; she is in his power; it is my belief that he would kill her if she resisted him. Mr. Wyant, I tremble for her life while she remains in that house!"

"Oh, come," said Wyant lightly, "they seem to understand each other well enough. But in any case, you must see that I can't interfere—at least you would if you were an Englishman," he added with an escape of contempt.

III

Wyant's affiliations in Siena being restricted to an acquaintance with his landlady, he was forced to apply to her for the verification of Count Ottaviano's story.

The young nobleman had, it appeared, given a perfectly correct account of his situation. His father, Count Celsi-Mongirone, was a man of distinguished family and some wealth. He was syndic of Orvieto, and lived either in that town or on his neighboring estate of Mongirone. His wife owned a large property near Siena, and Count Ottaviano, who was the second son, came there from time to time to look into its management. The eldest son was in the army, the youngest in the Church; and an aunt of Count Ottaviano's was Mother Superior of the Visitandine convent in Siena. At one time it had been said that Count Ottaviano, who was a most amiable and accomplished young man, was to marry the daughter of the strange Englishman, Doctor Lombard, but difficulties having arisen as to the adjustment of the young lady's dower, Count Celsi-Mongirone had very properly broken off the match. It was sad for the young man, however, who was said to be deeply in love, and to find frequent excuses for coming to Siena to inspect his mother's estate.

Viewed in the light of Count Ottaviano's personality the story had a tinge of opera bouffe; but the next morning, as Wyant mounted the stairs of the House of the Dead Hand, the situation insensibly assumed another aspect. It was impossible to take Doctor Lombard lightly; and there was a suggestion of fatality in the appearance of his gaunt dwelling. Who could tell amid what tragic records of domestic tyranny and fluttering broken purposes the little drama of Miss Lombard's fate was being played out? Might not the accumulated influences of such a house modify the lives within it in a manner unguessed by the inmates of a suburban villa with sanitary plumbing and a telephone?

One person, at least, remained unperturbed by such fanciful problems; and that was Mrs. Lombard, who, at Wyant's entrance, raised a placidly wrinkled brow from her knitting. The morning was mild, and her chair had been wheeled into a bar of sunshine near the window, so that she made a cheerful spot of prose in the poetic gloom of her surroundings.

"What a nice morning!" she said; "it must be delightful weather at Bonchurch."

Her dull blue glance wandered across the narrow street with its threatening house fronts, and fluttered back baffled, like a bird with clipped wings. It was evident, poor lady, that she had never seen beyond the opposite houses.

Wyant was not sorry to find her alone. Seeing that she was surprised at his reappearance he said at once: "I have come back to study Miss Lombard's picture."

"Oh, the picture—" Mrs. Lombard's face expressed a gentle disappointment, which might have been boredom in a person of acuter sensibilities. "It's an original Leonardo, you know," she said mechanically.

"And Miss Lombard is very proud of it, I suppose? She seems to have inherited her father's love for art."

Mrs. Lombard counted her stitches, and he went on: "It's unusual in so young a girl. Such tastes generally develop later."

Mrs. Lombard looked up eagerly. "That's what I say! I was quite different at her age, you know. I liked dancing, and doing a pretty bit of fancy-work. Not that I couldn't sketch, too; I had a master down from London. My aunts have some of my crayons hung up in their drawing-room now—I did a view of Kenilworth which was thought pleasing. But I liked a picnic, too, or a pretty walk through the woods with young people of my own age. I say it's more natural, Mr. Wyant; one may have a feeling for art, and do crayons that are worth framing, and yet not give up everything else. I was taught that there were other things."

Wyant, half-ashamed of provoking these innocent confidences, could not resist another question. "And Miss Lombard cares for nothing else?"

Her mother looked troubled.

"Sybilla is so clever—she says I don't understand. You know how self-confident young people are! My husband never said that of me, now—he knows I had an excellent education. My aunts were very particular; I was brought up to have opinions, and my husband has always respected them. He says himself that he wouldn't for the world miss hearing my opinion on any subject; you may have noticed that he often refers to my tastes. He has always respected my preference for living in England; he likes to hear me give my reasons for it. He is so much interested in my ideas that he often says he knows just what I am going to say before I speak. But Sybilla does not care for what I think—"

At this point Doctor Lombard entered. He glanced sharply at Wyant. "The servant is a fool; she didn't tell me you were here." His eye turned to his wife. "Well, my dear, what have you been telling Mr. Wyant? About the aunts at Bonchurch, I'll be bound!"

Mrs. Lombard looked triumphantly at Wyant, and her husband rubbed his hooked fingers, with a smile.

"Mrs. Lombard's aunts are very superior women. They subscribe to the circulating library, and borrow *Good Words* and the *Monthly Packet* from the curate's wife across the way. They have the rector to tea twice a year, and keep a page-boy, and are visited by two baronets' wives. They devoted themselves to the education of their orphan niece, and I think I may say without boasting that Mrs. Lombard's conversation shows marked traces of the advantages she enjoyed."

Mrs. Lombard colored with pleasure.

"I was telling Mr. Wyant that my aunts were very particular."

"Quite so, my dear; and did you mention that they never sleep in anything but linen, and that Miss Sophia puts away the furs and blankets every spring with her own hands? Both those facts are interesting to the student of human nature." Doctor Lombard glanced at his watch. "But we are missing an incomparable moment; the light is perfect at this hour."

Wyant rose, and the doctor led him through the tapestried door and down the passageway.

The light was, in fact, perfect, and the picture shone with an inner radiancy, as though a lamp burned behind the soft screen of the lady's flesh. Every detail of the foreground detached itself with jewel-like precision. Wyant noticed a dozen accessories which had escaped him on the previous day.

He drew out his note-book, and the doctor, who had dropped his sardonic grin for a look of devout contemplation, pushed a chair forward, and seated himself on a carved settle against the wall.

"Now, then," he said, "tell Clyde what you can; but the letter killeth."

He sank down, his hands hanging on the arm of the settle like the claws of a dead bird, his eyes fixed on Wyant's notebook with the obvious intention of detecting any attempt at a surreptitious sketch.

Wyant, nettled at this surveillance, and disturbed by the speculations which Doctor Lombard's strange household excited, sat motionless for a few minutes, staring first at the picture and then at the blank pages of the note-book. The thought that Doctor Lombard was enjoying his discomfiture at length roused him, and he began to write.

He was interrupted by a knock on the iron door. Doctor Lombard rose to unlock it, and his daughter entered.

She bowed hurriedly to Wyant, without looking at him.

"Father, had you forgotten that the man from Monte Amiato was to come back this morning with an answer about the bas-relief? He is here now; he says he can't wait."

"The devil!" cried her father impatiently. "Didn't you tell him—"

"Yes; but he says he can't come back. If you want to see him you must come now."

"Then you think there's a chance?—"

She nodded.

He turned and looked at Wyant, who was writing assiduously.

"You will stay here, Sybilla; I shall be back in a moment."

He hurried out, locking the door behind him.

Wyant had looked up, wondering if Miss Lombard would show any surprise at being locked in with him; but it was his turn to be surprised, for hardly had they heard the key withdrawn when she moved close to him, her small face pale and tumultuous.

"I arranged it—I must speak to you," she gasped. "He'll be back in five minutes."

Her courage seemed to fail, and she looked at him helplessly.

Wyant had a sense of stepping among explosives. He glanced about him at the dusky vaulted room, at the haunting smile of the strange picture overhead, and at the pink-and-white girl whispering of conspiracies in a voice meant to exchange platitudes with a curate.

"How can I help you?" he said with a rush of compassion.

"Oh, if you would! I never have a chance to speak to any one; it's so difficult—he watches me—he'll be back immediately."

"Try to tell me what I can do."

"I don't dare; I feel as if he were behind me." She turned away, fixing her eyes on the picture. A sound startled her. "There he comes, and I haven't spoken! It was my only chance; but it bewilders me so to be hurried."

"I don't hear any one," said Wyant, listening. "Try to tell me."

"How can I make you understand? It would take so long to explain." She drew a deep breath, and then with a plunge—"Will you come here again this afternoon—at about five?" she whispered.

"Come here again?"

"Yes — you can ask to see the picture, — make some excuse. He will come with you, of course; I will open the door for you — and — and lock you both in" — she gasped.

"Lock us in?"

"You see? You understand? It's the only way for me to leave the house — if I am ever to do it" — She drew another difficult breath. "The key will be returned — by a safe person — in half an hour — perhaps sooner — "

She trembled so much that she was obliged to lean against the settle for support.

Wyant looked at her steadily; he was very sorry for her.

"I can't, Miss Lombard," he said at length.

"You can't?"

"I'm sorry; I must seem cruel; but consider — "

He was stopped by the futility of the word: as well ask a hunted rabbit to pause in its dash for a hole!

Wyant took her hand; it was cold and nerveless.

"I will serve you in any way I can; but you must see that this way is impossible. Can't I talk to you again? Perhaps — "

"Oh," she cried, starting up, "there he comes!"

Doctor Lombard's step sounded in the passage.

Wyant held her fast. "Tell me one thing: he won't let you sell the picture?"

"No — hush!"

"Make no pledges for the future, then; promise me that."

"The future?"

"In case he should die: your father is an old man. You haven't promised?"

She shook her head.

"Don't, then; remember that."

She made no answer, and the key turned in the lock.

As he passed out of the house, its scowling cornice and façade of ravaged brick looked down on him with the startlingness of a strange face, seen momentarily in a crowd, and impressing itself on the brain as part of an inevitable future. Above the doorway, the marble hand reached out like the cry of an imprisoned anguish.

Wyant turned away impatiently.

"Rubbish!" he said to himself. "*She* isn't walled in; she can get out if she wants to."

IV

Wyant had any number of plans for coming to Miss Lombard's aid: he was elaborating the twentieth when, on the same afternoon, he stepped into the express train for Florence. By the time the train reached Certaldo he was convinced that, in thus hastening his departure, he had followed the only reasonable course; at Empoli, he began to reflect that the priest and the Levite had probably justified themselves in much the same manner.

A month later, after his return to England, he was unexpectedly relieved from these alternatives of extenuation and approval. A paragraph in the morning paper announced the sudden death of Doctor Lombard, the distinguished English dilettante who had long resided in Siena. Wyant's justification was complete. Our blindest impulses become evidence of perspicacity when they fall in with the course of events.

Wyant could now comfortably speculate on the particular complications from which his foresight had probably saved him. The climax was unexpectedly dramatic. Miss Lombard, on the brink of a step which, whatever its issue, would have burdened her with retrospective compunction, had been set free before her suitor's ardor could have had time to cool, and was now doubtless planning a life of domestic felicity on the proceeds of the Leonardo. One thing, however, struck Wyant as odd—he saw no mention of the sale of the picture. He had scanned the papers for an immediate announcement of its transfer to one of the great museums; but presently concluding that Miss Lombard, out of filial piety, had wished to avoid an appearance of unseemly haste in the disposal of her treasure, he dismissed the matter from his mind. Other affairs happened to engage him; the months slipped by, and gradually the lady and the picture dwelt less vividly in his mind.

It was not till five or six years later, when chance took him again to Siena, that the recollection started from some inner fold of memory. He found himself, as it happened, at the head of Doctor Lombard's street, and glancing down that grim thoroughfare, caught an oblique glimpse of the doctor's house front, with the Dead Hand projecting above its threshold.

The sight revived his interest, and that evening, over an admirable *frittata,* he questioned his landlady about Miss Lombard's marriage.

"The daughter of the English doctor? But she has never married, signore."

"Never married? What, then, became of Count Ottaviano?"

"For a long time he waited; but last year he married a noble lady of the Maremma."

"But what happened — why was the marriage broken?"

The landlady enacted a pantomime of baffled interrogation.

"And Miss Lombard still lives in her father's house?"

"Yes, signore; she is still there."

"And the Leonardo — "

"The Leonardo, also, is still there."

The next day, as Wyant entered the House of the Dead Hand, he remembered Count Ottaviano's injunction to ring twice, and smiled mournfully to think that so much subtlety had been vain. But what could have prevented the marriage? If Doctor Lombard's death had been long delayed, time might have acted as a dissolvent, or the young lady's resolve have failed; but it seemed impossible that the white heat of ardor in which Wyant had left the lovers should have cooled in a few short weeks.

As he ascended the vaulted stairway the atmosphere of the place seemed a reply to his conjectures. The same numbing air fell on him, like an emanation from some persistent will-power, a something fierce and imminent which might reduce to impotence every impulse within its range. Wyant could almost fancy a hand on his shoulder, guiding him upward with the ironical intent of confronting him with the evidence of its work.

A strange servant opened the door, and he was presently introduced to the tapestried room, where, from their usual seats in the window, Mrs. Lombard and her daughter advanced to welcome him with faint ejaculations of surprise.

Both had grown oddly old, but in a dry, smooth way, as fruits might shrivel on a shelf instead of ripening on the tree. Mrs. Lombard was still knitting, and pausing now and then to warm her swollen hands above the brazier; and Miss Lombard, in rising, had laid aside a strip of needlework which might have been the same on which Wyant had first seen her engaged.

Their visitor inquired discreetly how they had fared in the interval, and learned that they had thought of returning to England, but had somehow never done so.

"I am sorry not to see my aunts again," Mrs. Lombard said resignedly; "but Sybilla thinks it best that we should not go this year."

"Next year, perhaps," murmured Miss Lombard, in a voice which seemed to suggest that they had a great waste of time to fill.

She had returned to her seat, and sat bending over her work. Her hair enveloped her head in the same thick braids, but the rose color of her cheeks had turned to blotches of dull red, like some pigment which has darkened in drying.

"And Professor Clyde—is he well?" Mrs. Lombard asked affably; continuing, as her daughter raised a startled eye: "Surely, Sybilla, Mr. Wyant was the gentleman who was sent by Professor Clyde to see the Leonardo?"

Miss Lombard was silent, but Wyant hastened to assure the elder lady of his friend's well-being.

"Ah—perhaps, then, he will come back some day to Siena," she said, sighing. Wyant declared that it was more than likely; and there ensued a pause, which he presently broke by saying to Miss Lombard: "And you still have the picture?"

She raised her eyes and looked at him. "Should you like to see it?" she asked.

On his assenting, she rose, and extracting the same key from the same secret drawer, unlocked the door beneath the tapestry. They walked down the passage in silence, and she stood aside with a grave gesture, making Wyant pass before her into the room. Then she crossed over and drew the curtain back from the picture.

The light of the early afternoon poured full on it: its surface appeared to ripple and heave with a fluid splendor. The colors had lost none of their warmth, the outlines none of their pure precision; it seemed to Wyant like some magical flower which had burst suddenly from the mould of darkness and oblivion.

He turned to Miss Lombard with a movement of comprehension.

"Ah, I understand—you couldn't part with it, after all!" he cried.

"No—I couldn't part with it," she answered.

"It's too beautiful,—too beautiful,"—he assented.

"Too beautiful?" She turned on him with a curious stare. "I have never thought it beautiful, you know."

He gave back the stare. "You have never—".

She shook her head. "It's not that. I hate it; I've always hated it. But he wouldn't let me—he will never let me now."

Wyant was startled by her use of the present tense. Her look surprised him, too: there was a strange fixity of resentment in her innocuous eye. Was it possible that she was laboring under some delusion? Or did the pronoun not refer to her father?

"You mean that Doctor Lombard did not wish you to part with the picture?"

"No — he prevented me; he will always prevent me."

There was another pause. "You promised him, then, before his death — "

"No; I promised nothing. He died too suddenly to make me." Her voice sank to a whisper. "I was free — perfectly free — or I thought I was till I tried."

"Till you tried?"

"To disobey him — to sell the picture. Then I found it was impossible. I tried again and again; but he was always in the room with me."

She glanced over her shoulder as though she had heard a step; and to Wyant, too, for a moment, the room seemed full of a third presence.

"And you can't" — he faltered, unconsciously dropping his voice to the pitch of hers.

She shook her head, gazing at him mystically. "I can't lock him out; I can never lock him out now. I told you I should never have another chance."

Wyant felt the chill of her words like a cold breath in his hair.

"Oh" — he groaned; but she cut him off with a grave gesture.

"It is too late," she said; "but you ought to have helped me that day."

August 1904

"EDMUND KIRKE"

JAMES ROBERTS GILMORE

1822–1903

Quixotes are born singly; seldom do a brace of them perform in concert. This is the story of twin eccentrics who might have been Covenanters in Cromwell's New Model, enthusiasts both, reckless of danger, visionary, religious, playing their part as Christian soldiers with their minds made up to put a stop there and then to the Civil War.

James Roberts Gilmore who, under the pseudonym of Edmund Kirke, writes the record, was a man of restless ability. Too impetuous to go to college, he made an early fortune in cotton and, traveling about his business in the South, became very familiar with Southern speech, Southern manners, and Southern ambitions. Retiring with a competency in 1857, he wrote many books of Dixie and its people. Though without sympathy for the Confederate cause, he had an understanding of it and in his enthusiasm for peace held an early aversion regarding Lincoln which later evidence entirely reversed.

During the years before the Civil War, the cleavage between the states was paralleled by another schism within them. The Methodist Episcopal Church — both our heroes were ardent evangelicals — was cleft in two. As with the congregation so with its ministers who, in spite of the terrific tension, retained some measure of their brotherly love. To adventurous minds tinged with ardent zeal for the faith, it seemed that through the intercourse of Northern and Southern Methodists a natural channel would remain open for a discussion of Peace; and by 1864 many Northern politicians believed some overtures to the South an absolute necessity.

The first link in the chain of events which pulled Gilmore into the adventure of his life was forged out of his distrust of Lincoln. Horace Greeley, who flirted with the preposterous and hated the President, proposed to Gilmore that he should sound out General Rosecrans and determine whether that warrior might not be a likely candidate for the Republican nomination. This mission would have been unimportant had it not led to Gilmore's chance meeting with Colonel James F. Jaquess, Methodist Parson-Colonel of the Preachers' Regiment, the 73rd Illinois Volunteers. The two men, fired with the same enthusiasm and the same motive, coalesce like twin globules of quicksilver. After a single tentative experiment by Jaquess, the brothers-in-arms had but one purpose, Peace with Union. "No compromise with traitors but their immediate return to God and country." They formulated a plan and selected themselves as its emissaries. The utter sincerity of the two men won Lincoln's confidence, not in their plan but in themselves. With his usual wariness he declined to communicate with them in writing, or to give them the least semblance of authority, but unwilling to lose any conceivable opportunity, he did issue to them the passes necessary to their design, and in July '64 the two Quixotes started off to pay a personal call upon the Commander in Chief of the armies of Disunion, Jefferson Davis. With them it was neck or nothing.

The tale of their romantic adventure is printed below, but it may be interesting to complete the record by transcribing an interview between the President and Gilmore which occurred immediately after the latter's return from his hazardous and futile mission. Eager for any scrap of intelligence, Lincoln consented to receive Gilmore. I quote from Gilmore's notes.

> Arrived in Washington, I hurried to the White House. Mr. Sumner was closeted with the President, but my name was no sooner announced than a kindly voice said, "Come in. Bring him in." As I entered his room Lincoln rose and, grasping my hand, said: "I'm glad you're back. I heard of your return two nights ago, but they said you were non-committal. What is it, — as we expected?"
>
> "Exactly, sir," I answered. "There is no peace without separation. Coming down on the boat, I wrote out the interview to read to you when you are at leisure."
>
> "I am at leisure now," he replied. "Sumner, too, would be glad to hear it."
>
> When I had finished the reading, he said, "What do you propose to do with this?"

"*Put a beginning and an end to it, sir, on my way home, and hand it to the* Tribune."

"*Can't you get it into the* Atlantic Monthly?" *Lincoln asked.* "*It would have less of a partisan look there.*"[1]

"*No doubt I can, sir,*" *I replied;* "*but there would be some delay about it.*"

"*And it is important that Davis's position should be known at once,*" *said Mr. Lincoln.* "*It will show the country that I didn't fight shy of Greeley's Niagara business without a reason; and everybody is agog to hear your report. Let it go into the* Tribune."

"*Permit me to suggest,*" *said Mr. Sumner,* "*that Mr. Gilmore put at once a short card, with the separation declaration of Davis, into one of the Boston papers, and then, as soon as he can, the fuller report into the* Atlantic."

"*That is it,*" *said Mr. Lincoln.* "*Put Davis's 'We are not fighting for slavery; we are fighting for independence' into the card, — that is enough; and send me the proof of what goes into the* Atlantic. *Don't let it appear till I return the proof. Some day all this will come out, but just now we must use discretion.*"

As I rose to leave, Mr. Lincoln took my hand, and while he held it in his said, "*Jaquess was right, — God's hand is in it. This may be worth as much to us as half a dozen battles. Get the thing out as soon as you can; but don't forget to send me the proof of what you write for the* Atlantic. *Good-by. God bless you.*"

[1] *The aloofness of the* Atlantic *from the calorics of debate became a cardinal principle of my own editorship. E. S.*

Our Visit to Richmond in 1864

EDMUND KIRKE

I

Why my companion, the Rev. Dr. Jaquess, Colonel of the Seventy-Third Regiment of Illinois Volunteers, recently went to Richmond, and the circumstances attending his previous visit within the Rebel lines, — when he wore his uniform, and mixed openly with scores of leading Confederates, — I shall shortly make known to the public. It may now, however, be asked why I, a "civil" individual, and not in the pay of Government, became his travelling-companion, and, at a time when all the world was rushing North to the mountains and the watering-places, journeyed South for a conference with the arch-Rebel, in the hot and dangerous latitude of Virginia. So, now, in looking inward for the why and the wherefore which I know will be demanded of me at the threshold of this article, I find half a dozen reasons for my visit to Richmond, any one of which ought to prove that I am a sensible man, altogether too sensible to go on so long a journey, in the heat of midsummer, for the mere pleasure of the thing.

First: Very many honest people at the North sincerely believe that the revolted States will return to the Union, if assured of protection to their peculiar institution. The Government having declared that no State shall be readmitted which has not first abolished Slavery, these people hold it responsible for the continuance of the war. It is, therefore, important to know whether the Rebel States will or will not return, if allowed to retain Slavery. Mr. Jefferson Davis could, undoubtedly, answer that question; and that may have been a reason why I went to see him.

Second: On the second of July last, C. C. Clay, of Alabama, J. P. Holcombe, of Virginia, and G. N. Sanders, of nowhere in particular, appeared at Niagara Falls, and publicly announced that they were there to confer with the Democratic leaders in reference to the Chicago nomination. Very soon thereafter, a few friends of the Administration received intimations from those gentlemen that they were Commissioners from the Rebel Government, with authority to negotiate preliminaries of peace on something like the following basis, namely:

A restoration of the Union as it was; all negroes actually freed by the war to be declared free, and all negroes not actually freed by the war to be declared slaves.

These overtures were not considered sincere. They seemed concocted to embarrass the Government, to throw upon it the odium of continuing the war, and thus to secure the triumph of the peace-traitors at the November election. The scheme, if well managed, threatened to be dangerous, by uniting the Peace-men, the Copperheads, and such of the Republicans as love peace better than principle, in one opposition, willing to make a peace that would be inconsistent with the safety and dignity of the country. It was, therefore, important to discover — what was then in doubt — whether the Rebel envoys really had, or had not, any official authority.

Within fifteen days of the appearance of these "Peace Commissioners," Jefferson Davis had said to an eminent Secession divine, who, late in June, came through the Union lines by the Maryland back-door, that he would make peace on no other terms than a recognition of Southern Independence. (He might, however, agree to two governments, bound together by a league offensive and defensive, — for all external purposes *one,* for all internal purposes *two;* but he would agree to nothing better.)

There was reason to consider this information trustworthy, and to believe Mr. Davis (who was supposed to be a clear-minded man) altogether ignorant of the doings of his Niagara satellites. If this were true, and were proven to be true, — if the *great* Rebel should reiterate this declaration in the presence of a trustworthy witness, at the very time when the *small* Rebels were opening their Quaker guns on the country, — would not the Niagara negotiators be stripped of their false colors, and their low schemes be exposed to the scorn of all honest men, North and South?

I may have thought so; and that may have been another reason why I went to Richmond.

Third: I had been acquainted with Colonel Jaquess's peace-movements from their inception. Early in June last he wrote me from a battle-field in Georgia, announcing his intention of again visiting the Rebels, and asking an interview with me at a designated place. We met, and went to Washington together. Arriving there, I became aware that obstacles were in the way of his further progress. Those obstacles could be removed by my accompanying him; and that, to those who know the man and his "mission," which is to preach peace on earth and good-will among men, would seem a very good reason why I went to Richmond.

Fourth, — and this to very many may appear as potent as any of the preceding reasons, — I had in my boyhood a strange fancy for church-belfries and liberty-poles. This fancy led me, in school-vacations, to perch my small self for hours on the cross-beams in the old belfry, and to climb to the very top of the tall pole which still surmounts the little village-green. In my youth, this feeling was simply a spirit of adventure; but as I grew older it deepened into a reverence for what those old bells said, and a love for the principle of which that old liberty-pole is now only a crumbling symbol.

Had not events shown that Jeff. Davis had never seen that old liberty-pole, and never heard the chimes which still ring out from that old belfry? Who knew, in these days when every wood-sawyer has a "mission," but *I* had a "mission," and it was to tell the Rebel President that Northern liberty-poles still stand for Freedom, and that Northern church-bells still peal out, "Liberty throughout the land, to *all* the inhabitants thereof"?

If that *was* my mission, will anybody blame me for fanning Mr. Davis with a "blast" of cool Northern "wind" in this hot weather?

But enough of mystification. The straightforward reader wants a straightforward reason, and he shall have it.

We went to Richmond because we hoped to pave the way for negotiations that would result in peace.

If we should succeed, the consciousness of having served the country would, we thought, pay our expenses. If we should fail, but return safely, we might still serve the country by making public the cause of our failure. If we should fail, and *not* return safely, but be shot or hanged as spies, — as we might be, for we could have no protection from our Government, and no safe-conduct from the Rebels, — two lives would be added to the thousands already sacrificed to this Rebellion, but they would as effectually serve the country as if lost on the battle-field.

These are the reasons, and the only reasons, why we went to Richmond.

II

We went there in an ambulance, and we went together, — the Colonel and I; and though two men were never more unlike, we worked together like two brothers, or like two halves of a pair of shears. That we got *in* was owing, perhaps, to me; that we got *out* was due altogether to him; and a man more cool, more brave, more self-reliant, and more self-devoted than that quiet "Western parson" it never was my fortune to encounter.

When the far-away Boston bells were sounding nine, on the morning of Saturday, the sixteenth of July, we took our glorious Massachusetts General by the hand, and said to him, —

"Good bye. If you do not see us within ten days, you will know we have 'gone up.' "

"If I do not see you within that time," he replied, "I'll demand you; and if they don't produce you, body and soul, I'll take two for one, — better men than you are, — and hang them higher than Haman. My hand on that. Good bye."

At three o'clock on the afternoon of the same day, mounted on two raw-boned relics of Sheridan's great raid, and armed with a letter to Jeff. Davis, a white cambric handkerchief tied to a short stick, and an honest face, — this last was the Colonel's, — we rode up to the Rebel lines. A ragged, yellow-faced boy, with a carbine in one hand, and another white handkerchief tied to another short stick in the other, came out to meet us.

"Can you tell us, my man, where to find Judge Ould, the Exchange Commissioner?"

"Yas. Him and t'other 'Change officers is over ter the plantation beyont Miss Grover's. Ye'll know it by its hevin' nary door nur winder [the mansion, he meant]. They's all busted in. Foller the bridle-path through the timber, and keep your rag a-flyin', fur our boys is thicker'n huckleberries in them woods, and they mought pop ye, ef they didn't seed it."

Thanking him, we turned our horses into the "timber," and, galloping rapidly on, soon came in sight of the deserted plantation. Lolling on the grass, in the shade of the windowless mansion, we found the Confederate officials. They rose as we approached; and one of us said to the Judge, — a courteous, middle-aged gentleman, in a Panama hat, and a suit of spotless white drillings, —

"We are late, but it's your fault. Your people fired at us down the river, and we had to turn back and come overland."

"You don't suppose they saw your flag?"

"No. It was hidden by the trees; but a shot came uncomfortably near us. It struck the water, and ricochetted not three yards off. A little nearer, and it would have shortened me by a head, and the Colonel by two feet."

"That would have been a sad thing for you; but a miss, you know, is as good as a mile," said the Judge, evidently enjoying the "joke."

"We hear Grant was in the boat that followed yours, and was struck while at dinner," remarked Captain Hatch, the Judge's Adjutant, — a gentleman, and about the best-looking man in the Confederacy.

"Indeed! Do you believe it?"

"I don't know, of course"; and his looks asked for an answer. We gave none, for all such information is contraband. We might have told him that Grant, Butler, and Foster examined their position from Mrs. Grover's house, — about four hundred yards distant, — two hours after the Rebel cannon-ball danced a break-down on the Lieutenant-General's dinner-table.

We were then introduced to the other officials, — Major Henniken of the War Department, a young man formerly of New York, but now scorning the imputation of being a Yankee, and Mr. Charles Javins, of the Provost-Guard of Richmond. This latter individual was our shadow in Dixie. He was of medium height, stoutly built, with a short thick neck, and arms and shoulders denoting great strength. He looked a natural-born jailer, and much such a character as a timid man would not care to encounter, except at long range of a rifle warranted to fire twenty shots a minute, and to hit every time.

To give us a *moonlight view* of the Richmond fortifications, the Judge proposed to start after sundown; and as it wanted some hours of that time, we seated ourselves on the ground, and entered into conversation. The treatment of our prisoners, the *status* of black troops, and non-combatants, and all the questions which have led to the suspension of exchanges, had been good-naturedly discussed, when the Captain, looking up from one of the Northern papers we had brought him, said, —

"Do you know, it mortifies me that you don't hate us as we hate you? You kill us as Agassiz kills a fly, — because you love us."

"Of course we do. The North is being crucified for love of the South."

"If you love us so, why don't you let us go?" asked the Judge, rather curtly.

"For that very reason, — because we love you. If we let you go, with slavery, and your notions of 'empire,' you'd run straight to barbarism and the Devil."

"We'd take the risk of that. But let me tell you, if you are going to

Mr. Davis with any such ideas, you might as well turn back at once. He can make peace on no other basis than Independence. Recognition must be the beginning, middle, and ending of all negotiations. Our people will accept peace on no other terms."

"I think you are wrong there," said the Colonel. "When I was here a year ago, I met many of your leading men, and they all assured me they wanted peace and reunion, even at the sacrifice of slavery. Within a week, a man you venerate and love has met me at Baltimore, and besought me to come here, and offer Mr. Davis peace on such conditions."

"That may be. Some of our old men, who are weak in the knees, may want peace on any terms; but the Southern people will not have it without Independence. Mr. Davis knows them, and you will find he will insist upon that. Concede that, and we'll not quarrel about minor matters."

"We'll not quarrel at all. But it's sundown, and time we were 'on to Richmond.' "

"That's the 'Tribune' cry," said the Captain, rising; "and I hurrah for the 'Tribune,' for it's honest, and — I want my supper."

We all laughed, and the Judge ordered the horses. As we were about to start, I said to him, —

"You've forgotten our parole."

"Oh, never mind that. We'll attend to that at Richmond."

Stepping into his carriage, and unfurling the flag of truce, he then led the way, by a "short cut," across the cornfield which divided the mansion from the high-road. We followed in an ambulance drawn by a pair of mules, our shadow — Mr. Javins — sitting between us and the twilight, and Jack, a "likely darky," almost the sole survivor of his master's twelve hundred slaves, ("De ress all stole, Massa, — stole by you Yankees,") occupying the front-seat, and with a stout whip "working our passage" to Richmond.

Much that was amusing and interesting occurred during our three-hours' journey, but regard for our word forbids my relating it. Suffice it to say, we saw the "frowning fortifications," we "flanked" the "invincible army," and, at ten o'clock that night, planted our flag (against a lamp-post) in the very heart of the hostile city. As we alighted at the doorway of the Spotswood Hotel, the Judge said to the Colonel, —

"Button your outside-coat up closely. Your uniform must not be seen here."

The Colonel did as he was bidden; and, without stopping to register our names at the office, we followed the Judge and the Captain up to No. 60. It was a large, square room in the fourth story, with an unswept, ragged carpet, and bare, white walls, smeared with soot and tobacco-juice. Several chairs, a marble-top table, and a pine wash-stand and clothes-press straggled about the floor, and in the corners were three beds, garnished with tattered pillow-cases, and covered with white counterpanes, grown gray with longing for soapsuds and a wash-tub. The plainer and humbler of these beds was designed for the burly Mr. Javins; the others had been made ready for the extraordinary envoys (not envoys extraordinary) who, in defiance of all precedent and the "law of nations," had just then "taken Richmond."

A single gas-jet was burning over the mantel-piece, and above it I saw a "writing on the wall" which implied that Jane Jackson had run up a washing-score of fifty dollars!

I was congratulating myself on not having to pay that woman's laundry-bills, when the Judge said,—

"You want supper. What shall we order?"

"A slice of hot corn-bread would make *me* the happiest man in Richmond."

The Captain thereupon left the room, and shortly returning, remarked,—

"The landlord swears you're from Georgia. He says none but a Georgian would call for corn-bread at this time of night."

On that hint we acted, and when our sooty attendant came in with the supper-things, we discussed Georgia mines, Georgia banks, and Georgia mosquitoes, in a way that showed we had been bitten by all of them. In half an hour it was noised all about the hotel that the two gentlemen the Confederacy was taking such excellent care of were from Georgia.

The meal ended, and a quiet smoke over, our entertainers rose to go. As the Judge bade us good-night, he said to us,—

"In the morning you had better address a note to Mr. Benjamin, asking the interview with the President. I will call at ten o'clock, and take it to him."

"Very well. But will Mr. Davis see us on Sunday?"

"Oh, that will make no difference."

III

The next morning, after breakfast, which we took in our room with Mr. Javins, we indited a note—of which the following is a copy—to the Confederate Secretary of State.

Spotswood House, Richmond, Va.
July 17th, 1864.

Hon. J. P. Benjamin,
Secretary of State, etc.

Dear Sir, — The undersigned respectfully solicit an interview with President Davis.

They visit Richmond only as private citizens, and have no official character or authority; but they are acquainted with the views of the United States Government, and with the sentiments of the Northern people relative to an adjustment of the differences existing between the North and the South, and earnestly hope that a free interchange of views between President Davis and themselves may open the way to such *official* negotiations as will result in restoring peace to the two sections of our distracted country.

They, therefore, ask an interview with the President, and awaiting your reply, are

Truly and respectfully yours.

This was signed by both of us; and when the Judge called, as he had appointed, we sent it — together with a commendatory letter I had received, on setting out, from a near relative of Mr. Davis — to the Rebel Secretary. In half an hour Judge Ould returned, saying, — "Mr. Benjamin sends you his compliments, and will be happy to see you at the State Department."

We found the Secretary — a short, plump, oily little man in black, with a keen black eye, a Jew face, a yellow skin, curly black hair, closely trimmed black whiskers, and a ponderous gold watch-chain — in the northwest room of the "United States" Custom-House. Over the door of this room were the words, "State Department," and round its walls were hung a few maps and battle-plans. In one corner was a tier of shelves filled with books, — among which I noticed Headley's "History," Lossing's "Pictorial," Parton's "Butler," Greeley's "American Conflict," a complete set of the "Rebellion Record," and a dozen numbers and several bound volumes of the "Atlantic Monthly," — and in the centre of the apartment was a black-walnut table, covered with green cloth, and filled with a multitude of "state-papers." At this table sat the Secretary. He rose as we entered, and, as Judge Ould introduced us, took our hands, and said, —

"I am glad, very glad, to meet you, Gentlemen. I have read your note, and" — bowing to me — "the open letter you bring from ——. Your errand commands my respect and sympathy. Pray be seated."

As we took the proffered seats, the Colonel, drawing off his "duster," and displaying his uniform, said, —

"We thank you for this cordial reception, Mr. Benjamin. We trust you will be as glad to hear us as you are to see us."

"No doubt I shall be, for you come to talk of peace. Peace is what we all want."

"It is, indeed; and for that reason we are here to see Mr. Davis. Can we see him, Sir?"

"Do you bring any overtures to him from your Government?"

"No, Sir. We bring no overtures and have no authority from our Government. We state that in our note. We would be glad, however, to know what terms will be acceptable to Mr. Davis. If they at all harmonize with Mr. Lincoln's views, we will report them to him, and so open the door for official negotiations."

"Are you acquainted with Mr. Lincoln's views?"

"One of us is, fully."

"Did Mr. Lincoln, *in any way,* authorize you to come here?"

"No, Sir. We came with his pass, but not by his request. We say, distinctly, we have no official, or unofficial, authority. We come as men and Christians, not as diplomatists, hoping, in a frank talk with Mr. Davis, to discover some way by which this war may be stopped."

"Well, Gentlemen, I will repeat what you say to the President, and if he follows my advice, — and I think he will, — he will meet you. He will be at church this afternoon; so, suppose you call here at nine this evening. If anything should occur in the mean time to prevent his seeing you, I will let you know through Judge Ould."

Throughout this interview the manner of the Secretary was cordial; but with this cordiality was a strange constraint and diffidence, almost amounting to timidity, which struck both my companion and myself. Contrasting his manner with the quiet dignity of the Colonel, I almost fancied our positions reversed, — that, instead of our being in his power, the Secretary was in ours, and momently expecting to hear some unwelcome sentence from our lips. There is something, after all, in moral power. Mr. Benjamin does not possess it, nor is he a great man. He has a keen, shrewd, ready intellect, but not the *stamina* to originate, or even to execute, any great good or great wickedness.

After a day spent in our room, conversing with the Judge, or watching the passers-by in the street, — I should like to tell who they were and how they looked, but such information is just now contraband, — we called again, at nine o'clock, at the State Department.

Mr. Benjamin occupied his previous seat at the table, and at his right sat a spare, thin-featured man, with iron-gray hair and beard, and a clear, gray eye full of life and vigor. He had a broad, massive forehead, and a mouth and chin denoting great energy and strength of will. His face was emaciated, and much wrinkled, but his features were good, especially his eyes, — though one of them bore a scar, apparently made by some sharp instrument. He wore a suit of grayish-brown, evidently of foreign manufacture, and, as he rose, I saw that he was about five feet ten inches high, with a slight stoop in the shoulders. His manners were simple, easy, and quite fascinating; and he threw an indescribable charm into his voice, as he extended his hand, and said to us, —

"I am glad to see you, Gentlemen. You are very welcome to Richmond."

And this was the man who was Secretary of War for the United States under Franklin Pierce, and who is now the heart, soul, and brains of the Southern Confederacy!

His manner put me entirely at my ease, — the Colonel would be at his, if he stood before Cæsar, — and I replied, —

"We thank you, Mr. Davis. It is not often you meet men of our clothes, and our principles, in Richmond."

"Not often, — not so often as I could wish; and I trust your coming may lead to a more frequent and a more friendly intercourse between the North and the South."

"We sincerely hope it may."

"Mr. Benjamin tells me you have asked to see me, to" ——

And he paused, as if desiring we should finish the sentence. The Colonel replied, —

"Yes, Sir. We have asked this interview in the hope that you may suggest some way by which this war can be stopped. Our people want peace, — your people do, and your Congress has recently said that *you* do. We have come to ask how it can be brought about."

"In a very simple way. Withdraw your armies from our territory, and peace will come of itself. We do not seek to subjugate you. We are not waging an offensive war, except so far as it is offensive-defensive, — that is, so far as we are forced to invade you to prevent your invading us. Let us alone, and peace will come at once."

"But we cannot let you alone so long as you repudiate the Union. That is the one thing the Northern people will not surrender."

"I know. You would deny to us what you exact for yourselves, — the right of self-government."

"No, Sir," I remarked. "We would deny you no natural right. But we think Union essential to peace; and, Mr. Davis, *could* two people, with the same language, separated by only an imaginary line, live at peace with each other? Would not disputes constantly arise, and cause almost constant war between them?"

"Undoubtedly, — with this generation. You have sown such bitterness at the South, you have put such an ocean of blood between the two sections, that I despair of seeing any harmony in my time. Our children may forget this war, but *we* cannot."

"I think the bitterness you speak of, Sir," said the Colonel, "does not really exist. *We* meet and talk here as friends; our soldiers meet and fraternize with each other; and I feel sure, that, if the Union were restored, a more friendly feeling would arise between us than has ever existed. The war has made us know and respect each other better than before. This is the view of very many Southern men; I have had it from many of them, — your leading citizens."

"They are mistaken," replied Mr. Davis. "They do not understand Southern sentiment. How can we feel anything but bitterness towards men who deny us our rights? If you enter my house and drive me out of it, am I not your natural enemy?"

"You put the case too strongly. But we cannot fight forever; the war must end at some time; we must finally agree upon something; can we not agree now, and stop this frightful carnage? We are both Christian men, Mr. Davis. Can *you,* as a Christian man, leave untried any means that may lead to peace?"

"No, I cannot. I desire peace as much as you do. I deplore bloodshed as much as you do; but I feel that not one drop of the blood shed in this war is on *my* hands, — I can look up to my God and say this. I tried all in my power to avert this war. I saw it coming, and for twelve years I worked night and day to prevent it, but I could not. The North was mad and blind; it would not let us govern ourselves; and so the war came, and now it must go on till the last man of this generation falls in his tracks, and his children seize his musket and fight his battle, *unless you acknowledge our right to self-government.* We are not fighting for slavery. We are fighting for Independence, — and that, or extermination, we *will* have."

"And there are, at least, four and a half millions of us left; so you see you have a work before you," said Mr. Benjamin, with a decided sneer.

"We have no wish to exterminate you," answered the Colonel. "I believe what I have said, — that there is no bitterness between the

Northern and Southern *people*. The North, I know, loves the South. When peace comes, it will pour money and means into your hands to repair the waste caused by the war; and it would now welcome you back, and forgive you all the loss and bloodshed you have caused. But we *must* crush your armies, and exterminate your Government. And is not that already nearly done? You are wholly without money, and at the end of your resources. Grant has shut you up in Richmond. Sherman is before Atlanta. Had you not, then, better accept honorable terms while you can retain your prestige, and save the pride of the Southern people?"

Mr. Davis smiled.

"I respect your earnestness, Colonel, but you do not seem to understand the situation. We are not exactly shut up in Richmond. If your papers tell the truth, it is your capital that is in danger, not ours. Some weeks ago, Grant crossed the Rapidan to whip Lee, and take Richmond. Lee drove him in the first battle, and then Grant executed what your people call a 'brilliant flank-movement,' and fought Lee again. Lee drove him a second time, and then Grant made another 'flank-movement'; and so they kept on,—Lee whipping, and Grant flanking,—until Grant got where he is now. And what is the net result? Grant has lost seventy-five or eighty thousand men,—*more than Lee had at the outset,*—and is no nearer taking Richmond than at first; and Lee, whose front has never been broken, holds him completely in check, and has men enough to spare to invade Maryland, and threaten Washington! Sherman, to be sure, *is* before Atlanta; but suppose he is, and suppose he takes it? You know, that, the farther he goes from his base of supplies, the weaker he grows, and the more disastrous defeat will be to him. And defeat *may* come. So, in a military view, I should certainly say our position was better than yours.

"As to money: we are richer than you are. You smile; but admit that our paper is worth nothing,—it answers as a circulating-medium; and we hold it all ourselves. If every dollar of it were lost, we should, as we have no foreign debt, be none the poorer. But it *is* worth something; it has the solid basis of a large cotton-crop, while yours rests on nothing, and you owe all the world. As to resources: we do not lack for arms or ammunition, and we have still a wide territory from which to gather supplies. So, you see, we are not in extremities. But if we were, —if we were without money, without food, without weapons,—if our whole country were devastated, and our armies crushed and disbanded,—could we, without giving up our manhood, give up our right to govern ourselves? Would *you* not rather die, and feel yourself a man, than live, and be subject to a foreign power?"

"From your stand-point there is force in what you say," replied the Colonel. "But we did not come here to argue with you, Mr. Davis. We came, hoping to find some honorable way to peace; and I am grieved to hear you say what you do. When I have seen your young men dying on the battle-field, and your old men, women, and children starving in their homes, I have felt I could risk my life to save them. For that reason I am here; and I am grieved, grieved, that there is no hope."

"I know your motives, Colonel Jaquess, and I honor you for them; but what can I do more than I am doing? I would give my poor life, gladly, if it would bring peace and good-will to the two countries; but it would not. It is with your own people you should labor. It is they who desolate our homes, burn our wheat-fields, break the wheels of wagons carrying away our women and children, and destroy supplies meant for our sick and wounded. At your door lies all the misery and the crime of this war,—and it is a fearful, fearful account."

"Not all of it, Mr. Davis. I admit a fearful account, but it is not *all* at our door. The passions of both sides are aroused. Unarmed men are hanged, prisoners are shot down in cold blood, by yourselves. Elements of barbarism are entering the war on both sides, that should make us—you and me, as Christian men—shudder to think of. In God's name, then, let us stop it. Let us do something, concede something, to bring about peace. You cannot expect, with only four and a half millions, as Mr. Benjamin says you have, to hold out forever against twenty millions."

Again Mr. Davis smiled.

"Do you suppose there are twenty millions at the North determined to crush us?"

"I do,—to crush your *government*. A small number of our people, a very small number, are your friends,—Secessionists. The rest differ about measures and candidates, but are united in the determination to sustain the Union. Whoever is elected in November, he *must be* committed to a vigorous prosecution of the war."

Mr. Davis still looking incredulous, I remarked,—

"It is so, Sir. Whoever tells you otherwise deceives you. I think I know Northern sentiment, and I assure you it is so. You know we have a system of lyceum-lecturing in our large towns. At the close of these lectures, it is the custom of the people to come upon the platform and talk with the lecturer. This gives him an excellent opportunity of learning public sentiment. Last winter I lectured before nearly a hundred of such associations, all over the North,—from Dubuque to Bangor,—and I took pains to ascertain the feeling of the people. I found a unanimous determination to crush the Rebellion and save the Union at every sacrifice. The majority are in favor of Mr. Lincoln, and nearly all of those opposed to him are opposed to him because they think he does not fight you with enough vigor. The radical Republicans, who go for slave-suffrage and thorough confiscation, are those who will defeat him, if he is defeated. But if he is defeated before the people, the House will elect a worse man,—I mean, worse for you. It is more radical than he is,—you can see that from Mr. Ashley's Reconstruction Bill,—and the people are more radical than the House. Mr. Lincoln, I know, is about to call out five hundred thousand more men, and I can't see how you *can* resist much longer; but if you do, you will only deepen the radical feeling of the Northern people. They will now give you fair, honorable, *generous* terms; but let them suffer much more, let there be a dead man in every house, as there is now in every village, and they will give you *no* terms,—they will insist on hanging every Rebel south of —— Pardon my terms. I mean no offence."

"You give no offence," he replied, smiling very pleasantly. "I wouldn't have you pick your words. This is a frank, free talk, and I like you the better for saying what you think. Go on."

"I was merely going to say, that, let the Northern people once really feel the war,—they do not feel it yet,—and they will insist on hanging every one of your leaders."

"Well, admitting all you say, I can't see how it affects our position. There are some things worse than hanging or extermination. We reckon giving up the right of self-government one of those things."

"By self-government you mean disunion,—Southern Independence?"

"Yes."

"And slavery, you say, is no longer an element in the contest."

"No, it is not, it never was an *essential* element. It was only a means of bringing other conflicting elements to an earlier culmination. It fired the musket which was already capped and loaded. There are essential differences between the North and the South that will, however this war may end, make them two nations."

"You ask me to say what I think. Will you allow me to say that I know the South pretty well, and never observed those differences?"

"Then you have not used your eyes. My sight is poorer than yours, but I have seen them for years."

The laugh was upon me, and Mr. Benjamin enjoyed it.

"Well, Sir, be that as it may, if I understand you, the dispute between your government and ours is narrowed down to this: Union or Disunion."

"Yes; or to put it in other words: Independence or Subjugation."

"Then the two governments are irreconcilably apart. They have no alternative but to fight it out. But it is not so with the people. They are tired of fighting, and want peace; and as they bear all the burden and suffering of the war, is it not right they should have peace, and have it on such terms as they like?"

"I don't understand you. Be a little more explicit."

"Well, suppose the two governments should agree to something like this: To go to the people with two propositions: say, Peace, with Disunion and Southern Independence, as your proposition, — and Peace, with Union, Emancipation, No Confiscation, and Universal Amnesty, as ours. Let the citizens of all the United States (as they existed before the war) vote 'Yes,' or 'No,' on these two propositions, at a special election within sixty days. If a majority votes Disunion, our government to be bound by it, and to let you go in peace. If a majority votes Union, yours to be bound by it, and to stay in peace. The two governments can contract in this way, and the people, though constitutionally unable to decide on peace or war, can elect which of the two propositions shall govern their rulers. Let Lee and Grant, meanwhile, agree to an armistice. This would sheathe the sword; and if once sheathed, it would never again be drawn by this generation."

"The plan is altogether impracticable. If the South were only one State, it might work; but as it is, if one Southern State objected to emancipation, it would nullify the whole thing; for you are aware the people of Virginia cannot vote slavery out of South Carolina, nor the people of South Carolina vote it out of Virginia."

"But three-fourths of the States can amend the Constitution. Let it be done in that way, — in any way, so that it be done by the people. I am not a statesman or a politician, and I do not know just how such a plan could be carried out; but you get the idea, — that the PEOPLE shall decide the question."

"That the *majority* shall decide it, you mean. We seceded to rid ourselves of the rule of the majority, and this would subject us to it again."

"But the majority must rule finally, either with bullets or ballots."

"I am not so sure of that. Neither current events nor history shows that the majority rules, or ever did rule. The contrary, I think, is true. Why, Sir, the man who should go before the Southern people with such a proposition, with *any* proposition which implied that the North was to have a voice in determining the domestic relations of the South, could not live here a day. He would be hanged to the first tree, without judge or jury."

"Allow me to doubt that. I think it more likely he would be hanged, if he let the Southern people know the majority couldn't rule," I replied, smiling.

"I have no fear of that," rejoined Mr. Davis, also smiling most good-humoredly. "I give you leave to proclaim it from every house-top in the South."

"But, seriously, Sir, you let the majority rule in a single State; why not let it rule in the whole country?"

"Because the States are independent and sovereign. The country is not. It is only a confederation of States; or rather it *was:* it is now *two* confederations."

"Then we are not a *people,*—we are only a political partnership?"

"That is all."

"Your very name, Sir, '*United* States,' implies that," said Mr. Benjamin. "But, tell me, are the terms you have named—Emancipation, No Confiscation, and Universal Amnesty—the terms which Mr. Lincoln authorized you to offer us?"

"No, Sir, Mr. Lincoln did not authorize me to offer you any terms. But I *think* both he and the Northern people, for the sake of peace, would assent to some such conditions."

"They are *very* generous," replied Mr. Davis, for the first time during the interview showing some angry feeling. "But Amnesty, Sir, applies to criminals. We have committed no crime. Confiscation is of no account, unless you can enforce it. And Emancipation! You have already emancipated nearly two millions of our slaves,—and if you will take care of them, you may emancipate the rest. I had a few when the war began. I was of some use to them; they never were of any to me. Against their will you 'emancipated' them; and you may 'emancipate' every negro in the Confederacy, but *we will be free!* We will govern ourselves. We *will* do it, if we have to see every Southern plantation sacked, and every Southern city in flames."

"I see, Mr. Davis, it is useless to continue this conversation," I replied; "and you will pardon us, if we have seemed to press our views with too much pertinacity. We love the old flag, and that must be our apology for intruding upon you at all."

"You have not intruded upon me," he replied, resuming his usual manner. "I am glad to have met you, both. I once loved the old flag as well as you do; I would have died for it; but now it is to me only the emblem of oppression."

"I hope the day may never come, Mr. Davis, when *I* say that," said the Colonel.

A half-hour's conversation on other topics — not of public interest — ensued, and then we rose to go. As we did so, the Rebel President gave me his hand, and, bidding me a kindly good-bye, expressed the hope of seeing me again in Richmond in happier times, — when peace should have returned; but with the Colonel his parting was particularly cordial. Taking his hand in both of his, he said to him, —

"Colonel, I respect your character and your motives, and I wish you well, — I wish you every good I can wish you consistently with the interests of the Confederacy."

The quiet, straightforward bearing and magnificent moral courage of our "fighting parson" had evidently impressed Mr. Davis very favorably.

As we were leaving the room, he added, —

"Say to Mr. Lincoln from me, that I shall at any time be pleased to receive proposals for peace on the basis of our Independence. It will be useless to approach me with any other."

When we went out, Mr. Benjamin called Judge Ould, who had been waiting during the whole interview — two hours — at the other end of the hall, and we passed down the stairway together. As I put my arm within that of the Judge, he said to me, —

"Well, what is the result?"

"Nothing but war, — war to the knife."

"Ephraim is joined to his idols, — let him alone," added the Colonel, solemnly.

IV

It was not far from eleven o'clock at night when we took leave of the Rebel President, and, arm in arm with Judge Ould, made our way through the silent, deserted streets to our elevated quarters in the Spotswood Hotel at Richmond. As we climbed the long, rickety stairs which led to our room in the fourth story, one of us said to our companion, —

"We can accomplish nothing more by remaining here. Suppose we shake the sacred soil from our feet to-morrow?"

"Very well. At what hour will you start?" he replied.

"The earlier, the better. As near daybreak as may be, — to avoid the sun."

"We can't be ready before ten o'clock. The mules are quartered six miles out of town."

That sounded strange, for Jack, our ebony Jehu, had said to me only the day before, "Dem *is* mighty foine mules, Massa. I 'tends ter dem mules myself; *we keeps 'em right round de corner*." Taken together, the statements of the two officials had a bad look; but Mr. Davis had just given me a message to his niece, and Mr. Benjamin had just intrusted Colonel Jaquess with a letter — contraband, because three pages long — for delivery within the limits of the "United States"; therefore the discrepancy did not alarm me, for the latter facts seemed to assure our safe deliverance from Dixie. Merely saying, "Very well, — ten o'clock, then, let it be, — we'll be ready," — we bade the Judge good-night at the landing, and entered our apartment.

We found the guard, Mr. Javins, stretched at full length on his bed, and snoring like the Seven Sleepers. Day and night, from the moment of our first entrance into the Rebel dominions, that worthy, with a revolver in his sleeve, our door-key in his pocket, and a Yankee in each one of his eyes, had implicitly observed his instructions, — "Keep a constant watch upon them"; but overtasked nature had at last got the better of his vigilance, and he was slumbering at his post. Not caring to disturb him, we bolted the door, slid the key under his pillow, and followed him to the land of dreams.

It was a little after two o'clock, and the round, ruddy moon was looking pleasantly in at my window, when a noise outside awoke me. Lifting the sash, I listened. There was a sound of hurrying feet in the neighboring street, and a prolonged cry of murder! It seemed the wild, strangled shriek of a woman. Springing to the floor, I threw on my clothes, and shook Javins.

"Wake up! Give me the key! They're murdering a woman in the street!" I shouted, loud enough to be heard in the next world.

But he did not wake, and the Colonel, too, slept on, those despairing cries in his ears, as peacefully as if his great dream of peace had been realized. Still those dreadful shrieks, mingled now with curses hot from the bottomless pit, came up through the window. No time was to be lost, — so, giving another and a desperate tug at Javins, I thrust my hand under his pillow, drew out his revolver and the door-key, and, three steps at a time, bounded down the stairways. At the outer entrance a half-drunken barkeeper was rubbing his eyes, and asking, "What's the row?"—but not another soul was stirring. Giving no heed to him, I hurried into the street. I had not gone twenty paces, however, before a gruff voice from the shadow of the building called out,—

"Halt! Who goes thar'?"

"A friend," I answered.

"Advance, friend, and give the countersign."

"I don't know it."

"Then ye carn't pass. Orders is strict."

"What is this disturbance? I heard a woman crying murder."

The stifled shrieks had died away, but low moans, and sounds like hysterical weeping, still came up from around the corner.

"Oh! nothin',—jest some nigger fellers on a time. Thet's all."

"And you stood by and saw it done!" I exclaimed, with mingled contempt and indignation.

"Sor it? How cud *I* holp it? I hes my orders,—ter keep my eye on thet 'ar' door; 'sides, thar' war' nigh a dozen on 'em, and these Richmond nigs, now thet the white folks is away, is more lawless nor old Bragg himself. My life 'ou'dn't ha' been wuth a hill o' beans among 'em."

By this time I had gradually drawn the sentinel to the corner of the building, and looking down the dimly lighted street whence the sounds proceeded, I saw that it was empty.

"They are gone now," I said, "and the woman may be dying. Come, go down there with me."

"Carn't, Cunnel. I 'ou'dn't do it fur all the women in Richmond."

"Was your mother a woman?"

"I reckon, and a right peart 'un,—ye mought bet yer pile on thet."

"I'll bet my pile she'd disown you, if she knew you turned your back on a woman."

He gave me a wistful, undecided look, and then, muttering something about "orders," which I did not stop to hear, followed me, as I hurried down the street.

Not three hundred yards away, in a narrow recess between two buildings, we found the woman. She lay at full length on the pavement, her neat muslin gown torn to shreds, and her simple lace bonnet crushed into a shapeless mass beside her. Her thick, dishevelled hair only half-concealed her open bosom, and from the corners of her mouth the blood was flowing freely. She was not dead, — for she still moaned pitifully, — but she seemed to be dying. Lifting her head as tenderly as I could, I said to her, —

"Are you much hurt? Can't you speak to me?"

She opened her eyes, and staring at the sentinel with a wild, crazed look, only moaned, —

"Oh! don't! Don't, — any more! Let me die! Oh! let me die!"

"Not yet. You are too young to die yet. Come, see if you can't sit up."

Something, it may have been the tone of my voice, seemed to bring her to her senses, for she again opened her eyes, and, with a sudden effort, rose nearly to her feet. In a moment, however, she staggered back, and would have fallen, had not the sentinel caught her.

"There, don't try again. Rest awhile. Take some of this, — it will give you strength"; and I emptied my brandy-flask into her mouth. "Our General" had filled it the morning we set out from his camp; but two days' acquaintance with the Judge, who declared "*such* brandy contraband of war," had reduced its contents to a low ebb. Still, there was enough to do that poor girl a world of good. She shortly revived, and sitting up, her head against the sentinel's shoulder, told us her story. She was a white woman, and served as nursery-maid in a family that lived hard by. All of its male members being away with the army, she had been sent out at that late hour to procure medicine for a sick child, and, waylaid by a gang of black fiends, had been gagged and outraged in the very heart of Richmond! And this is Southern civilization under Jefferson I.!

At the end of a long hour, I returned to the hotel. The sentry was pacing to and fro before it, and, seating myself on the door-step, I drew him into conversation.

"Do such things often happen in Richmond?" I asked him.

"Often! Ye's strange yere, I reckon," he replied.

"No, — I've been here forty times, but not lately. Things must be in a bad way here, now."

"Wal, they is! Thar's nary night but thar's lots o' sech doin's. Ye see, thar' ha'n't more'n a corporal's-guard o' white men in the hull place, so the nigs they hes the'r own way, and ye'd better b'lieve they raise the Devil, and break things, ginerally."

"I've seen no other able-bodied soldier about town; how is it that you are here?"

"I ha'n't able-bodied," he replied, holding up the stump of his left arm, from which the sleeve was dangling. "I lost thet more'n a y'ar ago. I b'long ter the cavalry,—Fust Alabama,—and bein' 's I carn't manage a nag now, they's detailed me fur provost-duty."

"First Alabama? I know Captains Webb and Firman of that regiment."

"Ye does? What! old man Webb, as lives down on Coosa?"

"Yes, at Gadsden, in Cherokee County. Streight burnt his house, and both of his mills, on his big raid, and the old man has lost both of his sons in the war. It has wellnigh done him up."

"I reckon. Stands ter natur' it sh'u'd. The Yankees is all-fired fiends. The old man use' ter hate 'em loike ——. I reckon he hates 'em wuss'n uver now."

"No, he don't. His troubles seem to have softened him. When he told me of them, he cried like a child. He reckoned the Lord had brought them on him because he'd fought against the Union."

"Wal, I doan't know. This war's a bad business, anyhow. When d'ye see old Webb last?"

"About a year ago,—down in Tennessee, nigh to Tullahoma."

"Was he 'long o' the rigiment?"

That was a home question, for I had met Captain Webb while he was a prisoner, in the Court-House at Murfreesboro'. However, I promptly replied,—

"No,—he'd just left it."

"Wal, I doan't blame him. 'Pears loike, ef sech things sh'u'd come onter me, I'd let the war and the kentry go ter the Devil tergether."

My acquaintance with Captain Webb naturally won me the confidence of the soldier; and for nearly an hour, almost unquestioned, he poured into my ear information that would have been of incalculable value to our generals. Two days later I would have given my right hand for liberty to whisper to General Grant some things that he said; but honor and honesty forbade it.

A neighboring clock struck four when I rose to go. As I did so, I said to the sentinel,—

"I saw no other sentry in the streets; why are you guarding this hotel?"

"Wal, ye knows old Brown's a-raisin' Cain down thar' in Georgy. Two o' his men hes come up yere ter see Jeff, and things ha'n't quite satisfactory, so we's orders ter keep 'em tighter'n a bull's-eye in fly-time."

So, not content with placing a guard in our very bedchamber, the oily-tongued despot over the way had fastened a padlock over the keyhole of our outside-door! What *would* happen, if he should hear that I had picked the padlock, and prowled about Richmond for an hour after midnight! The very thought gave my throat a preliminary choke, and my neck an uneasy sensation. It was high time I sought the embrace of that hard mattress in the fourth story. But my fears were groundless. When I crept noiselessly to bed, Javins was sleeping as soundly and snoring as sweetly as if his sins were all forgiven.

When I awoke in the morning, breakfast was already laid on the centre-table, and an army of newsboys were shouting under our windows, " 'Ere's the 'En′quirer' and *the* 'Dis′patch.' Great news from the front. Gin'ral Grant mortally killed, — shot with a cannon." Rising, and beginning my toilet, I said to Javins, in a tone of deep concern, —

"When did that happen?"

"Why, o' Saturday. I hearn of it afore we left the lines. 'Twas all over town yesterday," he replied, with infinite composure.

"And you didn't tell us! That was unkind of you, Javins, — very unkind. How *could* you do it?"

"It's ag'in' orders to talk news with you; — besides, I thought you knowed it."

"How should we know it?"

"Why, your boat was only just ahead of his'n, comin' up the river. He got shot runnin' that battery. Hit in the arm, and died when they amputated him."

"Amputated him! Did they cut off his head to save his arm?"

Whether he saw a quiet twinkle in my eye, or knew that the news was false, I know not. Whichever it was, he replied, —

"I reckon. Then you don't b'lieve it?"

"Why should I doubt it? Don't your papers always tell the truth?"

"No, they never do; lyin's their trade."

"Then you suppose they're whistling now to keep up their courage? But let us see what they say. Oblige me with some of your currency."

He kindly gave me three dollars for one, and ringing the bell, I soon had the five dingy half-sheets which every morning, "Sundays excepted," hold up this busy world, "its fluctuations and its vast concerns," to the wondering view of beleaguered Richmond.

"Dey's fifty cents apiece, Massa," said the darky, handing me the papers, and looking wistfully on the poor specimen of lithography which remained after the purchase; "what shill I do wid dis?"

"Oh! keep it. I'd give you more, but that's all the lawful money I have about me."

He hesitated, as if unwilling to take my last half-dollar; but self soon got the better of him. He pocketed the shin-plaster, and said nothing; but "Poor gentleman! I's sorry for *you!* Libin' at de Spotswood, and no money about you!" was legible all over his face.

We opened the papers, and, sure enough, General Grant *was* dead, and laid out in dingy sheets, with a big gun firing great volleys over him! The cannon which that morning thundered Glory! Hallelujah! through the columns of the "Whig" and the "Examiner" no doubt brought him to life again. No such jubilation, I believe, disgraced our Northern journals when Stonewall Jackson fell.

Breakfast over, the Colonel and I packed our portmanteaus, and sat down to the intellectual repast. It was a feast, and we enjoyed it. I always have enjoyed the Richmond editorials. If I were a poet, I should study them for epithets. Exhausting the dictionary, their authors ransack heaven, earth, and the other place, and into one expression throw such a concentration of scorn, hate, fury, or exultation as is absolutely stunning to a man of ordinary nerves. Talk of their being bridled! They never had a bit in their mouths. Before the war they ran wild, and now they ride rough-shod over decorum, decency, and Davis himself. But the dictator endures it like a philosopher. "He lets it pass," said Judge Ould to me, "like the idle wind, which it is."

At last, ten o'clock — the hour when we were to set out from Dixie — struck from a neighboring steeple, and I laid down the paper, and listened for the tread of the Judge on the stairs. I had heard it often, and it had always been welcome, for he is a most agreeable companion, but I had not *listened* for it till then. Then I waited for it as "they that watch for the morning," for he was to deliver us from the "den of lions," — from "the hold of every foul and unclean thing." Ten, twenty, thirty minutes I waited, but he did not come! Why was he late, that prompt man, who was always "on time," — who put us through the streets of Richmond the night before on a trot, lest we should be a second late at our appointment?

At length eleven o'clock sounded, and I took out my watch to count the minutes. One, two, three, — how slow they went! Four, five, — ten, — fifteen, — twenty! What was the matter with the watch? Even at this day I could affirm on oath that it took five hours for that hour-hand to get round to twelve. But at last it got there, and then — each second seeming a minute, each minute an hour — it crept slowly on to one; but still no Judge appeared! Why did he not come? The reason was obvious. The mules were "quartered six miles out of town," because he had to see Mr. Davis before letting us go. And Davis had heard of my nocturnal rambling, and concluded we had come as spies. Or he had, from my cross-questioning the night before, detected *my* main object in coming to Dixie. Either way *my* doom was sealed. If we were taken as spies, it was hanging. If held on other grounds, it was imprisonment; and ten days of Castle Thunder, in my then state of health, would have ended my mortal career.

I had looked at this alternative before setting out. But then I saw it afar off; now I stood face to face with it, and — I thought of home, — of the brave boy who had said to me, "Father, I think you ought to go. If I was only a man, *I*'d go. If you never come back, *I*'ll take care of the children."

These thoughts passing in my mind, I rose and paced the room for a few moments, — then, turning to Javins, said, —

"Will you oblige me by stepping into the hall? My friend and I would have a few words together."

As he passed out, I said to the Colonel, —

"Ould is more than three hours late! What does it mean?"

All this while he had sat, his spectacles on his nose, and his chair canted against the window-sill, absorbed in the newspapers. Occasionally he would look up to comment on something he was reading; but not a movement of his face, nor a glance of his eye, had betrayed that he was conscious of Ould's delay, or of my extreme restlessness. When I said this, he took off his spectacles, and, quietly rubbing the glasses with his handkerchief, replied, —

"It looks badly, but — *I* ask no odds of them. We may have to show we are men. We have tried to serve the country. That is enough. Let them hang us, if they like."

"Colonel," I exclaimed, with a strong inclination to hug him, "you are a trump! the bravest man I ever knew!"

"I trust in God, — that is all," was his reply.

This was all he said, — but his words convey no idea of the sublime courage which shone in his eye and lighted up his every feature. I felt rebuked, and turned away to hide my emotion. As I did so, my attention was arrested by a singular spectacle in a neighboring street. Coming down the hill, hand in hand with a colored woman, were two little boys of about eight or nine years, one white, the other black. As they neared the opposite corner, the white lad drew back and struck the black boy a heavy blow with his foot. The ebony juvenile doubled up his fist, and, planting it behind the other's ear, felled him to the sidewalk. But the white lad was on his feet again in an instant, and showering on the black a perfect storm of kicks and blows. The latter parried the assault coolly, and, watching his opportunity, planted another blow behind the white boy's ear, which sent him reeling to the ground again. Meanwhile the colored nurse stood by, enjoying the scene, and a score or more of negroes of all ages and sizes gathered around, urging the young ebony on with cheers and other expressions of encouragement. I watched the combat till the white lad had gone down a third time, when a rap came at the door, and Judge Ould entered.

"Good evening," he said.

"Good evening," we replied.

"Well, Gentlemen, if you are ready, we'll walk round to the Libby," he added, with a hardness of tone I had not observed in his voice before.

My worst fears were realized! We were prisoners! A cold tremor passed over me, and my tongue refused its office. The Colonel stood, drawn up to his full height, looking at Ould. Not a feature of his fine face moved, but his large gray eye was beaming with a sort of triumph. I have met brave men, — men who have faced death a hundred times without quailing; but I never met a man who had the moral grandeur of that man. His look inspired me, for I turned to Ould, and, with a coolness that amazed myself, said, —

"Very well. We are ready. But here is an instructive spectacle"; and I pointed to the conflict going on in the street. "That is what you are coming to. Fight us another year, and that scene will be enacted, by larger children, all over the South."

"To prevent that is why we are fighting you at all," he replied, dryly.

We shook Javins by the hand, and took up our portmanteaus to go. Then our hotel-bill occurred to me, and I said to Ould, —

"You cautioned us against offering greenbacks. We have nothing else. Will you give us some Confederate money in exchange?"

"Certainly. But what do you want of money?" he asked, resuming the free and easy manner he had shown in our previous intercourse.

"To pay our hotel-bill."

"You have no bill here. It will be settled by the Confederacy."

"We can't allow that. We are not here as the guests of your Government."

"Yes, you are, and you can't help yourselves," he rejoined, laughing pleasantly. "If you offer the landlord greenbacks, he'll have you jugged, certain, — for it's against the law."

"That's nothing to us. We are jugged already."

"So you are!" and he laughed again, rather boisterously.

His manner half convinced me that he had been playing on our sensibilities; but I said nothing, and we followed him down the stairs.

At the outer door stood Jack and the ambulance! Their presence assured us a safe exit from Dixie, and my feelings found expression somewhat as follows: —

"How are you, Jack? You're the best-looking darky I ever saw."

"I's bery well, Massa, bery well. Hope you's well," replied Jack, grinning until he made himself uglier than Nature intended. "I's glad you tinks I's good-lookin'."

"Good-looking! You're better-looking than any man, black or white, I ever met."

"You've odd notions of beauty," said the Judge, smiling. "That accounts for your being an Abolitionist."

"No, it don't." And I added, in a tone too low for Jack to hear, "It only implies, that, until I saw that darky, I doubted our getting out of Dixie."

The Judge gave a low whistle.

"So you smelt a rat?"

"Yes, a very big one. Tell us, why were you so long behind time?"

"I'll tell you when the war is over. Now I'll take you to Libby and the hospitals, if you'd like to go."

We said we would, and, ordering Jack to follow with the ambulance, the Judge led us down the principal thoroughfare. A few shops were open, a few negro women were passing in and out among them, and a few wounded soldiers were limping along the sidewalks; but scarcely an able-bodied man was to be seen anywhere. A poor soldier, who had lost both legs and a hand, was seated at a street-corner, asking alms of the colored women as they passed. Pointing to him, the Judge said, —

"There is one of our arguments against reunion. If you will walk two squares, I'll show you a thousand."

"All asking alms of black women? That is another indication of what you are coming to."

He made no reply. After a while, scanning our faces as if he would detect our hidden thoughts, he said, in an abrupt, pointed way, —

"Grant was to have attacked us yesterday. Why didn't he do it?"

"How should we know?"

"You came from Foster's only the day before. That's where the attack was to have been made."

"Why wasn't it made?"

"*I* don't know. Some think it was because you came in, and were *expected out* that way."

"Oh! That accounts for your being so late! You think we are spies, sent in to survey, and report on the route?"

"No, I do not. I think you are honest men, and I've *said so*."

And I have no doubt it was because he "said so" that we got out of Richmond.

By this time we had reached a dingy brick building, from one corner of which protruded a small sign, bearing, in black letters on a white ground, the words, —

LIBBY AND SON,

SHIP-CHANDLERS AND GROCERS.

It was three stories high, and, I was told, eighty feet in width and a hundred and ten in depth. In front, the first story was on a level with the street, allowing space for a tier of dungeons under the sidewalk; but in the rear the land sloped away till the basement-floor rose aboveground. Its unpainted walls were scorched to a rusty brown, and its sunken doors and low windows, filled here and there with a dusky pane, were cobwebbed and weather-stained, giving the whole building a most uninviting and desolate appearance. A flaxen-haired boy, in ragged "butternuts" and a Union cap, and an old man, in gray regimentals, with a bent body and a limping gait, were pacing to and fro before it, with muskets on their shoulders; but no other soldiers were in sight.

"If Ben Butler knew that Richmond was defended by only such men, how long would it be before he took it?" I said, turning to the Judge.

"Several years. When these men give out, our women will fall in. Let Butler try it!"

Opening a door at the right, he led us into a large, high-studded apartment, with a bare floor, and greasy brown walls hung round with battle-scenes and cheap lithographs of the Rebel leaders. Several officers in "Secession gray" were lounging about this room, and one of them, a short, slightly-built, youthful-looking man, rose as we entered, and, in a half-pompous, half-obsequious way, said to Judge Ould, —

"Ah! Colonel Ould, I am very glad to see you."

The Judge returned the greeting with a stateliness that was in striking contrast with his usual frank and cordial manner, and then introduced the officer to us as "Major Turner, Keeper of the Libby." I had heard of him, and it was with some reluctance that I took his proffered hand. However, I did take it, and at the same time inquired,—

"Are you related to Dr. Turner, of Fayetteville?"

"No, Sir. I am of the old Virginia family." (I never met a negro-whipper nor a negro-trader who did not belong to that family.) "Are you a North-Carolinian?"

"No, Sir"——

Before I could add another word, the Judge said,—

"No, Major; these gentlemen hail from Georgia. They are strangers here, and I'd thank you to show them over the prison."

"Certainly, Colonel, most certainly. I'll do it with great pleasure."

We entered a room about forty feet wide and a hundred feet deep, with bare brick walls, a rough plank floor, and narrow, dingy windows, to whose sash only a few broken panes were clinging. A row of tin wash-basins, and a wooden trough which served as a bathing-tub, were at one end of it, and half a dozen cheap stools and hard-bottomed chairs were littered about the floor, but it had no other furniture. And this room, with five others of similar size and appointments, and two basements floored with earth and filled with *débris,* compose the famous Libby Prison, in which, for months together, thousands of the best and bravest men that ever went to battle have been allowed to rot and to starve.

At the date of our visit, not more than a hundred prisoners were in the Libby, its contents having recently been emptied into a worse sink in Georgia; but almost constantly since the war began, twelve and sometimes thirteen hundred of our officers have been hived within those half-dozen desolate rooms and filthy cellars, with a space of only ten feet by two allotted to each for all the purposes of living!

Overrun with vermin, perishing with cold, breathing a stifled, tainted atmosphere, no space allowed them for rest by day, and lying down at night "wormed and dovetailed together like fish in a basket,"—their daily rations only two ounces of stale beef and a small lump of hard corn-bread, and their lives the forfeit, if they caught but one streak of God's blue sky through those filthy windows,—they have endured there all the horrors of the middle-passage. My soul sickened as I looked on the scene of their wretchedness. If the liberty we are fighting for were not worth even so terrible a price, — if it were not cheaply purchased even with the blood and agony of the many brave and true souls who have gone into that foul den only to die, or to come out the shadows of men, — living ghosts, condemned to walk the night and to fade away before the breaking of the great day that is coming, — who would not cry out for peace, for peace on any terms?

And while these thoughts were in my mind, the cringing, foul-mouthed, brutal, contemptible ruffian who had caused all this misery stood within two paces of me! I could have reached out my hand, and, with half an effort, have crushed him, and —— I did not do it! Some invisible Power held my arm, for murder was in my heart.

"This is where that Yankee devil Streight, that raised hell so among you down in Georgia, got out," said Turner, pausing before a jut in the wall of the room. "A flue was here, you see, but we've bricked it up. They took up the hearth, let themselves down into the basement, and then dug through the wall, and eighty feet underground into the yard of a deserted building over the way. If you'd like to see the place, step down with me."

"We would, Major. We'd be right glad ter," I replied, adopting, at a hint from the Judge, the Georgia dialect.

We descended a rough plank stairway, and entered the basement. It was a damp, mouldy, dismal place, and even then — in hot July weather — as cold as an ice-house. What must it have been in midwinter!

The keeper led us along the wall to where Streight and his party had broken out, and then said, —

"It's three feet thick, but they went through it, and all the way under the street, with only a few case-knives and a dust-pan."

"Wal, they *war* smart. But, keeper, whar' wus yer eyes all o' thet time? Down our way, ef a man couldn't see twenty Yankees a-wuckin' so fur six weeks, by daylight, in a clar place like this yere, we'd reckon he warn't fit ter 'tend a pen o' niggers."

The Judge whispered, "You're overdoing it. Hold in." Turner winced like a struck hound, but, smothering his wrath, smilingly replied, —

"The place wasn't clear then. It was filled with straw and rubbish. The Yankees covered the opening with it, and hid away among it when any one was coming. I caught two of them down here one day, but they pulled the wool over my eyes, and I let them off with a few days in a dungeon. But that fellow Streight would outwit the Devil. He was the most unruly customer I've had in the twenty months I've been here. I put him in keep, time and again, but I never could cool him down."

"Whar' is the keeps?" I asked. "Ye's got lots o' them, ha'n't ye?"

"No,—only six. Step this way, and I'll show you."

"Talk better English," said the Judge, as we fell a few paces behind Turner on our way to the front of the building. "There are some schoolmasters in Georgia."

"Wal, thar' ha'n't,—not in the part I come from."

The dungeons were low, close, dismal apartments, about twelve feet square, boarded off from the remainder of the cellar, and lighted only by a narrow grating under the sidewalk. Their floors were incrusted with filth, and their walls stained and damp with the rain, which, in wet weather, had dripped down from the street.

"And how many does ye commonly lodge yere, when yer hotel's full?" I asked.

"I have had twenty in each, but fifteen is about as many as they comfortably hold."

"I reckon! And then the comfut moughtn't be much ter brag on."

The keeper soon invited us to walk into the adjoining basement. I was a few steps in advance of him, taking a straight course to the entrance, when a sentinel, pacing to and fro in the middle of the apartment, levelled his musket so as to bar my way, saying, as he did so,—

"Ye carn't pass yere, Sir. Ye must go round by the wall."

This drew my attention to the spot, and I noticed that a space, about fifteen feet square, in the centre of the room, and directly in front of the sentinel, had been recently dug up with a spade. While in all other places the ground was trodden to the hardness and color of granite, this spot seemed to be soft, and had the reddish-yellow hue of the "sacred soil." Another sentry was pacing to and fro on its other side, so that the place was completely surrounded! Why were they guarding it so closely? The reason flashed upon me, and I said to Turner,—

"I say, how many barr'ls hes ye in thar'?"

"Enough to blow this shanty to ——," he answered, curtly.

"I reckon! Put 'em thar' when thet feller Dahlgreen wus a-gwine ter rescue 'em,—the Yankees?"

"I reckon."

He said no more, but that was enough to reveal the black, seething hell the Rebellion has brewed. In this room, seated on the ground, or leaning idly against the walls, were about a dozen poor fellows who the Judge told me were hostages, held for a similar number under sentence of death by our Government. Their dejected, homesick look, and weary, listless manner disclosed some of the horrors of imprisonment.

"Let us go," I said to the Colonel; "I have had enough of this."

"No,—you must see the up-stairs," said Turner. "It a'n't so gloomy up there."

It was not so gloomy, for some little sunlight did come in through the dingy windows; but the few prisoners in the upper rooms wore the same sad, disconsolate look as those in the lower story.

"It is not hard fare, or close quarters, that kills men," said Judge Ould to me; "it is homesickness; and the strongest and the bravest succumb to it first."

In the sill of an attic-window I found a Minié-ball. Prying it out with my knife, and holding it up to Turner, I said,—

"So ye keeps this room fur a shootin'-gallery, does ye?"

"Yes," he replied, laughing. "The boys practise once in a while on the Yankees. You see, the rules forbid their coming within three feet of the windows. Sometimes they do, and then the boys take a pop at them."

"And sometimes hit 'em? Hit many on 'em?"

"Yes, a heap."

We passed a long hour in the Libby, and then visited Castle Thunder and the hospitals for our wounded. I should be glad to describe what I saw in those "institutions," but the limits of my paper forbid it.

It was five o'clock when we bade the Judge a friendly good-bye, and took our seats in the ambulance. As we did so, he said to us,—

"I have not taken your parole, Gentlemen. I shall trust to your honor not to disclose anything you have seen or heard that might operate against us in a military way."

"You may rely upon us, Judge; and, some day, give us a chance to return the courtesy and kindness you have shown to us. We shall not forget it."

We arrived near the Union lines just as the sun was going down. Captain Hatch, who had accompanied us, waved his flag as we halted near a grove of trees, and a young officer rode over to us from the nearest picket-station. We despatched him to General Foster for a pair of horses, and in half an hour entered the General's tent. He pressed us to remain to dinner, proposing to kill the fatted calf,—"for these my sons were dead and are alive again, were lost and are found."

We let him kill it, (it tasted wonderfully like salt pork,) and in half an hour were on our way to General Butler's head-quarters.

September, December, 1864

HETTY HEMENWAY

1890–

An editor's first passion and his last is, and ought to be, curiosity. In people, in persons rather, for the editor studies them one by one, he must be endlessly interested. For in every human record there is a story to be found, and it is with the solicitous scrutiny of a midwife that the editor should look into his visitor's face. Very often a story of quality is born without successors, but I know of few instances where a story so genuinely conceived, so sensitively told as this, remains almost the sole achievement of a gifted pen. In spite of the editor's remonstrances Hetty Hemenway married, and a succession of babies have formed a clamorous barrier against an admirable career.

It is often said of a story that it wrote itself. "Four Days" seems to me a literal example. It was written under the overpowering emotions of the First World War. For a brief season selfish worries of the daily round were swallowed up in generous and pitying thoughts.

In spite of humanitarianism, in the face of humanity itself, war abides as a spiritual paradox. William James's famous proposal "The Moral Equivalent of War" saps the wall of contradiction, but does not topple it. Nothing short of immolation, of self-destruction in a common cause, seems to satisfy the exalted spirit when every instinct, every compulsive ardor gives the charge.

Four Days

HETTY HEMENWAY

I

WITH savage pity Marjorie regarded a sobbing girl whose face was distorted, and whose palsied hands were trying to straighten her veil and push back stray wisps of hair. Marjorie thought: "What a fool she is to cry like that! Her nose is red; she's a sight. I can control myself. I can control myself."

An elderly man with an austere face, standing beside Marjorie, started to light a cigarette. His hands trembled violently and the match flickered and went out.

Marjorie's heart was beating so fast that it made her feel sick.

A locomotive shrieked, adding its voice to the roar of traffic at Victoria Station. There came the pounding hiss of escaping steam. The crowd pressed close to the rails and peered down the foggy platform. A train had stopped, and the engine was panting close to the gate-rail. A few men in khaki were alighting from compartments. In a moment there was a stamping of many feet, and above the roar and confusion in the station rose the eager voices of multitudes of boys talking, shouting, calling to each other.

Marjorie saw Leonard before he saw her. He was walking with three men — joking, laughing absent-mindedly, while his eyes searched for a face in the crowd. She waited a moment, hidden, suffocated with anticipation, her heart turning over and over, until he said a nonchalant good-bye to his companions, who were pounced upon by eager relatives. Then she crept up behind and put both her hands about his wrist.

"Hello, Len."

Joy leaped to his eyes.

"Marjie!"

Impossible to say another word. For seconds they became one of the speechless couples, standing dumbly in the great dingy station, unnoticed and unnoticing.

"Where's the carriage?" said Leonard, looking blindly about him.

"Outside, of course, Len."

A crooked man in black livery, with a cockade in his hat, who had been standing reverently in the background, waddled forward, touching his hat.

"Well, Burns, how are you? Glad to see you."

"Very well, sir, and thank you, sir. 'Appy, most 'appy to see you back, sir. Pardon, sir, this way." His old face twitched and his eyes devoured the young lieutenant.

A footman was standing at the horses' heads, but the big bays, champing their bits, and scattering foam, crouched away from the tall young soldier when he put out a careless, intimate hand and patted their snorting noses. He swaggered a little, for all of a sudden he longed to put his head on their arching necks and cry.

"You've got the old pair out; I thought they had gone to grass," he said in his most matter-of-fact tone to the pink-faced footman, who was hardly more than a child.

"Well, sir, the others were taken by the Government. Madam gave them all away except Starlight and Ginger Girl. There is only me and Burns and another boy under military age in the stables now, sir."

Inside the carriage Leonard and Marjorie were suddenly overawed by a strange, delicious shyness. They looked at each other gravely, like two children at a party, dumb, exquisitely thrilled. It was ten months ago that they had said a half-tearful, half-laughing good-bye to each other on the windy, sunny pier at Hoboken. They had been in love two months, and engaged two weeks. Leonard was sailing for England to keep a rowing engagement, but he was to return to America in a month. They were to have an early autumn wedding. Marjorie chose her wedding-dress and was busy with her trousseau. She had invited her bridesmaids. It was to be a brilliant, conventional affair — flowers, music, countless young people dancing under festoons and colored lights. In August the war broke out. Leonard had been in training and at the front from the first. Marjorie crossed the precarious ocean, to be in England for his first leave. It was now May: they were to be married at last.

"Marjie."

"Len."

"I have just four days, you know, darling. That's all I could get. We've been transferred to the Dardanelles; else I wouldn't have got off at all."

"Four days," murmured Marjorie. She looked up, and met his eyes, and stared, and could not look away. "It's a long, long time, four days," she said, without knowing what she was saying. All at once she put her hands over her eyes, and, pressing her head fiercely against Leonard's arm, she began to cry and to laugh, continuing to repeat, senselessly, "It's a long, long time."

And Leonard, trembling all over, kissed her on the back of her head, which was all he could reach.

They drew near to Richmond, the familiar avenues and the cool, trim lawn, and the great trees. Majorie's tongue all at once loosened; she chattered whimsically, like an excited child.

"It's home, home, home, and they're all waiting for us — mater and your father, and all the family. He's been in a perfect state all day, poor old dear, though he hasn't an idea any one's noticed it. Little Herbert's the only one that's behaved a bit natural — and old Nannie. I've been rushing about your room, sitting in all the chairs, and saying, 'To-night he'll be sitting in this chair; to-night he may be standing in this very spot before the fire; to-night he may be looking out of this window.' O, Len, we're to be married at half-past eight, and we're going in motors so as not to waste any time. I haven't even read over the marriage service. I haven't the vaguest idea what to do or say. But what difference does that make! Do you see, Len? Do you see?" She stopped and squeezed Leonard's hand, for she saw that he was suddenly speechless. "There they are," lifting the blind, "mother and little Herbert; and see the servants peeking from the wing."

They swept grandly around the bend in the avenue. The windows of the great house blazed a welcome. All the sky was mother-of-pearl and tender. In the air was the tang of spring. In the white light Marjorie saw Leonard's lips quiver and he frowned. She had a sudden twinge of jealousy, swallowed up by an immense tenderness.

"There's mother," he said.

"Hello, Len, old boy."

His father was on the steps. Leonard greeted him with the restraint and the jocose matter-of-factness that exist between men who love each other. He kissed his mother a little hungrily, just as he had when he was a small boy back from his first homesick term at Eton, and fluttered the heart of that frail, austere lady, who had borne this big, strapping boy — a feat of which she was sedately but passionately proud.

Little Herbert, all clumsiness and fat legs and arms, did a good deal of hugging and squealing, and Miss Shake, Leonard's old governess, wept discreetly and worshipfully in the background.

"Look at 'im! Ain't he grand? Glory be to God — bless 'im, my baby!"

cried Irish Nannie, who had suckled this soldier of England; and loudly she wept, her pride and her joy unrebuked and unashamed.

At the risk of annoying Leonard, they must follow him about, waiting upon him at tea-time, touching him wistfully, wonderingly, for was it not himself, their own Leonard, who had come back to them for a few days? And instead of himself, it might have been just a name,—Leonard Leeds,—one among a list of hundreds of others; and written opposite each name one of the three words, *Wounded, Missing, Dead.*

Jealously his own family drew aside and let Marjorie go upstairs with him alone. She had the first right; she was his bride. Mr. Leeds plucked little Herbert back by his sailor collar and put his arm through his wife's. Together they watched the two slender figures ascending the broad staircase. Each parent was thinking, "He's hers now, and they're young. We mustn't be selfish, they have such a short time to be happy in, poor dears."

"Looks fit, doesn't he?" said the father, cheerfully, patting his wife's arm. Inwardly he was thinking, "How fortunate no woman can appreciate all that boy has been through!"

"Do you think so? I thought he looked terribly thin," she answered, absently. To herself she was saying, "No one—not even his father—will ever know what that boy has seen and suffered."

Little Herbert, watching with big eyes, suddenly wriggled his hand from his father's grasp.

"Wait, Leonard, wait for me! I am coming!"

Upstairs old Nannie was officiating. She was struggling with Leonard's kit, which resembled, she thought, more the rummage box of a gypsy pedler than the luggage of a gentleman.

The young officer had taken off his great-coat and was standing with his back to the hearth. He loomed up very big in the demure room, a slender, boyish figure, still too slim for his shoulder-width and height, clad in a ragged uniform, a pistol bulging from one hip at his belt. He looked about him at the bright hangings, with a wandering gaze that reverted to a spot of sunlight on Marjorie's hair and rested there.

"I'm all spinning round," he said with a puzzled smile, "like a dream."

He continued to stare with dazed, smiling eyes on the sunbeam. His hair was cropped close like a convict's, which accentuated the leanness of his face and the taut, rigid lines about his mouth. Under his discolored uniform, the body was spare almost to the point of emaciation. Through a rent in his coat, a ragged shirt revealed the bare skin. He looked at it ruefully, still smiling. "I'm rather a mess, I expect," he said. "Tried to fix up in the cars, but I was too far gone in dirt to succeed much."

Marjorie, with the instinct of a kitten that comforts its master, went up to him and rubbed her head against the torn arm.

"Don't," he said, hoarsely; "I'm too dirty." He put out a hand, and softly touched her dress. "Is it pink?" he asked, "or does it only look so in this light? It feels awfully downy and nice."

She noticed that two of his nails were crushed and discolored, and the half of one was torn away. She bent down and kissed it, to hide the tears which were choking her. She felt his eyes on her, and she knew that look which made her whole being ache with tenderness — that numb, dazed look. She had seen it before in the eyes of very young soldiers home on their first leave — mute young eyes that contained the unutterable secrets of the battlefield, but revealed none. She had seen them since she came to England, sitting with their elders, gray-haired fathers who talked war, war, war, while the young tongues — once so easily braggart — remained speechless.

What had they seen, these silent youngsters — sensitive, joyous children, whom the present day had nurtured so cleanly and so tenderly? Their bringing-up had been the complex result of so much enlightened effort. War, pestilence, famine, slaughter, were only names in a history book to them. They thought hardship was sport. A blithe summer month had plunged them into the most terrible war of the scarred old earth. The battlefields where they had mustered, stunned, but tingling with vigor and eagerness, were becoming the vast cemeteries of their generation. The field where lay the young dead was their place in the sun. The still hospital where lay the maimed was their part in a civilization whose sincerity they had trusted as little children trust in the perfection of their parents.

Besides the army of maimed and fallen boys was another shadowy army of girls in their teens and sweet early twenties — the unclaimed contemporaries of a buried generation.

There was a fumbling at the door-handle, and a small, muffled voice came from the corridor: —

"I say, Len; I say, Marjorie, can I come in?" And in he walked, spotless and engaging, in a white sailor suit with baggy long trousers, his hair still wet from being tortured into corkscrew curls. "I'm all dressed for the party," he announced; "I'm not going to bed at all to-night."

Marjorie tried to draw him into her lap, but he eluded her with a resentful wiggle, and walking up to Leonard, whacked him on the thigh and looked up with a sly, beseeching glance which said, "Whack me back. You play with me. You notice me. I love you."

His eyes were on a level with Leonard's pistol; he put his little pink face close to it lovingly, but drew back again, puckering up his small nose.

"Oh, Leonard, you smell just like a poor man!" he exclaimed.

Leonard grinned. "You never got as near as this to any poor man who is half as dirty as I am, old dear."

"You've got just half an hour to dress for dinner, and we're due in the church at eight," said Marjorie.

She paused in the doorway, a slim figure in a crumpled white dress.

Leonard stared at her blankly, and then put out a bony arm and drew her to his side.

"It's awfully tough on you, honey, to have it this way; no new clothes or anything fixed up, and," he added, smiling and closing his eyes, "coming away across the ocean full of dirty little submarines to a bridegroom smelling like a poor man! Jove! I want a bath!"

"Just as I was about to take the liberty of remarking myself," old Nannie said. She was standing in the doorway, her arms akimbo and her sleeves rolled up. "Captain Leeds, it's all ready."

Leonard's arms were still about Marjorie. "Captain Leeds, otherwise known as Lieutenant Leeds," he said, "once known as Leonard, presents his compliments to Mrs. Bridget O'Garrity, née Flannagan, and wishes her to request Mr. Jakes, in the culinary regions, to draw his bath and lay out his things and generally make himself a nuisance. He will not permit Mrs. O'Garrity to dress him."

"Oh, now, Captain Leeds — well then, Leonard dearie, you bad boy," wailed the old woman reproachfully. "Mr. Jakes has gone to the war, as has likewise all the men in the house, and a good riddance it is, too. There was a time when you weren't too grand to let your poor old Nannie wait on you. Why, Miss Marjorie, I remember the time when he couldn't — "

"No reminiscences!" broke in Leonard, eyeing Nannie suspiciously. "You have had so much experience with men you ought to know how they hate it. Why, Marjorie, do you realize that Nannie has had five husbands?"

"Oh, Master Leonard, indade, it is only three!" cried Nannie, horrified.

"Seven," Leonard insisted; "it's a compliment. It only shows how fascinating you are with the polygamous sex. It was seven, only two never showed up after the wedding. I was to be the eighth, Marjie, only you came in between us."

"Master Leonard, I could smack you for talking like that! Don't listen to 'im, Miss Marjorie."

"Cheer up, old Nannie," continued Leonard; "there's still Kitchener. He's a bachelor and a woman-hater, but then, he's never met you, and he's even a greater hero than I am."

Nannie, aghast but delighted, advanced toward Leonard, shaking her gray curls. "H'm, h'm. Woman-haters, you say. I never met one, indade." Then, very coaxingly, "Didn't you bring your old Nannie a souvenir from the war?"

"Rather," said Leonard, indicating with his chin the rent on his shoulder. "How about this?"

"How about that?" said Nannie, her old eyes in their deep furrows gleaming with malice.

From behind her broad back she drew forth a round metal object that flashed in the firelight.

"It's a German helmet!" cried Marjorie.

"I want it!" shouted Herbert, stretching up his arms for the flashing plaything.

"It's mine," coaxed Marjorie, trying to wrest it from Nannie.

Leonard put out a swift hand, and held it aloft by the spike.

"Let me try it on," wheedled Marjorie, coaxing down his arm.

"You look like a baby Valkyrie," said Leonard, placing the helmet on her head; but he frowned.

Marjorie regarded herself in the mirror.

"This belonged to an officer of the Prussian guard," she said.

"It did. How did you know?"

Marjorie continued to stare at herself in the mirror as if she saw something there behind her own reflection. "The very first man who was ever in love with me wore a helmet like this," she said, suddenly, lifting enigmatic and mischievous eyes to Leonard.

"How many have there been since?" Leonard smiled, lazily.

"I can remember only the first and the last," said Marjorie.

Leonard laughed, but he could not see Marjorie's face. She was standing looking down at the gold eagle-crest, holding the helmet in both hands, carefully, timidly, as if it were a loaded weapon that might go off.

"Where did you get it, Len?" she asked, gravely.

"There's a crop of them coming up in France this summer," said Leonard.

"But seriously, Len?"

"Seriously, Marjorie." He took the helmet by the spike and put it on the mantel. "Lord knows, I'm not presenting that as a token of valor to any one. It belonged to a poor chap who died on the field the night I was wounded. My orderly packed it in my kit."

Marjorie drew a deep breath. "Oh, Len," she whispered, staring at the helmet. "How does it feel to kill a man?"

Leonard, smiling, shifted his position and answered, "No different from killing your first rabbit, if you don't sit down on the bank and watch it kick, and write poetry. Besides, you always have the pleasure of thinking it's a German rabbit."

"Oh, Len!"

"You're just one in a great big machine called England. It isn't your job to think," Leonard said. "For God's sake, lamb, don't cherish any fool Yankee pacifist notions. We are going to beat the Germans till every man Fritz of them is either dead or can't crawl off the field." His black fingers closed over Marjorie's. "Remember, after to-night you're an Englishwoman. You can't be a little American mongrel any more; not until I'm dead, anyway. Now I've got you, I'll never let you go!" He showed his teeth in a fierce, defiant smile, in which there was pathos. He knew what a life in the Dardanelles was worth. He put his cropped head close to Marjorie's. "Do you hate me for that, Marjie?"

Marjorie, pressing against him, felt the strength of his gaunt shoulder through his coat. A sense of delicious fear stole over her, and the savage which lies close to the surface in every woman leaped within her.

"I love you for it!" she cried.

"Don't rub your head against my coat," murmured Leonard; "there's bugs in it."

They both laughed excitedly.

II

Two hours later the wedding took place in the church where Leonard had been baptized and confirmed. Little Herbert thought he had never been to such a strange party. He didn't care if he never went to one again. No one was dressed up but himself. The church was dark, and it seemed to Herbert so vast and strange at this late hour. Candles gleamed on the altar, at the end of a long, shadowy aisle. Their footsteps made no sound on the velvet carpet as they walked under the dim arches to the front seat. His aunts and his uncles and his brother's big friends from the training camp seemed suddenly to appear out of the shadows and silently fill the front rows. In the queer light he kept recognizing familiar faces that smiled and nodded at him in the dimness. Nannie was dressed in her "day-off" clothes. She was crying. Herbert looked about him wonderingly: yes, Miss Shake was crying, too — and that lady in the black veil over there: oh, how she was crying! No; he didn't like this party.

Through a little space between his father's arm and a stone pillar he could see Leonard's back. Leonard was standing on the white stone steps, very straight. Then he kneeled down, and Herbert heard his sword click on the stone floor. The minister, dressed in a white and purple robe, with one arm outstretched, was talking to him in a sing-song voice. Herbert couldn't see Marjorie, the pillar was in the way; but he felt that she was there. Leonard's voice sounded frightened and muffled, not a bit like himself, but he heard Marjorie's voice just as plain as anything —

"Till death us do part."

Presently the choir began to sing, and his mother found the place in the hymn-book. Herbert couldn't read, but he knew the hymn. Each verse ended, —

Rejoice, rejoice,
Rejoice, give thanks, and sing.

Herbert looked on the hymn-book and pretended he was reading. The book trembled. Leonard and Marjorie were passing close to the pew. They looked, oh, so pleased! Leonard smiled at his mother, and she smiled back. She lifted Herbert up on the seat and he watched them pass down the dark aisle together and out through the shadowy door-way at the very end. The little boy felt a vague sensation of distress. He looked up at his mother and the distress grew. She was still singing, but her mouth kept getting queerer and queerer as she came to the line, —

— give thanks, and sing.

He had never seen his mother cry before. He didn't suppose she could cry. She was grown up. You don't expect grown-up people, like your mother, to cry — except, of course, Nannie and Miss Shake.

Rejoice, rejoice,
Rejoice, give thanks, and sing.

He sang it for her. The voices of the choir seemed suddenly to have traveled a long way off and the tones of the organ were hushed. He heard his own voice echoing in the silent church. The words seemed to come out all wrong. He felt a terrible sense of oppression in the region of his stomach, and he wondered if he were going to be ill. It was a relief to hear himself crying at the top of his lungs, and to have Nannie scolding him lovingly, and leading him out of the church. He drove home, sniffing but comforted, in his father's lap.

"He felt it," old Nannie said to Burns, as she lifted him out of the carriage. "The child understood, bless him!"

III

Ever, when it comes May, and the soft, chill breezes blow from the ocean across the sun-soaked sands, and the clouds run dazzling races with the sea gulls, Marjorie will feel herself running too, catching up breathless a few paces behind Leonard, as on that second afternoon on a wind-swept beach of the Kentish coast. Like mad things, their heads thrown back, hair flying, mouths open, the spray smiting their open eyes, with all the ecstasy of their new-found energy, they clambered over the slippery seaweed and leaped from rock to rock, swept along with the winds, daring the waves, shouting down the surf.

Marjorie, when those spring days come round again, will remember a little cove, sheltered from the wind, warmed by the fitful spring sunlight, where, panting, they threw themselves down on the sand, bodies glowing, faces to the sun.

"Hello, sun!" cried Marjorie.

"Hello, clouds!" cried Leonard.

"Hello, old sea gulls!" cried Marjorie, beginning to sneeze.

"God, but I feel fit; I feel glorious! Don't you, Marjie?"

"Don't I, though! I feel glorious. O God!" cried Marjorie, who did not know whether that was swearing or praying, and did not care.

Leonard ran his hands through the chill, warm sand, and watched a huge black spider promenading with bustling importance up his arm.

"The female spider eats the male as soon as he fertilizes the eggs, but he has to just the same," said Leonard, dreamily.

"Let's kill her," said Marjorie.

"No."

"Yes."

"Why?"

"She's a cannibal," said Marjorie.

"No, it's her instinct," said Leonard.

He opened an alleyway for the spider in the sand, and, with his head down close, watched it hustling away. "It's the same with us; we know we have every chance of being killed in this war, and we have to go, and we're glad to. It's not courage or sacrifice; it's instinct."

"You think so, Leonard?"

"It's not nice to lie alongside of a man you've killed and watch him die," said Leonard, inconsistently, eyes looking down into the sand, head pillowed on his arm.

"Did you have to, Len?"

"I didn't exactly mean to kill him. He was wounded," murmured Leonard, raising little white pools in the sand with his nostrils. "We had a rotten day and had taken a small position which didn't amount to anything when we got it. *Wasn't* I in a nasty sulk! Some of my green men had funked just at the crucial moment, and I had all but shot one. The ground was covered with wounded. Couldn't tell theirs from ours. Awful mess. I was coming back across the field over dead bodies, and cursing every one I stumbled across. I suppose I felt pretty sick. I saw a helmet gleaming in some burnt shrubbery. It was a nice shiny one, with an eagle crest. It occurred to me you'd written me to send you one, 'because all the girls had them'—remember?"

Leonard rolled over close beside her and his head went down into the sand again.

"I went to pick it up, but it seems I got something else with it. A great blonde fellow in gray, all powdered with dust and bleeding,—Jove! how he was bleeding!—came up with it. It surprised me and he managed to knife me, and over I went, on top of him. I had my pistol cocked, and I let him have it right in the chest. I must have fainted, because when I came to I was on my back and the moon was shining in my eyes. The man in gray was there alongside of me, supporting himself on one arm and looking at me.

" 'I am dying,' he said in German.

"That didn't seem very interesting to me. So is everybody else, I thought; and I didn't answer. Presently he said it again, in English: 'I'm dying.'

" 'Really?' said I.

" 'Yes,' he answered.

"There was something impersonal in his tone, and he looked eery there in the moonlight, I can tell you, leaning on one arm and bleeding. Awfully good-looking chap. Built like a giant. He reminded me of a statue called the Dying Gaul, or something."

"Oh, yes; I know that statue!"

"Well, he looked like that — with all the fight going out of him. Suddenly he smiled at me.

" 'Did you think you were playing your football when you came down on top of me that way, eh?'

"I say, I was a bit surprised. Football doesn't seem a very congenial subject for a dying man; but do you know, we sat there and talked for an hour at least about all kinds of sports and athletics. You should have seen the way he kept tossing the hair out of his eyes and saying, 'Fine, fine!' And then he'd boast, and tell me all about the things he'd done. I never saw a fellow built as he was. It seems that he was a champion in most everything. But after a while he seemed to get on to the fact that he was losing an awful lot of blood, and then he said again, 'Schade.' That was all. After two or three foolish tries I got up on my feet. The last I saw of him he was supporting himself on his arm, and looking for all the world like that statue.

"They'd cleared off all the wounded, and only the dead were left. It was terribly still, and I could hear him choking, a long way off, as I came back across the lines. The next day I happened to stumble across him. It was bright sunshine, and he was like marble, and the ground all about was sticky. He was staring up in the sun with his head thrown back and his eyes open, and the strangest look! Well, anyway, it made me think of a chap I saw once make a ripplingly clever catch at ball, with the sun shining straight in his eyes, while the crowds went wild, and he didn't know what had happened for a minute. — His helmet was still there beside him, keeping guard, sort of like a dog, and I took it back with me. I don't know why."

Leonard paused; then he said, suddenly, averting his eyes like a child caught in a wrong act, "That talk we had was so queer — I mean it was as if — don't you know? — as if we were — well, sort of the same at heart. I mean, of course, if he hadn't been German. War is queer," he continued, lamely, raising his cropped head and looking off at the horizon, "awfully queer."

Presently he spoke again.

"So many men have been killed — Englishmen I mean; almost all the men I went to school with." He started to count as if by rote: "Don and Robert, and Fred Sands, and Steve, and Philip and Sandy." His voice was muffled in the sand. "Benjamin Robb and Cyril and Eustis, Rupert and Ted and Fat — good old Fat!"

Lying close to Marjorie on the sand, his mighty young body still hot from the joyous contact of the noonday sun, his eyes, full of an uncomplaining and uncomprehending agony, sought hers; and Marjorie looked dumbly back with a feeling of desolation growing within her as vast and dreary as the gray expanse lapping beside them, for it seemed to her that Leonard was groping, pleading — oh, so silently — for an explanation, an inspiration deeper than anything he had known before — a something immense that would make it all right, this gigantic twentieth-century work of killing; square it with the ideals and ideas that this most enlightened century had given him.

Marjorie strangled a fierce tide of feeling that welled up within her, and her eyes, bent on Leonard, were fierce because she loved him most and she had nothing, nothing to give him. For he had to go back, oh, he had to go back to-morrow, and he hated it so — they all hated it — the best of them! How clearly she saw through the superb, pitiful bluff, that it was all sport, "wonderful"! Wonderful? She knew, but she would never dare let Leonard see that she knew.

And still Leonard counted, his head in his arms: "Arnold and Allen, and Rothwood, and Jim Douglas, and Jack and — Oh, Christ! I can't count them all!"

IV

They came up to London in a second-class compartment. Any one could have told they were on their honeymoon, for they wore perfectly new clothes, and on their knees between them they balanced a perfectly new tea-basket. They were making tea and sandwiches, and although it was all rather messy, it gave them the illusion of housekeeping. It was the afternoon of the fourth day. An old lady and gentleman, their only traveling companions, went tactfully to sleep. Leonard glanced warily at them, and turned his back on the flying landscape.

"Marjorie," he said, carefully peeling a hard-boiled egg; "Marjie."

"Yes, Len."

"Were you ever in love before this?"

Marjorie laughed. She was in the mood for laughter. She must be happy and light-hearted. Time enough later on to be serious.

"Sure," she replied gravely, mocking eyes on Leonard. "Weren't you?"

Leonard shook his head. "Just with actresses and things, when I was a kid. Never, really."

"I suppose," said Marjorie, pensively, "I ought to care if you've been bad or not, but I don't."

"But Marjie, darling," — Leonard brought her back and went straight to his point,—"were you ever really in love with that German chap you spoke of when I gave you the helmet?"

"He was my first love," said Marjorie, with wicked demureness. "I was fifteen and he was eighteen."

"You were just a flapper," said Leonard; "you couldn't be in love."

"A woman is never too young to adore some man," said Marjorie, sagely. "I was a miserable homesick wretch, spending the winter in a German boarding-school."

"A German school! What for?" said Leonard, frowning.

"In order to learn German—and culture."

Leonard gave a grunt.

"Yes, Len, dear, it was dreadful. You never could have stood it, you're so particular," Marjorie said, settling her head against Leonard's arm. "The girls only bathed once a year!"

"Dirty beasts!" muttered Leonard. "But what's that got to do with the point?"

"I'm preparing you for that by degrees. Len, dear, it was dreadful. No one spoke a word of English, and I couldn't speak a word of German, and it was such a long winter, and all the flowers and grass were dead in the garden, and at night a huge walnut tree used to rattle against my window and scare me; and they don't open their windows at night, and I nearly died of suffocation! They think in Germany that the night air is poisonous."

"They don't use it instead of gas. How about the man? Hurry up!"

He looked at his watch, but Marjorie chose to ignore him.

"We've got eleven hours," she said, with tragic contentment; "I'm coming to the man. The girls used to sit about indoors and embroider—oh, everlastingly! Hideous things. I was, oh, so restless! You know how you are at that age."

"I was playing football," said Leonard; "so ought the man to have been, instead of casting sheep's eyes at you."

"He had nice eyes," said Marjorie, pensively, "and lived next door, and," she added, as Leonard puffed stolidly at his pipe, "he was terribly good-looking."

"He was?" said Leonard, raising his eyebrows.

"So tall for his age, and his head always looked as if he were racing against the wind. He was always rumpling his hair as if in a sort of frenzy of energy, and he was awkward and graceful at the same time, like a big puppy who is going to be awfully strong. He was like a big, very young dog. So energetic, it was almost as if he were hungry."

"He's hungry along with the rest of 'em now, I hope," murmured Leonard.

"His name was Carl von Ehnheim. He lived in a very grand house next door," continued Marjorie, "and he used to come over and make formal calls on the pension Müller. He never looked at me, and whenever I spoke he looked down or out of the window, and that's how I knew he liked me."

"Most abominable case of puppy love," said Leonard.

"Oh, it was *so* puppy!" cried Marjorie; "but of course it made the winter pass less drearily."

"How so — 'of course'?"

"Because he would always happen to come down his steps when I came down mine. Or when I was in the garden walking on the frozen walk with huge German overshoes on, he would draw aside the curtain of his house and stand there pretending not to see me until I bowed, and then he would smile and pretend he had just noticed me. And then, when Christmas came, all the girls went home, and Frau Müller and I were asked over to his house to spend the day. Did you ever spend a Christmas in Germany, Len, dear?"

"No, but I hope to some day."

"It's so nice, it's like Christmas in a book. He used to come into the garden after that, and we'd play together. And we read German lesson-books in the summer-house. And then, sometimes, for no reason at all, we would run around the summer-house until we were all out of breath, and had messed up all the paths. One day he had to go away. It was time for him to go into the army to be made an officer, and I didn't see him for so long, and I forgot all about him, nearly. I would have if I hadn't been so lonely."

"Humph!" said Leonard; and Marjorie squeezed his fingers.

"Aren't you just a little bit jealous?" she pleaded.

"Jealous of a Hun?" answered Leonard, knocking the ashes from his pipe. "No." But he squeezed her hand somewhat viciously in return. "Not a bit. Stop wriggling! Not a bit. When did you see him again?"

"Not for a long time. One day I came home and on the hall table was a gold sword and a gold helmet with an eagle crest. Maybe I heard his voice in the parlor, maybe I didn't. Anyway, I put the helmet on my head and took the sword out of the scabbard. Oh, wasn't it shiny! I was admiring myself in the mirror when he came out. — Stop whistling, Leonard, or I won't go on.

"He was dressed all in blue and gold, and he wore a gray cape lined with red, and oh, he looked like a picture in a fairy book, I can tell you, and he just stood there and stared at me. And he said, in a very low voice, 'I didn't dare to kiss you under the mistletoe.' And I wanted to say something, but couldn't think of anything because he wouldn't take his eyes away; and then Frau Müller came out and said 'Good-bye' to him with great formality. And afterward she said it was very *unziemlich* to talk to a young officer alone in the hall, and, oh, I don't know—a whole lot of things I didn't listen to."

"And of course that only fanned your ardor and you continued to meet?" prompted Leonard.

He lighted a pipe and stuck it in the corner of his mouth, and never took his smiling eyes off Marjorie's thin little face, all animated in the dusk.

"Of course we met, but only on the avenue, when we girls were walking in a long line, dressed alike, two by two, guarded by dragons of teachers. But I'd lie awake every night and think of all kinds of things—his look, and the way his sword clanked against his boots. And twice I saw him at the opera, looking at me from one of the boxes filled with officers. You can't think how big I felt having him notice me—and you can't think how beautiful I thought he was. Little thrills ran up and down my spine every time I looked at him. Is that the way you felt when you looked at your silly actresses?"

"Maybe," said Leonard, grinning with the corner of his mouth unoccupied by the pipe, and staring out into the shadowy darkness. "Was that all?"

They were drawing near to London.

"Mostly," answered Marjorie, fingering the buttons on Leonard's sleeve. "Last time I saw him it was in the garden on the same bench in the sun. He came over the fence, and he told me that his regiment had been ordered to Berlin the next day."

"You knew more German then?" asked Leonard.

"Yes, I suppose so; but I didn't need to understand. It was all in the sun, and the air was all warm from the cut clovers, and his eyes were, oh, so blue! And—I don't know. He took off his helmet and put it on my head, and he took his sword out of the scabbard and he put it in my hand, and he said, oh, all kinds of things in German that I couldn't understand very well."

"He was probably asking you how much your dowry was."

"Maybe, but his eyes didn't ask me that. And that was all. I never saw him again, and I don't ever expect to."

"Should rather think not."

"Would you mind?"

"Certainly," said Leonard.

"They're horrible tyrants, English husbands," said Marjie, kissing his arm.

"Not so bad as German ones," he replied, putting his head down to hers.

The casements rattled. Into the little dark square of the compartment window peered a confusion of lights, the myriad eyes of a great city.

"Why, it's London!" cried Marjorie. "I'd lost all track of time. Hadn't you, Leonard?"

"No," he answered laconically, slamming down the lid of the tea-basket.

But Marjorie squeezed up against him and gave a little laugh. "Supposing it could be the same man, Leonard," she said.

"What man?" asked Leonard, snapping the lock.

"Why, the man of the Helmet — the Dying Gaul — and my man I've been telling you about."

Leonard looked at her, and for some reason his eyes flinched. "What difference would that make? He was German," was all he said.

It was a sultry evening. Flowers were being sold in profusion on street-corners. Hurdy-gurdies played war tunes in the gutter. The streets were filled with soldiers in khaki, and florid civilians in their summer clothes. Suddenly she remembered a passage in the Bible that always seemed beautiful to her, but now it seemed to have been specially written for her: —

"Where thou goest, I will go, And where thou lodgest, I will lodge. Thy people shall be my people, And thy God, my God."

She walked as close to Leonard as she dared: "Thy people shall be my people, And thy God, my God."

The passers-by smiled at her and turned and stared after. "Awfully hard on a girl," they thought, touched by the rapt look on the young face.

"Oh, Len," she whispered, pulling at his arm, "I love all these people; I love England."

He smiled indulgently.

"They're all right," he assented; "I don't mind strangers, but I hate the thought of all the relatives we've got to face when we get back. There'll be Aunt Hortense and Uncle Charles. Mater'll have all the uncles and the cousins and the aunts in to bid me a tender farewell.

Think of spending my last evening with you answering questions about how deep the mud is in the trenches, and what we get to eat, and what the names of all the officers in my mess are."

"And then they'll spend the rest of our precious time connecting them up to people of the same name in England," said Marjorie.

"Exactly," agreed Leonard. "Aren't grown-up relations beastly?"

"Horrible," said Marjorie, "but they've been awfully decent about letting me have you all of these four days."

To put off the evil moment of arrival they stopped at every shop-window and stared in, their faces pressed close to the glass. Finally, deliciously weary, and full of the languor of the summer night, they retraced their steps and took the two-penny tube.

They arrived home late. The family were at dinner.

"We've missed two courses," said Leonard gleefully; "the aunts must be raging."

"Shall I dress up?" said Marjorie.

"Good God!" answered Leonard, "I go to-morrow at five. Don't wear anything that will make them think we're going to sit round and converse with Aunt Hortense all the evening. I'm going up to say good-bye to the boy."

Marjorie found him there, stretched out on Herbert's little cot, completely covering the little mound under the pink coverlet.

"Don't you come near, Marjorie; I've got Leonard all to myself," cried Herbert, who, like all the others, was jealous of Marjorie, but did not scruple to show it.

"Ha-ha! Who's jealous now?" said Leonard, putting his head down on Herbert's. Marjorie lay down on the quilt at the foot of the bed. Her restless eyes watched a light from the driveway scurry across the bed and zig-zag over the faces of the two brothers. Like a sudden flame struck from a match it lit a metal object on the shelf over the bed. Ah, it looked grim and incongruous in that peaceful English nursery! Once it had been one among a golden sea of helmets, sweeping across a great plain like a river. The sun smote upon gleaming bayonets, passing with the eternal regularity of waves. Last autumn the world had shaken under the tread of the feet marching toward Paris.

The light clung to the glittering object, and then scudded away. Marjorie's eyes kept closing. Suddenly, and oh, so vividly, there came the memory of another garden; the cold, brooding stillness of the winter air, and the sun sifting through the diamond windows of the summer-house, and shining on the dancing letters of the lesson-book and on his yellow hair. Then she heard Leonard's laughter and was back again in the present. How could he laugh like that! It was because he was so young. They were all so young!

"Good night, old man," said Leonard, pulling himself up from Herbert's bed; "don't forget me."

Three times Herbert called him back, and when Leonard returned and stood beside him, the little boy wriggled apologetically.

"Play with me," he said, plaintively.

"Play with you! I'll stand you on your head instead," said Leonard, and put his arm around Marjorie.

But Herbert continued to call to the emptiness.

Leonard and Marjorie paused on the landing, and he reached up and spread his hand over the face of the clock.

"Stop moving!" he said.

"You're just about three years old to-night," said Marjorie.

"I know — I know," he said. Suddenly, with an impulse and gesture of childlike and terrible longing, he put both his arms about Marjorie. His face wore an expression that she could never forget. Looking up at him with wide, tearless eyes, she felt in that one uncontrolled moment that she knew him better than she ever would again. She felt wonderfully old, immeasurably older than Leonard, older than the whole world. With a love almost impersonal in its unconscious motherliness, she yearned with the mighty power of her woman's body and soul to protect this immature and inarticulate being who was faring forth to the peninsula of the "Dead English" to make his silent sacrifice. The great house seemed to be listening, hushed, to the sober ticking of the clock on the landing. Suddenly, with a preliminary shudder, its melodious voice rang out nine times. The two stole downstairs to the dining-room.

"Nine o'clock. We've missed three courses," whispered Leonard to Marjorie.

All through dinner he sulked. He could not forgive his Aunt Hortense for her very considerable bulk, which was situated between him and Marjorie. He squeezed his mother's hand under the table, till her rings cut into her flesh, and she had to smile; but toward all the flattering advances of his aunt, and her effort to ascertain his opinion on every aspect of the war, he remained dumb with the maddening imperturbability of a sulky boy, who refuses to be "pumped."

After dinner he was claimed by his father and remained in the smoking-room, detained by a certain wistfulness in his father's manner.

"We've missed you these four days, old boy," his father said. "But I hardly expect you missed us. Can't we have a talk now?"

"Yes, sir; of course," Leonard answered. He felt suddenly contrite. He noticed for the first time in his life that his father looked old and little, almost wizened, and there was something deferential in his manner toward his big son that smote Leonard. It was as if he were saying, apologetically, "You're the bone and sinew of this country now. I admire you inordinately, my son. See, I defer to you; but do not treat me too much like a back number." It was apparent even in the way he handed Leonard the cigars.

Desperately conscious of the hands on the clock's face, which kept moving forward, Leonard sat and conversed on the recent drive in France, the Dardanelles campaign, home politics, held simply by the pathos of his father's new manner. At every pause in the conversation he listened for Marjorie's voice in the drawing-room.

And Marjorie, in the drawing-room, was wondering desperately if he knew how the time was flying as he sat there quietly smoking and holding forth endlessly about transports and supplies and appropriations, and all the things which meant nothing to her. More wily than Leonard, she had escaped from Aunt Hortense, who, in true English fashion, had not appeared to be aware of her presence until well on toward the middle of the evening, after the men had left; then she turned to Marjorie suddenly, raising her lorgnette.

"Leonard's letters must have been very interesting to your friends in America."

"Oh, yes," stammered Marjorie; "but he never said very much about the war." She blushed.

"Ah," said the older woman; "I observed he was very silent on that subject. It's a code or custom among his set in the army, you may be sure of that. So many young officers' letters have been published," she continued, turning to Mrs. Leeds. "Lady Alice Fryzel was telling me the other day that she was putting all her son's letters into book form."

Marjorie had an inward vision of Leonard's letters published in book form! She knew them by heart, written from the trenches in pencil on lined paper — "servant paper," Leonard called it. They came in open envelopes unstamped, except with the grim password "war zone." Long, tired letters; short, tired letters, corrected by the censor's red ink, and full of only "our own business," as Leonard said. Sometimes at the end there would be a postscript hastily inserted: "I was in my first real battle to-day. Can't say I enjoyed it." Or, "Ronald Lambert, who was my chum at Eton, never turned up to-night. I feel pretty sick about it." She remembered the postscript of his first letter from the front; not a word about the thunder of the distant cannonading or the long line of returning ambulances that greeted the incoming soldier. It gave the first realistic smack of the filthy business of war. "I've had my head shaved," Leonard wrote. "P.P.S. Caught One." Marjorie wondered how that would look to Aunt Hortense, published in book form.

"Aren't the men a long while?" said Mrs. Leeds, for the fifth time; and Marjorie could endure it no longer. She could not bear to sit there and look at Mrs. Leeds's face. The fierce resignation of the mother's eyes seemed dumbly to accuse Marjorie, whose whole youth and passionate being protested: "I won't let her have Leonard this evening—I won't—I can't—it's his last! Why don't old people, like Aunt Hortense, fight wars, if they're so crazy about it?"

She crept unnoticed to the dark alcove, and slipped through the curtains of the French window. But the older woman's shrewd glance followed her; and all the while she was listening with apparent composure and concern to Hortense, she was saying to herself with bitter impatience,—

"Fool! Why did she have to come this evening!" And then, "O Leonard, is it possible that little young thing can love you as I do!" And, "O Leonard—O Leonard!"

Marjorie, in the garden, skirted the shrubs and stole between the flower-beds to the library window. Vividly she could see Leonard, stretched out in a chair, his cigarette in one hand, gesticulating, talking.

"He's happy; he's forgotten all about me," she thought; and swept by an absurd emotion of self-pity, she kissed her own arms in the darkness to comfort herself, till her eyes, which never left his face, saw him turn warily and desperately to the clock.

"Leonard," she whispered, pressing close to the glass.

Suddenly he saw her revealed in the pale halo of light cast by the window into the darkness. He looked at her for moments without moving. Then she saw him get up and say good-night to his father, putting his hand awkwardly and self-consciously on his sleeve. Minutes passed, and she knew he had gone to say good-night to his mother, and then she saw the light of his cigarette coming toward her across the lawn. She waited without moving for him to touch her. So many times she would feel him coming toward her in the moonlight, the outline of his dear form lost in the dusk, and when he put out his hand it would be only empty shadows.

"Marjorie, where are you?"

"Here, Len."

Some one came to the front door and called out,—

"Are you there, Leonard and Marjorie? Lock the door when you come in, Leonard."

From the darkness they saw his mother's form silhouetted against the light inside. She started as if to come toward them, and then suddenly shut the door and left them alone together in the white night.

V

A thick yellow fog lay over London; at five o'clock in the Victoria Station the dawn had not penetrated, and the great globes of electricity in the murky ceiling shed an uncertain light. Through the usual sombre and preoccupied din of the early morning traffic, came the steady, rhythmic tread of marching feet. Lost in the smoke and fog, a band was playing "Rule Britannia."

Marjorie and Leonard were standing in the very centre of the vast dingy shed. Heavy-eyed, they looked about them with an unseeing, bewildered gaze, that kept reverting to each other. Marjorie had both her hands about one of Leonard's, and was holding it convulsively in the pocket of his great-coat. Many times she had pictured this last scene to herself, anticipating every detail. Even in these nightmares, she had always seen herself, with a sick heart, bearing up bravely for Leonard's sake, making it easier for him.

A hunchback, dodging under the elbows of the crowd, stared at her, and smiled queerly and whispered to himself. Marjie shivered, then forgot him as a spasmodic gasp ran through the crowd; a sound suddenly seemed to envelope her like a wave, breaking, gathering itself, then breaking again—just two words:—"Good-bye—Good-bye—Good-bye."

She looked into Leonard's face, and saw that the moment had arrived; he was going. She was gripped with a sense of suffocation and panic. It was the same feeling that she had experienced as a child when she had gone in wading and had slipped into the water over her head. She clung to Leonard now just as she had clung to her rescuer then.

"Don't go! Don't go! I can't bear it! O Leonard!"

His hand, disengaging itself from her fingers, increased her panic. He put his arm about her.

"Marjie," he said, in a steady voice, which yet sounded unreal, not like his own, "I'm going. Good-bye. I love you with my whole soul; I always will. I shan't be able to hear from you, but I'll write you as often as I can. Don't worry if there are long intervals between letters. And, Marjie, don't believe too easily that I'm dead. If you hear I'm missing, there is still a good chance; even if I'm on the lists, keep on hoping. I'm coming back. Good-bye." He kissed her, then paused, and put his dark head close to hers. "Marjie, if we should have one, — if it's a boy, — I want it brought up in England; and in case we should — promise me to take the best care of yourself — promise! That's right. Now stop trembling."

Marjorie nodded, with white lips, but continued to tremble. Leonard's face became equally white. He set his quivering mouth and turned away, but Marjorie clutched wildly at his sleeve.

"I'm coming with you as far as the boat, Leonard, just as far as the boat. See, those women are going. Oh, let me, Leonard!"

He hesitated, and in that empty moment a voice behind them said, "The average life of an officer in the Dardanelles is eleven days."

Leonard frowned; then glared at the hunchback, who was still peering at them.

"O Leonard, please, *please!*"

"You couldn't come back with them," he said painfully, averting his eyes from hers.

"Eleven days!" repeated an incredulous voice.

"I *will* come — I *will* come!" gasped Marjorie, trying to squeeze past Leonard through the gates.

He pushed her back peremptorily. His boyish face was pitiful in its determination.

"You go back," he said. He beckoned to a young officer who was standing in the crowd. "Stuart," he said, "will you see my wife to her carriage? She doesn't feel well. I'm going."

The soldier advanced. Marjorie glared at him with the eyes of an animal who sees her young taken away from her, and he drew back, his face full of pity. She threw one last despairing look at Leonard as he turned down the platform, and in that last glimpse of his strangely numb face she saw how he was suffering. She had a revulsion of feeling; a sense of desolate shame swept over her which, for a moment, surmounted her terror.

She had failed him! Behaved like a coward. Made it terrible for him at the very last. Oh, if he would only look at her again! The whole force of her despair went into that wish — and Leonard turned. A few yards farther down the platform he swung suddenly about, and finding her face among the crowd, he tilted his chin and flashed his white smile at her while his eyes lighted and his lips framed the word "Smile."

The band, which had been gathering impetus for the last moment, pealed forth "Rule Britannia." Marjorie smiled, smiled as she never had before, and kissed her hand. He waved his cap. It was among a forest of caps. The whistle shrieked. The guards slammed the doors. Through the fog the train was moving.

Rule, Britannia, rule the waves,
Britons never shall be slaves!

The crowds cheered. There came an acrid rush of smoke, which swallowed up the moving train with its cargo of khaki-clad boys. Above the cheering the hunchback, still dodging under the elbows of the crowd, was calling loudly,

"I came that they might have Life—Life—Life!"

The people stared down at the little sardonic face.

"Crazy?" they muttered.

The cripple shouted with laughter.

"Life—Life—Life!" he said.

When the smoke had cleared again, the tracks were empty, stretching away into blackness.

May 1917

BARTOLOMEO VANZETTI

1888–1927

The world has good cause to remember the fifteenth of April, 1920. On that day a factory paymaster and his guard in Braintree, Massachusetts, were shot and the payroll of $16,000 stolen. Evidence of a disputed character pointed to Sacco and Vanzetti, a shoemaker and a fish peddler. Both were very poor. Both were political radicals. Both were condemned to death.

The case was appealed. Conservatives and radicals made it their chosen ground of battle. Never have I been so acutely conscious of what class warfare means. No incitement to hatred was wanting. Both men were evaders of the draft. Both were revolutionaries. The I.W.W. supported the defense. Subscriptions were taken up. It was reported that a fund of five hundred thousand dollars was raised by labor to fight the battle of radicalism. From that moment in the opinion of many of us the men were doomed. Seven years were consumed in delays which seemed calculated to throw all criminal procedure into contempt, and what two men were permitted to suffer during that eternity seemed to tens of thousands a punishment cruel beyond understanding. The poison spread through Massachusetts, through the United States, through the world. A vulgar murder, like ten thousand others in this turbulent country, became the sign and symbol of class hatred, and throughout those seven years two convicted felons in whose innocence half the world believed suffered the tortures of Hell.

In the sixth year of the war, for war it was, the Atlantic *published an article summarizing the whole case, quietly written but of the highest explosive character, by Felix Frankfurter, then a professor in the Harvard Law School. There had been hundreds of indignant protests, but Professor Frankfurter's contribution seemed to canalize them all. So deeply was popular interest stirred, so poignant was the reflection that we might be witnessing a terrible miscarriage of justice that the Governor of Massachusetts, in whose hands rested the power to pardon, appointed three notable citizens to examine the evidence and to report upon it. It was commonly thought this meant the* release of the prisoners. But to the relief of many conservatives and to the consternation of others who were far from being in the radical camp, the report reaffirmed the conviction, and on August 23, 1927, the men were executed.

All this is common knowledge. I have no wish to retell the gruesome story, but the part played by the Atlantic in the fateful drama was to the magazine as well almost a matter of life or death. By countless readers it was held a lawless act, a flagrant interference with a matter still sub judice, which placed the Atlantic directly in contempt of court. Many went further. The Daily Worker or the New Masses might have published it and welcome, but that a magazine devoted to literature, dedicated to good breeding, should rouse the rabble by such an article and assault the due and orderly process of the law — the outrage was intolerable.

Against this the editor could only reflect that to discuss the case after due process of the law had completed its orderly course and the men had been executed would be but to print a cynical epitaph for the world to read, and after all, if a magazine is a living thing, as certainly it ought to be, it has its own personal conscience to consult.

During the first four years of this tortuous history I had thought little of the case. Murders were common. But in 1925, suffering from the ravages of a streptococcus (which to my thinking proves beyond cavil the existence of a Personal Devil), I sailed for South America. One evening at dusk I climbed the hill of Montevideo and there in the public square came face to face with immense hoardings. In letters a foot high I spelled out EL CRIMEN DEL BOSTON, the Crime of Boston, and beneath was printed a ringing appeal to the workers of the world to unite and save Sacco and Vanzetti, two innocent men, from the horror of a political execution. MURDER was the word printed there.

Then for the first time I understood that what confronted us might be not a crime but a Cause, and through my travels the impression deepened. The next spring found me in London. The former Lord Chancellor, Lord Haldane, had for many years been a kind friend to me. One evening I was dining alone with him at Queen Anne's Gate and, as I smoked his delicious cigar, he spoke to me in words of great earnestness: "You are a journalist, and a journalist has great responsibilities. In America two men widely believed to be innocent have for six years been subject to the tortures of the damned. Study that case and then speak out."

The very next day I lunched with John Galsworthy to whom human suffering was ever an outrage worse than death. He spoke with bitter directness. "Think," he said, "of those six years. You would not hold rats in a trap and let them suffer so."

The lawyer and the artist had spoken. The very day I returned to Boston I called up the counsel for Sacco and Vanzetti, my familiar and conservative friend, William G. Thompson. Thompson was a Tory by nature. How strange the fate which transformed this accomplished and intellectual lawyer, bred to loyalties not dissimilar from those which animated Sir Walter Scott toward the Duke of Buccleuch, Chieftain of his clan, into the Promethean defender of human injustice! At this distance I cannot quote his words, but he recalled his native tendency to temperate opinion and his lifelong opposition to radicalism. Yet so intense was his belief in his clients' innocence he said he had come to feel it were better the whole world should be consumed rather than that two guiltless men be murdered to save it.

I told Thompson I would drop everything and study the record, and then he reminded me that so intricate was the case I could not hope to grasp it, for we were working against time. But for months, he said, Professor Frankfurter had been absorbed in the task and his findings now verged on completion. From that day I worked with Frankfurter and so "The Case of Sacco and Vanzetti" was published in the Atlantic for March 1927. The effect reached far. The Atlantic was damned to the depths and praised to the skies, but there was now a focus for the burning issue. The Governor acted. President Lowell of Harvard, Judge Robert Grant, and President Samuel W. Stratton of the Massachusetts Institute of Technology were appointed a Board to review the evidence and report to Governor Fuller. In view of the excoriation which followed the judgment rendered by the Board, I can add a word of accurate personal testimony regarding the attitude of at least two of these gentlemen.

After the publication of the Atlantic article I had taken care to avoid society and saw few friends, but just before the Board was appointed, I dropped in at the Saturday Club where old and staid

Bostonians lunch together once a month. Mr. Lowell beckoned me to a seat beside him. "Are you bitter against me?" I asked. "No," he replied with emphasis, "you did the right and the honest thing." A fews days later I found myself sitting at a familiar dining club next to Judge Grant. It was the lawyer in him who spoke: "You have done an outrageous thing," he said. "You have attempted to interfere with the orderly procedure of the court. No man can tell whether these men are innocent or guilty without months of study. You had no right to speak through the Magazine." I avoided the issue. "I came here," I said, "not to be vituperated but to drink with you." His bitterness passed and we spent a happy evening.

Were Sacco and Vanzetti, one or both, guilty? Whatever is our conviction, we must remember that three prudent, intelligent and courageous citizens sat long in judgment and then approved the verdict. Innocent or guilty, Sacco was of a dull, unimaginative type that could hardly arouse intellectual sympathy and Vanzetti by his personal choice had elected to be tried with him. For myself I have thought much about Vanzetti. I believed that he ought in justice to have had a separate trial, and felt bitterly that his earlier counsel, who seemed to care little for a human life if only it would feed the bonfire which the I.W.W. was forever seeking to kindle, should have insisted the two men should be tried together.

The very night before his execution his attorney, William G. Thompson, visited Vanzetti and with infinite care took down his last words. These which appeared in the Atlantic I reprint below. Can such words as these be the final message to the world of a man with murder on his soul, who, believing in no other, has in this world left all hope behind? I cannot bring myself to think so. To me the message seems not unworthy to run deep in the mind of a reader who, closing the last immortal page of the Phaedo thinks of the spirit of Socrates.

Vanzetti's Last Statement

Monday, August 22, 1927

A RECORD BY W. G. THOMPSON

[The following document has no bearing upon the official record of the tragic case to which it forms the natural epilogue. But in human records its extraordinary character gives it a place unlike any other known to us.]

SACCO and Vanzetti were in the Death House in the State Prison at Charlestown. They fully understood that they were to die immediately after midnight. Mr. Ehrmann and I, having on their behalf exhausted every legal remedy which seemed to us available, had retired from the active conduct of the case, holding ourselves in readiness, however, to help their new counsel in any way we could.

I was in New Hampshire, where a message reached me from Vanzetti that he wanted to see me once more before he died. I immediately started for Boston with my son, reached the prison in the late afternoon or early evening, and was at once taken by the Warden to Vanzetti. He was in one of the three cells in a narrow room opening immediately to the chair. In the cell nearest the chair was Madeiros, in the middle one Sacco, and in the third I found Vanzetti. There was a small table in his cell, and when I entered the room he seemed to be writing. The iron bars on the front of the cell were so arranged as to leave at one place a wider space, through which what he needed could be handed to him. Vanzetti seemed to be expecting me; and when I entered he rose from his table, and with his characteristic smile reached through the space between the bars and grasped me warmly by the hand. It was intimated to me that I might sit in a chair in front of the cell, but not nearer the bars than a straight mark painted on the floor. This I did.

I had heard that the Governor had said that if Vanzetti would release his counsel in the Bridgewater case from their obligation not to disclose what he had said to them the public would be satisfied that he was guilty of that crime, and also of the South Braintree crime. I therefore began the interview by asking one of the two prison guards who sat at the other end of the room, about fifteen feet from where we were, to come to the front of the cell and listen to the questions I was about to ask Vanzetti and to his replies. I then asked Vanzetti if he had at any time said anything to Mr. Vahey or Mr. Graham which would warrant the inference that he was guilty of either crime. With great emphasis and obvious sincerity he answered no. He then said, what he had often said to me before, that Messrs. Vahey and Graham were not his personal choice, but became his lawyers at the urgent request of friends, who raised the money to pay them. He then told me certain things about their relations to him and about their conduct of the Bridgewater case, and what he had in fact told them. This on the next day I recorded, but will not here repeat.

I asked Vanzetti whether he would authorize me to waive on his behalf his privilege so far as Vahey and Graham were concerned. He readily assented to this, but imposed the condition that they should make whatever statement they saw fit to make in the presence of myself or some other friend, giving his reasons for this condition, which I also recorded.

The guard then returned to his seat.

I told Vanzetti that although my belief in his innocence had all the time been strengthened, both by my study of the evidence and by my increasing knowledge of his personality, yet there was a chance, however remote, that I might be mistaken; and that I thought he ought for my sake, in this closing hour of his life when nothing could save him, to give me his most solemn reassurance, both with respect to himself and with respect to Sacco. Vanzetti then told me quietly and calmly, and with a sincerity which I could not doubt, that I need have no anxiety about this matter; that both he and Sacco were absolutely innocent of the South Braintree crime, and that he (Vanzetti) was equally innocent of the Bridgewater crime; that while, looking back, he now realized more clearly than he ever had the grounds of the suspicion against him and Sacco, he felt that no allowance had been made for his ignorance of American points of view and habits of thought, or for his fear as a radical and almost as an outlaw, and that in reality he was convicted on evidence which would not have convicted him had he not been an anarchist, so that he was in a very real sense dying for his cause. He said it was a cause for which he was prepared to die. He said it was the cause of the upward progress of humanity, and the elimination of force from the world. He spoke with calmness, knowledge, and deep feeling. He said he was grateful to me for what I had done for him. He asked to be remembered to my wife and son. He spoke with emotion of his sister and of his family. He asked me to do what I could to clear his name, using the words "clear my name."

I asked him if he thought it would do any good for me or any friend to see Boda. He said he thought it would. He said he did not know Boda very well, but believed him to be an honest man, and thought possibly he might be able to give some evidence which would help to prove their innocence.

I then told Vanzetti that I hoped he would issue a public statement advising his friends against retaliating by violence and reprisal. I told him that, as I read history, the truth had little chance of prevailing when violence was followed by counter-violence. I said that, as he well knew, I could not subscribe to his views or to his philosophy of life; but that, on the other hand, I could not but respect any man who consistently lived up to altruistic principles, and was willing to give his life for them. I said that if I were mistaken, and if his views were true, nothing could retard their acceptance by the world more than the hate and fear that would be stirred up by violent reprisal. Vanzetti replied that, as I must well know, he desired no personal revenge for the cruelties inflicted upon him; but he said that, as he read history, every great cause for the benefit of humanity had had to fight for its existence against entrenched power and wrong, and that for this reason he could not give his friends such sweeping advice as I had urged. He added that in such struggles he was strongly opposed to any injury to women and children. He asked me to remember the cruelty of seven years of imprisonment, with alternating hopes and fears. He reminded me of the remarks attributed to Judge Thayer by certain witnesses, especially by Professor Richardson, and asked me what state of mind I thought such remarks indicated. He asked me how any candid man could believe that a judge capable of referring to men accused before him as "anarchistic bastards" could be impartial, and whether I thought that such refinement of cruelty as had been practised upon him and upon Sacco ought to go unpunished.

I replied that he well knew my own opinion of these matters, but that his arguments seemed to me not to meet the point I had raised, which was whether he did not prefer the prevalence of his opinions to the infliction of punishment upon persons, however richly he might think they deserved it. This led to a pause in the conversation.

Without directly replying to my question, Vanzetti then began to speak of the origin, early struggles, and progress of other great movements for human betterment. He said that all great altruistic movements originated in the brain of some man of genius, but later became misunderstood and perverted, both by popular ignorance and by sinister self-interest. He said that all great movements which struck at conservative standards, received opinions, established institutions, and human selfishness were at first met with violence and persecution. He referred to Socrates, Galileo, Giordano Bruno, and others whose names I do not now remember, some Italian and some Russian. He then referred to Christianity, and said that it began in simplicity and sincerity, which were met with persecution and oppression, but that it later passed quietly into ecclesiasticism and tyranny. I said I did not think that the progress of Christianity had been altogether checked by convention and ecclesiasticism, but that on the contrary it still made an appeal to thousands of simple people, and that the essence of the appeal was the supreme confidence shown by Jesus in the truth of His own views by forgiving, even when on the Cross, His enemies, persecutors, and slanderers.

Now, for the first and only time in the conversation, Vanzetti showed a feeling of personal resentment against his enemies. He spoke with eloquence of his sufferings, and asked me whether I thought it possible that he could forgive those who had persecuted and tortured him through seven years of inexpressible misery. I told him he knew how deeply I sympathized with him, and that I could not say that if I were in the same situation I should not have the same feeling; but I said that I had asked him to reflect upon the career of One infinitely superior to myself and to him, and upon a force infinitely greater than the force of hate and revenge. I said that in the long run the force to which the world would respond was the force of love and not of hate, and that I was suggesting to him to forgive his enemies, not for their sakes, but for his own peace of mind, and also because an example of such forgiveness would in the end be more powerful to win adherence to his cause or to a belief in his innocence than anything else that could be done.

There was another pause in the conversation. I arose and we stood gazing at each other for a minute or two in silence. Vanzetti finally said that he would think of what I had said.[1]

I then made a reference to the possibility of personal immortality, and

[1] It is credibly reported that when, a few hours later, Vanzetti was about to step into the chair, he paused, shook hands with the Warden and Deputy Warden and the guards, thanked them for their kindness to him, and, turning to the spectators, asked them to remember that he forgave some of his enemies. — W. G. T.

said that, although I thought I understood the difficulties of a belief in immortality, yet I felt sure that if there was a personal immortality he might hope to share it. This remark he received in silence.

He then returned to his discussion of the evil of the present organization of society, saying that the essence of the wrong was the opportunity it afforded persons who were powerful because of ability or strategic economic position to oppress the simple-minded and idealistic among their fellow men, and that he feared that nothing but violent resistance could ever overcome the selfishness which was the basis of the present organization of society and made the few willing to perpetuate a system which enabled them to exploit the many.

I have given only the substance of this conversation, but I think I have covered every point that was talked about and have presented a true picture of the general tenor of Vanzetti's remarks. Throughout the conversation, with the few exceptions I have mentioned, the thought that was uppermost in his mind was the truth of the ideas in which he believed for the betterment of humanity, and the chance they had of prevailing. I was impressed by the strength of Vanzetti's mind, and by the extent of his reading and knowledge. He did not talk like a fanatic. Although intensely convinced of the truth of his own views, he was still able to listen with calmness and with understanding to the expression of views with which he did not agree. In this closing scene the impression of him which had been gaining ground in my mind for three years was deepened and confirmed — that he was a man of powerful mind, of unselfish disposition, of seasoned character, and of devotion to high ideals. There was no sign of breaking down or of terror at approaching death. At parting he gave me a firm clasp of the hand and a steady glance, which revealed unmistakably the depth of his feeling and the firmness of his self-control.

I then turned to Sacco, who lay upon a cot bed in the adjoining cell and could easily have heard and undoubtedly did hear my conversation with Vanzetti. My conversation with Sacco was very brief. He rose from his cot, referred feelingly though in a general way to some points of disagreement between us in the past, said he hoped that our differences of opinion had not affected our personal relations, thanked me for what I had done for him, showed no sign of fear, shook hands with me firmly, and bade me good-bye. His manner also was one of absolute sincerity. It was magnanimous in him not to refer more specifically to our previous differences of opinion, because at the root of it all lay his conviction, often expressed to me, that all efforts on his behalf, either in court or with public authorities, would be useless, because no capitalistic society could afford to accord him justice. I had taken the contrary view; but at this last meeting he did not suggest that the result seemed to justify his view and not mine.[2]

February 1928

[2] I afterward talked with the prison guard to whom I have referred in this paper. He told me that after he returned to his seat he heard all that was said by Vanzetti and myself. The room was quiet and no other persons were talking. I showed the guard my complete notes of the interview, including what Vanzetti had told me about Messrs. Vahey and Graham. He read the notes carefully and said that they corresponded entirely with his memory except that I had omitted a remark made by Vanzetti about women and children. I then remembered the remark and added it to my memorandum. — W. G. T.

ALICE BACHE GOULD
1868–

Daughter of a famous astronomer, Alice Gould early distinguished herself in mathematics, and during the First World War taught navigation to naval cadets on the Great Lakes. For the past quarter-century she has been living in Spain, consumed with an historian's passion to rescue for immortality the lives of the individual sailors who, with Columbus, found a new world. Scores of them, now snatched from oblivion through her efforts, are recorded in the footnotes of famous books.

Miss Gould's quest has led her to strange places. The ancient Castillo of Simáncas near Valladolid now serves as a prison. Crime had not flourished thereabouts with the usual Spanish luxuriance, and to make use of the empty cells, the thrifty townsmen had stuffed the place with waste paper in the form of huge bundles of ancient documents useful for starting fires and irreplaceable to historians. When Miss Gould asked for the privilege of examining them, the jailor explained the impossibility of granting such a request to a woman. At that very instant a murderer was confined there, caught red-handed, his butcher knife dripping with his victim's blood. "Why Señorita, were you to enter you would be locked in with this miscreant from eight in the morning till six in the evening." Quietly Miss Gould replied that those were her working hours, and so the rusty gate was double-locked behind her. Each day the murderer sat huddled, sobbing in one corner, while the historian sorted and deciphered memoranda bearing the Arrows and the Yoke, sign manuals of Los Reyes, Isabella and Ferdinand.

About the "waste paper" which forms the background of Miss Gould's adventure: the reader can form some estimate of her labors when he learns that it consisted, according to the records, of thirty-three million documents which have been preserved since the days of Cardinal Ximenes.

The following story represents a diverting interlude in Miss Gould's labors. The reader cannot but remark parenthetically how pathetic and how hopeless is the effort to escape the limelight once it blazes about a man. Furtive amusements are not made for heroes. Between immortality and the pleasures of this life, they have to make their choice.

The Adventure of the Missing Fortnight

ALICE BACHE GOULD

I

THIS is the story of a little adventure in the Spanish archives. It was an adventure, not so much in the writing of history proper, as in the humbler field of making tools for the historian's use; and the tool in this case was an Itinerary of the Emperor Charles V.

Itineraries, or time-tables, showing where important personages were at any given time, have proved their value again and again. They are especially useful in checking documents whose date or whose genuineness may be challenged. A really careful itinerary is an instrument of precision, like any other gauge, and it means much arduous laboring over facts in themselves as unimportant as any scratch upon a vernier scale.

The Emperor Charles V very nearly broke the record for royal travel. He was the heir of all four grandparents, some of whom did more than twofold balls and treble sceptres carry. To this was added the Holy Empire and the whole New World *plus ultra.* Small wonder that he moved from capital to capital, and that, even with the help of his secretary's journal and his own memoirs, it is hard to follow him exactly.

To make a complete and scientific itinerary of Charles V, from his cradle in Ghent to his coffin in San Yuste, — and indeed the book has finally exceeded a little at each extreme, — giving his whereabouts on every day of more than fifty-eight years, with reference to the ultimate authority for every statement, was the task set for himself by a modern Spanish scholar. Don Manuel Foronda — now Marquis of that ilk and member of the Royal Academy of History, but then merely a well-born young Spanish lawyer and counselor of embassy — began in youth the accumulation of facts which he has recently published at the age of seventy-five. He published many small works on the way to the large one, — Charles V in this place and Charles V in that place,

Charles V considered as doing this, that, and the other, — and also a skeleton itinerary which we wish he would republish corrected for use by workers. His *magnum opus* is a magnificent thing; but ten pounds avoirdupois and three pounds sterling are a disheartening combination for ready reference.

Of course, three quarters of such compiling is straightforward drudgery with steady advance. Then come the disputed or ignored dates which require investigation, and the archives begin to yield their more uninteresting secrets. Finally, there remain some outposts of ignorance, some days when all that can be said is that we have no reason to suppose that the protagonist has gone anywhere or done anything. We have to leave him *in statu quo* — but with the mark of interrogation required by the modern scientific conscience.

Years rolled by, as the melodramas sum it up. Years rolled, and D. Manuel Foronda toiled, and at last the life was complete but for one single interval of about a fortnight. One little group of hypocritic days refused to look straight and be classified. Under their solemn fillets they looked scorn at the historian.

See what is the conscience of the modern maker of "scientific" history! For fifteen years Foronda held that book back — for fifteen years — and he, the author, was over sixty when at last it was ready except for the abhorred vacuum of that fortnight. In those fifteen years he became known as *el bou de los archiveros* — the bogy lying in wait for young archivists. I have heard it whispered that his later appeals met with little except courtesy — at least, not with solid work. "Can we by searching find out what is not there? Pray try, señora; it is all open to you. But I, have I not tried? In years gone by, when Foronda wanted other dates, I found them for him. I tried long for that fortnight and now — I try no more."

The days wanted were in 1538. On July 26, 1538, Charles leaves Barcelona for Valladolid. In early August he arrives — at least, in the latter part of that month he has been there for some time, and Foronda suggested the 9th for his arrival. The Secretary, Vandenesse, tells us he went to Valladolid, traveling *par ses journées,* to join the Empress. This contented the old-fashioned compilers; but a careful modern worker by the day notices at once, both that the number of days in the interval is too great, and that we know nothing of the route followed.

Many other times Charles crosses the Spains between those two places, and his progress is always traceable. So, when nothing can be found in

1538, one naturally looks for some unusual route. But when letters to the archives, whether of church or town, in every littlest hamlet that suggested itself had yielded nothing, and reiterated search in the large deposits of state papers seemed to make it certain that Charles had transacted no business that required his signature, then the perturbed biographer began to ask himself strange questions. If other intervals had not been filled up at last, it would have been less disconcerting. But that over fifty-eight years should be traceable day by day, in peace and war, in rain and shine, in better and worse fortune, and yet one consecutive fortnight be baffling; that half a dozen transferences between the same two places should be readable long after, because of addresses by the loyal, largesses by the monarch, household accounts, letters, state papers, diaries, pardons; and yet that another journey should leave no trace at all — all this was certainly queer. On the negative evidence D. Manuel ventured only two opinions: that Charles had not passed through Lerida, nor yet through Saragossa. But there was growing in his mind a suspicion that more than met the eye might be shadowed here. Monarchs have wanted to disappear before now.

It was a suggestive time for a mystery, for Charles had just returned from a very important conference. There had been an attempt at a triple meeting of Pope and Emperor and French King; but although the Pope came to Nice and talked with Charles and talked with Francis, he never could inveigle his two sons-in-Christ into his presence at the same time. At last, he fairly gave it up and went home, escorted for some distance by the Emperor, who, having thus astutely got rid of the third party, turned back and overtook Francis at Aigues-Mortes. A dramatic moment of pause — and then the royal brothers-in-law seek each other's arms, and "register" complete confidence and affection, so straitly embraced that Eleanor the Queen puts her arms about the two at once. Chroniclers dwell with affectionate detail upon the precious vessels, the crystal and the napery of the splendid banquet that followed, at which Eleanor and her step-daughter, the French princess Marguerite, brought water to wash the imperial hands after eating, and offered the damask napkins. But Charles would accept no personal service from such noble ladies. With graceful courtesy, he elected to wipe his mouth on the tablecloth instead.

A treaty for a ten years' peace is drawn up; the monarchs embrace and part; and Charles sails across to the Spanish coast, landing at Barcelona. The Empress, his Regent, is at Valladolid, and for Valladolid he is to start on July 26. The rest is silence.

Now there are certain possibilities in this situation. No reader of melodrama but guesses at once that Charles has crossed the Pyrenees and is secretly seeing Francis again—in an interview unknown to history. If not—why then one begins to think of that little affair of Hernani. Is there another Doña Sol in 1538? Where is Charles, and what is he doing? Apparently it is something that he preferred should not be known, and to the modern scientific historian that seems reason enough for trying to know it.

So for fifteen long years Foronda's book lay waiting, and D. Manuel himself wrote and searched and wondered. Then it seems to have been a chance comment by a friend that brought him to the sticking-place. Many friends had urged publication, and been told, "Not yet." But some well-intentioned person said to Foronda,—apropos of his being seventy-five years old,—"Don Manuel, what a pity it would be *if anything should happen* to prevent your ever publishing at all!"

"He put it politely—*but I knew perfectly well what the man meant.*"

And the result of this crystallizing feather touch was the final publication of Foronda's weighty tome, with an appeal in the preface to all and sundry, and in the hope, as D. Manuel said, that the very fact of owning to ignorance of those few days would guarantee his trustworthiness about all other days.

II

When I first saw Foronda's book, I was studying the discovery of America in one of the larger Spanish archives; and I was somewhat disheartened by the lack of answer to the broader questions I was putting to the dusty bundles. Was it that no answer could be given? or that I personally could not handle an archive? I wanted to test myself on something neatly asked. Spanish policies, streams of tendency, motives of legislators—all these are slippery matters; but "Where was the Emperor on August 1, 1538?"—this is so definite and safe and clear an inquiry. Either you know the answer, or you don't.

Moreover, I was distinctly intrigued by the appeal in Foronda's introduction, and by the story of his unavailing persistence. Other people's affairs are so interesting. Of course, the real reason for their charm is that one sheds all responsibility when one strays into bypaths, and any primroses pulled by the path are pure gain. From the beginning, I think that I meant to try for those missing days, though I was half ashamed to confess it to myself, even with the excuse that a new eye on a problem is an advantage. I have often witnessed what the language of the moment would call the "mobilization of ignorance," which sends ignoramuses rushing in where scholars fear to tread. Sometimes they come out with surprisingly valuable results, just because of the naïve unexpectedness of their points of view. I was at least free from all prejudice about Charles's doings in 1538.

It occurred to me at once that the uncertain date of arrival in Valladolid could be checked by the Empress's signatures as Regent. When did she stop signing? Most routine papers were executed by the Council, but certain things, mostly appointments and commissions, carry the royal *Yo el rey*. I sought the bundles where such papers were on file, and started a tabulation of signatures, and an hour or two gave me what I wanted.

Charles himself seemed to have signed none of the routine papers until quite late in the month; evidently he took things easily for some time after his arrival. As to the Empress Isabel — since I write without any of my own notes at hand, I cannot give exact numbers; but, speaking loosely, it was rare to find a day with no signature at all from her, and there were usually two or three daily, until August 11, when she suddenly took to signing more than a score of papers, and then she never signed again!

Evidently Foronda had put Charles's arrival too early, when he guessed it to be on the 9th, for the Regent would never have signed in Valladolid with the Emperor already present. Moreover, if human nature in the sixteenth century was my human nature today, that woman expected her lord on August 12. The score of signatures on the 11th meant that the Empress was cleaning up her desk.

This was not enough to send to Foronda, and it made the time Charles spent on the journey even longer than before. So, after struggling for some hours among the state papers of 1538, to the great amusement of an archivist who had already spent many a weary day among those bundles, I dropped the matter, with an inward vow that I would try again in Barcelona.

I was going to Barcelona for some weeks of early spring, partly on pleasure bent and partly to visit the Archivo de la Corona de Aragon. Besides more serious matters, I wanted to look there for a little freak of a fact reported fifty years ago by Bergenroth, who says that Ferdinand gave to the Venetian ambassador an island found by Columbus, together with the title in perpetuity of Count of the Cannibal Isle. This is pleasant enough, and an alternative name for the island, "Of Cannibals or of Roses," really adds another touch. The whole affair seemed to me deliciously improbable, and Bergenroth gives no reference; but the context showed in what papers he had been grubbing, and I wanted to grub a little on my own account. Let me in passing beg pardon of Bergenroth's most scholarly ghost, for I found the grant exactly as he says. It is a long paper in mediæval Latin, and the only doubt that remains to me is whether "roses" should not be translated with reference to a man's name and not to a rose-bush, though one hates not to leave such a choice as that between cannibals and roses to the taste and fancy of the speller.

But all this is beside the mark. I was bound for the Archivo de la Corona de Aragon, and I was trying to keep it a secret from myself that, wherever I went, I meant to append to my own legitimate work a somewhat shamefaced inquiry after the year 1538.

III

The Aragonese archive is beautifully arranged and excellently administered. But papers may be in Latin, Catalan, or Spanish, to say nothing of other languages. Secular and religious matters are kept apart, and the different kingdoms — Aragon, Sicily, Navarre, and so on — are all separately filed. Moreover, when one gets down to the ultimate divisions and the papers themselves, one finds that they have been bound into an order roughly chronological, but not always exact within the limits of any given month. I saw at once that it was no quick and easy thing to say surely whether any signature of a given date existed. To get out all the proper bundles, to find the place on the page where each document was dated, and then to see whether it was signed by council or by king, would mean a deal of drudgery, of fussy, nervously irritating, meticulous, what the Scotch call "fikey" little labors, petty and persistent. To plod one's weary way through twenty or thirty pages in each of twenty or thirty books, would be so disagreeable that, if any of Foronda's searching had been done by copyists who search for a price, it was likely enough not to have been done thoroughly. With a certain furtiveness, telling myself that it was merely for amusement, I began to search a book or two in a day, in odds and ends of time.

There followed the reward that sometimes falls to one through sheer luck. One morning, as I was languidly turning over successive documents without even trying to read more than the endings, I suddenly sat up electrified. I was staring at an ending plainly written, as plain as if it had been in print — *De Lerida, último de Julio de 1538. Yo el Rey.*

Lerida! Directly on the road to Saragossa, and just the reasonable time after leaving Barcelona! The document itself was perfectly uninteresting — a letter about the affairs of some obscure person who had appealed to Cæsar; but I dropped the search for the Count of the Cannibals, whose Latin title had not yet gladdened my eyes; I dropped Columbus and all his companions; I came forward more than forty years, to 1538, and attacked the thing in earnest. A few days' livelier work yielded five signatures and three stopping-places, taking Charles as far as Saragossa on August 4. Here the trail was lost again. There was one straight road to Valladolid; but, if he arrived on the 12th, he was still taking too many days for the journey. Had he lingered in Saragossa? Was the key to the affair in that city?

The head of the archives, to whom I carried my trove, was very sympathetic and very much amused. From his professional point of view, the really funny thing was the emotion that would be felt by those who had assured Foronda that all the books had been thoroughly searched. He gave me the names of certain excellent investigators who had committed themselves to the nonexistence of any such dates. One such person — of national reputation — was even then downstairs. "Señora, he is not likely to think it as amusing as we think it!"

There was another person downstairs, a man who would take photostat prints, both good and cheap. This was luck, indeed, for such prints are not always to be had; and I promptly secured reproductions of all five documents.

Now for my own good reasons, connected with violets and blossoming groves of orange, with roses and the blue Mediterranean, I meant to go by Tarragona to Valencia, before turning north again. Valencia was much in my thoughts, and I instinctively noticed it whenever it came to the fore in my miscellaneous reading. I noticed for instance that just at this time, in July and August of 1538, the viceroy in Valencia was sore vexed by pirates off the coast making descents on little towns near by. It was not the famous pirate Barbarossa, whom Charles had himself chastised three years before; but just because of this recent fight with Barbarossa, Charles was likely to take much interest in the havoc wrought, and Saragossa was the point nearest Valencia, if one stopped on the direct road from Barcelona to Valladolid. Could it be that the Emperor had paused to send couriers to the south? If so, there would be letters in the Archivo Regional of Valencia. I meant to look in there at any rate, because I wanted some things about the Santangel family, whose persistent repetitions of a few Christian names (after christening began in that family) has confused many a good writer about Columbus's money affairs.

And in that archive I promptly found two other letters signed by Charles, both dated in Saragossa on August 4, with plenty of evidence of the anxiety of the Viceroy, the Duke of Calabria, who kept writing about those pirates both to Charles and to the Empress. Though the hearts of kings are bad guessing, I decided to adopt the theory that here we had at least one motive for a short delay in Saragossa, which would account for a lapse of days, and might be followed by travel at the ordinary speed.

Again my luck held. I received a call from a professor of history in the University of Valencia, who had run across my tracks so often that I had become a joke. "La mís" had always just preceded him. No Spanish peasant could pronounce my name, but "la mís," as who should say, the señorita, or the fräulein, was identification enough; and my tastes, whether *in re* manuscripts or meringues, amateur bull-fights or library hours, were continually brought out for comparison with his own. Indeed it is not from him alone that I know how the village confectioner in a certain upland village still urges the local *azucarillo* and a particular kind of cake as favorites with "la mís," therefore proper for all and any of these queer pilgrims of history who arrive from distant parts.

My caller had a keen sense of humor, as so many Spaniards have, and he invited me to consider my own existence dispassionately. I imagine he may have modified a first belief that there warn't no sich a person into an attempt to prove that "la mís" was a sun-myth, or perhaps some modern incarnation of the visiting moon. And when finally he heard (I don't know how) that "la mís" was actually in his own city, walking about his own library and university, it was too much for him. He presented himself at the desk of an archivist friend, and requested an immediate introduction to the mís-errant, who could even then be seen near the window, wrestling with the ramifications of the Santangel family.

When two writers-errant meet, they compare adventures. We were soon offering mutual sympathy on the way in which one finds all sorts of interesting things one doesn't want, while the longed-for things elude all capture. I was pursuing Christopher Columbus; the professor's subject just then was the Marquis of Brandenburg, second husband of Germaine de Foix. As far as I could gather, he had been selected because nobody knew anything about him. He was therefore what in my student days was called a good subject for a Ph.D. His own biographer assured me that he never did anything worth mention, except marry Germaine and attend a chapter of the Golden Fleece, both these things in Barcelona, in 1519. Germaine de Foix, let me remind the reader, is the young princess whom Ferdinand married after Isabella's death; she was, incidentally, his own great-half-niece,—or half-great-niece, if that sounds any better,—and naturally she outlived him. The marquis was a cadet of the electoral house of Brandenburg; and Charles may have turned an eye on the two Brandenburg votes of 1519, when he bestowed the hand of his step-grandmother and second-half-cousin on this one of his own young companions.

The marquis died early, and the Queen's third venture was a man of more importance, that very Duke of Calabria who was anxious about pirates in 1538. His tomb is one of the things to see in Valencia, though it is not the Queen, but a later duchess, who lies beside him. For my own satisfaction, I tried to formulate the connection between this last Duchess of Calabria and Isabella the Catholic. Spanish enables one to express neatly things like a brother's brother-in-law, or the other god-father of one's own godson, but Spanish saves me nothing if I want to say that one woman was the second wife of the third husband of the second wife of the only husband of the other. I might make the chain even longer, since the duchess too had been married before.

The professor had amassed a surprising amount of information about this so-frankly-uninteresting Brandenburg, husband *ad interim* of Queen Germaine; but queerly enough his marriage lines are not to be found, and even the exact day of the wedding is doubtful. We chatted on about this missing marriage record, and the many missing things I wanted, and the horrid probability that a little fact for which we toil and moil in vain may even then be lying, an unappreciated jewel, before some other scratcher-up of the heap. Bitterest of all, the little fact gets buried again, as if it had never come to the surface.

For my own part, I keep a collection of what I call staccato notes. For instance, is there anyone reading this who wishes to know that Isabella the Catholic bought an alarm-clock in 1496? Clocks are not in my line, but the books which I rather timidly consulted would seem to place the invention of portable alarm-clocks distinctly later than that. If anybody wants this fact, let me present it. The exact date and price have escaped my memory, but I have them in my notes the other side of the ocean.

My new friend and I felt alike on the moral obligation of keeping tab on what other folk are doing, in order that labor may not be wasted. Upon this hint I spoke of my latest adventure. "For instance," said I, not expecting to throw a thunderbolt, but merely illustrating the conversation, — "for instance, I have found documents signed by Charles in that interval for which Foronda has looked so long. Is it not whimsical in Fate to send them to me instead of to him?"

Tableau! My new-found professor was a personal friend of Foronda. I fancy he had himself pursued the hunt for those days in the same half-shamefaced way in which I had begun. At any rate, the effect upon him of this somewhat off-hand announcement was such as startled me.

"Señora!" he gasped after a speechless moment, "am I to understand that you know where Charles was during those days?"

I indicated that, simple as I sat there, at the service of God and of himself, I had my own opinion concerning Charles's whereabouts. "I have photographs of the documents," I added, becoming almost frightened by the man's expression.

"Señora! have you communicated with Foronda?"

"Not yet — I wanted to try a little longer — the record was not complete."

"Señora! for the love of God! Do you not know that Foronda takes his seat in the Academy of History within three weeks; that his inaugural discourse upon that itinerary must be printed beforehand! that he would rather have this information *now,* this week, than ever again — *now,* NOW!"

Truly I should have known it, and I could only plead that I had regarded Charles as a luxury, while Columbus and his companions were necessary business. The professor was polite, but he looked at me as I should look at a child whom I found playing with priceless first editions. "La mís," indeed! He went away, after bidding me lose no time in writing to Madrid, and offering to come and correct any Spanish letter for me at the hotel — this in answer to a feeble excuse which I proffered for doing things so slowly.

Accordingly I arranged my photographic reproductions, pasted the loose leaves together, and sketched my letter to Foronda, which was nearly ready when, on my return from another morning in the archives, I found the Professor of History with a minor archivist holding up the door of the hotel like a pair of caryatides. He had been told that I was not at home, but to avoid any possible chance of missing me, he had taken the liberty of posting himself in the entrance, instead of going to the drawing-room and calling on the other ladies in my party. He had a letter from Foronda!

Whether he had telegraphed, or merely written, I do not know. At any rate, he was taking no chances, and if one compares the Yankee and the Spaniard concerned in this matter, the national characteristics have got themselves rather mixed. Foronda's letter breathed amazement. For the love of God and his Holy Mother! is the classic exclamation — if he did not use those words, he meant them. If it were true that a person, an amateur, a foreigner, a Yanquí — and a woman! — was wandering about Spain, with his long-sought dates in her pocket! then for the love of heaven, while this lady was within reach, let his friend find out where she got them, how she knew! and *where* Charles was. Also, let him assure the lady that, if she would but share her knowledge, all glory and credit should be given her: he, Foronda, would — then followed, numbered (1), (2), (3), and so on, the things Foronda would do! He would announce it in print, he would proclaim it to the Academy; the name of that lady should, and so forth, and so forth.

The lady found herself inclined to laughter. Who was she, to be an accomplice, so long after the fact, in Charles's celebrated disappearance? But the solemnity of the occasion overwhelmed all temptation to be flippant. She assured the waiting historian that her constant intention had been to put that minute bit of information where it would do the most good. Certainly it would do no good to her or to Christopher Columbus, and she was deeply grateful for having been saved from further delay, even though the material was still so incomplete.

We had begun the business in the portal, to the great edification of the concierge, but we adjourned to a more fitting spot, and I went to fetch the evidence. I brought the photographs of the Barcelona documents, I produced the numbers of the Valencia documents. But might he take these photographs and see if he could get them off *certificados* in this evening's mail for Madrid? He might. He did. He returned to inspect and correct my own letter, and he declared — such was his agitation that it shook his judgment — that it was in faultless Spanish.

IV

I suppose I kept my rough draft of that letter, and I certainly have kept and treasured the answer to it, the first of many letters from my dear and honored friend the Marquis of Foronda. But both are on the other side of the Atlantic now, and I can reproduce only from memory. I developed with painful accuracy the case of Aladdin's window. When Aladdin wished to give the greatest possible pleasure to his father-in-law — so I began; but a foreign language made my would-be gracefulness rather elephantine — "on me," as the Irish would say, with their excellent feeling for the ethical dative. I remember explaining, "You, sir, must be Aladdin, and the public is in this case the father-in-law, and I" — here I found myself getting very much mixed as I proffered these few little inclosed gems to the detail of a jeweled pattern which even yet must be unfinished. I do not now remember how I managed to include myself in the compound father-in-law, but I do remember that I had no dictionary with me. I was traveling light, and I was supposed no longer to need a dictionary. At any rate, I know I ended with the reflection that, when the baffled sultan gave up the window, he had at least learned to appreciate the labor represented by the rest of the palace.

But where I flounder out of my depth in courtly tropes, a Spaniard glides serenely into port. The return letter addressed me by a combination of every title, French, English, and Spanish. "Señora of my utmost admiration and respect. The Spanish language is universally acknowledged to be the richest since the Tower of Babel. Nevertheless, señora, it does not contain sufficient words to express my gratitude. What an honor for my poor book, — nay, what an honor for history, for Charles, and for Spain herself, — that ladies traveling in her borders should be moved to occupy themselves with such matters!" There followed a kind and cordial invitation to come to Madrid at the time when he was to enter the Academy of History.

I did not go to the Academy meeting. I think I was alarmed at the prospect of the honor-giving hand, *monstrante digito,* under circumstances which would make it impossible for me to protest that I knew the size of a grain of sand, and knew the difference between productive erudition and sheer good luck. But I forthwith decided again to make the audacious attempt to find something in the great Archives of Simancas where so many had looked before me; and on the way there, to travel for myself from village to village, over the road from Saragossa to Valladolid, and see for myself whether anything remained in church or town records. This I did, in the company of two thrilled Spanish companions. The three white elephants, we used to call ourselves, as we noted the surprise we left in our wake. And it profited us nothing at all. Never a trace remained, so far as I could see, of the passage of the Emperor Charles; although perhaps four centuries hence someone may come upon traces of the passage of the three elephants.

We had a very good time, and were very courteously entreated, except by a single snappy old blind priest, who informed us that no one short of a *grande de España* ought to be interested in the doings of Charles the Emperor. But the results for history were just exactly nothing at all

— nothing externally, that is. Internally, I was revolving the question as never before, with the hope of taking it from some new angle.

And a new idea did come to me. The household accounts — expenses *de casa y boca* — have been a source of copious information, and if such royal accounts for 1538 had been extant, I believe that Foronda would not have experienced any difficulty. They are not to be found; but it occurred to me that there was a similar class of papers which had not been tried.

Some time before, when studying that very bundle in which I found the alarm-clock, I had noticed that couriers used to be paid by distance ridden, not by the time it took them to ride it. The bills used to state that they were sent from such a place to such a place, a distance of so many leagues, and they were then paid by the league. If this was true in 1538, and if Charles wrote to anybody about anything while on that journey; if, indeed, any of the secretaries accompanying him wrote any letters of importance, then, even though the letters themselves may have perished long ago, there is always the chance that the posting-bills are on file. Now I knew just where to call for such courier's accounts, although, indeed, anyone who has ventured on the vasty deep of archived papers feels like a Glendower calling for documents. Will they come? Would the postman's bills have gone where household bills go?

Reader, they had not gone! Perhaps because they were so totally uninteresting to anybody, there they were in duplicate, perfectly in order, absolutely easy to read. Heaven knows how long it was since anybody had opened that bundle, or "book" as the inventories call it. A "book" is distinguished by the simple and primitive binding process, which consists in punching a hole, putting a piece of string through it, and tying a looped knot. If you expect to be bound, you leave a little round blank spot in the upper left quarter of the page. If you fail to do this, a crescent cut is made, and the flap of each page is turned back. In years the round trap-door of course tears out, and little round bits of manuscript litter the shelves of every archive. Moreover, as the bundle is lifted by that string, of course it cuts through the paper in time. But so little had the couriers' books been touched that they were as if new.

And there — oh, triumph and delight! — I found exactly what I wanted. Charles's two principal secretaries, Los Cobos and Granvelle, were also crossing Spain, but farther to the north and slightly behind him, and from their three lines of route the couriers wove back and forth like shuttles, and then shot away for the courts of Hungary and

Bohemia. Above all, Charles was sending forward to the Empress at Valladolid, to tell her of his progress, and the Empress was sending couriers to greet him on his way, and it was always a payment for bearing our royal letters from such a place to such a place, on such a date. The whole route was perfectly clear; nay, heaven vouchsafed me one final reward, for I actually found a paper at Simancas which had been overlooked. It was a secretary's rough draft of a letter, — what would be replaced to-day by a press copy or typewritten duplicate, — and because it was full of corrections and was a mere rough unsigned copy, and had, moreover, its date tucked into a corner, no one had bothered to read it through. But it was another letter to the Duke of Calabria, who was still troubled about those pirates; it was sent from Aranda de Duero, the last stage before Valladolid, and it mentioned that they had been making forced marches in order to make up for the time lost, and that (if it were God's will) they would enter Valladolid to-morrow, August 12. It was written on the 11th — the very day when I had felt so sure that the Empress was clearing her desk. Truly, it was like the answer that proves the sum. Aladdin's tower was finished, and his window framed and glazed.

And will the reader please notice that the point of this story lies in its utter pointlessness? Charles was not doing anything at all. There was no mystery. It was the merest chance that had made those days recalcitrant; and if Foronda had published when he was only sixty, instead of waiting till he was seventy-five, his book would have served just as well for all historical purposes, but I should have missed one amusing episode of my life in Spain, and should have missed the friendship of the very most charming Spaniard whom I have known.

But what is the moral? Is it, "Do your work thoroughly"? or is it, "Scant your work sometimes"? Perhaps it is, "Trust the public, and appeal to 'Notes and Queries.'" "The thing that concerns you not, meddle not with" — this is an excellent maxim, but it doesn't seem to work out. "Mind your own business" (*ma non troppo*), would be a good motto for my collection of staccato notes.

Y así se escribe la historia — thus is history written. The Spaniard uses this little catchword with a shrug, but in its literal sense it indicates whole romances of modern adventure, when Pentapolin *del arremangado brazo* — he of the rolled up sleeves — prepares to dig the dust enclosed in archive cupboards.

July 1919

PHILIP CABOT

1872–1941

It was Philip Cabot's family which gave rise to the Bostonian aphorism of fifty years ago: "The Cabots are a tribe indigenous to Brookline. They have customs but no manners." Philip's father was the gentlest of philosophers, beloved companion and biographer of Emerson. His mother, a cousin of President Eliot, had both the penetration and the directness of her remarkable New England clan. Unassuaged by a single daughter, the seven sons were as rampageous a tribe of young barbarians as has disrupted family peace since the riots of Osbaldistone Hall. I speak from experience, for I cannot forget lunching with them on a Sunday when I was a freshman. Nobody answered the bell but shouts of war sounded from within. Pushing the door ajar, I came into violent collision with all seven engaged in the fraternal exercise of jamming one another's heads against the sharp pegs of coat hangers whilst, in the parlor beyond, I caught a glimpse of Mr. Elliot Cabot sitting beneath the bust of Emerson and as unruffled, motionless, and totally oblivious of the oaths and imprecations rising shrilly from the battle line. But out of the bedlam of their youth, grew stalwart men, and at least four of the seven sons turned into citizens of stature. Not the best known, Philip, to my thinking, was the most remarkable.

After careful preparation, Philip identified himself with public utilities. He threw his personal genius into solving the social problems to which they give rise, and developed a passion for righteousness such as I have hardly seen equaled. Success came to him. But almost at that instant he was struck by what all the doctors considered a fatal case of diabetes. "Phil has no business living," said his medical brother to me in Cabot phraseology. When I went to see him Philip told me of his predicament: "You see there were five of us in my diabetes class; four in the hospital, I at my desk. Two died last week, one is dying at this moment. I have just dismissed the doctor and I am taking active charge of my own case."

"Active" was an understatement. Everybody knows that sugar is

the end-all of diabetes cases, that insulin is their lifeline, and that the problem is to eat enough to support existence without trying to live a life. Cabot considered his own case. He had to work, he wanted to live, and suffering he could bear. Exercise, however painful, would tend to eliminate the sugar. He ate huge bowlfuls of unnourishing "roughage" which at least served as scaffolding to his empty belly, adding just enough nutriment to make activity possible. He rose at six, took an hour's horseback ride, drove himself to the edge of town, walked two miles to his work, then after a morning of intense concentration back again, and in the afternoon played eighteen holes of golf, creeping into bed almost crying aloud with hunger. Lest the outbursts of his agonized temper should antagonize her, he sent his daughter to lodge elsewhere. He hired a manservant on the express condition that the butler should close his ears to every cataract of involuntary curses. Throughout four hours daily given to his office he worked like a man possessed. His friends waited patiently for him to die, but die he would not. He could not afford to. Gradually his health improved and he lived on for twenty years.

During the most fruitful portion of his career Cabot served as professor at the Harvard Business School. There his influence was unique. Whatever his subject, it was righteousness he taught, righteousness and religion. The one sure basis of life, he preached, is to follow the will of God. Business must set itself squarely upon that foundation, and every business practice must be based on the eternities.

Cabot was a one-man revivalist, but always he was practical, always efficient. There was no rodomontade about him. He was the most popular lecturer on the staff. His classrooms were jammed, and upon one group he lavished particular attention. He gave a "refresher" course to proved executives of ten, twenty, thirty years' experience. Vice-Presidents of great corporations flocked to him each winter for a six-weeks session, and after his lecture, he was often found in the pulpit for a noonday service. It was during this period of white heat, the radiation of a human spirit which finds surcease for its own suffering in working for others, that I asked him to set down the story of his conversion. To many thousand people it came as water in a thirsty land.

The Conversion of a Sinner

PHILIP CABOT

I

This is a record of personal experience. It is not a system of philosophy nor a theological creed. I make no pretense of proof of the beliefs I state because they are not conclusions reached by conscious logical mental processes. I think them true for me because they produce certain results; they give me more vitality and power and a keener zest for life. They may not be true for any other man, but, unless I am wholly different from all other men, they must contain some truth or light for them.

I begin with the story of another man.

I knew him for several years only as we know our business associates, the men whom we see often at Directors' and Executive Committee meetings; a thin-faced, alert, courteous gentleman, with a deep wrinkle between the eyes and dark circles under them; a mind keen as a rapier, stored with knowledge of life and men, and illuminated with flashes of cynical humor. But it was not until I crossed the continent with him on a tour of corporation inspection that I saw the real man. Revelation began on the train with his humorous side-thrust at my third volume of Gibbon's *Decline and Fall,* which struck him, an up-state New Yorker, as typical of my Puritan descent, and for long thereafter he used to greet me daily with the question, "Still Declining and Falling?" To which I had no apt repartee in view of the undoubted fact that I found the volume of *The Devil's Paw,* by E. Phillips Oppenheim, to which he was wedded, far more amusing.

And then his game of bridge! It was of the fierce predatory type, for a high stake, which sent me "to the mat" in the second round, hopelessly outclassed. To miss a possible trick caused him a sharp pang, and he rarely did it. But I first caught him without his mask on a morning when, after a night in a small country hotel of western Oregon, I saw him get out of bed — or, rather, the ghost of him. Hollow-eyed, with cheeks fallen in and a temper about as genial as that of a bald hornet, he offered no vestige of a salutation until, after bolting three cups of black coffee and cursing the bellboy because it was not strong enough, he was moved to say, "Cabot, I can remember the time when one cup of coffee with my breakfast would set me up for the day. Now three on an empty stomach just bring my head above water."

That was the man without his mask, and I was shocked but hardly surprised to hear, three years later, that he was dead, having been killed by the overturning of his motor while running at the high speed habitual to him.

The incident was shocking but surprise was unwarranted, for the thing was not really an accident: it was implicit in his life. But ten years had elapsed before its full significance dawned upon me. Then, in that incident I saw myself and some millions of my fellow countrymen mirrored to the life. It was really the picture of a man whose world was not "God's perfect Universe," but, in sober fact, a Hell from which his craving to escape drove him to excitement in various forms, of which three cups of black coffee before breakfast were perhaps the most effective and the least harmful. As with most powerful business men in America to-day, his business was not a trade nor an intellectual pursuit, but a game of wild excitement, played day and night, not for money or the advancement of knowledge or the benefit of mankind, but for the excitement of the game itself; and his so-called amusements — bridge, literature, and motoring — were mere variations of the same thing. His whole life was one huge gamble — which he ultimately lost.

The class to which he belonged is limited, but the morbid craving which drove him on can be seen on every hand. Take, for example, the industrial worker. A large fraction of his time and all his savings are spent on strikes which, in the last analysis, amount to a declaration that *his* life, also, is in Hell and that he won't stand it any longer. And this in the face of the fact that his material condition or "standard of living" is unequaled in the world's history.

Nor is this condition confined to men. Their women-folk, whose natural life is housekeeping, homemaking, and the care of their children, are on strike, too, declaring such work to be "sordid and degrading," and seeking escape from it by every means in their power.

All these human souls exhibit the same craving to escape from the slavery of their lives, and they have tried every form of excitement to satisfy their craving, only to find that like all stimulants they make the craving worse.

No one will deny that relaxation and amusement are necessary for us all; but, in order to see clearly the change which has taken place, compare our forms of amusement with those of fifty years ago. In literature, painting, and music, the classics of our grandfathers are pronounced dull and slow to-day and things with "more snap to them," as we phrase it, have taken their place. Not beauty but excitement is what we crave, and this not alone in our sedentary relaxations. In the out-of-doors world our grandfathers, of a Sunday afternoon or on week-days, as opportunity offered, strolling in the woods and fields, acquired an intimacy with the trees, birds, and flowers, which they prized; or they hitched the fat old horse into the carryall, loaded in their children and women-folk, and jogged along the quiet roads at an average of four miles an hour. To-day the woods and fields are deserted, except for the hunter, strung with the thirst to kill, while ten million motor-cars whirl us at blinding speed, over crowded thoroughfares on which we dodge our neighbors with incredible agility and fierce irritation, returning home dazed and exhausted with a record of one hundred miles or so between luncheon and dinner.

If these things be relaxing to the nerves and elevating to the spirit, human nature has changed indeed! They have the earmarks of stimulants, not sedatives; of the fear of life, rather than the love of it. Foreign observers have often remarked with a touch of humor that Americans work hard and hurry over their play. But this is not hurry; it is hysteria—a sort of spiritual madness.

This is the condition of our world which all men recognized—all men, it seemed, except myself. Slower than most to see the obvious, I am, however, more impatient of a mystery. Most social phenomena have an ascertainable cause or origin. What is the origin of this universal madness?

Physicians and the public-health authorities do, it is true, report an increase in diseases of the nervous system and deaths from heart disease. But the increase is not very great and is wholly insufficient to account for such a condition of mind as we see about us. For this condition is nation-wide; a large fraction of our population is affected; clearly this is not exactly a case for the doctors of medicine. We must look elsewhere. Here are some straws that may show where the wind is.

II

A profound political observer is said to have remarked, many centuries ago, "He who believeth doth not make haste"; which, being interpreted, means that the man who has a clear purpose in his life, and a firm grasp upon his work, is the master of it, not the sport of circumstance, driven hither and yon by every change of wind. The man who is always in a hurry is the slave of his work.

A recent article by an eminent economist in a well-known quarterly has developed at some length the proposition that the mechanical devices which man has produced have now become so powerful that they have taken command of his material world and made him their servant and their slave. And this is true. Our machines do govern us; the material has overwhelmed the spiritual. The mechanical genius of America has evolved the marvel of "quantity production," by which wonderful combinations of machines turn out their product with incredible volume and cheapness. But the men who feed the machines do so at the price of body and soul. The destruction of these things which we cannot replace is not included in the cost of production. Our captains of industry figure depreciation on their machines, but not on their men. If the depreciation of human souls were included in the cost, "quantity production" would lose its charm for them, because it would not be cheap.

Quantity production and "the dominion of machines" are not, however, *inventions* of our Western world; they are *expedients* to which we have been forced by the drying-up of the springs of our spiritual life. The workingman from whom the "joy of labor" has taken flight, has sought refuge in high living — which he miscalls a high standard of living and which involves high wages to support it. It is in the struggle to avoid a "labor cost" so high that it would stop production and reduce us to beggary that our complex mechanical and industrial system originated. The root cause is our spiritual poverty, and if Labor now suffers from "the dominion of machines," the fault lies at its own door. But, unless some remedy for this can be devised, our machines will wreck our civilization by destroying the race.

And moreover it is clear that this poverty of spiritual life, or loss of Faith, is not confined to America. All Christendom is affected. For note well that the World War was not the special crime of any group of individuals, or of any one nation. Europe drifted into that war because of lack of leadership among nations whose material resources and power had wholly outgrown their spiritual control. And the civilization of Europe to-day, four years after the Armistice, is, according to the most competent observers, upon the verge of collapse. Without Faith the nations perish.

Here then perhaps we have our clue. The conditions which we see around us are conditions of disease, and it is disease of the soul rather than of the body.

Look now at a concrete example: the conditions, material and spiritual, in our American world which drove my friend to his death, had driven me, after twenty-five years of battle, to the verge of it. My soul, like his, had for many years been fed on stimulants and sawdust, and in a final revolt it wreaked its vengeance upon my body, which soon went down in defeat. For eight years more, however, I refused to see it so; fought stubbornly against disease with all the weapons which medical science could provide, but without any real success. I contrived, it is true, to keep myself alive by a system of fierce repression which required me to give up all the normal pleasures of life and almost all human society. But the achievement was of more than doubtful value, so far as I can see, and was due more to the instinct to cling to mere life than to an intelligible purpose.

Early last summer I became interested in considering the power and operation of the subconscious mind, and perceived how much more active, powerful, and important its processes are than those of which we are conscious, known as intellect and will. The examples of the stone and the bicycle and of the six-inch plank in the floor *vs.* the six-inch girder on the skyscraper as footpaths showed the superiority of the subconsciousness to the will; while the quest for the forgotten word demonstrated its faultless memory. The superior quality in some persons of the thinking processes during sleep interested me because it was not true apparently of every one. Then I learned that some healers made their "suggestions" at night, and remembered that hypnotic influence was based upon a condition resembling sleep in the patient. I read that M. Coué affirmed that cure by autosuggestion was highly effective; that the suggestions should be made night and morning, and without effort of will.

Of course, the reaction of the soul on the body (malignant or beneficent) had been observed and preached for two thousand years or more. In my own case, I found that if I instructed myself *in spoken words,* at night, just before going to sleep, as to the problems to be dealt with and the pitfalls to be avoided on the next day, great improvement in conduct and achievement could be produced.

After following this procedure for a short time, it came to me that what I was saying was tending to "degenerate" into prayer, a form of begging to which I had never fallen; and then, with a real shock, that the times of prayer from time immemorial had been morning and evening, the very times fixed by Coué for autosuggestion. Moreover, the method of Coué and the method of prayer taught by the Church were strikingly similar. Both rested their healing power on belief, conviction, *faith* — the surrender or subordination of the will being a first essential.

It then came to me that from the time of Zeno, at least, men of spiritual insight had perceived and declared that God was within us; that the human soul was a part of God; and that it should be sought and would be found within and not without.

With these notions in my head, I looked curiously about me for evidence which would refute or support these assumptions, and *this* struck me as significant. As a whole, the American people appear to fair-minded outsiders to be remarkably unspiritual, material, practical — far more so than their ancestors. In other words, the tendency of the nation — or, at least, of the upper classes — seemed to be toward materialism, toward building up the mind at the expense of the soul. Such a process would result from starving the soul and feeding the mind, and if, as it seemed to me, the soul and the so-called subconsciousness were closely allied, or were one, it was of vital importance how men spent the last hours before sleep.

Then the remarkable development and spread of the American newspaper struck me, and I realized that although, a hundred years ago, good men read their Bibles before going to bed, to-day they read the newspaper, play bridge or billiards at the Club or after overeating at a friend's house, and, in the morning, get up tired and cross and go to their city business. Obviously, if the soul is nocturnal and has to be fed night and morning, it is being fed on chaff, and the starvation or atrophy which our critics discern is exactly what we should expect.

This idea was supported in my own case by great increase in calmness and poise following a change of routine which put the evening paper before supper and the Bible or its spiritual equivalent after.

Toward the end of August, upon the verge of despair, I went up to my camp in the Connecticut Valley for two weeks of so-called rest, taking along a liberal supply of the "very light" novels on which I was accustomed to feed, and, by accident, a little book on *The Meaning of Prayer* which a dear friend had given me to read.

It was August, the weather was rather hot and muggy, life looked very bleak, though fortunately not very long, for me, and the novels for a space went well. But after a few days even E. Phillips Oppenheim could not hold my attention, and one hot morning, throwing down the book in despair, my eye fell on *The Meaning of Prayer*. I began to browse on it with a vacant mind which rapidly changed to an absorption so complete that I was keenly annoyed by the arrival of lunchtime, three hours later. That afternoon I went back to Oppenheim but, finding him intolerable, took up again *The Meaning of Prayer* with a rather sheepish feeling to be reading such a book. The hours of the afternoon, however, vanished as those of the morning, and supper was another unwelcome interruption — a remarkable fact for a man living on a starvation diet, in whom the pangs of hunger were never quenched.

After supper I sat down to think. This thing looked serious. Here was I for the first time in my life bored with novels and absorbed in worship. Was this the first stage of conversion or the madness which precedes death?

III

After a few days of this sort, during which I experimented and examined my sensations with scientific coldness, I was convinced that I was not mad. Something different was in process. It seemed that in worship, or prayer, and in my Bible, the solution to the riddle of my universe had been revealed to me; for I was living in a new world of peace, beauty, and gladness, such as I had never conceived. I was devouring the Sacred Books with the hunger of a starving man; the material world with its harassing duties, dangers, and excitements had faded on the horizon, and my wreck of a body (to maintain which in operation at all had been taking most of my time and all of my will-power) seemed a wholly secondary matter which was looking after itself very well.

That condition has continued except that I have returned to the world of men, taken up again my daily chores with the keenest interest and with a sureness of touch and an absence of worry and excitement to which all my associates can testify, and my health has continued to improve in a remarkable way. My experience was, I think, a sort of "conversion," though not of the usual type; for subsequent reading has taught me that the sensations of genuine conversion of the explosive type, such as often occurs to those in middle life, are so ecstatic and ineffable as to be beyond the power of man to describe. Certainly it has never been done. Adjective is piled on adjective, as Ossa on Pelion, but no clear picture results; and as to what might be called normal conversion, of the sort which comes to thousands during adolescence, it is apparently such an easy and painless process as to escape observation, and so descriptive analysis, in most cases. I conclude, therefore, that mine was not a genuine conversion, for the process was perfectly conscious and easily described.

Sitting in my great cool living-room, with the humming of the bees and the sound of the river in my ears; rowing on the river at sunrise; mowing my grass or weeding my garden, or even while putting on my boots, ideas would pop into my mind and automatically fit themselves in with other ideas like the pieces of a picture puzzle. Sometimes they took places apparently without reference to the ideas already there, and for days would hang so to speak in space. But gradually the gaps were filled in and the picture became complete.

At the time, the process seemed miraculous and I had the feeling of being controlled by an external power; but, as I was spending much time in reading the Bible, *The Meaning of Prayer, Varieties of Religious Experience,* and other books on philosophy, I now see that the ideas gleaned from these books and sinking into my subconscious mind were simply reappearing after the process of assimilation had reached a certain stage. My mind wandered very much, concentration was never achieved, and it is certain that no reasoning process produced the final result. It was mainly subconscious, but, by a gradual process extending over some weeks, a clear picture was produced, the picture of the relation of my soul to all other souls, and thus to the Whole, the Infinite, or God — Who is the sum of all.

I use the word picture and refer to it as "seen," but it is a thing of feeling and not of vision, a synthesis or harmony of the universe, which belongs rather in the realm of music. Life is like a great chorus in which each soul has its certain place. If it finds that place and fills it, it is happy and successful — it lives in Heaven; otherwise it is unhappy and lives in Hell.

Our modern world has its gains as well as its losses, and one of the gains is that it has accustomed us to miracles and we see them for what they are — merely as effects, of which we do not know the cause, but which produce results on which we can rely. My conversion, therefore, while miraculous, did not excite me, for even at first it seemed far more credible and normal than the atomic theory, for example, or electrical phenomena, such as alternating currents, telephones, and wireless; and, as I have examined at more leisure and with more thoroughness what took place, I think I see in it the normal working of cause and effect, based upon laws which are of twin birth with man; a part of the law of the universe, but one which each of us must painfully rediscover for himself. The truth which has always been known had just dawned upon me, namely, that there is a material body and a spiritual body; that the spiritual body, in other words the soul, must be tended and fed as well as the material body, and that worship of God by prayer is the method by which it is fed. Without such feeding it will die and, in my case, a starved or ill-nourished soul had produced almost fatal reactions upon my body. The results, therefore, which we see on every hand, of feeding our souls on stimulants and sawdust,—namely, disease and death,—seem to me exactly what we should expect, and the miracles of healing by Christian faith are the normal working of cause and effect. For I take the heart of that faith to be that belief in God, shown by love and obedience to His will, gives men the power to draw strength and life from God.

And there is another way of stating the same thing which I find useful. If I assume that God is Love, Goodness, and Truth,—or, if you prefer, the Harmony of the universe,—I find that He is also Life. For Love, Goodness, and true ideas in the mind do, I find, give me vitality and working power. I find, for example,—and so do other men,—that worship revives and invigorates me, while anger, hatred, and jealousy exhaust and depress. In short, God is Truth and Truth is Life, while sin and error are untruth and so "not Life." So far as action is governed by fear or sin it tends to become automatic, a reflex from a false premise in the subconscious, and to that extent the soul has atrophied and died; while action based on true spiritual motives makes the soul more alert, that is, more alive. Sin is a perversion of the soul, like cancer in the cells of the body, and if not eradicated it will slowly eat its way through the whole structure and kill it.

The Christian faith, put at its very lowest, is a working hypothesis like the law of gravity, the theories of electricity, astronomy, and physics. In all these cases, if the hypothesis works, by explaining the facts we observe, we adopt and use it. These are acts of faith and appear to me more questionable, far less supported by evidence and far more difficult to believe than the Christian's faith in God. Our faith in God, in the power of His love, and in the life-giving results of obedience and surrender to His will, is supported by the whole history and experience of man. It has been tested and proved, not hundreds but literally millions of times. If evidence from experience can prove anything, it has proved this. It is really amazing what hard work we make of it. Men are skeptical about God because they cannot see him. It is quite respectable to be so. But are they skeptical about an "alternating current," or a telephone message, or an atom, because they cannot see it? They would not dare to say so. Times have changed. Five hundred years ago the position was exactly reversed. To confess skepticism about God would send a man to the stake, while all respectable persons thought Columbus was crazy and that of course the world was flat. Now we seem to be ruled by science and machinery. A man may be as skeptical as he will about the power of God, or what is far worse, may not bother his head about it in any least degree; but to question the atomic theory or the law of gravity or the justice of the prevailing industrial system will cause his neighbors to shake their heads.

To-day we deify the intellect and are skeptical about God; but the mystic of the Middle Ages was an example of skepticism of another sort. We usually class as skeptics the men of high intelligence and learning who worship the mind and doubt the existence of God because the mind cannot grasp and express Him; while the mystic, seeing the proof of God in the whole universe about him, and the wisdom of yesterday proved the folly of to-day, was skeptical about the power of the intellect to grasp and describe the Infinite, but believed in God because he saw His works.

And, therefore, it is clear to me that the true remedy — in fact, the only one — for the ills from which we suffer is a revival of our faith in God. Our lives are torn to rags and tatters by the whirling nebulæ of disconnected activities which fill our days, resulting so often in a final explosion from the centrifugal forces generated by such rapid rotation. Vivid faith will centralize or polarize our lives, giving them a central motive — the service of God — which will unify our efforts, making them more effective and relieving us of the killing strain of heterogeneous action. Faith will construct for each of us the great girders binding the rim of the wheel to its centre, which will be strong enough to resist the pull of centrifugal forces and enable the machine to do its work.

The miracles of science are "seen" by their results, which we accept without question. We believe them, we say, because they work. But does not our belief in God "work"? I believe it to be the most dynamic thing in the world! It works more, and more powerfully, than all the works of man. Millions have put it to the test of experience and their lives testify to its truth. What more could be asked in God's name or the Devil's? No law of which we have any conception is so completely and convincingly proved. No rational man, therefore, it seems to me, *who will give his mind to it and will examine the evidence,* can remain in doubt that God is the source of life and that by faith — that is, love and obedience to His will — man can draw life from that source. The reason that so many men doubt is because they have never looked at the evidence. It is time they did.

IV

But how shall we achieve and hold to our faith? Discussions of this problem are as old as man, being discoverable in the oldest books of the Bible, in the teachings of the Greek philosophers, in the Neo-Platonists, in the writings of the Fathers of the Church, and of all the mystics. But each generation prefers to restate its truths, and the discussion best suited to the need of our times, as I see it, is in Hocking's book, *The Meaning of God in Human Experience.*

Briefly stated, what Hocking says is this. There is in this universe a God all-powerful and all-wise, and the existence of man depends upon so regulating or tuning the individual life as to act in harmony with the divine plan. It is the will of God that man should devote much of his time in this world to accomplishing material work; but God's universe is so devised that too great absorption in material ideas, as the result of which they come to be regarded as ends in themselves, produces a subtle poison, or toxin, which saps man's energy, makes these ends appear worthless and thus deprives life of its zest. This is a necessary result of the fact that man, being human, all his efforts must contain a certain coefficient of error which, if allowed to continue for too long a time without correction, will make his course wholly wrong and all his efforts futile. The way to correct the error, the antidote or antitoxin for the poison, is to set aside for a time all material work, and to concentrate attention on God, the spiritual centre of the universe. Just as the sea captain corrects his course by daily observations of the sun, the centre of the solar system, so man must correct his course at frequent intervals by transferring his attention to God by means of worship or prayer. After the corrections have been made — that is, after God has indicated to him his true course — man's attention must be retransferred to the temporal world and its material duties. This transfer and retransfer is the principle of alternation so illuminatingly stated in Hocking's book.

It seems to me, therefore, that the method or technique by which this is accomplished *must be* the most important study of man; for in proportion to the completeness of his success in devising a method for real communion with God will be his power to tune his life in harmony with the Law of God, with the consequent ability to draw that vitality and power to make himself a useful servant, which is the purpose of life and the only source of happiness and success.

Unfortunately the human soul is the most lonely thing of which we can conceive. No "communion of souls" is possible in the deepest sense — only communion with God. No human soul can touch any other soul except through the medium of God, so that the method of communion or worship must be unique for each individual and he must discover it for himself. But there are certain general principles which are of universal validity and which are the foundation on which the individual may build. All are as old as man and antiquity is the proof of their validity. But modern science has done much to explain their origin and force and should be accepted for what it can give. The fact that our material and mechanical discoveries may for the moment have overwhelmed us should not blind us to their value. An all-wise God has not willed these developments without a purpose. Our spiritual progress is temporarily in arrears, but the day will dawn when we shall have regained such spiritual mastery as will put these machines in their proper place.

Now the practice of worship by prayer can be approached in many ways, and nothing is more striking, or at first more baffling, than the different ways in which praying men approach it. One of the hindrances most often met with is the argument of those who think of prayer as asking for things, that a wise and loving God, knowing what we need before we ask for it, will give us if it is good for us. But we must remember that in communion with God, as with individuals, "the question which has not been asked cannot be answered." Until we are *prepared to receive* God's gift, that is, until the thing we ask for has become a dominant desire of our lives, our prayer for it *cannot* be answered. We may pray for an understanding of God's love, but until we have firmly grasped the meaning of the Commandment "Thou shalt love thy neighbor as thyself," and have an earnest desire to obey it, our prayer for the needful strength must go unanswered.

It is in this aspect of prayer that modern psychology can help us. From time immemorial men have prayed morning and evening and now we know the reason why. Most of our actions and all of the internal functions of our bodies are controlled, not by the intellect and the will, but by the subconscious. The spring of action, whether in our daily judgments or in our digestive metabolism, is inaccessible to the intellect and the will except through the subconscious. The subconscious holds the key. We can, in fact we must, communicate with the subconscious through the intellect controlled by will; all action by the subconscious must originate in the conscious mind, but the conscious mind cannot control the act. It is to the application of this law that the miracles of healing by suggestion and faith are due, and moreover it has recently been proved that there are what might be called tides in the subconscious; that is, that there are times at which it is nearer to the surface or more accessible than at others, and that for most people these times are morning and evening—the ancient times of prayer.

The value of this principle in its application to prayer is this: in order to get our dominant desire made effective in our lives, we *must use the subconscious;* an important aspect of prayer is the clear and explicit instruction of the subconscious as to what we intend to be our dominant desire in order that it may be accomplished. I find, therefore, that for me an important part of the preparation for worship is the soliloquy, night and morning, in which I definitely instruct my subconscious as to the results of my conscious thinking about my daily life. Before praying for grace to love our neighbors we must first grasp what we mean by that, wherein we fail, and what is in fact our dominant desire about it. This desire we must clearly communicate to the subconscious to be made effective. Then our prayer for the needed grace can be and will be answered—but not before.

And there is another way in which the new psychology has enlightened me. The great class of mental disorders from which men suffer, known as the phobias, can often, we are now told, be attacked successfully if the cause of the fear can be discovered. The destructive power of fear seems to be due to the fact that it originates in instinct and is not grasped by the mind. If the origin of the phobia can be dragged out into the sunlight of the mind, it loses its power and dies like the disease-germ when exposed to the sun. And this same principle can be applied, I think, to our sins and false ideas, by soliloquy or prayer. Self-examination and confession are in fact the ancient application and use of this principle which we have just discovered.

This is supported by what we know of the practice of the men who have made prayer the most powerful agent or working force in their lives. "Chinese" Gordon, for example, writes, "This morning I dragged Agag out into the presence of the Lord and hacked him to pieces"—Agag being used by him for a symbol of his own worldly ambitions.

Of course, soliloquy of this sort is not exactly prayer; it is rather the preparation for prayer by laying the foundation for dominant desire, but such a dominant desire, expressed in the constant work of our lives, is a prerequisite of worship and effective prayer.

I think we must admit that the verbal prayers of confession, humiliation, and self-abasement resemble soliloquy more than prayer, and they must be practised with discretion. For the sick soul to dwell upon its sickness is likely to make the sickness worse by concentrating too much attention on it. Mind cure, or the religion of healthy-mindedness is most vital for the sick — which explains the well-known fact that only the very saintly should dwell upon their sins. But that such prayers may be very helpful and profoundly important is proved by the calming and cleansing reaction which they certainly produce, so that perhaps we ought not to be too critical in making an exact distinction.

The miraculous cures that have been accomplished by the disciples of mind-cure, Christian Science, and autosuggestion seem to me to result from a method which is in fact common to all of them, although it has been obscured by superficial differences which have been overemphasized. Each of them has developed a formula or method by which the mind of the patient is concentrated on the conception of health, at times and in ways which successfully transfer this image to the seat of action in the subconscious. This concentration is the secret of their success, and I am tempted to believe that the miracles of healing of all times rest upon the same foundation. The simplest and perhaps most effective example is the formula of M. Coué repeated twenty times night and morning.

Now it is impossible for me to doubt that if the same concentration can be achieved in Christian prayer, similar but more far-reaching curative results will be produced. I hold that the great problem for each of us in developing the technique of prayer is to ascertain exactly by what method such concentration upon the symbols of his faith can be produced in his individual soul.

V

Our daily prayer, however, and the method of preparation for it, is not, I think, the most important form of worship by means of prayer. The deepest form of worship is communion with God in order that our souls may be fed and the course of our lives directed in true accord with His will. For this the "Seeing Eye" and the "Listening Ear" must be developed by an utter concentration of all our spiritual powers — which requires time. Silent attention, with every spiritual sense alert, is the attitude of the worshiper who would hear the word of God.

In developing individual technique, the practice of the great mystics in their preparation for revelation furnishes some guidance. It was a process, occupying days or even weeks, by which the worshiper divested himself one by one of all his bodily and material desires and interests, using the intellect and the will to their uttermost limits, until, having eliminated every thought but the love of God, and with his whole personality concentrated on that conception, he made the final leap, surrendering absolutely to the will of God and becoming merged in complete communion. Something of this sort must take place, I think, in every individual when, turning away from his material work, he seeks that alternation, or communion with his God, which is necessary for his soul's life. The method of preparation for this must be unique in every case. Some will find the best environment in their church, as the greatest symbol of their spiritual life; some in the star-lit heavens; some in gazing at the blue or snow-capped mountain, outlined against the sky, or the lonely desert, or the endless sea. It was the habit of Jesus, when he prayed, to go into the wilderness.

In the course of years, each man must learn, at the peril of his spiritual life, where and how best to develop the seeing eye and the listening ear and, having done so, he must frequently submerge himself in these conditions and surrender himself to silent worship. Obviously, however, this is not a condition of body and mind which can be attained by the worshiper in a few moments or a few hours. It is on a wholly different plane from the level of our daily lives. This process of "alternation," vital as it is, takes so long a time that it can be accomplished only at considerable intervals, and, for most men, can never become a part of their daily lives. The periods when we turn to God to adjust our spiritual courses must be systematic and periodic, but can hardly be daily. Such of us as are intended to do material rather than spiritual work must do it with such insight as our daily praying can afford, sustained and corrected *at intervals more or less widely separated* by periods of retirement and complete concentration on worship. Two things, therefore, become of vital import: that the technique of our daily prayer should be developed with such earnestness and intelligence as to make it as powerful as possible in the support and guidance of our daily work; and that the periodic "alternations" should be sacredly observed, adequately protected, and, by the use of the highest skill possible to us, rendered as fruitful as our spiritual power will permit. Special periods must be set aside for them, with which nothing, not even illness, should interfere. In fact, if we fall ill such an alternation may prove to be the proper cure.

As a nation we surely have the vacation habit; men in all walks of life, even to the lowest, now take vacations liberally. But how do we spend them? Some of us alternate our city lives with a few weeks at a "Summer Resort," where jazzing and the movies, with fireworks and violent exercise, constitute our "relaxations." Others pack their wives and children into a motorcar, grasp the wheel, and proceed to tear off more miles per hour for more hours per day than any normal being ever before imagined. There are a favored few who can retire to great and beautiful country estates, and who do so for months on end. But even then they do not seek a revival and reorientation of the soul. The same round of material occupation goes on. We live in a burdensome luxury and in a whirl of social dissipation. The great American country houses are as laborious to manage as a summer hotel. Such an environment is not the atmosphere of high spiritual life.

Something far removed from this must be devised. The wise old Roman Catholic Church has offered one solution. For laymen as well as for priests it provides places of retreat; places of dignified and spiritual symbolism, to which the spiritually exhausted man may retire for a period of fasting and prayer, to cleanse and call home his spirit and prepare himself to serve again his God in the material world. Something of this sort is obviously necessary for us all as a beginning, and from this each soul must build up for itself, with its highest skill and will-power, a method of cleansing and purification which shall make possible a true communion with God.

Such a method of developing and feeding the spiritual body seems to me to be the cure for that disease of the soul from which I and many of my fellow men are suffering. It will, I think, cure the spiritual madness which I tried at the beginning to describe, and may enable us to save our tottering civilization by regaining control of the great scientific, mechanical, and industrial processes which have deprived us of liberty, the pursuit of happiness, and, almost, of life itself.

August 1923

KATHARINE FULLERTON GEROULD

1879–1944

Katharine Fullerton Gerould had won a prize as far back as 1902, but by 1908 she had published nothing since, and when I took charge of the Atlantic she was wholly unknown to me. It happened that the very week before I had dropped in at the office and idly turned over the contents of the basket which stood on one corner of the editor's desk. A little paper lay there which attracted my attention. The miniature essay had a certain awareness of living in it that made me jot down the name of Gerould, and when I took possession of the editor's desk, almost my first inquiry was what had become of it. The ancient whose duty it was to give desks a semblance of dustlessness replied, "Oh that was sent back." I recovered it and "In Defense of the Verb" was printed without signature in "The Contributors' Club." That was the beginning of a long acquaintance, delightful to me, and of fame to the magazine.

Katharine Fullerton was the daughter of an Evangelical minister at Brockton, Massachusetts. Never was an odder flowerpot for such a bloom than that dismal birthplace of boots and shoes. In her there was nothing of Evangelicism, nothing suggestive of a narrow environment. She married a scholar and lived in Princeton. There the winds of a wide world blew about her, and there she wrote with her individual distinction and her intolerance of things which were not distinguished.

The Knight's Move

KATHARINE FULLERTON GEROULD

I

Havelock the Dane settled himself back in his chair and set his feet firmly on the oaken table. Chantry let him do it, though some imperceptible inch of his body winced. For the oak of it was neither fumed nor golden; it was English to its ancient core, and the table had served in the refectory of monks before Henry VIII decided that monks shocked him. Naturally Chantry did not want his friends' boots havocking upon it. But more important than to possess the table was to possess it nonchalantly. He let the big man dig his heel in. Any man but Havelock the Dane would have known better. But Havelock did as he pleased, and you either gave him up or bore it. Chantry did not want to give him up.

Chantry was a feminist; a bit of an æsthete but canny at affairs; good-looking, and temperate, and less hipped on the matter of sex than feminist gentlemen are wont to be. That is to say, while he vaguely wanted *l'homme moyen sensuel* to mend his ways, he did not expect him to change fundamentally. He rather thought the women would manage all that when they got the vote. You see, he was not a socialist: only a feminist.

Havelock the Dane, on the other hand, was by no means a feminist, but was a socialist. What probably brought the two men together—apart from their common likableness—was that each, in his way, refused to "go the whole hog." They sometimes threshed the thing out together, unable to decide on a programme, but always united at last in their agreement that things were wrong. Havelock trusted Labor, and Chantry trusted Woman; the point was that neither trusted men like themselves, with a little money and an inherited code of honor. Havelock wanted his money taken away from him; Chantry desired his code to be trampled on by innumerable feminine feet. But each was rather helpless, for both expected these things to be done for them.

Except for this tie of ineffectuality, they had nothing special in common. Havelock's life had been adventurous in the good old-fashioned sense: the bars down and a deal of wandering. Chantry had sown so many crops of intellectual wild oats that even the people who came for subscriptions might be forgiven for thinking him a mental libertine, good for subscriptions and not much else. Between them, they boxed the compass about once a week. Havelock had more of what is known as "personality" than Chantry; Chantry more of what is known as "culture." They dovetailed, on the whole, not badly.

Havelock, this afternoon, was full of a story. Chantry wanted to listen, though he knew that he could have listened better if Havelock's heel had not been quite so ponderous on the secular oak. He took refuge in a cosmic point of view. That was the only point of view from which Havelock (it was, by the way, his physical type only that had caused him to be nicknamed the Dane: his ancestors had come over from England in great discomfort two centuries since), in his blonde hugeness, became negligible. You had to climb very high to see him small.

"You never did the man justice," Havelock was saying.

"Justice be hanged!" replied Chantry.

"Quite so: the feminist slogan."

"A socialist can't afford to throw stones."

The retorts were spoken sharply, on both sides. Then both men laughed. They had too often had it out seriously to mind; these little insults were mere convention.

"Get at your story," resumed Chantry. "I suppose there's a woman in it: a nasty cat invented by your own prejudices. There usually is."

"Never a woman at all. If there were, I shouldn't be asking for your opinion. My opinion, of course, is merely the rational one. I don't side-step the truth because a little drama gets in. I am appealing to you because you are the average man who hasn't seen the light. I honestly want to know what you think. There's a reason."

"What's the reason?"

"I'll tell you that later. Now, I'll tell you the story." Havelock screwed his tawny eyebrows together for a moment before plunging in. "Humph!" he ejaculated at last. "Much good anybody is in a case like this.—What did you say you thought of Ferguson?"

"I didn't think anything of Ferguson—except that he had a big brain for biology. He was a loss."

"No personal opinion?"

"I never like people who think so well of themselves as all that."

"No opinion about his death?"

"Accidental, as they said, I suppose."

"Oh, 'they said'! It was suicide, I tell you."

"Suicide? Really?" Chantry's brown eyes lighted for an instant. "Oh, poor chap; I'm sorry."

It did not occur to him immediately to ask how Havelock knew. He trusted a plain statement from Havelock.

"I'm not. Or — yes, I am. I hate to have a man inconsistent."

"It's inconsistent for any one to kill himself. But it's frequently done."

Havelock, hemming and hawing like this, was more nearly a bore than Chantry had ever known him.

"Not for Ferguson."

"Oh, well, never mind Ferguson," Chantry yawned. "Tell me some anecdote out of your tapestried past."

"I won't."

Havelock dug his heel in harder. Chantry all but told him to take his feet down, but stopped himself just in time.

"Well, go on, then," he said, "but it doesn't sound interesting. I hate all tales of suicide. And there isn't even a woman in it," he sighed maliciously.

"Oh, if it comes to that, there is."

"But you said — "

"Not in it exactly, unless you go in for *post hoc, propter hoc*."

"Oh, drive on." Chantry was pettish.

But at that point Havelock the Dane removed his feet from the refectory table. He will probably never know why Chantry, just then, began to be amiable.

"Excuse me, Havelock. Of course, whatever drove a man like Ferguson to suicide is interesting. And I may say he managed it awfully well. Not a hint, anywhere."

"Well, a scientist ought to get something out of it for himself. Ferguson certainly knew how. Can't you imagine him sitting up there, cocking his hair" (an odd phrase, but Chantry understood), "and deciding just how to circumvent the coroner? I can."

"Ferguson hadn't much imagination."

"A coroner doesn't take imagination. He takes a little hard, expert knowledge."

"I dare say." But Chantry's mind was wandering through other defiles. "Odd, that he should have snatched his life out of the very jaws of what-do-you-call-it, once, only to give it up at last, politely, of his own volition."

"You may well say it." Havelock spoke with more earnestness than he had done. "If you're not a socialist when I get through with you, Chantry, my boy — "

"Lord, Lord! don't tell me your beastly socialism is mixed up with it all! I never took to Ferguson, but he was no syndicalist. In life *or* in death, I'd swear to that."

"Ah, no. If he had been! But all I mean is that, in a properly regulated state, Ferguson's tragedy would not have occurred."

"So it was a tragedy?"

"He was a loss to the state, God knows."

Had they been speaking of anything less dignified than death and genius, Havelock might have sounded a little austere and silly. As it was — Chantry bit back, and swallowed, his censure.

"That's why I want to know what you think," went on Havelock, irrelevantly. "Whether your damned code of honor is worth Ferguson."

"It's not my damned code any more than yours," broke in Chantry.

"Yes, it is. Or, at least, we break it down at different points — theoretically. Actually, we walk all round it every day to be sure it's intact. Let's be honest."

"Honest as you like, if you'll only come to the point. Whew, but it's hot! Let's have a gin-fizz."

"You aren't serious."

Havelock seemed to try to lash himself into a rage. But he was so big that he could never have got all of himself into a rage at once. You felt that only part of him was angry — his toes, perhaps, or his complexion.

Chantry rang for ice and lemon, and took gin, sugar, and a siphon out of a carved cabinet.

"Go slow," he said. He himself was going very slow, with a beautiful crystal decanter which he set lovingly on the oaken table. "Go slow," he repeated, more easily, when he had set it down. "I can think just as well with a gin-fizz as without one. And I didn't know Ferguson well; and I didn't like him at all. I read his books, and I admired him. But he looked like the devil — *the* devil, you'll notice, not *a* devil. With a dash of Charles I by Van Dyck. The one standing by a horse. As you say, he cocked his hair. It went into little horns, above each eyebrow. I'm sorry he's lost to the world, but it doesn't get me. He may have been a saint, for all I know; but there you are — I never cared particularly to know. I am serious. Only, somehow, it doesn't touch me."

And he proceeded to make use of crushed ice and lemon juice.

"Oh, blow all that," said Havelock the Dane finally, over the top of his glass. "I'm going to tell you, anyhow. Only I wish you would forget your prejudices. I want an opinion."

"Go on."

Chantry made himself comfortable.

II

"You remember the time when Ferguson didn't go down on the *Argentina*?"

"I do. Ferguson just wouldn't go down, you know. He'd turn up smiling, without even a chill, and meanwhile lots of good fellows would be at the bottom of the sea."

"Prejudice again," barked Havelock. "Yet in point of fact, it's perfectly true. And you would have preferred him to drown."

"I was very glad he was saved." Chantry said it in a stilted manner.

"Why?"

"Because his life was really important to the world."

Chantry might have been distributing tracts. His very voice sounded falsetto.

"Exactly. Well, that is what Ferguson thought."

"How do you know?"

"He told me."

"You must have known him well. Thank heaven, I never did."

Havelock flung out a huge hand. "Oh, get off that ridiculous animal you're riding, Chantry, and come to the point. You mean you don't think Ferguson should have admitted it?"

Chantry's tone changed. "Well, one doesn't."

The huge hand, clenched into a fist, came down on the table. The crystal bottle was too heavy to rock, but the glasses jingled and a spoon slid over the edge of its saucer.

"There it is — what I was looking for."

"What were you looking for?" Chantry's wonder was not feigned.

"For your hydra-headed Prejudice. Makes me want to play Hercules."

"Oh, drop your metaphors, Havelock. Get into the game. What is it?"

"It's this: that you don't think — or affect not to think — that it's decent for a man to recognize his own worth."

Chantry did not retort. He dropped his chin on his chest and thought for a moment. Then he spoke, very quietly and apologetically.

"Well — I don't see you telling another man how wonderful you are.

It isn't immoral, it simply isn't manners. And if Ferguson boasted to you that he was saved when so many went down, it was worse than bad manners. He ought to have been kicked for it. It's the kind of phenomenal luck that it would have been decent to regret."

Havelock set his massive lips firmly together. You could not say that he pursed that Cyclopean mouth.

"Ferguson did not boast. He merely told me. He was, I think, a modest man."

Incredulity beyond any power of laughter to express settled on Chantry's countenance. "Modest? and he *told* you?"

"The whole thing." Havelock's voice was heavy enough for tragedy. "Listen. Don't interrupt me once. Ferguson told me that, when the explosion came, he looked round — considered, for fully a minute, his duty. He never lost control of himself once, he said, and I believe him. The Argentina was a small boat, making a winter passage. There were very few cabin passengers. No second cabin, but plenty of steerage. She sailed, you remember, from Naples. He had been doing some work, some very important work, in the Aquarium. The only other person of consequence, — I am speaking in the most literal and un-snobbish sense, — in the first cabin, was Benson. No" (with a lifted hand), "*don't interrupt me*. Benson, as we all know, was an international figure. But Benson was getting old. His son could be trusted to carry on the House of Benson. In fact, every one suspected that the son had become more important than the old man. He had put through the last big loan while his father was taking a rest-cure in Italy. That is how Benson *père* happened to be on the Argentina. The newspapers never sufficiently accounted for that. A private deck on the Schrecklichkeit would have been more his size. Ferguson made it out: the old man got wild, suddenly, at the notion of their putting anything through without him. He trusted his gouty bones to the Argentina."

"Sounds plausible, but — " Chantry broke in.

"If you interrupt again," said Havelock, "I'll hit you, with all the strength I've got."

Chantry grunted. You had to take Havelock the Dane as you found him.

"Ferguson saw the whole thing clear. Old Benson had just gone into the smoking-room. Ferguson was on the deck outside his own stateroom. The only person on board who could possibly be considered as important as Ferguson was Benson; and he had good reason to believe that every one would get on well enough without Benson. He had just time, then, to put on a life-preserver, melt into his stateroom, and get a little pile of notes, very important ones, and drop into a boat. No, don't interrupt. I know what you are going to say. 'Women and children.' What do you suppose a lot of Neapolitan peasants meant to Ferguson — or to you, and me, either? He didn't do anything outrageous; he just dropped into a boat. As a result, we had the big book a year later. No" (again crushing down a gesture of Chantry's), "don't say anything about the instincts of a gentleman. If Ferguson hadn't been perfectly cool, his instincts would have governed him. He would have dashed about trying to save people, and then met the waves with a noble gesture. He had time to be reasonable; not instinctive. The world was the gainer, as he jolly well knew it would be — or where would have been the reasonableness? I don't believe Ferguson cared a hang about keeping his individual machine going for its own sake. But he knew he was a valuable person. His mind was a Kohinoor among minds. It stands to reason that you save the Kohinoor and let the little stones go. Well, that's not the story. Only I wanted to get that out of the way first, or the story wouldn't have meant anything. Did you wish," he finished graciously, "to ask a question?"

Chantry made a violent gesture of denial. "Ask a question about a hog like that? God forbid!"

"Um-m-m." Havelock seemed to muse within himself. "You will admit that if a jury of impartial men of sense could have sat, just then, on that slanting deck, they would have agreed that Ferguson's life was worth more to the world than all the rest of the boiling put together?"

"Yes, but — "

"Well, there wasn't any jury. Ferguson had to be it. I am perfectly sure that if there had been a super-Ferguson on board, our Ferguson would have turned his hand to saving him first. In fact, I honestly believe he was sorry there hadn't been a super-Ferguson. For he had all the instincts of a gentleman; and it's never a pleasant job making your reason inhibit your instincts. You can't look at this thing perfectly straight, probably. But if you can't, who can? I don't happen to want an enlightened opinion: I've got one, right here at home. You don't care about the State: you want to put it into white petticoats and see it cross a muddy street."

"I don't wonder the socialists won't have anything to do with you."

"Because I'm not a feminist? I know. Just as the feminists won't have anything to do with you because you're so reactionary. We're both out of it. Fifty years ago, either of us could have been a real prophet, for the price of a hall and cleaning the rotten eggs off our clothes. Now we're too timid for any use. But this is a digression."

"Distinctly. Is there anything more about Ferguson?"

"I should say there was. About a year ago, he became engaged. She's a very nice girl, and I am sure you never heard of her. The engagement wasn't to be announced until just before the marriage, for family reasons of some sort — cockering the older generation somehow. I've forgotten; it's not important. But they would have been married by now, if Ferguson hadn't stepped out."

"You seem to have been very intimate with Ferguson."

"He talked to me once — just once. The girl was a distant connection of my own. I think that was why. Now I've got some more things to tell you. I've let you interrupt a good lot, and if you're through, I'd like to start in on the next lap. It isn't easy for me to tell this thing in bits. It's an effort."

Havelock the Dane set down his second emptied glass and drew a long breath. He proceeded, with quickened pace.

III

"He didn't see the girl very often. She lives at some little distance. He was busy, — you know how he worked, — and she was chained at home, more or less. Occasionally he slipped away for a week-end, to see her. One time — the last time, about two months ago — he managed to get in a whole week. It was as near happiness as Ferguson ever got, I imagine; for they were able to fix a date. Good heaven, how he loved that girl! Just before he went, he told me of the engagement. I barely knew her, but, as I said, she's some sort of kin. Then, after he came back, he sent for me to come and see him. I didn't like his cheek, but I went as though I had been a laboratory boy. I'm not like you. Ferguson always did get me. He wanted the greatest good of the greatest number. Nothing petty about him. He was a big man.

"I went, as I say. And Ferguson told me, the very first thing, that the engagement was off. He began by cocking his hair a good deal. But he almost lost control of himself. He didn't cock it long: he ruffled it instead, with his hands. I thought he was in a queer state, for he seemed to want to give me, with his beautiful scientific precision, — as if he'd been preparing a slide, — the details of a country walk he and she had taken the day before he left. It began with grade-crossings, and I simply couldn't imagine what he was getting at. It wasn't his business to fight grade-crossings — though they might be a very pretty symbol for the kind of thing he was fighting, tooth and nail, all the time. I couldn't seem to see it, at first; but finally it came out. There was a grade-crossing, with a 'Look out for the Engine' sign, and there was a tow-headed infant in rags. They had noticed the infant before. It had bandy legs and granulated eyelids, and seemed to be dumb. It had started them off on eugenics. She was very keen on the subject; Ferguson, being a big scientist, had some reserves. It was a real argument.

"Then everything happened at once. Towhead with the sore eyes rocked onto the track simultaneously with the whistle. They were about fifty yards off. Ferguson sprinted back down the hill, the girl screaming pointlessly meanwhile. There was just time — you'll have to take my word for this; Ferguson explained it all to me in the most meticulous detail, but I can't repeat that masterpiece of exposition — for Ferguson to decide. To decide again, you understand, precisely as he had decided on the Argentina. Rotten luck, wasn't it? He could just have flung towhead out of the way by getting under the engine himself. He grabbed for towhead, but he didn't roll onto the track. So towhead was killed. If he had got there ten seconds earlier, he could have done the trick. He was ten seconds too late to save both Ferguson and towhead. So — once more — he saved Ferguson. Do you get the situation?"

"I should say I did!" shouted Chantry. "Twice in a man's life — good Lord! I hope you walked out of his house at that point."

"I didn't. I was very much interested. And by the way, Chantry, if Ferguson had given his life for towhead, you would have been the first man to write a pleasant little article for some damned highbrow review, to prove that it was utterly wrong that Ferguson should have exchanged his life for that of a little Polish defective. I can even see you talking about the greatest good of the greatest number. You would have loved the paradox of it: the mistaken martyr, self-preservation the greatest altruism, and all the rest of it. But because Ferguson did exactly what you would have said in your article that he ought to have done, you are in a state of virtuous chill."

"I should have written no such article. I don't see how you can be so flippant."

"Flippant — I? Have I the figure of a flippant man? Can't you see — honestly, now, can't you see? — that it was a hideous misfortune for that situation to come to Ferguson twice? Can't you see that it was about as hard luck as a man ever had? Look at it just once from his point of view."

"I can't," said Chantry frankly. "I can understand a man's being a coward, saving his own skin because he wants to. But to save his own skin on principle — humph! Talk of paradoxes: there's one for you. There's not a principle on earth that tells you to save your own life at some one else's expense. If he thought it was principle, he was the bigger defective of the two. Of course it would have been a pity; of course we should all have regretted it; but there's not a human being in this town, high or low, who wouldn't have applauded, with whatever regret — who wouldn't have said he did the only thing a self-respecting man could do. Of course it's a shame; but that is the only way the race has ever got on: by the strong, because they were strong, going under for the weak, because they were weak. Otherwise we'd all be living to this day, in hell."

"I know; I know." Havelock's voice was touched with emotion. "That's the convention — invented by individualists, for individualists. All sorts of people would see it that way, still. But you've got more sense than most; and I will make you at least see the other point of view. Suppose Ferguson to have been a good Catholic — or a soldier in the ranks. If his confessor or his commanding officer had told him to save his own skin, you'd consider Ferguson justified; you might even consider the priest or the officer justified. The one thing you can't stand is the man's giving himself those orders. But let's not argue over it now — let's go back to the story. I'll make you 'get' Ferguson, anyhow — even if I can't make him 'get' you.

"Well, here comes in the girl."

"And you said there was no girl in it!"

Chantry could not resist that. He believed that Havelock's assertion had been made only because he didn't want the girl in it — resented her being there.

"There isn't, as I see it," replied Havelock the Dane quietly. "From my point of view, the story is over. Ferguson's decision: that is the whole thing — made more interesting, more valuable, because the repetition of the thing proves beyond a doubt that he acted on principle, not on impulse. If he had flung himself into the life-boat because he was a coward, he would have been ashamed of it; and whatever he might have done afterwards, he would never have done that thing again. He would have been sensitive: not saving his own life would have turned into an obsession with him. But there is left, I admit, the murder. And murders always take the public. So I'll give you the murder — though it throws no light on Ferguson, who is the only thing in the whole accursed affair that really counts."

"The murder? I don't see — unless you mean the murdering of the towheaded child."

"I mean the murder of Ferguson by the girl he loved."

"You said 'suicide' a little while ago," panted Chantry.

"Technically, yes. She was a hundred miles away when it happened. But she did it just the same. — Oh, I suppose I've got to tell you, as Ferguson told me."

"Did he tell you he was going to kill himself?" Chantry's voice was sharp.

"He did not. Ferguson wasn't a fool. But it was plain as day to me after it happened, that he had done it himself."

"How — "

"I'm telling you this, am I not? Let me tell it, then. The thing happened in no time, of course. The girl got over screaming, and ran down to the track, frightened out of her wits. The train managed to stop, about twice its own length farther down, round a bend in the track, and the conductor and brakeman came running back. The mother came out of her hovel, carrying twins. The — the — thing was on the track, across the rails. It was a beastly mess, and Ferguson got the girl away; set her down to cry in a pasture, and then went back and helped out, and gave his testimony, and left money, a lot of it, with the mother, and — all the rest. You can imagine it. No one there considered that Ferguson ought to have saved the child; no one but Ferguson dreamed that he could have. Indeed, an ordinary man, in Ferguson's place, wouldn't have supposed he could. It was only that brain, working like lightning, working as no plain man's could, that had made the calculation and *seen*. There were no preliminary seconds lost in surprise or shock, you see. Ferguson's mind hadn't been jarred from its pace for an instant. The thing had happened too quickly for any one — except Ferguson — to understand what was going on. Therefore he ought to have laid that super-normal brain under the wheels, of course!

"Ferguson was so sane, himself, that he couldn't understand, even after he had been engaged six months, our little everyday madnesses. It never occurred to him, when he got back to the girl and she began all sorts of hysterical questions, not to answer them straight. It was by way of describing the event simply, that he informed her that he would just have had time to pull the creature out, but not enough to pull himself back afterwards. Ferguson was used to calculating things in millionths of an inch; she wasn't. I dare say the single second that had given

Ferguson time to turn round in his mind, she conceived of as a minute, at least. It would have taken her a week to turn round in her own mind, no doubt—a month, a year, perhaps. How do I know? But she got the essential fact: that Ferguson had made a choice. Then she rounded on him. It would have killed her to lose him, but she would rather have lost him than to see him standing before her, etc., etc. Ferguson quoted a lot of her talk straight to me, and I can remember it; but you needn't ask me to soil my mouth with it. 'And half an hour before, she had been saying with a good deal of heat that that little runt ought never to have been born, and that if we had decent laws it never would have been allowed to live.' Ferguson said that to me, with a kind of bewilderment. You see, he had made the mistake of taking that little fool seriously. Well, he loved her. You can't go below that: that's rock-bottom. Ferguson couldn't dig any deeper down for his way out. There *was* no deeper down.

"Apparently Ferguson still thought he could argue it out with her. She so believed in eugenics, you see—a very radical, compared with Ferguson. It was she who had had no doubt about towhead. And the love-part of it seemed to him fixed: it didn't occur to him that that was debatable. So he stuck to something that could be discussed. Then—and this was his moment of exceeding folly—he caught at the old episode of the Argentina. *That* had nothing to do with her present state of shock. She had seen towhead; but she hadn't seen the sprinkled Mediterranean. And she had accepted that. At least, she had spoken of his survival as though it had been one of the few times when God had done precisely the right thing. So he took that to explain with. The fool! The reasonable fool!

"Then—oh, then she went wild. (Yet she must have known there were a thousand chances on the Argentina for him to throw his life away, and precious few to save it.) She backed up against a tree and stretched her arms out like this"—Havelock made a clumsy stage-gesture of aversion from Chantry, the villain. "And for an instant he thought she was afraid of a Jersey cow that had come up to take part in the discussion. So he threw a twig at its nose."

IV

Chantry's wonder grew, swelled, and burst.

"Do you mean to say that that safety-deposit vault of a Ferguson told you all this?"

"As I am telling it to you. Only much more detail, of course—and much, much faster. It wasn't like a story at all: it was like — like a hemorrhage. I didn't interrupt him as you've been interrupting me. — Well, the upshot of it was that she spurned him quite in the grand manner. She found the opposites of all the nice things she had been saying for six months, and said them. And Ferguson — your cocky Ferguson — stood and listened, until she had talked herself out, and then went away. He never saw her again; and when he sent for me, he had made up his mind that she never intended to take any of it back. So he stepped out, I tell you."

"As hard hit as that," Chantry mused.

"Just as hard hit as that. Ferguson had had no previous affairs; she was very literally the one woman; and he managed, at forty, to combine the illusions of the boy of twenty and the man of sixty."

"But if he thought he was so precious to the world, wasn't it more than ever his duty to preserve his existence? He could see other people die in his place, but he couldn't see himself bucking up against a broken heart. Isn't that what the strong man does? Lives out his life when he doesn't at all like the look of it? Say what you like, he was a coward, Havelock — at the last, anyhow."

"I won't ask for your opinion just yet, thank you. Perhaps if Ferguson had been sure he would ever do good work again, he wouldn't have taken himself off. That might have held him. He might have stuck by on the chance. But I doubt it. Don't you see? He loved the girl too much."

"Thought he couldn't live without her," snorted Chantry.

"Oh, no — not that. But if she was right, he was the meanest skunk alive. He owed the world at least two deaths, so to speak. The only approach you can make to dying twice is to die in your prime, of your own volition." Havelock spoke very slowly. "At least, that's the way I've worked it out. He didn't say so. He was careful as a cat."

"You think" — Chantry leaned forward, very eager at last — "that he decided she was right? That I'm right — that we're all of us right?"

Havelock the Dane bowed his head in his huge hands. "No. If you ask me, I think he kept his own opinion untarnished to the end. When I told him I thought he was right, he just nodded, as if one took that for granted. But it didn't matter to him. I am pretty sure that he cared only what *she* thought."

"If he didn't agree with her? And if she had treated him like a criminal? He must have despised her, in that case."

"He never said one word of her — bar quoting some of *her* words — that wasn't utterly gentle. You could see that he loved her with his whole soul. And — it's my belief — he gave her the benefit of the doubt. In killing himself, he acted on the hypothesis that she had been right. It was the one thing he could do for her."

"But if no one except you thinks it was suicide — and you can't prove it — "

"Oh, he had to take that chance — the chance of her never knowing — or else create a scandal. And that would have been very hard on her and on his family. But there were straws she could easily clutch at — as I have clutched at them. The perfect order in which everything happened to be left — even the last notes he had made. His laboratory was a scientist's paradise, they tell me. And the will, made after she threw him over, leaving everything to her. Not a letter unanswered, all little bills paid, and little debts liquidated. He came as near suggesting it as he could, in decency. But I dare say she will never guess it."

"Then what did it profit him?"

"It didn't profit him, in your sense. He took a very long chance on her guessing. That wasn't what concerned him."

"I hope she will never guess, anyhow. It would ruin her life, to no good end."

"Oh, no." Havelock was firm. "I doubt if she would take it that way. If she grasped it at all, she'd believe he thought her right. And if he thought her right, of course he wouldn't want to live, would he? She would never think he killed himself simply for love of her."

"Why not?"

"Well, she wouldn't. She wouldn't be able to conceive of Ferguson's killing himself for merely that — with *his* notions about survival."

"As he did."

"As he did — and didn't."

"Ah, she'd scarcely refine on it as you are doing, Havelock. You're amazing."

"Well, he certainly never expected her to know that he did it himself. If he had been the sort of weakling that dies because he can't have a particular woman, he'd have been also the sort of weakling that leaves a letter explaining."

"What then did he die for? You'll have to explain to me. Not because he couldn't have her; not because he felt guilty. Why, then? You haven't left him a motive."

"Oh, haven't I? The most beautiful motive in the world, my dear fellow. A motive that puts all your little simple motives in the shade."

"Well, what?"

"Don't you see? Why, I told you. He simply assumed, for all practical purposes, that she had been right. He gave himself the fate he knew she considered him to deserve. He preferred — loving her as he did — to do what she would have had him do. He knew she was wrong; but he knew also that she was made that way, that she would never be right. And he took her for what she was, and loved her as she was. His love — don't you see? — was too big. He couldn't revolt from her: she had the whole of him — except, perhaps, his excellent judgment. He couldn't drag about a life which she felt that way about. He destroyed it, as he would have destroyed anything she found loathsome. He was merely justifying himself to his love. He couldn't hope she would know. Nor, I believe, could he have lied to her. That is, he couldn't have admitted in words that she was right, when he felt her so absolutely wrong; but he could make that magnificent silent act of faith."

Chantry still held out. "I don't believe he did it. I hold with the coroner."

"I don't. He came as near telling me as he could without making me an accessory before the fact. There were none of the loose ends that the most orderly man would leave if he died suddenly. Take my word for it, old man."

A long look passed between them. Each seemed to be trying to find out with his eyes something that words had not helped him to.

Finally Chantry protested once more. "But Ferguson couldn't love like that."

Havelock the Dane laid one hand on the arm of Chantry's chair and spoke sternly. "He not only could, but did. And there I am a better authority than you. Think what you please, but I will not have that fact challenged. Perhaps you could count up on your fingers the women who are loved like that; but, anyhow, she was. My second cousin once removed, damn her!" He ended with a vicious twang.

"And now" — Havelock rose — "I'd like your opinion."

"About what?"

"Well, can't you see the beautiful sanity of Ferguson?"

"No, I can't," snapped Chantry. "I think he was wrong, both in the beginning and in the end. But I will admit he was not a coward. I respect him, but I do not think, at any point, he was right — except perhaps in 'doing' the coroner."

"That settles it, then," said Havelock. And he started towards the door.

"Settles what, in heaven's name?"

"What I came to have settled. I shan't tell her. If I could have got one other decent citizen — and I confess you were my only chance — to agree with me that Ferguson was right, — right about his fellow passengers on the Argentina, right about towhead on the track, — I'd have gone to her, I think. I'd rather like to ruin her life, if I could."

A great conviction approached Chantry just then. He felt the rush of it through his brain.

"No," he cried. "Ferguson loved her too much. He wouldn't like that — not as you'd put it to her."

Havelock thought a moment. "No," he said in turn; but his "no" was very humble. "He wouldn't. I shall never do it. But, my God, how I wanted to!"

"And I'll tell you another thing, too." Chantry's tone was curious. "You may agree with Ferguson all you like; you may admire him as much as you say; but you, Havelock, would never have done what he did. Not even" — he lifted a hand against interruption — "if you knew you had the brain you think Ferguson had. You'd have been at the bottom of the sea, or under the engine-wheels, and you know it."

He folded his arms with a hint of truculence.

But Havelock the Dane, to Chantry's surprise, was meek. "Yes," he said, "I know it. Now let me out of here."

"Well, then," — Chantry's voice rang out triumphant, — "what does that prove?"

"Prove?" Havelock's great fist crashed down on the table. "It proves that Ferguson's a better man than either of us. I can think straight, but he had the sand to act straight. You haven't even the sand to think straight. You and your reactionary rot! The world's moving, Chantry. Ferguson was ahead of it, beckoning. You're an ant that got caught in the machinery, I shouldn't wonder."

"Oh, stow the rhetoric! We simply don't agree. It's happened before." Chantry laughed scornfully. "I tell you I respect him; but God Almighty wouldn't make me agree with him."

"You're too mediæval by half," Havelock mused. "Now, Ferguson was a knight of the future — a knight of Humanity."

"Don't!" shouted Chantry. His nerves were beginning to feel the strain. "Leave chivalry out of it. The Argentina business may or may not have been wisdom, but it certainly wasn't cricket."

"No," said Havelock. "Chess, rather. The game where chance hasn't a show — the game of the intelligent future. That very irregular and disconcerting move of his. — And he got taken, you might say. She's an irresponsible beast, your queen."

"Drop it, will you!" Then Chantry pulled himself together, a little ashamed. "It's fearfully late. Better stop and dine."

"No, thanks." The big man opened the door of the room and rested a foot on the threshold. "I feel like dining with some one who appreciates Ferguson."

"I don't know where you'll find him."

Chantry smiled and shook hands.

"Oh, I carry him about with me. Good-night," said Havelock the Dane.

February 1917

ELLEN TERRY

1848–1928

Not, I think, since Atalanta won her race has any woman run as Ellen Terry ran. Her motion was poetry, and her voice had the morning freshness of her favorite heroines. Without the intensity of a great actress, in comedy she was undiluted joy and in tragedy, a consolation — and one needed consolation when the powerful but stilted genius of Henry Irving stalked opposite her across the stage.

To write of Ellen Terry is to think of charm, but one must not use the word, for it was she who said "Blow that word, 'charm'! There is more in my acting than charm." And she was right. Of her inspiration there is no question. It came from Shakespeare with never a commentator between, and did she not tell Sir Henry that Shakespeare was the only man she ever really loved? "When I was sixteen or seventeen and very unhappy I forswore the society of men. Yet all the same, I was lonely. I wanted a sweetheart. Well Shakespeare became my sweetheart."

The Letters in Shakespeare's Plays

ELLEN TERRY

Some years ago, when I was asked to lecture on Shakespeare's heroines in the light of the knowledge which I had gained of their character through impersonating them on the stage, I wondered if it were possible to find anything to say that had not been said before. "If nothing is, that has not been before, how are our brains beguiled!" However, I found out, when I applied myself to the task, that even Shakespeare, about whom hundreds of books have been written, has a little of the unknown. For years it was my trade to find out, not what he had been to others, but what he was to *me,* and to make that visible in my acting. It was easier to describe what I saw through my own medium, than through one for which I have had no training; but I am glad that I tried, because it meant more study of the plays, and so, more delightful experiences.

In the course of this study for my lectures on the women in Shakespeare, I was struck by the fact that the letters in his plays have never had their due. Little volumes of the songs have been published; jewels of wit and wisdom have been taken out of their setting and reset in birthday books, calendars, and the rest; but, so far as I know, there is no separate collection of the letters. I found, when I read them aloud, that they were wonderful letters, and worth talking about on their merits. "I should like to talk about them as well as the heroines," I said. "But there are so few," the friend, to whom I suggested them as a subject for a *causerie,* objected. "I can't remember any myself beyond those in *The Merchant of Venice,* and *As You Like It.*" "That's splendid!" I thought. "If you, who are not at all ignorant, can't do better than that, there must be hundreds to whom it will be a surprise to learn that there are thirty letters, and all good ones!"

There is all the more reason for giving them our attention because they are the only letters written by Shakespeare that have survived. I doubt whether, as a man, he was a good correspondent. He crowded his great life's work, which has made England more honored throughout the world than the achievements of her great soldiers, sailors, and statesmen, into a score of years. He did not begin his career as a youthful prodigy, and he died when he was fifty-two. What with adapting plays, creating them, re-touching them at rehearsal, writing sonnets, acting, managing companies of actors, and having a good time with his friends, he could not have had much leisure for pouring out his soul in letters. The man who does that is, as a rule, an idle man, and Shakespeare, I feel sure, was always busy.

People often say we have no authority for talking about Shakespeare as a man at all. What do we know for certain about his life? But I quite agree with Georg Brandes (my favorite Shakespearean scholar) that, given the possession of forty-five important works by any man, it is entirely our own fault if we know nothing about him. But perhaps these works are not by Shakespeare, but by a syndicate, or by some fellow who took his name! Why should we pursue these tiresome theories? I wish we had just one authentic letter of Shakespeare's to put a stop to it. Otherwise, I should be glad that he left none behind for posterity to thumb. I don't like reading the private letters of a great man. Print is so merciless. Many things pass in hand-writing, which print "shows up." Print is so impertinent — flinging open the door of a little room, where, perhaps, two lovers are communing, and saying to the public, "Have a look at them — these great people in love! You see they are just as silly as little people." The Browning letters — ought they ever to have been published? The *Sonnets from the Portuguese* gave us the picture of a great love. The letters were like an anatomical dissection of it.

Now these letters in Shakespeare's plays were meant for the public ear — invented to please it; so we can examine them with a clear conscience. Yet they are true to life. We can learn from them how the man of action writes a letter, and how the poet writes a letter. We can learn that, when people are in love, they all use the same language. Whether they are stupid or clever, they employ the same phrases. "I love you," writes the man of genius — and "I love you," writes the fool. Hamlet begins his letter to Ophelia in the conventional rhymes which were fashionable with Elizabethan gallants: —

"To the celestial and my soul's idol, the most beautified Ophelia" — "In her excellent white bosom, these," and so on.

Doubt thou the stars are fire,
Doubt that the sun doth move,
Doubt truth to be a liar,
But never doubt I love.

So far he writes in his character of "the glass of fashion." But he does not like the artificial style and soon abandons it for simple, earnest prose: —

O DEAR OPHELIA, I am ill at these numbers. I have not art to reckon my groans; but that I love thee best, O most best, believe it. Adieu.

Thine evermore, most dear lady,
Whilst this machine is to him,
HAMLET.

Is this a sincere love-letter? Was Hamlet ever in love with Ophelia? I think he was, and found it hard to put her out of his life. At the very moment when the revelation of his mother's infidelity had made him cynical about woman's virtue, this girl acts in a way that fills him with suspicion. She hands his letters to her father, allows herself to be made a tool. His conclusion is: "You are like my mother; you could act as she did." But he loved her all the same.

I loved Ophelia. Forty thousand brothers
Could not, with all their quantity of love,
Make up my sum.

Proteus, in *The Two Gentlemen of Verona,* is one of those professional lovers who are never in love and never out of it. I can imagine him reeling off love-letters with consummate ease, not caring much to whom they were addressed so long as they contained enough beautiful epithets to satisfy *him!* Of his letter to Julia we hear only fragments: "Kind Julia"; "love-wounded Proteus"; "poor forlorn Proteus"; "passionate Proteus" — more of Proteus than of Julia, you see! — for Julia, like many another woman, has, for the sake of her self-respect, torn up the letter that she is burning to read! She pieces the torn bits together, but these incoherent exclamations are all that her pride has left legible. Proteus's letter to Silvia we hear complete. It is in the fashionable rhyme, affected, insincere, but quite pretty.

My thoughts do harbour with my Silvia nightly,
And slaves they are to me that send them flying:
O, could their master come and go as lightly,
Himself would lodge where senseless they are lying!
My herald thoughts in thy pure bosom rest them,
While I, their King, that hither them importune,
Do curse the grace that with such grace hath blessed them,
Because myself do want my servants' fortune.

I curse myself, for they are sent by me,
That they should harbour where their lord would be.

. . . . . .

Silvia, this night I will enfranchise thee.

How this letter-writer enjoyed playing with words! And how different this skill at pat-ball from the profound feeling in the letter from Antonio to Bassanio in *The Merchant of Venice!* Hear how a man, deeply moved, writes to the friend he loves.

SWEET BASSANIO, — My ships have all miscarried, my creditors grow cruel, my estate is very low, my bond to the Jew is forfeit, and since in paying it, it is impossible I should live, all debts are cleared between you and I, if I might but see you at my death. Notwithstanding, use your pleasure. If your love do not persuade you to come, let not my letter.

To my mind, in this letter human love at its greatest finds expression. This love has all the tenderness of a woman's love: "Sweet Bassanio!" the trustfulness of a child's "I have only to tell him and he will help me"; the generosity and manliness of a true friend's "Don't feel that you owe me anything. It's all right, but I would like to see you and grasp your hand"; the unselfishness with which wives and mothers love: "You mustn't think of coming all the same, if it puts you out." Of all the letters in the plays, this one of Antonio's is my favorite.

Our manner of expression is determined by the age in which we live, but in this letter it is the thing expressed that seems to have changed. It is impossible to study Shakespeare's plays closely without noticing that to him friendship was perhaps the most sacred of all human relations. Valentine offers to sacrifice Silvia to Proteus. Bassanio says that his wife matters less to him than the life of his friend. To an Elizabethan audience this exaltation of friendship did not seem strange. Two of Shakespeare's comrades, Beaumont and Fletcher, lived together "on the Bankside, not far from the playhouse," and had the same "clothes and cloak between them"; and there were many such all-sufficing friendships. That attractive old sinner, John Falstaff, was cut to the heart when his friend Prince Hal publicly denounced him. His affection for young Harry is a lovable trait in his character; and who does not feel sorry for him, worthless old waster as he is, when the Prince answers his, "God save thee my sweet boy," with "I know thee not, old man; fall to thy prayers"? But when Falstaff wrote the following letter, Harry was still unreformed and friendly: —

Sir John Falstaff, knight, to the son of the King nearest his father, Harry Prince of Wales, greeting: —

I will imitate the honourable Romans in brevity. I commend me to thee, I commend thee, and I leave thee. Be not too familiar with Poins; for he misuses thy favours so much, that he swears thou art to marry his sister Nell. Repent at idle times as thou mayest; and so, farewell.

Thine by yea and no, which is as much as to say, as thou usest him, Jack Falstaff with my familiars, John with my brothers and sisters, and Sir John with all Europe.

When we meet Sir John again in *The Merry Wives of Windsor,* — in which play Shakespeare had to bring him out of his grave, "by request," because he was so popular in the theatre that audiences wanted to see him in another play, — his wit is not quite so bright, but his epistolary style is much the same. You may remember that he writes two love-letters, word for word the same, to two women living in the same town, who, as he must have known, met often and exchanged confidences. This alone shows that the Falstaff of the *Merry Wives* is not quite the man he was in *Henry IV* — does not carry his sack as well, perhaps!

Ask me no reason why I love you; for though Love use Reason for his physician, he admits him not for his counsellor. You are not young, no more am I; go to then, there's sympathy. You are merry, so am I; ha, ha! then there's more sympathy. You love sack, and so do I; would you desire better sympathy? Let it suffice thee, Mistress Page, — at the least, if the love of a soldier can suffice, — that I love thee. I will not say, pity me; 'tis not a soldier-like phrase; but I say, love me. By me,

Thine own true knight,
By day or night,
Or any kind of light,
With all his might
For thee to fight,

John Falstaff.

This letter may not be very funny in print; but when it is read aloud on the stage, it provokes much laughter. Sometimes one thinks that a joke is the thing most affected by the time-spirit. Remove it from its place in time, and it ceases to exist as a joke. Our sense of what is tragic remains the same through the centuries; but our sense of humor — that changes. It is hard to believe that some Elizabethan comedies were ever amusing. In nothing does Shakespeare show himself "above the law" more clearly than in his fun. It is not always "nice," but it is mirth-provoking, that is, if it is not treated academically. If a modern audience does not laugh at Shakespeare's jokes, blame the actors! The letter that Maria, in *Twelfth Night,* palms off on Malvolio as Olivia's has all the material for making us laugh; but I have seen Malvolios who so handled the material as to justify the opinion that Shakespeare's comedy is no longer comic. Here again it is the situation that makes the letter good fun on the stage. It begins in verse of rather poor quality—

Jove knows I love;
But who?
Lips, do not move;
No man must know.
I may command where I adore;
But silence, like a Lucrece knife,
With bloodless stroke my heart doth gore.
M, O, A, I, doth sway my life!

Maria was not much of a poet, but when she takes to prose, she shines.

If this fall into thy hand, revolve. In my stars I am above thee, but be not afraid of greatness. Some are born great, some achieve greatness, and some have greatness thrust upon 'em. Thy Fates open their hands, let thy blood and spirit embrace them; and, to inure thyself to what thou art like to be, cast thy humble slough and appear fresh. Be opposite with a kinsman, surly with servants; let thy tongue tang arguments of state; put thyself into the trick of singularity: she thus advises thee that sighs for thee. Remember who commended thy yellow stockings, and wished to see thee ever cross-gartered. I say, remember. Go to, thou art made, if thou desirest to be so; if not, let me see thee a steward still, the fellow of servants, and not worthy to touch Fortune's fingers. Farewell. She that would alter services with thee,

THE FORTUNATE UNHAPPY.

Then follows the postscript; and Maria had reserved her great coup for the postscript (the only one, by the way, that is written in full in the plays):—

If thou entertainest my love, let it appear in thy smiling. Thy smiles become thee well; therefore in my presence still smile, dear my sweet, I prithee!

Shakespeare was no Puritan. He probably enjoyed bear-baiting, and yet, unlike many of his contemporaries, felt sorry for the bear. So after writing this scene, in which Malvolio is baited, and deluded, and made to look a fool, he is able to write another in which our sympathies are roused with the victim of Maria's "sport royal." Malvolio's letter to Olivia makes us see that the sport had its cruel side.

By the Lord, madam, you wrong me, and the world shall know it. Though you have put me into darkness and given your drunken cousin rule over me, yet have I the benefit of my senses as well as your ladyship. I have your own letter that induced me to the semblance I put on; with the which I doubt not but to do myself much right, or you much shame. Think of me as you please. I leave my duty a little unthought of and speak out of my injury.

THE MADLY-USED MALVOLIO.

Although written in circumstances calculated to make the best servant "a little forget his duty," this letter is full of the dignity of service, and a just rebuke to those who hold their "inferiors" up to ridicule.

From a letter from a steward in a gold chain, preserving his dignity in an undignified position, I turn to one from a groom. A plain fellow this. I see him sitting down, laboriously scratching out a few illegible sentences. But they are straight to the point, and they have their dramatic value in adding a touch to the portrait of Cardinal Wolsey in *Henry VIII*.

MY LORD, — The horses your lordship sent for, with all the care I had, I saw well chosen, ridden, and furnished. They were young and handsome, and of the best breed in the north. When they were ready to set out for London, a man of my Lord Cardinal's by commission and main power, took 'em from me, with this reason: His master would be served before a subject, if not before the King; which stopped our mouths, sir.

There is a tedious, pedantic letter in *Love's Labour's Lost,* which may have amused Shakespeare's contemporaries because it satirizes the affectations of their day. Armado's style in this letter is only a slight exaggeration of that in which people wrote to Queen Elizabeth. They used six long words when one short one would have conveyed their meaning, and racked their brains for pretentious and extravagant compliments. I used to read this letter in one of my lectures, and oh, what a job it was to get any fun out of it! Here is a sample of its humor: —

The magnanimous and most illustrate king Cophetua set eye upon the pernicious and indubitate beggar, Zenelophon; and he it was that might rightly say, *Veni, vidi, vici;* which to annothanize in the vulgar, — O base and obscure vulgar! — videlicet, He came, saw, and overcame: he came, one; saw, two; overcame, three. Who came? The king. Why did he come? To see. Why did he see? To overcome. To whom came he? To the beggar. What saw he? The beggar. Who overcame he? The beggar. The conclusion is victory; on whose side? The king's. The captive is enriched; on whose side? The beggar's. The catastrophe is a nuptial; on whose side? The king's; no, on both in one, or one in both.

And so forth.

But, of course, when the audience has seen the popinjay Armado and knows that this high-flown stuff is written to an illiterate peasant-girl, the letter makes a different impression, especially if Boyet, who has to read it, is a good actor! But if he is a wise one, he will probably beg for the effusion to be "cut."

"I say she never did invent this letter," exclaims Rosalind, after hearing the rhymed jingle that Phebe sends her under the impression that she is a handsome young man. This lets us into a little secret about these rhymed letters. They could be bought in many English villages, from the professional letter-writer of the parish. And this was the sort of letter that he turned out:—

If the scorn of your bright eyne
Have power to raise such love in mine,
Alack, in me what strange effect
Would they work in mild aspect!
Whiles you chid me, I did love;
How then might your prayers move?
He that brings this love to thee
Little knows this love in me;
And by him seal up thy minds,
Whether that thy youth and kind
Will the faithful offer take
Of me, and all that I can make;
Or else by him my love deny,
And then I'll study how to die.

In *All's Well that Ends Well,* we find that women of property commanded the services of their stewards when they wanted a letter written. Bertram's mother in this play instructs her steward, Rinaldo, to write to her son for her:—

Write, write, Rinaldo,
To this unworthy husband of his wife.
Let every word weigh heavy of her worth
That he does weigh too light. My greatest grief,
Though little he do feel it, set down sharply.

Rinaldo evidently obeyed this instruction faithfully, for we hear later on that the letter "stings Bertram's nature," and that on the reading of it "he changed almost into another man." Bertram ends his letter to his mother with "My duty to you." He is not on good terms with her, but he does not forget to be externally filial and polite. An odious young man, yet Helena, whom he treats so outrageously, is annoyingly fond of him.

> Thus, Indian-like,
> Religious in mine error, I adore
> The sun, that looks upon his worshipper,
> But knows of him no more.

My next letter-writer, Leonatus in *Cymbeline,* plays his wife a dirty trick. But in all ages a man whose jealousy is roused is forgiven much. Leonatus is devoted to Imogen, yet he can make her chastity the subject of a wager with a man who scoffs at the idea of any woman being chaste.

He writes and asks her to welcome this man of whom he has every reason to think ill. He goes so far as to describe Iachimo to her as "one of the noblest note, to whose kindnesses I am most infinitely tied. Reflect upon him accordingly, as you value your trust — " "So far I read aloud," says Imogen; and adds that the rest of the letter warms "the very middle of my heart" — a letter written by a husband who cannot believe in her without proof, and has sent a comparative stranger to make an assault on her virtue!

It is not surprising that, when Iachimo returns with his catalogue of all the furniture in Imogen's room, and a careful description of the mole on her left breast, "cinque-spotted, like the crimson drops i' the bottom of a cow-slip," Leonatus should "see red"; but there is really no excuse for his sitting down and writing a base falsehood to lure his wife to her death. How differently Imogen behaves when Iachimo traduces Leonatus to her! She is not only indignant; she is reasonable and sensible. When he urges her to be revenged, she says that, if it were true, — but she will not let her heart be abused in haste by her ears, — revenge would not help her. And what wisdom there is in her reply to Iachimo: —

> If thou wert honourable,
> Thou wouldst have told this tale for virtue, not
> For such an end thou seek'st.

She sees through this man, but naturally does not see through this letter from Leonatus.

> Justice, and your father's wrath, should he take me in his dominion, could not be so cruel to me, as you, O the dearest of creatures, would even renew me with your eyes. Take notice that I am in Cambria, at Milford-Haven; what your own love will out of this advise you, follow. So he wishes you all happiness, that remains loyal to his vow, and your increasing in love
>
> LEONATUS POSTHUMUS.

I never could read it on the stage without believing in its sincerity. A woman would have to be very suspicious to take it as "a trap." Imogen's love was so great that she forgave the man who wrote it to make her death sure. Did Shakespeare himself hold the opinion that a woman's love and a man's love have no common denominator? Leonatus shows his love by planning to kill his wife, when he is convinced that she is unfaithful. When he finds that he has been deceived, he calls himself "a credulous fool," and other harsh names. But Imogen refrains from petty reproaches. The worst she says is:—

> Why did you throw your wedded lady from you?
> Think that you are upon a rock, and now
> Throw me again.

To love when all goes well—that is easy. To love when the loved one behaves like Leonatus—that requires a self-abnegation which is apparently considered impossible except to women!

Macbeth's letter to his wife is interesting, not only because it is one of those rare tributes that a man sometimes pays to the share his wife has had in the making of his career, but because of the light it throws on the visionary element in Macbeth's character. The goal of his ambition is a material thing,—an earthly crown,—but he believes in the supernatural nature of his "call."

> They met me in the day of success; and I have learned by the perfectest report, they have more in them than mortal knowledge. When I burned in desire to question them further, they made themselves air, into which they vanished. Whiles I stood rapt in the wonder of it, came missives from the King, who all-hailed me "Thane of Cawdor"; by which title, before, these weird sisters saluted me, and referred me to the coming on of time, with "Hail, King that shalt be!" This have I thought good to deliver thee, my dearest partner of greatness, that thou mightest not lose the dues of rejoicing, by being ignorant of what greatness is promised thee. Lay it to thy heart, and farewell.

"My dearest partner of greatness!" Is not that a wonderful revelation of the relationship between this husband and his wife? Is not the whole letter a wonderful revelation of the man's character? a man who was driven by dreams into a common and cruel crime.

We could not have a better example than this of Shakespeare's use of the letter in his plays. Dramatists now condemn them, with soliloquies, as a clumsy expedient for letting the audience "know things." But Shakespeare employs both letters and soliloquies with a skill that strikes one more when one sees his plays in action than when one reads them. Bellario's letter to the Duke in *The Merchant of Venice,* besides being a model of what a letter should be, is a masterly preparation for Portia's entrance in the Court scene, and an instruction as to how the actress ought to handle that scene. She is not to behave with feminine inconsequence, and provoke laughter by her ignorance of legal procedure, but to conduct herself like a trained advocate. The letter makes Portia's eloquence and intelligence convincing to the audience.

Your Grace shall understand that at the receipt of your letter I am very sick; but in the instant that your messenger came, in loving visitation was with me a young doctor of Rome. His name is Balthazar. I acquainted him with the cause in controversy between the Jew and Antonio the merchant. We turned o'er many books together. He is furnished with my opinions; which, bettered with his own learning, the greatness whereof I cannot enough commend, comes with him, at my importunity, to fill up your Grace's request in my stead. I beseech you, let his lack of years be no impediment to let him lack a reverend estimation; for I never knew so young a body with so old a head. I leave him to your gracious acceptance, whose trial shall better publish his commendation.

What a lot of things there are to think over in this letter! And what pictures it conjures up! No Italian painter could make us see more clearly the learned Bellario receiving his young visitor and instructing her how to conduct her case. With the instinct of genius, the dramatist absorbed the spirit of the Renaissance in this play, as in *Julius Cæsar* he absorbed the spirit of ancient Rome. If Shakespeare knew "small Latin and less Greek," he was able to make this letter of warning to Cæsar typically Latin in its conciseness:—

Cæsar, beware of Brutus; take heed of Cassius; come not near Casca; have an eye to Cinna; trust not Trebonius; mark well Metellus Cimber; Decius Brutus loves thee not; thou hast wronged Caius Ligarius. There is but one mind in all these men, and it is bent against Cæsar. If thou beest not immortal, look about you; security gives way to conspiracy. The mighty gods defend thee! Thy lover,

ARTEMODORUS.

The whole plot of the play, and the guiding motive of each character, can be found in these short sentences.

If we compare this letter with the long-winded effusion from Armado to the King in *Love's Labour's Lost* (which I am not going to quote here, because it is so terribly long), we get a good idea of the infinite variety of style that the dramatist had at his command, and of his insight into the characteristics of different races at different times. He knew that the Romans were masters of brevity. And he knew that the affected Elizabethan courtier was a master of verbosity. Both he can imitate to the life.

In *Henry IV* Hotspur reads a letter, and this time it is the man who reads it, not the man who writes it, on whom our attention is concentrated. You see a quick-witted, courageous fellow, impatient of cautious people who see both sides of a question and are afraid of going too far. You see the "extremist," with all his good points and his bad ones.

He could be contented; why is he not, then? In respect of the love he bears our house: he shows in this, he loves his own barn better than he loves our house. . . . "The purpose you undertake is dangerous"; — why that's certain. 'Tis dangerous to take a cold, to sleep, to drink; but I tell you, my lord fool, out of this nettle, danger, we pluck this flower, safety. "The purpose you undertake is dangerous; . . . the friends you have named uncertain; and your whole plot too light for the counterpoise of so great an opposition." Say you so, say you so? I say unto you again, you are a shallow, cowardly hind, and you lie. What a lack-brain is this! By the Lord, our plot is a good plot as ever was laid; our friends true and constant: a good plot, good friends, and full of expectation; an excellent plot, very good friends. What a frosty-spirited rogue is this! Why, my Lord of York commends the plot and the general course of the action. 'Zounds, an I were now by this rascal, I could brain him with his lady's fan.

There is real "vinegar and pepper" in this outburst of Hotspur's. Compare it with the "vinegar and pepper" of Sir Andrew Aguecheek's fiery challenge to Viola in *Twelfth Night*. Sir Andrew is, as you know, a very devil of a fellow. He is quite sure that this letter is bold enough to strike terror into the heart of the most confident enemy: —

Youth, whatsoever thou art, thou art but a scurvy fellow. Wonder not, nor admire not in thy mind, why I do call thee so, for I will show thee no reason for't. Thou com'st to the lady Olivia, and in my sight she uses thee kindly. But thou liest in thy throat; that is not the matter I challenge thee for. I will waylay thee going home; where if it be thy chance to kill me, thou killest me like a rogue and a villain. Fare thee well, and God have mercy upon one of our souls! He may have mercy upon mine; but my hope is better, and so look to thyself.

Thy friend, as thou usest him, and thy sworn enemy,

ANDREW AGUECHEEK.

Besides Hamlet's letter to Ophelia, there are two other letters from him in the play which are often omitted in acting versions. The first is to Horatio, and it has its bright side in the complete confidence he places in his friend: —

Horatio, when thou shalt have overlooked this, give these fellows some means to the King; they have letters for him. Ere we were two days old at sea, a pirate of very warlike appointment gave us chase. Finding ourselves too slow of sail, we put on a compelled valour. In the grapple I boarded them. On the instant they got clear of our ship, so I alone became their prisoner. They have dealt with me like thieves of mercy, but they knew what they did: I am to do a good turn for them. Let the King have the letters I have sent, and repair thou to me with as much speed as thou wouldst fly death. I have words to speak in your ear will make thee dumb, yet are they much too light for the bore of the matter. These good fellows will bring thee where I am. Rosencrantz and Guildenstern hold their course for England; of them I have much to tell thee. Farewell.

He that thou knowest thine,

HAMLET.

The wording of the second letter, to the King, is simple and direct enough, yet it has a sinister and malevolent sound — its very civility is calculated to terrify the guilty conscience of the King: —

High and mighty, You shall know I am set naked on your kingdom. To-morrow shall I beg leave to see your kingly eyes, when I shall, first asking your pardon thereunto, recount the occasions of my sudden and more strange return.

HAMLET.

"And in a postscript here," says the King, who reads the letter, "he says, 'alone.'"

In *Antony and Cleopatra,* Shakespeare adopts the method of making someone give the substance of a letter, instead of reading the actual words of the writer. Twice Octavius Cæsar enters "reading a letter," and twice we have to trust to his honor that he is reporting it fairly.

The first, which brings news of Antony, is obviously colored by Octavius's jealousy of his great "competitor."

From Alexandria
This is the news: he fishes, drinks, and wastes
The lamps of night in revel; is not more manlike
Than Cleopatra; nor the Queen of Ptolemy
More womanly than he; hardly gave audience, or
Vouchsafed to think he had partners. You shall find there
A man who is the abstract of all faults
That all men follow.

You feel at once that Octavius reads this as a stroke of diplomacy. He wants to justify himself in the eyes of the world for hating Antony, and he does not trouble to be accurate. Half a truth is always more damning than a lie.

Antony was, as he is represented here, a pleasure-seeker; he had that reckless determination to enjoy the moment, which is not an uncommon attribute of great rulers and great artists. But he was, as well, a fine soldier, one who was at his best in defeat and misfortune. He loved luxury, but he could at times renounce all comfort for the sake of keeping up the courage of his men. But with Roman fortitude he had neither Roman restraint nor Roman simplicity. He loves striking an attitude. Twice he challenges Octavius to single combat, and in language so vain-glorious that Octavius exclaims: "He calls me boy" (this time he is too angry to misrepresent Antony, and we may take it that his version of the challenge is true):—

He calls me boy; and chides as he had power
To beat me out of Egypt. My messenger
He hath whipped with rods; dares me to personal combat,
Cæsar to Antony. Let the old ruffian know
I have many other ways to die.

Timon of Athens's last message to the world is melancholy reading! Its fierce and savage cynicism shows our gentle Shakespeare in a new light. Timon makes his grave on the "beached verge of the salt flood," and erects his own tomb,—

Entombed upon the very hem o' the sea.

A soldier takes an impression in wax of the inscription scratched on it, and brings it to Alcibiades:—

Here lies a wretched corse, of wretched soul bereft.
Seek not my name: a plague consume you wicked caitiffs left!
Here lie I, Timon, who, alive, all living men did hate.
Pass by and curse thy fill, but pass and stay not here thy gait.

Alcibiades, with a generosity that we should imitate, finds the noble element in this last effort after consistency of a consistent hater of men: —

These well express in thee thy latter spirits:
Though thou abhorr'dst in us our human griefs,
Scorn'dst our brain's flow and those our droplets which
From niggard nature fall, yet rich conceit
Taught thee to make vast Neptune weep for aye
On thy low grave, on faults forgiven.

Those are good words with which to bring this little study of a corner of the great world of Shakespeare's mind to an end!

December 1921

MARY WEBB

1881–1927

Of Mary Webb and of the gifts which Wenlock Edge bestowed upon her I have written at length in another book. Suffice it here to say that I have never known man or woman whose passion for Nature was so intimately bound to a single locality — the Shropshire of her youth. The Welsh mountains remained the boundary of her horizon, and no flower in Shropshire fields but stood in her mind for all the beauties of Creation. It was of the simple people she had known she loved best to write. For the drawing of character she had little gift. The men and women of her stories were born good or bad, and good or bad they obdurately remained, like puppets in the show. Yet in her stories you always felt her presence. Mary Webb had come from the land of little change and her style was filled with rhythms which those who love Seventeenth Century prose can readily detect. But the lasting value of her work lies in the intensities of her feelings. They are as real today as on the day she died.

The Prize

MARY WEBB

I

The vicarage lawn, bright green in the August sunshine, with beds of golden violas, had been galvanized into frantic gayety by the incursion of the entire village. It was the great day of the year in Cherrington Magna; for the school treat and the festival of the local club had been rolled into one enormous — and, to the hermit vicar, horrific — revel. A tea, a dance, and races were included in the programme. Tea was over and, with the lusty country scorn of digestion which prevails at such festivals, everybody was now prepared to run races. Their faces shone with pleasure, hope of useful prizes, and honest yellow soap. They were of the good but unemotional type produced by preoccupation with the material side of life, and they had the touch of harshness which comes from absorption in petty worries. The women's dresses, of homely stuffs, in neutral or primary colors, made dark or brilliant patches on the green grass.

Apart from the rest, in deepest black, stood a tall, rather harsh-featured woman, who seemed to have about her something of the atmosphere of the pariah. She leaned against the churchyard wall in the purple shadow of the yew tree, which spread its flat, dark masses over the daisied lawn from the dank enclosure of the churchyard, and she had the look of a creature at bay — sullen, and inexpressive. She was of the age that corresponds to the apple tree's time of hard, green fruit, half way between maturity and middle age. She had the spare angularity and weathered complexion of all field-workers. Yet, although she had no beauty, she was, in a curious subtle way, arresting. She had the air of remoteness that some people always take with them, so that their lives seem to move to a different rhythm from the lives around them, and one surprises in their eyes an impassioned secrecy, and feels in their presence the magnetism of great things forever unrevealed. She stood fronting a little crowd.

"I'll run for pig," she said.

"What?" cried Mrs. Parton of the shop, roundly, "d'you mean to tell me, Selina Stone, as you're going to run for pig, and your lawful 'usband lying by lonesome over the churchyard wall?"

A slight flicker of emotion lit Selina's face and passed. It might have been anger or scorn or even mirth.

"I'll run for pig," she repeated tonelessly.

The sexton's wife took up the argument as of inalienable right. "And poor Bobbie Stone only measured for coffin Friday was a week!"

"Scarce cold! Scarce cold!"

This was from Mrs. Marsh, the washerwoman, whose face was large and white, and had the appearance of perpetually reflecting the full moon, and whose hands were always bleached and wrinkled and water-logged. But her feet were, as she put it, "as the Lord made 'em," and she intended to compete for the pig, and would have been pleased to know that Selina, with her long tireless legs, was out of it.

"It's not what the vicar will like," said Miss Milling, the schoolmistress, very quiet in gray silk, and having the air of politely ignoring the world, the flesh, and the Devil.

Jane, the vicar's cook, whose hair was so tidy that it looked like black paint, said "That it inna!" She was going to run herself, as proxy for her sister, whose complaint it was that Providence, while giving her an enormous progeny and thus making her both need and deserve bacon at Christmas, saw fit every year to incapacitate her for competing for the pig by decreeing that she should be "in the family way." So Jane was to run for the family, and she felt that she was supremely in the right, and that this muscular Selina had "no call" to triumph over her slight stoutness (due to the generous living at the vicarage) by thus breaking all the laws of good taste.

Jane's sister looked up from suckling the latest addition to the family. "She's got no little uns to feed. She dunna need bacon," she said decisively.

A murmur that matched the wind in the yew tree ran over the group, a shocked, and withal an interested, sigh.

"Run she will!"

"Dear 'eart, to think on it!"

"Run for pig, and poor Bob not sodded!"

"You're a bad 'oman, Selina Stone!"

Selina's sallow face looked sallower. She swallowed hard, but she gazed unflinchingly into the moon-face of the washerwoman, and she remained self-poised, like a heavy pebble in a water-course. She held on to her own personality, though whelmed in the currents of public opinion.

Jane's sister tried the human note, looking up over the bundle that was her new, creased, enthralling baby.

"My dear, you've no need to do any such thing. Bob was insured, as I very well know. Think how my little uns could enjoy that dear little pig come Christmas. Dunna rob them! Of such is the kingdom of 'eaven."

"Amen!" said her husband.

Three or four girls, all more or less blooming and blossomy, looked at their young men and giggled. Save for these young men, the race would have been a "walk-over" for them, but the consciousness of admiring eyes seriously disturbed their breathing apparatus and, by the justice of things, gave the unromantic a chance.

"Selina! O Selina Stone!" quavered a very old man with an impressive falsetto voice. "You'll ne'er run, my wench?"

"Ah, I'll run."

"You'll fall afore the fall of the leaf if you do wrong by the dead."

"Oot give it up if Vicar says no?"

Selina, weary of repetition, merely shook her head and leaned back against the churchyard wall. Hostile eyes focused themselves upon her, hostile thoughts washed over her. A man pushed his way through the little crowd and came to her.

"My girl," he said, stooping so that she could hear his undertone, "best not! Looks queer-like. Ye can have a plenty of bacon when ye set up with me."

People nudged each other. This was Bill Jakeways, the hedger, to whom, it was said, Selina had given all he asked when, in sultry summer evenings, she had worked overtime, hoeing turnips, and he had done piecework at the hedges between hay harvest and corn harvest. What he had ever seen in her had always been a puzzle to the village. He might have taken his pick, it was said. He was the best-looking man in the place, a splendid creature, like a statue, minded like the naïve dumb things of wood and meadow. Like a dumb creature he had worked for Selina, carrying water, lugging wood, helping her in the fields.

"I won'er what Stone thinks of it!"

This was one of the village phrases. But Bobbie Stone, slight and frail and tired, coughing now and again over his bespoke boots in Selina's tidy kitchen, never divulged by any word or look what he thought. He and Selina lived like middle-aged people, far outside the scope of passion. He would look up and smile when she came in from the fields to get his tea of bacon and potatoes; and if she was late and more flushed than usual he never seemed to notice it. They were judged by the village to be well matched, for she had always been "poor favored" and he was "not much of a chap — a rickety piece."

So life went on until Bobbie, coughing a little more each month, became too tired to push the needle through the leather. The doctor ordered this and that. Selina sat up at night and often stayed away from the fields. Bill was sent here and there for medicines and delicacies. But none the less, when the hot weather came, Bobbie laid his weary head on the pillow, and smiled wistfully at Selina, and said, "I'm tired, lass. I'll sleep a bit."

And he slept on now under the ugly battened mound of brown earth. The pansies nodded golden heads as they did last year, the pig awaited the race with the same complacent ignorance as had the pig of last year.

Jakeways was rather shocked at this callousness of Selina's. "I doubt it's no good to fly in the face of folk. It's the same in pleachin' — yo mun lay the bough the way it wants to go," he said.

"Fine and pleased they be," remarked Mrs. Marsh to the sexton's wife, "and it wunna be above a month or so afore there's a wedding in Cherrington."

"She's a lucky woman, no danger!"

"Ah! A tidy chap. Keeps off the drink too. Never merry but of a Saturday night."

II

Meanwhile the competitors were gathering for the most exciting race of the day. Even the vicar and the doctor drew towards the course to see the ladies distinguish themselves. The vicar kept a deaf ear turned to the broad jokes and the betting among the young men, each of whom backed his own girl, speaking of her in racing terms.

The doctor, knowing everybody's constitution to a nicety, was entrusted with the handicapping. He gave Mrs. Marsh a tremendous start, because he knew she had incipient dropsy. Nobody else knew it, however, so there was a general groan. Mrs. Marsh decided to glaze the doctor's collars as no collars had ever been glazed. She stood far up the course, and the judge, at the winning-post, saw her round white face shining there like an argent shield. Jane, with her cheeks as suddenly red as those of a Dutch doll, and her neat black hair, also like a

Dutch doll's, was heavily handicapped; and so were the half-dozen giggling village girls.

Behind all the rest stood Selina.

"You're not in the race, of course, Mrs. Stone," said Dr. Pierce.

"Ah, sir, I be."

He looked surprised. The vicar was distressed.

"No, no, Selina! Think!"

"I be to run, sir."

"It's not wise, Mrs. Stone," murmured the doctor.

"No, already there are strange rumors afoot," said the vicar. "It would not take much to make them say you murdered poor Bob."

Selina flung her head back with the air of a savage queen.

"What do I care if they do, saving your presence, sir! Let 'em talk till their tongues shrivel! I shanna hear 'em."

"Ready!" shouted the starter.

The pig was placed in position by his owner's oddman, and firmly held in spite of expostulation. Mrs. Marsh took off her bonnet. So might Britannia, for some enormous conflict, temporarily doff her helmet. The girls flung their hats to their mothers or friends.

Selina turned to Jakeways with a smile of great sweetness and sadness. It came on her harsh face like dawn on a mountain side. It was clear from her smile that she loved him, but with an anguished love.

"I'm bound to run, lad," she said.

There was in her voice the mournful note that the wind raises about the shell of ruined masonry, its lament around old dead cities, its cry in the cornices of abandoned homes.

"Ready — Steady — Go!"

The oddman let the pig go, and tumult broke over the course — yells from the various backers, squeals from the pig, hands held out to snatch, flying feet, laughter, fury.

"Selina runs as if life and all was on it."

"I'll be bound she'll win."

"Go it, Mrs. Marsh!" shouted the doctor.

Like a nest of hungry birds, Jane's nephews and nieces lifted their voices: —

"Keep at it, a'ntie!" Then, jubilantly, "Mrs. Stone's fell down."

"But she's got the pig," wailed their mother.

Far up the course, with both arms round the pig, lay Selina. The roar of applause died away as she still lay there.

The crowd surged forward.

"It's a judgment."

"Ah! She's strook."

"Sarve un right."

"Being so desper't set on a pig! And poor Stone not sodded!"

"Well, seems like she's done for herself now, no danger."

"Struck down in 'er pride!"

"What is it?"

"What's took the woman?"

" 'Twas poor Bobbie Stone as come agen in the middle of the race and called 'er. They come agen very bad afore they're sodded, you mind."

Meanwhile, by the silent Selina and the shrieking pig knelt the doctor. She was coming round, but he knew the case was hopeless. It was heart-failure.

"You know what I told you after that influenza — about your heart, Mrs. Stone?"

"Yes."

"You knew what would happen. Why take such a risk for a pig?"

"A pig? What pig?"

The doctor was puzzled, but silent.

Jakeways elbowed through the crowd, and, seeing her deathly face, burst into tears. He knelt down and loosened her tense, unconscious fingers from the pig.

"There wunna no call for you to do it," he said mournfully. "I'd ha' seen as you'd enough o' meat, if you'd set up with me."

"I know ye would."

"I like ye right well, Selina."

"And I like you. Only I was sore set on poor Bob. Baby an' all was Bob to me."

Dr. Pierce returned with the vicar. "But if she didn't want the pig, what *did* she run for?" he was saying. "Ask her, vicar!"

The dreamy vicar stooped and took her hand. Their eyes met, and understanding flashed from one to the other. Then Selina's heavy lids came down, and the only reply the doctor ever had was her faint, enigmatic smile.

April 1924

SACHA GUITRY
1885–

The arc of light over the Théâtre Sarah Bernhardt has long been dimmed. Sacha Guitry who has spread more joy in the world than twenty, I might say one hundred, philanthropists, is paying the penalty for the qualities which made him famous. During the occupation of Paris he was guilty of amusing the Germans and to amuse an enemy is to give the aid and comfort which patriotism forbids. Poor Sacha! He has been amusing people all his life and the only thing he does not know about acting is how to act out of character. He is not a patriot by profession and his specialty is not the Moral Law. It has never been. Never has he deviated from the primrose path, throwing the blossoms promiscuously about himself and all the rest of the world.

In September of 1944, Fate caught up with Fancy. Guitry was arrested and in company with a number of other collaborationists was sent to await trial in the concentration camp at Drancy. This was misery enough, but I think he found it still more painful to read in the Temps *that he was one of a group consisting of "small fry." The Star had come to dust.*

The trial was not severe as trials go. His guilt of collaboration with the Germans was self-evident. But his importance was no longer great, his health was failing, and by the court's decree Guitry was given "provisional liberty" and permitted to enter a medical clinic. There he has occupied his melancholy leisure in writing "Ma Défense" for the Paris papers. His apology is less of a defense of his own crimes than a confession of human weakness to which all but heroes are subject. And it was never Sacha's ambition to be a hero, but to many of us who wrongfully go on believing that to the sinner who scatters happiness about him much should be forgiven it is a comfort to know that he is free and has talked, irresponsibly I fear, of coming to America.

Sacha's defense before the Tribunal was pitiful enough.

"I did not want Paris to die," he pleaded. "When a German general or Otto Abetz knocks at my dressing room door and I say, 'Entrez,' and then see who it is, do you expect me to throw him out?"

Then he passed to the personal world which is to him the only important one. "I have made many enemies," he went on. "I have written, directed, produced, and starred in 114 plays. The last N'écoutez Pas, Madame, *ran 600 consecutive performances. I made twenty-three million francs. People do not forgive that."*

Sacha's is not a pleasant story, but any American who recalls the paradise of Paris in the old days will think twice before condemning him altogether. To them the vision will return; the starry lights over the theater door proclaiming that M. Sacha Guitry and Mlle. Yvonne Printemps offer to entertain the public within. Then every old heart will feel within a little flame of gratitude for if ever marriage was made in heaven, it was of those two bright spirits of gaiety and laughter. The fracture of that perfect union was a blow at human happiness.

That is the crime of Sacha Guitry which will not be forgiven.

In the Wings

SACHA GUITRY

I

I HAVE often mentioned my mother's father, René de Pont-Jest, and I must speak of him again. My conscience demands it.

This excessively forgotten novelist — and to be forgotten so totally is a form of injustice — this journalist, this brave and gallant gentleman, is one whom my brother and I most stupidly underrated. He published over forty volumes in his lifetime, and some of them, like *The Trial of the Hindu Thugs,* were enormously successful. He used to say of that particular novel that, published as a serial, it had made the fortune of the daily *Petit Journal.* He maintained also that it was he who had invented the colored poster at the time when another of his books, *The River of Pearls, or the Red Spider,* was being advertised. The French Academy awarded a prize to this novel. He flattered himself that he had saved the city of Dunkerque, and that it was he, moreover, who had first had the idea of using the marine corps to defend Paris in 1870.

Unfortunately, my brother and I had acquired the reprehensible habit of ridiculing our grandfather. We had agreed once and for all that it would be stupid to believe a single word of the stories he told, thus blinding ourselves to the advantage we might have received from the conversation of a perfectly intelligent, instructive, witty, cultivated, and kindly man. You may wonder why we had got so firmly into our heads the notion that everything he said was untrue. It must have been because he spoke exactly as he wrote his novels — that is, constantly concerned to awaken interest, hold attention, captivate the listener. He took up the conversation as he might take up his pen — for a long session, and everything he said began like the first volume of an endless novel expressly intended for popularity. This was our excuse, our sole excuse. Between two mouthfuls, for no special reason, without particular provocation, he would lay down his knife as if it were a sword and begin: —

"On the eighteenth of April, 1865, on a day so cold that it nipped our ears, we arrived in Peking. . . ."

How could we but doubt the veracity of a story that began in this fashion? And besides, this charming man, like most writers who do not write extremely well, had an exaggerated respect for grammar, even in speaking. He spared us no imperfect of the subjunctive, and those with which he adorned his pompous sentences lent to his tales a flavor of artificiality which deprived them of all credibility.

Thus, having from childhood been convinced that Grandfather invented everything he said and never spoke the truth, we came easily to the conclusion that he had not written the novels that were mentioned, that he had not been awarded the decorations he spoke of, that he had not fought twelve duels, that he was neither a Bonapartist nor a royalist, that he had not managed the Indo-Chinese concession at the Exposition of 1900, and that he had not even been an officer of the marine corps. In short, we doubted everything we heard about or from him.

And to-day, by way of making full amends, I have gone through the trunk into which for the past thirty years I have thrown an enormous mass of family papers, and without trouble, though not without emotion, I have found evidence that everything Grandfather told us was true — the Indo-Chinese concession, the duels, everything. When Admiral Bouët-Willaumez recommended to Admiral Pothuau that René de Pont-Jest be awarded the Cross of the Legion of Honor, he did it "not only because of the services he had rendered the Baltic Squadron" during his command of it, but also because he was the first to "suggest the defense of Paris by the marine corps."

Going through these yellowing papers, I came upon a veritable mine of documents concerning the possible return of the monarchy in France. It appears that my grandfather had never been able to make up his mind between Prince Victor (Bonaparte) and the Duc d'Orléans. I was about to conclude from this that his political opinions were chiefly remarkable for their instability when it occurred to me that, on the contrary, there could be no more precise and impartial fashion of being simply anti-republican.

I have often heard it said that certain diseases and physical disabilities jump a generation. This seems to me reasonable. Since looking through my grandfather's papers I am certain that failings and weaknesses of character also have a tendency to jump a generation. I always knew that René de Pont-Jest loved gambling, and that he spent all his evenings and some of his nights at the Press Club tables. I knew that he ruined himself gambling; I knew how he had died; but what I did not know was that he had elaborated (with irrefutable demonstrations) a sort of infallible system for playing the squares about the zero, and that to his mind he would one day break the bank at Monte Carlo with this system. Now, for twenty years I have put down my money only in the neighborhood of zero. I concede that my system is fallible, but I am still hopeful of winning the chandeliers and carpets of the Casino one of these days.

My grandfather and I were walking in the Rue Royale one summer evening. At the corner of the Faubourg-Saint-Honoré a blind man sat on a folding stool, begging. Grandfather put his hand in his pocket and handed me four sous.

"Give this to the poor chap."

I dropped the coins in the man's hat and rejoined my grandfather. We walked on, and he said:—

"You ought to have touched your cap."

"To him?"

"Of course."

"Why?"

"One should always do that when giving alms."

I said, "But not this one: he's blind."

Not bad; but my grandfather, who always had a rejoinder to everything, had a rather pretty one for me that day.

"He may be a fraud," said he.

II

I must now tell about my first love. I was thirteen years old. She was ravishing. Ravishing, did I say? She was one of the prettiest women in Paris. But I didn't know that. I *thought* she was pretty, and it happened that she was, extremely. That was a mere coincidence.

She was the daughter of a famous painter and was married to the most successful of writers. He was one of my father's intimate friends and later became one of mine. I was then the constant companion of their son and was in their house almost every Sunday at tea time. All the family were handsome and their home life was happiness itself.

Her smile was adorable and her eyes were all tenderness. How could I but be in love with her? As for why I loved her, not to love her would have been monstrous, criminal, disquieting even. It was more than my right, it was my duty to love her, for at thirteen one cannot know what it is to love. I dreamed about her. Could I tell her so? I would have died first. What to do, then? Prove it to her: save my pennies during the week and commit a great folly the next Sunday. I saved my pennies and I committed the folly. Eight francs—an enormous bouquet of violets. It was the handsomest bouquet of violets ever known, and so big that I had to hold it in both hands.

My plan was to call at two o'clock and ask to see her instead of going directly up to her son's room. It turned out a little difficult. She was engaged. I insisted. The maid led me to her boudoir. She was putting on her hat and about to go out. I went in with beating heart.

"Hello, my dear. What do you want to see me about?"

She had not even turned round. She had not yet seen the bouquet. She could not understand.

I held out my eight francs' worth of violets.

"Oh, the beautiful violets!" she exclaimed.

It seemed to me the game was won.

I went toward her, trembling. She took my bouquet into her hands as if it were a baby's face and raised it up as if to kiss it.

"How good they smell!"

Then, indicating that I might go, she added:—

"Do tell your papa how much I thank him."

III

My father was playing in *L'Assommoir* at the Porte-Saint-Martin. I went into his dressing room between the acts one evening and found with him Mounet-Sully, who had come to see the play. I must have been about fifteen years old then and I was seeing Mounet-Sully off stage for the first time. He made a great impression upon me. He was a handsome man, his smile was attractive, and when he spoke in a low voice one heard a distant, very distant sort of thunder rumbling in his chest. He was handsome, indeed, but his eyes were already very bad, so that when his head was in profile one almost thought he was looking one straight in the face.

My father introduced me in these words: "My dear Mounet, this is my son Sacha, your future pupil."

It was a habit he had adopted when making me known to any celebrated actor, French or foreign.

Mounet-Sully, who took everything seriously and doubtless wanted to show that he liked me, opened his arms with a familiar majesty and said in a ringing voice, as if I had been fifty paces off and separated from him by a river, "Come! Come, my child! Allow me to embrace you."

It was impossible for me to refuse; and besides, he had already put his right hand to the nape of my neck and drawn me forward. Never in my life shall I forget the violence of the kiss he placed upon my forehead.

Then he resumed the conversation with my father which I had interrupted. They talked about the Comédie-Française and about Claretie, whom Mounet-Sully called "Monsieur Clarecie," holding on to the last syllable until he had transformed it into a sort of hiss. He left a few minutes later, forgetting to say good-bye to me as he passed before me to the door which my father's dresser was respectfully holding open. This dresser was very small and wore heavy moustaches. There was really no resemblance between him and me. Yet Mounet-Sully looked at him fixedly and exclaimed, "Once more, my child. I must kiss you once more." And on the forehead of the astounded and perhaps delighted dresser Mounet imprinted a swift but fervent kiss.

IV

My schoolmate Colin and I had between us thirty years of age and about fifty francs of money the day we determined to have an adventure. Our plan was very simple: it was to invite a pretty woman, an actress, to supper. Yes, only one: supper once over, she would choose between us.

An actress; but which one? There were almost too many to choose from, for didn't I know them all? Jane Hading, Andrée Mégard, Lavallière, Germaine Gallois, and the rest.

"They're all playing to-night," said I. "Let's go. We'll begin with . . ." I shall not say who, but I can swear that she thought the idea of supping with me very funny.

When I said to her, "Madame, I have come to ask if you will have the kindness to take supper with my friend Colin and me," she let out a "What!" and a gale of laughter that I could readily translate into, "Well, I'll be . . . The nerve of the kid!"

Our second try came to the same thing, and so did our third. Disgusted then with actresses, who seemed really lacking in imagination, we went off to the Moulin-Rouge. It was in the days of the famous quadrille — La Goulue, Grille d'Egout, I don't recall the name of the third, and Mélinite, the delightful Jane Avril. One of them in particular took our eye, and I went boldly up to her. It was between dances and she was out of breath and in a temper. My proposal that she sup with us brought no smile to her lips, for she could not look forward to it with a smile. She stared at me contemptuously and then said, "Later, maybe — if nobody else asks me."

At one o'clock in the morning we crossed the Place Blanche — she, Colin, and I. We were in an indescribable state of pride — not she, but Colin and I. She was still as ill-tempered as ever. Five minutes later we were in an upstairs room of a restaurant opposite the Moulin-Rouge. We were having supper with an actress, in a private room! But our joy was somewhat confined. Our conquest was lugubrious. High cheekbones; great, magnificent eyes with rings under them, eyes that burned up her face; too much make-up: she was a perfect Toulouse-Lautrec, and indeed he immortalized her on canvas. The conversation was dreary, our dancer avoiding taking any part in it. We were drinking champagne, *demi-sec,* and eating ham. Colin and I chattered on.

"Why don't you get your father to give us two seats at the Gymnase for next Sunday matinée?" asked Colin.

Idly she asked: "Is your father a ham?"

"Yes."

"What's his name?"

"Lucien Guitry."

She jumped in astonishment. "Is Guitry your father?"

"Of course."

"What are you doing out at this hour of the night?"

"Why, I . . ."

"Aren't you in school, you two?"

"Yes, but we sneaked out."

"And you come here and pick up the first woman you run into at the Moulin-Rouge, a woman you've never seen before? Don't you know the risk you run? To think that parents go to the trouble to bring their children up as best they know how — and you do this kind of thing! You finish eating that ham this minute and come along back to your school!"

And she took us back to the school door, to Mariaud's, to be sure that we should not go on when her back was turned.

V

Imagine what Lucien Guitry must have been at the age of thirty-two years, when he embarked upon his career. He seized life and embraced it, sought only to make it constantly more beautiful; and it was in those days that he began to gather about him that court of familiar friends in which new faces continued to appear throughout the whole of his sumptuous existence — the most sumptuous possible, since he always spent in advance all the money he was about to earn.

His homes changed with his theatres: going into the Renaissance in 1894, he stayed there until 1910, and from 1894 to 1910 he lived at 26, Place Vendôme.

His earliest friends were Forain, Edmond Haraucourt, de Maupassant, Georges and Henri Cain, and Messenger. Later came Noblet, Feydeau, Calmettes, and Maurice Donnay. Thereafter came the great collection, so to say, of all those whose plays he performed: François de Curel, Abel Hermant, Octave Mirbeau, Georges de Porto-Riche, Vandérem, Gustave Guiches, Anatole France, Edmond Rostand, Alfred Capus, Eugène Brieux, Jules Lemaître, Henri Lavedan, Paul Bourget, Henry Bataille, Henry Bernstein. One after the other, I saw all these men, all these eminent dramatists, seated at my father's table, and from the next room I heard all or nearly all of them read their manuscripts. And the absorbing and interesting conversations that followed the readings! The things said round that table! The advice given — and followed by the great! How many "curtains" I heard instantly rectified and played by my father — rectified as an expert shot rectifies the handling of a gun in the field. What promises of success given and kept! What plans and projects for the following season! After such readings life seemed very beautiful to those two men perpetually in search of each other, indispensable to one another — the author and the interpreter.

The reading of *L'Aiglon* was something which I shall never forget. It began one day toward noon in the apartment on the Place Vendôme, and because of it I still own the Louis XIV tabouret, upholstered in red velvet, on which Edmond Rostand laid his manuscript as he read.

He had come round, not without some apprehension, to ask my father to play the part of Flambeau. This part had been written originally for Coquelin, but there were reasons that were not mentioned why Coquelin was now not to play it. Rostand and my father sat in the study while I listened, enraptured, from the adjoining room. The first act was read very rapidly, Rostand having forewarned my father that he did not appear in it. It is probably the most dazzling first act ever written, and my father was enchanted with it. The second act also produced a great effect.

Indeed, Rostand did not read his play, he acted it. He imitated Sarah Bernhardt a little, and he acted admirably. He knew the play by heart and often forgot to turn the pages of his script. Everything about him was attractive — his recent celebrity, his sensitive face, his pleasing voice. When he reached the third act he read that less well than the first two, but the effect of the first two acts remained.

"Magnificent," my father said; "magnificent!"

"Well?" asked Rostand.

"Well . . . yes . . . I think so. I don't see why I might not do this admirable play."

But Rostand felt that my father had already sensed why he might not do it. The reason was the next two acts, the scene of the ball and of Wagram, and the last act, in which Flambeau does not appear. Not to be in the first act is bad enough; but to die before the last act . . .

Poor Rostand! As he read out, "Act Four," he seemed to swoon a little. I don't say he was pretending, but one could see that he was doing nothing to master himself. He closed his eyes, mopped his forehead, excused himself, and declared that he could not go on — he was too tired, and besides he was dying of hunger.

My father let it go at that and we three went to lunch at Prunier's. Obviously, my father had not been taken in by this little scene, and Rostand knew it. If the one had pretended to be overcome, the other had certainly pretended belief. I could feel in them both a like fear that their pleasure might be spoiled; and as Sarah Bernhardt had sent word that she wanted my father's answer by two o'clock, both feigned to believe it impossible that she be kept waiting. The result of this comedy was that by the end of luncheon it was agreed that Lucien Guitry would play Flambeau.

Amongst those friends of my father whom we saw only occasionally there was one who, at the time, impressed me more than all the rest. I could not guess that he was later to become my closest friend. He was a big man with red hair, bushy eyebrows, and sky-blue eyes. He did not chew his words, he chopped them; and he looked like a sheep dog. It was Octave Mirbeau.

He always arrived with terrifying news: Clemenceau had just told him so-and-so; Labori had just told him this-and-that; Colonel du Paty de Clam was a liar, and Scheurer-Kestner knew the truth well enough. I used to wonder what Mirbeau did. Was he an army officer in mufti? A politician? A lawyer? I had then seen him only three times, and each time he had talked only about the Dreyfus affair. In those days the Dreyfus affair was the sole subject of conversation.

Nobody born since 1885 can have any notion what the Dreyfus affair was. As I write, the Stavisky affair is a subject of interest, passion, and disgust throughout France, but compared with the Dreyfus affair it is very small beer. The reason is simply that the Stavisky case concerns guilty men, while the Dreyfus affair was built up round an innocent man.

Mirbeau, as I say, seemed to me a sort of politician. He arrived one day in a state of even greater effervescence than usual. What had happened, we wanted to know. Was Colonel Picquart to be executed? Not at all. Mirbeau had discovered Maeterlinck. The next week he was again in the same state, engaged in glorifying Rodin.

Renard used to say that every morning Mirbeau woke up furious. It was true. He would open his eyes convinced that in the course of the day a hundred injustices would be committed, and he was exasperated in advance of their commission. He took it for granted that his interlocutors were his adversaries, and he had a fashion of urging you to go to see an exposition of paintings by Monet which was like a challenge to mortal combat. This way of his — shall I say this oddity? — made some people detest him and others adore him. He was actually an adorable man. Like all extremely violent people, like all people ready to do battle for an idea, he must himself have committed injustices, but always in the service of justice and of a noble cause.

Many people in literary circles thought they disliked Mirbeau. They were wrong: it was he who disliked them.

VI

Everybody kept asking me what I was going to do when I grew up. It seemed to worry everybody, and to me it was unbearable. I knew no more than they did about it, and the thought of "doing something" became hateful to me.

It was only when I was about fourteen years old that I began to think seriously about going on the stage. You have to bear in mind that an actor's son does not look upon a career in the theatre quite as a son of the average citizen does. For a son of the average citizen the theatre is forbidden fruit; it is a sort of sin, and the temptation is the greater for this fact. For an actor's son it is also something forbidden — not forbidden in principle, but because one must be worthy of the career. Actor and average citizen use the same word, but in how different a tone! When the boy, taking his courage in both his hands, comes to his father and declares that he wants to be an actor, the average citizen cries out, "You, an actor!" by which he means, "You, a son of mine, to take an unspotted name and trail it in the mud!" As for the actor, he also cries out, "You, an actor!" but what he means is, "You, a son of mine, to run the risk of tarnishing the name you bear! Think twice about it, and make no mistake. The desire you feel to go on the stage is perfectly natural, but it is no indication of an irresistible vocation. One cannot buy one's way on to the stage."

And just as the average citizen will add, "Of course I can understand the son of an actor following in his father's steps," so the actor will say to his son, "There is more chance of the average citizen's son feeling a sincere vocation for the theatre than of an actor's son feeling it."

These words were not said to me, but I felt them nonetheless. They made me wonder if my desire to become an actor was justified by the gifts I possessed. It was natural that I should wonder. Despite this, to get it off my mind, I wrote my father of my desire. I was then spending the summer in Dieppe, separated from him. I have preserved his reply.

My dear boy, I have thought a good deal about the subject of your letter. We must talk about it together, and we shall.

Meanwhile, you ask me to suggest five or six scenes that you might learn. Learn anything that amuses you: men, women, princes, princesses, servants, mistresses, masters, valets — in a word, anything. To know one's part is not the important thing. One always knows it. The important thing is to be able to express everything. You see how simple it is!

Your very affectionate father,

L. G.

The letter was scarcely encouraging. "We must talk about it together," he said. That expressed less a promise to talk later than a wish not to talk at all. He was putting me off. That letter gave me a lot to think about. To embark by oneself upon a career other than one's father's was bad enough; but to embark by oneself upon one's father's own career might prove impossible. I was very afraid.

Besides, one cannot hide for the purpose of being an actor. Change one's name, yes; but not one's face—unless one wore a false beard on stage and off. One can write, or draw, without revealing the fact to anybody. That can be done at home. But the stage is something else again. To be an actor requires the consent of a producer, an author, other people in the cast—and the consent of the public. Well . . . I took to drawing.

I take it that one has the right to speak of the young man one was when one is no longer that young man. I had a talent for drawing and a certain feeling for caricature. Naturally, I did not work at it. I drew too quickly and was always in a hurry to finish what I had begun. This haste was so great that I never finished anything. When I had enough of a drawing, I signed it; and the fact of signing it made me believe it was finished. I may say that this is a characteristic of which I have never wholly cured myself: I have several times scamped the end of a play in ten minutes in order to read it to someone who was coming to lunch.

Meanwhile, although I drew, I drew only for my own pleasure and without thought of a future; but another reason might have been that I wanted people to stop asking me what I meant to do when I grew up. I had observed that, if one drew, one was not bothered by people. In order not to have to do anything, I drew constantly.

One Sunday, at one o'clock in the morning, I had just finished my first play and was engaged in writing out a clean copy on the dining-room table when my grandfather came in from his club.

"What are you doing there?"

"Working."

"You, working!"

"I've just written a play."

"A play! Read it to me right away."

He listened with grandfatherly emotion, congratulated me, confessed his astonishment, kissed me — and advised me to bury my one-act play in the bottom of my desk drawer.

This scarcely veiled opinion did not offend me, but it seemed to me to attach a great deal of importance to my little play, and even to myself.

I have wondered from time to time how I got the notion of writing a play, and I have never been able to recall. Because everybody had so often said of me that I could never do anything, I thought I could do anything, and I had written the play for the same reason that I drew — out of pure distraction. How could I possibly know then that I was to write a hundred more? Why, then, should I bury this one?

I did not follow my grandfather's advice (which was later given me a dozen times about *Berg-op-Zoom,* and *Jean de la Fontaine,* and *Le Veilleur de Nuit,* and other plays of mine). Instead, I took the little play to Francis de Croisset, whom I had recently met, and read it to him. I owe to him the fact that my play was performed. You may hold it against him if you like, but I owe thanks to the young man he then was, recently celebrated but already doing kindnesses to others and being loved by them — something that has been characteristic of him for thirty years. Thanks to him, the very next day Marguerite Deval accepted *Le Page* and it was performed at the Mathurins, which was later to be my theatre and bear my name from 1913 to 1920.

For twenty years I regretted not having preserved the manuscript of my first play. I would say to myself: After all, it was my first play. Maybe . . . Two years ago, on the thirtieth anniversary of my entry into the theatre, some of my friends planned a charming surprise. They found *Le Page* in the national archives where — I never knew this — manuscripts are deposited for censorship. They had it copied and presented the copy to me.

Alas, my dear friends, why did you not leave me with my illusions?

VII

Six months pass and I am beginning to be worried. My drawings fetch ten francs at the *Rire* or the *Sourire;* my play has brought me in perhaps three hundred francs; and there I am. Not very good.

What am I to do? Be an actor. Yes, but where shall I act? It was very hard. Wherever I went, I felt that people were fearful of displeasing my father by giving me a part. Nevertheless, one day a producer talked about engaging me. He even spoke of putting my name up in lights. That bothered me. The man did not like my father. I caught on just in time.

Then I thought of the phrase in my father's letter: "We must talk about this together." One evening we talked.

"But, my boy, if you really want to do it, why not? You know well enough that I shall do nothing to stop you. There is no finer profession in the world. Only, you'll have to work at it seriously. Recite something for me."

I can see the two of us: him in his armchair, smiling; me standing, paralyzed with fright, reciting Rodrigue's combat against the Moors, out of *Le Cid*. When Rodrigue had finished the tale of his exploits, my father said, "Look here, that's not bad. But since it could be better, you had best take some lessons. Only, with whom? I can't think."

"But, Father . . ."

He interrupted me. "No, anybody but me. I should be either too patient or not hard enough on you. I'll give you a note to Talbot."

"Very well, Father."

Noblet, however, had other advice: "Play, play! That's the best way to learn your job." A week later I made my first appearance at Versailles, in *Hernani*.

I did not play the part of Hernani, nor that of Don Carlos, nor the part of Don Ruy Gomez de Silva, but, with Pierre Juvenet, Mondolo, and a third actor called Guéguette, one of three other parts. Each of us was to be paid ten francs. Sogond, the tragedian, played Hernani, and Jeanne Morlet played Doña Sol.

The performance was a disaster from beginning to end, not so much because of us as because of my brother, who was in the theatre with a crowd of friends, male and female, who broke into thunders of applause every time I opened my mouth.

The producer had not respected Victor Hugo's directions concerning the opening of the last act of his masterpiece. The author indicates that "people in masks and dominoes, singly or in groups, cross the terrace here and there." By way of representing all these people, "singly or in groups," there were Pierre Juvenet, Mondolo, Guéguette, and I. And it wasn't only that this crowd was made up of four people: the management had forgotten to hire dominoes for us. We could hardly appear as noblemen in the conspirators' costumes we had worn in the preceding acts. Between the acts my brother had had an idea. He had gone to a neighboring house — which you will permit me not to designate more specifically — and had borrowed four pink and blue wrappers. Our entrance in these wrappers released a hilarity and then a riot such that at the end of the play the manager of the theatre, that worthy Félix Lagrange, said to me:—

"Not only will I not pay you your ten francs, but I'll be damned if I don't see that you never play Versailles again!"

He was right: I never did play Versailles again.

August 1935

LORD MOULTON

1844–1921

John Fletcher Moulton, first Baron of Bank, was a philosopher of the law. For many years he served as a Lord Justice of Appeal and broke new ground in the service of society as first chairman of the medical research committee under the National Insurance Act of Great Britain. At the outset of the First World War he became Minister of Munitions. His talent as an administrator and Parliamentarian were vividly recognized but, above all, men came to rely upon him as an exponent of human wisdom seldom equaled in his generation. This judgment was impressively confirmed by the Lord Chancellor who on Lord Moulton's death in 1921 paid this tribute to his services: —

"I choose my words carefully when I say that I greatly doubt whether it would have been possible for the war to have been brought to a successful conclusion when it was but for the part Lord Moulton took in it. I hope the country will not soon forget the extraordinary work of this most remarkable man, whose memory his colleagues will long cherish."

Lord Moulton was gifted with the power of thinking at great speed with entire accuracy, and of expressing his thoughts with complete lucidity. Incredible as it seems, I have been assured that this perfect speech was made on the issue of the instant, quite without preparation. But we remember the preparation had been lifelong.

One could cite but few instances parallel to this: the sureness of utterance, the largeness of the idea, the inspiration of the moment.

Law and Manners

THE RIGHT HONORABLE LORD MOULTON

In order to explain this extraordinary title I must ask you to follow me in examining the three great domains of Human Action. First comes the domain of Positive Law, where our actions are prescribed by laws binding upon us which must be obeyed. Next comes the domain of Free Choice, which includes all those actions as to which we claim and enjoy complete freedom. But between these two there is a third large and important domain in which there rules neither Positive Law nor Absolute Freedom. In that domain there is no law which inexorably determines our course of action, and yet we feel that we are not free to choose as we would. The degree of this sense of a lack of complete freedom in this domain varies in every case. It grades from a consciousness of a Duty nearly as strong as Positive Law, to a feeling that the matter is all but a question of personal choice. Some might wish to parcel out this domain into separate countries, calling one, for instance, the domain of Duty, another the domain of Public Spirit, another the domain of Good Form; but I prefer to look at it as all one domain, for it has one and the same characteristic throughout — it is the domain of Obedience to the Unenforceable. The obedience is the obedience of a man to that which he cannot be forced to obey. He is the enforcer of the law upon himself.

One of the reasons why I have chosen this as the subject on which to speak is that I have spent my life as a commissioner for delimiting the frontier line which divides this domain from the realm of Positive Law. I have had to decide so frequently whether Law could say, "You must," or regretfully to say, "I must leave it to you." This is the land in which all those whom the Law cannot reach take refuge. It might be thought from such a description that I wished to annex that country and bring it under the rule of Positive Law. That is not the case. The infinite variety of circumstances surrounding the individual and rightly influencing his action make it impossible to subject him in all things to rules rigidly prescribed and duly enforced. Thus there was wisely left the intermediate domain which, so far as Positive Law is concerned, is a land of freedom of action, but in which the individual should feel that he was not wholly free. This country which lies between Law and Free

Choice I always think of as the domain of Manners. To me, Manners in this broad sense signifies the doing that which you should do although you are not obliged to do it. I do not wish to call it Duty, for that is too narrow to describe it, nor would I call it Morals for the same reason. It might include both, but it extends beyond them. It covers all cases of right doing where there is no one to make you do it but yourself.

All these three domains are essential to the properly organized life of the individual, and one must be on one's guard against thinking that any of them can safely be encroached upon. That Law must exist needs no argument. But, on the other hand, the domain of Free Choice should be dear to all. This is where spontaneity, originality, and energy are born. The great movements which make the history of a country start there. It covers a precious land where the actions of men are not only such as they choose, but have a right to claim freedom even from criticism. Men must keep safely guarded this right to follow the bent of their nature in proper cases and act as they would without anyone having the right to utter a word of dictation or command. This country forms the other frontier of the domain of Manners and delimits it on the side farthest away from that of Positive Law.

The dangers that threaten the maintenance of this domain of Manners arise from its situation between the region of Absolute Choice and the region of Positive Law. There are countless supporters of the movements to enlarge the sphere of Positive Law. In many countries — especially in the younger nations — there is a tendency to make laws to regulate everything. On the other hand, there is a growing tendency to treat matters that are not regulated by Positive Law as being matters of Absolute Choice. Both these movements are encroachments on the middle land, and to my mind the real greatness of a nation, its true civilization, is measured by the extent of this land of Obedience to the Unenforceable. It measures the extent to which the nation trusts its citizens, and its existence and area testify to the way they behave in response to that trust. Mere obedience to Law does not measure the greatness of a Nation. It can easily be obtained by a strong executive, and most easily of all from a timorous people. Nor is the licence of behavior which so often accompanies the absence of Law, and which is miscalled Liberty, a proof of greatness. The true test is the extent to which the individuals composing the nation can be trusted to obey self-imposed law.

In the changes that are taking place in the world around us, one of those which is fraught with grave peril is the discredit into which this idea of the middle land is falling. I will give two examples. First, I will take freedom of debate in the houses of legislature such as our own House of Commons. For centuries the members had unrestricted freedom of debate, and no inconvenience was felt. But in recent times some members of this House have said to themselves: "We have unrestricted freedom of debate. We will use it so as to destroy debate. The absence of imposed restriction enables us to do it." This obstruction was developed, and it has destroyed freedom of debate, and, indeed, all useful debate in practically every legislature. The freedom due to absence of positive restriction has been treated by the individual members as leaving their use of debate a matter of Absolute Choice, fettered with no duty that they were bound to regard. They shut their eyes to the fact that the freedom was given to them in trust to help forward debate, and that it was incumbent on them so to use it. Clumsy and even mischievous regulations have necessarily been introduced which fetter debate but prevent its being absolutely stifled. The old freedom cannot now be entrusted to the members, because when they possessed it they did not respond to it by the exercise of that moral sense which would have led them to treat it as a trust, and not as an absolute possession, unburdened by obligations which they should compel themselves to regard.

It is not only the conduct of individual members of the legislature that furnishes an illustration. The conduct of the legislatures themselves furnishes an equally striking one. It is the fundamental principle of democracies to bow to the decision of the majority. But in accepting this we do not surrender ourselves to the rule of the majority in all things, but only in those things which are of a kind fit to be regulated by Government. We do not admit, for instance, the right of the majority to decide whom we should marry or what should be our religion. These are but types of a vast number of matters of great interest in life which we hold to be outside the decision of a majority, and which are for the individual alone to decide. But in form the power of a Government has no restrictions. It has the power to do everything, and too often it forgets that this limitless power does not leave the scope of its legislation a matter of absolute choice on its part, but a choice fettered by a duty to act according to the trust reposed in it, and to abstain from legislating in matters where legislation is not truly within its province. And what is true as to the scope of legislation is also true to a great extent as to the nature of that legislation. But there is a widespread tendency to regard the fact that they can do a thing as meaning that they may do it. There can be no more fatal error than this. Between "can do" and "may do" ought to exist the whole realm which recognizes the sway of duty, fairness, sympathy, taste, and all the other things that make life beautiful and society possible. It is this confusion between "can do" and "may do" which makes me fear at times lest in the future the worst tyranny will be found in democracies. Interests which are not strongly represented in parliament may be treated as though they had no rights by Governments who think that the power and the will to legislate amount to a justification of that legislation. Such a principle would be death to liberty. No part of our life would be secure from interference from without. If I were asked to define tyranny, I would say it was yielding to the lust of governing. It is only when Governments feel it an honorable duty not to step beyond that which was in reality, and not only in form, put into their hands that the world will know what true Freedom is.

The tendency of modern legislation is to extend the area ruled by Positive Law, and to diminish the area of action which is determined by the decision of the individual himself. But there is one great example in the opposite direction. In one instance the People have deliberately chosen to carve a domain out of that previously covered by Positive Law and to throw it into the domain where the individual can determine for himself his course of action. Take the legislation relating to Trades-Unions and Trade Disputes. Limitations on the power of combination have been swept away, and to a great extent that which was previously marked out by Law is now in the hands of the individuals themselves.

I am far from suggesting that this was a retrograde step, but to my mind the question whether it is dangerous, and whether it may and will become disastrous, depends on whether the masters of workmen who gained this freedom of action, not allowed them by the Common Law, look upon the change as justifying their treating the matters to which it relates as belonging to the realm of Absolute Choice, or whether as belonging to the realm where, though not restrained by Positive Law, they yet recognize the duty of obedience to the Unenforceable. Do they recognize that the increase of their freedom of action brings with it not unfettered choice but the corresponding responsibility of using that freedom? That many have failed to realize that this is the true effect of the change has already been made too clear. At the time of the general coal-strike many voices were heard which in a tone hitherto unknown to us cried: "We can by a universal strike bring the nation to its knees." It is a proof of the extent to which the sense of Duty ran in the nation, even at a time of such excitement, that this cry was not heeded, and that we came out of the crisis with little harm beyond some labor legislation which will probably have to be modified many, many times before it comes into working order — a very light price to pay for the experience.

I am not afraid to trust people — my fear is that people will not see that trust is being reposed in them. Hence I have no wish that Positive Law should annex this intermediate country. On the contrary, I dread it. Instead of the iron rule of law being thrown over it I would rather see it well policed by the inhabitants. I am too well acquainted with the inadequacy of the formal language of statutes to prefer them to the living action of public and private sense of Duty.

The great principle of Obedience to the Unenforceable is no mere ideal, but in some form or other it is strong in the hearts of all except the most depraved. If you wish to know how strong, remember the account of the Titanic disaster. The men were gentlemen to the edge of death. "Ladies first." Why was that? Law did not require it. Force could not have compelled it in the face of almost certain death. It was merely a piece of good Manners in the sense in which I have used the phrase. The feeling of obedience to the Unenforceable was so strong that at that terrible moment all behaved as, if they could look back, they would wish to have behaved. I have no fear of its strength, whatever be the class appealed to. Even if one takes the least educated, — the so-called lower classes, of whom so many are afraid, — one would find the same loyal obedience to unenforceable obligation in the relationships with which these classes are familiar. The danger lies in that by the growth of the democratic spirit they have newly come into much larger powers, and they have not yet learned that power has its duties as well as its rights. When they have become familiar with these powers, and when intercourse with those who have a wider outlook has taught them that the domain of obligation includes them in their use of them, I am satisfied that those who have been loyal to duty in the smaller lives that they have led will be loyal in the wider fields in which they are now able to exercise their power. It is this faith that makes me dread lest we should hurriedly let Positive Law come in and check the growth of self-reliance, check the growth of the sense of personal duty, and lead people to feel that, if they obey the Law, they have done all their duty. It is wiser to exercise patience and let them alone till increase of experience in life teaches them to appreciate better their true position, and to feel that it is still needful for them to see for themselves that they behave as worthy men should do.

Now I can tell you why I chose the title "Law and Manners." It must be evident to you that Manners must include all things which a man should impose upon himself, from duty to good taste. I have borne in mind the great motto of William of Wykeham—*Manners makyth Man.* It is in this sense—loyalty to the rule of Obedience to the Unenforceable, throughout the whole realm of personal action—that we should use the word "Manners" if we would truly say that "Manners makyth Man."

July 1924

THE MOONSHINER'S WIFE

I had ridden through the moonshiners' country and had sat on hickory logs passing the time of day with squirrel shooters over a pipe of rough-cut. I had followed trails past signboards warning "REVENOORS Keep Out" and had gasped what I thought my last breath as I washed down corn pone and bacon fat with a sip of liquid lightning. So it was a lively picture that rose in my mind when I heard the story of a young lady, educated and accomplished, leaving a New York home where every proper convention was observed to unite herself in marriage with an illiterate Kentucky mountaineer. A friend of hers told me the tale in barest outline, and at first I suspected exaggeration. Here was King Cophetua and the beggar maid with the rôles reversed and the riches of education substituted for the hoard of gold. From some anomalous condition of the head or heart the lady, but a year or two out of college, had left her family in New York and betaken herself to the Southern mountains, there to conduct social-service work and incidentally to teach a class of husky fellows, some much older than herself, to spell, write, and figure. That the schoolma'am had a way with her, it was evident, for rioting in the class was at an all time low, and during school hours even pistol-toting was utterly taboo. Now and then — it seemed a pretty touch — bunches of wild flowers were laid on teacher's desk according to the time-honored practice in schools of a more juvenile character.

But amongst all her pupils one was conspicuous for single-minded devotion to learning. He was a magnificent young savage (such was the story) a year or two older than his schoolmistress, and though far from being head of the class, he was the natural leader of the gang when hounds were belling on the fox's trail, or, as teacher suspected, some deviltry was cooking to add a little excitement to holiday evenings. In school hours no pupil gratified his instructress by closer questioning concerning the absurdity of spelling "wrong" with a "w" or the use of a zero "which didn't mean nuthin'." S. was always first at the log schoolhouse to kindle the fire in the airtight stove on an autumn morning; it was S. again who every morning brought in the bucket of spring water and hung the dipper above it, and he too who after school would bring his speller to the desk for a little additional instruction.

The class had run on for months. One day this tamed young wildcat raised his hand to ask for something special. "Teacher, may I see you for a spell after school? Suthin' pertickler's on my mind."

So the event came to pass, but there was tumult and much searching in the young lady's heart before she gave her consent. There were emotions also in the hearts of a New York family, but that's a different story.

Such was the tale as I heard it. Of its complete truth I could but guess and my editorial soul longed to find out. I secured the lady's address and wrote her a letter as free as possible from the outrage of impertinence. More intimate correspondence followed, and finally came the true story which is printed below. At the time I write of, "The Unsuitable Marriage" had brought unexpected trouble. Sensible of the risks of old companionships, the young wife persuaded her husband to go north, there to find employment as a miner while she added to the family budget by working as a secretary. In the evenings she would read to him and, as she tells in her story, romance was to him merely realities at high temperature. Her letters added to the vividness of her description of reading Ivanhoe aloud. The nurse would glance nervously at the temperature chart when she came to the excellent passage describing Locksley, when Torquilstone was stormed. "Curse on his Spanish steel coat! Had English smith forged it, these arrows had gone through an as if it had been silk or sandal." How Sir Walter would have delighted in his appreciation!

Such happiness was not to last. After the bright dry air of the mountains, the dark of the mines oppressed the mountaineer, the dust settled in his lungs. Symptoms of phthisis appeared. He grew very sick and their little world shrank to a hall bedroom.

At this point let the moonshiner's wife take up the story.

Our Unsuitable Marriage

BY A MOONSHINER'S WIFE

I

THERE is no primrose path to success. The triteness of this remark does not invalidate its truth, and it holds even truer of marriage than of other undertakings. If you are going to succeed in your married life, you must quite literally put your heart and soul into it; you must give it study and attention; you must make the same sacrifices for it that you make as a matter of course for any important work upon which you are engaged. If you undertake marriage at all, you should undertake it seriously — not sadly, but soberly and in good earnest.

That both S. and I share and even put into practice the above-described sentiment accounts for the fact that an apparently foolhardy marriage has so far proved a success. It may be that disaster will eventually overtake our matrimonial venture; but inasmuch as we have weathered three difficult years, we consider our chances of lasting happiness to be good.

There was only one reason why S. and I should have married each other, and every reason why we should have fled fast and far in opposite directions to avoid such a contingency. By inheritance and upbringing, in temperament, religion, and experience, we differ from each other as completely as a bird does from a fish. We do not even belong to the same period in history, for S. is late sixteenth century, and I am early twentieth. My family is of the kind that is generally described as being "good." My mother was born and bred near the classic shades of an Eastern university. My father is a fine old conservative, with a long legal ancestry behind him. We never had much money, but we always had books — and the decencies of life if not all the comforts. I grew up in a highly intellectual atmosphere, went to college, read constantly, kept up with the topics of the day, voted in a Presidential election the year I was twenty-one — in short I typified the latest human product of civilization, a modern woman. In all my multifarious activities I did not forget that the proper study of even the new woman is man. Eventually I was engaged to a young author admirably suited to me — or so everyone said. He was complex, highly developed, supercivilized, doing adequate justice to all the shibboleths of that not very remote period — the pre-war days. His one primitive emotion, jealousy, suddenly came to the surface, displayed in such fashion that our engagement ended, leaving me with a hearty distaste for "suitable" men.

Post-war restlessness rendered me out of harmony with the pleasant but somewhat monotonous life of the suburb where we lived. After six months of swimming, tennis, motoring, bridge-playing, and so forth, I developed an overwhelming dislike for the inanity and conventionality of my life. It and I were both useless and hedged in by "they say" and "one does." The "Pentecost of Calamity" had passed, leaving the world distinctly untransfigured. Disillusionment was complete.

In this frame of mind I procured a difficult piece of social-service work — a post-war activity among a group of Service men, chiefly West Virginia and Kentucky mountaineers who had been transplanted from their native hills. It was my lot to have charge of a small community-house for these men. Somewhat inadequately assisted by books and magazines (useless for the most part), a wheezy and antique Victrola, and games, in my single person I was supposed to furnish attractions enough to wean these boys away from the various sinks of iniquity which seemed to abound in the village. This was the first time I had ever come in contact with the Southern mountaineer, and I found him intensely interesting. Illiterate, crude, and reckless though he might be, he was undoubtedly genuine.

While I was new and the men were shy, everything went very smoothly; but before long a change crept into the atmosphere. I had allowed cards in the clubhouse, but of course gambling was forbidden. I suspected that money was illegitimately changing owners, but several evenings passed before I was able to catch the boys red-handed. When the gambling was quelled, a fad for wearing more or less concealed revolvers to the clubhouse took its place. Realizing that some influence less orderly than mine was dominating the boys, I began looking about to see who my rival was, and discovered S., who had hitherto remained modestly in the background. Vivid memories of our first encounter crowd upon me. The edict against carrying revolvers had gone forth, but I personally had said nothing to any of the boys. I was waiting for their leader. Leaving word that I wanted to see S. as soon as he came in, I retired to my office. Presently came a tap at the door.

"The boys told me ye sent fer me."

I looked up and for the first time really saw S. Somewhat above medium height, slender, lithe, with a plume of fair hair tossed back from a broad forehead, a head noticeably well-shaped, with ears small and close, a quick-tempered nose, a boyish mouth set in most unboyishly bitter lines — all these sufficiently individual characteristics faded into insignificance compared to his eyes: brown, I thought at first, but a closer look showed me that they were dark blue, very big, far apart, and direct, with amazingly large pupils. At least, that is how they looked that night. Never in the course of a wide experience have I seen eyes like S.'s. Sometimes they are the color of a sunny sea, sometimes the hard, shiny gray of a granite tombstone, sometimes the slit green of a hunting cat's, sometimes hazel, and sometimes even black, for his pupils expand and contract according to the light much more than do the average. But the first time I saw his eyes they were as I have described them, and in them was a look of quiet amusement which was the last thing I expected to see. It came to me with a little shock that of all the men by whom I was surrounded, S. was the only one who encountered me on equal terms. The others accepted me, without question or understanding, as one in an official position, but S. looked beyond the official position and saw only the person. Instinctively I stood up and faced him, and as I did so I noticed the outline of a revolver under his blouse.

"S.," I asked quietly, "why do you carry a gun when it's against orders?"

"Why do ye think I do?" he countered.

I pointed to the gun-butt.

"Do you suppose I can't tell a revolver when I see one sticking out?"

He looked a very little disconcerted and I followed up my advantage by asking him if I was going to have to call in a military policeman to help me keep order. The upshot of the conversation was that S. persuaded me to keep his 45-automatic for him, alleging that it was sure to be stolen if he left it in his quarters.

Theoretically the victory was on my side, but the fact that S.'s concession to my wiles was somewhat ironical made it impossible for me lightly to dismiss him from my attention. There was some quality that set him apart from his fellows. After some study I made out this difference to be twofold. First was a deep-rooted unhappiness, more vital by far than my petty discontent. This unhappiness resulted in a recklessness which I had never seen equaled, or even faintly imagined.

Before I knew S. I had not realized how even twentieth-century deeds are generally restricted by ideas and opinions, rules and regulations, which are not the doer's own but which come to him from various outside sources. No outside pronouncement hampered S.'s freedom of action. Law was literally nothing to him. Conventions were not even a name. No penalty of man could increase his suffering. Consequently he lived entirely by his own code — a code which, though it might lack some articles that we consider important, was nevertheless worthy of respect because it was entirely his own, wrought out of his own inner consciousness and tested by his own experience. This quality of recklessness made him leader among the men and it soon became evident that I must have him on my side if my work was to succeed. To win him over was not difficult: an appeal to fair play, the first article in his code, was sufficient, and from then on clubhouse manners and morals were unexceptionable.

II

S. never relapsed into the background. Subsequently he was my chief mainstay in my somewhat anomalous position. We became friends and at last he took me into his full confidence. In picturesque dialect he told me of his mother's early death, of his stormy upbringing, and of the feud that was his father's sole legacy to his four sons. Finally he even confided to me that before he entered the army he had been the leader of a somewhat notorious gang of moonshiners.

"I reckon moonshinin' was in my blood," he told me. "Grandpappy and pappy had allus done it, so it just come natural to me. After pappy died I got a bunch of boys tergither, an' we went to making whisky with pap's and Uncle Steven Smith's still. I never seed a better place for a still than the one we picked, fer there was two ways of gittin' out and only one of gittin' in, 'less you packed a rope ladder with hooks. Hit was a cave in under a cliff and had a spring right handy to the still. By usin' a rope ladder, — an' we allus had two-three in the cave, — we could go down over the cliff inter a big tree and then climb down the tree. But we used the trail up the holler except when the officers was after us. Day an' night we guarded this trail. We used a red bandanna fer a danger signal daytimes. Nights the signal was two shots fired close tergither. We had passwords, too, which we changed each month. When we was in a crowd like at a fair er an apple-peelin', we'd use these words to warn each other of danger. Most gen'ally the words was some little silly old saying that everybody but us tuck fer nonsense. The last one we had was, 'Oh, no, you never!'

"I was in a church-house oncet when, just as they started to take the collection, my first cousin stuck his head in the door and shouted, 'Oh, no, you never!' I didn't wait to explain nor fer no hat to be passed, but

I clumb through the nearest window jest as a deputy sheriff come in the door with a warrant fer me in one hand and a gun in the other. The meetin' was considerable upsot, but nobody was hurt except the winder, fer the deputy put a bullet-hole through hit firin' at me. He never was no great of a shot and he come nigher hittin' Aunt Mary Nichols than he did me."

Excitement was the air they breathed. "I was gettin' from eight to twelve dollars a quart when I jined up, fer I made good stuff, but't weren't the money we keered about — it was the excitement. Lord, how I did *love* layin' along a branch watchin' the revenoo men tryin' to trail me! Why I've been so clost to them when they was argyin' about which way I'd gone that I could a dropped a bullet plumb on Joker Dingus's old, high-crowned hat; but the leaves was so thick that, even if they had looked up, they wasn't likely to have seed me."

Thus S. in his happier moments — eyes blue and alive with laughter — gleefully recalled various escapades. But there was another side to the shield. There were occasional days when S. barely spoke at all, when his boyish mouth was set in bitter lines, and his eyes were hard and cold and dangerous. When he was in these moods, the boys dared not speak to him, and I have seen a sudden hush fall over a cheerful "kidding" group if S. happened to turn those cold, hard eyes that way.

Believing that his bitterness was a shield for heartfelt misery I determined to try to break through his reserve, and accordingly the next time S. came in gloomy and morose, I sought him out — on these occasions he invariably shunned me — and asked him to come with me to the office. For a moment I thought he was going to refuse, but presently he followed me listlessly.

"S.," I said as he stood before me with his head bent and one hand restlessly tapping my desk, "Can't you tell a friend what makes you so unhappy?"

There was an instant's pause and then he raised his eyes to mine. I could hardly repress an audible gasp. For a moment the inscrutable curtain which hides the spirit was withdrawn, and I saw a soul in pain so indescribable that my conventional consolation was struck to silence.

"Unhappy?" he said bitterly. "What have I got to make me happy? All my life since I was two year old I've had ter fight fer everythin' I got. Fer three years I've been hunted like a dog. I've never knowed what it was to lay down in peace. I've allus slept in my clothes with my gun in my hand. My life has depended on my bein' quicker than Government's hired gunmen or the coal companies' deputies. My *life!*

What good is life ter me? I've prayed it might be ended. I've stood up when bullets was a-flyin' and a-rattlin' and begged them ter hit me. I've worked in the mines pullin' pillars when all the other miners was out and the roof was crackin' and bucklin' till the foremen sont in ter have me fotched out, and nothin' never happened. What does life hold fer me? I cain't even read them magazines ye've got there. I'm ashamed to talk to ye, fer ever' time I speak I show my ignorance. I've never had a home, ner never will — ner life like other people. God! — only there ain't none! When I think of what I've gone through and what I am, I wonder that I keep on living."

With that he was gone — out of the office, and out of the house, leaving me overwhelmed by a vicarious sorrow deeper than any I had ever before experienced.

Eventually I realized that this terrible unhappiness, almost despair, was merely the longing of a powerful personality for a more extended and loftier sphere of activity. His extraordinarily keen mind had absolutely nothing on which to feed. As he had said, he could neither read nor write, and his ignorance of the most common facts of history, science, and politics was amazing. Except for his lack of education and the possession of a sense of humor, S. at this period uncommonly resembled the Byronic hero of a bygone generation. Byronic heroes have always more or less fascinated women, and the twentieth century could not save me from the fatal spell. His recklessness fascinated me, entirely weary of convention. His haunting unhappiness won my pity; the crude, untamed force of his personality compelled my admiration.

The next few months were indescribably strange ones. S. and I were both hundreds of miles away from our settings. That nobody noticed any unusual increase of interest in each other shows that we must have gone through the motions of our daily routine adequately; but for all the part other people played in our real lives, we might have been on a desert island, or even dead. We did not exactly meet in the immemorial clash of the sexes, but more as two disembodied personalities. Opposed as our temperaments are, we are both blessed or cursed with strong wills, and life at that time was a series of semiconscious contests, not so much to dominate the other as to resist the other's domination over ourselves.

III

Though our subconscious antagonism was mutual and similar, the emotions behind it were different. Before I had even seen S., my dissimilarity to the other women of his experience had caused him to fall passionately in love with me. But love, the last emotion he wished to undergo, did not cause him to lose his head. For some weeks he struggled against his feelings, and then, finding that he could not overcome them, he decided to win my affections. Before I was at all aware of his existence, he had made a careful study both of me and of the possibilities afforded by the situation, and laid his plans accordingly. The change of atmosphere in the clubhouse was part of a carefully arranged scheme to attract my attention. Everything worked out exactly as he intended, except that my influence over him grew stronger as my interest in him increased. He had expected, in waking my interest, to establish his domination, but he had underrated the power of my personality even as I underrated his. For when I first became aware of his feeling for me, I determined to make it the lever to lift him from his unhappy circumstances. Not once did it occur to me that this inexperienced mountain boy could threaten my hard-won peace of mind. Had S. been other than he was, or had exterior events taken ever so slightly different a course, I might have escaped unscathed. As it was, I did what I still think any woman would have done who "had a heart and in that heart courage to make love known."

Even the mutual acknowledgment of our feelings did not at first lessen the antagonism. Our temperaments were so utterly different that we strove almost passionately to keep our own identities from losing their individuality. But as our knowledge of each other grew, we learned that our fundamental principles were the same, and from that time on the tension grew less. In spite of the easing-up of the psychological strain, however, the situation was serious. Here we were, products of two utterly contrasted environments, total strangers in each other's worlds, yet loving each other with a deep and genuine emotion. Feeling unable to live apart, we yet were unable to live together and stay in our respective orbits. S., realizing fully that I could never be happy in his sphere, agreed to enter mine.

Now this business of changing one's world is no trivial affair. It involves considerably more than mere book-learning, important though that is. Not only ways of speech, but ways of thought, had to be changed; for his manner of thought as well as of speech belonged to the spacious times of great Elizabeth.

There was a brief probation during which we tested S.'s ability to re-date himself. When we were both convinced that he could, we were married — very quietly, because the translation was not complete, and S., realizing the situation as keenly as I, declined to put me in a position in which I might be forced to feel apologetic on his behalf. So it happens that very few know of our marriage, and we have been able to work out our destiny.

IV

For four years we have dwelt in a new world — neither S.'s nor mine, but sufficiently foreign to us both: a world peopled only by ourselves and by vague shadows that affect our lives without impinging on our consciousness. So much of our time and strength has gone into earning our living and making our marriage a success, that we have had nothing left for outsiders. Fortunately, most of our conflicts ended when our engagement graduated into marriage. I imagine that most engaged couples quarrel occasionally, but I think few encounter so wholeheartedly as did we. The result of our well-foughten fields was that we entered on our married life with a clear comprehension of each other's limits in temper and temperament. An additional factor for peace was a sort of "contract" that we framed before we were married. This contract detailed what each expected of the other, and though it has been often invoked, it has never yet been violated.

The first year of marriage, which many people find so trying, was to us sufficiently difficult but even more interesting. Our antagonism was ended, our interests, aims, and hopes were identical. There was to be a year or two of work for both of us and study for S., and then, hand-in-hand, we would return to my world and live happily ever afterwards. There was nothing impossible about this programme, but Something certainly does dispose of what man proposes. The transition from the silence and freedom of S.'s hills to the roar and confinement of New York would have been quite trying enough without the translation from a spacious, simpler, and more leisurely age to the crowded, complex, jazzing present. S.'s spirit was willing, his mind was adequate, but his flesh was weak. Shortly after our marriage a heavy cold settled on his lungs and grew worse instead of better. As I still held a position, his illness was not the complete *bouleversement* it would otherwise have been, but it contracted our scale of living painfully. That was my first experience of what it meant to be really poor.

By day I held down my job as best I could, considering that my mind was chiefly on the little hall bedroom where my invalid lay. There was nobody to look after him, for we could not afford a nurse, and S.'s painful dread of the hospital and strangers caused the doctor to believe that the ward would harm more than it helped. All day long I was never free from the fear of what I might find when I reached home.

When half-past five released me from my desk, I would hold my breath until I reached the narrow, semirespectable house where our tiny living-quarters were. With my heart in my mouth I would run up the three flights of stairs and down the dark hallway that led to our room. Often with my hand on the door-knob I have paused listening, until a rustle or a cough showed me that life was still in the room. For S. was as sick as that. Once sure that he was still alive, I would open the door to find him eagerly watching for me.

I never failed to feel a fresh pang at seeing him so changed. His eyes, always large, were enormous in his thin face. His lithe strength was changed to pathetic weakness. His hasty temper was transformed into surprising patience. Only in spirit did the S. of New York resemble the S. of Kentucky. His courage was undaunted, his smile as gay as ever, and his eyes were always blue. All day long, as he lay in his narrow, none-too-soft bed, surrounded by the most dreary liver-colored walls I ever saw, in imagination he had been roaming in a new and wonderful world; and as soon as each of us had learned how the day had gone with the other, his speech was all of other days, and of men to whom he was infinitely more akin, albeit they had long been dead, than to the men who thronged the pavements or hurled themselves into the crowded subways of New York. During my absence he had wandered with the Disinherited Knight or battled in the lists with the unknown hero whose mere presence struck terror to the unknightly heart of Prince John.

When supper, which was ready for me except when S. was at his worst, had been eaten, the real day for both of us began. For a few hours we could forget my desk and S.'s temperature, the smell of onions from the room down the hall, and the clang of the elevated two or three houses away. Together we wandered through a land and time into which S. fitted perfectly, the England of Cœur-de-Lion. Till he knew me, his sole acquaintance with literature had been *Jesse James's Blackest Crime,* read to him by his sister-in-law. *Ivanhoe* was his first introduction to the books of my world. His vivid imagination rendered the story and the characters in the novel infinitely more real to him than the scenes and people of New York. Night after night, propped up in bed, gazing at me with eyes feverishly bright, he hung breathlessly on my lips as the tale unfolded. How deeply he sympathized with Ivanhoe when he lay stricken during the siege of Torquilstone! Later, when he began to gain strength and the doctor permitted him to read to himself, I selected *St. Ives* for his first attempt. I have never seen anyone so oblivious to what was going on around him as was S. when reading. Part of my world S. dislikes or considers futile, but its books he wholeheartedly assimilates.

This illness kept us from making the most of New York's opportunities. In the eighteen months we were there, we were never able to go to the theatres. As S. has never seen a play, I was particularly anxious to see how he reacted to some of the great dramas; but that experience is still in store for us. Motion-pictures as a whole do not appeal to him.

I must admit that I entered upon his education with fear and trembling. I preferred, on the whole, to have him remain an untutored savage rather than to have him develop a liking for all the wrong things. I need not have been afraid, however. His instincts are correct if not catholic, and second-rate things do not attract him. This ensures a permanent and increasing congeniality of intellectual interest which is an important factor in a happy marriage.

To my surprise, as soon as S. assumed the responsibilities of a member of society, he developed a decided tendency toward conventionality. So strongly did he revert to the ideas and traditions of his people, that a conflict threatened to ensue. S. desired to confine my activities to my home, but the "contract" and his illness overbore him, and by degrees he has abandoned the prejudices of the mountains and adopted—I fancy with some mental reservations—the ways of more up-to-date communities. He has almost completely left his old world behind, but he has not yet altogether found his bearings in this new one.

Whether our marriage will withstand *all* the tests of time we, of course, cannot yet tell. It has come off triumphant from one great test—poverty. Babies, strikes, and S.'s ill-health have made our very existence a struggle, especially during the last year. The coal strike caught us before the first baby was paid for. Somehow we survived the strike; but only a few weeks after S. went back in the mines, he was ordered out forever. His lungs are solid with coal-dust—a fate which late or soon overtakes every miner of coal. Since that time his health has steadily declined and our fortunes with it. But no one could wish for a better companion in poverty than S. Except when too keen a realization of how completely I am at present barred from my own world sweeps over him, he is unfailingly light-hearted, making a game out of our wolf-dodging; and indeed I do not know of any game so keenly exciting as this same sport of baffling the wolf. Everyone would do well to try the game, for what it teaches can be learned in no other way. If it had not been for the discipline of this last most difficult year, trivial misunderstandings might have come between us. Poverty drives selfish love out of the window, and doubtless neither of us would ever have realized the depth and unselfishness of the other's feeling if poverty had not revealed them to us.

I have marveled how a man with S.'s wild background could in so short a time develop such a keen comprehension of what the minor discomforts of our circumstances mean to me. Most men with his upbringing would accept these unpleasantnesses as a matter of course. Perhaps a concrete instance will make clearer what I mean. Chief among the household duties that I loathe is the washing, which, however, I am willing to perform as part of my share of the burden. Sick or well, S. has always insisted on doing it for me and making a good job of it. No matter whether he was getting up at four in the morning to work in the mines, or whether his head was racked with pain (the aftermath of a sun-stroke early this summer), washing clothes for the babies has been as regular a duty as brushing his teeth. When one considers that often the water has had to be carried up one or two flights of stairs, or painfully hauled up hand over hand from a deep well, one realizes that keeping two babies clean is no light matter. Cooking, scrubbing, even mending — chores that most mountain men and perchance some city men would consider either too menial or too unimportant — he has performed voluntarily and capably. He is as skillful with the babies as a trained nurse could be — feeds them, bathes them, puts them to sleep. When I reflect that I might never otherwise have known his infinite possibilities for tenderness and self-forgetfulness, I am not sorry for the bitter struggle through which we are passing.

Poverty our marriage can endure triumphantly, but another test even greater may be in store for it. If some modern miracle should enable us to go home, — back to my world, — what then? S. is of opinion that this return will prove the real test. Civilization with him will never be of the soul. Underneath a sufficiently modern surface burn all his old passions, "nowise cool for being curbed." First of these is a jealousy that once or twice nearly ended our engagement. It is not so vulgar as jealousy of men, but it is more dangerous. It is a jealousy of anything and everything that attracts my interest. Dwelling for three years in a world strange to us both, we have literally been all in all to each other. What will happen when we enter a world foreign to S. but familiar and dear to me, we can only surmise. There is a mountain song beloved of S. that he quotes whenever this subject is under discussion.

I wish I had me a golden box
  To put my true love in.
I'd take her out and kiss her twice
  And put her back again.

Inasmuch as S. realizes his weakness and faces it fairly, and inasmuch as he has overcome disabilities which seemed infinitely greater, I believe that we shall come off triumphantly from this test, too. Study and natural adaptability have equipped S. to encounter my world on equal terms; and surely the past three years of toil, privation, and sacrifice, cheerfully and ungrudgingly borne, have forged a link between us which cannot be broken by the less soul-searching routine of comfortable life.

There is not one of my friends, married or unmarried, who is not comfortably ensconced in that pleasant world I once knew; there is not one of my married friends who has not made a more "suitable" match than I have. There is not one whom I envy.

January 1924

Here her Atlantic story closes, but not her own. That was disclosed in later letters. At first her correspondence was cheerful, filled with hopes and plans. But soon it took on a somber hue. Very gradually health of body returned to S. but his mind grew heavy with foreboding. Hallucinations seemed to beset him. He spoke constantly of being followed, of men dogging his trail. He would start violently when the door opened. His wife knew the familiar phobia and to her it seemed a portent. The mountaineer could not stand transplantation. Civilization was killing him, and she determined to take her husband back to his own country.

How to do it? Money there was next to none, and two babies added to the family complications. But the greater the difficulty, the higher rose the courage of the Moonshiner's Wife. Friends helped, and presently she wrote saying that an outworn Dodge car was hers. The tonneau piled high with babies and household goods, they started south back to the mountains.

I had helped in her decision and was eager to know the result, but the next letter did not quiet my apprehensions. True, they were safely back among the mountains in their cabin of roughhewn logs. The familiar landscape and the faces of old friends were soothing to the sufferer's nerves. He would start less involuntarily when a visitor crossed the run and came up the narrow path; but there was still the strained tired look in his eyes. He hadn't thrown the dogs off the trail, he said, and as for a doctor, he would not see one but turned instead to his old uncle, the village herbalist, for a brew of some sovereign remedy of mountain folk. Something was deeply wrong. The husband would sit quiet and moody, then suddenly he would be up and off on a long ramble with old friends, the very rapscallions from whom his wife would like to keep him away. Sometimes he would stay out all night. He was settling back into old and dangerous ways and more often than ever he would mutter something about men on his trail.

Succeeding months continued the story. The illusions came more often now, and more and more nights he spent away from home almost as if he feared his own bed. The mountains were not curing him and the fragments of education, taught with such loving patience, were slipping away. She saw what he needed; sunshine and quiet days far removed from the rough companionship of his mates.

Again she made her plan and stuck to it. Out came the old car. In went the babies and the battered belongings. For a week they traveled and at last reached journey's end — a tiny cottage in a lovely California town. To her the place seemed part of Heaven. Quiet and peace were there. Healthy labor for him in the garden, and for her everything she loved.

They were poor, but without a debt in the world. Life was beginning again, and again content shone in her face. The babies flourished. She picked up some stenographic work. Port after stormy seas, it seemed, and then the gathering tempest broke.

One afternoon as she watched him setting out some plants, smiling as she saw the hillbilly pattern of his work, she noticed that his eyes were full of fear. He came in for supper nervous and excited. Men were shadowing him again. He knew it. All through life he was being pursued. His wife tried to comfort him. It was indigestion. It was fancy. It was nothing. Why should anyone wish to do him injury? No one who knew him hated him. They loved him. What more did he want in the world than he had now? Then as they were talking there came a sharp rap at the door. She opened it and in walked two men in plain clothes. They showed their badges and then and there her husband was taken into custody for robbing a post office.

There had been no phobia. The case had been plain, unadulterated terror. Several months before his marriage S. had been on the loose with a party of friends. Any tenderfoot who has tasted white lightning remembers the effect. Vitriol could do little more. I have watched a mountaineer pour a tall glass of it into his asbestos stomach; that it intoxicated him was no surprise, but that he survived was a miracle. On that unhappy night the young desperadoes had shared a bottle and wanted more. They had broken into a grocery store and found what they wanted. Unluckily they found more than whiskey. The rear of the store was partitioned off, and the ominous sign U. S. POST OFFICE over the little window gave them no pause. S. pulled out a drawer, breaking the lock. Stamps and a few dollars were lying there. Drunk as he was he swept the contents into his pocket and when the lark was over took that as the end of the matter.

But with the Federal Government in matters like this there is but one end. After careful search S. had been identified. Detectives followed him to New York. There they lost the scent, but came on it again and trailed him back to Kentucky. They pursued him to California, and now after four years they had him.

It was a plain case. S. was tried, convicted, and sent to prison. This was the end of the long road to which the Moonshiner's Wife had come, yet even in this extremity her courage did not desert her. She saw the whole tragedy in its true light. She saw the wild adventurous youth without schooling, without work, without responsibility, accustomed from childhood to look upon officers of the law as intruders to be tricked and fought and thwarted, and she asked herself how much of the guilt was really his. When her husband had served some months of his sentence, she went straight to the judge in his chambers and told him the whole story of their marriage. He listened attentively and not unkindly, but when she had finished with a passionate appeal for mercy, his face was rigid. "That story is not true," he said, "you are lying to me."

She caught her breath. "I never lie," she said.

The judge continued, "I have read that story with my own eyes in the Atlantic. It was there you read it."

"It is my story," she replied, "I wrote it for the Atlantic."

The judge was moved. "I will do what I can," he said.

The Moonshiner's Wife had won her case. The judge strongly recommended pardon, and in due course S. was released.

Here the story ends, but the year before a curious sidelight had been shed for me upon it. "Our Unsuitable Marriage" by a Moonshiner's Wife had just been published. I went West to see something of one of my sons in a Californian school. I had been a schoolmaster myself and there is a freemasonry among teachers which established a certain intimacy between me and the headmaster and his staff. One evening at Faculty Supper a young teacher of Spanish came up to me and said, "Mr. Sedgwick, if you are not going right to bed, won't you stroll out with me?" We walked out past the baseball diamond toward the open country. My companion was silent and spoke in monosyllables. Then of a sudden he remarked, "That was an extraordinarily interesting story you printed in the Atlantic." I knew at once to what he referred. "Yes," I replied, "I found it very interesting." He stopped, faced about, and then said with intensity: "To me it was the most interesting story I ever heard in my life. You see . . . she is my sister."

When I returned to the schoolhouse I found the headmaster still up. I told him my story. "True," said he, "it is all quite true. The Moonshiner's Wife is his sister. Their father was a graduate of Harrow and of Oxford and their grandfather was an Archbishop of Canterbury."

WALTER D. EDMONDS

1903–

When Walter Edmonds left college he was determined to write — and to marry. That last was a deep secret, but it complicated his problem and the equation had to be solved. His uncle had been a close friend of mine at Harvard, so to me he came for advice. Now in the generation before mine it was unusual for men, even of talent, to depend for their living upon writing, at least during their early decades. Prose and poetry were flavoring for the pudding, but nine to five at the office desk paid for the flour and the plums. Thus, when Walter asked me whether I would advise his going into writing, my face took on all the rigidity of a prospective employer. The conversation went something like this.

"Certainly not."

"But I have written a good deal in college. I think I could do it."

"Well, you say you're twenty-one. If you go into an office you will make two years' worth of mistakes. Possibly you have two years to bet on yourself. But remember it is bread you will eat, and rye at that, and veal loaf on Sundays only. So long that is (and I glanced straight at him) as you've made up your mind not to marry."

Walter came to life. "Marry! That's just what I'm going to do. I've got the girl."

We both laughed. There was something about the boyish Edmonds that gave me not confidence but hope for confidence. I asked him to leave the scripts he had brought, and told him to come back a week later.

That evening I read his story. Something there is about talent that gives color even to an ill-typed page. I could hardly miss this, and though I did not see in my mind's eye the advertisement of half a million copies of Drums Along the Mohawk by Walter D. Edmonds, all serious doubt disappeared. But worry never leaves an editor, and soon my concern was centering about how much of his work I could get hold of before the prehensile grip of the Philadelphia Octopus closed about him.

Death of Red Peril

WALTER D. EDMONDS

I

JOHN brought his off eye to bear on me:—

What do them old coots down to the store do? Why, one of 'em will think up a horse that's been dead forty year and then they'll set around remembering this and that about that horse until they've made a resurrection of him. You'd think he was a regular Grattan Bars, the way they talk, telling one thing and another, when a man knows if that horse hadn't've had a breeching to keep his tail end off the ground he could hardly have walked from here to Boonville.

A horse race is a handsome thing to watch if a man has his money on a sure proposition. My pa was always a great hand at a horse race. But when he took to a boat and my mother, he didn't have no more time for it. So he got interested in another sport.

Did you ever hear of racing caterpillars? No? Well, it used to be a great thing on the canawl. My pa used to have a lot of them insects on hand every fall, and the way he could get them to run would make a man have his eyes examined.

The way we raced caterpillars was to set them in a napkin ring on a table, one facing one way and one the other. Outside the napkin ring was drawed a circle in chalk three feet acrost. Then a man lifted the ring and the handlers was allowed one jab with a darning needle to get their caterpillars started. The one that got outside the chalk circle the first was the one that won the race.

I remember my pa tried out a lot of breeds, and he got hold of some pretty fast steppers. But there wasn't one of them could equal Red Peril. To see him you wouldn't believe he could run. He was all red and kind of stubby, and he had a sort of a wart behind that you'd think would get in his way. There wasn't anything fancy in his looks. He'd just set still studying the ground and make you think he was dreaming about last year's oats; but when you set him in the starting ring he'd hitch himself up behind like a man lifting on his galluses, and then he'd light out for glory.

Pa came acrost Red Peril down in Westernville. Ma's relatives resided there, and it being Sunday we'd all gone in to church. We was riding back in a hired rig with a dandy trotter, and Pa was pushing her right along and Ma was talking sermon and clothes, and me and my sister was setting on the back seat playing poke your nose, when all of a sudden Pa hollers, "Whoa!" and set the horse right down on the breeching. Ma let out a holler and come to rest on the dashboard with her head under the horse. "My gracious land!" she says. "What's happened?" Pa was out on the other side of the road right down in the mud in his Sunday pants, a-wropping up something in his yeller handkerchief. Ma begun to get riled. "What you doing, Pa?" she says. "What you got there?" Pa was putting his handkerchief back into his inside pocket. Then he come back over the wheel and got him a chew. "Leeza," he says, "I got the fastest caterpillar in seven counties. It's an act of Providence I seen him, the way he jumped the ruts." "It's an act of God I ain't laying dead under the back end of that horse," says Ma. "I've gone and spoilt my Sunday hat." "Never mind," says Pa; "Red Peril will earn you a new one." Just like that he named him. He was the fastest caterpillar in seven counties.

When we got back onto the boat, while Ma was turning up the supper, Pa set him down to the table under the lamp and pulled out the handkerchief. "You two devils stand there and there," he says to me and my sister, "and if you let him get by I'll leather the soap out of you."

So we stood there and he undid the handkerchief, and out walked one of them red, long-haired caterpillars. He walked right to the middle of the table, and then he took a short turn and put his nose in his tail and went to sleep.

"Who'd think that insect could make such a break for freedom as I seen him make?" says Pa, and he got out a empty Brandreth box and filled it up with some towels and put the caterpillar inside. "He needs a rest," says Pa. "He needs to get used to his stall. When he limbers up I'll commence training him. Now then," he says, putting the box on the shelf back of the stove, "don't none of you say a word about him."

He got out a pipe and set there smoking and figuring, and we could see he was studying out just how he'd make a world-beater out of that bug. "What you going to feed him?" asks Ma. "If I wasn't afraid of constipating him," Pa says, "I'd try him out with milkweed."

Next day we hauled up the Lansing Kill Gorge. Ned Kilbourne, Pa's driver, come aboard in the morning, and he took a look at that caterpillar. He took him out of the box and felt his legs and laid him down on the table and went clean over him. "Well," he says, "he don't look like a great lot, but I've knowed some of that red variety could chug along pretty smart." Then he touched him with a pin. It was a sudden sight.

It looked like the rear end of that caterpillar was racing the front end, but it couldn't never quite get by. Afore either Ned or Pa could get a move Red Peril had made a turn around the sugar bowl and run solid aground in the butter dish.

Pa let out a loud swear. "Look out he don't pull a tendon," he says. "Butter's a bad thing. A man has to be careful. Jeepers," he says, picking him up and taking him over to the stove to dry, "I'll handle him myself. I don't want no rum-soaked bezabors dishing my beans."

"I didn't mean harm, Will," says Ned. "I was just curious."

There was something extraordinary about that caterpillar. He was intelligent. It seemed he just couldn't abide the feel of sharp iron. It got so that if Pa reached for the lapel of his coat Red Peril would light out. It must have been he was tender. I said he had a sort of a wart behind, and I guess he liked to find it a place of safety.

We was all terrible proud of that bird. Pa took to timing him on the track. He beat all known time holler. He got to know that as soon as he crossed the chalk he would get back safe in his quarters. Only when we tried sprinting him across the supper table, if he saw a piece of butter he'd pull up short and bolt back where he come from. He had a mortal fear of butter.

Well, Pa trained him three nights. It was a sight to see him there at the table, a big man with a needle in his hand, moving the lamp around and studying out the identical spot that caterpillar wanted most to get out of the needle's way. Pretty soon he found it, and then he says to Ned, "I'll race him agin all comers at all odds." "Well, Will," says Ned, "I guess it's a safe proposition."

II

We hauled up the feeder to Forestport and got us a load of potatoes. We raced him there against Charley Mack, the bank-walker's, Leopard Pillar, one of them tufted breeds with a row of black buttons down the back. The Leopard was well liked and had won several races that season, and there was quite a few boaters around that fancied him. Pa argued for favorable odds, saying he was racing a maiden caterpillar; and there was a lot of money laid out, and Pa and Ned managed to cover most of it. As for the race, there wasn't anything to it. While he was putting him in the ring — one of them birchbark and sweet grass ones Indians make — Red Peril didn't act very good. I guess the smell and the crowd kind of upset him. He was nervous and kept fidgeting with his front feet; but they hadn't more'n lifted the ring than he lit out under the edge as tight as he could make it, and Pa touched him with the needle just as he lepped the line. Me and my sister was supposed to be in bed, but Ma had gone visiting in Forestport and we'd snuck in and was under the table, which had a red cloth onto it, and I can tell you there was some shouting. There was some couldn't believe that insect had been inside the ring at all; and there was some said he must be a cross with a dragon fly or a side-hill gouger; but old Charley Mack, that'd worked in the camps, said he guessed Red Peril must be descended from the caterpillars Paul Bunyan used to race. He said you could tell by the bump on his tail, which Paul used to put on all his caterpillars, seeing as how the smallest pointed object he could hold in his hand was a peavy.

Well, Pa raced him a couple of more times and he won just as easy, and Pa cleared up close to a hundred dollars in three races. That caterpillar was a mammoth wonder, and word of him got going and people commenced talking him up everywhere, so it was hard to race him around these parts.

But about that time the lock keeper of Number One on the feeder come across a pretty swift article that the people round Rome thought high of. And as our boat was headed down the gorge, word got ahead about Red Peril, and people began to look out for the race.

We come into Number One about four o'clock, and Pa tied up right there and went on shore with his box in his pocket and Red Peril inside the box. There must have been ten men crowded into the shanty, and as many more again outside looking in the windows and door. The lock tender was a skinny bezabor from Stittville, who thought he knew a lot about racing caterpillars; and, come to think of it, maybe he did. His name was Henry Buscerck, and he had a bad tooth in front he used to suck at a lot.

Well, him and Pa set their caterpillars on the table for the crowd to see, and I must say Buscerck's caterpillar was as handsome a brute as you could wish to look at, bright bay with black points and a short fine coat. He had a way of looking right and left, too, that made him handsome. But Pa didn't bother to look at him. Red Peril was a natural marvel, and he knew it.

Buscerck was a sly, twirpish man, and he must've heard about Red Peril — right from the beginning, as it turned out; for he laid out the course in yeller chalk. They used Pa's ring, a big silver one he'd bought secondhand just for Red Peril. They laid out a lot of money, and Dennison Smith lifted the ring. The way Red Peril histed himself out from under would raise a man's blood pressure twenty notches. I swear you could see the hair lay down on his back. Why, that black-pointed bay was left nowhere! It didn't seem like he moved. But Red Peril was just gathering himself for a fast finish over the line when he seen it was yeller. He reared right up; he must've thought it was butter, by Jeepers, the way he whirled on his hind legs and went the way he'd come. Pa begun to get scared, and he shook his needle behind Red Peril, but that caterpillar was more scared of butter than he ever was of cold steel. He passed the other insect afore he'd got halfway to the line. By Cripus, you'd ought to've heard the cheering from the Forestport crews. The Rome men was green. But when he got to the line, danged if that caterpillar didn't shy agin and run around the circle twicet, and then it seemed like his heart had gone in on him, and he crept right back to the middle of the circle and lay there hiding his head. It was the pitifullest sight a man ever looked at. You could almost hear him moaning, and he shook all over.

I've never seen a man so riled as Pa was. The water was running right out of his eyes. He picked up Red Peril and he says, "This here's no race." He picked up his money and he says, "The course was illegal, with that yeller chalk." Then he squashed the other caterpillar, which was just getting ready to cross the line, and he looks at Buscerck and says, "What're you going to do about that?"

Buscerck says, "I'm going to collect my money. My caterpillar would have beat."

"If you want to call that a finish you can," says Pa, pointing to the squashed bay one, "but a baby could see he's still got to reach the line. Red Peril got to wire and come back and got to it again afore your hayseed worm got half his feet on the ground. If it was any other man owned him," Pa says, "I'd feel sorry I squashed him."

He stepped out of the house, but Buscerck laid a-hold of his pants and says, "You got to pay, Hemstreet. A man can't get away with no such excuses in the city of Rome."

Pa didn't say nothing. He just hauled off and sunk his fist, and Buscerck come to inside the lock, which was at low level right then. He waded out the lower end and he says, "I'll have you arrested for this." Pa says, "All right; but if I ever catch you around this lock again I'll let you have a feel with your other eye."

Nobody else wanted to collect money from Pa, on account of his build, mostly, so we went back to the boat. Pa put Red Peril to bed for two days. It took him all of that to get over his fright at the yeller circle. Pa even made us go without butter for a spell, thinking Red Peril might know the smell of it. He was such an intelligent, thinking animal, a man couldn't tell nothing about him.

III

But next morning the sheriff comes aboard and arrests Pa with a warrant and takes him afore a justice of the peace. That was old Oscar Snipe. He'd heard all about the race, and I think he was feeling pleasant with Pa, because right off they commenced talking breeds. It would have gone off good only Pa'd been having a round with the sheriff. They come in arm in arm, singing a Hallelujah meeting song; but Pa was polite, and when Oscar says, "What's this?" he only says, "Well, well."

"I hear you've got a good caterpillar," says the judge.

"Well, well," says Pa. It was all he could think of to say.

"What breed is he?" says Oscar, taking a chew.

"Well," says Pa, "well, well."

Ned Kilbourne says he was a red one.

"That's a good breed," says Oscar, folding his hands on his stummick and spitting over his thumbs and between his knees and into the sandbox all in one spit. "I kind of fancy the yeller ones myself. You're a connesewer," he says to Pa, "and so'm I, and between connesewers I'd like to show you one. He's as neat a stepper as there is in this country."

"Well, well," says Pa, kind of cold around the eyes and looking at the lithograph of Mrs. Snipe done in a hair frame over the sink.

Oscar slews around and fetches a box out of his back pocket and shows us a sweet little yeller one.

"There she is," he says, and waits for praise.

"She was a good woman," Pa said after a while, looking at the picture, "if any woman that's four times a widow can be called such."

"Not her," says Oscar. "It's this yeller caterpillar."

Pa slung his eyes on the insect which Oscar was holding, and it seemed like he'd just got an idee.

"Fast?" he says, deep down. "That thing run! Why, a snail with the string-halt could spit in his eye."

Old Oscar come to a boil quick.

"Evidence. Bring me the evidence."

He spit, and he was that mad he let his whole chew get away from him without noticing. Buscerck says, "Here," and takes his hand off'n his right eye.

Pa never took no notice of nothing after that but the eye. It was the shiniest black onion I ever see on a man. Oscar says, "Forty dollars!" And Pa pays and says, "It's worth it."

But it don't never pay to make an enemy in horse racing or caterpillars, as you will see, after I've got around to telling you.

Well, we raced Red Peril nine times after that, all along the Big Ditch, and you can hear to this day — yes, sir — that there never was a caterpillar alive could run like Red Peril. Pa got rich onto him. He allowed to buy a new team in the spring. If he could only've started a breed from that bug, his fortune would've been made and Henry Ford would've looked like a bent nickel alongside of me to-day. But caterpillars aren't built like Ford cars. We beat all the great caterpillars of the year, and it being a time for a late winter, there was some fast running. We raced the Buffalo Big Blue and Fenwick's Night Mail and Wilson's Joe of Barneveld. There wasn't one could touch Red Peril. It was close into October when a crowd got together and brought up the Black Arrer of Ava to race us, but Red Peril beat him by an inch. And after that there wasn't a caterpillar in the state would race Pa's.

He was mighty chesty them days and had come to be quite a figger down the canawl. People come aboard to talk with him and admire Red Peril; and Pa got the idea of charging five cents a sight, and that made for more money even if there wasn't no more running for the animile. He commenced to get fat.

And then come the time that comes to all caterpillars. And it goes to show that a man ought to be as careful of his enemies as he is lending money to friends.

IV

We was hauling down the Lansing Kill again and we'd just crossed the aqueduct over Stringer Brook when the lock keeper, that minded it and the lock just below, come out and says there was quite a lot of money being put up on a caterpillar they'd collected down in Rome.

Well, Pa went in and he got out Red Peril and tried him out. He was fat and his stifles acted kind of stiff, but you could see with half an eye he was still fast. His start was a mite slower, but he made great speed once he got going.

"He's not in the best shape in the world," Pa says, "and if it was any other bug I wouldn't want to run him. But I'll trust the old brute," and he commenced brushing him up with a toothbrush he'd bought a-purpose.

"Yeah," says Ned. "It may not be right, but we've got to consider the public."

By what happened after, we might have known that we'd meet up with that caterpillar at Number One Lock; but there wasn't no sign of Buscerck, and Pa was so excited at racing Red Peril again that I doubt if he noticed where he was at all. He was all rigged out for the occasion. He had on a black hat and a new red boating waistcoat, and when he busted loose with his horn for the lock you'd have thought he wanted to wake up all the deef-and-dumbers in seven counties. We tied by the upper gates and left the team to graze; and there was quite a crowd on hand. About nine morning boats was tied along the towpath, and all the afternoon boats waited. People was hanging around, and when they heard Pa whanging his horn they let out a great cheer. He took off his hat to some of the ladies, and then he took Red Peril out of his pocket and everybody cheered some more.

"Who owns this here caterpillar I've been hearing about?" Pa asks. "Where is he? Why don't he bring out his pore contraption?"

A feller says he's in the shanty.

"What's his name?" says Pa.

"Martin Henry's running him. He's called the Horned Demon of Rome."

"Dinged if I ever thought to see him at my time of life," says Pa. And he goes in. Inside there was a lot of men talking and smoking and drinking and laying money faster than leghorns can lay eggs, and when Pa comes in they let out a great howdy, and when Pa put down the Brandreth box on the table they crowded round; and you'd ought to've heard the mammoth shout they give when Red Peril climbed out of his box. And well they might. Yes, sir!

You can tell that caterpillar's a thoroughbred. He's shining right down to the root of each hair. He's round, but he ain't too fat. He don't look as supple as he used to, but the folks can't tell that. He's got the winner's look, and he prances into the centre of the ring with a kind of delicate canter that was as near single footing as I ever see a caterpillar get to. By Jeepers Cripus! I felt proud to be in the same family as him, and I wasn't only a little lad.

Pa waits for the admiration to die down, and he lays out his money, and he says to Martin Henry, "Let's see your ring-boned swivel-hocked imitation of a bug."

Martin answers, "Well, he ain't much to look at, maybe, but you'll be surprised to see how he can push along."

And he lays down the dangedest lump of worm you ever set your eyes on. It's the kind of insect a man might expect to see in France or one of them furrin lands. It's about two and a half inches long and stands only half a thumbnail at the shoulder. It's green and as hairless as a newborn egg, and it crouches down squinting around at Red Peril like a man with sweat in his eye. It ain't natural nor refined to look at such a bug, let alone race it.

When Pa seen it, he let out a shout and laughed. He couldn't talk from laughing.

But the crowd didn't say a lot, having more money on the race than ever was before or since on a similar occasion. It was so much that even Pa commenced to be serious. Well, they put 'em in the ring together and Red Peril kept over on his side with a sort of intelligent dislike. He was the brainiest article in the caterpillar line I ever knowed. The other one just hunkered down with a mean look in his eye.

Millard Thompson held the ring. He counted, "One — two — three — and off." Some folks said it was the highest he knew how to count, but he always got that far anyhow, even if it took quite a while for him to remember what figger to commence with.

The ring come off and Pa and Martin Henry sunk their needles — at least they almost sunk them, for just then them standing close to the course seen that Horned Demon sink his horns into the back end of Red Peril. He was always a sensitive animal, Red Peril was, and if a needle made him start you can think for yourself what them two horns did for him. He cleared twelve inches in one jump — but then he sot right down on his belly, trembling.

"Foul!" bellers Pa. "My 'pillar's fouled."

"It ain't in the rule book," Millard says.

"It's a foul!" yells Pa; and all the Forestport men yell, "Foul! Foul!"

But it wasn't allowed. The Horned Demon commenced walking to the circle — he couldn't move much faster than a barrel can roll uphill, but he was getting there. We all seen two things, then. Red Peril was dying, and we was losing the race. Pa stood there kind of foamy in his beard, and the water running right out of both eyes. It's an awful thing to see a big man cry in public. But Ned saved us. He seen Red

Peril was dying, the way he wiggled, and he figgered, with the money he had on him, he'd make him win if he could.

He leans over and puts his nose into Red Peril's ear, and he shouts, "My Cripus, you've gone and dropped the butter!"

Something got into that caterpillar's brain, dying as he was, and he let out the smallest squeak of a hollering fright I ever listened to a caterpillar make. There was a convulsion got into him. He looked like a three-dollar mule with the wind colic, and then he gave a bound. My holy! How that caterpillar did rise up. When he come down again, he was stone dead, but he lay with his chin across the line. He'd won the race. The Horned Demon was blowing bad and only halfway to the line. . . .

Well, we won. But I think Pa's heart was busted by the squeal he heard Red Peril make when he died. He couldn't abide Ned's face after that, though he knowed Ned had saved the day for him. But he put Red Peril's carcase in his pocket with the money and walks out.

And there he seen Buscerck standing at the sluices. Pa stood looking at him. The sheriff was alongside Buscerck and Oscar Snipe on the other side, and Buscerck guessed he had the law behind him.

"Who owns that Horned Demon?" says Pa.

"Me," says Buscerck with a sneer. "He may have lost, but he done a good job doing it."

Pa walks right up to him.

"I've got another forty dollars in my pocket," he says, and he connected sizably.

Buscerck's boots showed a minute. Pretty soon they let down the water and pulled him out. They had to roll a couple of gallons out of him afore they got a grunt. It served him right. He'd played foul. But the sheriff was worried, and he says to Oscar, "Had I ought to arrest Will?" (Meaning Pa.)

Oscar was a sporting man. He couldn't abide low dealing. He looks at Buscerck there, shaping his belly over the barrel, and he says, "Water never hurt a man. It keeps his hide from cracking." So they let Pa alone. I guess they didn't think it was safe to have a man in jail that would cry about a caterpillar. But then they hadn't lived alongside of Red Peril like us.

November 1928

WOODROW WILSON

1856–1924

One does not think of him mulling over literary essays. Yet there were years when his friends knew him as a Wordsworthian in spirit, a passionate pilgrim to Grasmere and Dove Cottage. Those were happy days in a life not destined to serenity, the heights unclimbed, the depths unplumbed, and mere literature to gambol in.

"Mere Literature"

WOODROW WILSON

A SINGULAR phrase this, "mere literature,"—the irreverent invention of a scientific age. Literature we know, but "mere" literature? We are not to read it as if it meant *sheer* literature, literature in the essence, stripped of all accidental or ephemeral elements, and left with nothing but its immortal charm and power. "Mere literature" is a serious sneer, conceived in all honesty by the scientific mind, which despises things which do not fall within the categories of demonstrable knowledge. It means *nothing but literature,* as who should say, "mere talk," "mere fabrication," "mere pastime." The scientist, with his head comfortably and excusably full of knowable things, takes nothing seriously and with his hat off except human knowledge. The creations of the human spirit are, from his point of view, incalculable vagaries, irresponsible phenomena, to be regarded only as play, and, for the mind's good, only as recreation,—to be used to while away the tedium of a railway journey, or to amuse a period of rest or convalescence; mere byplay, mere make-believe.

And so very whimsical things sometimes happen, because of this scientific and positivist spirit of the age, when the study of the literature of any language is made part of the curriculum of our colleges. The more delicate and subtle purposes of the study are put quite out of countenance, and literature is commanded to assume the phrases and the methods of science. It would be very painful if it should turn out that schools and universities were agencies of Philistinism; but there are some things which should prepare us for such a discovery. Our present plans for teaching everybody involve certain unpleasant things quite inevitably. It is obvious that you cannot have universal education without restricting your teaching to such things as can be universally understood. It is plain that you cannot impart "university methods" to thousands, or create "investigators" by the score, unless you confine your university education to matters which dull men can investigate, your laboratory training to tasks which mere plodding diligence and submissive patience can compass. Yet, if you do so limit and constrain what you teach, you thrust taste and insight and delicacy of perception out of the schools, exalt the obvious and the merely useful above the things which are only imaginatively or spiritually conceived, make education an affair of tasting and handling and smelling, and so create Philistia, that country in which they speak of "mere literature." I suppose that in Nirvana one would speak in like wise of "mere life."

The fear, at any rate, that such things may happen cannot fail to set us anxiously pondering certain questions about the systematic teaching of literature in our schools and colleges. How are we to impart classical writings to the children of the general public? "Beshrew the general public!" cries Mr. Birrell. "What in the name of the Bodleian has the general public got to do with literature?" Unfortunately, it has a great deal to do with it; for are we not complacently forcing the general public into our universities, and are we not arranging that all its sons be instructed how they may themselves master and teach our literature? You have nowadays, it is believed, only to heed the suggestions of pedagogics in order to know how to impart Burke or Browning, Dryden or Swift. There are certain practical difficulties, indeed; but there are ways of overcoming them. You must have strength so that you can handle with real mastery the firm fibre of these men; you must have a heart, moreover, to feel their warmth, an eye to see what they see, an imagination to keep them company, a pulse to experience their delights. But if you have none of these things, you may make shift to do without them. You may count the words they use, note the changes of phrase they make in successive revisions, put their rhythm into a scale of feet, run their allusions—particularly their female allusions—to cover, detect them in their previous reading. Or if none of these things please you, or you find the big authors difficult or dull, you may drag to light all the minor writers of their time, who are easy to understand.

By setting an example in such methods you render great services in certain directions. You make the higher degrees of our universities available for the large number of respectable men who can count, and measure, and search diligently; and that may prove no small matter. You divert attention from thought, which is not always easy to get at, and fix attention upon language, as upon a curious mechanism, which can be perceived with the bodily eye, and which is worthy to be studied for its own sake, quite apart from anything it may mean. You encourage the examination of forms, grammatical and metrical, which can be quite accurately determined and quite exhaustively catalogued. You bring all the visible phenomena of writing to light and into ordered system. You go further, and show how to make careful literal identification of stories somewhere told ill and without art with the same stories told over again by the masters, well and with the transfiguring effect of genius. You thus broaden the area of science; for you rescue the concrete phenomena of the expression of thought — the necessary syllabification which accompanies it, the inevitable juxtaposition of words, the constant use of particles, the habitual display of roots, the inveterate repetition of names, the recurrent employment of meanings heard or read — from their confusion with the otherwise unclassifiable manifestations of what had hitherto been accepted, without critical examination, under the lump term "literature," simply for the pleasure and spiritual edification to be got from it.

An instructive differentiation ensues. In contrast with the orderly phenomena of speech and writing, which are amenable to scientific processes of examination and classification, and which take rank with the orderly successions of change in nature, we have what, for want of a more exact term, we call "mere literature," — the literature which is not an expression of form, but an expression of spirit. This is a troublesome thing, and perhaps does not belong in well-conceived plans of universal instruction; for it offers many embarrassments to pedagogic method. It escapes all scientific categories. It is not pervious to research. It is too wayward to be brought under the discipline of exposition. It is an attribute of so many different substances at one and the same time that the consistent scientific man must needs put it forth from his company, as without responsible connections. By "mere literature" he means mere evanescent color, wanton trick of phrase, perverse departures from categorical statement, — something *all* personal equation, such stuff as dreams are made of.

We must not all, however, be impatient of this truant child of fancy.

When the schools cast her out, she will stand in need of friendly succor, and we must train our spirits for the function. We must be free-hearted in order to make her happy, for she will accept entertainment from no sober, prudent fellow who shall counsel her to mend her ways. She has always made light of hardship, and she has never loved or obeyed any save those of her own mind, — those who were indulgent to her humors, responsive to her ways of thought, attentive to her whims, content with her "mere" charms. She already has her small following of devotees, like all charming, capricious mistresses. There are some still who think that to know her is better than a liberal education.

There is but one way in which you can take mere literature as an education, and that is directly, at first hand. Almost any media except her own language and touch and tone are non-conducting. A descriptive catalogue of a collection of paintings is no substitute for the little areas of color and form themselves. You do not want to hear about a beautiful woman, simply, — how she was dressed, how she bore herself, how the fine color flowed sweetly here and there upon her cheeks, how her eyes burned and melted, how her voice thrilled through the ears of those about her. If you have ever seen a woman, these things but tantalize and hurt you, if you cannot see her. You want to be in her presence. You know that only your own eyes can give you direct knowledge of her. When once you have seen her, you know her in her habit as she lived; nothing but her presence contains her life. 'T is the same with the authentic products of literature. You can never get their beauty at second hand, or feel their power except by direct contact with them.

It is a strange and occult thing how this quality of "mere literature" enters into one book, and is absent from another; but no man who has once felt it can mistake it. I was reading the other day a book about Canada. It is written in what the reviewers have pronounced to be an "admirable spirited style." By this I take them to mean that it is grammatical, orderly, and full of strong adjectives. But these reviewers would have known more about the style in which it is written if they had noted what happens on page 84. There a quotation from Burke occurs. "There is," says Burke, "but one healing, catholic principle of toleration which ought to find favor in this house. It is wanted not only in our colonies, but here. The thirsty earth of our own country is gasping and gaping and crying out for that healing shower from heaven. The noble lord has told you of the right of those people by treaty; but I consider the right of conquest so little, and the right of human nature so much, that the former has very little consideration with me. I look upon the people of Canada as coming by the dispensation of God under the British government. I would have us govern it in the same manner as the all-wise disposition of Providence would govern it. We know he suffers the sun to shine upon the righteous and the unrighteous; and we ought to suffer all classes to enjoy equally the right of worshiping God according to the light he has been pleased to give them." Now, the peculiarity of such a passage as that is, that it needs no context. Its beauty seems almost independent of its subject matter. It comes on that eighty-fourth page like a burst of music in the midst of small talk,—a tone of sweet harmony heard amidst a rattle of phrases. The mild noise was unobjectionable enough until the music came. There is a breath and stir of life in those sentences of Burke's which is to be perceived in nothing else in that volume. Your pulses catch a quicker movement from them, and are stronger on their account.

It is so with all essential literature. It has a quality to move you, and you can never mistake it, if you have any blood in you. And it has also a power to instruct you which is as effective as it is subtle, and which no research or systematic method can ever rival. 'T is a sore pity if that power cannot be made available in the classroom. It is not merely that it quickens your thought and fills your imagination with the images that have illuminated the choicer minds of the race. It does indeed exercise the faculties in this wise, bringing them into the best atmosphere, and into the presence of the men of greatest charm and force; but it does a great deal more than that. It acquaints the mind, by direct contact, with the forces which really govern and modify the world from generation to generation. There is more of a nation's politics to be gotten out of its poetry than out of all its systematic writers upon public affairs and constitutions. Epics are better mirrors of manners than chronicles; dramas oftentimes let you into the secrets of statutes; orations stirred by a deep energy of emotion or resolution, passionate pamphlets that survive their mission because of the direct action of their style along permanent lines of thought, contain more history than parliamentary journals. It is not knowledge that moves the world, but ideals, convictions, the opinions or fancies that have been held or followed; and whoever studies humanity ought to study it alive, practice the vivisection of reading literature, and acquaint himself with something more than anatomies which are no longer in use by spirits.

There are some words of Thibaut, the great jurist, which have long seemed to me singularly penetrative of one of the secrets of the intellectual life. "I told him," he says, — he is speaking of an interview with Niebuhr, — "I told him that I owed my gayety and vigor, in great part, to my love for the classics of all ages, even those outside the domain of jurisprudence." Not only the gayety and vigor of his hale old age, surely, but also his insight into the meaning and purpose of laws and institutions. The jurist who does not love the classics of all ages is like a post-mortem doctor presiding at a birth, a maker of manikins prescribing for a disease of the blood, a student of masks setting up for a connoisseur in smiles and kisses. In narrating history, you are speaking of what was done by men; in discoursing of laws, you are seeking to show what courses of action and what manner of dealing with one another men have adopted. You can neither tell the story nor conceive the law till you know how the men you speak of regarded themselves and one another; and I know of no way of learning this but by reading the stories they have told of themselves, the songs they have sung, the heroic adventures they have conceived. I must know what, if anything, they revered; I must hear their sneers and gibes; must learn in what accents they spoke love within the family circle, with what grace they obeyed their superiors in station; how they conceived it politic to live, and wise to die; how they esteemed property, and what they deemed privilege; when they kept holiday, and why; when they were prone to resist oppression, and wherefore, — I must see things with their eyes, before I can comprehend their law books. Their jural relationships are not independent of their way of living, and their way of thinking is the mirror of their way of living.

It is doubtless due to the scientific spirit of the age that these plain, these immemorial truths are in danger of becoming obscured. Science, under the influence of the conception of evolution, devotes itself to the study of forms, of specific differences, of the manner in which the same principle of life manifests itself variously under the compulsions of changes of environment. It is thus that it has become "scientific" to set forth the manner in which man's nature submits to man's circumstances; scientific to disclose morbid moods, and the conditions which produce them; scientific to regard man, not as the centre or source of power, but as subject to power, a register of external forces instead of an originative soul, and character as a product of man's circumstances rather than a sign of man's mastery over circumstance. It is thus that it has become "scientific" to analyze language as itself a commanding element in man's life. The history of word roots, their modification under the influences of changes wrought in the vocal organs by habit or by climate, the laws of phonetic change to which they are obedient, and their persistence under all disguises of dialect, as if they were full of a self-originated life, a self-directed energy of influence, is united with the study of grammatical forms in the construction of scientific conceptions of the evolution and uses of human speech. The impression is created that literature is only the chosen vessel of these forms, disclosing to us their modification in use and structure from age to age. Such vitality as the masterpieces of genius possess comes to seem only a dramatization of the fortunes of words. Great writers construct for the adventures of language their appropriate epics. Or, if it be not the words themselves that are scrutinized, but the style of their use, that style becomes, instead of a fine essence of personality, a matter of cadence merely, or of grammatical and structural relationships. Science is the study of the forces of the world of matter, the adjustments, the apparatus, of the universe; and the scientific study of literature has likewise become a study of apparatus, — of the forms in which men utter thought, and the forces by which those forms have been and still are being modified, rather than of thought itself.

The essences of literature of course remain the same under all forms, and the true study of literature is the study of these essences, — a study, not of forms or of differences, but of likenesses, likenesses of spirit and intent under whatever varieties of method, running through all forms of speech like the same music along the chords of various instruments. There is a sense in which literature is independent of form, just as there is a sense in which music is independent of its instrument. It is my cherished belief that Apollo's pipe contained as much eloquent music as any modern orchestra. Some books live; many die: wherein is the secret of immortality? Not in beauty of form, nor even in force of passion. We might say of literature what Wordsworth said of poetry, the most easily immortal part of literature: it is "the impassioned expression which is in the countenance of all science; it is the breath of the finer spirit of all knowledge." Poetry has the easier immortality because it has the sweeter accent when it speaks, because its phrases linger in our ears to delight them, because its truths are also melodies. Prose has much to overcome, — its plainness of visage, its less musical accents, its homelier turns of phrase. But it also may contain the immortal essence of truth and seriousness and high thought. It too may clothe conviction with the beauty that must make it shine forever. Let a man but have beauty in his heart, and, believing something with his might, put it forth arrayed as he sees it, the lights and shadows falling upon it on his page as they fall upon it in his heart, and he may die assured that that beauty will not pass away out of the world.

Biographers have often been puzzled by the contrast between certain men as they lived and as they wrote. Schopenhauer's case is one of the most singular. A man of turbulent life, suffering himself to be cut to exasperation by the petty worries of his lot, he was nevertheless calm and wise when he wrote, as if the Muse had rebuked him. He wrote at a still elevation, where small and temporary things did not come to disturb. 'T is a pity that for some men this elevation is so far to seek. They lose permanency by not finding it. Could there be a deliberate regimen of life for the author, it is plain enough how he ought to live, not as seeking fame, but as deserving it.

> Fame, like a wayward girl, will still be coy
> To those who woo her with too slavish knees;
> But makes surrender to some thoughtless boy,
> And dotes the more upon a heart at ease.
>
> . . . .
>
> Ye love-sick bards, repay her scorn with scorn;
> Ye love-sick artists, madmen that ye are,
> Make your best bow to her and bid adieu:
> Then, if she likes it, she will follow you.

It behooves all minor authors to realize the possibility of their being discovered some day, and exposed to the general scrutiny. They ought to live as if conscious of the risk. They ought to purge their hearts of everything that is not genuine and capable of lasting the world a century, at least, if need be. Mere literature is made of spirit. The difficulties of style are the artist's difficulties with his tools. The spirit that is in the eye, in the pose, in mien or gesture, the painter must find in his color box; as he must find also the spirit that nature displays upon the face of the fields or in the hidden places of the forest. The writer has less obvious means. Word and spirit do not easily consort. The language that the philologists set out before us with such curious erudition is of very little use as a vehicle for the essences of the human spirit. It is too sophisticated and self-conscious. What you need is, not a critical knowledge of language, but a quick feeling for it. You must recognize the affinities between your spirit and its idioms. You must immerse your phrase in your thought, your thought in your phrase, till each becomes saturated with the other. Then what you produce is as necessarily fit for permanency as if it were incarnated spirit.

And you must produce in color, with the touch of imagination which lifts what you write away from the dull levels of mere exposition. Black-and-white sketches may serve some purposes of the artist, but very little of actual nature is in mere black-and-white. The imagination never works thus with satisfaction. Nothing is ever conceived completely when conceived so grayly, without suffusion of real light. The mind creates, as great Nature does, in colors, with deep chiaroscuro and burning lights. This is true not only of poetry and characteristically imaginative writing, but also of the writing which seeks nothing more than to penetrate the meaning of actual affairs, — the writing of the greatest historians and philosophers, the utterances of orators and of the great masters of political exposition. Their narratives, their analyses, their appeals, their conceptions of principle, are all dipped deep in the colors of the life they expound. Their minds respond only to realities, their eyes see only actual circumstance. Their sentences quiver and are quick with visions of human affairs, — how minds are bent or governed, how action is shaped or thwarted. The great "constructive" minds, as we call them, are of this sort. They "construct" by seeing what others have not imagination enough to see. They do not always know more, but they always realize more. Let the singular reconstruction of Roman history and institutions by Theodor Mommsen serve as an illustration. Safe men distrust this great master. They cannot find what he finds in the documents. They will draw you truncated figures of the antique Roman state, and tell you the limbs cannot be found, the features of the face have nowhere been unearthed. They will cite you fragments such as remain, and show you how far these can be pieced together toward the making of a complete description of private life and public function in those first times when the Roman commonwealth was young; but what the missing sentences were they can only weakly conjecture. Their eyes cannot descry those distant days with no other aids than these. Only the greatest are dissatisfied, and go on to paint that ancient life with the materials that will render it lifelike, — the materials of the constructive imagination. They have other sources of information. They see living men in the old documents. Give them but the torso, and they will supply head and limbs, bright and animate as they must have been. If Mommsen does not quite do that, another man, with Mommsen's eye and a touch more of color on his brush, might have done it, — may yet do it.

It is in this way that we get some glimpse of the only relations that scholarship bears to literature. Literature can do without exact scholarship, or any scholarship at all, though it may impoverish itself thereby; but scholarship cannot do without literature. It needs literature to float it, to set it current, to authenticate it to the race, to get it out of closets, and into the brains of men who stir abroad. It will adorn literature, no doubt; literature will be the richer for its presence; but it will not, it cannot, of itself create literature. Rich stuffs from the East do not create a king, nor costly trappings a conqueror. There is, indeed, a natural antagonism, let it be frankly said, between the standards of scholarship and the standards of literature. Exact scholarship values things in direct proportion as they are verifiable; but literature knows nothing of such tests. The truths which it seeks are the truths of self-expression. It is a thing of convictions, of insights, of what is felt and seen and heard and hoped for. Its meanings lurk behind nature, not in the facts of its phenomena. It speaks of things as the man who utters it saw them, not necessarily as God made them. The personality of the speaker runs throughout all the sentences of real literature. That personality may not be the personality of a poet: it may be only the personality of the penetrative seer. It may not have the atmosphere in which visions are seen, but only that in which men and affairs look keenly cut in outline, boldly massed in bulk, consummately grouped in detail, to the reader as to the writer. Sentences of perfectly clarified wisdom may be literature no less than stanzas of inspired song, or the intense utterances of impassioned feeling. The personality of the sunlight is in the keen lines of light that run along the edges of a sword no less than in the burning splendor of the rose or the radiant kindlings of a woman's eye. You may feel the power of one master of thought playing upon your brain as you may feel that of another playing upon your heart.

Scholarship gets into literature by becoming part of the originating individuality of a master of thought. No man is a master of thought without being also a master of its vehicle and instrument, style, that subtle medium of all its evasive effects of light and shade. Scholarship is material; it is not life. It becomes immortal only when it is worked upon by conviction, by schooled and chastened imagination, by thought that runs alive out of the inner fountains of individual insight and purpose. Colorless, or without suffusion of light from some source of light, it is dead, and will not twice be looked at; but made part of the life of a great mind, subordinated, absorbed, put forth with authentic stamp of currency on it, minted at some definite mint and bearing some sovereign image, it will even outlast the time when it shall have ceased to deserve the acceptance of scholars, — when it shall, in fact, have become "mere literature."

Scholarship is the realm of nicely adjusted opinion. It is the business of scholars to assess evidence and test conclusions, to discriminate values and reckon probabilities. Literature is the realm of conviction and of vision. Its points of view are as various as they are oftentimes unverifiable. It speaks individual faiths. Its groundwork is not erudition, but reflection and fancy. Your thorough-going scholar dare not reflect. To reflect is to let himself in on his material; whereas what he wants is to keep himself apart, and view his materials in an air that does not color or refract. To reflect is to throw an atmosphere about what is in your mind, — an atmosphere which holds all the colors of your life. Reflection summons all associations, and they throng and move so that they dominate the mind's stage at once. The plot is in their hands. Scholars, therefore, do not reflect; they label, group kind with kind, set forth in schemes, expound with dispassionate method. Their minds are not stages, but museums; nothing is done there, but very curious and valuable collections are kept there. If literature use scholarship, it is only to fill it with fancies or shape it to new standards, of which of itself it can know nothing.

True, there are books reckoned primarily books of science and of scholarship which have nevertheless won standing as literature: books of science such as Newton wrote, books of scholarship such as Gibbon's. But science was only the vestibule by which such a man as Newton entered the temple of nature, and the art he practiced was not the art of exposition, but the art of divination. He was not only a scientist, but also a seer; and we shall not lose sight of Newton because we value what he was more than what he knew. If we continue Gibbon in his fame, it will be for love of his art, not for worship of his scholarship. We some of us, nowadays, know the period of which he wrote better even than he did; but which one of us shall build so admirable a monument to ourselves, as artists, out of what we know? The scholar finds his immortality in the form he gives to his work. It is a hard saying, but the truth of it is inexorable: be an artist, or prepare for oblivion. You may write a chronicle, but you will not serve yourself thereby. You will only serve some fellow who shall come after you, possessing, what you did not have, an ear for the words you could not hit upon, an eye for the colors you could not see, a hand for the strokes you missed.

Real literature you can always distinguish by its form, and yet it is not possible to indicate the form it should have. It is easy to say that it should have a form suitable to its matter; but how suitable? Suitable to set the matter off, adorn, embellish it, or suitable simply to bring it directly, quick and potent, to the apprehension of the reader? This is the question of style, about which many masters have had many opinions; upon which you can make up no safe generalization from the practice of those who have unquestionably given to the matter of their thought immortal form, an accent or a countenance never to be forgotten. Who shall say how much of Burke's splendid and impressive imagery is part and stuff of his thought, or tell why even that part of Newman's prose which is devoid of ornament, stripped to its shining skin, and running bare and lithe and athletic to carry its tidings to men, should promise to enjoy as certain an immortality? Why should Lamb go so quaintly and elaborately to work upon his critical essays, taking care to perfume every sentence, if possible, with the fine savor of an old phrase, if the same business could be as effectively done in the plain and even cadences of Mr. Matthew Arnold's prose? Why should Gibbon be so formal, so stately, so elaborate, when he had before his eyes the example of great Tacitus, whose direct, sententious style had outlived so many hundred years the very language in which he wrote? In poetry, who shall measure the varieties of style lavished upon similar themes? The matter of vital thought is not separable from the thinker; its forms must suit his handling as well as fit his conception. Any style is author's stuff which is suitable to his purpose and his fancy. He may use rich fabrics with which to costume his thoughts, or he may use simple stone from which to sculpture them, and leave them bare. His only limits are those of art. He may not indulge a taste for the merely curious or fantastic. The quaint writers have quaint thoughts; their material is suitable. They do not merely satisfy themselves as virtuosi, with collections of odd phrases and obsolete meanings. They needed twisted woods to fit the eccentric patterns of their thought. The great writer has always dignity, restraint, propriety, adequateness; what time he loses these qualities he ceases to be great. His style neither creaks nor breaks under his passion, but carries the strain with unshaken strength. It is not trivial or mean, but speaks what small meanings fall in its way with simplicity, as conscious of their smallness. Its playfulness is within bounds, its laugh never bursting too boisterously into a guffaw. A great style always knows what it would be at, and does the thing appropriately, with the larger sort of taste.

This is the condemnation of tricks of phrase, devices to catch the attention, exaggerations and loud talk to hold it. No writer can afford to strive after effect, if his striving is to be apparent. For just and permanent effect is missed altogether, unless it be so completely attained as to seem like some touch of sunlight, perfect, natural, inevitable, wrought without effort and without deliberate purpose to be effective. Mere audacity of attempt can, of course, never win the wished-for result; and if the attempt be successful, it is not audacious. What we call audacity in a great writer has no touch of temerity, sauciness, or arrogance in it. It is simply high spirit, a dashing and splendid display of strength. Boldness is ridiculous unless it be impressive, and it can be impressive only when backed by solid forces of character and attainment. Your plebeian hack cannot afford the showy paces; only the full-blooded Arabian has the sinew and proportion to lend them perfect grace and propriety. The art of letters eschews the bizarre as rigidly as does every other fine art. It mixes its colors with brains, and is obedient to great Nature's same standards of right adjustment in all that it attempts.

You can make no catalogue of these features of great writing; there is no science of literature. Literature in its essence is mere spirit, and you must experience it rather than analyze it too formally. It is the door to nature and to ourselves. It opens our hearts to receive the experiences of great men and the conceptions of great races. It awakens us to the significance of action and to the singular power of mental habit. It airs our souls in the wide atmosphere of contemplation. "In these bad days, when it is thought more educationally useful to know the principle of the common pump than Keats's 'Ode on a Grecian Urn,'" as Mr. Birrell says, we cannot afford to let one single precious sentence of "mere literature" go by us unread or unpraised. If this free people to which we belong is to keep its fine spirit, its perfect temper amidst affairs, its high courage in the face of difficulties, its wise temperateness and wide-eyed hope, it must continue to drink deep and often from the old wells of English undefiled, quaff the keen tonic of its best ideals, keep its blood warm with all the great utterances of exalted purpose and pure principle of which its matchless literature is full. The great spirits of the past must command us in the tasks of the future. Mere literature will keep us pure and keep us strong. Even though it puzzle or altogether escape scientific method, it may keep our horizon clear for us, and our eyes glad to look bravely forth upon the world.

December 1893

ELLERY SEDGWICK

1872–

One piece of my own I venture to introduce, although it may invite the contumely of the right thinking to whom it is infamous, once to have loved Japan. I confess I did love Japan for I have never been happier than in that beautiful country. I seemed to find there a more refined, and a less material civilization than any I had been privileged to know. No visitor to Japan in those days ever saw the military men who plotted and achieved the ruin of their country. But one did see astonishingly pacific admirals, statesmen, merchants, collectors, and men of affairs who wished to live and let live and were sensible of the worlds visible and invisible, and who lived in simplicity utterly unknown in the Western World.

Even during the war a neutral might have pointed to certain redeeming qualities here and there to be observed. Very recently I have come upon an authenticated instance of conduct which even an American officer might emulate. On one of the Pacific atolls a large force of Japanese surrendered. It became the duty of the Japanese Vice-Admiral lately in Command to co-operate with the conquerors. This repugnant service he performed with a completeness, a dignity and a self-respecting courtesy which greatly struck his American conqueror. Wishing to show appreciation of his attitude our senior officer, a Vice-Admiral, offered personally to take a letter from the prisoner to his wife and thus relieve her dreadful anxiety concerning her husband's fate. It was explained to the Japanese that the letter would be properly censored and every regulation of the service scrupulously enforced so that he might be assured there would be nothing clandestine about the transaction. This invitation, graciously offered, was as graciously declined. The Japanese expressed his high appreciation, but declared he must refuse. The American knew how poignantly the proposed favor must appeal to the prisoner and after an interval, our Admiral renewed his offer. He gave absolute assurance that no smuggling was in question. He would take the letter, after examination by the censor, in his own pocket and would transport it himself to its destination. He even gave his word that in case of difficulty, he would burn the letter rather than have a change of hands open any opportunity for a mistake or any attendant publicity.

The Japanese bowed gravely in recognition of a courtesy from the enemy, of which he was deeply sensible, and then after a moment, he said: "I fully understand all that you promise and I hope you understand that I have no lack of appreciation of all you offer to do. But now that you tell me how you propose to do it, may I, with equal candor, explain why it is impossible for me to accept your kindness? In my command there are thirty-nine thousand junior officers and enlisted men. For them, you obviously cannot do the same great service. The fate of these men is my fate. Their misfortunes are my misfortunes. You see why I cannot accept."

I tell this story for there is about it a certain scrupulous delicacy of which I myself have seen many, many instances.

There is another side, also, to Japanese nature, much travestied in the United States. Even in ruin, the nation wears a smile. We think this fatuous and out of place, but they think differently. A smile can be more imperturbable than gravity and any display of feeling seems to an educated Japanese unsuitable exposure of his personality. To us nakedness of the body is an affront to human dignity; to them to strip the mind naked is the great offense.

Much might be written of the Japanese smile. It is an index of a unique civilization. To the Japanese, courtesy demands a smile and while some of us think truth-telling important in the small give-and-take of social life, they would hold that the supreme infraction of the code of manners is to wound the feelings. In familiar association, a Japanese will gloze over the unpleasant. "Out with it," makes no appeal to him. He holds it not a virtue, but a flagrant fault. The story I have to tell, while it ranks primarily as a major adventure in the life of a respectable old gentleman, requires for its understanding some conception of what Japan was and will never be again.

A Tale of Old Japan

ELLERY SEDGWICK

I

THE impression grew and flourished that Fuji was an innkeeper's legend. Of course, there were pictures in every shop of this chiefest miracle of nature, but there is no sect in Japan which can boast more devotees than that which troops after the God of Advertising, and the story grew that, like the imperious dragons with curly tails and the Thousand-armed Buddhas, the sweep and lift of Fuji was the vision of some supreme artist which Hokusai and Hiroshige had translated into the vernacular of everyday life. Every morning, it is true, the newly arrived were told to look southwest from Tokyo, for a northerly breeze would part the clouds and disclose the heaven-pointing pyramid; but each day clouds, thick with rain, where Fuji ought to be, confirmed the suspicion of a profitable and patriotic hoax. It was all of a piece with Santa Claus. Once you were let into the secret you joined the conspiracy.

Now, if any man were responsible, it was obviously mine host at Miyanoshita, Mr. Yamagouchi. His delectable inn, the Fuji-ya, where the splash of water tumbling into a camellia-shaded pool all but drowns the tinkle of cocktail glasses on the verandah, is dedicated to pilgrims searching for Fuji-san — Fuji-Sir, as the Japanese say in affectionate respect. Never was hostelry more nicely calculated to assuage disappointment. Food, bed, service, all tempt the visitor to stay one more day when it "will be sure to clear"; and Fuji after rain, you are told, is the supremely perfect Fuji.

How satisfying are these best inns of Japan! How fastidiously they minister to the sentimental traveler! The maid, in her gay kimono and gayer obi, comes in to bring you tea.

"What a charming view you have given me from my window," you say. "How beautiful it would be to see the sun."

She looks out, lost for an instant in the loveliness of young willows bursting into leaf.

"Yes," she says with a smile, "a beautiful place to see the sun, but it is a more beautiful place still to see the moon."

Where else among chambermaids radiates the soft influence of Diana?

Mr. Yamagouchi is a necromancer, but even his lively wit and the majesty of his moustache, eighteen inches from tip to tip, cannot drive from the visitor's mind the thought that Fuji, one sight of Fuji, is the hope that lured him to Miyanoshita. Still, that moustache is no trivial eccentricity lightly to be passed over. Not merely does it give our host primacy in the Moustache Club, where you may see, from authentic photographic records, mustachios rampant, couchant, undulant, recessive, rococo, flamboyant, sometimes with beards, sometimes in solitary magnificence of line, black, white, and gray; mustachios in the structural harmony of flying buttresses or in delicate finials pointed to the airy filament of a single hair — from such competition one may not lightly bear away the capillary crown. Not only, I say, does this masculine achievement divert one's thoughts from the pursuit of Fuji; it elevates one's standards from the dandified mustachios of Paris to purer and nobler forms, where, freeing itself from parasitical adornments, it becomes its own triumphant vindication.

Three days of rain had been followed by three days of cloud, but the wind still blew from the northeast. If you do not know what that means, you have only to walk down the streets of a Japanese city and note the precautions which the architect whose site is the northeast corner of a block must take if the devil of that quarter (the most exasperating, I am told, of all devils in Hell or out of it) is to be barred out. The devil is smart, but the architect is smarter, and, instead of constructing the ordinary right-angled corner, he folds the corner inward in a sharp recessive angle, thus:  This is unexpected, and to the devil looks so remarkably like a trap that he follows the way of prudence and makes no attempt to enter.

Well, we were out to know the secret of Fuji, and after a day of blackest cloud we awoke the second morning to broad sunshine. All things were auspicious. The line of little bowing boys in the hall smiled in unison. The waitress, her kimono bright with plum blossoms, brought us coffee and toast, and the promise of a lovely "cherry day," while Mr. Yamagouchi twisted the fierce extremities of his mustachios and said we had brought the south wind in our valises — which meant that this day we were to be let into the secret of Fuji-san, whatever that might be.

II

Have you ever noticed that when a traveler tells of Fuji he attempts to describe the incredible? You learn that the peak is 12,365 feet above sea level, a figure you were obviously intended to remember on account of the days of the year, but after that single intelligible remark the pilgrim becomes rapturously mystical. Fuji-san is a dream, a vision, a symbol of the unattainable, an exhalation of the Divine Spirit returning again to God, the single perfect abstraction in Nature. This is not description. This is rhetoric, and the reason is that the indescribable cannot be described. You can speak of the mists circling about the base of the peak, now white as snow, now golden with the sun, now purpling under the passing shadow of a cloud, but all this might be said of other mountains, and Fuji is no more like the Alps, or the Rockies, or the Andes, than the Grand Canyon is like a muddy gulch. Prose is futile. Painting tells of it only what is in the mind's eye, but Fuji is the vision, not of what is, but of what might be.

Mr. Yamagouchi was on the porch to welcome us when we returned from our all-day drive about the five lakes which lie, the posters tell us, in a great circle about the mountain. We were in his secret. We complimented him on the compact completeness of his lunch boxes — chicken, beef, ham, tongue, salad, bamboo knife and fork, bamboo salts and peppers, bamboo sprouts to eat, and bamboo to pack them in; and he complimented us on knowing what we knew.

That evening a seven-course dinner meandering pleasantly from caviar to strawberries and cream, and that current of loving-kindness toward all men that comes from half a bottle of Burgundy and a glass of port! Then my wife left me with the injunction to be careful not to wake her when I came up, for we had driven that day from nine to six.

Now a lonely cigar is not the way to end a day of days. Seeking out Mr. Yamagouchi, I found him in expansive mood, and baited my hook for his story. The Japanese, I remarked, are not a people of individual achievement. They work in pairs, or groups, or crowds. In fact, one of the constant miracles of a miraculous country is the continual transition from individual incompetence to collective genius. Watch the helplessness of the man called to mend your water pipe, but note the swift dispatch of the business when his mates rally to his aid. Every Cabinet Minister has his Vice Minister, every executive his alter ego, but if now and then you come on an individual Japanese who has "done it all himself," depend upon it he has a story to tell well worth your attentive ear. This is the story that Mr. Yamagouchi told me.

His father and, for that matter, his father's father had been innkeepers in Japan. They were a stiff, unbending race, who had found that there was one right way to do everything, and cared not to learn another. They had made a success of their business, and it was the duty of the sons to plant their small footprints precisely in their father's confident tracks. But Mr. Yamagouchi — it was before his adoption, and his name was Kanaya then — had a will and ideas of his own, and when he left school to enter the hotel kitchen as an apprentice, although he was quick to learn every detail of the Japanese style of cooking, serving, and living, he was acutely aware of the changing world about him, and knew that when the hordes of the West swarmed over his country they would cry out to be fed with their own food and to sleep in their own beds — and incidentally would pay well for the trouble. Month in and month out, the boy pleaded with his father to be allowed to cross the ocean and study Western ways. But always his father repulsed him, not too gently, and thrust him back into the kitchen to keel the pots and fill the *hibachis* with fresh charcoal.

The Japanese boy does not disobey, but by persistence he can make a father's life unendurable. I suspect that it was by pressing his talent in this direction that this particular boy finally wormed out of his father permission to go to England, if he could pay for the journey. It was a prudent promise to make to a penniless boy of sixteen, whose wages were three meals of rice with a *bonne bouche* of raw squid or eels on festal occasions. But where there is a Japanese will, there is an ultimate way, and the boy, who had picked up some knowledge of English, contrived to make himself so useful to a prospective traveler that his new friend agreed to pay his transportation to San Francisco in return for service assiduously rendered.

So the first barrier was crossed, but once in America the boy was left to his own devices. Everywhere he sought for work, and everywhere he was refused. His dollars dwindled to pennies; he lived on bananas, and slept in the open. His foot was in the doorway, but the door was slamming in his face.

Very close to despair, the little stranger sat on a San Francisco pier, gazed toward the home he had longed to leave, and idly watched a big ship warp into the dock. Then came the miracle which, whatever pessimists say, never fails him who waits patiently, wisely, and courageously. A certain great lady, now on her way to London in advance of her husband, who had been named ambassador, chanced to be amongst the passengers. The boy had seen her at his father's inn, and now came forward, bowing and smiling, to make her welcome. He poured out his story. "How fortunate!" she said. "A sick friend of my husband, now on his way to London, needs an interpreter and guide." And so it was that the young pilgrim reached his Promised Land.

But for him that land flowed not with honey, neither with milk. London was larger than San Francisco, and food cost less, but it costs something even for an appetite nourished on rice and porridge. The boy starved and shivered, but at last in the Savoy he found a scullion's job. Now he had English pots to clean, instead of Japanese ones, but all the while he watched how things were done. When work failed at the Savoy, he found a job at the Cecil, and, before the year was out, all there was to know below-stairs in the great West End hotels he knew.

But times grew hard again, and work faded away. Now was his chance to perform his own miracle. He called again on the ambassadress who had helped him in his despair. Starvation is a liberal education for the wits, and he addressed her with confidence. "I have heard," said he, "you need a diligent Japanese in your service, really versed in English. That is no longer accurate, for here he is." The lady demurred, hesitated, accepted, and Yamagouchi was on his way.

Still the boy's salary was tiny, and none of his native astrologers could have called his future bright. But, earning money by hook and crook, within two years he was attending lectures at Cambridge. And then came the third miracle. It chanced that at Cambridge there was another Japanese boy, homeless, friendless, and poor. In childhood he had been a chum of Yamagouchi's, and now the two small exiles took to roaming the countryside together. One day, in better spirits than usual and needing exercise, they proposed a bout of jiujitsu, in which Yamagouchi was proficient and his friend hardly an ignoramus. Taking off their shoes on a Cambridge green for the same reason that leads young Westerners to put on gloves for their bouts, the boys fell to, and in an instant Yamagouchi tossed his friend over his shoulder.

Again they went at it. The novelty of the show — this was early in the nineties — brought a crowd, and in the thick of it a tall young Cambridge boxer who looked on in amazement. A third time Yamagouchi flicked his friend over his shoulder as if he had been a feather pillow. The crowd huzzaed, but the watching athlete, six feet two of brawn and muscle, who, every inch of him, lived for sport and understood it, gave vent to his incredulity: "It's all very well for little codgers, but that's no man-size game."

"Come on," said Yamagouchi.

The Englishman hesitated, as an Englishman might before an

antagonist sixty pounds under his weight and twelve inches under his height.

"Try it on," said Yamagouchi.

Off came the athlete's coat and shoes. He started to spar, but in less than thirty seconds went flying through the air for a fall, heavy as on the hunting field.

"You don't drop right," said Yamagouchi.

"I say," panted the Englishman, "that's too good for you Japanese to keep to yourselves. You teach me and I will pay you a pound an hour."

So it came to pass that Yamagouchi became the first master of jiujitsu in England. In a day his reputation was established in Cambridge. In a month the young bloods in London knew of the strange new sport. With the backing of his English friend he formed classes. His gift for organization asserted itself. He taught his own instructors, and supervised their work in a long chain of classes. Within a year his income had jumped from ten shillings a week to a hundred pounds.

It was time to write home, now that he could write with dignity, but his father's reply was disconcerting: "Come home, my son, I need you." In vain the son expostulated. A fortune was in his grasp. His work was organized. It was interesting. It was rewarding. He wrote with patience, setting forth the facts.

To understand this story you must realize that this young man was now of age. He had received nothing from his father. His success was due to himself alone. Now he was asked to give up an independent fortune and to return to servitude. But as the teller of the tale remarked by way of simple comment, "We Japanese obey our fathers."

So back he went, back to the drudgery of his father's inn, back with only the memories of his independence; but he had taught himself to be the master of circumstance, and to-day he and his brother have a whole string of hotels, both native and foreign. Of these latter two are, I verily believe, the most comfortable and satisfying inns in the world. So perhaps his father was right after all.

III

The Fuji-ya Inn at Miyanoshita owes part, at least, of its comfortable air to the extreme irregularity of its form. Its general ground plan is a half circle, but wing after wing has been added, one detail of ornament or structure nicely assimilated to another, corridor joined to corridor, and one walks upstairs and down, over bridges and up inclines, in the daily round. To go to bed that night involved something between a stroll and a walk. My route was unconsciously familiar, and as I strolled down the long halls and through the series of swinging doors I pondered on the relations of fathers and sons, Western education, jiujitsu, the teaching of initiative, and quite a number of other philosophic matters which resolved themselves into extremely complex equations. But all the time the subconscious part of me was taking note: be sure to count the number of swinging doors, bear left through this corridor, then sharp left, then right, now up a flight of broad stairs, turn left again, note the bell-shaped windows of ground glass which mark the particular hallway and give an unmistakable sense of rightness to one's direction, then on through a corridor, — this time a short one, — face left before the last door, and there you are!

There I undoubtedly was, but I pride myself on the meticulousness of my observation, and it annoyed me to note that the young Boots, usually so careful, had misplaced my wife's shoes and substituted therefor certain imitations of lace in leather which to a man of my upbringing are peculiarly obnoxious. I must not wake my wife. I made no fuss over the shoes. I turned the knob with infinite care, opened the door silently, slipped within, and turned the key in the lock with so noiseless a precision that the final click as the bolt caught was absolutely inaudible. A faint light filtered dimly through the narrow transom, but I knew the terrain; the bathroom was directly to my left, while a step beyond opened out our vast room with four windows, two to the south, two to the west, and two beds, one in the far corner where I could just discern the shrouded outline of my partner as she lay in her first deep, refreshing slumber.

I am a considerate husband, well used to going to bed in the dark, and with the geography of the room I was familiar to the last detail. Slipping my feet out of my pumps, I took six stealthy steps which brought me to the bureau. It had, as I well remembered, a glass top, and I ran my hand over it seeking an unencumbered place for my keys and loose change. It was annoying to me to find a continuous litter of small objects effectually covering its surface. I do wish, thought I, my wife would leave me my share of bureau space. But knowing the feminine axiom that a man's belongings, being few and simple, require at most two hooks and a corner of a shelf, I felt for the drawers.

The first was chock-full. In the second I felt the fluff of skirts. In the third was a considerable series of nondescript articles which my wandering fingers could not identify, but which seemed associated with the charm of woman. But the fourth and lowest was empty. Triumph! To prevent the indiscretion of a rattle, I refolded my silk handkerchief and laid upon it my keys, money, knife and pocketbook. I then pushed the drawer home, and, standing upright, relieved myself of my coat and waistcoat. These I hung over the back of the chair, which, as I congratulated myself, I had drawn conveniently to the foot of my bed against just such a contingency. I wound my watch, and slipped it under my pillow. The details stick in my memory. Then, removing my trousers and shirt, I draped them over my coat, and was sitting on the bed taking off my socks when of a sudden there was an unmistakable rattle at the door. Someone was trying to get in.

The wandering idiot, thought I, will wake my wife; but after a twist or two the handle was silent, and I continued my undressing. One by one I rid myself of my remaining garments, and was shivering in the night wind, which filtered through the shutters, when an unpleasant thought struck me — suppose my wife had not laid out my pyjamas. I felt along the bed — not there. Under the pillow — not there either. On one of the pegs above the washstand — again, no. Upon my soul, it was careless of my wife, of whose comfort I was so careful.

Now this counsel has frequently been given me: when something is missing, do not look aimlessly in unlikely places; think out carefully where the missing object probably is. So I took thought, and while I was thinking, as a mere mechanical activity, I felt for my toothbrush. To go into domestic detail, my toothbrush has a curved bone handle, my wife's a handle of some translucent fabrication which I never patronize. Now in the neighboring toothbrush mugs were two brushes with two fabricated handles. How miserably awkward! My wife had obviously noticed that one was missing, and had supplied a substitute from her store of replacements. But in toothbrushes it is not probabilities, but certainties, that one seeks, and I did feel that she might have left some explanatory signal. However, selecting the one which I felt was still dry, I was crossing to the bathroom with it to make absolutely sure, when I was startled by a sudden and violent shaking of the door. The lunatic was at it again. Surely my wife would wake. But the breathing from the further bed was perfectly regular, and the noise stopped as suddenly as it was begun.

My irritation was growing. The innocence of my physical condition absolutely precluded my going to the door. Where were those pyjamas? Well, if they were still packed, I could slip into my dressing gown. Thank goodness that was still where I had hung it! I could feel the refreshing crispness of the poplin suspended from the hook. I seized it and was about to slip it on, when, like the first ominous crash of a thunderstorm, my door was violently shaken, and I heard an English voice shout, "*He is in there!*"

I am a forbearing man, but my temper was up — this British cheek in informing me at midnight that I was in my own room! I wound the dressing gown round my middle, and, still grasping the toothbrush in my left hand, unlocked the door with my right and threw it angrily open. A gentleman in clothes of English cut was standing in the hall, one arm in the air in a gesture of violent amazement, his face the color of claret, and behind him were ranged, rank on rank, eight little Japanese bellboys. I could see their scared white faces.

I held my temper in control. "I should like to ask, sir," I said, "the meaning of this unwarranted interruption."

The stranger made no direct reply, but his ejaculation had a peculiar intensity. "By God," he cried, "he's got my toothbrush, too!"

Never was there so shattering an irrelevancy. My complacence, even my anger, dissolved like mist. In a flash the whole horror of my situation flooded over me. The wronged husband in every French drama fleeted across my mind. There I was, my clothes dispersed, clad in the most temporary of loincloths, in a room precisely like my own, but in a different wing. Stretched on a couch by my side was an unconscious lady, while her husband gave voice to his indignation. For a full second I was speechless. Then I cried out, "Sir, my mortification will last through life! It is a mistake, sir, a hideous mistake!"

He looked as if he were gazing at some terrible apparition.

"My wish, sir, is to explain."

"And my wish, sir, is that you would get out."

The advice was excellent — and I took it.

March 1937

A. P. HERBERT

1890–

Like all great humorists, Herbert has a passionately serious side. The strait jacket of Divorce Laws, equality of opportunity for all, peril to his country, have in turn stirred him to high, higher, and highest pitches of moral enthusiasm. I remember a walk with him when his soul was outraged by the discrimination which enabled the liquor bar of the Houses of Parliament to keep open half an hour after closing time for the public. At his own expense — and large expense is inconvenient to him — he had engaged the most noted barrister in England to plead the public's cause, and in the spirit of Pym and Eliot, dragged the admirable Lord Robert Cecil, whom he had reason to believe enjoyed but the vaguest idea of what a bar is, to watch, as a reliable witness, the destructive spectacle of sherry circulating after hours.

I owe Herbert much for the joy of laughter — exists there a larger debt? — both from his company and his books. Lovers of the ludicrous will remember the agitation which swept Britain from John O'Groat's to the Solent when Topsy, his recalcitrant heroine in Punch, *was confined to the Tower for contempt of the Speaker and the Mother of Parliaments was kept in doubt lest its uppish ward should become the mother of twins. Successive chapters prolonged the intolerable anxiety.*

In especial I recall a telephone invitation from him to attend a mighty banquet to the Premiers of the Empire at the conclusion of an Imperial Conference, I think in 1925. It is a social axiom that a dinner is pleasant in inverse proportion to the number of the guests. More than the Graces, less than the Muses, is the golden rule, and here the guests numbered a thousand. Food and wine follow the mathematical formula of invited guests, and a kind of Gresham's Law governs the excellence of comestibles; so the fare on this multitudinous occasion offered little to fortify body and soul against unlimited oratory.

Each Premier spoke in turn and each was ever mindful of the home papers. When the speeches began, the spirits at our table were at an all-time low. The clarion call of a veteran orator sent them lower. On and on he went. Twenty minutes passed and he showed no sign of fatigue. South Africa, New Zealand, Irish Free State, Rhodesia, Newfoundland were all in the offing, God knows how many more. It was ten o'clock at the moment. Four hours later, it would be two, and there was no machinery for cloture.

The boredom grew intolerable. Herbert alone roused himself from the common despair. "It all depends," he said, "how you look at things. Forget this is an Empire show, consider it a horse race." He seized the menu cards, tore them into slips of varying lengths, and wrote on each the name of a Prime Minister. "Make your bets, gentlemen!" he cried. "Two and six it costs each of you for the kitty." And then, holding out a bundle of slips so that we should make our selections blind, "Now," said he, "these are the rules of the gate. Two slips for everybody. First and second prizes. Long slip, longest speaker — first prize, two pounds. Short slip, shortest speaker — second prize, one pound. The Treasurer keeps the balance." We held our slips and riveted our eyes, each on his favorite. Herbert's was a famous Premier, and he held the long slip with the great man's name on it. His Prime Minister droned on — thirty minutes, thirty-one minutes. There was fire in Herbert's eye. This must be a record. But the audience was comatose and the statesman showed tiny signs of flagging. Suddenly he paused for breath and seemed to weaken in the knees. It was a moment when Will could triumph. Herbert rose, leapt upon his chair, waved his napkin in an ecstasy of enthusiasm. "Hurrah!" he shouted, "more, more, MORE!" The startled tables took up the cry. From all over the hall came huzzahs. The orator caught the energy of applause and went to work with a will, while the audience slipped off again into half-insensible despair. For ten minutes of eternity the orator talked on. Forty full minutes had passed when he sank back in his chair. Everybody knew the tape had been breasted and the race won, but second money still claimed our attention. On the speeches went. Thirty-eight minutes — but the grand prize had been missed. Twenty — eighteen — eleven — that looked like a record on the short side, but now the Prime Minister of Newfoundland was on his feet. He was in trouble at nine minutes flat, faltering at ten. Another sixty seconds and second prize was lost. Then of a sudden the glories of Empire swept over him and he went indomitably on. It was ten and a half — a matter of seconds now for second money and Herbert knew it. Again he sprang upon his chair. "Down!" he cried, "DOWN!" The Premier collapsed into his seat, and Herbert had coppered the entire gate.

Of all his pieces "Two Gentlemen of Soho" is my prime favorite. I keep wondering if my Shakespeare holds anything more Shakespearian than this.

Two Gentlemen of Soho[1]

A. P. HERBERT

(It now appears that Shakespeare is best when played in modern clothes. Perhaps the themes of modern life would be better dressed in Shakespearean costume? Some may think the play wordy, but there are brutes who think Shakespeare wordy. The acting version is certainly shorter, though much less beautiful.)

CHARACTERS

THE DUCHESS OF CANTERBURY
LADY LÆTITIA, her daughter
HUBERT, her dancing partner
LORD WITHERS
TOPSY
SNEAK, a private detective
PLUM, a public detective
A WAITER

SCENE: *A night club. Three tables. The middle table empty.* TOPSY, *reading a book, at Table One.* PLUM, *suspicious, at Table Three. Music in the ballroom, off.*

PLUM Ho, girl, look up! A goblet of champagne?

TOPSY I thank you, no. Indeed, 'tis after hours.

(Returns to book)

[1] See caution notice p. 681.

PLUM (*downcast — aside*)
I am an officer from Scotland Yard,
Dressed in the likeness of an English lord,
And night by night, while seven weeks swung by,
Have I to this lewd haunt made pilgrimage
In search of some irregularity,
Cheating an entrance with a lusty lie
(But all's forgiven in a noble cause),
Sometimes disguisèd as a gentleman,
And sometimes in the costume of a virgin.
But nothing happens. I have offered bribes,
I have been suppliant for sweet wine or opium
After the hours by Parliament provided,
But like the fabulous Mongolian drop
Of water, on strong rock forever falling,
I have made no impression. I believe
There is no falsehood practised here but mine,
There is no jot nor tittle of the law
By these respectable impostors broken.
Well, this is hard. Only the dear old Duchess
Has with my bitterness some sweet compounded
Of nimble dances and beguiling looks.
But she engagèd with another is.
So, gentle sleep, upon my eyelids press,
And let me wake to catch some wickedness.
(*Sleeps. Music*)

(*Enter* LADY LÆTITIA *and* LORD WITHERS. *They sit at Table Two*)

LÆTITIA What is this place?
WITHERS My dear Lætitia,
I do misdoubt I do it too much honor,
And you too little, by this introduction.
It is a night club. You have seen a stone
Turned by a ploughman on the hills of Kent,
And the foul, creeping, many-leggèd things
Which dart from under, blinking in the light?
So from this den snatch suddenly the lid
Between the midnight and the milkman's hour,
You will see slink and scutter about Soho

The very dregs and sediment of London.
Here the hot cits of Wimbledon and Streatham
With busy rakes from Kensington combine
In obscene alchemy to make the night
One long invention in debauchery.
Wine, women, drugs—

LÆTITIA In that case, Algernon—
Pardon my *ab*surd curiosity,
But what is't brings you to this hell-hole?

WITHERS Well,
I am a writer, and as some physician,
Searching the secrets of the human body,
Doth not the healthy but the sick pursue,
And is more happy 'midst unique distempers,
Growths, fevers, tumors, abscesses, and boils
Than with the strong and undefilèd flesh,
So in the study of these diseasèd minds
Do I seek knowledge not to be explorèd
In the dull wits of the respectable,
Sucking a sweetness from the poisoned flower,
And, like the wombat, savoring the cheese
When 'tis corrupted.

LÆTITIA Well, I cannot say
That I see any signs of dissipation.

WITHERS (*indicating* TOPSY *and* PLUM)
Mark then this lout, which in a rustic stupor
Is dead till morning, when it swills again.
Mark too this maiden that with vestal eye
Seems to see nothing but the book she reads not.
Here's what they call a woman of the half-world—
That is, she is not one thing nor the other,
Dubs herself "dancing partner," and for hire
She will with any pursy sot that offers
Waltz, fox-trot, Charleston,—the whole catalogue
Of modern antics,—and the evening through
Will counterfeit with some strange stockbroker
A mercenary satisfaction. Pah!

(*Observes dancers off*)

And yet some follies may adorn the young
Which to the old must be disfigurement.

How yonder matron wallows in the dance,
A loaded wagon, creaking down the hill
Of years and adiposity! The traffic
Bounds and rebounds unheeded from her flanks
Or, pausing careless in her path, is crushed.
And on her breast is like a pendant hung
A slim, fair, pallid, and perspiring youth
That smiles and smiles and smiles, and is in torture.
How like a milit'ry balloon she looks
That is entangled in an aspen tree!
Do you not think so, dear?

LÆTITIA That is my mother.

WITHERS Is't so? So 'tis!

LÆTITIA And that *her* dancing partner!

WITHERS I never saw her here before, Lætitia!
These hands should quicker have torn out these eyes
Than these harsh lips have spoken, or these legs
Have carried me to these conclu-si-ons!

LÆTITIA It is not easy to avoid Mamma.
On summer evenings she is everywhere.
There is no saxophone doth not salute her,
With other mothers rounder than herself,
Like baby elephants that after twilight
Jump in the jungle.

WITHERS 'Tis the Age of Age.

LÆTITIA How true! Age will be served, and this pale youth
Must for a salary — how much I know not —
The nightly partner of her gambols be.
Oh me, 'tis pitiful to see one's mother
Go to the dogs!

WITHERS Weep not, Lætitia,
But let us have a dry Martini. Ho!

(*Enter a* WAITER. PLUM *wakes up*)

PLUM This is a viscount, and I never saw
A lord that did not love to break the law.

(*Watches*)

WITHERS Pluck me ten berries from the juniper
And in a beaker of strong barley spirit
The kindly juices of the fruit compress.

This is our Alpha. Next clap on your wings,
Fly south for Italy, nor come you back
Till in the cup you have made prisoner
Two little thimblefuls of that sweet syrup
The Romans call Martini. Pause o'er Paris
And fill two eggshells with the French vermuth.
Then home incontinent, and in one vessel
Cage your three captives, but in nice proportions,
So that no one is master, and the whole
Sweeter than France, but not so sweet as Italy.
Wring from an orange two bright tears, and shake,
Shake a long time the harmonious trinity.
Then in two cups like angels' ears present them,
And see there swims an olive in the bowl,
Which when the draught is finished shall remain
Like some sad emblem of a perished love.
This is our Omega. Go, fellow!

WAITER Sir,
It is too late. I cannot serve you.

PLUM Damn!

(*Music. Exit* WAITER)

WITHERS Oh, that in England might be born a man,
Sprung from the loins of English liberty,
To rise and sweep, twice daily, like old Thames,
In a strong tide 'gainst petty tyrannies;
And though at evening he be beaten back,
Flood in at morning to clean the channel again
Of busy women, and suck out to sea
Bans, prohibitions, interferences,
Movements, societies, government departments,
Such as curtail, diminish, and cut down
The antique privilege of true-born Englishmen
To take their pleasure in what way they please,
When, how, which, where, whatever, and with whom!

(*Chord*)

Was it for this I joined the infantry
And took up arms against a Continent,
To have my eating and my drinking times
Fixed by old maids and governed by policemen?

(PLUM, *with dignity, passes out to ballroom*)

I think, were Germany the master here,
We should at least be certain of our beer.
But see, the Duchess finds new company,
In age and form more fitter to her own!

LÆTITIA It is the fellow who was here asleep.

WITHERS Then I have wronged him, for the man is sober.

LÆTITIA He would not else have undertaken Mother.

(Enter HUBERT, *exhausted and mopping his brow. He sinks into a chair beside* TOPSY, *who sits up and takes notice)*

WITHERS And here, like some slim carack long distressed
In the rough storm and tempest of the ocean,
Comes the frail consort of her voyaging,
His sails awrack, his rigging in disorder,
And the proud pennant drooping at the peak!
Thankful, he creeps into the nearest port,
Nor is there barge, punt, fishing boat so humble
He will not gladly berth beside her.

TOPSY Sir,
You are distempered, and your breathing labors,
As I have seen some baby grampus pant
After a heavy supper. Why is this?

HUBERT Oh, it were better to be bound with vipers
To the great stone of Sisyphus, and roll
All day forever up and down the hill,
Than to be fastened to a human mountain
Aping the antics of an early lamb!
For one is punishment, pure, unmistaken,
But this—this is the sacrilege of Pleasure.
I do a treason to my youth. I am
Not Sisyphus, not Tantalus, but both!
It were enough to caper with a whale,
Or spin a waltz with a rhinoceros,
But to be jostled in the dance by fairies,
Young, unattainable, locked i' the arms
Of men not better but more blest than I am,
And on their soft and tantalizing lips
See the slow smile that mocks my servitude—
This is my torture and damna-ti-on!

(Is overcome)

TOPSY Be easy, sir. This is my own employment.
I too must foot it and be gay for gold
With such as can get nobody for nothing.

HUBERT Aye, but with many. I am bound to one.

TOPSY Life is a most extraordinary thing.

HUBERT Man, like a pebble on a glacier,
Moves imperceptibly, but always down.

TOPSY Life is a looking-glass, in which we see
Only the dull reflection of ourselves,
And every day 'tis less attractive.

HUBERT Come,
This is no time for dismal metaphor!
My monster's busy. While I have the chance,
Come, fellow slave, console me in the dance!
(They get up, get out, and get off. Music)

WITHERS I think between them there's a seed of love
Which shall grow up into a goodly tree. *(Kneels)*
And you, Lætitia, so frosty-proud,
Like to those castles of cold loveliness
Which scare the shipping on the North Atlantic,
So that old captains sniff the sky and mutter,
"There is an iceberg sixty miles away."
Hushed are the passengers, and no more now
The merry quoit rings lightly on the deck,
But when the wonder bursts upon the view
Fear is forgotten. O Lætitia,
You are so beautiful that I am bold
And dare defy the miracle with wooing.
Will you not swim a moment in the sun
Of my affection — from the Arctic waters
Of dumb indifference drift southward soon,
Hang in the middle latitudes, and then
Melt into matrimony? Oh, I know
'Tis not the mode to speak of marrying,
And this warm sentiment which now inflames me
Is but a mock and madness to the young.
No more the sweet confusions of the simple,
Rings, tokens, pledges, clutchings of the hands,
Partings and moons and memories, are holy.
Nay, I have heard some yearling split his sides
At roses clustered round a cottage door,

Or the fond statement of a Negro's passion.
For now is devotion the stale jest of fools,
And that wild ecstasy the poets sang
Is but a livelihood and theme for doctors,
Policemen, clowns, and psychoanalysts,
While he that boldly on his knees professes
A fixed affection for a single person
Calls down the cackle of the continents.
Yet, though to speak these shameful syllables
Names me a ninny, feeble in the mind,
In soul suburban — *will you marry me?*

LÆTITIA I am too much upset about my dam.
I think I shall not marry anyone,
But take my mother to a nunnery
And there with a little needlework convert her
From the vain fancies of the world. But look!
I would not have her see me. Let us fetch
A circuit to the ballroom, and from there
Play spy to the event.

WITHERS It shall be so.

(*They go off, right. Enter, left, the* DUCHESS, *with* PLUM. *Fairy music*)

PLUM I hope, Your Grace, I have not wearied you?

DUCHESS There are the wings of swallows on your feet
And in your arms the potency of lions.
It is not dancing when I dance with you —
I have no mind, no body; I am nothing
But a swift ghost that soars a prisoner
In the embraces of a flying bear.

PLUM It is a pleasure to give satisfaction.

DUCHESS Are you a member?

PLUM Duchess, I am not.

DUCHESS Then with what member — nay, in this poor house
What member moves with such a dignity,
Hath such a grace and nimbleness of wit,
That he dare vouch for such a visitor?

PLUM I did not come with any, but alone.

DUCHESS Is not a member, yet alone he came.
Strange!

(*Chord. Enter* SNEAK, *cloaked and masked. Chord*)

SNEAK (*darkly — apart*)

So. She's there. And this gross gentleman
Should be that paramour my daughter spoke of,
The constant prop of ducal indiscretion.
I will lie close and watch the giddy scene.
Waiter!

WAITER What would you?

SNEAK I am a detective —
Nay, do not tremble! Not His Majesty's,
But the sworn servant of an agency
Skilled to pursue, see, tabulate, record,
And in the courts most cunningly describe
All the sly naughtiness of faithless wives,
Or peccant husbands, as the case may be;
Looks, nods, and greetings, holding-on of hands
After the space by decency commanded,
Meetings and partings, secret matinées,
The sigh drawn upward or the blinds drawn down,
Gifts, letters, notes — But are you listening?

WAITER Aye.

SNEAK Well, His Grace the Duke of Canterbury
Has of our house required information
Touching the acts, deeds, conduct, and behavior
Of that loose elephant he calls his wife.
Whether in truth he doth suspect her virtue,
Whether the wish was father to the thought
And the old dog would find some cause for parting
Such as himself he doth not dare to furnish,
I cannot tell you. But I do persever
Here is the reason, cause, and circumstance
Why I sit here instead of somewhere else;
And now that all lies naked as the noon
In the hot deserts of Australia,
Nor doth one leaf of artful stratagem,
Lies, counterfeit, deception, subterfuge,
Ingenious accent, or oblique suggestion
O'er the bare truth project one inch of shadow,
And if there be a person here alive
Who doth not now know better than his mother

My name, my calling, and my secret business,
Then it were better for the loon to be
Boiled in ammonia till his wits return.
Well, if all's clear, known, plain, and manifest,
Then there is nothing I would say but this:
What *I* should like would be a spot of whiskey.

PLUM (*hearing, characteristically, last line only, pricks up ears*)
Now surely shall some misdemeanor follow!

DUCHESS They say the antelope on summer nights
Halts at the margin of the stream to drink.

PLUM Fellow, we thirst! Bring port and lemonade!

WAITER God made the lemon and the grape together,
But man, milady, has divided them,
And at this hour, by our wise Parliament,
The lemon's lawful, but the grape's a crime.

DUCHESS (*unstrung*)
What is this talk of Parliaments and lemons?
Am I a Duchess, to be fed on *lemons?*
Was there not somebody who died of lemons?
Did none arrest him nor none prosecute?
Is there no law against excessive lemons,
Or too much sugar, or intemperate tea,
Or the vile craving for hot-water bottles?
What! Lemons? Parliaments? As I'm a Duchess,
Bring me the article!

WAITER (*cowed*) It shall be done.

(*He takes bottle of port from pocket and places it on table*)

PLUM Ho! Bar the doors! Sound the alarm without!
(*Exit* WAITER)
Let none make entrance or emergencies!

WITHERS What's here?

LÆTITIA How?

TOPSY So!

HUBERT What is't?

SNEAK Ha!

DUCHESS Who are you, sir?
(*Picture*)

PLUM I am the Metropolitan Police,
And this my warrant. Let a trumpet sound! (*Chord*)

DUCHESS Oh, viper!
HUBERT Judas!
LÆTITIA Mother!
DUCHESS Oh, my daughter! (*Sobs*)
PLUM Oh, it is anguish for a horse to suffer
The opposing reins of office and affection,
Which right and left distract the tender mind!
But this no Englishman has done, nor shall:
Make duty servant to his inclinations.
Take you these papers and at once write down
Your names and callings, titles, dignities,
Estates and mansions, orders, decorations,
Whether in wedlock you be joined or no,
How many children, houses, wives, convictions,
With all such details and appendages
As shall be pertinent. And in the morning
At Bow Street presently make apparition.
Now to your homes go softly.
DUCHESS Oh, the shame!
HUBERT I will not!
WITHERS Insolent!
LÆTITIA My mother!
SNEAK HOLD!
PLUM Who's this that rudely doth resist the tide
Of our proceedings?
SNEAK I am a detective,
Now by the Duke of Canterbury charged
To see, watch, notice, and at dawn discover
The nightly conduct of this noblewoman.
DUCHESS Now open, earth, and hide me!
SNEAK "Sneak," said he,
"Good, honest Sneak, if you have any skill
Or any pity for a poor old man,
Find me that snake and serpent in the grass
Which hath drawn off my Duchess from her duty,
So that in naughtiness and vain delights
She doth dishonor the evening of our days
And utterly neglects the housekeeping.
Find me this worm, good Sneak, that I may split him!"
Thus the old Duke, with bloody, fearful oaths,

Cleaning a pistol by his lonely bed
Or whetting some great knife upon a stone;
And thus at daybreak shall I answer him:
"Duke, he is found, your ravisher of homes,
Snake in the grass and cuckoo in the nest,
A little, round, unpleasant, portly thing
Which crawls, part trespasser and part policeman,
Into the childish revels of the rich,
Toys with their wives and tramples on their toes,
Eats of their salt and presently arrests them
For some sly spinster's quibble in the law,
And while he smiles contaminates the air
With artful ruse and mean suspi-ci-on;
Will call for wine to catch a flunky out,
And drink with women only to denounce them.
This, Duke, is he that, doubly double-faced,
Has the pure spirit of your wife corrupted,
Night after night, entwinèd in the dance,
Which I with evidence can justify.
This scheming, slow, constabulary lump,
This is your libertine and co-respondent!

PLUM (*enraged, takes truncheon from trousers*)
Peace, caitiff!

SNEAK Ha!

PLUM Thou dog of Houndsditch!

DUCHESS Oh!

(*They fight. Hurry music*)

SNEAK What, bully?

PLUM Sot!

SNEAK Hog!

PLUM Bastard!

DUCHESS Oh! I swoon!

SNEAK Ah, would you?

WITHERS Peace!

LÆTITIA Oh, gentlemen!

PLUM Die, villain!

(SNEAK *dies. Chord*)

TOPSY (*prostrates self on body of* SNEAK)
Oh, sir, you have killed my father! Why was this?
I had no life, no being, but in him,

And, now he's not, I am not either. Oh!
(*Dies of grief. Chord*)

HUBERT (*kneels beside body of* TOPSY)
Oh, Topsy, Topsy, could you not have waited?
I did not think that you would leave me thus,
Without one word nor tender beckoning
To bid me follow you. Yet I will follow,
And make one date of all eternity.
(*He strikes self on head with truncheon and dies. Chord*)

PLUM This was an issue not to be expected.

WITHERS Yet I have heard some countryman remark,
Clapping the swallows from a field of corn,
"It is not seldom, in the course of nature,
After a drought not in light showers only
Falls and descends the gentle rain of heaven,
But in a spate and tempest."

PLUM But what's here?

DUCHESS (*kneeling*)
Now, earth, receive me, for I die of shame!

WITHERS (*apart*)
What does this bode?

LÆTITIA She spoke of death.

WITHERS I heard her.

LÆTITIA This must be hindered.

WITHERS Aye.

PLUM But mark what follows!

DUCHESS Farewell to revelry, farewell the dance,
And the gay trappings of my second youth!
Farewell the music,—and, sweet saxophone,
Thou art not music, yet I wish thee well,—
With all late suppers and hot gala nights,
The colored streamer and the blue balloon,
Fans, rattles, dolls, and India-rubber dogs,
And wicked kippers eaten in the dawn,
And those fierce rhythmic and delicious tunes
Which light a fever in the veins and set
The feet, the soul, fermenting—fare you well!
Oh, it is selfish in the young to grudge us
The little joys of our declining days!
Have they not Love and Happiness their servants,

And must all Pleasure bow to them as well?
This were ungenerous. And I think in Heaven,
If there be saxophones as well as harps,
They are not only for the young. But here
I shall not see a gala night again.

(*Dies of shame. Fairy music*)

LÆTITIA Oh, she is dead!

WITHERS Life, like a butterfly,
Hath from the window of this flesh departed.
I think I never did nor never shall
See any woman so impeccable.
She was a person of extreme distinction,
She had discretion, grace, nobility,
Beauty and strength, taste, wit, intelligence,
Was kind to animals, by children worshiped;
I think I never saw a woman—

LÆTITIA Peace!
Mother, shall any other lips but mine
Tell the long catalogue of your great virtues?
I was your child, and if in anything
From the straight furrow of the good you strayed,
I do accuse myself. I should have told you
The snares and dangers of this wicked world,
And nursed you always with a daughter's love.
For you were too much guarded in your youth,
And knew not everything, as we know now,
Who by experience of all temptation
Against temptation are inoculated;
But you, poor innocent, were an easy prey.
The first shrill saxophone that squeaked in London
Was your undoing. And where'er you be,
Whether 'tis harps or saxophones or timbrels
That now make mischief in your neighborhood,
You shall not face that music quite alone.

(*Dies of remorse. Chord*)

WITHERS Thou too, Lætitia, art thou dead?

PLUM She is.

WITHERS Then there is no more virtue in the world!
Fire hath no heat, and the congealèd sun
Swims like a frozen orange in the sky;

There is not any meaning anywhere,
And to no purpose the great stars revolve!
O my dear Tish, unique Lætitia,
I will not in this wilderness delay,
Where, without you, I am the one thing living,
Like some lone seaman left upon an island,
Who beats his head against an emptiness
And so goes mad. Give me the knife! I die!
(*Stabs self and dies. Chord*)

PLUM This is a most strange consequence and finish
Of one quite simple action. Ho! Without!
(*Enter* WAITER)
Where are the officers of this society?

WAITER Sir, they are drinking.

PLUM Then disturb them not,
But with all speed call ministers and surgeons.
Reverently then these bodies disentangle
And in two chambers decently dispose them,
Not in one vague and ill-considered heap,
As men store pheasants, cock and hen together,
But with due awe distinguishing the sexes.
And this poor body, which shall top the pile,
Cause in a cylinder to be cremated
Not far from Winchester, where I was born.
This is the end. Go, fellow! I have done.

WAITER Sir, from my birth I was a nervous child,
This way and that swung weakly by suggestion,
And could not see my fellow creatures weep
But I must echo them with noisy tears.
Speak of an earthquake, and I fly the house;
Hang o'er the bulwarks, I am sick myself.
And now, i' the presence of these diminished figures,
By their own act, I take it, brought to nought,
I feel the prickings of mortality.
Thoughts of destruction, fatal inclinations,
Throng in my arteries—

PLUM It is enough.
I see far off the goal to which you stumble.
Die, and have done with it, for I am waiting.
(WAITER *knocks head thrice on floor and dies. Chord*)

Now do the morning and the evening meet
To kiss the midnight in the noon of death.

(*Stabs self. Music*)

Now is the circle of our questionings
Completed in an equilateral triangle,
Whereof, like children in a labyrinth,
At the perimeter we wander dumbly
Groping for truth, nor can one path discover
Which is not soon concluded in a point
That hath not magnitude, nor space, nor nothing,
But down the windy parallels of Time
Echoes again that interrogative
Which mocked our entrances. Now, Plum, go off!

(*Stabs self*)

Now shall the nighthawk to the trees report,
"Plum is no more, poor Plum that used to hang
High in the branches of authority;
Poor Plum is fallen from the bough unripened,
Shook off too soon by unkind circumstance."

(*Stabs self*)

Now popes and persons, majesties and powers,
Dominions, sunsets, kings and macaroons,
Violets, marigolds, and moonlight falling
Like children's kisses on the mountain top.

(*Stabs self*)

Dukes, ferns, and shellfish, and all gentle things
In the high argument of love suspended,
Firelight at evening and the dawn of day,
Redwings and walnuts, oak, mahogany,
Lancaster, York, great Salisbury and Monmouth,
Hereford, Leicester, Northumberland, and Kent,
King's Cross, St. Pancras, Euston, Waterloo—
All noble-sounding and capacious words,
Come and be mourners at my funeral,
For I am in the vestibule of death.

(*Stabs self*)

This is the gate and portal of my ending,
I think there doth not any word remain,
But silence and still quiet touch my lips
With the mute harmony of things unspoken.

I never was of that loud company
Which seek their harvest in a waste of words;
"DO" was my dictionary. And my sword
Leaped from the sheath ere I could mention it.
(Stabs self)

As you may see in some great orchestra
A little lonely fellow at the end
Sits by the cymbals, and the instruments
Thunder around him their tempestuous din,—
Flutes, horns, and oboes, harp and clarinet,
And the wild fiddles like the forest swaying
On Swedish mountains when the storm is high,—
But he, that could with one most royal clash
Startle the city and make all that music
Like the small twittering of birds appear,
Sits with his brasses, but doth make no sound
Till the conductor shall command him so,
And leaves his cymbals and goes home at last,
Still with no sound, nor kindly thanks, nor notice,
For the conductor hath forgotten him—
So sit I here, and die without a word.
(Stabs self and surveys scene)
Well, this will puzzle them at Scotland Yard.
(Dies. Chord)

[CURTAIN]

May 1927

ANNE DOUGLAS SEDGWICK

1873–1935

When Arthur Balfour spoke of Anne Douglas Sedgwick as the most distinguished storyteller of her age, he gave a picture of the civilization of contemporary writers. Born an American, she lived her life in the English countryside. Far End, Kingham, lies beyond Oxford, and thither I often journeyed. In Miss Sedgwick's person there was a delicate loveliness. Her expressive face was crowned with whitest hair, and one who judges character from the hands could not take his eyes off hers, however diverting the talk.

I remember our first meeting. At a New York dinner, perhaps in 1903, I was quite aware I had an attractive partner, though I had not caught her name. There it lay on the card by her plate, "Miss Sedgwick." I knew that she was English and I felt it would make our conversation more amusing if at the opening I avoided the obvious. Taking for granted that I knew who she was, she ran admirably on about a hundred things and before the fruit was passed I felt that we were friends. As we rose I said to her, "Sedgwicks used to come from Woburn, England. Where was it you were born?" She smiled: "The Sedgwicks keep company. I was 'raised' in Great Barrington, Massachusetts, just six miles from where you were brought up." That was my first realization that we were kin, but never was I in her company that I did not feel it.

Daffodils

ANNE DOUGLAS SEDGWICK

I

Though he knew that he was going to die, Marmaduke Follett, as he lay in the hospital on the French coast, had never in his life been so happy. Until these last days he had not been able to feel it in its completeness. Of the great engagement where he had fallen he remembered only the overwhelming uproar, the blood and mud; and after that, torments, apathies, dim awakenings to the smell of ether and relapses to quieter sleep. Now the last operation had failed,—or, rather, he had failed to recover from it,—and there was no more hope for him; but he hardly suffered and his thoughts were emerging into a world of cleanliness, kindness, and repose.

The hospital, before the war, had been a big hotel, and his was one of the bedrooms on the second floor, its windows crossed by two broad blue bands of sea and sky. As an officer, he had a room to himself. The men were in the wards downstairs.

One of his nurses—both were pleasant girls, but this was the one who, with a wing of black hair curving under her cap, reminded him of his cousin Victoria—had put a glass of daffodils beside his bed—not garden daffodils, but the wild ones that grow in woods; and if she made him think of Victoria, how much more they made him think of the woods in spring at Channerley!

He was dying after a gallant deed. It was a fitting death for a Follett, and so little in his life had been at all fitted to that initial privilege: it was only in the manner of his death that his life matched at all those thoughts of Victoria and Channerley.

He did not remember much of the manner; it still remained cloaked in that overwhelming uproar; but, as he lay there, he seemed to read, in the columns of the London papers, what all the Folletts were so soon to read—because of him:—

"His Majesty the King has been graciously pleased to award the Victoria Cross to the under-mentioned officers, non-commissioned officers and men:—

"Sec. Lt. Marmaduke Everard Follett. For most conspicuous bravery.

"He was directed with 50 men to drive the enemy from their trench, and under intense shell and machine-gun fire he personally led three separate parties of bombers against a captured 325 yards of trench; attacking the machine-gun, shooting the firer with his revolver, and destroying gun and *personnel* with bombs. This very brave act saved many lives and ensured the success of the attack. In carrying one of his men back to safety, Sec. Lt. Follett was mortally wounded."

He felt himself smile, as he soberly spaced it out, to remember that the youths at the office used to call him Marmalade. It was curious that he most felt his present, and his present transfigured self, when he thought of Cauldwell's office, where so many years of his past had been spent. When he thought of that, of the jocund youths, of the weary hours and wasted years, it was to feel himself transfigured; when he thought of the Folletts and of Channerley, to feel that he matched them; it was, at last, to feel as if he had come home. What to the grimy, everyday world counted as transfiguration, counted as the normal, the expected, to the world of Channerley.

He wondered, lying there and looking out past the daffodils, where Victoria was; he had heard that she was nursing, too, somewhere in France; and again, as he had smiled over the contrast of "Sec. Lt. Marmaduke Everard Follett" and the "Marmalade" of Cauldwell's office, he smiled in thinking of the difference between Victoria and the nice young nurse who, for all her resembling curve of hair, was also second-rate. It would have been very wonderful to have been nursed by Victoria, and yet his thought turned from that. There had never been any sweetness, never even any kindness for him, in Victoria's clear young gaze: when it came to nursing, he could imagine her being kind to a Tommy, but not to him, the dull, submerged cousin; and the nice though second-rate nurse was very kind. He would rather die under her eyes than under Victoria's.

And he would rather think of Victoria as he had last seen her at the big London dance to which, most unexpectedly, he had found himself asked last spring — the spring before the war. He had decided, as with nervous fingers he tied his white cravat, — how rarely disturbed was that neat sheaf lying in his upper drawer! — that he must have been confused with some other Follett, for he was so seldom asked anywhere, where he would be likely to meet Victoria. However, it was a delight to see her in her snowy dress, her beautiful hair bound with silver, and to feel, as he watched her dancing, that she belonged, in a sense, to him; for he, too, was a Follett.

How much more did she belong to him now! And not only Victoria, but all of them, these Folletts of his and the Folletts of past generations; and Channerley, centre of all his aching, wistful memories. It had been for him, always, part of the very structure of his nature, that beautiful old house where he had spent his boyhood. Perhaps it was because he had been turned out of the nest so early that he never ceased to miss it. His thought, like a maimed fledgling, had fluttered round and round it, longing, exiled, helpless.

If, now, he could have survived, his eldest brother, he felt sure, must have asked him oftener to stay at Channerley. It still gave him a pang, or, rather, the memory of many pangs, to recall that Robert had not asked him for two years, and had seemed to forget all about him after that. They had all seemed to forget about him, — that was the trouble of it, — and almost from the very beginning: Robert, who had Channerley; Austin, who had gone into the army and was now in Mesopotamia; Griselda, married so splendidly up in her northern estate; and Amy, the artistic bachelor-girl of the family, whom he associated with irony and cigarette-smoke and prolonged absences in Paris. Even cheerful Sylvia, of South Kensington, with her many babies and K.C. husband, whom he always thought of, for all her well-being, as very nearly as submerged as himself, — even Sylvia saw little of him and asked him only to family dinners, — Mr. Shillington's family, not hers, — at depressingly punctual intervals.

But Sylvia, the one nearest him in years, was the one who had forgotten least, and she had, after her fashion, done her best for him. Confused at study, clumsy at games, shy and tongue-tied, he had not in any way distinguished himself at a rather second-rate public school; and to distinguish himself had been the only hope for him. The Folletts had never had any money to spare, and Eton and Oxford for Robert and Sandhurst for Austin fulfilled a tradition that became detached and terse where younger sons who could not distinguish themselves were concerned. Still, he had always felt that, had his father lived, something better would have been found for him than to be bundled, through the instrumentality of Mr. Shillington, into a solicitor's office. There he had been bundled, and there he had stuck for all these years, as clumsy, as confused as ever; a pallid, insignificant little fellow (oh, he had no illusions about himself!), with the yellow hair and small yellow moustache which, together with his name, had earned for him his sobriquet.

They had not disliked him, those direfully facetious companions of his. *Noblesse oblige* was an integral part of his conception of himself, however little they might be aware of his unvarying courtesy toward them as its exercise. He suspected that they thought of him as merely inoffensive and rather piteous; but shyness might give that impression; they could not guess at the quiet aversion that it covered. He was aware sometimes, suddenly, that in the aloofness and contemplative disdain of his pale sidelong glance at them, he most felt himself a Follett. If his mind, for most practical purposes, was slow and clumsy, it was sharp and swift in its perceptions. He judged the young men in Cauldwell's office as a Follett must judge them. In the accurate applying of that standard he was as instinctively gifted as any of his race; and if he knew, from his first look at her, that the nice young nurse was second-rate, how coldly and calmly, for all these years, he had known that the young men who called him Marmalade were third-rate. And yet they none of them disliked him, and he wondered whether it was because, when he most felt disdain, he most looked merely timid, or because they recognized in him, all dimly as it might be, the first-rateness that was his inherently and inalienably.

Just as the third-rate young men might recognize the first-rate but dimly, he was aware that to the world the Folletts, too, were not important. It was not one of the names, in spite of centuries of local lustre, to conjure with; and he liked it all the better because of that. They had never, it was true, distinguished themselves; but they were people of distinction, and that was, to his quiet, reflective savoring, an even higher state. He sometimes wondered if, in any of them, the centring of family consciousness was as intense as in himself. If they were aloof about third-rate people, it was not because they were really very conscious about themselves. They took themselves for granted, as they took Channerley and the family history; and only Amy was aware that some of the family portraits were good.

The history — it was not of course accurate to call it that, yet it seemed more spacious and significant than mere annals — pored over in long evenings, in faded parchments, deeds, and letters, was known in every least detail to him. How the Folletts had begun, very soberly but very decorously, in the fifteenth century, and how they had gone on: rooting more deeply into their pleasant woodlands and meadows; flowering, down the centuries, now in a type of grace — that charming Antonia who had married so well at James the First's court; and of gallantry — a Follett had fallen at Naseby, and a Follett had fought at Waterloo; or of good-humored efficiency, as in the eighteenth-century judge and the nineteenth-century bishop. And he, who was neither graceful nor gallant nor good-humored (sour and sad he felt himself), never could resist the warming, revivifying influence of these recognitions, stretching himself, sighing, smiling happily before his Bloomsbury fire on a winter's evening, as he laid down the thick pile of yellowed manuscripts to think it all over and feel himself, in spite of everything, a link with it all.

Robert had always been very decent about letting him have and keep the documents as long as he liked.

It was strange to think that he was never to see his Bloomsbury lodgings again, and stranger, really, that a certain tinge of regret was in the thought; for how, for years, he had hated them, place of exile, of relegation, as he had always felt them! Yet he had come to be fond of his little sitting-room, just because, to his eye, with its mingled comfort and austerity, it was so significant of exile. If a Follett couldn't have what he wanted, that was all he would have — his rack of pipes, his shelves of books, his little collection of mostly marginless mezzotints ranged along the dark, green walls. The room was a refuge and did not pretend to be an achievement, and in that very fact might, to an eye as sharp as his for such significance, suggest the tastes that it relinquished. He had, indeed, all the tastes and none of the satisfactions of Channerley.

There it was; he had come back to it again, as, indeed, he had, in spirit, never left it — never for a moment. He felt himself, lying there in the hospital on the French coast, with the soft spring sea lapping upon the beach under his window — he felt himself drop, drop, softly, sweetly, deeply, back to his childhood. From his high nursery-window he saw the dewy tree-tops, — the old hawthorn that grew so near the house, and the old mulberry, — and the rooks wheeling on a spring sky so many years ago. The dogs, at that early hour, just released, might be racing over the lawns: idle, jovial Peter, the spaniel, and Jack, the plucky, hot-tempered little Dandy-Dinmont.

Below the lawns were the high gray garden walls, and above, rising a little from the flagged rose-garden, were the woods where the daffodils grew, daffodils like those beside him now, tall and small, their pale, bright poetry set in warrior spears of green. Little bands of them ran out upon the lawn from under the great trees, and one saw their gold glimmering far, far among the woodlands. Oh, the beauty of it! and the stillness, the age and youth, the smile and the security! How he had always loved it, shambling about the woods and gardens; creeping rather — he always saw himself as creeping somehow — about the dear, gay, faded house! Always such an awkward, insignificant little boy; even his dear old Nanna had felt dissatisfied with his appearance; and he had always known it, when she sent him down with the others to the drawing-room; and his mother, she had made it very apparent, had found him only that.

He shrank from the thought of his mother; perhaps it was because of her, of her vexed and averted eyes, her silken rustle of indifference as she passed him by, that he saw himself as creeping anywhere where she might come. He only remembered her in glimpses: languidly and ironically smiling at her tea-table (Amy had her smile), the artificial tone of her voice had even then struck his boyish ear; reading on a summer afternoon, with bored brows and dissatisfied lips, as she lay on a garden chair in the shade of the mulberry tree; querulously arguing with his father, who, good-humored and very indifferent, strolled about the hall in his pink coat on a winter morning, waiting for the horses to be brought round; his mother's yellow braids shining under her neatly tilted riding-hat, her booted foot held to the blaze of the great log-fire. A hard, selfish, sentimental woman; and—wasn't it really the only word for what he felt in her?—just a little shoddy. He distinguished it from the second-rate nicely: it was a more personal matter; for his mother, though certainly not a Follett, was of good stock; he knew, of course, all about her stock. It always grieved him to think that it was from her he had his yellow hair and the pale gray of his eyes; his stature, too, for she had been a small woman; all the other Folletts were tall; but she had given him nothing more: not a trace of her beauty was his, and he was glad of it.

It was curious, since he had really had so little to do with him, as little, almost, as with his mother, how blissfully his sense of his father's presence pervaded his childish memories. He was so kind. The kindest thing he remembered at Channerley, except his dear old Nanna and Peter the spaniel. It used to give him a thrill of purest joy when, meeting him, his father, his hands clasped behind his back after his strolling wont, would stop and bend amused and affectionate eyes upon him; rather the eyes, to be sure, that he bent upon his dogs; but Marmaduke always felt of him that he looked upon his children, and upon himself, too, as parts of the pack; and it was delightful to be one of the pack, with him.

"Well, old fellow, and how goes the world with you to-day?" his father would say.

And after that question the world would go in sunshine.

He had always believed that, had his father lived, he would never have been so forgotten; just as he had always believed that his father would never have allowed one of his pack to be bundled into a solicitor's office. For that he had to thank, he felt sure, not only Sylvia's negative solicitude, but his mother's active indifference. Between them both they had done it to him.

And he never felt so to the full his dispossession as in thinking of Robert. He had always intensely feared and admired Robert. He did not know what he feared, for Robert was never unkind. But Robert was everything that he was not: tall and gay and competent, and possessing everything needful, from the very beginning, for the perfect fulfillment of his type. The difference between them had been so far more than the ten years that had made of Robert a man when he was still only a little boy. There had been, after all, a time when they had been a very big and a very little boy together, with Austin in between; yet the link had seemed always to break down after Austin. Robert, in this retrospect, had always the air of strolling away from him — for Robert, too, was a stroller. Not that he himself had had the air of pursuit; he had never, he felt sure, from the earliest age, lacked tact; tact and reticence and self-effacement had been bred into him. But his relationship with Robert had seemed always to consist in standing there, hiding ruefulness, and gazing at Robert's strolling back.

The difference with Austin had perhaps been as great, but it had never hurt so much, for Austin, though with his share of the Follett charm, had never had the charm of Robert. A clear-voiced and clear-eyed, masterful boy, Austin's main contact with others was in doing things with them, and that sort of contact did not mean congeniality. Austin had made use of him; had let him hold his ferrets and field for him at cricket; and a person whom one found useful did not, for the time being, bore one.

But he had bored Robert always — that was apparent; and beautiful Griselda, who was older than either of them, and Amy, who was younger. Griselda had gazed rather sadly over his head; and Amy had smiled and teased him so that he had seldom ventured on a remark in her presence. Even fat little Sylvia, the baby, had always preferred any of the others to him as she grew up; had only not been bored because, while she was good-humored, she was also rather dull. And at the bottom of his heart, rueful always, sore, and still patiently surprised, he knew that, while he found them all a little brutal, he could not admire them the less because of it. It was part of the Follett inheritance to be able to be brutal, unconsciously, and therefore with no loss of bloom.

And now, at last, he was not to bore them any longer; at last, he was not to be forgotten. How could he not be happy,—it brought back every blissful thrill of boyhood, his father's smile, the daffodil woods in spring, heightened to ecstasy,—when he had at last made of himself one of the Folletts who were remembered? He would have his place in the history beside the Follett who fell at Naseby. No family but is glad of a V.C. in its pages. They could no longer stroll away. They would be proud of him; he had done something for all the Folletts forever.

II

The nice young nurse came in. She closed the door gently, and, with her smile, calm before accustomed death, and always, as it were, a little proud of him,—that was because they were both English,—she took his wrist and felt his pulse, holding her watch in the other hand, and asked him, presently, how he felt. Only after that did she say, contemplating him for a moment,—Marmaduke wondered how many hours—or was it perhaps days?—she was giving him to live,—

"A gentleman has come to see you. You may see him if you like. But I've told him that he is only to stay for half an hour."

The blood flowed up to Marmaduke's forehead. He felt it beating hard in his neck and behind his ears, and his heart thumped down there under the neatly drawn bed-clothes.

"A gentleman? What's his name?"

Was it Robert?

"Here is his card," said the nurse.

She drew it from her pocket and gave it to him. It couldn't have been Robert, of course. Robert would only have had to come up. Yet he was dizzy with the disappointment. It was as if he saw Robert strolling away for the last time. He would never see Robert again.

Mr. Guy Thorpe was the name. The address was a London club that Marmaduke placed at once as second-rate, and "The Beeches, Arlington Road," in a London suburb. On the card was written in a neat scholarly hand: "May I see you? We are friends."

It was difficult for a moment to feel anything but the receding tide of his hope. The next thing that came was a sense of dislike for Mr. Guy Thorpe and for the words that he had written. Friends? By what right, since he did not know his name?

"Is he a soldier?" he asked. "How did he come? I don't know him."

"You needn't see him unless you want to," said the nurse. "No; he's not a soldier. An elderly man. He's driving a motor for the French Wounded Emergency Fund, and came on from the Alliance because he heard that you were here. Perhaps he's some old family friend. He spoke as if he were."

Marmaduke smiled a little. "That's hardly likely. But I'll see him, yes; since he came for that."

When she had gone, he lay looking again at the blue bands across the window. A flock of sea-gulls flew past — proud, swift, and leisurely, glittering in the sun. They seemed to embody the splendor and exultation of his thoughts, and, when they had disappeared, he was sorry, almost desolate.

Mr. Guy Thorpe. He took up the card again in his feeble hand and looked at it. And now, dimly, it seemed to remind him of something.

Steps approached along the passage, the nurse's light foot-fall and the heavier, careful tread of a man. An oddly polite, almost a deprecating tread. He had gone about a great many hospitals and was cautious not to disturb wounded men. Yet Marmaduke felt again that he did not like Mr. Guy Thorpe, and as they came in, he was conscious of feeling a little frightened.

There was nothing to frighten one in Mr. Thorpe's appearance. He was a tall, thin, ageing man, travel-worn, in civilian clothes, with a dingy Red-Cross badge on the sleeve of his water-proof overcoat. Baldish and apparently near-sighted, he seemed to blink toward the bed, and, as if with motoring in the wind, his eyelids were moist and reddened. He sat down, murmuring some words of thanks to the nurse.

A very insignificant man, for all his height and his big forehead. Altogether of The Beeches, Arlington Road. Had he turned gray, he might have looked less shabby; but dark thin locks still clustered above his high crown and behind his long-lobed ears. His eyes were dark, his moustache drooped, and he had a small, straight nose. Marmaduke saw that he was the sort of man who, in youth, might have been considered very handsome. He looked like a seedy poet and some sort of minor civil servant mingled, the civil servant having got the better of the poet. Marmaduke also imagined that he would have a large family and a harassed but ambitious wife, with a genteel accent — a wife a little below himself. His tie was of a dull red silk. Marmaduke did not like him.

Mr. Thorpe glanced round, as if cautiously, to see if the nurse had closed the door, and then, it was really as if more cautiously still, looked at Marmaduke, slightly moving back his chair.

"I'm very grateful to you, very grateful indeed," he said in a low voice, "for seeing me."

"You've come a long way," said Marmaduke.

"Yes. A long way. I had heard of your being here. I hoped to get here. I felt that I must see you. We are all proud of you; more proud than I can say."

He looked down now at the motoring-cap he held, and Marmaduke became aware that the reddened eyes were still more suffused and that the mouth under the drooping moustache twitched and trembled. He could think of nothing to say, except to murmur something about being very glad—though he didn't want to say that; and he supposed, to account for Mr. Thorpe's emotion, that he must be a moving sight, lying there, wasted, bandaged, and dying.

"You don't remember my name, I suppose," said Mr. Thorpe after a moment, in which he frankly got out his handkerchief and wiped his eyes.

"No, I'm afraid I don't," said Marmaduke very politely. He was glad to say this. It was the sort of thing he did want to say.

"Yet I know yours very, very well," said Mr. Thorpe, with a curious watery smile. "I lived at Channerley once. I was tutor there for some time—to Robert, your brother, and Griselda. Yes," Mr. Thorpe nodded, "I know the Folletts well; and Channerley, the dear old place."

Now the dim something in memory pressed forward, almost with a physical advance, and revealed itself as sundry words scratched on the school-room window-panes and sundry succinct drawings in battered old Greek and Latin grammars. Robert had always been very clever at drawing, catching with equal facility and accuracy the swiftness of a galloping horse and the absurdities of a human profile. What returned to Marmaduke now, and as clearly as if he had the fly-leaf before him, was a tiny thumb-nail sketch of such a galloping horse unseating a lank, crouching figure, of whom the main indications were the angles of acute uncertainty taken by the knees and elbows; and a more elaborate portrait, dashed and dotted as if with a ruthless boyish grin—such an erect and melancholy head it was, so dark the tossed-back locks, so classical the nose and unclassical the moustache, and a brooding eye indicated in a triangular sweep of shadow. Beneath was written in Robert's clear, boyish hand, "Mr. Guy Thorpe, Poet, Philosopher and Friend. Vale." Even the date flashed before him, 1880;

and with it, strange, in appropriate association — the daffodils running out upon the lawn, as no doubt he had seen them as he leaned from the schoolroom window, with the Greek grammar under his elbow on the sill.

So that was it. Mr. Guy Thorpe, placed, explained, disposed of — poor dear! He felt suddenly quite kindly toward him, quite touched by his act of loyalty to the old allegiance in coming; and flattered, too, — yes, even by Mr. Thorpe, — that he should be so recognized as a Follett who had done something for the name; and smiling very benevolently upon him, he said, —

"Oh, of course; I remember perfectly now — your name, and drawings of you in old schoolbooks, you know. All tutors and governesses get those tributes from their pupils, don't they? But I myself couldn't remember, could I? for it was before I was born that you were at Channerley."

There was a moment of silence after this, and in it Marmaduke felt that Mr. Thorpe did not like being so placed. He had no doubt imagined that there would be less ambiguous tributes, and that his old pupils would have talked of him to the younger generation.

And something of this chagrin certainly came out in his next words as, nodding and looking round at the daffodils, he said, —

"Yes, yes. Quite true. No, of course you couldn't yourself remember. I was more though, I think I may fairly say, than the usual tutor or governess. I came, rather, at Sir Robert's instance." — Sir Robert was Marmaduke's father. — "We had met, made friends, at Oxford; his former tutor there was an uncle of mine, and Sir Robert, in my undergraduate days, used to visit him sometimes. He was very keen on getting me to come. Young Robert wanted something of a firm hand. I was the friend rather than the mere man of books in the family."

"Poet, Philosopher and Friend" — Marmaduke had it almost on his lips, and almost with a laugh, his benevolence deepened for poor Mr. Thorpe, so self-revealed, so entirely Robert's portrait of him. Amusing to think that even the quite immature first-rate can so relegate the third. But perhaps it was a little unfair to call poor Mr. Thorpe third. The Folletts would not be likely to choose a third-rate man for a tutor; second was kinder, and truer. He had, obviously, come down in the world.

"I see. It's natural I never heard, though: there's such a chasm between the elders and the youngers in a big family, isn't there?" he said. "Griselda is twelve years older than I am, and Robert ten, you remember. She was married by the time I began my Greek. You never came back to Channerley, did you? I hope things have gone well with you since those days?"

He questioned, wanting to be very kind; wanting to give something of the genial impression of his father smiling, with his, "And how goes the world with you to-day?" But he saw that, while Mr. Thorpe's evident emotion deepened, it was with a sense of present grief as well as of retrospective pathos.

"No; I never came, — that is — No; I passed by: I never came to stay. I went abroad; I traveled, with a pupil, for some years before my marriage." Grief and confusion were oddly mingled in his drooping face. "And after that — life had changed too much. My dear old friend Sir Robert had died. I could not have faced it all. No, no; when some chapters are read, it is better to close the book; better to close the book. But I have never forgotten Channerley, nor the Folletts of Channerley; that will always remain for me the golden page; the page," said Mr. Thorpe, glancing round again at the daffodils, "of friendship, of youth, of daffodils in spring-time. I saw you there," he added suddenly, "once, when you were a very little lad. I saw you. I was passing by; bicycling; no time to stop. You remember the high road skirts the woods to the north. I came and looked over the wall; and there you were — in your holland pinafore and white socks — digging up the daffodils and putting them into your little red-and-yellow cart. A beautiful spring morning. The woods full of sunshine. You wouldn't remember."

But he did remember — perfectly. Not having been seen, but the day; the woods; the daffodils. He had dug them up to plant in his own little garden, down below. He had always been stupid with his garden; had always failed where the others succeeded. And he had wanted to be sure of daffodils. And they had all laughed at him for wanting the wild daffodils like that for himself, and for going to get them in the wood. And why had Mr. Thorpe looked over the wall and not come in? He hated to think that he had been watched on that spring morning — hated it. And, curiously, that sense of fear with which he had heard the approaching footsteps returned to him. It frightened him that Mr. Thorpe had watched him over the wall.

His distaste and shrinking were perhaps apparent in his face, for it was with a change of tone and hastiness of utterance, as though hurrying away from something, that Mr. Thorpe went on: —

"You see, — it's been my romance, always, Channerley — and all of you. I've always followed your lives — always — from a distance —

known what you were up to. I've made excuses to myself — in the days when I used to go a good deal about the country — to pass by Channerley and just have a glimpse of you. And when I heard that you had done this noble deed, — when I heard what you had done for England, for Channerley, for us all, — I felt I had to come and see you. You must forgive me if I seem a mere intruder. I can't seem that to myself. I've cared too much. And what I came for, really, was to thank you, — to thank you, my dear boy, — and to tell you that because of you, life must be nobler, always, for all of us."

His words had effaced the silly, groping fear. It was indeed, since his colonel's visit, the first congratulation he had had from the outer world. The nurses, of course, had congratulated him, and the surgeons; but no one who knew him outside; the kindly telegrams from Robert and Sylvia did not count as congratulations. And in a way poor Mr. Thorpe did know him, and though it was only from him, it had its sweetness. He felt himself flush as he answered, "That's very kind of you."

"Oh, no!" said Mr. Thorpe, shaking his head and swinging his foot — Marmaduke knew that from the queer movement of his body as he sat with very tightly folded arms. "Not kind! That's not the word — from us to you! Not the word at all!"

"I'm very happy, as you may imagine," said Marmaduke. And he was happy again, and glad to share his happiness with poor Mr. Thorpe. "It makes everything worth while, doesn't it, to have brought it off at all?"

"Everything, everything — it would; it would, to you. So heroes feel," said Mr. Thorpe. "To give your life for England. I know it all — in every detail. Yes, you are happy in dying that England may live. Brave boy! Splendid boy!"

Now he was weeping. He had out his handkerchief and his shoulders shook. It made Marmaduke want to cry, too, and he wondered confusedly if the nurse would soon come back. Had not the half hour passed?

"Really — it's too good of you. You mustn't, you know; you mustn't," he murmured, while the word, "boy — boy," repeated, made tangled images in his mind, and he saw himself in the white socks and with the little red-and-yellow cart, and then as he had been the other day, leading his men, his revolver in his hand and the bullets flying about him. "And I'm not a boy," he said; "I'm thirty-four; absurdly old to be only a second lieutenant. And there are so many of us. Why," — the thought came fantastically, but he seized it, because Mr. Thorpe was crying so and he must seize something, — "we're as common as daffodils!"

"Ah! not for me! not for me!" Mr. Thorpe gulped quickly. Something had happened to him. Something had given way in him — as if the word "daffodils" had pressed a spring. He was sobbing aloud, and he had fallen on his knees by the bed and put up his hand for Marmaduke's. "I cannot keep it from you! Not at this last hour! Not when you are leaving me forever! — My son! My brave son! I am your father, Marmaduke! I am your father, my dear, dear boy!"

III

It was the stillest room. The two calm bands of blue crossed the window. In the sunlight the gulls came flying back. Marmaduke looked out at them. Were they the same sea-gulls or another flock? Then quietly he closed his eyes. Stillness — calm. But something else was rising to him from them. Darkness; darkness; a darkness worse than death. Oh! death was sweet compared to this. Compared to this all his life had been sweet; and something far dearer than life was being taken from him. He only knew the terrible confusion of his whole nature. He opened his eyes again with an instinct of escape. There were the bands of blue, and, still passing in their multitudes, leaving him forever, the proud, exultant sea-gulls. The man still knelt beside him. He heard his own voice come: —

"What do you mean?"

"I never meant to tell you! I never meant to tell you!" a moan answered him. "But — seeing you lying there! — dying! — my son! — who has given his life for England! — And how I have longed for you for all these years! — My romance, Marmaduke — How could I be silent? Forgive me! Forgive me, my boy. Yes, mine. My known children are dear to me, but how far dearer the unknown son, seen only by stealth, in snatched glimpses! It is true, Marmaduke, true. We were lovers. She loved me. Do not ask. Do not question. We were young. She was very beautiful. It was spring-time; daffodils were in the woods. She said that she had never known anyone like me. She said that her life was hollow, meaningless. I opened doors to her. I read to her. Browning — I read Browning," he muttered on, "in the woods; among the daffodils. It was a new life to her — and to me. And we were swept away. Don't blame us, Marmaduke. If there was wrong, there was great beauty — then. Only then, for after, she was cruel — very cruel.

She turned from me; she crushed and tore my heart. Oh! — I have suffered! But no one knew. No one ever dreamed of it. Only she and I. My God! — I see her in your hair and eyes!"

It was true. It was absolutely true. Through his whole being he felt its inevitability. Everything was clear, with a strange, black, infernal clearness. His life lay open before him, open from beginning to end: that beginning of tawdry sentiment and shame — with daffodils; and this end, with daffodils again, and again with tawdry sentiment and shame.

He was not a Follett. He had no part in the Folletts. He had no part in Channerley. He was an interloper, a thief. He was the son of this wretched man, in whose very grief he could detect the satisfaction — oh, who more fitted to detect such satisfaction! — of his claim upon a status above his own. He was all that he had always most despised, a second-rate, a third-rate little creature; the anxious, civil, shrinking Marmalade of Cauldwell's office. Why (as the hideous moments led him on, point by point, his old lucidity, sharpened to a needle fineness, seemed to etch the truth in lines of fire upon the blackness), hadn't he always been a pitiful little snob? Wasn't it of the essence of a snob to over-value the things one hadn't and to fear the things one was? It hadn't been other people, it had been himself, what he really was, of whom he had always been afraid. He saw himself reduced to the heretofore unrecognized, yet always operative, element in his own nature — a timid, watchful humility.

Oh, Channerley! Channerley! The wail rose in his heart and it filled the world. Oh, his woods, his daffodils, his father's smile — gone — lost for ever! Worse than that — smirched, withered, desecrated!

A hideous gibbering of laughter seemed to rise around him, and pointing fingers. Amy's eyes passed with another malice in their mockery; and Robert would never turn to him now, and Griselda would never look at him. He saw it all, as they would never see it. He was not one of them, and they had always felt it; and oh, — above all, — he had always felt it. And now, quite close it seemed, softly rustling, falsely smiling, moved his loathsome mother: not only as he remembered her in her youth, but in her elegant middle years, as he had last seen her, with hard eyes and alien lips and air of brittle, untouched exquisiteness.

Suddenly fury so mounted in him that he saw himself rising in bed, rending his dressings, to seize the kneeling man by the throat and throttle him. He could see his fingers sinking in on either side among the clustered hair, and hear himself say, "How dare you! How dare you! You hound! You sniveling, sneaking hound! You look for pity from me, do you! — and tenderness! Well, take this, this! Everything, everything I am and have that's worth being and having, I owe to them. I've hated you and all you mean, always — yes, your fear and your caution and your admiration and your great high forehead. Oh, I see it! I see it! — it's my own! And though I am only that in myself, then take it from me that I hate myself along with you and curse myself with you!"

It came to him that he was slowly panting, and that after the fever-fury an icy chill crept over him. And a slow, cold smile came with it, and he saw Jephson, the wit of the office, wagging his head and saying, "Little Marmalade take a man by the throat! Ask me another!"

No; little Marmalade might win the V.C.; but only when he thought he was a Follett. Was that what it all came to, really? Something broke and stopped in his mind.

He heard his father's voice. How long ago it had all happened. He had known for years, hadn't he, that this was his father.

"Marmaduke! Mr. Follett! What have I done? Shall I call somebody? Oh, forgive me!"

His father was standing now beside him and bending over him. He looked up at him and shook his head. He did not want anyone to come.

"Oh what have I done?" the man repeated.

"I was dying anyway, you know," he heard himself say.

What a pitiful face it was, this weary, loosened, futureless old face! What a frightened face! What long years of slow disgarnishing lay behind it: youth, romance, high hopes, all dropped away. He had come to-day with their last vestiges, still the sentimental, romancing fool, self-centred and craving; but nothing of that was left. He was beaten, at last, down into the very ground. It was a haggard, humiliated, frightened face, and miserable. As he himself had been. But not even death lay before this face. For how many years must it go on sinking down until the earth covered it? Marmaduke seemed to understand all about him, as well as if he had been himself.

"Sit down," he said. He heard that his voice was gentle, though he was not aware of feeling anything, only of understanding. "I was rather upset. No; I don't want anyone. Of course I forgive you. Don't bother about it, I beg."

His father sat down, keeping his swollen eyes on the motoring-cap which, unseeingly, he turned and turned in his hands.

"Tell me about yourself a little," said Marmaduke, with the slow, spaced breaths. "Where do you live? How? Are you fairly happy?"

He knew that he was not happy; but he might, like most people with whom life had not succeeded, often imagine himself so, and Marmaduke wanted to help him, if possible, to imagine it.

"I live near London. I used to do a good deal of University Extension lecturing. I've a clerkship in the Education Office now." Mr. Thorpe spoke in a dead, obedient voice. "A small salary, not much hope of advance; and I've a large family. It's rather up-hill, of course. But I've good children; clever children. My eldest boy's at Oxford; he took a scholarship at Westminster; and my eldest girl's at Girton. The second girl, Winnie, has a very marked gift for painting; she is our artist; we're going to send her to the Slade next year when she leaves the High School. Good children. I've nothing to complain of."

"So you're fairly happy?" Marmaduke repeated. Oddly, he felt himself comforted in hearing about the good and happy children, in hearing about Winnie, her father's favorite.

"Happy? Well, just now, with this terrible war, one can't be that, can one? It is a great adventure for me, however, this work of mine, motoring about France. I don't think I've ever done anything I cared so much about since — for years," said Mr. Thorpe. "It's a beautiful country, isn't it? and the soldiers are such splendid fellows! One gets a lot out of it. But happy? No, I don't suppose I am. I'm pretty much of a failure, and I started life with great imaginings about myself. One doesn't get over that sort of disappointment; one never really gets over it in a way." Mr. Thorpe was looking at him now, and it was as if there were a kindliness between them. "Things have been rather gray and disagreeable on the whole," he said.

"They can be very gray and disagreeable, can't they?" said Marmaduke, closing his eyes.

He was very tired, and as he lay there quietly, having nothing further to know or to suffer, having reached the very limits of conscious dissolution, something else began to come to him. It seemed born of the abolition of self and of the acceptance of the fact that he was dead to all that had given life, worth or beauty. It would have been very good to be a Follett, though; he saw it now, he had over-prized that special sort of goodness — with so much else from which he had been, as really, shut out; but he was not a Follett; nor was he merely this poor, insignificant father. He did not quite make out in what the difference lay and he did not rejoice in it, for there was no rejoicing left in him. But, even if the difference were only an acquired instinct (dimly the terms of his complacent readings in biology and sociology returned to him), even it if were only that, not anything inherent and transmissible, it was, all the same, his own possession; something that he and the Folletts had made together; so that it was as true to say that he had won the V.C. as to say that they had. The lessened self that was left to him had still its worth. To see the truth, even if it undid one, was worthy; to see so unwaveringly that it was good to be a Follett even when one wasn't one, had the elements of magnanimity; and to accept the fact of being second-rate proved, did it not? — if one still cared to prove it; he felt himself smile as gently at the relinquished self as he had smiled at his father, — that one was not merely second-rate.

There was now a sound of stumbling movement; doors opening and shutting, nurses, surgeons in the room; and his father's face, far away, against the blue bands, looking at him, still so frightened and so miserable that he tried again to smile at him and to say, "It's all right. Quite all right."

At all events he had been decent to the poor old fellow. His thoughts came brokenly, but he was still seeing something, finding something; it was like a soft light growing. At all events, he had behaved as a Follett would wish to behave even when brought to such a pass. No — but it wasn't quite that, either; it was something new. He had behaved as anyone decent should wish to behave. And the daffodils glimmering to his vision seemed to light him further still. "We are as common as daffodils," came back to him. Daffodils were for everybody. Foolish little boy who, on the distant spring morning in the woods of Channerley, dug them up to take them to his own garden!

He was there among them with his little red-and-yellow cart, and the thrush was singing high above him, in the rosy topmost branches of an elm.

Beautiful woods. Beautiful flowers of light and chivalry. How the sunshine streamed among them!

"Dear Channerley," he thought. For again he seemed to belong there.

Gentle hands were tending him and, as he turned his cheek on the pillow, it was with the comfort — almost that of the little boy at Channerley being tucked up in the warm nursery to go to sleep — of knowing that he was dying, and that, in spite of everything, he had given something to the name.

August 1918

HENRY MERWIN

1853–1929

You remember Burns's poem on the twa doggies who "Rejoic'd they were na men but dogs." Henry Merwin felt the truth of that, and just below dogs, just above men, he put horses. While he lived there was in Boston an annual parade of work horses all glorious in burnished collars, with the six dappled Percherons of the Brewers' Wain drawing the plaudits of the crowd. A memorial seat on Commonwealth Avenue marks the place where, whenever his pen was not scratching for a living, Merwin used to sit and meditate on what heaven might be with all but lovers of dog and horse rigidly excluded.

On Dogs and Men

HENRY C. MERWIN

THERE are men and women in the world who, of their own free will, live a dogless life, not knowing what they miss; and for them this essay, securely placed in the dignified *Atlantic,* there to remain so long as libraries and books shall endure, is chiefly written. Let them not pass it by in scorn, but rather stop to consider what can be said of the animal as a fellow-being entitled to their sympathy, and having, perhaps, a like destiny with themselves.

As to those few persons who are not only dogless but dog-haters, they should excite pity rather than resentment. The man who hates a good dog is abnormal, and cannot help it. I once knew such a man, a money-lender long since passed away, whose life was largely a crusade against dogs, carried on through newspapers, pamphlets, and in conversation. He used to declare that he had often been bitten by these animals, and that, on one occasion, a terrier actually jumped on the street-car in which he was riding, took a small piece out of his leg (a mere soupçon, no doubt), and then jumped off, — all without apparent provocation, and in a moment of time. Probably this story, strange as it may sound, was substantially true. The perceptions of the dog are wonderfully acute. A recent occurrence may serve as the converse of the money-lender's story. A lost collie, lame and nearly starved, was taken in, fed, and cared for by a household of charitable persons, who, however, did not like or understand dogs, and were anxious to get rid of this one, provided that a good home could be found for him. In the course of a week there came to call upon them in her buggy an old lady who is extremely fond of dogs, and who possesses that combination of a masterful spirit with deep affection which acts like witchcraft upon the lower animals. The collie was brought out, and the story of his arrival was related at length. Meanwhile the old lady and the dog looked each other steadfastly in the eye. "Do you want to come with me, doggie?" she said at last, not really meaning to take him. Up jumped the dog, and sat down beside her, and could not be dislodged by any entreaties or commands, — and all parties were loath to use force. She took him home, but brought him back the next day, intending to leave him behind her. Again, however, the dog refused to be parted from his new and real friend. He bestowed a perfunctory wag of the tail upon his benefactors, — he was not ungrateful; but, like all dogs, he sought not chiefly meat and bones and a comfortable place by the fire, but affection and caresses. The dog does not live that would refuse to forsake his dinner for the companionship of his master.

The mission of the dog — I say it with all reverence — is the same as the mission of Christianity, namely, to teach mankind that the universe is ruled by love. Ownership of a dog tends to soften the hard hearts of men. There are two great mysteries about the lower animals: one, the suffering which they have to endure at the hands of man; the other, the wealth of affection which they possess, and which for the most part is unexpended. All animals have this capacity for loving other creatures, man included. Crows, for example, show it to a remarkable degree. "As much latent affection goes to waste in every flock of crows that flies overhead as would fit a human household for heaven." A crow and a dog, if kept together, will become almost as fond of each other as of their master. Surely this fact, this capacity of the lower animals to love, not only man, but one another, is the most significant, the most deserving to be pondered, the most important in respect to their place in the universe, of all the facts that can be learned about them. Compared with it how trivial is anything that the zoölogist or biologist or the physiologist can tell us about the nature of the lower animals!

The most beautiful sight in the world, I once heard it said (by myself, to be honest), is the expression in the eyes of an intelligent, sweet-tempered pup,—a pup old enough to take an interest in things about him, and yet so young as to imagine that everybody will be good to him; so young as not to fear that any man or boy will kick him, or that any dog will take away his bone. In the eyes of such a pup there is a look of confiding innocence, a consciousness of his own weakness and inexperience, a desire to love and be loved, which are irresistible. In older dogs one is more apt to notice an eager, anxious, inquiring look, as if they were striving to understand things which the Almighty had placed beyond their mental grasp; and the nearest approach to a really human expression is seen in dogs suffering from illness. Heine, who, as the reader well knows, served a long apprenticeship to pain, somewhere says that pain refines even the lower animals; and all who are familiar with dogs in health and in disease will see the truth of this statement. I have seen in the face of an intelligent dog, suffering acutely from distemper, a look so human as to be almost terrifying; as if I had accidentally caught a glimpse of some deep-lying trait in the animal which nature had intended to conceal from mortal gaze.

The dog, in fact, makes a continual appeal to the sympathies of his human friends, and thus tends to prevent them from becoming hard or narrow. There are certain families, especially perhaps in New England, and most of all, no doubt, in Boston, who need to be regenerated, and might be regenerated by keeping a dog, provided that they went about it in the proper spirit. A distinguished preacher and author, himself a Unitarian, remarked recently in an address to Unitarians that they were usually the most self-satisfied people that he ever met. It was a casual remark, and perhaps neither he nor those who heard it appreciated its full significance. However, the preacher was probably thinking not so much of Unitarians as of a certain kind of person often found in this neighborhood, and not necessarily professing any particular form of religion. We all know the type. When a man *invariably* has money in the bank, and is respectable and respected, was graduated at Harvard, has a decorous wife and children, has never been carried away by any passion or enthusiasm, knows the right people, and conforms strictly to the customs of good society; and when this sort of thing has been going on for, perhaps, two or three generations, then there is apt to creep into the blood a coldness that would chill the heart of a bronze statue. Such persons are really degenerates of their peculiar kind, and need to be saved, perhaps by desperate measures. Let them elope with the cook; let them get religion of a violent Methodistic, or of an intense Ritualistic, kind (the two have much in common); or if they cannot do that, let them get a dog, give him the run of the house, love him and spoil him, and so, by the blessing of Providence, their salvation may be effected.

Reformers and philanthropists should always keep dogs, in order that the spontaneous element may not wholly die out of them. Their tendency is to regard the human race as a problem, and particular persons as "cases" to be dealt with, not according to one's impulses, but according to certain rules approved of by good authority, and supposed to be consistent with sound, economic principles. To my old friend ——, who once liked me for myself, without asking why, I have long ceased to be an individual, and am now simply an item of humanity to whom he owes such duty as my particular wants or vices would seem to indicate. But if he had a dog he could not regard him in that impersonal way, or worry about the dog's morals; he would simply take pleasure in his society, and love him for what he was, without considering what he might have been.

I know and honor one philanthropist who, in middle life or thereabout, became for the first time the possessor of a dog; and thenceforth there was disclosed in him a genuine vein of sentiment and affection which many years of doing good and virtuous living had failed to eradicate. Often had I heard of his civic deeds and of his well-directed charities, but my heart never quite warmed toward him, until I learned that, with spectacles on nose and comb in hand, he had spent three laborious hours in painfully going over his spaniel, and eliminating those parasitic guests which sometimes infest the coat of the cleanest and most aristocratic dog. I am not ashamed to say that I have a confidence in his wisdom now which I did not have before, knowing that his head will never be allowed to tyrannize over his heart. His name should be recorded here, were it not that his modesty might be offended by the act. (Three letters would suffice to print it.)

In speaking of the dog as a kind of missionary in the household, I mean, it need hardly be said, something more than mere ownership of the animal. It will not suffice to pay a large sum for a dog of fashionable breed, to equip him with a costly collar, and then to relegate him to the stable or the kitchen. He should be one of the family, living on equal terms with the others, and their constant companion. The dog's life is short at the best, and every moment of it will be needed for his development. It is wonderful how year by year the household pet grows in intelligence, how many words he learns the meaning of, how quick he becomes in interpreting the look, the tone of voice, the mood of the person whom he loves. He is old at ten or eleven, and seldom lives beyond thirteen or fourteen. If he lived to be fifty, he would know so much that we should be uneasy, perhaps terrified, in his presence.

A certain amount of discipline is necessary for a dog. If left to his own devices, he is apt to become somewhat dissipated, to spend his evenings out, to scatter among many the affection which should be reserved for a few. But, on the other hand, a dog may easily receive too much discipline; he becomes like the child of a despotic father. A dog perfectly trained, from the martinet point of view,—one who never "jumps up" on you, never lays an entreating paw upon your arm, never gets into a chair, nor enters the drawing-room,—such a dog is a sad sight to one who really knows and loves the animal. It is against his nature to be so repressed. Over-careful housewives, and persons who are burdened with costly surroundings, talk of injury to carpets and other furniture if the dog has a right of entry everywhere in the house. But what is furniture for? Is it for display, is it a guaranty of the wealth of the owners, or is it for use? Blessed are they whose furniture is so inexpensive or so shabby that children and dogs are not excluded from its sacred precincts. Perhaps the happiest household to which I ever had the honor of being admitted was one where it was sometimes a little difficult to find a comfortable vacant chair: the dogs always took the arm-chairs. Alas, where are those hospitable chairs now? Where the dogs that used to sit up in them, and wink and yawn, and give their paws in humorous embarrassment?

"'The drawing-room was made for dogs, and not dogs for the drawing-room,' would be Lady Barnes's thesis, did she formulate it." It was this same Lady Barnes (Rhoda Broughton's) who once said, "'I have no belief in Eliza, the housemaid I leave in charge here. When last I came down from London the dogs were so unnaturally good that I felt sure she bullied them. I spoke very seriously to her, and this time, I am glad to say, they are as disobedient as ever, and have done even more mischief than when I am at home.' And she laughs with a delicate relish of her own folly."

Of all writers of fiction, by the way, is there any whose dogs quite equal those of Rhoda Broughton? Even the beloved author of *Rab and His Friends,* even Sir Walter himself, with his immortal Dandie Dinmonts, has not, it seems to me, given us such life-like and home-like pictures of dogs as those which occur in her novels. They seem to be there, not of set purpose, but as if dogs were such an essential part of her own existence that they crept into her books almost without her knowing it. No room in her novels is complete without a dog or two; and every remark that she makes about them has the quality of a caress. Even in a tragic moment, the heroine cannot help observing, that "Mink is lying on his small hairy side in a sunpatch, with his little paws crossed like a dying saint's." "Mr. Brown," that dear, faithful mongrel, is forever associated with the unfortunate Joan; and Brenda's "wouff" will go resounding down the halls of time so long as novels are read.

Perhaps the final test of anybody's love of dogs is willingness to permit them to make a camping-ground of the bed. There is no other place in the world that suits the dog quite so well. On the bed he is safe from being stepped upon; he is out of the way of draughts; he has a commanding position from which to survey what goes on in the world; and, above all, the surface is soft and yielding to his outstretched limbs. No mere man can ever be so comfortable as a dog looks.

Some persons object to having a dog on the bed at night; and it must be admitted that he lies a little heavily upon one's limbs; but why be so base as to prefer comfort to companionship! To wake up in the dark night, and put your hand on that warm soft body, to feel the beating of that faithful heart,—is not this better than undisturbed sloth? The best night's rest I ever had was once when a cocker spaniel puppy, who had just recovered from stomach-ache (dose one to two soda-mints), and was a little frightened by the strange experience, curled up on my shoulder like a fur tippet, gently pushed his cold, soft nose into my neck, and there slept sweetly and soundly until morning.

Companionship with his master is the dog's remedy for every ill, and only an extreme case will justify sending him away or boarding him out. To put a dog in a hospital, unless there is some surgical or other necessity for doing so, is an act of doubtful kindness. Many and many a dog has died from homesickness. If he is ill, keep him warm and quiet, give such simple remedies as you would give a child, pour beef tea or malted milk down his throat, or even a little whiskey, if he is weak from want of food; and let him live or die, as did our fathers and our fathers' dogs,—at home.

The worst evil that can befall a dog, it need not be said, is to be lost. The very words "lost dog" call up such pictures of canine misery as can never be forgotten by those who have witnessed them. I have seen a lost dog, lame, emaciated, wounded, footsore, hungry, and thirsty, and yet suffering so intensely from fear, and loneliness, and despair,—from the mere sense of being lost,—as to be absolutely unconscious of his bodily condition. The mental agony was so much greater that it swallowed up the physical pain. A little Boston terrier, lost in a large city for two or three days, became so wrecked in his nervous system that no amount of care or petting could restore him to equanimity, and it was found necessary to kill him. Oh, reader, pass not by the lost dog! Succor him if you can; preserve him from what is worse than death. It is easy to recognize him by the look of nervous terror in his eye, by his drooping tail, by his uncertain movements.

There is a remorseful experience of my own, of which I should be glad to unburden myself to the reader. It once became my duty to kill a dog afflicted with some incurable disease. Instead of doing it myself, as I should have done, I took him to a place where lost dogs are received, and where those for whom no home can be found are mercifully destroyed. There, instead of myself leading him to the death-chamber, as, again, I should have done, I handed him over to the executioner. The dog was an abnormally nervous and timid one; and as he was dragged most unwillingly away, he turned around, as nearly as he could, and cast back at me a look of horror, of fear, of agonized appeal, — a look that has haunted me for years.

Whether he had any inkling of what was in store for him, I do not know, but it is highly probable that he had. Dogs and other animals are wonderful mind-readers. I have known two cases in which some discussion about the necessity of killing an old dog, held in his presence, was quickly followed by the sudden, unaccountable disappearance of the animal; and no tidings of him could ever be obtained, although the greatest pains were taken to obtain them. Horses are inferior only to dogs in this capacity. Often, especially in the case of vicious or half-broken horses, an intention will flash from the mind of the horse to the mind of the rider or driver, and *vice versa,* without the slightest indication being given by horse or man. Men who ride race-horses have told me that a sudden conviction in their own minds, in the course of a race, that they could not win has passed immediately to the horse, and caused him to slacken his speed, although they had not ceased to urge him. It is notorious that faint-hearted and pessimistic drivers often lose races which they ought to win.

As to the remarkable stories about this or that animal, perhaps it might be said that they are probably true when they illustrate the animal's perceptive abilities, and are probably false when they depend upon his power to originate. There appeared lately an account of a race between loons in the wild state: how the loons got together and arranged the preliminaries (whether they made books on the event or adopted the pool system of betting was not stated), how the race was run, or rather flown, amid intense loon excitement, and how the victor was greeted with screams of applause!

Some power of origination animals, and dogs especially, certainly have. There is the familiar trick which dogs play when one, to get a bone away from another, rushes off a little space, gives the bark which signifies the presence of an intruder, then comes back and quietly runs away with the bone which the other dog, in his curiosity to see who is coming, has impulsively dropped. This is an example not only of reasoning, but of origination.

In general, however, when dogs surprise us, as they frequently do, it is by the delicacy and acuteness of their perceptive powers. How unerringly do they distinguish between different classes of persons, as, for example, between the members of the family and the servants; and again, between the servants and the friends of the household! Unquestionably the dog has three sets of manners for these three classes of persons. He will take liberties in the kitchen that he would never dream of taking in the dining-room. We have known our cook to fly in terror from the kitchen because Figaro, a masterful cocker spaniel, threatened to bite her, if she did not give him a piece of meat forthwith. Figaro reasoned that the cook was partly *his* cook, and that he had a right to bully her if he could.

As for the different members of the family, the dog will "size them up" with an unerring instinct. It is impossible to conceal any weakness of character from him; and if you are strong, he will know that too. As I write these lines, the vision of "Mr. Guppy" rises before me. Mr. Guppy was a very small Boston terrier with a white head, but otherwise of a brindle color. He had a beautiful "mug," much like that of a bull dog, with a short nose, wide jaws, and plenty of loose skin hanging about his stout little neck. It must be admitted that he was somewhat self-indulgent, being continually on the watch for a chance to lie close by the fire,—a situation considered by his friends to be unwholesome for him. Mr. Guppy understood me very well. He knew that I was a poor, weak, easy-going, absent-minded creature, with whom he could take liberties; and accordingly, when we were alone together, the rogue would lie sleeping with his head on the hearth, while I was absorbed in my book. But hark! there is a step on the stairs, of one whom Mr. Guppy both loved and feared more than any dog ever loved or feared me; and forthwith the little impostor would rise, and crawl softly back to his place on a rug in the corner; and there he would be found lying and winking, with an expression of perfect innocence, when the disciplinarian entered the room.

Dogs have the same sensitiveness that we associate with well-bred men and women. Their politeness is remarkable. Offer a dog water when he is not thirsty, and he will almost always take a lap or two, just out of civility, and to show his gratitude. I know a group of dogs that never forget to come and tell their mistress when they have had their dinner, feeling sure that she will sympathize with them; and if they have failed to get it, they will notify her immediately of the omission. If you happen to step on a dog's tail or paw, how eagerly — after one irrepressible yelp of pain — will he tell you by his caresses that he knows you did not mean to hurt him and forgives you!

In their relations with one another, also, dogs have a keen sense of etiquette. A well-known traveler makes this unexpected remark about a tribe of naked black men, living on one of the South Sea Islands: "In their every-day intercourse there is much that is stiff, formal, and precise." Almost the same remark might be made about dogs. Unless they are on very intimate terms, they take great pains never to brush against or even to touch one another. For one dog to step over another is a dangerous breach of etiquette unless they are special friends. It is no uncommon thing for two dogs to belong to the same person, and live in the same house, and yet never take the slightest notice of each other. We have a spaniel so dignified that he will never permit another member of the dog family to pillow his head on him; but, with the egotism of a true aristocrat, he does not hesitate to make use of the other dogs for that purpose.

Often canine etiquette is so subtle that one has much difficulty in following it out. In our household are two uncongenial dogs, who, in ordinary circumstances, completely ignore each other, and between whom any familiarity would be resented fiercely. And yet, when we are all out walking, if I am obliged to scold or punish one of these two, the other will run up to the offender, bark at him, and even jostle him, as if he were saying, "Well, old man, you got it that time; aren't you ashamed of yourself?" And the other dog, feeling that he is in the wrong, I suppose, submits meekly to the insult.

A family of six dogs used to pair off in couples, each couple being on terms of special intimacy and affection; and besides these relationships there were many others among them. For example, they all deferred to the oldest dog, although he was smaller and weaker than the rest. If a fight began, he would jump in between the contestants and stop it; if a dog misbehaved, he would rush at the offender with a warning growl; and this exercise of authority was never resented. The other dogs seemed to respect his weight of years, his character, which was of the highest, and his moral courage, which was undoubted. This same dog had many human traits. He and his companions slept together on a sofa upstairs, where, of a cold night, they would curl up together in an indistinguishable heap. Sometimes the old dog would put himself to bed before the others, and then, finding that he needed the warmth and companionship of their presence, he would go into the hall, put his head between the balusters, and whine softly until they came upstairs to join him.

Have dogs any sense of right and wrong? They have, as every one agrees, a sense of humor, and they have also a sense of shame, perfectly distinct from the fear of punishment. Of their sense of shame let me give one example. The dog's eyesight, so far at least as stationary objects are concerned, is very poor, his real reliance being upon his sense of smell, and I have often seen a dog mistake one of his own family for a strange animal, run toward him, with every sign of hostility, and then, when he came within a few feet of the other dog, suddenly drop his tail between his legs, and slink away, as if he feared that somebody had noticed his absurd mistake.

Can it be that an animal should possess a sense of humor and a sense of shame, without having also some elementary sense of right and wrong? But even if it be thought that he is devoid of that sense, it is certain that he has those kindly impulses from which it has been developed. All that is best in man springs from something which is practically the same in the dog that it is in him, namely, the instinct of pity or benevolence. To that instinct, as it exists in the lower animals, Darwin attributed the origin of conscience in man; and there are now few, if any, philosophers who would give a different account of it. I have seen a pup not six months old run to comfort another pup that cried out from pain; and the impulse that prompted this act was essentially the same which impels the noblest of mankind when they befriend the poor or the afflicted. We are akin to the lower animals morally, as well as physically and mentally.

But this is a modern discovery. It is astonishing and confusing to realize how little organized Christianity has done for the lower animals. The ecclesiastical conception of them was simply that they were creatures without souls, and therefore had no rights as against, or at the hands of, mankind. To this day that conception remains, although it is qualified, of course, by other and more humane considerations. Even Cardinal Newman said,—

"We have no duties toward the brute creation; there is no relation of justice between them and us. Of course, we are bound not to treat them ill, for cruelty is an offense against the holy law which our Maker has written on our hearts, and it is displeasing to Him. But they can claim nothing at our hand; into our hand they are absolutely delivered. We may use them, we may destroy them at our pleasure: not our wanton pleasure, but still for our own ends, for our own benefit and satisfaction, provided that we can give a rational account of what we do."

This position, though not perhaps cruel in itself, inevitably results in unlimited cruelties. When an English traveler remonstrated with a Spanish lady for throwing a sick kitten out of the window, she justified herself by saying that the kitten had no soul; and that is the national point of view.

Protestantism has been almost as indifferent as Catholicism to the lower animals. In fact, the conscience which exists outside of the church, Catholic or Protestant, has in this matter, outstripped the conscience of the church. "Cruelty," said Du Maurier, "is the only unpardonable sin"; and the world is slowly but surely coming to that opinion. The long deferred awakening of mankind to the sufferings of dumb animals was not due to a decline of the ecclesiastical conception of them, although it has declined; nor even to the new knowledge concerning the common origin of man and beast; indeed, it slightly preceded that knowledge; but it was due to the gradual enlightenment and moral improvement of the race, especially of the English-speaking race. The nineteenth century, as we are often told, saw more discoveries and inventions than had been made in the preceding six thousand years; but I believe that in future ages not one of those discoveries and inventions; nor all together, will bulk so large as factors in the development and uplifting of man, as will those humane laws and societies which first came into existence in that century.

The progress of mankind is far more moral than intellectual. Competent authorities tell us that the Anglo-Saxon of to-day is mentally inferior to the Greek who lived two thousand years ago: and if the human race has improved during that time it is not so much because man has advanced in knowledge as because he has acquired more sympathy with his inferiors, be they brute or human, more generosity, more mercy toward them. Not Stevenson, nor Faraday, nor Morse, nor Fulton, nor Bell, did so much for the human race, to say nothing of the brutes, as did that dueling Irishman who, in the year 1822, proposed in the English Parliament, amidst howls and shrieks of derision, what afterward became the first law for the protection of dumb animals ever placed on the statute-book of any country. Every movement for the relief of the brute creation has originated in England; and when we damn John Bull for one thing and another, let us remember this fact to his eternal honor!

It is hard to part from an old dog-friend with no hope of ever meeting him again, hard to believe that the spirit of love which burned so steadfastly in him is quenched forever. But for those who hold what I have called the ecclesiastical conception of the lower animals, no other view is possible. That devout Catholic and exquisite poet, Dr. Parsons, has beautifully expressed this fact:—

> When parents die there's many a word to say—
> Kind words, consoling—one can always pray;
> When children die 'tis natural to tell
> Their mother, "Certainly with them 'tis well!"
> But for a dog, 'twas all the life he had,
> Since death is end of dogs, or good or bad.
> This was his world, he was contented here;
> Imagined nothing better, naught more dear,
> Than his young mistress; sought no higher sphere;
> Having no sin, asked not to be forgiven;
> Ne'er guessed at God nor ever dreamed of heaven.
> Now he has passed away, so much of love
> Goes from our life, without one hope above!

But is there no hope? Is there not as much—or, if the reader prefers, as little—hope for the dog as there is for man? Years ago I remember reading in a prominent magazine the statement that doubtless a few men, the very wickedest, will become extinct at death, whereas the rest of mankind will be immortal. This view had some adherents then, but would now be regarded by almost everybody as irrational. Who can believe that between the best and the worst man there is any such gulf as would justify so diverse a fate! Moreover we have learned that there are no chasms or jumps in nature. One thing slides into another; every creature is a link between two others, and man himself can be traced back physically, mentally, and morally, to the lower animals. Is it not then reasonable to suppose that immortality belongs to all forms of life or to none, that if man is immortal, the dog is immortal, too? Even to speculate upon this subject seems almost ridiculous, our knowledge is so limited; and yet it is hard to refrain from speculating. The transmigration of souls may be a fact, or men and dogs and all other forms of life may be simply forms, temporary phases, proceeding from one source, and returning thereto. But alas, every supposition that we can make is rendered almost, if not quite untenable, by the mere fact that the human intellect has conceived of it, — it is so unlikely that we should hit upon the right solution!

In this situation, what we seem bound to do is to refrain from hasty, and especially from egotistic conclusions, to keep our minds open, to regard the lower animals not only with pity but with a certain reverence. We do not know what or whence they are; but we do know that their nature resembles ours; that they have Individuality, as we have it; that they feel pain, both physical and mental, that they are capable of affection; that, although innocent, as we believe, their sufferings have been, and are, unspeakable. Is there no mystery here?

To many men, to most men, perhaps, a dog is simply an animated machine, developed or created for the convenience of the human race. It may be so; and yet again it may be that the dog has his own rightful place in the universe, irrespective and independent of man, and that an injury done to him is an insult to the Creator.

January 1910

AGNES REPPLIER

1858–

The discipline most essential to American letters comes from France. Individualism is our genius, but there is a time when individualism becomes a riot and then lucidity, clarity, and the sense of a compulsive past gives healing, order, and sobriety to the ranks. Miss Repplier's intelligence is descended from the French as directly as her family line. Hers is an astringent gift, curbing enthusiasms not so much with humor as with the rarer wit, while ever at her command a pinch of malice serves as a most salutary correction. For an essayist she has the perfect tone and temper. Unique is a foolish word. Ever since Noah discarded the idea behind it, the word has been misapplied, but among all the friendships of a lifetime, I have enjoyed Miss Repplier's, with the most constant sense that no furthest search could bring me another like it. Such civilization as is my share, I feel that in a definite measure, I owe to her.

Perhaps Miss Repplier could not write so well had she not suffered. The ills of life have been heaped tumultuously upon her, but her religion is proof against them. Religion is a protective armor. There must be courage within it, and Miss Repplier has a quiet courage which I have never seen surpassed.

I recall an incident when she stopped to see me for a few moments. She was on her way to the hospital, and though she gave no slightest hint of it, I knew that the danger present in her imagination was the most terrible of the afflictions of the flesh — cancer.

She talked wittily of neutral things, of people and their obsessions, of contemporary books and their misdirection. Then, looking suddenly at her watch, she said, "Good-bye, my friend." In return I said, "Good-bye, Heroine." The faintest flush came over her face. She turned and went without another word.

It is a dangerous thing to offer Miss Repplier compliments. One touch of insincerity and she will laugh in your face. Only once have I been able to please her with a tribute. It chanced I had been lunch-

ing in London with Mr. Augustine Birrell, whose Obiter Dicta proved the definitive perfection of his taste and judgment. He had asked me if I knew Miss Repplier, and then went on to remark that she was "the first essayist of the contemporary English-speaking world." These words I brought to her, and Mr. Birrell's accolade brought her completest satisfaction.

I know of no remarkable talent which has not been fostered by the sympathy of some understanding friend. Miss Repplier's childhood made a slow start. Not until she was ten had she learned to read, nor was it necessary for her to do so. Through all the years between, her mother had recited endless poetry to the child, ballads and songs, English and French, and before she could print a letter her mind was steeped in "literature." Growing older, she was sent to the Sacred Heart Convent near Philadelphia, and it happened that in attendance there was a remarkable priest whose influence is still unforgotten. Father Hecker was attracted to the girl of nineteen, and, telling her she was a "bookish person," bade her turn to the essay form.

A "bookish person" she is, living in her library and reading unceasingly until a tragic illness overcame her will, good books, wise books, and occasional books not free from naughtiness. High on the topmost shelf, so high one must reach for them, is an irregular row of volumes, thick and thin. While she had strength, to run her hand along their lengthening rank ceased not to amuse her. They are the complete works of Agnes Repplier.

Agrippina

AGNES REPPLIER

SHE is sitting on my desk, as I write, and I glance at her with deference, mutely begging permission to begin. But her back is turned to me, and expresses in every curve such fine and delicate disdain that I falter and lose courage at the very threshold of my task. I have long known that cats are the most contemptuous of creatures, and that Agrippina is the most contemptuous of cats. The spirit of Bouhaki, the proud Theban beast that sat erect, with gold earrings in his ears, at the feet of his master, King Hana; the spirit of Muezza, whose slumbers Mahomet himself was not bold enough to disturb; the spirit of Micetto, Châteaubriand's ecclesiastical pet, dignified as a cardinal, and conscious ever that he was the gift of a sovereign pontiff,—the spirits of all arrogant cats that have played scornful parts in the world's great comedy look out from Agrippina's yellow eyes and hold me in subjection. I should like to explain to her, if I dared, that my desk is small, littered with many papers, and sadly overcrowded with the useful inutilities which affectionate friends delight in giving me at Christmas time. Sainte-Beuve's cat, I am aware, sat on his desk, and roamed at will among those precious manuscripts which no intrusive hand was ever permitted to touch; but Sainte-Beuve probably had sufficient space reserved for his own comfort and convenience. I have not; and Agrippina's beautifully ringed tail flapping across my copy distracts my attention and imperils the neatness of my penmanship. Even when she is disposed to be affable, turns the light of her countenance upon me, watches with attentive curiosity every stroke I make, and softly, with curved paw, pats my pen as it travels over the paper,—even in these halcyon moments, though my self-love is flattered by her condescension, I am aware that I should work better and more rapidly if I denied myself this charming companionship.

But in truth it is impossible for a lover of cats to banish these alert, gentle, and discriminating little friends, who give us just enough of their regard and complaisance to make us hunger for more. M. Fée, the naturalist, who has written so admirably about animals, and who understands, as only a Frenchman can understand, the delicate and subtle organization of a cat, frankly admits that the keynote of its character is independence. It dwells under our roof, sleeps by our fire, endures our blandishments, and apparently enjoys our society, without for one moment forfeiting its sense of absolute freedom, without acknowledging any servile relation to the human creature who shelters it. "The cat," says M. Fée, "will never part with its liberty; it will neither be our servant, like the horse, nor our friend, like the dog. It consents to live as our guest; it accepts the home we offer and the food we give; it even goes so far as to solicit our caresses, but capriciously, and when it suits its humor to receive them."

Rude and masterful souls resent this fine self-sufficiency in a domestic animal, and require that it should have no will but theirs, no pleasure that does not emanate from them. They are forever prating of the love and fidelity of the dog, of the beast that obeys their slightest word, crouches contentedly for hours at their feet, is exuberantly grateful for the smallest attention, and so affectionate that its demonstrations require to be curbed rather than encouraged. All this homage is pleasing to their vanity; yet there are people, less magisterial perhaps, or less exacting, who believe that true friendship, even with an animal, may be built up on mutual esteem and independence; that to demand gratitude is to be unworthy of it; and that obedience is not essential to agreeable and healthy intercourse. A man who owns a dog is, in every sense of the word, its master; the term expresses accurately their mutual relations. But it is ridiculous when applied to the limited possession of a cat. I am certainly not Agrippina's mistress, and the assumption of authority on my part would be a mere empty dignity, like those swelling titles which afford such innocent delight to the Freemasons of our severe republic. If I call Agrippina, she does not come; if I tell her to go away, she remains where she is; if I try to persuade her to show off her one or two little accomplishments, she refuses, with courteous but unswerving decision. She has frolicsome moods, in which a thimble, a shoe-buttoner, a scrap of paper, or a piece of string will drive her wild with delight; she has moods of inflexible gravity, in which she stares solemnly at her favorite ball rolling over the carpet, without stirring one lazy limb to reach it. "Have I seen this foolish toy before?" she seems to be asking herself with amusing austerity; "and can it be possible that there are cats who run after such frivolous trifles? Vanity of vanities, and all is vanity, save only to lie upon the hearth-rug, and be warm, and 'think grave thoughts to feed a serious soul.'" In such moments of rejection and humiliation, I comfort myself by recalling the words of one too wise for arrogance. "When I play with my cat," says Montaigne, "how do I know whether she does not make a jest of me? We entertain each other with mutual antics; and if I have my own time for beginning or refusing, she, too, has hers."

This is the spirit in which we should approach a creature so reserved and so utterly self-sufficing; this is the only key we have to that natural distinction of character which repels careless and unobservant natures. When I am told that Agrippina is disobedient, ungrateful, cold-hearted, perverse, stupid, treacherous, and cruel, I no longer strive to check the torrent of abuse. I know that Buffon said all this, and much more, about cats, and that people have gone on repeating it ever since, principally because these spirited little beasts have remained just what it pleased Providence to make them, have preserved their primitive freedom through centuries of effete and demoralizing civilization. Why, I wonder, should a great many good men and women cherish an unreasonable grudge against one animal because it does not chance to possess the precise qualities of another? "My dog fetches my slippers for me every night," said a friend triumphantly, not long ago. "He puts them first to warm by the fire, and then brings them over to my chair, wagging his tail, and as proud as Punch. Would your cat do as much for you, I'd like to know?" Assuredly not! If I waited for Agrippina to fetch me shoes or slippers, I should have no other resource save to join as speedily as possible one of the bare-footed religious orders of Italy. But, after all, fetching slippers is not the whole duty of domestic pets. As La Fontaine gently reminds us,

Tout animal n'a pas toutes propriétés.

We pick no quarrel with a canary because it does not talk like a parrot, nor with a parrot because it does not sing like a canary. We find no fault with a King Charles spaniel for not flying at the throat of a burglar, nor with a St. Bernard because we cannot put it in our pocket. Agrippina will never make herself serviceable, yet nevertheless is she of inestimable service. How many times have I rested tired eyes on her graceful little body, curled up in a ball and wrapped round with her tail like a parcel; or stretched out luxuriously on my bed, one paw coyly covering her face, the other curved gently inwards, as though clasping an invisible treasure! Asleep or awake, in rest or in motion, grave or gay, Agrippina is always beautiful; and it is better to be beautiful than to fetch and carry from the rising to the setting of the sun. She is droll, too, with an unconscious humor even in her most serious and sentimental moods. She has quite the longest ears that ever were seen on so small a cat, eyes more solemn than Athene's owl blinking in the sunlight, and an air of supercilious disdain that would have made Diogenes seem young and ardent by her side. Sitting on the library table, under the evening lamp, with her head held high in air, her tall ears as erect as chimneys, and her inscrutable gaze fixed on the darkest corner of the room, Agrippina inspires in the family sentiments of mingled mirthfulness and awe. To laugh at her in such moments, however, is to incur her supreme displeasure. I have known her to jump down from the table and walk haughtily out of the room, because of a single half-suppressed but wholly indecorous giggle.

Schopenhauer has said that the reason domestic pets are so lovable and so helpful to us is because they enjoy, quietly and placidly, the present moment. Life holds no future for them, and consequently no care; if they are content, their contentment is absolute; and our jaded and wearied spirits find a natural relief in the sight of creatures whose little cups of happiness can so easily be filled to the brim. Walt Whitman expresses the same thought more coarsely when he acknowledges that he loves the society of animals because they do not sweat and whine over their condition, nor lie awake in the dark and weep for their sins, nor sicken him with discussions of their duty. In truth, that admirable counsel of Sydney Smith's, "Take short views of life," can be obeyed only by the brutes; for the thought that travels even to the morrow is long enough to destroy our peace of mind, inasmuch as we know not what the morrow may bring forth. But when Agrippina has breakfasted, and washed, and sits in the sunlight blinking at me with affectionate contempt, I feel soothed by her absolute and unqualified enjoyment. I know how full my day will be of things that I don't want particularly to do, and that are not particularly worth doing; but for her time and the world hold only this brief moment of contentment. Slowly the eyes close, gently the little body is relaxed. Oh, you who strive to relieve your overwrought nerves, and cultivate power through repose, watch the exquisite languor of a drowsy cat, and despair of imitating such perfect and restful grace! There is a gradual yielding of every muscle to the soft persuasiveness of slumber; the flexible frame is curved into tender lines, the head nestles lower, the paws are tucked out of sight; no convulsive throb or start betrays a rebellious alertness; only a faint quiver of unconscious satisfaction, a faint heaving of the tawny sides, a faint gleam of the half-shut yellow eyes, and Agrippina is asleep. I look at her for one wistful moment, and then turn resolutely to my work. It were ignoble to wish myself in her place, and yet how charming to be able to settle down to a nap, *sans peur et sans reproche,* at ten o'clock in the morning!

These, then, are a few of the pleasures to be derived from the society of an amiable cat; and by an amiable cat I mean one that, while maintaining its own dignity and delicate reserve, is nevertheless affable and condescending in the company of human beings. There is nothing I dislike more than newspaper and magazine stories about priggish pussies—like the children in Sunday-school books—that share their food with hungry beasts from the back alleys, and show touching fidelity to old blind masters, and hunt partridges in a spirit of noble self-sacrifice for consumptive mistresses, and scorn to help themselves to delicacies from the kitchen tables, and arouse their households so often in cases of fire that I should suspect them of starting the conflagrations in order to win applause by giving the alarm. Whatever a real cat may or may not be, it is never a prig, and all true lovers of the race have been quick to recognize and appreciate this fact.

"I value in the cat," says Châteaubriand, "that independent and almost ungrateful temper which prevents it from attaching itself to any one; the indifference with which it passes from the salon to the housetop. When you caress it, it stretches itself out and arches its back, indeed; but that is caused by physical pleasure, and not, as in the case of the dog, by a silly satisfaction in loving and being faithful to a master who returns thanks in kicks. The cat lives alone, has no need of society, does not obey except when it likes, pretends to sleep that it may see the more clearly, and scratches everything that it can scratch."

Here is a sketch spirited enough and of good outline, but hardly correct in every detail. A cat seldom manifests affection, yet is often distinctly social, and likes to see itself the petted minion of a family group. Agrippina, in fact, so far from living alone, will not, if she can help it, remain for a moment in a room by herself. She is content to have me as a companion, perhaps in default of better; but if I go upstairs or downstairs in search of a book, or my eyeglasses, or any one of the countless things that are never where they ought to be, Agrippina follows closely at my heels. Sometimes, when she is fast asleep, I steal softly out of the door, thinking to escape her vigilance; but before I have taken a dozen steps she is under my feet, mewing a gentle reproach, and putting on all the injured airs of a deserted Ariadne. I should like to think such behavior prompted by affection rather than by curiosity; but in my candid moments I find this "pathetic fallacy" a difficult sentiment to cherish. There are people, I am aware, who trustfully assert that their pets love them; and one such sanguine creature has recently assured the world that "no man who boasts the real intimacy and confidence of a cat would dream of calling his four-footed friend 'puss.'" But is not such a boast rather ill-timed at best? How dare any man venture to assert that he possesses the intimacy and confidence of an animal so exclusive and so reserved? I doubt if Cardinal Wolsey, in the zenith of his pride and power, claimed the intimacy and confidence of the superb cat that sat in a cushioned armchair by his side, and reflected with mimic dignity the full-blown honors of the Lord High Chancellor of England. Agrippina, I am humbly aware, grants me neither her intimacy nor her confidence, but only her companionship, which I endeavor to receive modestly, and without flaunting my favors to the world. She is displeased and even downcast when I go out, and she greets my return with delight, thrusting her little gray head between the banisters the instant I open the house door, and waving a welcome in mid-air with one ridiculously small paw. Being but mortal, I am naturally pleased with these tokens of esteem, but I do not, on that account, go about with arrogant brow and boast of my intimacy with Agrippina. I should be laughed at, if I did, by everybody who is privileged to possess and appreciate a cat.

As for curiosity, that vice which the Abbé Galiani held to be unknown to animals, but which the more astute Voltaire detected in every little dog that he saw peering out of the window of its master's coach, it is the ruling passion of the feline breast. A closet door left ajar, a box with half-closed lid, an open bureau drawer, — these are the objects that fill a cat with the liveliest interest and delight. Agrippina watches breathlessly the unfastening of a parcel, and tries to hasten matters by clutching actively at the string. When its contents are shown her, she examines them gravely, and then, with a sigh of relief, settles down to repose. The slightest noise disturbs and irritates her until she discovers its cause. If she hears a footstep in the hall, she runs out to see whose it is, and, like certain troublesome little people I have known, she dearly loves to go to the front door every time the bell is rung. From my window she surveys the street with tranquil scrutiny, and, if boys are playing below, she follows their games with a steady scornful stare, very different from the wistful eagerness of a friendly dog, quivering to join in the sport. Sometimes the boys catch sight of her, and shout up rudely at her window; and I can never sufficiently admire Agrippina's conduct upon these trying occasions, the well-bred composure with which she affects neither to see nor to hear them, nor to be aware that there are such objectionable creatures as children in the world. Sometimes, too, the terrier that lives next door comes out to sun himself in the street, and, beholding my cat sitting well out of reach, he dances madly up and down the pavement, barking with all his might, and rearing himself on his short hind legs, in a futile attempt to dislodge her. Then the spirit of evil enters Agrippina's little heart. The window is open, and she creeps to the extreme edge of the stone sill, stretches herself at full length, peers down smilingly at the frenzied dog, dangles one paw enticingly in the air, and exerts herself with quiet malice to drive him to desperation. Her sense of humor is awakened by his frantic efforts, and by her own absolute security; and not until he is spent with exertion, and lies panting and exhausted on the bricks, does she arch her graceful back, stretch her limbs lazily in the sun, and with one light bound spring from the window to my desk. Wisely has Moncrif observed that a cat is not merely diverted by everything that moves, but is convinced that all nature is occupied exclusively with catering to her diversion.

There is a charming story told by M. Champfleury, who has written so much and so admirably about cats, of a poor hermit whose piety and asceticism were so great that in a vision he was permitted to behold his place in heaven, next to that of St. Gregory, the sovereign pontiff of Christendom. The hermit, who possessed nothing upon earth but a female cat, was abashed by the thought that in the next world he was destined to rank with so powerful a prince of the Church; and perhaps—for who knows the secret springs of spiritual pride?—he fancied that his self-inflicted poverty should win for him an even higher reward. Whereupon a second revelation made known to him that his detachment from the world was by no means so complete as he imagined, for that he loved and valued his cat, the sole companion of his solitude, more than St. Gregory loved and valued all his earthly possessions. The Pope on his throne was the truer ascetic of the two.

This little tale conveys to us, in addition to its excellent moral,—never more needed than at present,—a pleasing truth concerning the lovability of cats. While they have never attained, and never deserve to attain, the widespread and somewhat commonplace popularity of dogs, their fascination is a more potent and irresistible charm. He who yields himself to the sweet seductiveness of a cat is beguiled forever from the simple, honorable friendship of the more generous and open-hearted beast. The small domestic sphinx whose inscrutable eyes never soften with affection; the fetich animal that comes down to us from the far past, adored, hated, and feared, — a god in wise and silent Egypt, a plaything in old Rome, a hunted and unholy creature, suffering one long martyrdom throughout the half-seen, dimly-fathomed Middle Ages, — even now this lovely, uncanny pet is capable of inspiring mingled sentiments of horror and devotion. Those who are under its spell rejoice in their thralldom, and, like M. Champfleury's hermit, grow strangely wedded to this mute, unsympathetic comradeship. Those who have inherited the old, half-fearful aversion render a still finer tribute to the cat's native witchery and power. I have seen middle-aged women, of dignified and tranquil aspect, draw back with unfeigned dismay at the sight of Agrippina, a little ball of gray and yellow fur, curled up in peaceful slumber on the hearth-rug. And this instinctive shrinking has nothing in common with the perfectly reasonable fear we entertain for a terrier snapping and snarling at our heels, or for a mastiff the size of a calf, which our friend assures us is as gentle as a baby, but which looks able and ready to tear us limb from limb. It may be ignominious to be afraid of dogs, but the emotion is one which will bear analysis and explanation; we know exactly what it is we fear; while the uneasiness with which many people behold a harmless and perfectly indifferent cat is a faint reflection of that superstitious terror which the nineteenth century still borrows occasionally from the ninth. We call it by a different name, and account for it on purely natural principles, in deference to progress; but the mediæval peasant who beheld his cat steal out, like a gray shadow, on St. John's Eve, to join in unholy rites, felt the same shuddering abhorrence which we witness and wonder at to-day. He simplified matters somewhat and eased his troubled mind by killing the beast; for cats that ventured forth on the feast of St. John, or on Halloween, or on the second Wednesday in Lent, did so at their peril. Fires blazed for them in every village, and even quiet stay-at-homes were too often hunted from their chimney-corners to a cruel death. There is a receipt signed in 1575 by one Lucas Pommoreux, — abhorred forever be his name! — to whom has been paid the sum of a hundred *sols parisis* "for having supplied for three years all the cats required for the fire on St. John's Day"; and be it remembered that the gracious child afterwards Louis XIII. interceded with Henry IV. for the lives of these poor animals, sacrificed to wicked sport and an unreasoning terror.

Girt around with fear and mystery and subtle associations of evil, the cat comes down to us through the centuries; and from every land fresh traditions of sorcery claim it for their own. In Brittany is still whispered the dreadful tale of the cats that danced with sacrilegious glee around the crucifix until their king was killed; and in Sicily men know that if a black cat serve seven masters in turn he carries the soul of the seventh into hell. In Russia black cats become devils at the end of seven years, and in southern Europe they are merely serving their apprenticeship as witches. Norwegian folk lore is rich in ghastly stories like that of the wealthy miller whose mill has been twice burned down on Whitsun night, and for whom a traveling tailor offers to keep watch. The tailor chalks a circle on the floor, writes the Lord's prayer around it, and waits until midnight, when a troop of cats rush in and hang a great pot of pitch over the fireplace. Again and again they try to overturn this pitch, but every time the tailor frightens them away; and when their leader endeavors stealthily to draw him outside of his magic circle, he cuts off her paw with his knife. Then they all fly howling into the night, and the next morning the miller sees with joy his mill standing whole and unharmed. But the miller's wife cowers under the bedclothes, offering her left hand to the tailor, and hiding as best she can her right arm's bleeding stump.

Finer even than this tale is the well-known story which "Monk" Lewis told to Shelley of a gentleman who, late one night, went to visit a friend living on the outskirts of a forest in east Germany. He lost his path, and, after wandering aimlessly for some time, beheld at last a light streaming from the windows of an old and ruined abbey. Looking in, he saw a procession of cats lowering into a grave a small coffin with a crown upon it. The sight filled him with horror, and, spurring his horse, he rode away as fast as he could, never stopping until he reached his destination, long after midnight. His friend was still awaiting him, and at once he recounted what had happened; whereupon a cat that lay sleeping by the fire sprang to its feet, cried out, "Then I am the king of the cats!" and disappeared like a flash up the chimney.

For my part, I consider this the best cat story in all literature, full of suggestiveness and terror, yet picturesque withal, and leaving ample room in the mind for speculation. Why was not the heir apparent bidden to the royal funeral? Was there a disputed succession, and how are such points settled in the mysterious domain of cat-land? The notion that these animals gather in ghost-haunted churches and castles for their nocturnal revels is one common to all parts of Europe. We remember how the little maiden of the Mountain Idyl confides to Heine that the innocent-looking cat in the chimney-corner is really a witch, and that at midnight, when the storm is high, she steals away to the ruined keep, where the spirits of the dead wait spellbound for the word that shall waken them. In all scenes of impish revelry cats play a prominent part, although occasionally, by virtue of their dual natures, they serve as barriers against the powers of evil. There is the old story of the witch's cat that was grateful to the good girl who gave it some ham to eat, — I may observe here, parenthetically, that I have never known a cat that would touch ham; and there is the fine bit of Italian folk lore about the servant maid who, with no other protector than a black cat, ventures to disturb a procession of ghosts on the dreadful Night of the Dead. "It is well for you that the cat lies in your arms," the angry spirit says to her; "otherwise what I am you also would be." The last pale reflex of a universal tradition I found two years ago in London, where the bad behavior of the Westminster cats — proverbially the most dissolute and profligate specimens of their race — has given rise to the pleasing legend of a country house whither these rakish animals retire for nights of gay festivity, and whence they return in the early morning, jaded, repentant, and forlorn.

Of late years there has been a rapid and promising growth of what disaffected and alliterative critics call the "cat cult," and poets and painters vie with one another in celebrating the charms of this long-neglected pet. Mr. M. H. Spielmann's beautiful volume in praise of Madame Henriette Ronner and her pictures is a treasure upon which many an ardent lover of cats will cast wandering and wistful glances. It is impossible for even the most disciplined spirit not to yearn over these little furry darlings, these gentle, mischievous, lazy, irresistible things. As for Banjo, that dear and sentimental kitten, with his head on one side like Lydia Languish, and a decorous melancholy suffusing his splendid eyes, let any obdurate scorner of the race look at his loveliness and be converted. Mrs. Graham R. Tomson's pretty anthology, Concerning Cats, is another step in the right direction; a dainty volume of selections from French and English verse, where we may find old favorites like Cowper's Retired Cat and Calverly's Sad Memories, graceful epitaphs on departed pussies, some delightful poems from Baudelaire, and three, no less delightful, from the pen of Mrs. Tomson herself, whose preface, or "foreword," is enough to win for her at once the friendship and sympathy of the elect. The book, while it contains a good deal that might well have been omitted, is necessarily a small one; for poets, English poets especially, have just begun to sing the praises of the cat, as they have for generations sung the praises of the horse and dog. Nevertheless, all English literature, and all the literatures of every land, are full of charming allusions to this friendly animal, — allusions the brevity of which only enhances their value. Those two delicious lines of Herrick's, for example,

> And the brisk mouse may feast herself with crumbs,
> Till that the green-eyed kitling comes

are worth the whole of Wordsworth's solemn poem The Kitten and Falling Leaves. What did Wordsworth know of the innate vanity, the affectation and coquetry, of kittenhood? He saw the little beast gamboling on the wall, and he fancied her as innocent as she looked, — as though any living creature *could* be as innocent as a kitten looks! With touching simplicity he believed her all unconscious of the admiration she was exciting.

> What would little Tabby care
> For the plaudits of the crowd?
> Over happy to be proud,
> Over wealthy in the treasure
> Of her own exceeding pleasure!

Ah, the arrant knavery of that kitten! The tiny impostor, showing off her best tricks, and feigning to be occupied exclusively with her own infantile diversion! We can see her now, prancing and paddling after the leaves, and all the while peeping out of "the tail o' her ee" at the serene poet and philosopher, and waving her naughty tail in glee over his confidence and condescension.

Heine's pretty lines,

> And close beside me the cat sits purring,
> Warming her paws at the cheery gleam;
> The flames keep flitting, and flicking, and whirring;
> My mind is wrapped in a realm of dream,

find their English echo in the letter Shelley writes to Peacock, describing, half wistfully, the shrines of the Penates, "whose hymns are the purring of kittens, the hissing of kettles, the long talks over the past and dead, the laugh of children, the warm wind of summer filling the quiet house, and the pelting storm of winter struggling in vain for entrance." How incomplete would these pictures be, how incomplete is any fireside sketch, without its purring kitten or drowsy cat!

> The queen I am o' that cozy place;
> As with ilka paw I dicht my face,
> I sing an' purr with mickle grace.

This is the sphinx of the hearthstone, the little god of domesticity, whose presence turns a house into a home. Even the chilly desolation of a hotel may be rendered endurable by these affable and discriminating creatures; for one of them, as we know, once welcomed Sir Walter Scott, and softened for him the unfamiliar and unloved surroundings. "There are no dogs in the hotel where I lodge," he writes to Abbotsford from London, "but a tolerably conversable cat *who* eats a mess of cream with me in the morning." Of course it did, the wise and lynx-eyed beast! I make no doubt that, day after day and week after week, that cat had wandered superbly amid the common throng of lodgers, showing favor to none, and growing cynical and disillusioned by constant contact with a crowd. Then, one morning, it spied the noble, rugged face which neither man nor beast could look upon without loving, and forthwith tendered its allegiance on the spot. Only "tolerably conversable" it was, this reserved and town-bred animal; less urbane because less happy than the much-respected retainer at Abbotsford, Master Hinse of Hinsefeld, whom Sir Walter called his friend. "Ah, mon grand ami, vous avez tué mon autre grand ami!" he sighed, when the huge hound Nimrod ended poor Hinse's placid career. And if Scott sometimes seems to disparage cats, as when he unkindly compares Oliver le Dain to one, in *Quentin Durward,* he atones for such indignity by the use of the little pronoun "who" when writing of the London puss. My own habit is to say "who" on similar occasions, and I am glad to have so excellent an authority.

It were an endless though a pleasant task to recount all that has been said, and well said, in praise of the cat by those who have rightly valued her companionship. Théophile Gautier's charming pages are too familiar for comment. Who has not read with delight of the Black and White Dynasties that for so long ruled with gentle sway over his hearth and heart; of Madame Théophile, who thought the parrot was a green chicken; of Don Pierrot de Navarre, who deeply resented his master's staying out late at night; of the graceful and fastidious Seraphita; the gluttonous Enjolras; the acute Bohemian, Gavroche; the courteous and well-mannered Éponine, who received M. Gautier's guests in the drawing-room and dined at his table, taking each course as it was served, and restraining any rude distaste for food not to her fancy. "Her place was laid without a knife and fork, indeed, but with a glass, and she went regularly through dinner, from soup to dessert, awaiting her turn to be helped, and behaving with a quiet propriety which most children might imitate with advantage. At the first stroke of the bell she would appear, and when I came into the dining-room she would be at her post, upright on her chair, her forepaws on the edge of the table-cloth; and she would present her smooth forehead to be kissed, like a well-bred little girl who was affectionately polite to relatives and old people."

I have read this pretty description several times to Agrippina, who is extremely wayward and capricious about her food, rejecting plaintively one day the viands which she had eaten with apparent enjoyment the day before. In fact, the difficulty of catering to her is so well understood by tradesmen that recently, when the housemaid carried her on an errand to the grocery, — Agrippina is very fond of these jaunts and of the admiration she excites, — the grocer, a fatherly man, with cats of his own, said briskly, "Is this the little lady who eats the biscuits?" and presented her on the spot with several choice varieties from which to choose. She is fastidious, too, about the way in which her meals are served; disliking any other dishes than her own, which are of blue and white china; requiring that her meat should be cut up fine and all the fat removed, and that her morning oatmeal should be well sugared and creamed. Milk she holds in scorn. My friends tell me sometimes that it is not the common custom of cats to receive so much attention at table, and that it is my fault Agrippina is so exacting; but such grumblers fail to take into consideration the marked individuality that is the charm of every kindly treated puss. She differs from her sisters as widely as one woman differs from another, and reveals varying characteristics of good and evil, varying powers of intelligence and adaptation. She scales splendid heights of virtue, and, unlike Sir Thomas Browne, is "singular in offenses." Even those primitive instincts which we believe all animals hold in common are lost in acquired ethics and depravity. No heroism could surpass that of the London cat that crawled back five times under the stage of the burning theatre to rescue her litter of kittens, and, having carried four of them to safety, perished devotedly with the fifth. On the other hand, I know of a cat that drowned her three kittens in a water-butt, for no reason, apparently, save to be rid of them, and that she might lie in peace on the hearth-rug, — a murder well planned, deliberate, and cruel.

So Tiberius might have sat,
Had Tiberius been a cat.

Only in her grace and beauty, her love of comfort, her dignity of bearing, her courteous reserve, and her independence of character does puss remain immutable and unchanged. These are the traits which win for her the warmest corner by the fire, and the unshaken regard of those who value her friendship and aspire to her affection. These are the traits so subtly suggested by Mrs. Tomson in a sonnet which every true lover of cats feels in his heart *must* have been addressed to his own particular pet: —

Half gentle kindliness, and half disdain,
Thou comest to my call, serenely suave,
With humming speech and gracious gestures grave,
In salutation courtly and urbane;
Yet must I humble me thy grace to gain,
For wiles may win thee, but no arts enslave;
And nowhere gladly thou abidest, save
Where naught disturbs the concord of thy reign.

Sphinx of my quiet hearth! who deignst to dwell
Friend of my toil, companion of mine ease,
Thine is the lore of Ra and Rameses;
That men forget dost thou remember well,
Beholden still in blinking reveries,
With sombre sea-green gaze inscrutable.

June 1892

JEAN KENYON MACKENZIE

1874–1936

Who would own to a prejudice? Yet I admit that on some early journeys I was inoculated with a deep distrust of missionaries. It was my fault and my misfortune too, for the missionaries I had taken up with for unescapable half hours, sailing both East and West, were bedeviled with that exasperating sort of miseducation which, knowing it knows, cannot conceive that much of what it knows is nonsense. As I grew older and more philosophical it became evident that with missionaries even more than the rest of us opinions immutably held give granite to character. Still what the opinions are does make a difference, and the quality of the person who holds them makes all the difference in the world.

It was Jean Mackenzie who converted me to missionaries. She was a wisp of a woman, girlish, pale, and slender, with a laugh like the tinkle of a silver bell and an instant sympathy which in time came to make me almost as dear to her as the blacks of the Congo. Her father was a Scotch Divine, and at their simple house in Riverdale the last evening of every week was the counterpart of "The Cotter's Saturday Night." So quiet, so natural was the scene of unaffected piety it made the heart stick in the throat. Never have I so strongly felt the charm of natural goodness as when it lived and wrought in Jean Mackenzie.

I had heard of her talent for letter writing and called upon her. Obviously she was startled by an editor's visit, and told me she was no writer. "You have written letters home," said I, "and my guess is that your father and mother have kept them." "Yes," she replied, "isn't it absurd, there is a whole trunkful upstairs."

I had what I wanted. The trunkful went back to Boston with me and out of that faithful record came a clearer picture of the hearts of black men and women than I have ever known. There came beside the realization of what goodness can accomplish.

I can see her now on a visit to my own woods in Beverly, walking noiselessly among the leaves with the flat forest tread of a wild creature. I would tease her with the ancient superiority of the missionary caste: —

> Shall we whose souls are lighted
> With wisdom from on high,
> Shall we to men benighted
> The lamp of life deny?

And in return her laughter filled the wood. Hers was no spirit of Lady Bountiful giving of her largess. She was merely a sister sharing with sisters and with brothers too.

She told me stories of her work. Once near the African coast she heard of a village hidden twenty miles away in the depths of the forest where help was needed. Off she went with a single Negro guide for company. When she reached her destination it was black night and coming out of the forest she rubbed her eyes at a huge bonfire blazing in the clearing. Some jubilation was in progress. That she knew, for women were not in evidence and the young bucks were cavorting about the blaze singing their witching songs. They received her with respect, but she thought best to insist on going supperless to bed and was shown to her quarters — a huge barnlike room reached by an outside ladder which formed the upper chamber of the Powwow house where the central celebration was being held. She spread her blankets but could not sleep. The noise below which had first been hushed broke out into spasms of laughter and then into a wild chorus of excited catcalls. Very quietly Jean groped her way to a knothole in the floor. There she could see the whole scene. A score of glistening black bodies were circled round a keg of whiskey and, as the dipper circulated, the hubbub rose. Instantly her resolve was taken. Straight down the ladder she climbed and walked to the center of the hall.

"Take me home," she said. "Where whiskey is, white women do not go. I start at once."

The effect was instantaneous. Three or four blacks seized the keg and spilled the entire contents on the ground. "No whiskey here," they said, "do white woman stay."

It was a temperance story without the unction.

Exile and Postman

JEAN KENYON MACKENZIE

It used to make me homesick, in our little African clearing, to see the albino woman. She would move about among her brown companions like a flame — and her white body, that flickered in the sun and glimmered in the shade, used to knock at the door of nostalgia. Homesick people always long for a visit, and that albino was so white!

Once, to our neighborhood, where in those days white women did not come, there came a white woman. She did not lodge with us; she lodged with the white officer because she was an officer's wife. We used to wonder if she would call upon us. One of us had a pair of field-glasses, and we used to watch her little figure coming and going about the clearing on the government hill. When one day she was seen to come down into our valley by the zigzag trail, we thought we had a Visit. I cannot tell you how anxious we were, in that little bark house, to make a good appearance — or what fresh disposals were made, with our eyes upon that descent, of our properties. I do not wish to make you too sad, but that white woman did not visit us. She went away. She did not know about us, or about exiles — that they are always dreaming of a Visit.

It seems a hard thing, sometimes, when night closes the doors of all the little trails, that the day has passed without a visitor. It is true of exiles that they have the most unreasonable expectations of the sort, based perhaps upon the migrations of swallows, and not relinquished until the hour of dusk. Yes, then the little trails of the forest are perceived by the mind's eye — which like a cat's eyes sees them better for the dark — to wander away into an infinite distance and a solitude.

Dusk is altogether the most illuminating hour for the exile; he then knows so exactly where he is; he has a perfectly visual sense of his surroundings. He sees where he is, but how came he to be there? The geography of his circumstance is plain, but not the logic. He who has no other companions than himself suspects this companion, in that hour of dusk, to be a fool. It must be a poor fool, he thinks, who has drifted into such a clearing by such a river!

The forest of the Cameroon is as good a place as any to be homesick; but I will not be saying that the members of my profession — and I am a missionary — are chronic sufferers. Missionaries are, in the main, gay, and for excellent reasons — some of them pagan reasons, for they are little brothers of Antæus; some of them Christian reasons, for they are of the company of successful fishermen. A fisherman with a good catch can defy even the dusk; his string of silver fish is a lantern to his feet.

No, if there were an altar and a service to placate nostalgia it would not be that fisherman who would most attend that service. The path to that altar would be worn brown by the feet of the trader. I think the trader is lonelier than the missionaries are; he is better versed in solitude. He goes into the forest with a backward look; he comes out of the forest sometimes with a secret and a stricken countenance. More than missionaries do, he does. More often than they, he builds out of his lonely horror and the license of solitude a perverse habitation for his soul. Sometimes — and this is very sad — he is afraid. He lingers and lingers on the margin of that green sea of forest.

"The heart," say the Bulu, "has gone to hide in the dark." And this is a Bulu way of saying that the heart is not worn upon the sleeve. Well, upon the sleeve of the white-drill suits that beach-traders wear there is, I will agree, no device of hearts. But those lonely inland traders, — those that have traveled ten, twenty, thirty days from their kind, — what is that they sometimes seem to wear upon the sleeve of their singlets? And who cares where he wears his heart if there is never a white man's eye to fall upon it! In those little bark huts on the trading posts, where young white men pale with the passing hours, there comes to be a careless fashion in wear, whether of hearts or of collars. In the warm dusk of those little houses, where there is an earthen floor, where there are tin trade-boxes as bright as jockeys' jackets, where there are trade-cloths printed with violent designs, where there is salt fish and cheap scent and tobacco, — where all these desirable things may be had for ivory and rubber, — there the trader may wear his heart upon his sleeve without shame. None of those brilliant eyes, set in those dark faces, know a white man's heart when they see it. There in his hut is a monotony of brown bodies quick with vehement gestures; there is a tumult of controversy in a tongue he does not know. The sudden glitter of brass ornament is there and the glitter of brass spears. There are fantastic head-dresses studded with buttons and shells and beads, and scented with the odor of wood-fires. Between those brown bodies and the body of the white man lies the counter. More lies between them than this. There are between them such barriers that the white man is not more lonely when he is alone.

Yet how still it is of an idle day under the thatched leaves of that little house! The sun does its exaggerated violence to the yellow earth of the clearing; the forest hangs its arras over its secret. How far it is, in this place not named on the map, from Manchester! How, when the rain falls, it is other than rainfall on the Clyde! How the pale fruit that hangs high on the *ajap* tree is not like the apples that ripen in Wishaw!

Do not speak of apples! Nostalgia in her cruel equipment carries a scented phantom apple.

At night there is about that young trader a trouble of drums that never rest. There is the sharp concerted cry of the dancers. There is the concerted wail for the dead. There is about him all the rhythmic beating of the mysterious life of his neighborhood, tormenting him where he lies under his mosquito net. For this he will rise and walk about, the ember of his pipe drifting back and forth in the dark, and his gramophone, roused by himself, making its limited obedient effort.

There is this about a gramophone: it is a thing that speaks the home tongue. I have seen him sitting under the eaves of his little hut, by his little table spread with a checkered cloth, his gramophone beside him, trying, with its tale of the old grouse gunroom, to divert that lonely meal. Now that I think of it, the gramophone is a kind of hero of my little piece — a kind of David with five tunes to do battle with nostalgia. Back in the tent broods Saul, and this poor patient David plays the endless round of five tunes. Until some day there is a javelin in the wall, and a proud black man goes away with a gramophone into the wilderness.

The night sky does more permanent ministry to the homesick, and of all the bright ministers the moon is the most effectual. It is the great reflector of lights; there it comes, swinging up its old path in the sky, and the fires of home are mirrored on its disk. You who read have spread your hands, in your hour of homesickness, to those phantom fires — and other hands are always spread. Some of us were sitting on our heels about a little flame in a new clearing; all of us were alien in that clearing; one of us was white. And the black women said to the white woman when the moonlight fell upon all those women faces, —

"The moon looks upon the villages and upon the home village. We black people, when we sit in the towns of strangers and the moon shines, we say, 'Now by the light of this same moon the people at home dance to the drums!' However far we walk, we look upon the moon and we remember our friends at home."

Upon another moonlight night, sitting in a forest camp with young black girls for companions, these sang for me a little set of songs — the songs, they told me, of the moon: —

Ah, moné zip, alu a danéya! Ah, moné zip!

This little refrain they sang, clapping their hands ever so lightly, and the meaning of the singing was a warning:

Ah, little gazelle, the night has deepened! Ah, little gazelle!

It was a song of the moon, a song for wanderers. And the moon on that remembered night, dragging its net of broken silver cords in among the trees of the forest, caught everywhere the wandering hearts and drew them back on the little rough trails to the home fires. Every night that is a moonlight night there is the casting of that silver net upon far rivers and forests deeper than rivers — wherever aliens make a bed of leaves or sleep on a canvas cot.

On such a night, and caught in such a net, I have met the postman. Yes, on just such a night, when the world appeared as it hangs in space, a crystal globe, and when so observed from a little clearing in an African forest, it was seen to be charted for voyagers, and all its little paths ran readily about the globe to that gilt side which is home. On such a night, and upon such a path, I met the postman.

To hang upon a little wicket gate under the moon at the end of a moon-filled clearing in a breach of the forest, — to see the black body of the postman suddenly darken the checkered light upon the path from the west, — how to speak of this adventure with moderation! How to speak of postmen at all with moderation! And of those postmen who thread the lonely forests of the world, their loads upon their backs, their rations of salt fish on top of their loads; how to recall their aspects, their monthly or bi-monthly or semi-annual arrivals, the priceless treasures they carry! how speak of these things to men and women who have never followed the little gazelle into those forests where the night has deepened; who have never felt the divinity in postmen!

Imagine that there is a people in this world who let a postman walk up the path unattended, and who wait until he knocks on the door! Who do not shout to their neighbors when they receive a letter, and who receive one every day! These items alone prove the truth of the Bulu proverb that there are tribes and tribes, and customs and customs.

And I will agree that there are, even on the trails of the wilderness, postmen and postmen. There are even, though I hate to dwell upon it, postmen whom I do not trust. Not all postmen have wings upon their heels. The ideal postman does of course fly. He is like

The bird let loose in eastern skies
When hastening fondly home.

He avoids idle wanderers. But they do not all do so. I remember to have been wakened one night in a village by the gossip of two old headmen. They had met before my tent; there in the moonlight they chatted together. All the little life of the village was sleeping; the two old men alone were abroad. They were about the business of the post. It is a pioneer custom in Africa, east and west, that the white man's local letter is franked from town to town. The black man to whom the white man gives his letter carries it to the headman of the next settlement, who carries it in turn to his brother headman down the trail; and so from hand to hand, by day and by night, with a glance from any passing white man, the letter goes forward. Such a letter—carried as the custom is, in a split rod from which there hung, like a flag, a bit of turkey red—changed hands that night before my tent. And now I write it in a white man's book that the postmen loitered.

To stand and chat there in the moonlight with the exile's letter in your hands—how could you do that, you two old heartless headmen? I watched you from my little green tent. It is remembered of you that you so delayed, while in some lonely hamlet under that same moon a white man sickened for a letter. And when one gave the forked stick to the other, it was then too late. If indeed, as you would say, you spoke no more than five words of gossip one to the other, those words were five too many. It is remembered of you, and a thousand nights since when I have waited for the mail, if it were a moonlight night, I have told myself with an extreme self-pity and a bitterness, "The carrier is gossiping in some clearing." I have seen in my heart that man with the load of mail upon his back, standing for hours by a friend of his, laughing and asking news one of the other. This conjured vision of two black men holding up the mail is the sad issue of an imagination infected beyond cleansing. You see, *I saw them do it.*

Some postmen have come in late because their feet were sore. And some, in passing through their home town, have permitted themselves an illness or a marriage. Some have waited, with the mail in their loads, to bury the dead. Such a postman, so given to misadventures and clumsy ill-timed tragedies, was once late to the tune of eleven days. Who remembers what delayed him or what exquisite reasons he gave? And who of us in that little clearing forgets the long hours of that year of days?

Another postman, of an extreme beauty and an extreme speed, arrived before his time. There was a shouting when he came. All the inhabitants of that little settlement of white men called to each other; the four or five of them filled a room of a bark house — those white faces that were growing daily like the face of the Asra, "bleich und bleicher," were all lit by the flame of the mail. In all that little commonwealth, with its pioneer trades and its pioneer gardens and its pioneer hospital and school and church — in all that settlement all the busy crude wheels of industry slackened and stood still while the white men opened the load of the mail.

"Now they will be reading the *books* from home!"

And of Ebengé, that young carrier, it is still remembered that he arrived before he was due. "Ah, Ebengé," you still say to him from time to time, "that was a fine walking you walked that walk so long ago when you slept but three nights with the mail!"

Another postman, never to be forgotten by those exiles whom he served, never came at all. This was a boy, too young, you would think, for his great office. The letters in his little pack were from husbands to wives, and they must travel a hundred miles of forest-trail in time of war. Not twenty miles they traveled when the postman, surrounded by black soldiers, was called to deliver. He did not deliver. He could not give the white man's letters to another hand. He said, No, he could not. And for this they killed him. That young body tarried forever upon the trail, witnessing in that interminable delay — as Ebengé had witnessed in his swift coming — to the sacred element in the mail.

Here is the king's touch for the king's evil — the hand of the postman dropping a letter. For this the victims of nostalgia do long service. For this they scribble, in their lonely and various dwellings, their letters. There is a night, in those alien settlements all about the world, that is unlike other nights. It is the night before the mail is closed. The lamp is full of oil that night, and the cup of coffee is at the elbow. On and on, while the stars march, the white man's hand runs upon the page. In villages where there are no street lamps, the white man's window is a lamp all night of the night before the mail. From steamers that are tied to trees among the rushes, in rivers that you do not know, the officer on watch may look all night through such a window at such a man writing, writing a long, long letter — the beating heart of man, articulate in all that heartless darkness.

How quick a seed, you would say, the seed in such a letter! How such a letter must bear, some sixty-, some an hundred-fold! Yet myself I saw this: I saw the harbor-master of Kabinda, a settlement of white men on the west coast of Africa, come aboard the monthly steamer to get the mail. He was an old Portuguese, coffee-colored in his gray linen suit. A long time he had been harbor-master, and many times he had taken the brown bag of mail ashore. This day, when he lifted his bag, he "hefted" it: the lightness of it in his hand made him smile. Some irony that was the fruit of his long experience of exiles and their letters made that old indifferent man curl the lip. I think that in Kabinda that night there went white men hungry to bed. I would not like to live in Kabinda, where the postman is so old and so wise. These white postmen know too much; they can count more than ten. And other things they know: they know a thing too sad to tell. Better Ebengé, who ran so swiftly with his load, or little Esam, who thought that for a load of letters some would even dare to die.

January 1917

KATHERINE PEABODY GIRLING

1861–1938

This unpretentious story not easily forgotten was sent the Atlantic *by an author not otherwise represented in the magazine. It is entirely veracious, but no tale of genii or of fairy is more wonderful, so far has imagination lagged behind the realities.*

When Hannah Var Eight Yar Old

KATHERINE PEABODY GIRLING

"WERE you a little girl, Hannah, when you came to America?" I asked.

"No," she replied, letting her sewing fall in her lap as her grave eyes sought mine slowly, "I var a big girl eight yar old."

"Eight years old? How big you must have been! Can you tell me about it? Why you came?"

The recent accounts of people driven to America by tragedy, or drawn by a larger hope of finding a life to live in addition to earning a living, had colored my thoughts for days. Have all immigrants — the will-less, leaden people who pass in droves through our railway stations; the patient, indifferent toilers by the roadside; the maids who cook and mend for us; this girl who sits sewing with me to-day — a memory and a vision? Is each of them in some degree a Mary Antin? So I closed the magazine and asked her. — "A big girl eight yar old," she said.

"Oh, well," Hannah explained, "in Old Country if you are eight yar old and comes younger child'n in familie, you are old woman; you gotta be, or who shall help de moder?"

"Yes? Did your father and mother bring you?" I continued, probing for the story.

"No, — fader and moder var daid. My h'aunt, my fader's broder's wife, se came for us. It cost her twenty-eight dollar, but se do it."

"But surely you can't go to Sweden and return for twenty-eight dollars!"

"Seventeen yar ago, yes, but of course you must to take your own providings. It don't require much." Hannah's shoulders drew together expressively. "Madam knows she is apt to miss her appetite at sea!"

"But too well." I shrugged sympathetically. Then we both laughed.

"I can to tell you how it is I came on Ahmericah, but"—Hannah waited for words to express her warning—"it will make you a sharp sadness."

"Please."

"I don't know if I can tell it to you good, but I tell it so good as I can. My fader he var Swedish fisherman vat h'own his boat and go away by weeks and weeks, and sometimes comes strong wedder and he can't make it to get home quick. My moder se var German." Hannah hesitated, and then in lowered tones of soft apology added, "Se var a ver' pretty woman. Var three child'n more as me—Olga var six yar old, and Hilda four, and Jens—well, Jens var just a baby, suppose yar and half. We live in a little house close on by de sea. It is yust a little house, but it can to have a shed with a floor of stone. The door of de shed is broken so it is like a window mitout glass.

"The house is close on by a big dock where in somer-time comes big excursion-steamer mit—suppose hundert tourist people who climb on de mountain up de road. My moder se sell dem hot coffee, also bread and cheese, but dat is not de reason why we live in de little so lonesome house. It is de big dock is de reason. My fader he can to come home from late fishings mitout needing dat he sall walk on de roads. In Sweden in winter de roads swallow snow till it makes dangersome to you to walk because hides holes to step in. We live dare all somer, but in late autumn my fader he say, 'What about de winter?'

"My moder se say, 'I don't know, but anyway ve try it vonce.'

"Den my fader he go avay in his boad and my moder se get bad cold and comes sickness on her, and ven se couldn't to keep care on us by reason se is too weak, se lay on de cot in de kitchen-room and vatch on me dat I sall learn to keep care on de child'n."

"But what did you live on? How did you keep warm?"

"Oh,—is plenty fuel, and ve make hot stew of dried meat mit rice and raisins.

"One day my moder se say me, 'Hannah,' se say, 'you bain a big girl. I must to tell you sometings. You fader is very late, it seems, and winter comes now. I cannot to wait much more. It is soon I got to go.

You mustn't take a fear of me if I come all white like de snow and don't talk mit you any more. De little child'n dey will take a fear and cry. I cannot to bring a fear on my little child'n.'

"So se tell me what I shall do — I sall close bot' her eyes up and tie her hands togeder and lock de shed door."

"The shed door!"

"Ya."

Hannah had resumed her sewing. Her thread fairly snapped as stitch fell by even stitch with monotonous rhythm. In quiet, uneventful tone she continued, —

"So one night pretty soon se make dat I sall bring her best nightgown and help her mit to put it on. Den se kiss de little child'n in dair sleepings and se sit on a stool by de fire and say I sall put Jens in her arms. Se try to rock back and fort' and se sing on him a little hymn. But se is too weak, and I must to take him. Den se put on me a shawl and tie it behind under my arms, and se lean heavy on me, and we go out into de shed. My moder se do her bare feet on de stone floor. Se have yust but her nightgown on, but it is her best one with crocheted lace at de neck and wrists. Se tell me I sall put de ironing-board across two chair-seats, but it is too heavy and se sall try to help me, but comes coughing on her and se must to hold on by de shed door. Se look out across de road and de mountain all mit snow white and mit moonlight cold. And blood is on her lips but se wipe it away mit a snow bunch. Well, anyway, we do de ironing-board across de chair-seats and I spread a white sheet and put a head-cushion and my moder lie down and I cover her mit a more other sheet over.

"'Oh, moder,' I say, 'let me make some warm coverings on you.'

"'No,' se say, so soft dat I listen mit my ear, 'I must to come here while I yet have de stren'th, but I want to go quick away, and in de cold I go more quick. Oh, Hannah!' se say, 'my big daughter! You are so comfortable to me!'

"So I hold my moder's hand. Pretty soon it comes cold. I klapp it mit mine, but it comes more cold. I crumple it up and breathe my hot breath in it, but it comes not warm any more. So mit my fader's Sunday handkerchief I bind her eyes like if you play Blindman mit de child'n, and mit an apron-string I tie her hands together. Den I go back and make my hands warm in de kitchen-room and I take de comb down off de string, and I go back to my moder and make her hair in two braids like as I did all when se was sick. My moder se haf very strong hair; it is down by her knees on and so yellow, — so yellow as a copper tea-kettle! It could to haf been red but it yust are not. Den I lock de shed door and crawl in bed mit de child'n to make me warm.

"Next day I tell de child'n dat moder is gone away. Dey cry some, but pretty soon dey shut up. Anyway, it is so long se haf lain on de cot in de kitchen-room dat dey don't haf to miss her.

"So I keep care on de child'n and play wid dem, and some days go by. Comes stronger wedder mit storms of sleet and snow, and de wind sob and cry. Comes nobody on. At night when de child'n are sleeping I unlock de shed door and go to see if it makes all right mit my moder. Sometimes it is by the moonlight I see on her, but more often it is by a candle-glimmer."

Hannah broke the subdued tone of her narrative to add in a lower, more confiding note, "It is mit me now dat when I see a candle on light I haf a sharp sadness.

"Pretty soon de wedder is more better, and comes a man trompling troo de snow to tell my moder dat her husband can't come home yust yet — he is drowned in de sea. When he see how it is mit my moder and mit me and de little child'n, de water stands in his eyes — ya. And he go on, troo de snow, tree, four mile nearer on de city to de big castle where live de lady wat h'own all de land and se come in sleigh mit four horsen and big robes of fur and yingling bells. Se see on my moder and se go quick away, but so soon as it can, se come again and se do on my moder a white robe, heavy mit lace, most beautiful! and white stockings of silk and white slippers broidered mit pearlen. Se leaf my moder's hair, as I fix it, in two braids, but se put a wreath of flowers, white and green, yust like de real ones. Is few real flowers in Sweden in winter. Anyway, dese var like de flowers a girl vat gets married should to wear. Den my lady se send her sleigh dat all de people should come and see on de so brave woman vat couldn't to bring a fear on her little child'n. And de people dey make admiration on my moder. Dey say it is de prettiest dey ever see it, and dey make pity dat se couldn't to see it herself." She paused and breathed deeply. "I wish se could have to see dose slippers!"

"And did no one tell you that you were a wonderful little girl?"

"Oh, vell — I var eight yar old."

"But what became of you all?"

"My lady took us home in her sleigh mit — I want to stay mit my moder, but se say I sall come to keep care on de child'n dat dey don't cry. And dey don't cry — dey laugh mit de yingling bells. De need was on me strong, but I don't cry before my lady. Se var great dame vat go in de court mit de queen. Se sent men and dey do my moder in a coffin and carry her to a little chapel house in cemetaire and in de spring ven de snow is gone dey bury her. My lady se put a white stone mit my moder's name and some poetry — I can't to say it good in English, but it says, 'The stren'th in the heart of her poor is the hope of Sweden.' "

"And then did your aunt come?"

"Ya; my lady se wrote on my fader's broder vat var in Ahmericah. Se say we can to stay mit her, but my onkle he send his wife, and we come back mit her on Ahmericah, und dat is all how I came to be here."

June 1913

HAVELOCK ELLIS

1859–1939

Reformers may be gratefully remembered, but the gratitude is apt to be not at the moment but in remembrance. The trail Ellis blazed has become a broad highway. Through most of his life his work was persecuted, and what is worse, prosecuted. His Studies in the Psychology of Sex, *of which the first volume was begun in 1891, did more than mention the unmentionable. It pursued a detailed inquiry in which the proprieties had no place. Banned in England, it came to life — God knows how — in these United States, where its effect on the study of sexual psychology was immediate and lasting. Ellis's profounder studies led him to the consideration of phenomena along the fringes of his central problem, and this paper on dancing offers a pleasant example of his imaginative reasoning.*

The Philosophy of Dancing

HAVELOCK ELLIS

I

DANCING and architecture are the two primary and essential arts. The art of dancing stands at the source of all the arts that express themselves first in the human person. The art of architecture is the beginning of all the arts that lie outside the person. Music, acting, poetry, proceed in the one mighty stream; sculpture, painting, all the arts of design, in the other. There is no primary art outside these two arts, for their origin is far earlier than man himself; and dancing came first.

That is one reason why dancing, however it may at times be scorned by passing fashions, has a profound and eternal attraction even for those one might suppose furthest from its influence. The philosopher and the child are here at one. The joyous beat of the feet of children, the cosmic play of philosophers' thoughts, rise and fall to the same rhythm. If we are indifferent to the art of dancing we have failed to understand, not merely the supreme manifestation of physical life, but also the supreme symbol of spiritual life.

The significance of dancing, in the wide sense, thus lies in the fact that it is simply an intimate concrete appeal of that general rhythm which marks all the physical and spiritual manifestations of life. Dancing is the primitive expression alike of religion and of love, — of religion from the earliest human times we know of, and of love from a period long anterior to the coming of man. The art of dancing, moreover, is intimately entwined with all human traditions of war, of labor, of pleasure, of education, while some of the wisest philosophers and the most ancient civilizations have regarded the dance as the pattern in accordance with which the moral life of man must be woven. To realize, therefore, what dancing means for mankind, — the poignancy and the many-sidedness of its appeal, — we must survey the whole sweep of human life, both at its highest and at its deepest moments.

II

"What do you dance?" When a man belonging to one branch of the great Bantu division of mankind met a member of another, said Livingstone, that was the question he asked. What a man danced, that was his tribe, his social customs, his religion; for, as an anthropologist has recently put it, "a savage does not preach his religion, he dances it." There are peoples in the world who have no secular dances, only religious dances, and some investigators believe that every dance was of religious origin. That view seems too extreme, even if we admit that some even of our modern dances, like the waltz, may have been originally religious. It is more reasonable to suppose, with Wundt, that the dance was, in the beginning, the expression of the whole man.

Yet among primitive peoples religion is so large a part of life that the dance inevitably becomes of supreme religious importance. To dance was at once both to worship and to pray. Just as we still find in our Prayer Books that there are divine services for all the great fundamental acts of life, for birth, for marriage, for death, as well as for the cosmic procession of the world as marked by ecclesiastical festivals, and for the great catastrophes of nature, such as droughts, so also it has ever been among primitive peoples. For all the solemn occasions of life, for bridals and for funerals, for seed-time and for harvest, for war and for peace, for all these things, there were fitting dances.

To-day we find religious people who in church pray for rain or for the restoration of their friends to health. Their forefathers also desired these things but, instead of praying for them, they danced for them the fitting dance which tradition had handed down, and which the chief or the medicine-man solemnly conducted. The gods themselves danced, as the stars dance in the sky, — so at least the Mexicans, and we may be sure many other peoples, have held, — and to dance is therefore to imitate the gods, to work with them, perhaps to persuade them to work in the direction of our own desires. "Work for us!" is the song-refrain, expressed or implied, of every religious dance. In the worship of solar deities in various countries it was customary to dance around the altar, as the stars dance around the sun. Even in Europe the popular belief that the sun dances on Easter Sunday has perhaps scarcely yet died out. To dance is to take part in the cosmic control of the world. Every sacred dionysian dance is an imitation of the divine dance.

All religions, and not merely those of primitive character, have been at the outset, and sometimes throughout, in some measure saltatory. This is the case all over the world. It is not more pronounced in early Christianity and among the ancient Hebrews who danced before the ark, than among the Australian aborigines whose great *corroborees* are religious dances conducted by the medicine-men with their sacred staves in their hands. Every American Indian tribe seems to have had its own religious dances, varied and elaborate, often with a richness of meaning which the patient study of modern investigators has but slowly revealed. The Shamans in the remote steppes of Northern Siberia have their ecstatic religious dances, and in modern Europe the Turkish dervishes — perhaps of related stock — still dance in their cloisters similar ecstatic dances, combined with song and prayer, as a regular part of devotional service.

These religious dances, it may be realized, are sometimes ecstatic, sometimes pantomimic. It is natural that this should be so. By each road it is possible to penetrate toward the divine mystery of the world. The auto-intoxication of rapturous movement brings the devotee, for a while at least, into that self-forgetful union with the not-self which the mystic ever seeks. Pantomimic dances, on the other hand, with their effort to heighten natural expression and to imitate natural processes, bring the dances into the divine sphere of creation and enable them to assist vicariously in the energy of the gods. The dance thus becomes the presentation of a divine drama, the vital reënactment of a sacred history in which the worshiper is enabled to play a real part. In this way ritual arises.

It is in this sphere — highly primitive as it is — of pantomimic dancing crystallized in ritual, rather than in the sphere of ecstatic dancing, that we may to-day in civilization witness the survivals of dance in religion. The Divine Services of the American Indian, said Lewis Morgan, took the form of "set dances, each with its own name, songs, steps, and costume." At this point the early Christian worshiping the Divine Body was able to enter into spiritual communion with the ancient Egyptian or the American Indian. They are all alike privileged to enter, each in his own way, a sacred mystery, and to participate in the sacrifice of a heavenly Mass.

What by some is considered to be the earliest known Christian ritual — the "Hymn of Jesus," assigned to the second century — is nothing but a sacred dance. Eusebius in the third century stated that Philo's description of the worship of the Therapeuts agreed at all points with Christian custom, and that meant the prominence of dancing, to which indeed Eusebius often refers in connection with Christian worship. It has been supposed by some writers that the Christian Church was originally a theatre, the choir being the raised stage, — even the word *choir,* it is argued, meaning an enclosed space for dancing. It is certain that at the Eucharist the faithful gesticulated with their hands, danced with their feet, flung their bodies about. Chrysostom, who referred to this behavior round the Holy Table at Antioch, only objected to drunken excesses in connection with it; the custom itself he evidently regarded as traditional and right.

While the central function of Christian worship is a sacred drama, a divine Pantomime, the associations of Christianity and dancing are by no means confined to the ritual of the Mass and its later more attenuated transformations. The very idea of dancing had a sacred and mystic meaning to the early Christians, who had meditated profoundly on the text, "We have piped unto you and ye have not danced." Origen prayed that above all things there may be made operative in us the mystery "of the stars dancing in Heaven for the salvation of the Universe." St. Basil, who was enamored of natural things, described the angels dancing in Heaven, and later the author of the *Dieta Salutis* (said to have been St. Bonaventura), which is supposed to have influenced Dante in assigning so large a place to dancing in the *Paradiso,* described dancing as the occupation of the inmates of Heaven, and Christ as the leader of the dance. Even in more modern times an ancient Cornish carol sang of the life of Jesus as of a dance, and represented him as declaring that he died in order that man "may come unto the general dance."

This attitude could not fail to be reflected in practice. Genuine and not merely formalized and unrecognizable dancing, such as the traditionalized Mass, must have been frequently introduced into Christian worship in early times. Until a few centuries ago it remained not uncommon, and it still persists in remote corners of the Christian world. In English cathedrals dancing went on until the fourteenth century. At Paris, Limoges, and elsewhere in France, the priests danced in the choir at Easter up to the seventeenth century; in Roussillon up to the eighteenth century. Roussillon is a province with Spanish traditions, and it was in Spain that religious dancing took deepest root and flourished longest. In the cathedrals of Seville, Toledo, Valencia, and Xeres there was formerly dancing, although it now survives only at a few special festivals in the first. At Alaro in Majorca, also, at the present day, a dancing company called Els Cosiers, on the festival of St. Roch, the patron saint of the place, dance in the church, in fanciful costumes, with tambourines, up to the steps of the high altar, immediately after Mass, and then dance out of the church. In another part of the Christian world, in the Abyssinian Church, — an offshoot of the Eastern Church, — dancing is said still to form a part of the worship.

Dancing, we may see throughout the world, has been so essential, so fundamental a part of all vital and undegenerate religion, that whenever a new religion appears, a religion of the spirit and not merely an anæmic religion of the intellect, we should still have to ask of it the question of the Bantu: What do you dance?

III

Dancing is not only intimately associated with religion, it has an equally intimate association with love. Here indeed the relationship is even more primitive, for it is far older than man. Dancing, said Lucian, is as old as love. Among insects and among birds, for instance, it may be said that dancing is often an essential part of courtship. The male dances, sometimes in rivalry with other males, in order to charm the female; then, after a short or long interval, the female is aroused to share his ardor and join in the dance; the final climax of the dance is in the union of the lovers. This primitive love-dance of insects and birds reappears among savages in various parts of the world, notably in Africa, and in a conventionalized and symbolized form it is still danced in civilization to-day. It is indeed in this aspect that dancing has so often aroused reprobation, from the days of early Christianity until the present, among those for whom the dance has merely been, in the words of a seventeenth-century writer, a series of "immodest and dissolute movements by which the cupidity of the flesh is aroused."

But in Nature and among primitive peoples it has its value precisely on this account. It is a process of courtship and, even more than that, it is a novitiate for love, and a novitiate which was found to be an admirable training for love. Among some peoples, indeed, as the Omahas, the same word meant both to dance and to love. Here we are in the sphere of sexual selection. By his beauty, his energy, his skill, the male must win the female, so impressing the image of himself on her imagination that finally her desire is aroused to overcome her reticence. That is the task of the male throughout nature, and in innumerable species besides man it has been found that the school in which the task may best be learned is the dancing school. The moths and the butterflies, the African ostrich, and the Sumatran Argus pheasant, with their fellows innumerable, have been the precursors of man in the strenuous school of erotic dancing, fitting themselves for selection by the females of their choice as the most splendid progenitors of the future race.

From this point of view, it is clear, the dance performed a double function. On the one hand, the tendency to dance, arising under the obscure stress of this impulse, brought out the best possibilities the individual held the promise of; on the other hand, at the moment of courtship, the display of the activities thus acquired developed, on the sensory side, all the latest possibilities of beauty which at last became conscious in man. That this came about we cannot easily escape concluding. How it came about, how it happens that some of the least intelligent of creatures thus developed a beauty and a grace that are enchanting even to our human eyes, is a miracle effected by the mystery of sex, which we cannot yet comprehend.

When we survey the human world, the erotic dance of the animal world is seen not to have lost but rather to have gained influence. It is no longer the males alone who are thus competing for the love of the females. It comes about by a modification in the method of sexual selection that often not only the men dance for the women, but the women for the men, each striving in a storm of rivalry to arouse and attract the desire of the other. In innumerable parts of the world the season of love is a time which the nubile of each sex devote to dancing in each other's presence, — sometimes one sex, sometimes the other, sometimes both, in the frantic effort to display all the force and energy, the skill and endurance, the beauty and grace, which at this moment are yearning within them to be poured into the vital stream of the race's life.

From this point of view of sexual selection we may better understand the immense ardor with which every part of the wonderful human body has been brought into the play of the dance. The men and women of races spread all over the world have shown a marvelous skill and patience in imparting rhythm and music to the most unlikely, the most rebellious regions of the body, all wrought by desire into potent and dazzling images. To the vigorous races of Northern Europe in their cold damp climate, dancing comes naturally to be dancing of the legs, so naturally that the English poet, as a matter of course, assumes that the dance of Salome was a "twinkling of the feet." But on the opposite side of the world, in Japan and notably in Java and Madagascar, dancing may be exclusively dancing of the arms and hands, in some of the South Sea islands even of the hands and fingers alone. Dancing may even be carried on in the seated posture, as occurs at Fiji in a dance connected with the preparation of the sacred drink, *ava.* In some districts of Southern Tunisia dancing, again, is dancing of the hair, and all night long, till they perhaps fall exhausted, the marriageable girls will move their heads to the rhythm of a song, maintaining their hair in perpetual balance and sway. Elsewhere, notably in Africa, but also sometimes in Polynesia, as well as in the dances that had established themselves in ancient Rome, dancing is dancing of the body, with vibratory or rotatory movements of breasts or flanks.

The complete dance along these lines is, however, that in which all the play of all the chief muscle-groups of the body is harmoniously interwoven. When both sexes take part in such an exercise, developed into an idealized yet passionate pantomime of love, we have the complete erotic dance. In Spain the dance of this kind has sometimes attained its noblest and most harmoniously beautiful expression. It is in the relation of these dances to the primitive mystery of sexual selection that their fascination lies. From the narratives of travelers, it would appear that it was especially in the eighteenth century that among all classes in Spain dancing of this kind was immensely popular. The Church tacitly encouraged it, as an Aragonese canon told Baretti in 1770, in spite of its occasional indecorum, as a useful safety-valve for the emotions. It was not less seductive to the foreign spectator than to the people themselves. The grave traveler Peyron, toward the end of the century, growing eloquent over the languorous and flexible movements of the dance, the bewitching attitudes, the voluptuous curves of the arms, declares that when one sees a beautiful Spanish woman dance one is inclined to fling all philosophy to the winds. And even that highly respectable Anglican clergyman, the Reverend Joseph Townsend, was constrained to state that he could "almost persuade myself" that if the fandango were suddenly played in church the gravest worshipers would start up to join in that "lascivious pantomime."

There we have the rock against which the primitive dance of sexual selection suffers shipwreck as civilization advances. And that prejudice of civilization becomes so ingrained that it is brought to bear even on the primitive dance. The Pygmies of Africa are described by Sir H. H. Johnston as a very decorous and highly moral people, but their dances, he adds, are not so. Yet these dances, though in Johnston's eyes, blinded by European civilization, "grossly indecent," he honestly, and inconsistently, adds. are "danced reverently."

IV

From the vital function of dancing in love, and its sacred function in religion, to dancing as an art, a profession, an amusement, may seem, at the first glance, a sudden leap. In reality the transition is gradual, and it began to be made at a very early period in diverse parts of the globe. All the matters that enter into courtship tend to fall under the sway of art; their æsthetic pleasure is a secondary reflection of their primary vital joy. Dancing could not fail to be first in manifesting this tendency. But even religious dancing swiftly exhibited the same transformation; dancing, like priesthood, became a profession, and dancers, like priests, formed a caste. This, for instance, took place in old Hawaii. The *hula* dance was a religious dance; it required a special education and an arduous training; moreover, it involved the observance of important taboos and the exercise of sacred rites; therefore it was carried out by paid performers, a professional caste.

In India, again, the Devadasis, or sacred dancing girls, are at once both religious and professional dancers. They are married to gods, they are taught dancing by the Brahmins, they figure in religious ceremonies, and their dances represent the life of the god they are married to, as well as the emotions of love they experience for him. Yet at the same time, they also give professional performances in the houses of rich private persons who pay for them. It thus comes about that to the foreigner the Devadasis scarcely seem very unlike the Ramedjenis, the dancers of the street, who are of very different origin, and mimic in their performances the play of merely human passions. The Portuguese conquerors of India called both kinds of dancers indiscriminately Balheideras (or dancers) which we have corrupted in Bayaderes.

In our modern world professional dancing as an art has become altogether divorced from religion, and even, in any vital sense, from love; it is scarcely even possible, so far as western civilization is concerned, to trace back the tradition to either source. If we survey the development of dancing as an art in Europe, it seems to me that we have to recognize two streams of tradition which have sometimes merged, but yet remain in their ideals and their tendencies essentially distinct. I would call these traditions the Classical, which is much the more ancient and fundamental, and may be said to be of Egyptian origin, and the Romantic, which is of Italian origin, chiefly known to us as the ballet. The first is, in its pure form, solo dancing, and is based on the rhythmic beauty and expressiveness of the simple human personality when its energy is concentrated in passionate movement. The second is concerted dancing, mimetic and picturesque, wherein the individual is subordinated to the wider and variegated rhythm of the group. It may be easy to devise another classification, but this is simple and instructive enough for our purpose.

There can scarcely be a doubt that Egypt has been for many thousands of years, as indeed it still remains, a great dancing centre, the most influential dancing-school the world has ever seen, radiating its influence south and east and north. We may perhaps even agree with the historian of the dance, who terms it "the mother-country of all civilized dancing." We are not entirely dependent on the ancient wall-pictures of Egypt for our knowledge of Egyptian skill in the art. Sacred mysteries, it is known, were danced in the temples, and queens and princesses took part in the orchestras that accompanied them. It is significant that the musical instruments still peculiarly associated with the dance were originated or developed in Egypt; the guitar is an Egyptian instrument, and its name was a hieroglyphic already used when the Pyramids were being built; the cymbal, the tambourine, triangles, and castanets, in one form or another, were all familiar to the ancient Egyptians, and with the Egyptian art of dancing they must have spread all round the shores of the Mediterranean, the great focus of our civilization, at a very early date. Even beyond the Mediterranean, at Cadiz, dancing that was essentially Egyptian in character was established, and Cadiz became the dancing-school of Spain. The Nile and Cadiz were thus the two great centres of ancient dancing, and Martial mentions them both together, for each supplied its dancers to Rome. This dancing, alike whether Egyptian or Gaditanian, was the expression of the individual dancer's body and art; the garments played but a small part in it, they were frequently transparent, and sometimes discarded altogether. It was, and it remains, simple, personal, passionate dancing; classic, therefore, in the same sense as, on the side of literature, the poetry of Catullus is classic.

Ancient Greek dancing was essentially classic dancing as here understood. On the Greek vases, as reproduced in Emmanuel's attractive book on Greek dancing and elsewhere, we find the same play of the arms, the same sideward turn, the same extreme backward extension of the body, which had long before been represented in Egyptian monuments. Many supposedly modern movements in dancing were certainly already common both to Egyptian and Greek dancing, as well as the clapping of hands to keep time, which is still an accompaniment of Spanish dancing.

It seems clear, however, that, on this general classic and Mediterranean basis, Greek dancing had a development so refined and so special that it exercised no influence outside Greece. Dancing became indeed the most characteristic and the most generally cultivated of Greek arts. It may well be that the Greek drama arose out of dance and song, and that the dance throughout was an essential and plastic element in it. It is said that Æschylus developed the technique of dancing, and that Sophocles danced in his own dramas. In these developments, no doubt, Greek dancing tended to overpass the fundamental limits of classic dancing and fore-shadowed the ballet.

The real germ of the ballet, however, is to be found in Rome, where the pantomime with its concerted and picturesque method of expressive action was developed; and Italy is the home of Romantic dancing. The same impulse which produced the pantomime, produced more than a thousand years later, in the same Italian region, the modern ballet. In both cases, one is inclined to think, we may trace the influence of the same Etruscan and Tuscan race which so long has had its seat here, a race with a genius for expressive, dramatic, picturesque art. We see it on the walls of Etruscan tombs and again in pictures of Botticelli and his fellow Tuscans. The modern ballet, it is generally believed, had its origin in the spectacular pageants at the marriage of Galeazzo Visconti, Duke of Milan, in 1489.

The popularity of such performances spread to the other Italian courts, including Florence; and Catherine de Medici, when she became Queen of France, brought the Italian ballet to Paris. Here it speedily became fashionable. Kings and queens were its admirers, and even took part in it; great statesmen were its patrons. Before long it became an established institution with a vital life and growth of its own, maintained by distinguished musicians, artists, and dancers.

Romantic dancing, to a much greater extent than what I have called classic dancing, which depends so largely on simple personal qualities, tends to be vitalized by transplantation and the absorption of new influences, provided that the essential basis of technique and tradition is preserved in the new development. Lulli in the seventeenth century brought women into the ballet; Camargo discarded the fashionable unwieldy costumes, so rendering possible all the freedom and airy grace of later dancing; Noverre elaborated plot unraveled by gesture and dance alone, and so made the ballet a complete art-form.

In the French ballet of the eighteenth century a very high degree of perfection seems thus to have been reached, while in Italy, where the ballet had originated it decayed, and Milan which had been its source became the nursery of a tradition of devitalized technique carried to the finest point of delicate perfection.

The influence of the French school was maintained as a living force into the nineteenth century, overspreading the world, by the genius of a few individual dancers. When they had gone the ballet slowly and steadily declined. As it declined as an art, so also it declined in credit and in popularity; it became scarcely respectable even to admire dancing. Thirty years ago, the few who still appreciated the art of dancing — and how few they were! — had to seek for it painfully and sometimes in strange surroundings. A recent historian of dancing, in a book published so lately as 1906, declared that "the ballet is now a thing of the past, and, with the modern change of ideas, a thing that is never likely to be resuscitated." That historian never mentioned Russian ballet, yet his book was scarcely published before the Russian ballet arrived, to scatter ridicule over his rash prophecy by raising the ballet to a pitch of perfection it can rarely have surpassed, as an expressive, emotional, even passionate form of living art.

The Russian ballet was an offshoot from the French ballet, and illustrates once more the vivifying effect of transplantation on the art of romantic dancing. The Empress Anna introduced it toward the middle of the eighteenth century, and appointed a French ballet master and a Neapolitan composer to carry it on; it reached a high degree of technical perfection during the following hundred years, on the traditional lines, and the principal dancers were all imported from Italy. It was not until recent years that this firm discipline and these ancient traditions were vitalized into an art-form of exquisite and vivid beauty by the influence of the soil in which they had slowly taken root. This contact, when at last it was effected, involved a kind of revolution; for its outcome, while genuine ballet, has yet all the effect of delicious novelty. The tradition by itself was in Russia an exotic without real life, and had nothing to give to the world; on the other hand a Russian ballet apart from that tradition, if we can conceive such a thing, would have been formless, extravagant, bizarre, not subdued to any fine æsthetic ends.

What we see here, in the Russian ballet as we know it to-day, is a splendid and arduous technical tradition, brought at last—by the combined genius of designers, composers, and dancers—into real fusion with an environment from which during more than a century it had been held apart: Russian genius for music, Russian feeling for rhythm, Russian skill in the use of bright color, and, perhaps, above all, the Russian orgiastic temperament and the general Slav passion for folk-dancing, shown in all branches of the race, Polish, Bohemian, Bulgarian and Servian. The result has been that our age sees one of the most splendid movements in the whole history of romantic dancing.

V

Dancing as an art, we may be sure, cannot die out but will always be undergoing a re-birth. Not merely as an art but also as a social custom, it perpetually emerges afresh from the soul of the people. Less than a century ago the polka thus arose, extemporized by the Bohemian servant girl, Anna Slezakova, out of her own head for the joy of her own heart, and only rendered a permanent form, apt for world-wide popularity, by the accident that it was observed and noted down by an artist. Dancing had forever been in existence as a spontaneous custom, a social discipline. Thus it is, finally, that dancing meets us, not only as love, as religion, as art, but also as morals.

All human work, under natural conditions, is a kind of dance. In a large and learned work, supported by an immense amount of evidence, Karl Bücher has argued that work differs from the dance not in kind but only in degree, since they are both essentially rhythmic. In the memory of those who have ever lived on a sailing ship—that loveliest of human creations now disappearing from the world—there will always linger the echo of the chanties which sailors sang as they hoisted the topsail yard or wound the capstan or worked the pumps. That is the type of primitive combined work, and it is indeed difficult to see how such work can be effectively accomplished without such a device for regulating the rhythmic energy of the muscles.

The dance-rhythm of work has thus acted socializingly in a parallel line with the dance-rhythms of the arts, and indeed in part as their inspirer. Thus, as Bücher points out, poetic metre may be conceived as arising out of work; metre is the rhythmic stamping of feet, as in the technique of verse it is still metaphorically so called; iambics and trochees, spondees and anapæsts and dactyls may still be heard among blacksmiths smiting the anvil or navvies wielding their hammers in the streets. In so far as they arose out of work, music and singing and dancing are naturally a single art. Herein the ancient ballad of Europe is a significant type. It is, as the name indicates, a dance as much as a song, performed by a singer who sang the story and a chorus who danced and shouted the apparently meaningless refrain; it is absolutely the chanty of the sailors, and is equally apt for the purposes of concerted work. And yet our most complicated musical forms are evolved from similar dances. The symphony is but a development of a dance-suite, — in the first place folk-dances, — such as Bach and Händel composed. Indeed a dance still lingers always at the heart of music, and even at the heart of the composer. Mozart used often to say, so his wife stated, that it was dancing, not music, that he really cared for. Wagner believed that Beethoven's seventh symphony — to some of us the most fascinating of all of them, and the most purely musical — was an apotheosis of the dance, and even if that belief throws no light on the intention of Beethoven it is at least a revelation of Wagner's own feeling for the dance.

It is, however, the dance itself, apart from work and apart from the other arts, which, in the opinion of many to-day, has had a decisive influence in socializing, that is to say in moralizing, the human species. Work showed the necessity of harmonious rhythmic coöperation, but the dance developed that rhythmic coöperation and imparted a beneficent impetus to all human activities. It was Grosse, in his *Beginnings of Art,* who first clearly set forth the high social significance of the dance in the creation of human civilization. The participants in a dance, as all observers of savages have noted, exhibit a wonderful unison; they are, as it were, fused into a single being stirred by a single impulse. Social unification is thus accomplished. Apart from war, this is the chief factor making for social solidarity in primitive life; it was indeed the best training for war, as for all the other coöperative arts of life. All our most advanced civilization, Grosse insisted, is based on dancing. It is the dance that socialized man.

Thus, in the large sense, dancing has possessed peculiar value as a method of national education. As civilization grew self-conscious this was realized. "One may judge of a King," according to an ancient Chinese maxim, "by the state of dancing during his reign." So also among the Greeks: it has been said that dancing and music lay at the foundation of the whole political and military as well as the religious organization of the Dorian states.

In the narrow sense, in individual education, the great importance of dancing came to be realized, even at an early stage of human development, and still more in the ancient civilizations. "A good education," Plato declared in the *Laws,* the final work of his old age, "consists in knowing how to sing well and dance well." And in our own day one of the keenest and most enlightened of educators has lamented the decay of dancing. The revival of dancing, Stanley Hall declares, is imperatively needed to give poise to the nerves, schooling to the emotions, strength to the will, and to harmonize the feelings and the intellect with the body which supports them.

It can scarcely be said that these functions of dancing are yet generally realized and embodied afresh in education. For if it is true that dancing engendered morality, it is also true that in the end, by the irony of fate, morality, grown insolent, sought to crush its own parent, and for a time succeeded only too well. Four centuries ago dancing was attacked by that spirit, in England called Puritanism, which at that time spread over the greater part of Europe, just as active in Bohemia as in England, and which has indeed been described as a general onset of developing Urbanism against the old Ruralism. It made no distinction between good and bad, nor paused to consider what would come when dancing went. So it was that, as Rémy de Gourmont remarks, the drinking-shop conquered the dance, and alcohol replaced the violin.

But when we look at the function of dancing in life from a higher and wider standpoint, this episode in its history ceases to occupy so large a place. The conquest of dancing has never proved in the end a matter for rejoicing, even to morality, while an art which has been so intimately mixed with all the finest and deepest springs of life has always asserted itself afresh. For dancing is the loftiest, the most moving, the most beautiful of the arts, because it is no mere translation or abstraction from life; it is life itself. It is the only art, as Rahel Varnhagen said, of which we ourselves are the stuff.

It thus comes about that, beyond its manifold practical significance, dancing has always been felt to possess also a symbolic significance. Marcus Aurelius was accustomed to regard the art of life as like the dancer's art, though that Imperial Stoic could not resist adding that in some respects it was more like the wrestler's art. In our own time, Nietzsche, from first to last, showed himself possessed by the conception of the art of life as a dance, in which the dancer achieves the rhythmic freedom and harmony of his soul beneath the shadow of a hundred Damoclean swords. The dance lies at the beginning of art, and we find it also at the end. The first creators of civilization were making the dance, and the philosopher of to-day, hovering over the dark abyss of insanity, with bleeding feet and muscles strained to the breaking-point, still seems to himself to be weaving the maze of the dance.

February 1914

NORA WALN

1895–

If you are disillusioned with mankind, seek out a Quaker; there will be virtue in him. The miracle of his goodness is that it never stands in the way of what he has set his mind to do. Most of us are helpless in the clutch of moral excellence. Not so a Friend. He has visions of Heaven, and here below he gets on. So it is with Nora Waln. She does what she wants and the world profits.

In one of the best of books in foreign fields she has told her story. We all remember how for a hundred years the Walns of Philadelphia and the Lins of Canton had been trading and corresponding to their mutual satisfaction. Nora was fresh from college when old Mr. Lin, thinking it courteous after a century of intimacy, knocked at the Waln front door. His call was fruitful, and when he returned to China, Nora followed him to grow in grace with a daughter of his household. For years the Lins were her family and her home, "The House of Exile," so called because hundreds of years ago a Lin had married without his father's consent and had built his own fortunes in the remote province of Hopei, far from the ancestral acres.

It was from The House of Exile that Nora Waln sent her first writing to the Atlantic, *for with Walns, the magazine is a tradition, and when in 1929 I happened to be in Peking, we were already old friends. She wrote me asking me to visit her in Tienstin where her husband, then an official in the famous Postal Service inaugurated by Sir Robert Hart, had his headquarters. My schedule unfortunately did not admit of that, but learning from the timetable that my train would stop for twenty minutes, I telegraphed her and for those twenty minutes we walked up and down the platform cementing a friendship which has never been interrupted.*

Many years later, I was sick and alone in my Boston house, my spirits at low ebb, when at seven in the morning my telephone rang. "Is thee well?" I heard in a soft voice. "Nora Waln!" I exclaimed, and the voice went on. "If thee is not well I will come to thee." That day she came on and cured me. In after days I saw much of her.

Over the bookcase in my study there hangs a Chinese motto beautifully embroidered against black silk. Nora had had an artist copy a legend which had for generations hung in The House of Exile. Its meaning is "When the entire family is gathered together, joy springs up all of itself." That is today my children's motto. And in my garden is a new variety of Tree Peony. If you ask what difference there is between an ordinary and a Tree Peony, I will answer you in the words of a Chinese sage, "Precisely the difference between the Emperor and his Viziers." That is an accurate description, for in the realm of flowers, there is no blossom so glorious as this of the Tree Peony. Firm yet delicate in texture, its great petals carved like Chinese ivory, its glowing heart intensifying its color whether that be carmine or purple or shadowy white. When the blossom is palest, that heart flushes the whole flower like the last ray of sunset. The Tree Peony is indeed Emperor of the Flowery Kingdom. Each variety has its poetic name, "Moon World," "Companion of Serenity," "Poet of China," or other sweet and languorous designation. One, I have, a sport, different from the rest, simpler and with a certain wilfulness about its growth. I call it "House of Exile."

Fragments from a Flower Diary

NORA WALN

Habits and customs differ, but all peoples have the love of flowers in common.
— Chinese Proverb

I

It was in northern Hopei. The clouds had failed to gather in their season, and the time of showers had passed without rain. Parched by the midsummer sun, the earth was a dull beige in color. We had traveled three days over plains, valleys, and hills and seen nothing green except in the artificially irrigated plots near hamlets.

The ancient stone-paved trail led up along a narrow ledge. We waited at the foot for a line of pack coolies to come down. They were heavily laden with inland produce which they were transporting to the coast for foreign export. The containers roped on their backs towered high above their heads. Yet, despite his burden, the foremost man swerved out suddenly to the very edge of the cliff, and, as they came on, each of the nine men behind him did the same.

When they had passed us, we began our climb. My pack coolie was before me. When I came up to the place round which the others had swerved, he had squatted down and was pouring the last of the contents of his drinking canteen into a crevice in the paving. There, through the dust between the stones, a wild rose had grown — a slender fragile tendril with five pale leaves and an open flower. A perfect flower, beautifully tinted, and sweetly fragrant. "It is from such a one as this," my coolie said, "that we learn fortitude."

II

It was in the province of Kwangtung. The temple had once been beautifully furnished, but was now dirty and neglected. I chided the abbot concerning the dust on a Buddha's face. He did not answer me immediately. He led me across two courtyards and along a dark narrow passage.

At the end of the passage he opened a door and motioned to me to pass him and go through it. Beyond the door, I stood in a tiny garden above a deep ravine. All was neat and tidy there. No weeds grew in the rich, much-worked loam. A low wall of carefully placed rocks kept the garden from sliding down the mountain side.

In his garden, the abbot spoke to me, saying, "The furniture on an altar is but the symbol of religion . . . in the face of a flower the heart of God is revealed."

I had no answer. At my feet were tall white lilies, each with a golden heart. Over my head a magnolia was in bloom.

Lifting a clump of pansies with a careful trowel, the abbot planted them in an earthen pot. "Take this home," he said. "If you are one who sincerely seeks the truth, by living with a flower you will find it."

III

Bald-the-third, my serving matron, was stiff with anger. A filthy beggar had erected a mat shed against the wall of our residence at Nanking, and settled down to live just by the gate which led from our garden to the hill path.

He would have to go, she declared. Disease would be carried over the wall by every breeze. We should all be sick. Probably Small Girl would die of cholera.

Bald-the-third went out to clear him away. Sometime later I discovered her seated on the sewing-room floor hemstitching a sheet, an occupation she often uses to calm herself when she has been overwrought.

"Has the beggar gone?" I asked.

"No — he is still there," she answered.

"Oh! He defeated you in argument, did he?" I pressed her.

"I did not speak to him," she said. "He has a sprig of jasmine growing in a broken pot, and has given it the least drafty place in his miserable shelter. He certainly hadn't much tea, but he was sharing what he had with the flower. I do not think that such a man will do us any harm. People can be too concerned regarding physical health and neglect the health of the spirit. I've sent him out a gift of rice and fish."

IV

The Chinese love of flowers has been rewarded by genius in their cultivation. Certainly theirs is a transcendent capacity for taking trouble. Aided by their lovers' patient skill, blossoms open for their festivals all over the land despite the diversity of climate which makes the weather below zero in some districts when it is swelteringly hot in others.

Flowers are coddled, nursed, and coaxed. They are fed religiously. There is a vast lore of wisdom passed orally from generation to generation concerning the whims and peculiarities of different plants — also a voluminous detailed gardening literature in which the observations of centuries are garnered. In the House of Exile library there are forty books, considered classics, on the culture of chrysanthemums only, and nearly as many relating to dwarf trees.

In heat, plants are sheltered in the coolest places in the homestead, and shades are erected for blossoming trees, vines, and flowers which are stationary. I have seen people sit all through the breathless tropic noon fanning a drooping flower. In cold, plants are housed in paper shelters, their roots set in loam warmed by subterranean air pipes heated by buried charcoal.

These are constructed to-day exactly as decreed by a ruler of the state of Wei who lived more than two thousand years ago. He ordered that they should be so simply designed that even the poorest and the stupidest of his people might make one. In the most severe weather, florists clothe buds in little paper coats perforated with breathing holes.

Although they perform an infinite amount of toil in bringing their flowers to perfection, florists charge astonishingly low prices. A florist once explained this to me. He told me that a country in which flowers — a necessity for the refinement of the heart — were priced so as to make them a luxury was a country which had yet to learn the first principles of civilization.

V

According to Chinese legend, a flower presides over each month of the year, celebrating her anniversary on the fifth day after the rise of the new moon. It is usual for a minstrel, when he knocks at a homestead gate on a flower birthday, to ask to come in and sing the flower's ballads. Many tea shops have a story-teller as an attraction to patrons; and, passing on a flower's day, I have often heard the blind-man entertaining the laborers, who gather round him when the day's toil is done, with the flower's fables.

Narcissus is hostess of the first month, violet of the second, peach blossom of the third, which is a favorite month for weddings. In China the peach blossom is the wedding flower as the orange blossom is in America, and in ancient times marriage was celebrated with a festival at the season of the flowering of the peach orchards. Peony gives her name to the fourth month, but rose presides over the month. This is because "the peony is the millionaire's flower, symbol of riches and power; but the lovely rose belongs to everyone, as she graces cottage and palace impartially with her beauty."

The gentle jasmine is hostess of the fifth month. The lotus, symbol of purity because she grows out of the mud and is not soiled, reigns over the sixth month; balsam, famous for healing virtues, over the seventh; cassia flower, so small but so fragrant, over the eighth; chrysanthemum, beloved of scholars, over the ninth. Bright cheerful marigold is hostess of the tenth month; camellia of the eleventh; the flowering winter plum, whose petals are like the snowflakes, of the twelfth.

And that no flower shall feel neglected, just because there are not enough months for all, a Birthday of All Flowers is celebrated on the twelfth day of the second month.

On All Flowers' Day it is polite to make "flower calls," taking gifts of seeds and slips to one's friends. Every flower birthday is an appropriate occasion for a party. It is not even necessary to possess a garden to give a blossom tea. I know a Chinese lady in Peking, an invalid with neither the means nor the strength to achieve a garden, who has a blossom tea every year. A branch of her neighbor's wisteria extends over her courtyard wall, and each spring, when the wisteria flowers, she asks her friends to come. One year the wisteria did not bloom. She had her party, gay as the previous ones, in memory of the blossoms.

Wealthy families, who can, often give parties which are magnificent flower shows. These usually begin in the morning and last until well into the evening. After sunset the homestead is lit with silk lanterns placed to show each plant or flowering tree to the best advantage. Good manners permit one to go for as long or as short a time as one chooses.

Chinese people do not like to cut their flowers, and seldom do. The flowers displayed at a party are growing, either in pots or in the ground. Poetry and art through the centuries have endowed each tree, vine, and plant with a symbolic significance, and the cultured are guided by this in their arrangement. In the home of a scholar one is certain to see the "three friends" — that is, the bamboo, the pine, and the plum — grouped together.

The purpose of a flower party is to view the flowers, and tables for cards or mah jongg are considered in bad taste. Sometimes there is an open-air stage on which actors play the flower classics. At one party I attended, the little children of the house, dressed in flower costumes, danced a flower ballet of their own improvisation. Often someone who reads well is asked to read flower poetry.

Flower picnics are also popular. The Lins give an orchard party when the fruit trees bloom each year. Friends make up travel parties and go from all over China to admire the azaleas near Ningpo. When the lovely lotus opens her tulip-shaped blossoms in the shallow bays of the water highways, families in every province give boat picnics.

When I was preparing to attend the first flower festival to which I was invited, my mother-by-affection spoke to me about my dress. "One should honor the occasion by care in one's costume," Shun-ko said. "But according to an ancient rule of decorum observed by the refined of heart, it is impolite to outdress the flowers. The flower-party gown should be dainty, clean, delicate in color, and fashioned on simple lines. A new fashion, however lovely, is out of place at a flower's party. The courteous hostess and her guests remember that it is to celebrate the flowers that people are gathered, and to wear a gown which distracts attention from the blossoms is rude."

VI

I had been abroad for six months. Shortly after my return I needed a length of silk. I went to the place where Shih, the silk merchant, had opened a new shop just before I went away. The place was closed and appeared uninhabited. I made inquiry and I was told that he had gone back to his old address, where his father and his grandfather before him had done business.

I found him there. When I had made my selection and my bargain, over a cup of tea, I asked why he had left the Big Horse Road. He replied that it was not a good location.

"It is such a prominent place," I said in astonishment. "Didn't you find that you had more customers there than here?"

"A merchant," he informed me, "lives the major part of his life with his customers. The place was too prominent. Many came in just because it was convenient. They had long purses and they paid, but money is not everything."

The merchant's son, a boy of fourteen and heir to the business, further enlightened me. "This place is better for the future of our house," he said. "On the Big Horse Road there was one who came who let the breath of February blow in on a flowering plum tree which we had set on the counter for the delight of gentlefolk."

VII

I had lost my way and I had need to ask a policeman for direction. I drew my car up to the curb and waited. The policeman was occupied. Dressed in the splendid uniform copied from the city of San Francisco in which the American-educated governor of the town had clad all his republican police, this one was busy. Using his teapot as a watering can, he was watering the phlox which he had placed around his stance on the modern concrete road.

When he had finished, he gave me the information I requested. But before he signaled the permission for me to move on into the traffic he made a statement and asked a question: "There is no day in the year when flowers fail to bless China with their lovely charm," and, "Is this also so in the Outer World?"

July 1934

ALFRED NORTH WHITEHEAD

1861–

When you approach Professor Whitehead the first impression is pure benevolence. Talk with him, and the second is wisdom. Pull your chair alongside and spend an hour, and you will say this is the most modern of men. Age certainly cannot wither him. His voice is lower and his friends enunciate less clearly than they once did; but his outlook is hopeful as it was in his youth. The only change lies in the serenity settled upon it.

Most men of my generation think of "cultivation" as literary. Mathematics, speculative but rigid in its logic, is the core of his training. All the imagination of music is there, but the fabric is solid and there the inexpressible finds expression.

There are no short journeys in philosophy, but Professor Whitehead's seems infinite since he started eighty-six years ago from the little parsonage on the Island of Thanet endowed with an Anglican inheritance. His first distinguished career culminated as Professor of Mathematics in London University, gradually broadening mathematics into the enveloping world of philosophy. Sixty-two was the age of retirement and when his terminal birthday came, friends everywhere crowded about congratulating him on the quiet promised his remaining years. But then it was that Professor Whitehead's liveliest career began. He came to Harvard and took his place in the heart of the University's affection. In all excepting his stoop and his wisdom he was a young man. He took to Americans and believed in us; and he still thinks that young Lochinvars from the Middle West will pull us out of our slough.

Philosophy is the human expression of infinitude. My comprehension of Whitehead is small, personal, and circumscribed. I read his books with ever deepening incomprehension, but I am aware there is greatness in them. Baffled by his terminology which seeks to strait-jacket familiar words, deprive them of their range and connotation, and metamorphose them into integers of scientific calculation, I seek refuge among the commentators. But there too, no rest is to be found. For each critic has his personal view. Whitehead's long journey is an unresting search for God, but when I ponder over The Availability of Whiteheads' God for Religious Purposes *of one critical commentator, I cannot but smile, for it is borne in on me that every critic and philosopher, like each man-jack of the rest of us, has a private God of his own. In the sanctuary of every thinking man an altar is raised to the Unknown God.*

This has been so, longer than people think, reluctant as its expression habitually is. Centuries ago in the days of Charles II it is implicit in a famous story. When an insistent lady pressed the sceptical Shaftesbury to explain his religious beliefs, that cynic gave the perfect answer: "Madam, men of sense are really but of one religion." "What is that?" persisted the inquisitive fair one, all animation. "That, Madam, men of sense never tell."

Religion and Science

ALFRED NORTH WHITEHEAD

I

The difficulty in approaching the question of the relation between Religion and Science is that its elucidation requires that we have in our minds some clear idea of what we mean by either of the terms, "religion" and "science." Also I wish to speak in the most general way possible, and to keep in the background any comparison of particular creeds, scientific or religious. We have to understand the type of connection which exists between the two spheres, and then to draw some definite conclusions respecting the existing situation which at present confronts the world.

The *conflict* between religion and science is what naturally occurs to our minds when we think of this subject. It seems as though, during the last half-century, the results of science and the beliefs of religion had come into a position of frank disagreement, from which there can be no escape, except by abandoning either the clear teaching of science or the clear teaching of religion. This conclusion has been urged by controversialists on either side. Not by all controversialists, of course, but by those trenchant intellects which every controversy calls out into the open.

The distress of sensitive minds, and the zeal for truth, and the sense of the importance of the issues, must command our sincerest sympathy. When we consider what religion is for mankind, and what science is, it is no exaggeration to say that the future course of history depends upon the decision of this generation as to the relations between them. We have here the two strongest general forces (apart from the mere impulse of the various senses) which influence men, and they seem to be set one against the other—the force of our religious intuitions, and the force of our impulse to accurate observation and logical deduction.

A great English statesman once advised his countrymen to use large-scale maps as a preservative against alarms, panics, and general misunderstanding of the true relations between nations. In the same way, in dealing with the clash between permanent elements of human nature, it is well to map our history on a large scale, and to disengage ourselves from our immediate absorption in the present conflicts. When we do this, we immediately discover two great facts. In the first place, there has always been a conflict between religion and science; and in the second place, both religion and science have always been in a state of continual development. In the early days of Christianity there was a general belief among Christians that the world was coming to an end in the lifetime of people then living. We can make only indirect inferences as to how far this belief was authoritatively proclaimed; but it is certain that it was widely held, and that it formed an impressive part of the popular religious doctrine. The belief proved itself to be mistaken, and Christian doctrine adjusted itself to the change. Again, in the early Church, individual theologians very confidently deduced from the Bible opinions concerning the nature of the physical universe. In the year A.D. 535, a monk named Cosmas wrote a book which he entitled *Christian Topography*. He was a traveled man who had visited India and Ethiopia; and finally he lived in a monastery at Alexandria, which was then a great centre of culture. In this book, basing himself upon the direct meaning of Biblical texts as construed by him in a literal fashion, he denied the existence of the antipodes, and asserted that the world is a flat parallelogram whose length is double its breadth.

In the seventeenth century the doctrine of the motion of the earth was condemned by a Catholic tribunal. A hundred years ago the extension of time demanded by geological science distressed religious people, Protestant and Catholic. And to-day the doctrine of evolution is an equal stumblingblock. These are only a few instances illustrating a general fact.

But all our ideas will be in a wrong perspective if we think that this recurring perplexity was confined to contradictions between religion and science, and that in these controversies religion was always wrong and science always right. The true facts of the case are very much more complex, and refuse to be summarized in these simple terms.

Theology itself exhibits exactly the same character of gradual development, arising from an aspect of conflict between its own proper ideas. This fact is a commonplace to theologians, but is often obscured in the stress of controversy. I do not wish to overstate my case, so I will confine myself to Roman Catholic writers. In the seventeenth century a learned Jesuit, Father Petavius, showed that the theologians of the first three centuries of Christianity made use of phrases and statements which since the fifth century would be condemned as heretical. Also Cardinal Newman devoted a treatise to the discussion of the development of doctrine. He wrote it before he became a great Roman Catholic ecclesiastic, but throughout his life it was never retracted and continually reissued.

Science is even more changeable than theology. No man of science could subscribe without qualification to Galileo's beliefs, or to Newton's beliefs, or to all his own scientific beliefs of ten years ago.

In both regions of thought, additions, distinctions, and modifications have been introduced. So that now, even when the same assertion is made to-day as was made a thousand or fifteen hundred years ago, it is made subject to limitations or expansions of meaning which were not contemplated at the earlier epoch. We are told by logicians that a proposition must be either true or false, and that there is no middle term. But in practice we may know that a proposition expresses an important truth, but that it is subject to limitations and qualifications which at present remain undiscovered. It is a general feature of our knowledge that we are insistently aware of important truths; and yet that the only formulations of these truths which we are able to make presuppose a general standpoint of conceptions which may have to be modified. I will give you two illustrations, both from science.

Galileo said that the earth moves and that the sun is fixed; the Inquisition said that the earth is fixed and that the sun moves; and Newtonian astronomers, adopting an absolute theory of space, said that both the sun and the earth move. But now we say that any one of these three statements is equally true, provided that you have fixed your sense of "rest" and "motion" in the way required by the statement adopted. At the date of Galileo's controversy with the Inquisition, Galileo's way of stating the facts was, beyond question, the fruitful procedure for the sake of scientific research. But in itself it was not more true than the formulation of the Inquisition. But at that time the modern concepts of relative motion were in nobody's mind, so that the statements were made in ignorance of the qualifications required for their more perfect truth. Yet this question of the motions of the earth and the sun expresses a real fact in the universe, and all sides had got hold of important truths concerning it. But, with the knowledge of those times, the truths appeared to be inconsistent.

Again I will give you another example taken from the state of modern physical science. Since the time of Newton and Huyghens in the seventeenth century there have been two theories as to the physical nature of light. Newton's theory was that a beam of light consists of a stream of very minute particles, or corpuscles, and that we have the sensation of light when these corpuscles strike the retinas of our eyes. Huyghens's theory was that light consists of very minute waves of trembling in an all-pervading ether, and that these waves are traveling along a beam of light. The two theories are contradictory. In the eighteenth century Newton's theory was believed, in the nineteenth century Huyghens's theory was believed. Today there is one large group of phenomena which can be explained only on the wave theory, and another large group which can be explained only on the corpuscular theory. Scientists have to leave it at that, and wait for the future, in the hope of attaining some wider vision which reconciles both.

We should apply these same principles to the questions in which there is a variance between science and religion. We should believe nothing in either sphere of thought which does not appear to us to be certified by solid reasons based upon the critical research either of ourselves or of competent authorities. But, granting that we have honestly taken this precaution, a clash between the two on points of detail where they overlap should not lead us hastily to abandon doctrines for which we have solid evidence. It may be that we are more interested in one set of doctrines than in the other. But, if we have any sense of perspective and of the history of thought, we shall wait and refrain from mutual anathemas.

We should wait; but we should not wait passively, or in despair. The clash is a sign that there are wider truths and finer perspectives within which a reconciliation of a deeper religion and a more subtle science will be found.

II

In one sense, therefore, the conflict between science and religion is a slight matter which has been unduly emphasized. A mere logical contradiction cannot in itself point to more than the necessity of some readjustments, possibly of a very minor character, on both sides. Remember the widely different aspects of events which are dealt with in science and in religion respectively. Science is concerned with the general conditions which are observed to regulate physical phenomena, whereas religion is wholly wrapped up in the contemplation of moral and æsthetic values. On the one side there is the law of gravitation, and on the other the contemplation of the beauty of holiness. What one side sees the other misses, and vice versa.

Consider, for example, the lives of John Wesley and of Saint Francis of Assisi. For physical science you have in these lives merely ordinary examples of the operation of the principles of physiological chemistry, and of the dynamics of nervous reactions; for religion you have lives of the most profound significance in the history of the world. Can you be surprised that, in the absence of a perfect and complete phrasing of the principles of science and the principles of religion which apply to these specific cases, the accounts of these lives from these divergent standpoints should involve discrepancies? It would be a miracle if it were not so.

It would, however, be missing the point to think that we need not trouble ourselves about the conflict between science and religion. In an intellectual age there can be no active interest which puts aside all hope of a vision of the harmony of truth. To acquiesce in discrepancy is destructive of candor and of moral cleanliness. It belongs to the self-respect of intellect to pursue every tangle of thought to its final unravelment. If you check that impulse, you will get no religion and no science from an awakened thoughtfulness. The important question is, In what spirit are we going to face the issue? There we come to something absolutely vital.

A clash of doctrines is not a disaster — it is an opportunity. I will explain my meaning by some illustrations from science. The weight of an atom of nitrogen was well known. Also it was an established scientific doctrine that the average weight of such atoms in any considerable mass will be always the same. Two experimenters, the late Lord Rayleigh and the late Sir William Ramsay, found that if they obtained nitrogen by two different methods, each equally effective for that purpose, they always observed a persistent slight difference between the average weights of the atoms in the two cases. Now I ask you, would it have been rational of these men to have despaired because of this conflict between chemical theory and scientific observation? Suppose that for some reason the chemical doctrine had been highly prized throughout some district as the foundation of its social order—would it have been wise, would it have been candid, would it have been moral, to forbid the disclosure of the fact that the experiments produced discordant results? Or, on the other hand, should Sir William Ramsay and Lord Rayleigh have proclaimed that chemical theory was now a detected delusion?

We see at once that either of these ways would have been a method of facing the issue in an entirely wrong spirit. What Rayleigh and Ramsay did do was this. They at once perceived that they had hit upon a line of investigation which would disclose some subtlety of chemical theory that had hitherto eluded observation. The discrepancy was not a disaster—it was an opportunity to increase the sweep of chemical knowledge. You all know the end of the story: finally argon was discovered, a new chemical element which had lurked undetected, mixed with the nitrogen. But the story has a sequel which forms my second illustration. This discovery drew attention to the importance of observing accurately minute differences in chemical substances as obtained by different methods. Further researches of the most careful accuracy were undertaken. Finally another physicist, Ashton, working in the Cavendish Laboratory at Cambridge in England, discovered that even the same element might assume two or more distinct forms, termed "isotopes," and that the law of the constancy of average atomic weight holds for each of these forms, but as between the different isotopes differs slightly. The research has effected a great stride in the power of chemical theory, far transcending in importance the discovery of argon, from which it originated. The moral of these stories lies on the surface, and I will leave to you their application to the case of religion and science.

In formal logic a contradiction is the signal of a defeat, but in the evolution of real knowledge it marks the first step in progress toward a victory. This is one great reason for the utmost toleration of variety of opinion. Once and forever this duty of toleration has been summed up in the words, "Let both grow together until the harvest." The failure of religious Christians to act up to this precept, of the highest authority, is one of the curiosities of religious history. But we have not yet exhausted the discussion of the moral temper required for the pursuit of truth. There are short cuts leading merely to an illusory success. It is easy enough to find a theory, logically harmonious and with important applications in the region of fact, provided that you are content to disregard half your evidence. Every age produces people with clear logical intellects, and with the most praiseworthy grasp of the importance of some sphere of human experience, who have elaborated, or inherited, a scheme of thought that exactly fits those experiences which claim their interest. Such people are apt resolutely to ignore, or to explain away, all evidence which confuses their scheme with contradictory instances. What they cannot fit in is for them nonsense. An unflinching determination to take the whole evidence into account is the only method of preservation against the fluctuating extremes of fashionable opinion. This advice seems so easy, and is in fact so difficult to follow.

One reason for this difficulty is that we cannot think first and act afterward. From the moment of birth we are immersed in action, and can only fitfully guide it by taking thought. We have, therefore, in various spheres of experience to adopt those ideas which seem to work within those spheres. It is absolutely necessary to trust to ideas which are generally adequate, even though we know that there are subtleties and distinctions beyond our ken. Also, apart from the necessities of action, we cannot even keep before our minds the whole evidence except under the guise of doctrines which are incompletely harmonized. We cannot think in terms of an indefinite multiplicity of detail; our evidence can acquire its proper importance only if it comes before us marshaled by general ideas. These ideas we inherit — they form the tradition of our civilization. Such traditional ideas are never static. They are either fading into meaningless formulæ or gaining power by the new lights thrown by a more delicate apprehension. They are transformed by the urge of critical reason, by the vivid evidence of emotional experience, and by the cold certainties of scientific perception. One fact is certain: you cannot keep them still. No generation can merely reproduce its ancestors. You may preserve the life in a flux of form, or preserve the form amid an ebb of life. But you cannot permanently enclose the same life in the same mould.

III

The present state of religion among the European races illustrates the statements which I have been making. The phenomena are mixed. There have been reactions and revivals. But on the whole, during many generations, there has been a gradual decay of religious influence in European civilization. Each revival touches a lower peak than its predecessor, and each period of slackness a lower depth. The average curve marks a steady fall in religious tone. In some countries the interest in religion is higher than in others. But in those countries where the interest is relatively high it still falls as the generations pass. Religion is tending to degenerate into a decent formula wherewith to embellish a comfortable life. A great historical movement on this scale results from the convergence of many causes. I wish to suggest for consideration two of them which lie within the scope of this article.

In the first place, for over two centuries religion has been on the defensive, and on a weak defensive. The period has been one of unprecedented intellectual progress. In this way a series of novel situations has been produced for thought. Each such occasion has found the religious thinkers unprepared. Something, which has been proclaimed to be vital, has finally, after struggle, distress, and anathema, been modified and otherwise interpreted. The next generation of religious apologists then congratulates the religious world on the deeper insight which has been gained. The result of the continued repetition of this undignified retreat, during many generations, has at last almost entirely destroyed the intellectual authority of religious thinkers. Consider this contrast: when Darwin or Einstein proclaims theories which modify our ideas, it is a triumph for science. We do not go about saying that there is another defeat for science, because its old ideas have been abandoned. We know that another step of scientific insight has been gained.

Religion will not regain its old power until it can face change in the same spirit as does science. Its principles may be eternal, but the expression of those principles requires continual development. This evolution of religion is in the main a disengagement of its own proper ideas from the adventitious notions which have crept into it by reason of the expression of its own ideas in terms of the imaginative picture of the world entertained in previous ages. Such a release of religion from the bonds of imperfect science is all to the good. It stresses its own genuine message. The great point to be kept in mind is that normally an advance in science will show that statements of various religious beliefs require some sort of modification. It may be that they have to be expanded or explained, or, indeed, entirely restated. If the religion is a sound expression of truth, this modification will only exhibit more adequately the exact point which is of importance. This process is a gain. In so far, therefore, as any religion has any contact with physical facts, it is to be expected that the point of view of those facts must be continually modified as scientific knowledge advances. In this way the exact relevance of these facts for religious thought will grow more and more clear. The progress of science must result in the unceasing modification of religious thought, to the great advantage of religion.

The religious controversies of the sixteenth and seventeenth centuries put theologians into a most unfortunate state of mind. They were always attacking and defending. They pictured themselves as the garrison of a fort surrounded by hostile forces. All such pictures express half-truths. That is why they are so popular. But they are dangerous. This particular picture fostered a pugnacious party spirit that really expresses an ultimate lack of faith. They dared not modify, because they shirked the task of disengaging their spiritual message from the associations of a particular imagery.

Let me explain myself by an example. In the early mediæval times Heaven was in the sky, and Hell was underground; volcanoes were the jaws of Hell. I do not assert that these beliefs entered into the official formulations, but they did enter into the popular understanding of the general doctrines of Heaven and Hell. These notions were what everyone thought to be implied by the doctrine of the future state. They entered into the explanations of the most influential exponents of Christian belief. For example, they occur in the Dialogues of Pope Gregory the Great, a man whose high official position is surpassed only by the magnitude of his services to humanity. I am not saying what we ought to believe about the future state. But, whatever be the right doctrine, in this instance the clash between religion and science, which has relegated the earth to the position of a second-rate planet attached to a second-rate sun, has been greatly to the benefit of the spirituality of religion by dispersing these mediæval fancies.

Another way of looking at this question of the evolution of religious thought is to note that any verbal form of statement which has been before the world for some time discloses ambiguities, and that often such ambiguities strike at the very heart of the meaning. The effective sense in which a doctrine has been held in the past cannot be determined by the mere logical analysis of verbal statements, made in ignorance of the logical trap. You have to take into account the whole reaction of human nature to the scheme of thought. This reaction is of a mixed character, including elements of emotion derived from our lower natures. It is here that the impersonal criticism of science and of philosophy comes to the aid of religious evolution. Example after example can be given of this motive force in development. For instance, the logical difficulties inherent in the doctrine of the moral cleansing of human nature by the power of religion rent Christianity in the days of Pelagius and Augustine—that is to say, at the beginning of the fifth century. Echoes of that controversy still linger in theology.

So far my point has been this: that religion is the expression of one type of fundamental experiences of mankind; that religious thought develops into an increasing accuracy of expression, disengaged from adventitious imagery; that the interaction between religion and science is one great factor in promoting this development.

IV

I now come to my second reason for the modern fading of interest in religion. This involves the ultimate question which I stated in my opening sentences. We have to know what we mean by religion. The churches, in their presentation of their answers to this query, have put forward aspects of religion which are expressed in terms either suited to the emotional reactions of bygone times or directed to excite modern emotional interests of a non-religious character. What I mean under the first heading is that religious appeal is directed partly to excite that instinctive fear of the wrath of a tyrant which was inbred in the unhappy populations of the arbitrary empires of the ancient world, and in particular to excite that fear of an all-powerful arbitrary tyrant behind the unknown forces of nature. This appeal to the ready instinct of brute fear is losing its force. It lacks any directness of response, because modern science and modern conditions of life have taught us to meet occasions of apprehension by a critical analysis of their causes and conditions. Religion is the reaction of human nature to its search for God. The presentation of God under the aspect of power awakens every modern instinct of critical reaction. This is fatal; for religion collapses unless its main positions command immediacy of assent. In this respect the old phraseology is at variance with the psychology of modern civilizations. This change in psychology is largely due to science, and is one of the chief ways in which the advance of science has weakened the hold of the old religious forms of expression.

The nonreligious motive which has entered into modern religious thought is the desire for a comfortable organization of modern society. Religion has been presented as valuable for the ordering of life. Its claims have been rested upon its function as a sanction to right conduct. Also the purpose of right conduct quickly degenerates into the formation of pleasing social relations. We have here a subtle degradation of religious ideas, following upon their gradual purification under the influence of keener ethical intuitions. Conduct is a by-product of religion — an inevitable by-product, but not the main point. Every great religious teacher has revolted against the presentation of religion as a mere sanction of rules of conduct. Saint Paul denounced the Law, and Puritan divines spoke of the filthy rags of righteousness. The insistence upon rules of conduct marks the ebb of religious fervor. Above and beyond all things, the religious life is not a research after comfort. I must now state, in all diffidence, what I conceive to be the essential character of the religious spirit.

Religion is the vision of something which stands beyond, behind, and within, the passing flux of immediate things; something which is real, and yet waiting to be realized; something which is a remote possibility, and yet the greatest of present facts; something which gives meaning to all that passes, and yet eludes apprehension; something whose possession is the final good, and yet is beyond all reach; something which is the ultimate ideal, and the hopeless quest.

The immediate reaction of human nature to the religious vision is worship. Religion has emerged into human experience mixed with the crudest fancies of barbaric imagination. Gradually, slowly, steadily, the vision recurs in history under nobler form and with clearer expression. It is the one element in human experience which persistently shows an upward trend. It fades and then recurs. But when it renews its force it recurs with an added richness and purity of content. The fact of the religious vision, and its history of persistent expansion, is our one ground for optimism. Apart from it, human life is a flash of occasional enjoyments lighting up a mass of pain and misery, a bagatelle of transient experience.

The vision claims nothing but worship; and worship is a surrender to the claim for assimilation, urged with the motive force of mutual love. The vision never overrules. It is always there, and it has the power of love presenting the one purpose whose fulfillment is eternal harmony. Such order as we find in nature is never force — it presents itself as the one harmonious adjustment of complex detail. Evil is the brute motive force of fragmentary purpose, disregarding the eternal vision. Evil is overruling, retarding, hurting. The power of God is the worship He inspires. That religion is strong which in its ritual and its modes of thought evokes an apprehension of the commanding vision. The worship of God is not a rule of safety — it is an adventure of the spirit, a flight after the unattainable. The death of religion comes with the repression of the high hope of adventure.

August 1925

LORD DUNSANY

1878–

Napoleon was wont to remark on the prevalence of genius in children — until they went to school. Conventional education has a heavy hand and often dulls a shining talent. Among my friends there is no one who has kept the flame of childhood so clear and bright as Dunsany. No tutor has made his candle smoke or gutter, and the life of strenuous adventure he has led, hunting the breakneck country about Dunsany Castle, killing Germans in Europe or wild beasts in Africa, and writing fairy tales between, has trimmed the wick and let the flame burn clean. His stories are full of the delicious horror which affrights children as it enthralls them. He walks forever along the very edge of wonderland Dwarfs and ogres are his familiars, and no ghost nor goblin but is his friend.

As I write I see him at a desk in my own parlor, my children swarming about him. At his elbow are ranged four immense sticks of colored sealing wax, and beside him a lighted taper. Before the fascinated eyes about him flow on the paper marvelous contraptions of melting wax, dragons and octopuses, jabberwock and bandersnatch. Sometimes he picks up a big lump of clay. "Here," he says, "is the man determined to say 'No.'" Or, "Here's a gent on pleasure bent." Then right under your eyes come to life the comic features expressing precisely the titles he gives them.

One night Dunsany was to give a Boston lecture. It was billed for eight-fifteen. At six he had not turned up at my house, nor at seven. Seven-fifteen came as I hung nervously by the front door. Seven-thirty passed. It was seven-forty-five when up the street his car drove furiously. He had come from a visit to the naval station at Portsmouth, New Hampshire, and had miscalculated a bit. Out he threw his bag, leapt after it, and without one word except "I'm late and I'm hungry," dashed up the stairs through the drawing room and, without pause, straight into the dining room. On the table a comfortable supper was laid out, dominated by a roast chicken. Dunsany seized the bird, tore off a drumstick and, munching it, rushed upstairs to dress while his wife, mine and I stood by roaring with laughter. Oddities were not over for that day. "The one thing I want," he had written, "is a warm theatre. I have a cold. I must be warm." Since I was responsible for the performance I had that afternoon visited the theater and bribed the janitor to keep a hot furnace. Yet when we reached the foyer at eight-fourteen precisely, it was cold, indubitably cold. I felt trouble in my bones.

In a moment Dunsany made his appearance, laughing and delightful, and began his lecture. He seemed warming up and I relaxed. Then of a sudden I saw him shiver visibly. A page or two he turned and then, to the consternation of the audience, almost shouted, "I'm cold, I'm cold!" and, without ado, disappeared into the wing. A second later back he came bundled in his overcoat and around his neck a thick wool scarf. The informal lecture went on to the nervous applause of the audience, and when all was well over, it was with a thankful heart that I crept to bed.

Dunsany is like that. His is a child's genius, enduring and unspoiled. About it shades of the prison-house have never closed.

The Return

LORD DUNSANY

CAN you all hear me? I am speaking on the wireless. And I believe that I am in touch with you.

I thought that perhaps you might care to hear a ghost story. An actual personal experience, with nothing secondhand about it. A thing that occurred actually to myself, perhaps the most personal ghost story that any of you may have heard.

Well, to begin with, I was a long way away, when there came over me very suddenly an irresistible feeling to return to the old haunts that I had known a long while ago. I say "to begin with," for one must begin somewhere; and my long wanderings, and the remote parts to which I had come, are not much concerned with this tale. Sufficient that I turned at once for home, borne by a longing so strong that it seemed to leave me no choice, and I came in the course of time to that very village whose every chimney I knew. Every path I knew there too, and every little track running off from the paths the width of a single footstep, by which children ran to gardens of their own that they had found or made among weeds; but some of these paths had altered in the long time since I was there. It was a long, long time. The old public house was the sáme, the Green Man at the corner. And there I drifted, almost aimlessly, and yet with a feeling that there as much as anywhere I might find the life of the old village throbbing away. It was as I passed over the fields on the way to the Green Man that I first heard people talking about a ghost. I was passing a wheat field, over the stubble, brushing by a line of sheaves, when two men at work there, taking the sheaves away, began to talk of the ghost all of a sudden. "They say it comes every hundred years," said one. I knew at once they were speaking about a ghost.

"Yes," said the other, looking up at the leaves turning with the earliest touch of autumn, "and it should be about the very day."

"It is," said the first; and I heard them say no more, and passed on feeling sure I should hear more at the inn. At the inn I knew none of them, not one; and, where once I thought I did, it was only some old family likeness. So I sat all by myself in a corner beside a curtain and listened to what they said. And, just as I came in, their talk took the same turn as what I had heard in the cornfield. There was a ghost, it seemed, that came to that village once in a hundred years, and the hundred years were up. "Might be coming soon," said one, who looked like a gamekeeper.

"Aye, if there's any truth in it," said a farmer.

"True enough, by all accounts," said some.

"And there's been a look about the shadows lately," the keeper said, "like what my grandmother told me of."

"Your grandmother?" one of them asked.

"Yes, she saw it," he said.

"Must have been an old woman," said a man, looking round from the bar, on which he was leaning.

"Saw it as a child," said the keeper.

"I wouldn't walk near the stream to-night," said another, "not if any mist was rising. You'd meet it, all damp in the mist."

I sat there quietly in the shade of the curtain listening to all they said.

"Wonder where it comes from," said the farmer.

"Ah," they all said, and shook their heads, and no one even ventured to guess about that.

"Drifts over the fields where it used to walk, I expect, and up to the old house," said the bartender. "But as to where it comes from — ah."

And then their talk died away, as though it were somehow chilled by a draft blowing out of eternity. And when I saw I should get no more of this story from them I slipped quietly out of the room.

Two women were talking on a door-step as I passed the next house; they seemed to be talking about the price of tea. And suddenly I heard one say: "It will be about the hundred years."

"Aye," said the other one, "I shouldn't wonder." And one of them went inside the house at that, and the other hurried away along the street, and I was all alone once more.

I passed a group of children in the road; and saw from a certain hush that came over their playing, and from the way that a few of them put their heads together and glanced up towards the old house, that they too were talking of the ghost. It left no doubt that that house was the seat of the mystery, and that there these ends of tales one heard in the village would be all gathered together. But when would it be? Was it the hundred years? It hardly seemed to me that it could be yet. The air seemed somehow not quite sufficiently haunted, though it hardly seems worth telling you so airy a fancy. Partly to see the old village again, and partly to get more facts, if I could, about this tale of the ghost, I hung about the village. I went to the village green. It delighted me to see the calm old space again — altered, but not out of knowledge; and there were geese on it, just as of old. And then a young man and a girl came by, going along a path that slanted across the green, the same path that there had been in my time. And by some strange chance they too, as soon as they came within hearing, began to speak of the end of the hundred years, and that visitor that all of them were expecting. Half believing and half wondering, they passed away out of hearing.

One is moved by impulses more than by reason when one comes to old haunts that one knew. Had reason moved me alone, I should have gone at once to the old house on the hill beyond the village, and satisfied my curiosity there. But stronger than curiosity, stronger than any other emotion within me, I found the lure of the great willows, standing in their strange attitudes by the long-remembered stream. To them I went as evening began to draw in. A white mist rose as I came, and began to creep slowly through fields that sloped to the stream. I went with it, glad of its company, and loitered about those fields whose every boundary was unchanged by even a yard since the days when I knew them. And there the old haystacks stood, dark in the same corners, as though they had never been used since last I saw them; and the mist came up and touched them, and flowed about them, till they stood amongst it like islands. I seemed to know every one of them, not only by their positions, but by the size of them. You see, nothing could ever have happened in the years since I was there to make each field give more hay, or any less, or to find a better place for the haystack to stand in each field. It was this that made me see, what I already profoundly felt, that I still had my share in this village. Much had changed, but the fundamental things were there as ever. Indeed it could not have been otherwise. And it made me feel more friendly with the mist, with which I was sauntering amongst these remembered nooks, to reflect that it was another of those things that would be in that valley always. Or if it wandered away in the warm weather, carried off by some stray wind, it would return like myself.

Couples walking late, or men traveling lonely, turned now away from the mist, as though they found something ominous in its waving and wandering whiteness; they turned suddenly for the uplands, and we were left quite alone. And I knew they were right to avoid the stream at this hour, for there was a most haunted feeling about it, and that feeling slowly increased as the evening grew stiller and later. Rooks passed, and all the singing birds were asleep. A few wild ducks came over, and circled once, and dropped past me down to their home in a patch of irises; they alone seeming unperturbed by whatever was making the mist so unmistakably eerie. And then a silence fell that nothing disturbed at all, and all the while the eeriness was increasing.

It was like that till the moon rose. But when the moon came huge and yellow and magical and very nearly full, almost with a leap over a ridge of the downland that showed just clear of the osiers, I suddenly knew that the hundred years were up, and that whatever haunted the old house over the meadows, on the opposite side from the moon, would be now on its way if ever. So I left the stream at once and turned for the hill, to see what was to be seen. I went, all the way, over fields every one of which I had carried so long in my memory that I knew my way unmistakably. Sometimes they differed from the picture of them that I had treasured so long, but only by being a little duller, by shining a little less vividly, as must be the way with heavy solid earth when compared with an old memory. Voices were rising now in the village behind me, as though the large moon coming over the ridges, or the end of the hundred years, had awoken all of a sudden uneasy apprehensions; and not only human voices rose in a hum, but there came sharply through them the outcry of dogs, which clearly shared the vague fear that seemed haunting their masters. The sound of the voices grew low as I moved away from them, but never ceased to fill the night with fear. At what moment the hundred years would end I knew not, but it seemed to me that as the moon rose higher the very last hours of the century were falling away.

I crossed a road, and a couple walking down it paused suddenly and looked up to the old house on the hill. I saw the shape of it, dark, with no windows lit, though now and then the moon flashed curiously upon panes. And this bulk in the night, with flashes upon the windows, I knew for the end of my journey. In this house my life had begun, and to it I returned. It was this house that had called me, through all the length of my wanderings, and that I felt drawing me now, as the Pole draws the needles of magnets. I paid no heed any more to that uneasy hum that came quavering up from voices astir in the village, but left them to whatever troubled them in the mist, and made straight for that house. Far down below me now were the mist and its fears, and the slope of the hill steepened. I swept up it; and just as I came to the edge of the lawns I knew, as I know no other lawns, I found a high wall before me. They had built it since the days when I knew those lawns. There seemed something about the moon and about the hour that told me not to loiter before this wall, and I pressed on to the house.

The lawns were the same as ever, and all the dew was glittering under the moon, and a hush was heavy upon them, and the house was deep in sleep. Not a sound came from the black bulk of the house, not a movement of door or window, though I had returned to my home from so far and after so long. It stood there black and silent, but the chill and the hush and the darkness of the house were to stop me no more than the wall. I had come from so far to see those lawns again, and the old house standing amongst them. I went round to the door, and the glass which there was in its panels stared blankly at me, with shutters behind them; and all the bolts were locked. There a dog saw me. It had been lying down in a barrel, guarding the door, when it suddenly saw me and howled. But still no sound or movement came from the house.

I knew I was very near to the end of my long journey now, the old wainscot of oak on an upper landing, carved with the curious heads of ancient kings, dark with the years and darkening all the corridor, that ran to the door of a room that was once my nursery. I knew now that this carved oak was the end of my journey. I entered the house, and the dog howled once more. Before me, all in the dark, were the stairs I knew. I needed no light. I knew every turn of those stairs, and every step of them, and the very flight of the echoes that used to rise from the creak of each different board. I sped up them, and the dog was howling now with one long quivering howl. I came to the landing, and there was the old dark corridor, and there were the ancient heads with their curious faces that seemed to look at me with the first welcome I had had since my long journey began. The howling of the dog, which was louder now, seemed at last to disturb the house, for far away I heard the thudding of footsteps. And the steps were coming towards me.

Can you hear me? I feel that you can. I believe I am near you. A door opened some way off. The steps were nearer. A woman came along the corridor, holding a candle, walking slowly, and looking about her anxiously as she came. And just then clearly out of the tower of the old church of the village the notes of midnight floated over the mist; and it felt to me at that moment that the hundred years were over. And all of a sudden the woman holding the candle saw me. She seemed to see me more clearly than any had done in the village: I noticed that in her eyes as her mouth opened slowly. And then she screamed.

This is a personal experience. Nothing secondhand, as so often there is in such stories. I turned from the woman's white face to the dark of the old carved wainscot, whose every panel and every figure I knew; and, sinking far into that venerable timber, sinking home to the deeps of the oak, I knew that *I* was the ghost.

June 1935

ERNEST HEMINGWAY

1898–

A prime principle of Nature seems to be separation. Rigorously she divides species, separates one element from another, seems to draw a fixed line between plant and animal life. This classification she has taught men. When we read or study it is natural for us to think of things in schools and ranks and classes. So it is that when we come on a new force in literature we try at once to pigeonhole it with a convenient label. Nothing is wholly original of course. Everything has a precedent, but once in a considerable while comes a book that seems to come from the void. What inconvenience, then, had the critics to put up with in the early years of Ernest Hemingway! They have got him classified now, but at the outset he seemed a "sport" in the works of creation. New tricks he certainly has. He will fill whole pages with conversation which might be phonograph records of familiar talk. Then out of it he will conjure great effects. And the familiar matter gives assurance of its genuineness in that it is never expurgated. Often it comes rough and raw. My friend, Owen Wister, who was no upstanding prude himself, once wrote to Hemingway asking why he found it necessary to introduce unwonted and unwanted words, ugly in themselves and embarrassing to read aloud. Hemingway's reply was characteristic. He could not see why the words were unwonted, for the conversation to which Wister objected was merely a transcript of what he himself had listened to at the Captain's table when a Governor-General was chatting with a Bishop across the board!

There may have been a bit of spoofing in the answer. But if any man takes his art seriously, it is Hemingway. Sometimes the talk in his books may be dull, but that is when he wants to make it so; neutral colors are made to heighten the violence of a large design. But with Hemingway it is not only in language but the outrageous has no terrors. He is an artist utterly without compunction and sins willingly against human sympathy, brutalizing the reader's feelings with about the same degree of respect that Nature exhibits when she puts on her own shows.

We are used to Hemingway. We may not have his accurate measure now, but in earlier days people were aghast, for it was only a little while before that Reticence had been repealed. The world moves fast and it is almost incredible that one generation ago the story I have chosen for this book was a bugaboo to magazines. It went the rounds of the large circulations. Editors had fine phrases for it and courteous explanations for the author, but the agent came to think it unprintable, when news of it came to the Atlantic. We swooped down on that manuscript. In this office there were no doubts. The superb masculine lines of the story were like a Bellows etching of a pair of brutes within the squared circle. In all literature I myself can think of nothing quite comparable to the calcium light it casts on the darker psychology of the Prize Ring. But of course if you will have a fight in all its glory, Lavengro's bout with the Flaming Tinman remains supreme. Not such a battle as that has been fought since Homer, nor was Helen herself a more compulsive inspiration to victory than Isopel Berners with her "Fear God and take your own part."

Fifty Grand

ERNEST HEMINGWAY

I

"How are you going yourself, Jack?" I asked him.

"You seen this Walcott?" he says.

"Just in the gym."

"Well," Jack says, "I'm going to need a lot of luck with that boy."

"He can't hit you, Jack," Soldier said.

"I wish to hell he couldn't."

"He couldn't hit you with a handful of birdshot."

"Birdshot'd be all right," Jack says. "I wouldn't mind birdshot any."

"He looks easy to hit," I said.

"Sure," Jack says, "he ain't going to last long. He ain't going to last like you and me, Jerry. But right now he's got everything."

"You'll left-hand him to death."

"Maybe," Jack says. "Sure. I got a chance to."

"Handle him like you handled Kid Lewis."

"Kid Lewis," Jack said. "That kike!"

The three of us, Jack Brennan, Soldier Bartlett, and I, were in Handley's. There were a couple of broads sitting at the next table to us. They had been drinking.

"What do you mean, kike?" one of the broads says. "What do you mean, kike, you big Irish bum!"

"Sure," Jack says. "That's it."

"Kikes," this broad goes on. "They're always talking about kikes, these big Irishmen. What do you mean, kikes?"

"Come on. Let's get out of here."

"Kikes," this broad goes on. "Whoever saw you ever buy a drink? Your wife sews your pockets up every morning. These Irishmen and their kikes. Ted Lewis could lick you, too."

"Sure," Jack says. "And you give away a lot of things free, too, don't you?"

We went out. That was Jack. He could say what he wanted to when he wanted to say it.

Jack started training out at Danny Hogan's health farm over in Jersey. It was nice out there, but Jack didn't like it much. He didn't like being away from his wife and the kids, and he was sore and grouchy most of the time. He liked me and we got along fine together; and he liked Hogan, but after a while Soldier Bartlett commenced to get on his nerves. A kidder gets to be an awful thing around a camp if his stuff goes sort of sour. Soldier was always kidding Jack, just sort of kidding him all the time. It wasn't very funny and it wasn't very good, and it began to get to Jack.

It was sort of stuff like this. Jack would finish up with the weights and the bag and pull on the gloves. "You want to work?" he'd say to Soldier.

"Sure. How you want me to work?" Soldier would ask. "Want me to treat you rough like Walcott? Want me to knock you down a few times?"

"That's it," Jack would say. He didn't like it any, though.

One morning we were all out on the road. We'd been out quite a way and now we were coming back. We'd go along fast for three minutes and then walk a minute, and then go fast for three minutes again. Jack wasn't ever what you would call a sprinter. He'd move around fast enough in the ring if he had to, but he wasn't any too fast on the road. All the time we were walking Soldier Bartlett was kidding him. We came up the hill to the farmhouse.

"Well," says Jack, "you better go back to town, Soldier."

"What do you mean?"

"You better go back to town and stay there."

"What's the matter?"

"I'm sick of hearing you talk."

"Yes?" says Soldier.

"Yes," says Jack.

"You'll be a damn sight sicker when Walcott gets through with you."

"Sure," says Jack, "maybe I will. But I know I'm sick of you."

So Soldier went off on the train to town that same morning. I went down with him to the train. He was good and sore.

"I was just kidding him," he said. We were waiting on the platform. "He can't pull that stuff with me, Jerry."

"He's nervous and crabby," I said. "He's a good fellow, Soldier."

"The hell he is. The hell he's ever been a good fellow."

"Well," I said, "so long, Soldier."

The train had come in. He climbed up with his bag.

"So long, Jerry," he says. "You be in town before the fight?"

"I don't think so."

"See you then."

He went in and the conductor swung up and the train went out. I rode back to the farm in the cart. Jack was on the porch writing a letter to his wife. The mail had come and I got the papers and went over on the other side of the porch and sat down to read. Hogan came out the door and came over to me.

"Did he have a jam with Soldier?"

"Not a jam," I said. "He just told him to go back to town."

"I could see it coming," Hogan said. "He never liked Soldier much."

"No. He don't like many people."

"He's a pretty cold one," Hogan said.

"Well, he's always been fine to me."

"Me too," Hogan said. "I got no kick on him. He's a cold one, though."

Hogan went in through the screen door and I sat there on the porch and read the papers. It was just starting to get fall weather and it's nice country there in Jersey up in the hills, and after I read the paper through I sat there and looked out at the country and the road down below against the woods, with a car going along it, lifting the dust up. It was fine weather and pretty nice-looking country. Hogan came to the door and I said, "Say, Hogan, haven't you got anything to shoot out here?"

"No," Hogan said. "Only sparrows."

"Seen the paper?" I said to Hogan.

"What's in it?"

"Sande booted three of them in yesterday."

"I got that on the telephone last night."

"You follow them pretty close, Hogan?" I asked.

"Oh, I keep in touch with them."

"How about Jack?" I says. "Does he still play them?"

"Him?" said Hogan. "Can you see him doing it?"

Just then Jack came around the corner with the letter in his hand. He's wearing a sweater and an old pair of pants and boxing shoes.

"Got a stamp, Hogan?" he asks.

"Give me the letter," Hogan said. "I'll mail it for you."

"Say, Jack," I said. "Didn't you used to play the ponies?"

"Sure."

"I knew you did. I knew I used to see you out at Sheepshead."

"What did you lay off them for?" Hogan asked.

"Lost money."

Jack sat down on the porch by me. He leaned back against a post. He shut his eyes in the sun.

"Want a chair?" Hogan asked.

"No," said Jack. "This is fine."

"It's a nice day," I said. "It's pretty nice out in the country."

"I'd a damn sight rather be in town with the wife."

"Well, you only got another week."

"Yes," Jack says. "That's so."

We sat there on the porch. Hogan was inside at the office.

"What do you think about the shape I'm in?" Jack asked me.

"Well, you can't tell," I said. "You got a week to get around into form."

"Don't stall me."

"Well," I said, "you're not right."

"I'm not sleeping," Jack said.

"You'll be all right in a couple of days."

"No," says Jack, "I got the insomnia."

"What's on your mind?"

"I miss the wife."

"Have her come out."

"No. I'm too old for that."

"We'll take a long walk before you turn in, and get you good and tired."

"Tired!" Jack says. "I'm tired all the time."

He was that way all week. He wouldn't sleep at night and he'd get up in the morning feeling that way — you know, when you can't shut your hands.

"He's stale as poorhouse cake," Hogan said. "He's nothing."

"I never seen Walcott," I said.

"He'll kill him," said Hogan. "He'll tear him in two."

"Well," I said, "everybody's got to get it sometime."

"Not like this, though," Hogan said. "They'll think he never trained. It gives the farm a black eye."

"You hear what the reporters said about him?"

"Didn't I! They said he was awful. They said they oughtn't to let him fight."

"Well," I said, "they're always wrong, ain't they?"

"Yes," said Hogan. "But this time they're right."

"What the hell do they know about whether a man's right or not?"

"Well," said Hogan, "they're not such fools."

"All they did was pick Willard at Toledo. This Lardner, he's so wise now, ask him about when he picked Willard at Toledo."

"Aw, he wasn't out," Hogan said. "He only writes the big fights."

"I don't care who they are," I said. "What the hell do they know? They can write, maybe, but what the hell do they know?"

"You don't think Jack's in any shape, do you?" Hogan asked.

"No. He's through. All he needs is to have Corbett pick him to win for it to be all over."

"Well, Corbett'll pick him," Hogan says.

"Sure. He'll pick him."

That night Jack didn't sleep any either. The next morning was the last day before the fight. After breakfast we were out on the porch again.

"What do you think about, Jack, when you can't sleep?" I said.

"Oh, I worry," Jack says. "I worry about property I got up in the Bronx. I worry about property I got in Florida. I worry about the kids. I worry about the wife. Sometimes I think about fights. I think about that kike Ted Lewis and I get sore. I got some stocks and I worry about them. What the hell don't I think about?"

"Well," I said, "to-morrow night it'll all be over."

"Sure," said Jack. "That always helps a lot, don't it? That just fixes everything all up, I suppose. Sure."

He was sore all day. We didn't do any work. Jack just moved around a little to loosen up. He shadow-boxed a few rounds. He didn't even look good doing that. He skipped the rope a little while. He couldn't sweat.

"He'd be better not to do any work at all," Hogan said. We were standing watching him skip rope. "Don't he ever sweat at all any more?"

"He can't sweat."

"Do you suppose he's got the con? He never had any trouble making weight, did he?"

"No, he hasn't got any con. He just hasn't got anything inside any more."

"He ought to sweat," said Hogan.

Jack came over skipping the rope. He was skipping up and down in front of us, forward and back, crossing his arms every third time.

"Well," he says, "what are you buzzards talking about?"

"I don't think you ought to work any more," Hogan says. "You'll be stale."

"Wouldn't that be awful?" Jack says and skips away down the floor, slapping the rope hard.

II

That afternoon John Collins showed up out at the farm. Jack was up in his room. John came out in a car from town. He had a couple of friends with him. The car stopped and they all got out.

"Where's Jack?" John asked me.

"Up in his room, lying down."

"Lying down?"

"Yes," I said.

"How is he?"

I looked at the two fellows that were with John.

"They're friends of his," John said.

"He's pretty bad," I said.

"What's the matter with him?"

"He don't sleep."

"Hell," said John. "That Irishman could never sleep."

"He isn't right," I said.

"Hell," John said. "He's never right. I've had him for ten years and he's never been right yet."

The fellows with him laughed.

"I want you to shake hands with Mr. Morgan and Mr. Steinfelt," John said. "This is Mr. Doyle. He's been training Jack."

"Glad to meet you," I said.

"Let's go up and see the boy," the fellow called Morgan said.

"Let's have a look at him," Steinfelt said.

We all went upstairs.

"Where's Hogan?" John asked.

"He's out in the barn with a couple of his customers," I said.

"He got many people out here now?"

"Just two."

"Pretty quiet, ain't it?" Morgan said.

"Yes," I said. "It's pretty quiet."

We were outside Jack's room. John knocked on the door. There wasn't any answer.

"Maybe he's asleep," I said.

"What the hell's he sleeping in the daytime for?"

John turned the handle and we all went in. Jack was lying asleep on the bed. He was face down and his face was in the pillow. Both his arms were around the pillow.

"Hey, Jack!" John said to him.

Jack's head moved a little on the pillow. "Jack!" John says, leaning over him. Jack just dug a little deeper in the pillow. John touched him on the shoulder. Jack sat up and looked at us. He hadn't shaved and he was wearing an old sweater.

"Hell! Why can't you let me sleep?" he says to John.

"Don't be sore," John says. "I didn't mean to wake you up."

"Oh no," Jack says. "Of course not."

"You know Morgan and Steinfelt," John said.

"Glad to see you," Jack says.

"How do you feel, Jack?" Morgan asks him.

"Fine," Jack says. "How the hell would I feel?"

"You look fine," Steinfelt says.

"Yes, don't I?" says Jack. "Say," he says to John. "You're my manager. You get a big enough cut. Why the hell didn't you come out here when the reporters was out? You want Jerry and me to talk to them?"

"I had Lew fighting in Philadelphia."

"What the hell's that to me?" Jack says. "You're my manager. You get a big enough cut, don't you? You aren't making me any money in Philadelphia, are you? Why the hell aren't you out here when I ought to have you?"

"Hogan was here."

"Hogan," Jack says. "Hogan's as dumb as I am."

"Soldier Bahtlett was out here wukking with you for a while, wasn't he?" Steinfelt says, to change the subject.

"Yes, he was out here," Jack says. "He was out here, all right."

"Say, Jerry," John said to me. "Would you go and find Hogan and tell him we want to see him in about half an hour?"

"Sure," I said.

"Why the hell can't he stick around?" Jack says. "Stick around, Jerry."

Morgan and Steinfelt looked at each other.

"Quiet down, Jack," John said to him.

"I better go find Hogan," I said.

"All right, if you want to go," Jack says. "None of these guys are going to send you away, though."

"I'll go find Hogan," I said.

Hogan was out in the gym in the barn. He had a couple of his health-farm patients with the gloves on. They neither one wanted to hit the other for fear the other would come back and hit him.

"That'll do," Hogan said when he saw me come in. "You can stop the slaughter. You gentlemen take a shower and Bruce will rub you down."

They climbed out through the ropes and Hogan came over to me.

"John Collins is out with a couple of friends to see Jack," I said.

"I saw them come up in the car."

"Who are the two fellows with John?"

"They're what you call wise boys," Hogan said. "Don't you know them two?"

"No," I said.

"That's Happy Steinfelt and Lew Morgan. They got a pool room."

"I been away a long time," I said.

"Sure," said Hogan. "That Happy Steinfelt's a big operator."

"I've heard his name," I said.

"He's a pretty smooth boy," Hogan said. "They're a couple of sharp-shooters."

"Well," I said, "they want to see us in half an hour."

"You mean they don't want to see us until a half an hour?"

"That's it."

"Come on in the office," Hogan said. "To hell with those sharpshooters."

After about thirty minutes or so Hogan and I went upstairs. We knocked on Jack's door. They were talking inside the room.

"Wait a minute," somebody said.

"To hell with that stuff," Hogan said. "When you want to see me I'm down in the office."

We heard the door unlock. Steinfelt opened it.

"Come on in, Hogan," he says. "We're all going to have a drink."

"Well," says Hogan, "that's something."

We went in. Jack was sitting on the bed. John and Morgan were sitting on a couple of chairs. Steinfelt was standing up.

"You're a pretty mysterious lot of boys," Hogan said.

"Hello, Danny," John says.

"Hello, Danny," Morgan says and shakes hands.

Jack doesn't say anything. He just sits there on the bed. He ain't with the others. He's all by himself. He was wearing an old blue jersey and an old pair of pants and had on boxing shoes. He needed a shave. Steinfelt and Morgan were dressers. John was quite a dresser, too. Jack sat there looking Irish and tough.

Steinfelt brought out a bottle and Hogan brought in some glasses and everybody had a drink. Jack and I took one and the rest of them went on and had two or three each.

"Better save some for your ride back," Hogan said.

"Don't you worry. We got plenty," Morgan said.

Jack hadn't drunk anything since the one drink. He was standing up and looking at them. Morgan was sitting on the bed where Jack had sat.

"Have a drink, Jack," John said and handed him the glass and the bottle.

"No," Jack said, "I never liked to go to these wakes."

They all laughed. Jack didn't laugh.

They were all feeling pretty good when they left. Jack stood on the porch when they got into the car. They waved to him.

"So long," Jack said.

We had supper. Jack didn't say anything all during the meal except "Will you pass me this?" or "Will you pass me that?" The two health-farm patients ate at the same table with us. They were pretty nice fellas. After we finished eating we went out on the porch. It was dark early.

"Like to take a walk, Jerry?" Jack asked.

"Sure," I said.

We put on our coats and started out. It was quite a way down to the main road, and then we walked along the main road about a mile and a half. Cars kept going by and we would pull out to the side until they were past. Jack didn't say anything. After we had stepped out into the bushes to let a big car go by, Jack said, "To hell with this walking. Come on back to Hogan's."

We went along a side road that cut up over the hill and cut across the fields back to Hogan's. We could see the lights of the house up on the hill. We came around to the front of the house and there, standing in the doorway, was Hogan.

"Have a good walk?" Hogan asked.

"Oh, fine," Jack said. "Listen, Hogan. Have you got any liquor?"

"Sure," says Hogan. "What's the idea?"

"Send it up to the room," Jack says. "I'm going to sleep to-night."

"You're the doctor," Hogan says.

"Come on up to the room, Jerry," Jack says.

Upstairs Jack sat on the bed with his head in his hands.

"Ain't it a life?" Jack says.

Hogan brought in a quart of liquor and two glasses.

"Want some ginger ale?"

"What do you think I want to do—get sick?"

"I just asked you," said Hogan.

"Have a drink?" said Jack.

"No, thanks," said Hogan. He went out.

"How about you, Jerry?"

"I'll have one with you," I said.

Jack poured out a couple of drinks. "Now," he said, "I want to take it slow and easy."

"Put some water in it," I said.

"Yes," Jack said. "I guess that's better."

We had a couple of drinks without saying anything. Jack started to pour me another.

"No," I said, "that's all I want."

"All right," Jack said. He poured himself out another big shot and put water in it. He was lighting up a little.

"That was a fine bunch out here this afternoon," he said. "They don't take any chances, those two."

Then a little later, "Well," he says, "they're right. What the hell's the good in taking chances?"

"Don't you want another, Jerry?" he said. "Come on, drink along with me."

"I don't need it, Jack," I said. "I feel all right."

"Just have one more," Jack said. It was softening him up.

"All right," I said.

Jack poured one for me and another big one for himself.

"You know," he said, "I like liquor pretty well. If I hadn't been boxing I would have drunk quite a lot."

"Sure," I said.

"You know," he said, "I missed a lot, boxing."

"You made plenty of money."

"Sure, that's what I'm after. You know I miss a lot, Jerry."

"How do you mean?"

"Well," he says, "like about the wife. And being away from home so much. It don't do my girls any good. 'Who's your old man?' some of those society kids'll say to them. 'My old man's Jack Brennan.' That don't do them any good."

"Hell," I said. "All that makes a difference is if they got dough."

"Well," says Jack, "I got the dough for them all right."

He poured out another drink. The bottle was about empty.

"Put some water in it," I said. Jack poured in some water.

"You know," he says, "you ain't got any idea how I miss the wife."

"Sure."

"You ain't got any idea. You can't have an idea what it's like."

"It ought to be better out in the country than in town."

"With me now," Jack said, "it don't make any difference where I am. You can't have an idea what it's like."

"Have another drink."

"Am I getting soused? Do I talk funny?"

"You're coming on all right."

"You can't have an idea what it's like. They ain't anybody can have an idea what it's like."

"Except the wife," I said.

"She knows," Jack said. "She knows, all right. She knows. You bet she knows."

"Put some water in that," I said.

"Jerry," says Jack, "you can't have an idea what it gets to be like."

He was good and drunk. He was looking at me steady. His eyes were sort of too steady.

"You'll sleep, all right," I said.

"Listen, Jerry," Jack says. "You want to make some money? Get some dough down on Walcott."

"Yes?"

"Listen, Jerry." Jack put down the glass. "I'm not drunk now, see? You know what I'm betting on him? Fifty grand."

"That's a lot of dough."

"Fifty grand," Jack says, "at two to one. I'll get twenty-five thousand bucks. Get some money on him, Jerry."

"It sounds good," I said.

"How can I beat him?" Jack says. "It ain't crooked. How can I beat him? Why not make money on it?"

"Put some water in that," I said.

"I'm through after this fight," Jack says. "I'm through with it. I got to take a beating. Why shouldn't I make money on it?"

"Sure."

"I ain't slept for a week," Jack says. "All night I lay awake and worry my can off. I can't sleep, Jerry. You ain't got an idea what it's like when you can't sleep."

"Sure."

"I can't sleep. That's all. I just can't sleep. What's the use of taking care of yourself all these years when you can't sleep?"

"It's bad."

"You ain't got an idea what it's like, Jerry, when you can't sleep."

"Put some water in that," I said.

Well, about eleven o'clock Jack passes out and I put him to bed. Finally he's so he can't keep from sleeping. I helped him get his clothes off and got him into bed.

"You'll sleep, all right, Jack," I said.

"Sure," Jack says, "I'll sleep now."

"Good night, Jack," I said.

"Good night, Jerry," Jack says. "You're the only friend I got."

"Oh, hell," I said.

"You're the only friend I got," Jack says. "The only friend I got."

"Go to sleep," I said.

"I'll sleep," Jack says.

Downstairs Hogan was sitting at the desk in the office reading the papers. He looked up.

"Well, you get your boy friend to sleep?" he asks.

"He's off."

"It's better for him than not sleeping," Hogan said.

"Sure."

"You'd have a hell of a time explaining that to these sport writers, though," Hogan said.

"Well, I'm going to bed myself," I said.

"Good night," said Hogan.

III

In the morning I came downstairs about eight o'clock and got some breakfast. Hogan had his two customers out in the barn doing exercises. I went out and watched them.

"One! Two! Three! Four!" Hogan was counting for them. "Hello, Jerry," he said. "Is Jack up yet?"

"No. He's still sleeping."

I went back to my room and packed up to go in to town. About nine-thirty I heard Jack getting up in the next room. When I heard him go downstairs I went down after him. Jack was sitting at the breakfast table. Hogan had come in and was standing beside the table.

"How do you feel, Jack?" I asked him.

"Not so bad."

"Sleep well?" Hogan asked.

"I slept, all right," Jack said. "I got a thick tongue, but I ain't got a head."

"Good," said Hogan. "That was good liquor."

"Put it on the bill," Jack says.

"What time you want to go in to town?" Hogan asked.

"Before lunch," Jack says. "The eleven o'clock train."

Hogan went out.

"Sit down, Jerry," Jack said.

I sat down at the table. Jack was eating a grapefruit. When he'd find a seed he'd spit it out in the spoon and dump it on the plate.

"I guess I was pretty stewed last night," he started.

"You drank some liquor."

"I guess I said a lot of fool things."

"You weren't bad."

"Where's Hogan?" he asked. He was through with the grapefruit.

"He's out in front in the office."

"What did I say about betting on the fight?" Jack asked. He was holding the spoon and sort of poking at the grapefruit with it.

The girl came in with some ham and eggs and took away the grapefruit.

"Bring me another glass of milk," Jack said to her. She went out.

"You said you had fifty grand on Walcott," I said.

"That's right," Jack said.

"That's a lot of money."

"I don't feel too good about it," Jack said.

"Something might happen."

"No," Jack said. "He wants the title bad. They'll be shooting with him, all right."

"You can't ever tell."

"No. He wants the title. It's worth a lot of money to him."

"Fifty grand is a lot of money," I said.

"It's business," said Jack. "I can't win. You know I can't win anyway."

"As long as you're in there you got a chance."

"No," Jack says. "I'm all through. It's just business."

"How do you feel?"

"Pretty good," Jack said. "The sleep was what I needed."

"You might go good."

"I'll give them a good show," Jack said.

After breakfast Jack called up his wife on the long distance. He was inside the booth telephoning.

"That's the first time he's called her up since he's out here," Hogan said.

"He writes her every day."

"Sure," Hogan says. "A letter only costs two cents."

Hogan said good-bye to us, and Bruce, the nigger rubber, drove us down to the train in the cart.

"Good-bye, Mr. Brennan," Bruce said at the train. "I sure hope you knock his can off."

"So long," Jack said. He gave Bruce two dollars. Bruce had worked on him a lot. He looked kind of disappointed. Jack saw me looking at Bruce holding the two dollars.

"It's all in the bill," he said. "Hogan charged me for the rubbing."

On the train going into town Jack didn't talk. He sat in the corner of the seat with his ticket in his hatband and looked out of the window. Once he turned and spoke to me.

"I told the wife I'd take a room at the Shelby to-night," he said. "It's just around the corner from the Garden. I can go up to the house to-morrow morning."

"That's a good idea," I said. "Your wife ever see you fight, Jack?"

"No," Jack says. "She never seen me fight."

I thought, he must be figuring on taking an awful beating if he doesn't want to go home afterward. In town we took a taxi up to the Shelby. A boy came out and took our bags and we went in to the desk.

"How much are the rooms?" Jack asked.

"We only have double rooms," the clerk says. "I can give you a nice double room for ten dollars."

"That's too steep."

"I can give you a double room for seven dollars."

"With a bath?"

"Certainly."

"You might as well bunk with me, Jerry," Jack says.

"Oh," I said, "I'll sleep down at my brother-in-law's."

"I don't mean for you to pay it," Jack says. "I just want to get my money's worth."

"Will you register, please?" the clerk says.

He looked at the names. "Number 238, Mr. Brennan."

We went up in the elevator. It was a nice big room with two beds and a door opening into a bathroom.

"This is pretty good," Jack says.

The boy who brought us up pulled up the curtains and brought in our bags. Jack didn't make any move, so I gave the boy a quarter. We washed up and Jack said we better go out and get something to eat.

We ate a lunch at Jimmy Handley's place. Quite a lot of the boys were there. When we were about half through eating, John came in and sat down with us. Jack didn't talk much.

"How are you on the weight, Jack?" John asked him. Jack was putting away a pretty good lunch.

"I could make it with my clothes on," Jack said. He never had to worry about taking off weight. He was a natural welterweight and he'd never gotten fat. He'd lost weight out at Hogan's.

"Well, that's one thing you never had to worry about," John said.

"That's one thing," Jack says.

We went around to the Garden to weigh in after lunch. The match was made at a hundred forty-seven pounds at three o'clock. Jack stepped on the scales with a towel around him. The bar didn't move. Walcott had just weighed and was standing with a lot of people around him.

"Let's see what you weigh, Jack," Freedman, Walcott's manager, said.

"All right, weigh *him* then," Jack jerked his head toward Walcott.

"Drop the towel," Freedman said.

"What do you make it?" Jack asked the fellows who were weighing.

"Hundred and forty-three pounds," the fat man who was weighing said.

"You're down fine, Jack," Freedman says.

"Weigh *him,*" Jack says.

Walcott came over. He was a blonde with wide shoulders and arms like a heavyweight. He didn't have much legs. Jack stood about half a head taller than he did.

"Hello, Jack," he said. His face was plenty marked up.

"Hello," said Jack. "How you feel?"

"Good," Walcott says. He dropped the towel from around his waist and stood on the scales. He had the widest shoulders and back you ever saw.

"One hundred and forty-six pounds and twelve ounces."

Walcott stepped off and grinned at Jack.

"Well," John says to him, "Jack's spotting you about four pounds."

"More than that when I come in, Kid," Walcott says. "I'm going to go and eat now."

We went back and Jack got dressed. "He's a pretty tough-looking boy," Jack says to me.

"He looks as though he'd been hit plenty of times."

"Oh yes," Jack says. "He ain't hard to hit."

"Where are you going?" John asked when Jack was dressed.

"Back to the hotel," Jack says. "You looked after everything?"

"Yes," John says. "It's all looked after."

"I'm going to lie down a while," Jack says.

"I'll come around for you about a quarter to seven and we'll go and eat."

"All right."

Up at the hotel Jack took off his shoes and his coat and lay down for a while. I wrote a letter. I looked over a couple of times and Jack wasn't sleeping. He was lying perfectly still, but every once in a while his eyes would open. Finally he sits up.

"Want to play some cribbage, Jerry?" he says.

"Sure," I said.

He went over to his suitcase and got out the cards and the cribbage board. We played cribbage and he won three dollars off me. John knocked at the door and came in.

"Want to play some cribbage, John?" Jack asked him.

John put his kelly down on the table. It was all wet. His coat was wet, too.

"Is it raining?" Jack asks.

"It's pouring," John says. "The taxi I had got tied up in the traffic and I got out and walked."

"Come on, play some cribbage," Jack says.

"You ought to go and eat."

"No," says Jack. "I don't want to eat yet."

So they played cribbage for about half an hour and Jack won a dollar and a half off him.

"Well, I suppose we got to go eat," Jack says. He went to the window and looked out.

"Is it still raining?"

"Yes."

"Let's eat in the hotel," John says.

"All right," Jack says. "I'll play you once more to see who pays for the meal."

After a little while Jack gets up and says, "You buy the meal, John," and we went downstairs and ate in the big dining room.

After we ate we went upstairs and Jack played cribbage with John again and won two dollars and a half off him. Jack was feeling pretty good. John had a bag with him with all his stuff in it. Jack took off his shirt and collar and put on a jersey and a sweater, so he wouldn't catch cold when he came out, and put his ring clothes and his bathrobe in a bag.

"You all ready?" John asks him. "I'll call up and have them get a taxi."

Pretty soon the telephone rang and they said the taxi was waiting.

We rode down in the elevator and went out through the lobby, and got in the taxi and rode around to the Garden. It was raining hard, but there was a lot of people outside on the streets. The Garden was sold out. As we came in on our way to the dressing room I saw how full it was. It looked like half a mile down to the ring. It was all dark. Just the lights over the ring.

"It's a good thing, with this rain, they didn't try and pull this fight in the ball park," John said.

"They got a good crowd," Jack says.

"This is a fight that would draw a lot more than the Garden could hold."

"You can't tell about the weather," Jack says.

John came to the door of the dressing room and poked his head in. Jack was sitting there with his bathrobe on; he had his arms folded and was looking at the floor. John had a couple of handlers with him. They looked over his shoulder. Jack looked up.

"Is he in?" he asked.

"He's just gone down," John said.

We started down. Walcott was just getting into the ring. The crowd gave him a big hand. He climbed through between the ropes and put his two fists together and smiled and shook them at the crowd, first at one side of the ring, then at the other, and then sat down. Jack got a good hand coming down through the crowd. Jack is Irish, and the Irish always get a pretty good hand. An Irishman don't draw in New York like a Jew or an Eyetalian, but they always get a good hand. Jack climbed up and bent down to go through the ropes, and Walcott came over from his corner and pushed the rope down for Jack to go through. The crowd thought that was wonderful. Walcott put his hand on Jack's shoulder and they stood there just for a second.

"So you're going to be one of these popular champions," Jack says to him. "Take your goddam hand off my shoulder."

"Be yourself," Walcott says.

This is all great for the crowd. How gentlemanly the boys are before the fight! How they wish each other luck!

Solly Freedman comes over to our corner while Jack is bandaging his hands and John is over in Walcott's corner. Jack put his thumb through the slit in the bandage and then wrapped his hand nice and smooth. I taped it around the wrist and twice across the knuckles.

"Hey," Freedman says. "Where do you get all that tape?"

"Feel of it," Jack said. "It's soft, ain't it? Don't be a hick."

Freedman stands there all the time while Jack bandages the other hand, and one of the boys that's going to handle him brings the gloves and I pull them on and work them around.

"Say, Freedman," Jack asks. "What nationality is this Walcott?"

"I don't know," Solly says. "He's some sort of a Dane."

"He's a Bohemian," the lad who brought the gloves said.

The referee called them out to the centre of the ring and Jack walks out. Walcott comes out smiling. They met and the referee put his arm on each of their shoulders.

"Hello, Popularity," Jack says to Walcott.

"Be yourself."

"What do you call yourself Walcott for," Jack says. "Didn't you know he was a nigger?"

"Listen — " says the referee, and he gives them the same old line. Once Walcott interrupts him. He grabs Jack's arm and says, "Can I hit when he's got me like this?"

"Keep your hands off me," Jack says. "There ain't no moving picture of this."

They went back to their corners. I lifted the bathrobe off Jack and he leaned on the ropes and flexed his knees a couple of times and scuffed his shoes in the rosin. The gong rang and Jack turned quick and went out. Walcott came toward him and they touched gloves, and as soon as Walcott dropped his hands Jack jumped his left into his face twice. There wasn't anybody ever boxed better than Jack. Walcott was after him, going forward all the time with his chin on his chest. He's a hooker and he carries his hands pretty low. All he knows is to get in there and sock. But every time he gets in there close, Jack has the left hand in his face. It's just as though it's automatic. Jack just raises the left hand up and it's in Walcott's face. Three or four times Jack brings the right over, but Walcott gets it on the shoulder or high up on the head. He's just like all these hookers. The only thing he's afraid of is another one of the same kind. He's covered everywhere you can hurt him. He don't care about a left hand in his face.

After about four rounds Jack has him bleeding bad and his face all cut up, but every time Walcott's got in close he's socked so hard he's got two big red patches on both sides just below Jack's ribs. Every time he gets in close, Jack ties him up, then gets one hand loose and uppercuts him, but when Walcott gets his hands loose he socks Jack in the body so they can hear it outside in the street. He's a socker.

It goes along like that for three rounds more. They don't talk any. They're working all the time. We worked over Jack plenty, too, in between the rounds. He don't look good at all, but he never does much work in the ring. He don't move around much, and that left hand is just automatic. It's just like it was connected with Walcott's face and Jack just had to wish it in every time. Jack is always calm in close, and he doesn't waste any juice. He knows everything about working in close, too, and he's getting away with a lot of stuff. While they were in our corner I watched him tie Walcott up, get his right hand loose, turn it, and come up with an uppercut that got Walcott's nose with the heel of the glove. Walcott was bleeding bad and leaned his nose on Jack's shoulder so as to give Jack some of it, too, and Jack sort of lifted his shoulder sharp and caught him against the nose, and then brought down the right hand and uppercut him again.

Walcott was sore as hell. By the time they'd gone five rounds he hated Jack's guts. Jack wasn't sore; that is, he wasn't any sorer than he always was. He certainly did used to make the fellows he fought hate boxing. That was why he hated Kid Lewis so. He never got the Kid's goat. Kid Lewis always had about three new dirty things Jack couldn't do. Jack was as safe as a church all the time he was in there as long as he was strong. He certainly was treating Walcott rough. The funny thing was, it looked as though Jack was an open classic boxer. That was because he had all that stuff, too.

After the seventh round Jack says, "My left's getting heavy."

From then he started to take a beating. It didn't show at first. But instead of him running the fight it was Walcott was running it. Instead of being safe all the time, now he was in trouble. He couldn't keep Walcott out with the left hand now. It looked as though it was the same as ever, only now, instead of Walcott's punches just missing him, they were just hitting him. He took an awful beating in the body.

"What's the round?" Jack asked.

"The eleventh."

"I can't stay," Jack says. "My legs are going bad."

Walcott had been just hitting him for a long time. It was like a baseball catcher pulls the ball and takes some of the shock off. From now on Walcott commenced to land solid. He certainly was a socking machine. Jack was just trying to block everything now. It didn't show what an awful beating he was taking. In between the rounds I worked on his legs. The muscles would flutter under my hands all the time I was rubbing them. He was sick as hell.

"How's it go?" he asked John, turning around, his face all swollen.

"It's his fight."

"I think I can last," Jack says. "I don't want this bohunk to stop me."

It was going just the way he thought it would. He knew he couldn't beat Walcott. He wasn't strong any more. He was all right, though. His money was all right and now he wanted to finish it off right to please himself. He didn't want to be knocked out.

The gong rang and we pushed him out. He went out slow. Walcott came right out after him. Jack put the left in his face and Walcott took it, came in under it, and started working on Jack's body. Jack tried to tie him up and it was just like trying to hold on to a buzz saw. Jack broke away from it and missed with the right. Walcott clipped him with a left hook and Jack went down. He went down on his hands and knees and looked at us. The referee started counting. Jack was watching us and shaking his head. At eight John motioned to him. You couldn't hear on account of the crowd. Jack got up. The referee had been holding Walcott back with one arm while he counted.

When Jack was on his feet Walcott started toward him.

"Watch yourself, Jimmy," I heard Solly Freedman yell to him.

Walcott came up to Jack looking at him. Jack stuck the left hand at him. Walcott just shook his head. He backed Jack up against the ropes, measured him, and then hooked the left very light to the side of Jack's head and socked the right into the body as hard as he could sock just as low as he could get it. He must have hit him five inches below the belt. I thought the eyes would come out of Jack's head. They stuck way out. His mouth come open.

The referee grabbed Walcott. Jack stepped forward. If he went down, there went fifty thousand bucks. He walked as though all his insides were going to fall out.

"It wasn't low," he said. "It was a accident."

The crowd were yelling so you couldn't hear anything.

"I'm all right," Jack says. They were right in front of us.

The referee looks at John and then he shakes his head.

"Come on, you dirty Polack," Jack says to Walcott.

John was hanging on to the ropes. He had the towel ready to chuck in. Jack was standing just a little way out from the ropes. He took a step forward. I saw the sweat come out on his face like somebody had squeezed it, and a big drop went down his nose.

"Come on and fight," Jack says to Walcott.

The referee looked at John and waved Walcott on.

"Go in there, you slob," he says.

Walcott went in. He didn't know what to do either. He never thought Jack could have stood it. Jack put the left in his face. There was all this yelling going on. They were right in front of us. Walcott hit him twice. Jack's face was the worst thing I ever saw — the look on it. He was holding himself and all his body together, and it all showed on his face. All the time he was thinking and holding his body in where it was busted.

Then he started to sock. His face looked awful all the time. He started to sock with his hands low down by his side, swinging at Walcott. Walcott covered up and Jack was swinging wild at Walcott's head. Then he swung the left and it hit Walcott in the groin and the right hit Walcott right bang where he'd hit Jack. Way low. Walcott went down and grabbed himself there and rolled and twisted around.

The referee grabbed Jack and pushed him toward his corner. John jumps into the ring. There was all this yelling going on. The referee was talking with the judges and then the announcer got into the ring with the megaphone and says, "Walcott on a foul."

The referee is talking to John and he says, "What could I do? Jack wouldn't take the foul. Then when he's groggy he fouls him."

"He'd lost it anyway," John says.

Jack's sitting on the chair. I've got his gloves off and he's holding himself in down there with both hands.

"Go over and say you're sorry," John says into his ear. "It'll look good."

Jack stands up and the sweat comes out all over his face. I put the bathrobe around him and he holds himself in with one hand under the bathrobe and goes across the ring. They've picked Walcott up and they're working on him. There's a lot of people in Walcott's corner. Nobody speaks to Jack. He leans over Walcott.

"I'm sorry," Jack says. "I didn't mean to foul you."

Walcott doesn't say anything. He looks too damned sick.

"Well, you're the champion now," Jack says to him. "I hope you get a hell of a lot of fun out of it."

"Leave the kid alone," Solly Freedman says.

"Hello, Solly," Jack says. "I'm sorry I fouled your boy."

Freedman just looks at him.

Jack went over to his corner walking that funny jerky way, and we got him down through the ropes and through the reporters' tables and out down the aisle. A lot of people want to slap Jack on the back. He goes out through all that mob in his bathrobe to the dressing room. It's a popular win for Walcott. That's the way the money was bet in the Garden.

Once we got inside the dressing room Jack lay down and shut his eyes.

"We want to get to the hotel and get a doctor," John says.

"I'm all busted inside," Jack says.

"I'm sorry as hell, Jack," John says.

"It's all right," Jack says.

He lies there with his eyes shut.

"They certainly tried a nice double cross," John said.

"Your friends Morgan and Steinfelt," Jack said. "You got nice friends."

He lies there; his eyes are open now. His face has still got that awful drawn look.

"It's funny how fast you can think when it means that much money," Jack says.

"You're some boy, Jack," John says.

"No," Jack says. "It was nothing."

July 1927

JOHN JAY CHAPMAN

1862–1933

When he was agitated, and he usually was, Jack Chapman was a minor convulsion of nature. Inspiration he had in great things and folly in things less great. He was a gadfly of the Socratic order and made it his business in life to bludgeon those whom he could not persuade. His high-mindedness I recognized, his genius I admired, but I confess that an acquaintance of forty years left me not without sympathy for the citizens who drove Socrates to the hemlock.

Yet he was noble; there is no doubt of that. From his Jay ancestors he inherited a detestation of slavery which a generation earlier would have made him a second John Brown. In manhood he acquired other hates, all piping hot: Big Business of which he had an infant's knowledge, the Roman Catholic Church which he egregiously misunderstood, and Harvard College which he hated after the manner of Catullus execrating the woman he adored.

There are many things to fight in this bad world but Chapman never gave sufficient attention to any one of them to knock it down and out. Perhaps his solidest achievements were his interpretations of Garrison and Emerson. There his understanding was of a high order.

"Garrison," he wrote, "set a great brazen trumpet to his lips and blew; and the walls of Jericho fell. Garrison dies, and his trumpet sounds no more. Nevertheless, the small, inner, silver trumpet of Emerson caught and sounded the same note, and it continues to sound the note, shaking down the walls of inner Jerichos in men of later and ever later generations."

Among his friends and in society Chapman was a fountain of delight. His humor was burly and Falstaffian. An early picture in my memory is of Jack at a large New York dinner party. In his set the conversation was commonly on a plane of philosophic theory. I don't remember what the talk turned on that evening, probably it was a debate as to whether Hamlet really had the feelings of a gentleman or something of that sort. At any rate, it was pungent enough and punctuated with bursts of humor. I speak of "conversation" but it was really Chapman talking. An English gentleman on the opposite side of the table, conspicuous for his courteous and restrained manners and obviously unaccustomed to the American temperament, made several futile attempts to check the torrent and inject a word of needed correction into Chapman's vehement monologue. The argument rose to great heights and when finally the speaker leveled a bolt against some convention which seemed to pass the bounds of reason, the Englishman half rose in polite protest. At the first sight of this insubordination Jack leapt upon the seat of his chair and, in that commanding position, waved his napkin over the assembled company like the banner of a conqueror, shouting, "Down, Towser, down!" The Englishman collapsed and the whole dinner table shook with laughter.

Chapman's appearance was notable. He might have stalked across Israel as one of the lesser prophets. He wore a long black beard. His left sleeve was empty and this threw about his person a certain impressive austerity.

The story of that left sleeve is a legend which might have come down to us from the early Christians.

While Chapman was at the Harvard Law School he fell in love. According to his own testimony he had not asked the lady the accustomed question nor had he even interpreted his own feeling to himself. But he had read Dante with her and from her intensity he knew she loved someone. That she was in love with him, himself, he could not and did not credit.

That he was in love with her he may not have known but young men do suspect such things when they feel called upon to watch over and protect a young woman against dangers unseen by her natural guardians. At any rate Chapman was convinced that an interloper was attempting to trifle with her affections. Young Percival Lowell was older by half a dozen years. He was not yet an astronomer nor had he made himself famous by writing his wonderful books on Japan, books so good that they inspired Lafcadio Hearn to accomplish his life's best work, but Percival Lowell was a highly attractive man of the world and the carefree attentions he gave Miss Minna Timmins became in Chapman's mind a diabolical plot designed to steal the *lady's affections. Over this peril Chapman brooded. Then he acted in a manner that seems bordering on madness.*

There was, it happened, an evening party in Brookline at the house of Mrs. Walter C. Cabot, which stood on a hill overlooking Sevenells, where the seven Lowells were brought up. Percival, walking to the party in evening dress, was sauntering toward the Cabot steps when suddenly Chapman emerged from the house carrying in his hand a heavy cane he had seized from the family umbrella stand. He rushed on his unsuspecting victim and beat him brutally over the head. It was an act of semi-insanity and very soon Chapman came to the full realization of his iniquity. His hand had offended and he would cut it off and cast it from him. After dinner in the little house he shared with classmates at the Law School he went upstairs to his room ostensibly to study his law books. Close friends who sat below had noticed nothing unusual in his demeanor, but Chapman had an expiation to make. He knelt before the open grate and wrapping a pair of suspenders tight round the forearm, thrust his left hand into the living coals and held it there rigidly with his right until it was consumed.

Through his life the empty sleeve, telling a story strange and but half understood, cast an aura about Chapman's figure. He was a man apart. Of this the stranger was ever conscious, and to a friend it intensified the impression of a personality different from every other. Always with Chapman the thought of sin was coupled with the thought of expiation. Religion was a main current of his character, but it sprang not from the New Testament but the Old. The awful consequences of sin touched his vivid imagination, and kept turning it from the gay to the austerely grave.

In 1912 there occurred a striking illustration of this Biblical quality. The year before at Coatesville in Pennsylvania an atrocious crime had been committed under circumstances of peculiar horror. A Negro had been burned alive by a crowd which included numbers of "respectable" citizens. Lynching had invaded the North! The metropolitan papers blazed with indignation. Hardly had the deed been done when the people of Coatesville became conscious of the full frightfulness of it. But they did nothing. Not one man would come forth to testify against his neighbor. All waited with the miserable hope that the crime would be forgotten. To Chapman with his historic sense and his religious conviction that upon the children of the third and the fourth generation must the sins of the fathers be visited, it was intolerable to sit idly by. The crime had been committed at the unimportant little town of Coatesville. The sin was the sin of Slavery, and in the blackness of that guilt every American had his share. As the dreadful anniversary approached, Chapman went to Coatesville and engaged a room at the squalid hotel. As he walked the streets, a commanding figure with black beard and empty sleeve, a tremor of fear — fear of they knew not what — came over the people. Chapman answered no questions, but rumor ran wild. On Friday, August sixteenth, the following notice appeared in the Coatesville Record: —

In Memoriam

A Prayer Meeting will be held
On Sunday morning at eleven o'clock
At the Nagel Building.
Silent and aral [sic] *prayer:*
Reading of the Scriptures:
Brief address by John Jay Chapman.
In memory of the Tragedy of August 13, 1911
Oh Lord, receive my prayer!

The community waited. That Sunday morning the doors of the hall were thrown wide open that all could see what was going on within. People crowded in the streets, but when Chapman walked in, the hall was empty except for two persons, one an ancient Negress from Boston, the other an unidentified spectator whom Chapman took to be a stool pigeon. *Chapman, whose instinct for psychology was invariably wrong, expected a crowd, but, entirely unperturbed, he walked to the desk, read certain poignant passages from the Bible and made his address. Not the least interesting fact of this extraordinary occasion is that the sermon preached that day had nothing in it of violence, nothing of hate. It was solemn and profoundly sad. He spoke of a sinful world. I quote the final paragraphs.*

This whole matter has been a historic episode; but it is a part, not only of our national history, but of the personal history of each one of us. With the great disease (slavery) came the climax (the war), and after the climax gradually began the cure, and in the process of cure comes now the knowledge of what the evil was. I say that our need is new life, and that books and resolutions will not save us, but only such disposition in our hearts and souls as will enable the new life, love, force, hope, virtue, which surround us always, to enter into us.

This is the discovery that each man must make for himself — the discovery that what he really stands in need of he cannot get for himself, but must wait till God gives it to him. I have felt the impulse to come here today to testify to this truth.

The occasion is not too small; the occasion looks back on three centuries and embraces a hemisphere. Yet the occasion is small compared with the truth it leads us to. For this truth touches all ages and affects every soul in the world.

There is greatness in a human being who can do and say these things, but in this brief sketch I do not wish to leave the impression that Chapman was a man wholly dedicated and cut off from the world. He was fond of life, fond of friends. He overflowed with humor. His versatility, his learning, the brilliance of his talk had in them an electric contagion which made him the center of every group. The comfortable fortune which cut him off from material anxiety made him little charitable to other men's difficulties and temptations. That was his misfortune. God gave him talents. He did not lay them in a napkin, yet he never used them for the work he might have done. Wide wisdom is the salt of life. That was denied him. He kindled many flickering flames. He never lighted a bonfire and now the light that once seemed so brilliant is out almost to the final spark.

Learning

JOHN JAY CHAPMAN

An expert on Greek art chanced to describe in my hearing one of the engraved gems in the Metropolitan Museum. He spoke of it as "certainly one of the great gems of the world," and there was something in his tone that was even more thrilling than his words. He might have been describing the Parthenon, or Beethoven's Mass, — such was the passion of reverence that flowed out of him as he spoke. I went to see the gem afterwards. It was badly placed, and for all artistic purposes was invisible. I suppose that even if I had had a good look at it, I should not have been able to appreciate its full merit. Who could — save the handful of adepts in the world, the little group of gem-readers, by whom the mighty music of this tiny score could be read at sight?

Nevertheless it was a satisfaction to me to have seen the stone. I knew that through its surface there poured the power of the Greek world; that not without Phidias and Aristotle, and not without the Parthenon, could it have come into existence. It carried in its bosom a digest of the visual laws of spiritual force; and was as wonderful and as sacred as any stone could well be. Its value to mankind was not to be measured by my comprehension of it, but was inestimable. As Petrarch felt toward the Greek manuscript of Homer which he owned but could not read, so did I feel toward the gem.

What is Education? What are Art and Religion and all those higher interests in civilization which are always vaguely held up to us as being the most important things in life? These things elude definition. They cannot be put into words except through the interposition of what the Germans call a "metaphysic." Before you can introduce them into discourse, you must step aside for a moment and create a theory of the universe; and by the time you have done this, you have perhaps befogged yourself and exhausted your readers. Let us be content with a more modest ambition. It is possible to take a general view of the externals of these subjects without losing reverence for their realities. It is possible to consider the forms under which art and religion appear, — the algebra and notation by which they have expressed themselves in the past, — and to draw some general conclusion as to the nature of the subject, without becoming entangled in the subject itself.

We may deal with the influence of the gem without striving exactly to translate its meaning into speech. We all concede its importance. We know, for instance, that the admiration of my friend the expert was no accident. He found in the design and workmanship of the intaglio the same ideas which he had been at work on all his life. Greek culture long ago had become a part of this man's brain, and its hieroglyphs expressed what to him was religion. So of all monuments, languages, and arts which descend to us out of the past. The peoples are dead, but the documents remain; and these documents themselves are part of a living and intimate tradition which also descends to us out of the past, — a tradition so familiar and native to the brain that we forget its origin. We almost believe that our feeling for art is original with us. We are tempted to think there is some personal and logical reason at the back of all grammar, whether it be the grammar of speech or the grammar of architecture, — so strong is the appeal to our taste made by traditional usage. Yet the great reason of the power of art is the historic reason. "In this manner have these things been expressed; in similar manner must they continue to be said." So speaks our artistic instinct.

Good usage has its sanction, like religion or government. We transmit the usage without pausing to think why we do so. We instinctively correct a child, without pausing to reflect that the fathers of the race are speaking through us. When the child says "Give me a apple," we correct him. "You must say 'an apple.' " What the child really means, in fact, is an apple.

All teaching is merely a way of acquainting the learner with the body of existing tradition. If the child is ever to have anything to say of his own, he has need of every bit of this expressive medium to help him do it. The reason is, that, so far as expressiveness goes, only one language exists. Every experiment and usage of the past is a part of this language. A phrase or an idea rises in the Hebrew, and filters through the Greek or Latin and French, down to our own time. The practitioners who scribble and dream in words from their childhood up, — into whose habit of thought language is kneaded through a thousand reveries, — these are the men who receive, reshape, and transmit it. Language is their portion: they are the priests of language.

The same thing holds true of the other vehicles of idea, — of painting, architecture, religion, etc.; but since we have been speaking of language, let us continue to speak of language. Expressiveness follows literacy. The poets have been tremendous readers always, — Petrarch, Dante,

Chaucer, Shakespeare, Milton, Goethe, Byron, Keats; those of them who possessed not much of the foreign languages had a passion for translations. It is amazing how little of a foreign language you need if you have a passion for the thing written in it. We think of Shakespeare as of a lightly-lettered person; but he was ransacking books all day to find plots and language for his plays. He reeks with mythology; he swims in classical metaphor; and, if he knew the Latin poets only in translation, he knew them with that famished intensity of interest which can draw the meaning through the walls of a bad text. Deprive Shakespeare of his sources, and he could not have been Shakespeare.

Good poetry is the echoing of shadowy tongues, the recovery of forgotten talent, the garment put up with perfumes. There is a passage in the *Tempest* which illustrates the freemasonry of artistic craft, and how the weak sometimes hand the torch to the mighty. Prospero's apostrophe to the spirits is, surely, as Shakespearean as anything in Shakespeare and as beautiful as anything in imaginative poetry.

> Ye elves of hills, brooks, standing lakes and groves;
> And ye that on the sands with printless foot
> Do chase the ebbing Neptune, and do fly him,
> When he comes back; you demi-puppets that
> By moonshine do the green sour ringlets make,
> Whereof the ewe not bites; and you, whose pastime
> Is to make midnight mushrooms; that rejoice
> To hear the solemn curfew; by whose aid
> (Weak masters though ye be) I have bedimm'd
> The noontide sun, call'd forth the mutinous winds,
> And 'twixt the green sea and the azured vault
> Set roaring war: to the dread rattling thunder
> Have I given fire, and rifted Jove's stout oak
> With his own bolt: the strong-based promontory
> Have I made shake; and by the spurs pluck'd up
> The pine and cedar: graves, at my command,
> Have waked their sleepers; oped, and let them forth
> By my so potent art.

Shakespeare borrowed this speech from Medea's speech in Ovid, which he knew in the translation of Arthur Golding; and really Shakespeare seems almost to have held the book in his hand while penning Prospero's speech. The following is from Golding's translation, published in 1567.

Ye Ayres and windes: ye Elves of Hilles, of Brookes, of Woods alone,
Of standing Lakes, and of the Night, approche ye everychone,
Through helpe of whom (the crooked bankes much wondring at the thing)
I have compelled streames to run cleane backward to their spring.
By charmes I make the calme Seas rough, and make the rough Seas plaine
And cover all the Skie with Cloudes, and chase them thence againe.
By charmes I rayse and lay the windes, and burst the Vipers jaw,
And from the bowels of the Earth both stones and trees doe drawe.
Whole woods and Forestes I remove: I make the Mountaines shake,
And even the Earth it selfe to grone and fearfully to quake.
I call up dead men from their graves: and thee O lightsome Moone
I darken oft, though beaten brasse abate thy perill soone.
Our Sorcerie dimmes the Morning faire, and darkes the Sun at Noone.
The flaming breath of firie Bulles ye quenchèd for my sake.
And causèd there unwieldie necks the bended yokes to take.
Among the Earthbred brothers you a mortall war did set
And brought a sleepe the Dragon fell whose eyes were never shet.

There is, and is to be, no end of this reappearance of old metaphor, old trade secrets, old usage of art. No sooner has a masterpiece appeared, that summarizes all knowledge, than men get up eagerly the next morning with chisel and brush, and try again. Nothing done satisfies. It is all in the making that the inspiration lies; and this endeavor renews itself with the ages, and grows by devouring its own offspring.

The technique of any art is the whole body of experimental knowledge through which the art speaks. The glazes of pottery become forgotten and have to be hit upon over again. The knack of Venetian glass, the principle of effect in tiles, in lettering, in the sonnet, in the fugue, in the tower, — all the prestidigitation of art that is too subtle to be named or thought of, must yet be acquired and kept up by practice, held to by constant experiment.

Good artistic expression is thus not only a thing done: it is a way of life, a habit of breathing, a mode of unconsciousness, a world of being which records itself as it unrolls. We call this world Art for want of a better name; but the thing that we value is the life within, not the shell of the creature. This shell is what is left behind in the passage of time, to puzzle our after study and make us wonder how it was made, how such complex delicacy and power ever came to coexist. I have often wondered over the *Merchant of Venice,* as one wonders over a full-blown transparent poppy that sheds light and blushes like a cloud. Neither the poppy nor the play was exactly hewn out: they grew, they expanded and bloomed by a sort of inward power, — unconscious, transcendent. The fine arts blossom from the old stock, — from the poppy-seed of the world.

I am here thinking of the whole body of the arts, the vehicles through which the spirit of man has been expressed. I am thinking also of the sciences, — whose refractory, belligerent worshipers are even less satisfied with any past expression than the artists are, for their mission is to destroy and to rearrange. They would leave nothing alive but themselves. Nevertheless, science has always been obliged to make use of written language in recording her ideas. The sciences are as much a part of recorded language as the arts. No matter how revolutionary scientific thought may be, it must resort to metaphysics when it begins to formulate its ultimate meanings. Now, when you approach metaphysics, the Greek and the Hebrew have been there before you; you are very near to matters which perhaps you never intended to approach. You are back at the beginning of all things. In fact, human thought does not advance, it only recurs. Every tone and semitone in the scale is a key-note; and every point in the universe is the centre of the universe; and every man is the centre and focus of the cosmos, and through him passes the whole of all force, as it exists and has existed from eternity; hence the significance which may at any moment radiate out of anything.

The different arts and devices that time hands to us are like our organs. They are the veins and arteries of humanity. You cannot rearrange them or begin anew. Your verse-forms and your architecture are chosen for you, like your complexion and your temperament. The thing you desire to express is in them already. Your labors do no more than to enable you to find your own soul in them. If you will begin any piece of artistic work in an empirical spirit and slave over it until it suits you, you will find yourself obliged to solve all the problems which the artists have been engaged on since the dawn of history. Be as independent as you like, you will find that you have been anticipated at every point; you are a slave to precedent, because precedent has done what you are trying to do, and ah, how much better! In the first place the limitations, the horrible limitations of artistic possibility, will begin to present themselves: few things can be done; they have all been tried; they have all been worked to death; they have all been developed by immortal genius and thereafter avoided by lesser minds, — left to await more immortal genius. The field of endeavor narrows itself in proportion to the greatness of the intellect that is at work. In ages of great art every one knows what the problem is and how much is at stake. Masaccio died at the age of twenty-seven, after having painted half a dozen pictures which influenced all subsequent art, because they showed to Raphael the best solution of certain technical questions. The Greeks of the best period were so very knowing that everything appeared to them ugly except the few attitudes, the few arrangements, which were capable of being carried to perfection.

Any one who has something to say is thus found to be in one sense a slave; but a rich slave who has inherited the whole earth. If you can only obey the laws of your slavery, you become an emperor; you are only a slave in so far as you do not understand how to use your wealth. If you have but the gift of submission, you conquer. Many tongues, many hands, many minds, a traditional state of feeling, traditional symbols,— the whole passed through the eyes and soul of a single man,—such is art, such is human expression in all its million-sided variety.

II

I have thrown together these remarks in an elliptical and haphazard way, hoping to show what sort of thing education is, and as a prologue to a few reflections upon the educational conditions in the United States.

It is easy to think of reasons why the standards of general education should be low in America. Almost every influence which is hostile to the development of deep thought and clear feeling has been at the maximum of destructive power in the United States. We are a new society, made of a Babel of conflicting European elements, engaged in exploiting the wealth of a new continent, under conditions of climate which involve a nervous reorganization for Europeans who come to live with us. Our history has been a history of quiet colonial beginnings, followed by a national life which from its inception has been one of social unrest. And all this has happened during the great epoch of the expansion of commerce, the thought-destroying epoch of the world.

Let us take a rapid glance at our own past. In the beginning we were settlers. Now, the settlement of any new continent plays havoc with the arts and crafts. Let us imagine that among the Mayflower pilgrims there were a few expert wood-carvers, a violin-player or two, and a master architect. These men, upon landing in the colony, must have been at a loss for employment. They would have to turn into backwoodsmen. Their accomplishments would in time have been forgotten. Within a generation after the landing of the pilgrims there must have followed a decline in the fine arts, in scholarship, and in certain kinds of social refinement. This decline was, to some extent, counteracted in our colonial era by the existence of wealth in the colonies and by the constant intercourse with Europe, from which the newest models were imported by every vessel. Nevertheless, it is hard for a colony to make up for its initial loss; and we have recently seen the United States government making efforts on a large scale to give to the American farmer those practices of intensive cultivation of the soil which he lost by becoming a backwoodsman and has never since had time to recover for himself.

The American Revolution was our second serious set-back in education. So hostile to culture is war that the artisans of France have never been able to attain to the standards of workmanship which prevailed under the old monarchy. Our national culture started with the handicap of a seven-years' war, and was always a little behindhand. During the nineteenth century the American citizen was buffeting the waves of new development. His daily life was an experiment. His moral, social, political interests and duties were indeterminate. Nothing was settled for him by society. Was a man to have an opinion? Then he must make it himself. This demands a more serious labor than if he were obliged to manufacture his own shoes and candlesticks. No such drafts upon individual intellect are made in an old country. You cannot get a European to understand this distressing over-taxing of the intelligence in America. Nothing like it has occurred before, because in old countries opinion is part of caste and condition; opinion is the shadow of interest and of social status.

But in America the individual is not protected against society at large by the bulwark of his class. He stands by himself. It is a noble idea that a man should stand by himself, and the conditions which force a man to do so have occasionally created magnificent types of heroic manhood in America. Lincoln, Garrison, Emerson, and many lesser athletes are the fruits of these very conditions which isolate the individual in America and force him to think for himself. Yet their effect upon general cultivation has been injurious. It seems as if character were always within the reach of every human soul; but men must have become homogeneous before they can produce art.

We have thus reviewed a few of the causes of our American loss of culture. Behind all these causes, however, was the true and overmastering cause, namely, that sudden creation of wealth for which the nineteenth century is noted, the rise all over the world of new and uneducated classes. We came into being as a part of that world-movement which has perceptibly retarded culture, even in Europe. How then could we in America hope to resist it? Whether this movement is the result of democratic ideas, or of mechanical inventions, or of scientific discovery, no one can say. The elements that go to make up the movement cannot be unraveled. We only know that the world has changed: the old order has vanished with all its charm, with all its experience, with all its refinement. In its place we have a crude world, indifferent to everything except physical well-being. In the place of the fine arts and the crafts, we have business and science. Business is, of course, devoted to the increase of physical well-being; and science is, in all except its highest reaches of thought, a mere extension of business. Science is the theory of world-business, race-business, cosmic business. Science saves lives and dominates the air and the sea, science does a hundred wonders, and all of us are incredibly in debt to science, and we should not be ungrateful. But science does not express spiritual truth. It neither sings nor jokes, it neither prays nor rejoices, it neither loves nor hates. It respects only its own language and its own habits of thought, and puts trust only in what is in its own shop-window.

"What is science?" you ask. Now, science is anything which the scientific men of the moment are studying. In one decade science means the discussion of spontaneous variation, in the next of plasm, in the next of germs or of electrodes. I do not undervalue the accomplishments of science; but I deprecate the contempt which science expresses for anything that does not happen to be called science. Imperial and haughty science proclaims its occupancy of the whole province of human thought; yet, as a matter of fact, science deals in a language of its own, in a set of formulæ and conceptions which cannot cover the most important interests of humanity. It does not understand the value of the fine arts, and is always at loggerheads with philosophy. Is it not clear that science, in order to make good her claim to universality, must adopt a conception of her own function that shall leave to the fine arts and to religion their languages? She cannot hope to compete with these languages, nor to translate nor to expound them. She must accept them. At present she tramples upon them.

There are, then, in the modern world these two influences which are hostile to education,—the influence of business and the influence of science. In Europe these influences are qualified by the vigor of the old learning. In America they dominate remorselessly, and make the path of education doubly hard. Consider how they meet us in ordinary social life. We have all heard men bemoan the time they have spent over Latin and Greek, on the ground that these studies did not fit them for business, — as if a thing must be worth less if it can be neither eaten nor drunk. It is hard to explain the value of education to men who have forgotten the meaning of education: its symbols convey nothing to them.

The situation is very similar in dealing with scientific men, — at least with that large class of them who have little learning and no religion, and who are thus obliged to use the formulæ of modern science as their only vehicle of thought. These men regard humanity as something which started up in Darwin's time. They do not listen when the humanities are mentioned; and if they did they would not understand. When Darwin confessed that poetry had no meaning for him, and that nothing significant was left to him in the whole artistic life of the past, he did not know how many of his brethren his words were destined to describe.

We can forgive the business man for the loss of his birthright; he knows no better. But we have it against a scientist if he undervalues education. Surely the Latin classics are as valuable a deposit as the crustacean fossils or the implements of the stone age. When science shall have assumed her true relation to the field of human culture, we shall all be happier. To-day science knows that the silkworm must be fed on the leaves of the mulberry tree, but does not know that the soul of man must be fed on the Bible and the Greek classics. Science knows that a queen bee can be produced by care and feeding, but does not as yet know that every man who has had a little Greek and Latin in his youth belongs to a different species from the ignorant man. No matter how little it may have been, it reclassifies him. There is more kinship between that man and a great scholar than there is between the same man and some one who has had no classics at all; he breathes from a different part of his anatomy. Drop the classics from education? Ask rather, Why not drop education? for the classics are education. We cannot draw a line and say, "Here we start." The facts are the other way. We started long ago, and our very life depends upon keeping alive all that we have thought and felt during our history. If the continuity is taken from us, we shall relapse.

When we discover that these two tremendous interests — if indeed, business and science be not parts of the same interest — have arisen in the modern world and are muffling the voice of man, we tremble for the future. If these giants shall continue their subjugation of the gods, the whole race, we fear, may relapse into dumbness. By good fortune, however, there are other powers at work. The race is emotionally too rich and too much attached to the past to allow its faculties to be lost through disuse. New and spontaneous crops will soon be growing upon the mould of our own stubbly, thistle-bearing epoch.

In the mean time we in America must do the best we can. It is no secret that our standards of education are below those of Europe. Our art, our historical knowledge, our music and general conversation, show a stiffness and lack of exuberance, a lack of vitality and of unconscious force, — the faults of beginners in all walks of life. During the last twenty-five years much improvement has been made in those branches of cultivation which depend directly upon wealth. Since the Civil War there seems to have been a decline in the higher literature, accompanied by an advance in the plastic arts. And more recently still, there has been a literary reawakening, perhaps not of the most important kind, yet signifying a new era. If I may employ an obvious simile, I would liken America to a just-grown young man of good impulses, who has lacked early advantages. He feels that cultivation belongs to him; and yet he cannot catch it nor hold it. He feels the impulse of expression, and yet he can neither read nor write. He feels that he is fitted for general society; and yet he has no current ideas or conversation. And, of course, — I say it with regret, but it is a part of the situation, — of course, he is heady and proud of himself.

What do we all desire for this ingenuous youth on whom the postponed expectation of the world, as Emerson called it, has waited so long? We desire only to furnish him with true advantages. Let us take a simultaneous survey of the two extremities of the youth's education, namely, of nursery training and the higher education. The two are more intimately dependent upon each other than is generally suspected. With regard to the nursery, early advantages are the key to education. The focus of all cultivation is the fireside. Learning is a stove-plant that lives in the cottage and thrives during the long winter in domestic warmth. Unless it be born into children in their earliest years, there is little hope for it. The whole future of the world depends upon what is read to children before they can read to themselves. The world is powerless to reconvey itself through any mind that it has not lived in from the beginning, — so hard is the language of symbols, whether in music, or in poetry, or in painting. The arts must expand with the heart, as a hot rod of glass is touched by the gold-leaf and is afterwards blown into dusty stars and rainbows of mantling irradiation. If the glass expand before it has been touched by the metal, there is no means of ever getting the metal into it.

The age of machinery has peopled this continent with promoters and millionaires, and the work of a thousand years has been done in a century. The thing has, however, been accomplished at some cost. An ignorant man makes a fortune and demands the higher education for his children. But it is too late: he should have given it to them when he was in his shirtsleeves. All that they are able to receive now is something very different from education. In receiving it they drag down the old standards. School and college are filled with illiterates. The whole land must wait patiently till Learning has warmed back to life her chilled and starved descendants. Perhaps the child or grandchild of the fortune-builder will teach the children on his knee what he himself learned too late in life to stead him much.

Hunger and thirst for learning is a passion that comes, as it were, out of the ground; now in an age of wealth, now in an age of poverty. Young men are born whom nothing will satisfy except the arts and the sciences. They seek out some scholar at a university and aim at him from boyhood. They persuade their parents to send them to college. They are bored and fatigued by everything that life offers except this thing. Now, society does not create this hunger. All that society can do is to provide nourishment of the right kind, good instruction, true learning, the best scholarship which history has left behind. I believe that to-day there is a spirit of learning abroad in America, — here and there, in the young, — the old insatiable passion. I feel as if men were arising — most of them still handicapped by the lack of early training — to whom life has no meaning except as a search for the truth. This exalted famine of the young scholar is the hope of the world. It is religion and art and science in the chrysalis. The thing that society must beware of doing is of interposing between the young learner and his natural food some mechanical product or patent food of its own. Good culture means the whole of culture in its original sources; bad culture is any substitute for this.

Let us now examine the higher departments of education, the university, the graduate school, the museum, — the learned world in America. There is one function of learned men which is the same in every age, namely, the production of text-books. Learned men shed text-books as the oak sheds acorns, and by their fruits ye shall know them. Open almost any primary text-book or school-book in America, and you will, on almost every page of it, find inelegancies of usage, roughnesses, inaccuracies and occasional errors of grammar. The book has been written by an incompetent hand. Now, what has the writer lacked? Is it grammar? Is it acquaintance with English literature, with good models, with the Bible, with history? It is all these things, and more. No school-room teaching can make a man write good English. No school-teaching ever made an educated man, or a man who could write a good primary text-book. It requires a home of early culture, supplemented by the whole curriculum of scholarship and university training. Nothing but this great engine will produce that little book.

The same conditions prevail in music. If you employ the nearest excellent young lady music-teacher to teach your boys to play the piano, she will bring into the house certain child's music written by American composers, in which the rules of harmony are violated, and of which the sentiment is vulgar. The books have been written by incompetent people. There is a demand for such books, and they are produced. They are the best the times afford; let us be glad that they exist at all, and that they are no worse. But note this: it will require the whole musical impulse of the age, from the oratorio society and the musical college down to the street-organ, to correct the grammar of that child's music-book. Ten or twenty years from now a like book will perhaps be brought into your home, filled with better harmony and with truer musical feeling; and the change will have been wrought through the influence of Sebastian Bach, of Beethoven, — of the masters of music.

It is the same with all things. The higher culture must hang over the cradle, over the professional school, over the community. If you read the lives of the painters of Italy or of the musicians of Germany, you will find that, no matter where a child of genius was born, there was always an educated man to be found in the nearest village — a priest or a schoolmaster — who gave the child the rudiments himself, and became the means of sending him to the university. Without this indigent scholar, where would have been the great master?

It is familiarity with greatness that we need, — an early and first-hand acquaintance with the thinkers of the world, whether their mode of thought be music or marble or canvas or language. Their meaning is not easy to come at, but in so far as it reaches us it will transform us. A strange thing has occurred in America. I am not sure that it has ever occurred before. The teachers wish to make learning easy. They desire to prepare and peptonize and sweeten the food. Their little books are soft biscuit for weak teeth, easy reading on great subjects; but these books are filled with a pervading error; they contain a subtle perversion of education.

Learning is not easy, but hard; culture is severe. The steps to Parnassus are steep and terribly arduous. This truth is often forgotten among us; and yet there are fields of work in which it is not forgotten, and in such fields art springs up. Let us remember the accomplishments of our country. The art in which we now most excel is architecture. America has in it many beautiful buildings and some learned architects. And how has this come about? Through severe and conscientious study of the monuments of art, through humble, old-fashioned training. The architects have had first-rate text-books, generally written by Europeans, the non-peptonized, gritty, serious language of masters in the craft. Our painters have done something of the same sort. They have gone to Europe, and are conversant with what is being done in Europe. If they are developing their art here, they do it not ignorantly but with experience, with consciousness of the past.

I do not recommend subservience to Europe, but subservience to intellect. Recourse to Europe we must have; our scholars must absorb Europe, without themselves becoming absorbed. It is a curious thing that the American who comes in contact with the old world exhibits two opposite faults: he is often too much impressed, and loses stamina; or he is too little impressed, and remains a barbarian. Contact with the past and hard work are the cure for both tendencies. Europe is merely an incidental factor in the problem of our education; and this is very well shown in the conduct of our law schools. The Socratic method of instruction in law schools was first introduced at Harvard, and since then it has spread to many parts of the world. This is undoubtedly one of our best achievements in scholarship; and Europe had, so far as I know, no hand in it. The method consists in the *viva voce* discussion of leading cases, text-books being used merely as an auxiliary. The student thus attacks the sources for himself. Here we have American scholarship at its best, and it is precisely the same thing as the European article; it is simply scholarship.

If we can exhibit this spirit in one branch of learning, why not in all? The Promethean fire is one single element. A spark of this fire is all that is needed to kindle this flame. The glance of a child of genius at an Etruscan vase leaves the child a new being. That is why museums exist: not only for the million who get something from them, but for the one young person of intelligence to whom they mean everything.

Our American universities exhibit very vividly all the signs of retardation in culture which are traceable in other parts of our social life. A university is always a stronghold of the past, and is therefore one of the last places to be captured by new influence. Commerce has been our ruler for many years; and yet it is only quite recently that the philosophy of commerce can be seen in our colleges. The business man is not a monster; but he is a person who desires to advance his own interests. This is his occupation, and, as it were, his religion. The advancement of material interests constitutes civilization to him. He unconsciously infuses the ideas and methods of business into anything that he touches. It has thus come about in America that our universities are beginning to be run as business colleges. They advertise, they compete with one another, they pretend to give good value to their customers. They desire to increase their trade, they offer social advantages and business openings to their patrons. In some cases they boldly conduct intelligence offices, and guarantee that no hard work done by the student shall be done in vain; a record of work is kept during the student's college life, and the college undertakes to furnish him at any time thereafter with references and a character which shall help him in the struggle for life.

This miscarriage of education has been developed and is being conducted by some of our greatest educators, through a perfectly unconscious adaptation of their own souls to the spirit of the age. The underlying philosophy of these men might be stated as follows: "There is nothing in life nobler than for a man to improve his condition and the condition of his children. Learning is a means to this end." Such is the current American conception of education. How far we have departed from the idea of education as a search for truth, or as the vehicle of spiritual expression, may be seen herein. The change of creeds has come about innocently, and the consequences involved in it are, as yet, perceived by hardly any one. The skepticism inherent in the new creed is concealed by its benevolence. You wish to help the American youth. This unfortunate, benighted, ignorant boy, who has from his cradle heard of nothing but business success as the one goal of all human effort, turns to you for instruction. He comes to you in a trusting spirit, with reverence in his heart, and you answer his hope in this wise: "Business and social success are the best things that life affords. Come to us, my dear fellow, and we will help you toward them." Your son asks you for bread and you give him a stone, for fish and you give him a serpent. It would have been better for that boy if he had never come to your college; for then he might have retained a belief that somewhere in the world there existed ideas, art, enthusiasm, unselfishness, inspiring activity.

In so far as our universities have been turning into business agencies, they have naturally lost their imaginative importance. Our professors seem to be of little more consequence in the community than the department managers of other large shops. If learning is a useful commodity which is to be distributed for the personal advantage of the recipients, it is a thing to be paid for rather than worshiped. To be sure, the whole of past history cannot be swept away in a day, and we have not wholly discarded a certain conventional and rhetorical reverence for learning. A dash and varnish of education are thought to be desirable, — the wash that is growing every year more thin.

Now, the truth is that the higher education does not advance a man's personal influence except under special circumstances. What it gives a man is the power of expression; but the ability to express himself has kept many a man poor. Let no one imagine that society is likely to reward him for self-expression in any walk of life. He is much more likely to be punished for it. The question of a man's success in life depends upon society at large. The more highly an age is educated, the more highly it rewards education in the individual. In an age of indifference to learning, the educated man is at a disadvantage. Thus the thesis that education advances self-interest — that thesis upon which many of our colleges are now being conducted — is substantially false. The little scraps and snatches of true education which a man now gets at college often embarrass his career. Our people are finding this out year by year; and as they do so, they naturally throw the whole conception of the higher education overboard. If education is to break down as a commercial asset, what excuse have they for retaining it at all? They will force the colleges to live up to the advertisements, and to furnish the kind of education that pays its way. It is clear that if the colleges persist in the utilitarian view, the higher learning will disappear. It has been disappearing very rapidly, and can be restored only through the birth of a new spirit and of a new philosophic attitude in our university life.

There are ages when the scholar receives recognition during his lifetime, and when the paths which lead to his lecture-room are filled with men drawn there by his fame. This situation arises in any epoch when human intellect surges up and asserts itself against tyranny and ignorance. In the past the tyrannies have been political tyrannies, and these have become well understood through the struggles of intellect in the past; but the present commercial tyranny is a new thing, and as yet little understood. It lies like a heavy fog of intellectual depression over the whole kingdom of Mammon, and is fed by the smoke from a million factories. The artist works in it, the thinker thinks in it. Even the saint is born in it. The rain of ashes from the nineteenth-century Vesuvius of business seems to be burying all our landscape.

And yet this is not true. We shall emerge, even we who are in America and suffer most. The important points to be watched are our university classrooms. If our colleges will but allow something unselfish, something that is true for its own sake, something that is part of the history of the human heart and intellect, to live in their classrooms, the boys will find their way to it. The museum holds the precious urn, to preserve it. The university, in like manner, stands to house the alphabets of civilization, — the historic instruments and agencies of intellect. They are all akin to each other, as the very name and function of the place imply. The presidents and professors who sit beside the fountains of knowledge bear different labels and teach subjects that are called by various names. But the thing which carries the label is no more than the shell. The life you cannot label; and it is to foster this life that universities exist. Enthusiasm comes out of the world and goes into the university. Toward this point flows the current of new talent that bubbles up in society; here is the meeting-place of mind. All that a university does is to give the poppy-seed to the soil, the oil to the lamp, the gold to the rod of glass before it cools. A university brings the spirit in touch with its own language, that language through which it has spoken in former days and through which alone it shall speak again.

July 1910

JAMES MILLING WITHEROW

1867–1934

When President Wilson and Divine Providence dispatched Walter Page to London, it was the Ambassador's duty on a momentous occasion to visit Edinburgh. Standing on the steep slope of Arthur's Seat, he interpreted to a vast concourse our sympathy with Scotsmen to whom America owes so great a debt. Assuming to the amusement of his audience the roughest of Scotch burrs, he epitomized their democratic ideals, "Liberrty, Equality," and — after a long pause — "Fr-r-rugality." This trinity, the inheritance of every Scot, belonged in full measure to the Reverend Doctor Witherow. Curious it was that he was born in Londonderry for he was Scottish as the oatmeal which nourished him. He lectured in many colleges; his "Honours" were all "First Class." A moral philosopher, he probed deep into human nature with a degree of logic which in other hands would have seemed out of place in that most illogical of all fields of inquiry. He lectured for a season at Harvard and gave the Atlantic *a chance to recognize his quality. Like L. P. Jacks he liked to illustrate his problems by a story which served as framework for an idea. For such tales Never-Never Land is the convenient background, and the narrative which flows has something of the verisimilitude of Aesop.*

Americans like a puzzle and a thousand answers came in to the Atlantic *in reply to this little examination into the moralities. To me it does not seem difficult to attain a passing grade, but readers are apt to read their own thoughts into other men's instructions. Let everyone, then, formulate his own answer and check it against the author's, which is printed at the end of the story.*

The Test

J. M. WITHEROW

Mr. Julius Fairleigh Stern owned a palace on the St. Lawrence not far from Grindstone, a mansion on Fifth Avenue, New York, and a castle near Fiesole in Italy. Some of his friends were trying to persuade him to make his real home amid the romantic scenery of Cold Spring Harbor, Long Island, but Mr. Stern refused, as he preferred to give away his surplus income for the endowment of education rather than add further to his many luxuries. For some reason that no one could discover he took special interest in Tarrytown on the Hudson.

A report had just reached him from the principal of the Tarrytown High School saying that three pupils had tied for the prize of $200 which Mr. Stern had presented for the best year's work done by pupils in their final year at the school. The percentage attained by the three equal firsts was 88, a record figure for the Stern Prize Competition. Mr. Stern replied that he would himself be present at the next graduation, as he wished to meet the three young men, and enclosed his check for $400, so that each might receive the same amount as their predecessors in previous years.

So at the June graduation at Tarrytown High School the Stern Exhibitioners of 1920—Mr. Gerald Daly, Mr. Eric Arthur Hamlet, and Mr. Charles Burke Brookfield—were presented to Mr. Stern, who at the close of the day's proceedings carried off the young men to dinner at his hotel. In conversation there the rich man soon discovered that the three boys were keenly set upon a university career, but were all very poor.

"Very well," said Mr. Stern. "That is just what I had hoped. I am interested in the result of university education. I make a proposition to you. I will bear all your expenses at the university—traveling, board, books, fees, and personal allowances—for four years. You will choose each the university you prefer and the line of study you like best. My conditions are two—that you will all promise to do your best at college in your own line, and that four years hence you will all come to me and undergo earnestly and loyally"—Mr. Stern repeated these two adverbs slowly and with emphasis—"a test which I will then describe to you. The test will be nothing vexatious or unreasonable."

The young fellows expressed their thanks as best they could, being rather overwhelmed by what they had just heard, and gladly and enthusiastically assented to the conditions laid down. "Isn't he a jolly old chap?" said Brookfield, as the three sauntered home that night. "Isn't he splendid? And by the way, did you read his article in *Harper's* on the 'Castles of the Loire'?"

"No," said Daly, "but I have been in his castle on the St. Lawrence, and in his library there is the finest collection of British and American poets you ever saw, bound in blue morocco; and what's more, he reads them. Every volume I opened had something marked."

"My father," said Hamlet, "was once in his house on Fifth Avenue fixing the telephone wires, and the housekeeper showed him pictures by Maris and Corot and Sargent that would drive most art collectors crazy."

Time passed on, and in June 1924 three distinguished graduates appeared by appointment on a certain day in that same princely mansion on Fifth Avenue. Daly came from Yale, first-class honor man in history and law; Hamlet came from Harvard, first-class honor man in the classics; Brookfield came from Johns Hopkins, with first-class honors in German, French, and Spanish.

Mr. Stern met them and greeted them warmly. He then took them separately to his private room, gave each one a long sealed envelope on which his name was written in large letters, marked "Private," and said to each in turn: "Give me your word of honor you will not open this till you are at home and quite alone. It contains all instructions for the test."

Each promised, took his envelope, and went home to Tarrytown.

And that evening in Tarrytown each of the three young men was gazing at a check for $5000, and a sheet of paper bearing these words: —

THIS IS YOUR TEST

1. You shall visit, within the next twelve months, Holland or Switzerland, Germany or France, Italy or Greece, and Egypt.

2. You shall write a report on what you think important in the countries visited and send your report to me within twelve months.

3. You will bring or send me a match box filled with sand from the desert at the foot of the Great Pyramid.

N.B. No questions shall be asked by you regarding the meaning of these instructions, either verbally or in writing, directly or indirectly. You shall not consult with anyone regarding the contents of this document or your intentions or methods in obeying it.

This is your test. Remember your promise.

Julius Fairleigh Stern

June 18, 1924

Mr. Gerald Daly, of Yale University, first-class honor man in law and history, fastened on the phraseology, grammar, and punctuation of the document with all his faculties of meticulous scrutiny thoroughly aroused. To prevent himself from overlooking any qualifying word or clause, he slowly read aloud the whole composition sentence by sentence and then memorized it till he was word perfect — an expedient he had found helpful in solving many a legal puzzle.

Subconsciously Mr. Daly whispered to himself, "I promised to meet this test 'earnestly and loyally,' and I will. I will do what J. F. Stern wants done and I will do it with the utmost fidelity at my command. He does not require for his own need anything from me — neither words nor deeds nor gifts. But to test me, as he has every right to do, he tells me to obey him in certain matters. The best compliment I can render him is to respect his wishes in every particular. It is for me to understand him and then do exactly — no more, no less — whatever he has expressed or implied; no more, for that would be misusing his money; no less, for that would be disloyalty."

In this spirit Mr. Daly studied his instructions and obeyed them with scrupulous sincerity.

He saw at his first reading the effect of "or" and "and" in No. 1 — no country compulsory except Egypt, and yet a restricted choice. Very soon he had decided that his itinerary must be through Holland, France, and Italy to Egypt, and thence home. He sailed in a Dutch liner for Rotterdam, which called at Southampton, but Mr. Daly would not set foot on shore even for a few hours. Britain was not mentioned in No. 1. It was not till he had visited Leyden, Alkmaar, Utrecht, Dordrecht, and began to arrange for his departure to France, that a scruple arose in his mind about going there by rail. If he did so he must report passing through Belgium, and that would look careless. He felt he could not. It was not playing the game. So, after trying in vain to get a passenger steamer, he decided to go from Amsterdam to Paris by aeroplane, and thus recovered peace of mind.

His traveling was continued with the same carefulness to Italy, Egypt, and home again. A liner was obtained at Alexandria bound for

New York, but Daly refused to go ashore at Malta or Gibraltar or the Azores.

Instruction No. 2 gave him very few qualms. "What you think important," Daly repeated to himself again. "Well, I am free from challenge there. It cannot mean *all* that I think important — it would be unreasonable to ask that. I will choose one thing which I think important, health, and report on whatever I think benefits or injures public health."

In harmony with this view of his duty, Daly examined the duration-of-life statistics in the various countries and wrote little notes of observations on athletics, drainage, ventilation, and cookery, and so drew up a short but businesslike account of public health in the lands he had seen.

Instruction No. 3, of course, was the clearest and easiest of all. At the second reading Daly pounced on the change from "you shall" to "you will," and said, "Quite so, quite so — a request, not an injunction; but in this matter Stern's wishes are law as much as his commands."

On reaching the Pyramids he was tempted to bring also a match box full of sand labeled "From between the giant paws of the Sphinx," but eventually refrained. He had not sufficient authority for that.

And so Mr. Gerald Daly, of Yale University, having carefully executed all that was prescribed, drew up his report and sent it along with a carefully packed match box, filled with sand from the base of the Great Pyramid, by registered post to the house on Fifth Avenue at the end of May, 1925.

On reaching his home in Tarrytown, however, Daly found that he had still in his pocketbook $523.75 unexpended out of his $5000 check. Murmuring to himself, "This is your test," he wrote an explanatory letter and mailed the money to Mr. Stern.

Mr. Eric Arthur Hamlet, of Harvard University, first-class honor man in Greek and Latin, also read his test paper of instructions with extreme care, but he took a somewhat different view from that of Mr. Daly.

"This is some test," Hamlet murmured to himself; and then, after a second reading and a long pause, "The snag is in No. 3."

He secured a berth on a transatlantic liner at the earliest possible date, spending the few days before sailing in New York libraries. Crossing the ocean, he went straight to London and took rooms near the British Museum, where for a whole month he read as hard as he had ever done at college, taking careful notes. Then followed a hurried visit to Holland and three months in Germany, three months in Italy, and three in Egypt.

The result of his investigations he embodied in three of the most brilliant essays he or any other Harvard graduate ever wrote. He selected certain aspects of the industrial, the educational, and the religious conditions of the three countries, and on a basis of carefully ascertained causes and consequences deduced the probable effect on Europe and America generally of the new movements in Germany, Italy, and Egypt. His incisive remarks on the decay of religion in the two former countries, his reasoned prediction that Fascism would survive Mussolini and effectually ruin Italian literature, and that Egypt would ere long alter both the commercial and the religious position in the Orient, astonishing Manchester as much as Constantinople — these reports sent in by Mr. Hamlet, when published a year afterward, attracted universal attention, evoked long-continued discussion, and are likely to retain a permanent place among the prose classics of British and American literature.

"Stern has practically asked me for my best," said Hamlet to himself. "He had a right to ask it, and I am giving it. He said he was interested in testing university culture, and every line of Orders 1 and 2 shows he wishes to test wisdom of judgment, insight, power of forming opinion, and discrimination between the really momentous and the trivial. Order 3 — but is it an order? — is the catch. Did he add this to see if we should have the common sense to omit it? And in any case a match box is a poor thing to pack sand in."

Very strongly inclined to take no notice of No. 3, Hamlet consulted various authorities on the geological characteristics of Egyptian sand in the hope of discovering some overlooked value or rare property, but without success. Finally he returned home and sent in his reports, and after much hesitation sent in also a small bag of sand, frankly confessing his fear that he must have misunderstood instruction No. 3.

Mr. Charles Burke Brookfield, of Johns Hopkins University, first-class honor man in German, French, and Spanish, gazed one moment in stupefied silence with open mouth after reading his test paper and his check. Then he gave forth his college yell. His mother barely saved herself from a heart attack by recognizing the "tune." Hardly had the martial strain died away when Brookfield sprang to his desk, whipped out his fountain pen, and wrote the following letter.

Tarrytown, *June* 18, 1924

Dear Mr. Stern: —

How to thank you for your colossal gift of a whole year of joy after all you have given already is a problem that knocks me helpless. I have dreamed again and again of at last being able to manage one month in Europe. And now a year! A whole year free of cost! Sir, you are a prince. Thank you again and again.

Yours most devotedly,

C. B. Brookfield

"The dear, delicious old humbug," he said to himself more than once, as he sealed and addressed and mailed the letter, "he nearly bamboozled me with his 'shalls' and 'wills' and 'musts' and 'must nots.' But his check and his match box gave him away. What a heart of gold! Giving and giving all the time what will help us best and please us most, and then trying to save our faces with his 'tests' and 'promises' and 'shalls' and 'musts.' Oh, the kindness of it all! If he were only a girl I should love to kiss him and call him a peach and a darling."

Brookfield started again on his college yell, but stopped abruptly as he awoke to the fact that he was coming through the front doorway of the post office.

"Are you hurt?" said an elderly man, turning around suddenly.

"No, thank you. I was just thinking."

"Thinking — thinking you were a steamer lost in a fog."

"Steamer!" shouted Brookfield. "Of course. Thank you — that is just what I ought to be thinking about," and hurried off to the nearest shipping agent, leaving the man muttering, "Crazy ass."

In England Brookfield carefully examined the National Gallery, the Tate Gallery, and the Wallace Collection, and after a day at the Tower and Westminster Abbey hurried off to Oxford, where he made copious sketches and notes. His next stay was at Amsterdam and his next at Nuremberg, and there he wrote his first report, dwelling chiefly on the development of portraiture from Rembrandt to Sargent and a study of mediæval architecture, exemplified in Nuremberg and Oxford. The latter subject he continued in a study of Lisieux, and a playful comparison of the majestic Mont St.-Michel with the Renaissance splendor of Chantilly.

His third report consisted of an almost lyrical dialogue between the Rigi, Pilatus, and the Rochers de Naye, each proudly claiming the grandest prospect of the dawn to be seen anywhere in the world.

With truly American energy he hurried from Switzerland to the

South of Spain, pausing only to make a careful survey of the Pont du Gard and Carcassonne. A small steamer carried him from Gibraltar to Palermo, where amid the golden glories of Monreale and the Capella Palatina he wrote an enthusiastic essay on the respective merits of the Moors, the Normans, and the Saracens.

Girgenti and Syracuse were not forgotten; but at Taormina, in front of the indescribable magnificence of Etna, snow-robed, against the burning Sicilian blue, Brookfield laid down both brush and pen. "Oh, Mr. Stern, I can't — I can't tell you what I see and feel. How can we ever thank God for giving us a world like this?"

And so the enthusiast passed on, drinking deep drafts of the loveliness of Rome and Naples, Florence and Venice, Athens and Delphi, and writing out, as he was able, something of the overflowing joy of his heart, till at length he arrived in Egypt. There he saw the principal sights of interest, but dwelt chiefly on all that threw light on Akhenaten, the one original mind that appeared in the long procession of Pharaohs. He made some pretty sketches of boats on the Nile, but expressed his regret that he had "no art that would sketch the awesome silence of the desert."

Brookfield reached New York on the first of June. He had spent every cent of his $5000. But twenty exquisite sketches of scenes in Athens, Cairo, and Thebes brought him $150 from a Broadway art dealer, and after making a certain purchase he drove to the Stern mansion. The secretary told him the great man was at Grindstone. Brookfield said he wished to write a note and leave a small parcel for him. Shown into the library, he wrote as follows: —

New York, *June* 1, 1925

Dear Sir: —

I return at the close of the most joyous twelve months of my life — a gift from you under the guise of what you called my "test." Well, I have tried earnestly and loyally to satisfy my examiner. I have visited all the countries you mentioned and more. I have reported what I thought "important" — namely, the truth and the beauty in art and nature that your writings taught me to see and love, and everything that seemed likely to give a little pleasure to one who had given so much pleasure to me. Your third instruction I divined was meant to find out if in the midst of all my enjoyment I remembered the giver. My dear friend, I remembered you with loving gratitude every day. In proof of this I ask you to accept the enclosed match box with its Egyptian sand, and believe me

Yours ever faithfully,

C. B. Brookfield

Having signed his name, Brookfield drew a small packet out of his pocket and opened it. It was an exquisitely carved little match box of pure gold. But alas, through careless packing most of the sand had oozed out into the paper and through the paper into Brookfield's pocket and through a tiny hole in the pocket had been steadily leaking since he left the jeweler's shop on Broadway. Scarcely a teaspoonful remained. In much distress he had to add a postscript, describing what had happened and bewailing his failure to do what he had been asked to do.

Mr. Julius Fairleigh Stern, a man without near relatives and with few intimates, died suddenly in January 1926. He left by will his three residences on Fifth Avenue, at Grindstone, and at Fiesole, with all their contents and all his invested property, amounting to $20,000,000, to the one of the three young men "who on being tested had shown the highest quality of careful, intelligent, and noble obedience."

Was it the graduate of Yale or of Harvard, or of Johns Hopkins?

If you can judge reasonably between Saint Paul and the Pharisees, or between Erasmus and Luther, or between Fundamentalists and Modernists — you can answer the question.

October, 1926

Note

Of the interpretation of Mr. Stern's directions, it seemed to the editor there could be little question. In fact he was confident that had he been privileged to enter the competition, he would have brought back the bacon. But so great was the volume of inquiry that followed the publication of this story and so divergent the explanations offered that I append Professor Witherow's own key to the mystery. Whether it really fits the lock, that desirable friend of mine, the reader, must decide for himself.

". . . But I hope," says Professor Witherow's letter, "I have brought out the point that Mr. Daly deserved the prize if Mr. Stern was a mere martinet, a mere drill-sergeant or a petty-fogging attorney; also that Mr. Hamlet deserved the prize if Mr. Stern took delight only in a man's best service, the putting forth to the utmost of all that the brain of man can furnish in insight, originality, and industry. This view of Mr. Stern and his test was a higher and truer view than Mr. Daly's and the author confesses that he has a warm spot in his own

mind for gallant Mr. Hamlet. Mr. Brookfield, however, saw what Mr. Hamlet saw and something more which Mr. Hamlet missed. There was a hungering in the rich man's heart for gratitude. The test was all that Mr. Daly and Mr. Hamlet found in it, but it was also a call of spirit to spirit, and Brookfield alone heard and responded to that note."

"Summing it up in more abstract terms, to obey you must not only know the command but the commander. The truest idea of Stern gave the best clue to the finest execution of Stern's behests. . . ."

SALVADOR DE MADARIAGA

1886–

Professional diplomat and diplomatic professor, Salvador de Madariaga is cosmopolite by education and Spaniard by pure descent. As a historian he has listened with credulity to the whispers of fancy, but as an excellent European, he has persistently explored paths to peace devious and straight both through the League and his own efforts. Of paradox he is the consummate master, while the ironic spirit which hovers over his work makes it a safe refuge from the botheration of the commonplace.

Professor de Madariaga has lived in England during the internecine struggle in Spain. He still lingers away from his country. A man of peace, he longs for quiet in his native land.

Englishman, Frenchman, Spaniard

SALVADOR DE MADARIAGA

I

TELL a man that the three angles of a triangle are worth two rights. If he answers, "Prove it," and, when satisfied, adds, "Very well; I know now how all triangles behave in all circumstances," he is a Frenchman. If he answers, "That may be *more or less* so, but when I come up against a triangle I will see for myself," he is an Englishman. And if he answers, "The triangle will be worth what I want it to be," he is a Spaniard.

I have been looking at the English, the French, and the Spaniards these twenty years. I have been looking at *them,* not at the facts about them. Facts are carcasses of dead ideas thought by others. I have turned away from facts, my hand on my nose.

Three nations — by which I mean three peoples fascinating to watch. No three clearer types could be found on the face of the earth. This distinctiveness of their respective natures was the first hint which I received from them as I observed their movements. What was it exactly which made them to me like three mutually independent, mutually equidistant samples of human nature?

My instinct told me that England, France, and Spain were like the three points of a psychological triangle. The ignorant, the superficial, or the "fact"-bound observer would talk to me about the "Latin" and the Anglo-Saxon peoples; more keen-eyed persons would ask, "Don't you think there is more affinity between Spaniards and Englishmen than between the French and either of them?" My instinct answered, "Just as much — that is, just as little." And with that intimate conviction I resumed my watch.

What is the spontaneous attitude of each of these three peoples toward life? What is the spontaneous criterion which determines their actions or abstentions? This question called forth three answers, represented by three untranslatable terms: *fair play; droit; honor*. These words describe three psychological entities as clear to the intuition as the elm, the wolf, or aluminium.

Fair play is an instinct which manifests itself in action, and, determining action, is determined by it. The fair play of a cricket match is not the fair play of a parliamentary election. Fair play is simultaneous with action, consubstantial with it. In fact, fair play is action.

Droit — so pitiably translated (?) as "law" — is an abstraction, a diagram, an idea. It is a map of the possibilities of the citizen in a world of citizens, a network of definitions and limitations drawn out beforehand. *Droit* is an idea. It is of the stuff of thought.

Honor is a more evasive species. The word is also untranslatable. For neither "honor" nor *honneur* conveys what the Spanish word *honor* means. *Honor* is a subjective criterion. It is admirably illustrated in the old ballad of the Count of León. Courtiers and ladies are conversing in a gallery of the Royal Palace overlooking the yard in which can be seen the lions presented to the King of Castile by the King of Morocco. Doña Ana lets fall her glove in the lions' cage, wishing to test the valor of the men present. The Count of León rescues the glove from the lions' cage, but, before giving it back to its owner, he strikes the fair face of the frivolous lady with her glove in order to teach her not to play with the good name of gallant men; then, turning to the knights present, he adds, "If anyone disagrees with what I have done, let him come out to the field of *honor,* where I shall maintain it." Such is the criterion of *honor*. Synthetic and subjective. The individual may do what he likes — violate even that supreme law of chivalry which forbids striking a woman; but he must be noble in his own subjective standards; and, as a pledge of nobility, he must be ready to give his life. *Honor* is, therefore, essentially individual and synthetic. It is of the nature of passion.

I mean by "action" the exercise of the will, and by "thought" that of the intellect. I mean by "passion" the state in which man lets the life stream flow through him in its wholeness and spontaneity, without interfering with it.

II

Let us, then, risk an hypothesis. The Englishman is above all a man of action, the Frenchman a man of thought, and the Spaniard a man of passion. By which, of course, we do not mean that each of the types is devoid of the faculties which are typical of the other two, but merely that the typical faculty in each case rules the others and makes them serve its ends. Thus Cromwell, by no means lacking in intellect or in passion, was preëminently a man of action; Voltaire, certainly an active man and one who knew what passions are, was nevertheless a man of thought; and Saint Theresa, a prodigy of action and an intelligent woman, was nevertheless a woman whose life was lived in the realm of passion.

This submission of two of the primary human tendencies to the third has been observed in one only of our three cases — that of the Englishman. It goes in English psychology by the name of utilitarianism. This uncouth word really means that the Englishman expects fruits of action from every investment of vital energy. Thought for the sake of thinking, passion for the sake of experiencing, are mere "indulgences" which the Englishman spurns. Thought and passion must yield results in terms of action. English utilitarianism, therefore, is but the direct outcome, indeed, the very definition of the type as a man of action.

Such an argument suggests a line of thought along which utilitarianism can be generalized in order to cover the other two types. Just as the Englishman, man of action, subordinates thought and passion to action, so the Frenchman, man of thought, must be expected to subordinate action and passion to thought; and the Spaniard, man of passion, will be found to subordinate action and thought to passion. French utilitarianism will, therefore, consist in exacting a yield in thought from action and passion, and Spanish utilitarianism in exacting a yield in passion from action and thought.

What each type seeks in life is the satisfaction of his main tendency.

Outside this tendency the type becomes "utilitarian." But within his own tendency the type is disinterested, since, living his own life, he lives it for nothing, as we all live. Hence what is naturally disinterested in the English is action—sports; in the French, thought—culture; in the Spaniards, passion—contemplation.

A man of action may be thinking; a man of passion may be acting. We have, therefore, to consider nine cases which, for purposes of comparison, could be grouped in table form.

1a Action in the man of action	1b Action in the man of thought	1c Action in the man of passion
2a Thought in the man of action	2b Thought in the man of thought	2c Thought in the man of passion
3a Passion in the man of action	3b Passion in the man of thought	3c Passion in the man of passion

This table shows a number of symmetries and analogies. The line crossing it from the left top corner to the right bottom corner is its axis of symmetry. The three cases on this line—namely, 1a, 2b, 3c—are analogous. In each of these cases, the type is in his own element. They are cases of satisfaction, cases without inner strife, cases of success. They lead us to anticipate that, in each of them, the type will be found at his best. Then there are three groups of two cases each which are symmetrically placed, both in geometry and in psychology: 1b and 2a; 1c and 3a; 2c and 3b.

Too often parallels between any two of these three peoples fail through an insufficient understanding of the position as revealed by the above table. It is evident that a comparison between French and English action must fail, as unfair to the Frenchman, since in action the Englishman is in his element and the Frenchman out of it. Similarly the parallel between French thought and English thought is unfair to the Englishman, since in thought the Frenchman is at home while the Englishman is an uncomfortable and shy guest.

Self-control in the individual and the spirit of coöperation in the community are two psychological features of the tendency to action in the Englishman. By means of his self-control he keeps his will fit and apt to command the forces of the individual. The spirit of coöperation is a collective virtue acting in each individual for the benefit of the group. It explains the genius for spontaneous organization which is the greatest asset of the British nation. Every Englishman carries in him the spirit of the community, the living voice and inspiration of the racial group. A discourteous wag has said, "One Englishman, a fool; two Englishman, a match; three Englishmen, the British Empire." The first term of this epigram is as foolish as it is discourteous, and yet it is not altogether without justification, as may be shown hereafter; the second term is good, in as much as a match, living example of the working of fair play, is an apt symbol of English life; as for the third, it only sins on the side of modesty: contrary to what the author of the epigram seems to think, three Englishmen are not necessary to make up the British Empire — one is enough.

While the Englishman is bent on doings things, the Frenchman seeks to understand them. His main preoccupation is with truth. He wants to see. He treats himself as an optical apparatus and often speaks and thinks of *mise au point*. This expression describes the operation whereby the object is placed at the best distance for vision. The Frenchman, therefore, places himself instinctively at a certain distance from life in order the better to see it. Clarity and intellectual courage are his mental virtues. No prejudice is allowed to interfere with the free working of his mind. Thought values attain in France a national scope. The natural abode of the Frenchman's mind is in the universal and abstract. His aim consists in establishing a scheme of the world appealing to the intellect.

The Spaniard is neither moved to action nor on the watch for thought. He simply waits and contemplates. Passively letting the life stream flow through his being as on a river bed, he acquires experience by living. His virtues are spontaneity and the sense of wholeness. The "sense of life" which is the subject of Miguel de Unamuno's great work is the ruling factor in the Spaniard's existence. It means union between life as a whole and the individual. The individual is thus the ultimate aim for the Spaniard. It takes the place which the community occupies for the Englishman and the mental scheme of the world for the Frenchman.

So much for the Englishman in action, the Frenchman in thought, and the Spaniard in passion — states in which they are each in his own element, happy and apt. All other phases are out of balance and give rise to inner conflicts due to the fact that the type is no longer in his element. The inherent symmetries which link together every two of these six cases into three groups provide a reliable criterion of comparison. The most illuminating parallels that can be made between these three peoples result from a comparison of the Englishman in thought with the Frenchman in action; the Frenchman in passion with the Spaniard in thought; and the Spaniard in action with the Englishman in passion.

III

The Englishman in thought is not at home. His home is in action and, while thinking, he is homesick. He is supposed to be unintelligent and inclined to be proud of it. Yet his mind, needless to say, is of the very first order. Even if we were to admit — as Englishmen sometimes seem to suggest — that the British Empire is due to a series of fits of absent-mindedness, the mind, though absent, exists, and the fits in question could hardly be those of a half-witted people. The fact is that the English have a mind but do not like to use it. They spare it for action. They do not plan beforehand, lest thought might cripple their freedom of action. They do not prejudge — that is, they do not imprison future action in present thought. The Englishman's thought must be applied to action. It is, therefore, the brightest, not before or after action, but on that very spot of the present when thought and action touch.

His thinking, moreover, is not done in his head. "Brainy" is not a word of praise in English. "Clever" is positively insulting. "He is so clever," says the Englishman, and he shakes his head. When he must think, the Englishman thinks with his whole body. He emits a cloud of thought through his knees, elbows, chest, and abdomen. And the curious thing is that, unless his head meddles with it, his thought is generally sound. Sound, please notice — that is, healthy. For he judges thought, not on dialectical principles (Is it correct or erroneous?), but on vital grounds (Is it sound or unsound?). He therefore refuses to grant to all thought an equal right to expression. There are zones of thought which the Englishman does not explore, thoughts of a corrosive nature which might undermine the springs of action. The Englishman guards against such mind adventures by means of inhibitions, reservations, prejudices, and all kinds of devices which may prune thought of its more dangerous growths.

The Frenchman in action is no more at home than the Englishman in thought. He is apt to consider action as an excellent opportunity for setting problems before his mind. Hence that sense of elaborate preparation which prospective action tends to produce in him. We have seen English thought weakest before and after the spot on the present where action and thought touch and live; symmetrically, French action is at its best before and after that spot — when action, unborn, has not yet emerged out of thought, or else when, dead, it is being devoured by thought in that vulture-like operation known as criticism. Just as the Englishman judges thought not on dialectical principles but on vital grounds, so the Frenchman judges action not on vital grounds but on dialectical principles. The question debated is not so much what is to be done as how, and in the name of which principles, it is to be done.

The Frenchman, moreover, premeditates, foresees, and preregulates his action; he endeavors to catch future action in a network of present thought. The Englishman does not foresee, because he trusts action but mistrusts thought, while the Frenchman foresees, because he trusts thought but mistrusts action. Similarly, while the Englishman, by inhibitions, reservations, and prejudices, prunes thought of all the growths which might be dangerous to action, the Frenchman, by abstractions, definitions, and limitations, prunes life of all irrational elements dangerous to thought. Finally, just as the Englishman muddles through, — that is, succeeds in action while keeping a confused mind, — the Frenchman, bent on seeing everything with a clear mind, is apt to lose his temper while engaged in the throes of action.

The Frenchman in passion is not, of course, in his element. We know that as an intellectual he places himself at a distance from nature in order to look at it. Distant, he is cool. Intellectual, he is reasonable. He governs his passions, not in order to act, but because in him the hierarchy of the faculties is safely established with reason at the head. He thus remains outside his passions and watches their play, as a man the play of his favorite dogs, knowing he can always bring them back to order when he wishes. The Frenchman analyzes his passions and dissociates the animal and the intellectual factors in them, losing, however, in the process, all the imponderabilia of irrational and ineffable elements which are, perhaps, the very essence of life. He excels in the chemistry of the passions.

The Spaniard in thought presents features in symmetry with those of the Frenchman in passion. For the wholeness and the spontaneity of the man of passion check all tendencies to split and fracture the life stream. And therefore thought in the Spaniard is wholesale, integral, intuitional — a feature in contrast with the analytical and dissociated character of French passion. The Spaniard is, so to say, sunk in his thought, while the Frenchman is outside his passion. To the coolness of the French passion corresponds the human warmth of Spanish thought, which springs from the recesses of the being in which it is formed. And the intellectual consciousness which distinguishes French passion is symmetrical with the subconscious character of Spanish intuition, true form of Spanish thought.

The Englishman in passion is hindered by his self-control and by his group sense. Group sense is the corollary of his genius for spontaneous organization, which presupposes the existence of the group. That is why all English collective virtues are, so to say, "refracted" on crossing the racial border, just as a ray of light is broken when it passes from air to water. Self-control and the group sense penetrate deep into the life stream of the individual Englishman, canalizing it toward the mills of social service, dividing it into all kinds of currents and subcurrents. The life stream in the Englishman is, therefore, neither spontaneous nor homogeneous. The pressure of the group forces on individual passions the stamp and color of the group. It drives underground all those passions which resist the group action. Thus, under the armor of self-control, the strong passions of the Englishman live a secluded life — if anything, stronger for their seclusion.

Just as the Englishman keeps off passions for fear of lowering his value as a unit in the group team, so the Spaniard keeps off action lest through action the group enslave him as an individual. His apparent laziness, his passivity, his indifference, his contemplation, are but forms of a selective instinct which evades all action dangerous to individual liberty. It is, therefore, an instinct in strict symmetry with English self-control. So that, to the pressure inward wherewith the group enslaves the Englishman and drives deep trouble into his life stream, corresponds the pressure outward which the Spanish individual exerts on the group, depriving it of its order and efficiency. Spanish actions are ultra-individualistic, just as English passions are ultra-collective. (Hamlet and Don Quixote might be considered as the two characters which personify this contrast. Hamlet — despite incomprehensive critics — is a man of action. His swift decision in everything but the main problem he has to solve is evident. But he feels the strong pressure of the group in the tradition which bids him avenge his father. He is sick with group pressure. Don Quixote is a man of passion — a lover, a reader of books — who goes out and imposes his own individual visions on the outside world. He is mad with an excessive individual pressure outward, which he exerts on the world.) Under Spanish indifference, stores of human energy are accumulated by time, and now and then the feat, the exploit, is accomplished when they are released. Similarly, under the cold crust of self-control, the heat of English passions rises unseen, and now and then bursts into exceptional flames. Thus the true symmetrical types of the great Spaniards of action — Hernán Cortés, Balboa, Pizarro — are the great English poets — Shakespeare, Shelley, Byron — rising above English calm as the *conquistadores* rise above Spanish indifference. The true parallel of the English genius for spontaneous organization, which guarantees the full life of the group, is Spanish spontaneity of the passions, which guarantees full life to the individual.

Faithful to action, the Englishman is empirical. Faithful to thought, the Frenchman is theoretical. Faithful to passion, the Spaniard is individualistic. The first rules his life by moral-social standards; the second by intellectual principles; the third by individual experience. The Englishman's virtue is wisdom; the Frenchman's is reason; the Spaniard's serenity. A gap between standards and behavior is covered by a bridge of fiction called hypocrisy. Hypocrisy is, therefore, an English vice. Yet it can be generalized by extending it to other than moral standards. English standards are moral; so is English hypocrisy. French standards are intellectual; so is French hypocrisy. Spanish standards are of the passions; so is Spanish hypocrisy. The Englishman feigns when he does not behave; the Frenchman when he does not understand; the Spaniard when he does not experience. But, as hypocrisy is proportional to the strength of the group, the three hypocrisies differ in intensity as well as in quality.

IV

The structure of the community is aristocratic in England, bourgeois in France, and popular in Spain.

In the people of action, the community is spontaneously organized in a natural hierarchy. The aristocracy is not a self-appointed leading and privileged class, but the outcome of a traditional evolution. All Englishmen rejoice in their aristocracy. When the Duke of Devonshire gives his daughter in marriage, all English homes enjoy the taste of wedding cake; when the Duke of Richmond rides with his hounds, all Englishmen blow their horns.

French social structure is built on a theoretical conception of intellectual order. It is superimposed rather than grown, architectural rather than natural. Rather than a nation, France is a state. The French hierarchy rests on an intellectual criterion. Not pedigree but intelligence is what gives prestige and authority to men. The respect and public admiration which are bestowed in England on dukes and princes go in France to *membres de l'Institut*.

In Spain there is an instinctive rebellion against all social structure. So far as there is a social structure, it is based on the all-pervading influence of the popular element in the country. The standard in England is the aristocrat, and so English charwomen do their best to dress like duchesses; in France, the bourgeoisie, and every Frenchwoman dresses like a bourgeoise; in Spain, the people, and when a Spanish duchess wants to look smart she imitates the dress and manners of a Seville cigarette maker.

England is a political but not a social democracy; France is both a political and a social democracy; Spain is not a political democracy, but she is the most democratic of the three in actual life. English political life is built on liberty, but neglects equality and has no conception of fraternity.[1] French political life is built on equality, but tends to over-regulate liberty and to understand fraternity as a theoretical idea rather than to feel it as a cordial fact. Spain is such a fanatic about individual liberty that she is unable to evolve the adequate conditions for ensuring it, and her sense of equality is so profound that it amounts to cordial fraternity.

Politics are regulated in England by ethics, economics, and fair play; in France by intellectual creeds and theories; in Spain by the free play of individual ambitions judged by the remainder of the nation in virtue of dramatic standards. In England an increase in the income tax or a private scandal may ruin a political career. In France a lively episode of the *cherchez la femme* type would, if anything, add distinction to a

[1] It is, however, rich in charity. But charity differs from fraternity in that charity is active and fraternity may or may not be active, and, moreover, charity looks downward, while fraternity looks level. — AUTHOR

public man, but a difference in political creed will suffice to drive anyone from office. In Spain a prominent man, a *prohombre,* has an inherent right to appear on the political stage whether he is a good or a bad statesman, just as in a novel the hero and the villain are equally interesting for the reader.

A parliamentary debate in England is like a cricket match. Good humor and coöperation on both sides; enjoyment of good batting and bowling, whatever side be the winner; and an all-round respect of the wigged umpire, the Speaker — so called, of course, because he is the only member who does not speak. The parliamentary system is run for business and not for ideas and opinions. In France, on the contrary, ideas matter in themselves and business must wait till the battle of principles has been fought out. It is a fierce battle, in which arguments are hurled with fury and seek the political death of the adversary. Yet the passion of French debates is not an original source of energy — it is the by-product and waste of intellectual strife. In Spain a parliamentary debate is a show.

The English language is an empirical chaos. Words are monosyllabic; for the present, tense of the man of action, leaves no room for more. Verbs, nouns, adjectives, have all one shape, which means that the Englishman does not prejudge their function and meaning before actual use calls for them. By themselves, moreover, words have not much personality, and it is the phrase accent and stress which give them their true value, just as society gives his true value to the Englishman. The language is led by the upper classes. Hence its chaotic spelling and mannerisms. The language of poetry and letters is artificial, and popular language has no value. English has but one vowel, a cloud of a vowel which remains indefinite and changeable, ever ready to compromise, as reserved and reticent as the Englishman himself, and so successful in the art of dodging that it can remain unrevealed for several syllables, hidden behind screens of consonants — for instance, in the word "particularly," which is pronounced "p't'c'l'ly."

The French language is a black-and-white image of Latin. Every Latin word, in passing into French, collapses like an opera hat, losing its mass, color, and relief. Most words, whatever their vowels in Latin, take a French shape dominated by the letter *e,* the middle vowel, the vowel without color or mass, the vowel which suggests moderation and measure. Thus all the Latin words of the *honor* family pass into *eur* endings, — *couleur, douleur,* — forms which suggest moderation and measure; all except *amour,* in which case, of course, moderation and measure would be evidently out of keeping. French grammar is rigid. It does not admit inversions. It follows strictly its own rules. The literary language differs from the language of the people, but less than in the case of England. The ruling form in France is the language of the middle classes, and the immense majority of Frenchmen write it well.

The Spanish language is spontaneous, energetic, and popularly led. It retains the mass and the color of the Latin, but makes it more luminous by dropping the *m* endings and by increasing the number of full vowels, particularly *o* and *a.* It is rebellious to rules, apt to produce its sentences synthetically rather than in logical order, and contemptuous of grammar. Its most exquisite flowers of poetry are often grown on pure popular soil.

Art begins as a passion; it is formed and refined by the intellect and consumed and absorbed by society and convention. Spanish art is therefore strongest in its first impulse — inspiration; French art in the middle phase — formation; English art in the last phase — actual production and consumption. Subconscious in Spain, art is conscious in France and self-conscious in England. Purely æsthetic in Spain, it is apt to take on intellectual prejudices in France and ethical prejudices in England. In Spain it is free and individualistic; in France it is classified in "schools" and "generations"; in England it is aristocratic and conventional.

Religion is in Spain an individual passion, and the Spaniard is apt to absorb into his being the divine beings he worships. In France religion is mainly a school of thought, often leading to incredulity; in England, mostly an ethical force devoted to social service. Individual and concrete in Spain, it is abstract and universal in France, national and racial in England. The world is covered with English churches and English churchyards, so that Englishmen, no doubt, when the parting signal comes, sail in English coffins and land at last in an English eternity which is but another dominion beyond the seas of death.

The man of action; the man of thought; the man of passion — so different and yet so identical. Their existence is a brilliant proof of the delightful imagination of the Divine Artist.

April 1928

RALPH BARTON PERRY

1876–

In the history of intellectual America there are few more interesting passages than the early comradeship of William James and Oliver Wendell Holmes, Jr. It is the story of perfect understanding and gradual estrangement. Not that these friends quarreled; it is simply that their sympathies diverged. Each followed the dictates of his own nature. To James, the path of legalism, of logic, of cool appraisal of the aspirations of men, was wholly foreign. To Holmes, hot enthusiasm, experimentation, and the faith that leaps from probabilities to possibilities and from possibilities into the Empyrean, were alike distasteful. The friends went on to great careers, wide as the world asunder. The question, which has made the more precious addition to the common heritage, will be answered by each of us according to his individual measuring rule. It involves in a way the comparative importance of harnessing men's energies to the task of promoting orderly progress in this world, or of releasing them for flights into the unknown and unknowable. One path is practical and has an end. The other is impractical and leads to infinity; but it is the endless journey which unfetters the human spirit.

Professor Perry's history of the James family is a model for biographers to follow. Henry James, Sr., William James, and Henry James, Jr., are the sum of divergent qualities. Their family history is a challenge to some future Galton to plunge deeper into the mystery of inheritance. From his complete story of William James's life this chapter is a thing apart, but no passage which has passed under the editorship of Professor Perry seems to me more illuminating than the following correspondence.

The Common Enemy

Early Letters of Oliver Wendell Holmes, Jr., and William James

RALPH BARTON PERRY

In writing the Preface of his *Principles of Psychology* in 1890, William James recorded his indebtedness to Chauncey Wright and Charles Peirce for "their intellectual companionship in old times." Adding Oliver Wendell Holmes, Jr., there were three of these old-time intellectual companionships which must be taken account of in any discussion of James's early philosophical orientation, and which bear directly on the issue between science and religion. All of these men were of a relatively rigorous or skeptical turn of mind, and by exposure to their criticism James's germinating metaphysics became a hardier plant.

The intimacy with Holmes began while the latter was a student in the Harvard Law School (1864–1866). In Brazil in 1865 James longed for Holmes, and after he returned to his medical studies in 1866 he "wrangled" with Holmes by the hour. In the winter of 1866–1867 the two were deep in a continuing metaphysical discussion, echoes of which are preserved in a memorandum on "materialism," addressed by James to Holmes. It contained a defense of optimism against the negations of agnosticism — a defense which he "was groping for the other evening," but "could not say" until Holmes was gone and he was in bed. On April 16, 1867, James sailed from New York on the *Great Eastern* — bound for his long voyage of exile and discovery. Suffering from mortification that he should be so unreliable in health and so vacillating in will, he had kept his plan a secret even from his family and friends. But on the eve of his departure he must hold a farewell session at the Holmes house on Charles Street: "Dear Wendy boy, — I will go in tomorrow night, and we will evolve cosmos out of chaos for positively the last time."

During all the time of his homesickness and heart-searching in Germany, James felt that Holmes and Tom Ward were his "best friends so far." In September 1867, he wrote from Berlin complaining of Holmes's silence, inquiring after the results of his "study of the *vis viva* question," and referring familiarly to their "dilapidated old friend the Cosmos." He received this reply:—

BOSTON, Dec. 15, 1867

DEAR BILL,—

I shall begin with no apologies for my delay in writing except to tell you that since seeing you I have written three long letters to you at different intervals on *vis viva,* each of which I was compelled to destroy because on reflection it appeared either unsound or incomplete. But I was talking yesterday with Fanny Dixwell and she told me to fire away anyhow—that she thought it would please you to hear from me even without *vis viva.* So here goes. Writing is so unnatural to me that I have never before dared to try it to you unless in connection with a subject. Ah! dear Bill, do me justice. My expressions of esteem are not hollow nor hyperbolical—nor put in to cover my neglect. In spite of my many friends I am almost alone in my thoughts and inner feelings. And whether I ever see you much or not, I think I can never fail to derive a secret comfort and companionship from the thought of you. I believe I shall always respect and love you whether we see much or little of each other. . . .

For two or three months I debauched o' nights in philosophy. But now it is law—law—law. My *magnum opus* was reading the *Critique of Pure Reason* and Schulze's *éclaircissement*—which on the whole, though an excellent abridgment, doesn't much by way of *éclaircissements.* . . .

Assumed that logic exhaustively classifies judgments according to their possible forms, it [Kant's *Critique*] has then implicitly classified concepts in like manner. But all experience to be thought must be thought through concepts. The forms of concepts, then, are inherent in all organised experience as an *a priori* element. Hence it is explained *inter alia* why, given phenomenon *A,* we say it must have had a cause in an antecedent phenomenon. The phenomenon only became thinkable through that form and others. You see how ingenious and audacious was his attempt—yet its fallacy seems obvious when the reasoning by which it was arrived at is grasped.

Thus, the logical categories have reference only to the form in which judgments are expressed. The conceptions of substance, causal relation, etc., belong to the content and are not given in the form. Thus, take the hypothetical judgment, "if *A* then *B.*" This form is not coterminous with the causal judgment, as Thomson (reasoning *alio intuitu*) points out; *e.g.,* "if this be poetry, poetry is worthless," is as much hypothetical in form as "if the moon attracts in the same line as the sun the tides are at their highest." Thomson says the only case of causal relation is when the four terms are all different: "if *A* is *B* then *C* is *D.*" But whether even this last is always so may be doubted—*e.g.,* "if I am right then tomorrow will be warm." Again, he and Mansel have both shown—I should think successfully, but I am no logician—that all of these can be reduced to categorical judgments. And then what becomes of a theory based on their fundamental distinctions? But the other objection is, I think, insuperable — that if the concept cause and effect be only a form of thought corresponding to the hypothetical judgment, that judgment ought never to express any but causal relations. . . . It's puerile stuff enough, I admit, to waste energy on. But it seems necessary to read a good deal of useless stuff, in order to know that it is so and not to depend only on a surmise. At present, I say it's nothing but law; though, by the by, I am reading Tyndall's book on *Heat* — what a yellow-whiskered, healthy, florid-complected, pleasant English book it is, to be sure. Aren't the foreigners simpler than we? See what one of the great lights of English law says in the preface to a book I'm reading (he is speaking of Savigny): "I have used great exertions, but without effect, to make myself sufficiently master of the German language to read this work in the original." If a man here had three cents' worth of second-hand knowledge would he confess that he didn't know anything under the sun? Talking of Britons, there have been a lot here of late — one, a Mr. Henry Cowper — brother of the present Earl C., made a decided impression on me. He had the cosmos at heart, it seemed to me, and we hammered at it late into the night several times. . . .

Oh! Bill, my beloved, how have I yearned after thee all this long time. How I have admired those brave, generous and magnanimous traits of which I will not shame thee by speaking. I am the better that I have seen thee and known thee, — let that suffice. Since I wrote the last word I have been to see your father. By a rather remarkable coincidence, your last letter referred to Kant and to Schulze's books. It is rather strange, isn't it? It is now evening and the whole day has been yours with the exceptions noted and meals. I expect Gray directly. May this get to you in time to wish you a Happy New Year. By Heaven I do, — *vis viva* must wait. There are stickers I can't answer. But I rather think you found difficulty — at least I did — in the insufficiency of facts. As one is shaping his views he wants to say, Is this experiment so or so? I got more out of Cooke on terms by way of translating mathematics into English than anyone else. But I found my first explanations in great measure *chimæra bombinans in vacuo* when I went into the matter a second time in order to write you. As it is I just see that force isn't destroyed, without having mastered the formulæ. What a passion your father has in writing and talking his religion! Almost he persuadeth me to be a Swedenborgian, but I can't go it so far — will see whether the other scheme busts up first, I think.

Good-bye, dear Bill — don't forget me quite.

Affectionately yours,

O. W. Holmes

BERLIN, Jan. 3, 1868

MY DEAR WENDLE, —

Ich weiss nicht was soll es bedeuten, dass ich so traurig bin, tonight. The ghosts of the past all start from their unquiet graves and keep dancing a senseless whirligig around me so that, after trying in vain to read three books, to sleep, or to think, I clutch the pen and ink and resolve to work off the fit by a few lines to one of the most obtrusive ghosts of all — namely the tall and lank one of Charles Street. Good golly! how I would prefer to have about twenty-four hours' talk with you up in that whitely lit-up room — without the sun rising or the firmament revolving so as to put the gas out, without sleep, food, clothing or shelter except your whiskey bottle, of which, or the like of which, I have not partaken since I have been in these longitudes! I should like to have you opposite me in any mood, whether the facetiously excursive, the metaphysically discursive, the personally confidential, or the jadedly *cursive* and argumentative — so that the oyster-shells which enclose my being might slowly turn open on their rigid hinges under the radiation, and the critter within loll out his dried-up gills into the circumfused ichor of life, till they grew so fat as not to know themselves again. I feel as if a talk with you of any kind could not fail to set me on my legs again for three weeks at least. I have been chewing on two or three dried-up old cuds of ideas I brought from America with me, till they have disappeared, and the nudity of the Kosmos has got beyond anything I have as yet experienced. . . .

I don't know how it is I am able to take so little interest in reading this winter. I marked out a number of books when I first came here, to finish. What with their heaviness and the damnable slowness with which the Dutch still goes, they weigh on me like a haystack. I loathe the thought of them; and yet they have poisoned my slave of a conscience so that I can't enjoy anything else. I have reached an age when practical work of some kind clamors to be done — and I must still wait!

There! Having worked off that pent-up gall of six weeks' accumulation I feel more genial. I wish I could have some news of you — now that the postage is lowered to such a ridiculous figure (and no letter is double) there remains no *shadow* of an excuse for not writing — but, still, I don't expect anything from you. I suppose you are sinking ever deeper into the sloughs of the law — yet I ween the Eternal Mystery still from time to time gives her goad another turn in the raw she once established between your ribs. Don't let it heal over yet. When I get home let's establish a philosophical society to have regular meetings and discuss none but the very tallest and broadest questions — to be composed of none but the very topmost cream of Boston manhood. It will give each one a chance to air his own opinion in a grammatical form, and to sneer and chuckle when he goes home at what damned fools all the other members are — and may grow into something very important after a sufficient number of years. . . .

I'll now pull up. I don't know whether you take it as a compliment that I should only write to you when in the dismalest of dumps — perhaps you ought to — you, the one emergent peak, to which I cling when all the rest of the world has sunk beneath the wave. Believe me, my Wendly boy, what poor possibility of friendship in the crazy frame of W. J. meanders about thy neighborhood. Good-bye! Keep the same bold front as ever to the Common Enemy — and don't forget your ally,

W. J.

P.S. Jan. 4 [Written on the outside of the envelope]. By a strange coincidence, after writing this last night, I received yours this morning. Not to sacrifice the postage stamps which are already on the envelope (Economical W!) I don't reopen it. But I will write you again soon. Meanwhile, bless your heart! thank you! *Vide* Shakespeare: Sonnet XXIX.

Boston, April 19, 1868

Dear Bill, —

The icy teeth have melted out of the air and winter has snapped at us for the last time. Now are the waters beneath my window of a deeper and more significant blue than heretofore. Now do the fields burn with green fire — the evanescent hint of I know not what hidden longing of the earth. Now all the bushes burgeon with wooly buds and the elm trees have put on bridal veils of hazy brown. Now to the chorus of the frogs answers the chorus of the birds in antiphony of morning and evening. Now couples, walking round Boston Common Sundays after sunset, draw near to each other in the dark spaces between the gas lights and think themselves unseen. Now are the roads around Cambridge filled with collegians with new hats and sticks and shining schoolboy faces. Now the young man seeks the maiden nothing loath to be pursued. Spring is here, Bill, and I turn to thee, — not with more affection than during the long grind of the winter, but desiring if it may be to say a word to thee once more.

Since I wrote in December I have worked at nothing but the law. Philosophy has hibernated in torpid slumber, and I have lain "sluttishly soaking and gurgling in the devil's pickle," as Carlyle says. It has been necessary, — if a man chooses a profession he cannot forever content himself in picking out the plums with fastidious dilettantism and give the rest of the loaf to the poor, but must eat his way manfully through crust and crumb — soft, unpleasant, inner parts which, within one, swell, causing discomfort in the bowels. Such has been my cowardice that I have been almost glad that you weren't here, lest you should be disgusted to find me inaccessible to ideas and impressions of more spiritual significance but alien to my studies. Think not, however, that I distrust the long enduring of your patience. I know that you would be the last of all to turn away from one in whom you discerned the possibility of friendship because his vigils were at a different shrine, knowing it was the same Divinity he worshipped. And the winter has been a success, I think, both for the simple discipline of the work and because I now go on with an ever increasing conviction that law as well as any other series of facts in this world may be approached in the interests of science and may be studied, yes and practised, with the preservation of one's ideals. I should even say that they grew robust under the regimen, — more than that I do not ask. To finish the search of mankind, to discover the *ne plus ultra* which is the demand of ingenuous youth, one finds is not allotted to an individual. To reconcile oneself to life — to dimly apprehend that this dream disturbing the sleep of the cosm is not the result of a dyspepsy, but is well — to suspect some of the divine harmonies, though you cannot note them like a score of music — these things, methinks, furnish vanishing points which give a kind of perspective to the chaos of events. Perhaps I am fortunate in what I have often made a reproach to myself.

Harry never lets up on his high aims, — somehow it connects itself with the absence of humor in him which himself avows. *I do.* There are not infrequent times when a bottle of wine, a good dinner, a girl of some trivial sort can fill the hour for me. So for longer spaces, work, — of which only at the beginning and the end do I perceive the philosophic *nexus,* and while performing forget the Great Task Master's Eye. This makes life easier though perhaps it does not deserve approval.

Let me give another example of "if *A* is *B,* then *C* is *D*" (in my last letter) which does not denote a causal connection — the one I gave was open to objection as standing on peculiar grounds. Take all judgments of universal or assumed universal concomitants: "If the barometer falls suddenly, there will be a gale"; "If the sun shines in Boston, the stars are out in China." In these, etc., there is no causal connection between protasis and apodosis, although *by going outside of the judgment* to an induction we may say with more or less confidence that where two facts are always found together, if one is not the cause of the other then they are both (probably) referable to a common cause. . . . Is it not clear that . . . the relation of the *if* and the *then* to a common cause is not in any way given in the form of the judgment, and that said *if* and *then* don't stand to each other in the relation of cause and effect? . . .

Dear old Bill, I haven't said anything about your illness to you — there is nothing, perhaps, which particularly belongs to me to say. But for God's sake don't lose that courage with which you have faced "the common enemy" (as you well have it). Would that I could give back the spirits which you have given to me so often. At all events doubt not of my love.

Let me not be sad, — at least for this letter. There is a new fire in the earth and sky. I, who through the long winter have felt the wrinkles deepening in my face and a stoop settling in my back — I, who have said to myself that my life henceforth must and should be given only to severe thought, and have said to youth, "*procul esto,*" — I feel the mighty quickening of the spring.

The larches have sprouted.

I saw a butterfly today just loosed from the bondage of winter, and a bee toiling in sticky buds half opened.

O! passionate breezes! O! rejoicing hills! How swells the soft full chorus — for this earth which slept has awakened and the air is tremulous with multiplied joyous sound.

Sing, sparrow — kissing with thy feet the topmost tassels of the pines.

Cease not thy too much sound, O! robin. Squirrels, grind thy scissors in the woods. Creak, blackbirds. Croak, frogs. Caw, high-flying crows, who have seen the breaking of the ice in northern rivers and the seaward moving booms.

A keen, slender, stridulous vibration — almost too fine for the hearing, weaving in and out, and in the pauses of the music dividing the silence like a knife — pierces my heart with an ecstasy I cannot utter. Ah! what is it? Did I ever hear it? Is it a voice within, answering to the others, but different from them — and like a singing flame not ceasing with that which made it vocal?

Dear Bill, to whom should I vent this madness but to you? Good-bye. You know my sentiments — I will not repeat them.

Affectionately yours,
O. W. Holmes

Apr. 25. It is snowing again. S' help me.

Dresden, May 15, 1868

My dear Wendell, —

Your unexpected letter has just burst into my existence like a meteor into the sphere of a planet, and here I go for an answer while the heat developed by the impact is at its highest. I have got so accustomed to thinking of you as not a writing animal that such an event rather dislocates my mind from its habitual "sag" in contemplating the world. I have of late been repeatedly on the point of writing to you but have paused ere slipping o'er the brink. It is easy to write people whom you have been steadily writing to, for one letter seems to continue the previous ones. But to fire off a letter point blank at a man once in six months has an arbitrary savor. There are so many things of about equal importance for you to tell him that there is no reason for you to begin with any particular one and leave off the rest. Consequently you don't begin at all. However, heaven reward you for this inspired effusion and help you to another some time. It runs through the whole circle of human energy, Shelley, Kant, Goethe, Walt Whitman, all being fused in the unity of your fiery personality. Were I only in the vein, O! friend, I would answer in the same high strain, but today I grovel in prose. That you firmly embrace like a *Bothriocephalus latus* the very bowels of the law and grapple them to your soul with hooks of steel, is good. That the miasmas thence arising do not forever hide the blue Jove above, is better. I am firmly convinced that by going straight in almost any direction you can get out of the woods in which the young mind grows up, for I have an idea that the process usually consists of a more or less forcible reduction of the other elements of the chaos to a harmony with the terms of the one on which one has taken his particular stand. I think I might have fought it out on the line of practical medicine quite well. Your image of the ideals being vanishing points which give a kind of perspective to the chaos of events, tickleth that organ within me whose function it is to dally with the ineffable. I shall not fail to remember it, and if I stay long enough in Germany to make the acquaintance of ary a philosopher, I shall get it off as my own, you bet!

Your letter last winter I got and acknowledged on the cover of one I had just written you. Your criticism of Kant seems perfectly sound to me. I hoped to have got at him before now but have been interfered with. I have read only his *Prolegomena* and his little *Anthropology* (a marvellous, biting little work), and Cousin's exposé of him (and of himself at the same time, darn him and the likes of him! — he is a mere politician). I hope soon to begin with the *Kritik*, for which I feel myself now quite prepared. And I reserve any half-ripe remarks I may have made on Kant till after that is done. I think a good five hours' talk with you would probably do me more good than almost any other experience I can conceive of. I have not had any contact out of books with any soul possessed of *reason* since I left home, except, perhaps, Grimm — and I did not, owing to the linguistic wall between us, succeed in putting myself into communication with him. And in personal contact, Wendell, lies a deep dark power. I say "reason," but I have no idea what the thing is. I have slipped so gradually out of sight of it in people that I did not know any particular thing was gone, till the day before yesterday I made the acquaintance of a young female from New York who is here in the house, and suddenly noticed that an old long-forgotten element was present (I mean in her way of accepting the world). It has been a beneficent discovery, and the suddenness and quasi-definiteness of it almost shatters one's empirical philosophy. But probably it, too, may be resolved into other more vulgar elements.

The fact is, my dear boy, that I feel more as if you were my ally against what you call "the common enemy" than anyone I know. As I am writing a grave statement of facts and not an effusion of friendliness, I may say that Tom Ward seems to me to have as great an intuition of the length and breadth of the enemy (which is the place in which most people fail), and perhaps a greater animal passion in his feeling about it, but poor Tom is so deficient in power of orderly thought that intercourse with him hardly ever bears fruit. With Harry and my Dad I have a perfect sympathy "personally," but Harry's orbit and mine coincide but part way, and Father's and mine hardly at all, except in a general feeling of philanthropy in which we both indulge. I have no idea that the particular point of view from which we spy the fiendish enemy has *per se* any merit over that of lots of other men. Such an opinion we recognize in other people as "conceit." But merely because it is common to both of us, I have an esteem for you which is *tout particulier,* and value intercourse with you. You have a far more logical and orderly mode of thinking than I (I stand between you and T. Ward), and whenever we have been together I have somehow been conscious of a reaction against the ascendancy of this over my ruder processes — a reaction caused by some subtle deviltry of egotism and jealousy, whose causes are untraceable by myself, but through whose agency I put myself involuntarily into a position of self-defense, as if you threatened to overrun my territory and injure my own proprietorship. I don't know whether you ever noticed any such thing, — it is hard to define the subtleness of it. *Some* of it may have been caused by the feeling of a too "cosmocentric" consciousness in you. But most of it was pure meanness. I *guess* that were we to meet now I should be less troubled with it. I have grown into the belief that friendship (including the highest half of that which between the two sexes is united under the single name of love) is about the highest joy of earth, and that a man's rank in the general scale is well indicated by his capacity for it. So much established, I will try in a few brief strokes to define my present condition to you. If asked the question which all men who pretend to know themselves ought to be able to answer, but which few probably could offhand, — "What reason can you give for continuing to live? What ground allege why the thread of your days should not be snapped *now?*"

May 18th. Wendell of my entrails! At the momentous point where the last sheet ends I was interrupted by the buxom maid calling to tea and through various causes have not got back till now. As I sit by the open window waiting for my breakfast and look out on the line of *Droschkes* drawn up on the side of the Dohna Platz, and see the coachmen, red-faced, red-collared, and blue-coated, with varnished hats, sitting in a variety of indolent attitudes upon their boxes, one of them looking in upon me and probably wondering what the devil I am, — when I see the big sky with a monstrous white cloud battening and bulging up from behind the houses into the blue, with a uniform copper film drawn over cloud and blue, which makes one anticipate a soaking day — when I see the houses opposite with their balconies and windows filled with flowers and greenery — Ha! on the topmost balcony of one stands a maiden, black-jacketed, red-petticoated, fair and slim under the striped awning, leaning her elbow on the rail and her peach-like chin upon her rosy finger tips! Of whom thinkest thou, maiden, up there aloft? Here *here!* beats that human heart for which in the drunkenness of the morning hour thy being vaguely longs, and tremulously, but recklessly and wickedly, posits elsewhere, over those distant housetops which thou regardest. Out of another window hangs the form, seen from behind and centre of gravity downwards, of an intrepid servant girl, washing the window. Blue frocked is she, and like a spider fast holding to his thread, or one that gathers samphires on dizzy promontory, she braves the danger of a fall. Against the lamp-post leans the *Dienstmann* or *commissionnaire,* cross-legged and with tin-badged cap, smoking his cheap morning cigar. Far over the *Platz* toils the big country wagon with high-collared horses, and the still pavement rings with the shuffling feet of broad-backed wenches carrying baskets, and of short-necked, wide-faced men. The day has in fact begun, and when I see all this and think that at the same moment thou art probably in a dead sleep whirled round through the black night with rocks and trees and monuments like an inanimate thing, when I think all this, I feel — *how?* — I give it up myself! After this interruption, which on the ground of local color and my half-awake condition you will excuse, I return to the former subject. But here's the breakfast! Excuse me! Man eats in Germany a very light breakfast, chocolate and dry bread, so it won't take me long.

'Tis done, and a more genial glow than ever fills my system. Having read over what I wrote the day before yesterday I feel tempted not to send it, for I cannot help thinking it does not represent with perfect sincerity the state of the case. Still, if I do not write to you now, it may postpone itself a good while, and I let it go for the general spirit which animates it rather than for the particular propositions it contains. The point which seems to me unwarranted was my assumption of any special battle I was fighting against the powers of darkness, and of your being allied with me therein as the ground of my esteem for you. The truth is painfully evident to me that I am but little interested in any particular battle or movement of progress, and the ground of my friendship for you is more a sort of physical relish for your wit and wisdom, and passive enjoyment of the entertainment they afford, than anything else. Much would I give for a constructive passion of some kind. As it is, I am in great measure in the hands of Chance. Your metaphysical industry and the artistic satisfaction you take in the exercise of it, gives you an immeasurable advantage. In the past year if I have learned little else, I have at least learned a good deal that I previously did not suspect about the limits of my own mind. They are not exhilarating. I will not annoy you by going into the details but they all conspire to give my thoughts a vague emptiness wherever feeling is, and to drive feeling out wherever the thought becomes good for anything. Bah! My answer to the question I asked at the end of sheet two would be vague indeed; it would vary between the allegation of a dogged desire to assert myself, at certain times, and the undermined hope of making *some* nick, however minute, in the pile which humanity is fashioning, at others. Of course I would beg for a *temporary* respite from the inevitable shears, for different reasons at different times. If a *particular* and passionate reason for wishing to live for four hours longer were *always* forthcoming, I should think myself a very remarkable man, and be quite satisfied. But in the intervals of absence of such a reason, I could wish that my general grounds are more defined than they are. . . .

I am tending strongly to an empiristic view of life. I don't know how far it will carry me, or what rocks insoluble by it will block my future path. Already I see an ontological cloud of absolute idealism waiting for me far off on the horizon, but I have no passion for the fray. I shall continue to apply empirical principles to my experiences as I go on and see how much they fit. One thing makes me uneasy. *If* the end of all is to be that we must take our sensations as simply given or as preserved by natural selection for us, and interpret this rich and delicate overgrowth of ideas, moral, artistic, religious and social, as a mere mask, a tissue spun in happy hours by creative individuals and adopted by other men in the interests of their sensations, — how long is it going to be well for us not to "let on" all we know to the public? How long are we to indulge the "people" in their theological and other vagaries so long as such vagaries seem to us more beneficial on the whole than otherwise? How long are we to wear that uncomfortable "air of suppression" which has been complained of in Mr. Mill? Can any men be trusted to dole out from moment to moment just that measure of a doctrine which is consistent with utility? I know that the brightest jewel in the crown of Utilitarianism is that every notion hatched by the human mind receives justice and tolerance at its hands. But I know that no mind can trace the far ramifications of an idea in the mind of the public; and that any idea is at a disadvantage which cannot enlist in its favor the thirst for conquest, the love of absoluteness, that have helped to found religions; and which cannot open a *definite* channel for human sympathies and affections to flow in. It seems exceedingly improbable that any new *religious* genius should arise in these days to open a fresh highway for the masses who have outgrown the old beliefs. Now ought not we (supposing we become indurated sensationalists) to begin to smite the old, hip and thigh, and get, if possible, a little enthusiasm associated with our doctrines? If God is dead or at least irrelevant, ditto everything pertaining to the "Beyond." If happiness is our Good, ought we not to try to foment a passionate and bold will to attain that happiness among the multitudes? Can we not conduct off upon our purposes from the old moralities and theologies a beam which will invest us with some of the proud absoluteness which made them so venerable, by preaching the doctrine that Man is his own Providence, and every individual a real God to his race, greater or less in proportion to his gifts and the way he uses them? The sentiment of philanthropy is now so firmly established and apparently its permanence so guaranteed by its beneficent nature, that it would be bold to say it could not take its place as an ultimate motive for human action. I feel no *confidence* (even apart from my doubts as to the theoretical finality of "sensationalism") that society is as yet ripe for it as a popular philosophy and religion combined, but as I said above, no one can measure the effects of an idea, or distribute exactly the shares which different ideas have in our present social order. And certainly there is something disheartening in the position of an esoteric philosopher. The conscientious prudence which would wish to educate mankind gradually instead of throwing out the line, and letting it educate itself, may be both presumptuous and timid. Do you take? I only throw out these as doubts, and would like to know whether you have been troubled by any similar ones on the matter of policy. The breath of my nostrils is doubt, and that is what makes me so the slave of chance. . . .

I have been reading lately in Teplitz in Schiller and Goethe. The possession of those two men's lives and works by a people gives them a great advantage over neighboring nations. Goethe at last has shot into distinct individual shape for me, which is a great relief, and an enormous figure he is. . . . I am sensible to your expression of sympathy with my stove-in condition of back. I shall *endeavor* (by jerks) to keep the upper lip rigid even if the vertebral column yields. An account of a man in a western settlement which I heard from a traveler on the ship coming over has afforded me much satisfaction ever since, and served as a good example. The traveler stopped at a grocery store to get some whiskey, and alarmed at the woebegone appearance of the storekeeper, asked him what was the matter. "Do you see that man sitting in the back shop?" said the other. "He's the sheriff, and has attached all my goods." He then went on to tell his other misfortunes, ending with the story of his wife having run away the day before with another man, but presently wiped his eyes, and with a smile of sweet recollection said: "I don't know, though, as I have any right to complain — I've done pretty well on the whole since I came to this settlement." Comment is needless.

There, my dear boy, I hope you have not begun to thank your stars I don't write oftener, since I write at such length. I wanted to give you a report of my mental condition, I have done so more or less, and trust you will respect the affection and confidence which dictated it. I'd rather my father should not see it. Use your own judgment about showing it to Harry. I leave here in a month or so for Heidelberg. Get my address from Harry whenever you write. And for God's sake do so again before too long. I got a letter in Teplitz from Miss Fanny Dixwell which was a great godsend. Please remember me to all your family, and believe me thy friend

Wm. James

As is intimated in this letter, James's affection for Holmes was not untroubled. He felt a certain constraint in his presence, which was perhaps due at bottom to a difference of emotional "wave length." James would let himself go, and then recoil when he felt that the circuit was not completed. He was more impulsive, headlong, self-forgetful — Holmes more firmly resolute and self-contained, as well as more ironical. James was sometimes led by this experience to attribute a certain hardness and self-seeking to Holmes. The latter is said to have remarked of another of his friends, "I'm afraid Brandeis has the crusading spirit. He talks like one of those upward-and-onward fellows." So did James, and he never wholly relished the air of flippancy or dry cynicism with which Holmes masked his own service of mankind. After James's return from Europe, Holmes continued to be a familiar intimate of the James household. "W. Holmes rings the bell as usual at eight and one-half o'clock on Saturday evenings, and we are all falling into our old ways," wrote the elder Mrs. James to her son Henry. But James was constantly baffled by him — found him "composed of at least two and a half distinct human beings."

That there was something about Holmes's very adherence to his chosen task which was appalling to the other members of the James family, as well as to William, will be seen in this paragraph from a letter written to Henry James by his mother in 1873: "Wendell Holmes dined with us a few days ago. His whole life, soul and body, is utterly absorbed in his *last* work upon his Kent. He carries about his manuscript in his green bag and never loses sight of it for a moment. He started to go to Will's room to wash his hands, but came back for his bag, and when we went to dinner, Will said, 'Don't you want to take your bag with you?' He said, 'Yes, I always do so at home.' His pallid face, and this fearful grip upon his work, makes him a melancholy sight."

As time went on there was a weakening of the philosophical bond that united the two men. Already, as early as 1868, James had felt that their divergent specialization had seriously diminished their community of interest. He had remarked to Ward that "the mystery of the *Total* is a rather empty platform to be the only one to meet a man on." And even within the field of this common interest there was a profound difference which was bound to widen with the years. James and Holmes had been drawn together chiefly through their common negations and defiances, and through their participation in the common problems of youthful emancipation. When James recovered from his weakness he recovered from his doubts; sensationalism and utilitarianism, as is clearly to be seen in all of his momentary avowals of them, were never more than a counsel of desperation. As he grew more constructive and speculative, as his beliefs multiplied, he traveled farther and farther from that crossroads where he and Holmes had met. The latter never lost his philosophical interest, and when James became a writer of books Holmes read them and sent his comment. But he could rarely agree on any point of doctrine. The two men were divided, morally and metaphysically. Their deepest and most durable bond was that "physical relish" for one another's "wit and wisdom" to which James had alluded in his youthful confession.

September 1935

JEAN COCTEAU

1891–

He began as a Classicist but those were the days of his "waking" books as he called them, for there came a time when his artistic life seemed to fall into a trance. For that "somnambulism" is his word, and his long sleep has brought queer dreams. He has experimented ferociously in every direction. The five traditional arts satisfy most of their practitioners. But Cocteau burst their bounds, and cinema, ballet, jazz, and the circus joined his Thespian troop. As he observed, to his comprehensive satisfaction, "After all art must satisfy all the nine Muses," and five and four make nine.

Jean Cocteau was dowered with all the talents but he has jumbled them into a little personal chaos of his own. Along with Dali and all the other vertiginous coruscations of our generation, he explodes like a fragmentary bomb. Before the echo came from Japan, the Atomic Age had begun.

Over the Wire

A Drama

JEAN COCTEAU

[The scene of the action, framed in a drop painted to imitate red draperies, shows the corner of a woman's bedroom — a sombre room, in bluish tones. To the left, a bed in disorder; to the right, a door opening into a white bathroom ablaze with light; in the centre, leaning forward from a panel, the photographic enlargement of some great picture, or possibly a family portrait — in a word, a disheartening room. In front of the prompter's box stand an easy-chair and a table with telephone, books, and a lamp throwing out merciless light.

The curtain rises on what seems to be a room where a murder has been committed. On the floor by the bed lies a woman in a long negligee, stretched out as if assassinated. Dead silence. The woman sits up, and becomes motionless again. Finally she makes up her mind, gets to her feet, takes a cloak from the bed, and moves toward the door, after stopping a moment by the telephone. Just as she reaches the door, the telephone bell rings. She drops the cloak and hastens to answer the call, kicking the cloak out of her way as she goes. She takes down the receiver.

From now on she talks — standing, sitting, facing the audience, turning away from it, kneeling behind the easy-chair, leaning over its back, pacing up and down the room with the cord trailing after her — until the very end, when she falls face-down across the bed. Then her head drops dead over the edge, and the receiver falls like a stone.

Each pose the woman takes serves some particular phase of the monologue-dialogue (the dog phase, the lie phase, and so forth). Her nervousness is not revealed by haste, but by this succession of poses, each seeming to embody the very climax of distress.

The woman's negligee, the ceiling, door, easy-chair, furniture covers, lamp shade — all are white. By some device a shadow must be projected from the prompter's box high above the woman, in order to emphasize the light streaming from the lamp.

As the style of this play excludes everything resembling cleverness, the author advises any actress attempting to play it without his guidance to put into the rôle none of the sarcasm of a wounded woman — no bitterness. The character is merely a commonplace victim, in love from head to heels; she attempts only a single ruse, when she gives the man a chance to admit he has lied to her, in order that she shall not be left with this tawdry memory of him. The actress should give the impression of bleeding — of losing her blood like a wounded animal — of bringing the act to a close in a room full of blood.]

Hello! hello! hello! . . . No, no, this is a party line; will you please hang up? . . . Hello! . . . This is my call. . . . Oh! . . . Hello. . . . Hang up yourself. . . . Hello, operator, hello! . . . Kindly let us talk. . . . No, this is *not* Dr. Schmidt's. . . . 18 J, not 18 W. . . . Hello! . . . This is absurd. . . . Someone was trying to get me, I don't know who. (*She hangs up, with her hand still on the receiver. The bell rings.*) Hello! . . . Hello, what can I do about it? . . . You are very rude. . . . What, *my* fault? . . . Certainly not . . . certainly not. . . . Hello! . . . Hello, operator! . . . Someone is trying to get me and I can't hear them. Another person is trying to cut in. Please ask that lady to hang up. (*She hangs up. The bell rings.*) Hello! Is that you? . . . Is that you? . . . Yes. . . . I can hardly hear you. You sound far away, very far. . . . Hello! . . . This is too much! . . . Somebody is trying to cut in. . . . Ask for my number again. Hello! *Ask-for-my-num-ber-a-gain!* . . . I said, ask for my number again! . . . Will you *please* get off the line? I told you that I am not Dr. Schmidt. . . . Hello! (*She hangs up the receiver. The bell rings.*)

Ah, at last! . . . At last it's you. . . . Yes . . . I'm all right. . . . Hello! . . . Yes. . . . It was maddening to hear you trying to talk against all those other people . . . yes . . . yes. . . . No. . . . How lucky! . . . I only came in ten minutes ago. . . . You didn't call me up before? . . . Ah! . . . No, no. . . . I was dining out. . . . At Marthe's. . . . It must be about quarter past eleven. . . . Aren't you at home? . . . Well, then, look at your electric clock. . . . That's what I thought. . . . Yes, yes, dearest. . . . Last night? Last night I went right to bed, and when I found I couldn't sleep I took a powder . . . No . . . only one . . . about nine o'clock. . . . I did have a little headache, but I soon shook that off. Then Marthe came in. She had lunch with me. I did some errands, then I came home. I've put all the letters in the yellow bag. I have . . . What? . . . Oh, very strong! . . . I give you my word . . . I have lots and lots of courage. . . . After that? After that I got dressed, Marthe called for me, and that's that! . . . I've just come back from her house. She was perfect — simply perfect. . . . Very, very sweet. . . . She looks that way, but she isn't! You were right; you always are. . . . My pink dress, with the fur. . . . My black hat . . . I still have my hat on. . . . No, no, I'm not smoking. I've only smoked three cigarettes. . . . Yes, honor bright! . . . Yes, it is. . . . You're very dear. . . . And have you just come in? . . . You stayed home? . . . Which trial? . . . Oh, of course! . . . You mustn't get too tired . . . Hello, hello! Don't cut me off. Hello! . . . Hello, dearest . . . Hello! . . . If they cut off, call me back right away . . . of course. . . . Hello! No, here I am. . . . The bag? . . . Your letters and mine. You can send for them whenever you like. . . . It's a little hard. . . . I understand. . . . Oh, my darling, don't make any excuses; it's perfectly natural; I was the stupid one. . . . You are a dear . . . you're a perfect dear. . . . I didn't, either; I didn't think I was strong enough. . . . No, I'm nothing so wonderful. I go around like a woman walking in her sleep. I dress, I go out, I come in again like a piece of machinery. Perhaps to-morrow I won't be so brave. . . . You? . . . of course not! . . . Why, dearest, I don't blame you the least bit in the world. . . .

I . . . I . . . Don't say that! . . . What? . . . Perfectly natural. . . . On the contrary. . . . It was . . . it was always understood we'd be frank with each other, and it would have been wicked if you'd let me go without telling me anything till the last minute. That would have been too much to bear. As it was, I had time to get used to it, to understand. . . . Acting? . . . Hello! You say that I'm acting? Me? . . . You know perfectly well I'm not that sort of person. . . . Not at all, not at all! . . . Certainly not! . . . Perfectly calm. . . . You'd hear it if I did. . . . I say you'd hear it if I did. I don't sound like a person trying to hide something. . . . No, I made up my mind to be brave, and I'm going to be . . . no, please! . . . That wasn't the same. . . . That's possible; but it doesn't matter how much you think you're prepared for the bad news, it knocks you out just the same. . . . Don't exaggerate. . . . Yes, but all the same I had time to get used to it. You *tried* to make it painless for me. . . . Our love never had a chance. I either had to resist it and refuse five years of happiness or take the risk. I never thought it would come out right. I'm paying dear now, but what I had was worth it. . . . Hello! . . . I say, was worth it and I don't regret. . . . I don't regret . . . I don't regret anything, anything, anything! . . . You . . . you're mistaken! . . . You're . . . you're mistaken. I've got . . . Hello! . . . I've got what I deserve. I wanted to throw everything to the winds and have the happiness of madness . . . darling . . . listen . . . Hello! . . . darling . . . please! . . . Hello! . . . let me speak. Don't blame yourself. It's all my fault. Yes, it is. . . . Do you remember that Sunday at Versailles and the telegram? . . . Ah! . . . Well, then . . . It was *I* who wanted to come, it was I who wouldn't listen to you, it was I who said I didn't care what happened. . . . No . . . no . . . no. . . . Now you're being unfair. . . . I . . . I was the first to telephone. . . . No, Tuesday . . . Tuesday, I'm sure of it. Tuesday the twenty-seventh. Your telegram came Monday evening, the twenty-sixth. Don't you suppose I know those dates by heart? . . . Your mother? Why? . . . It's hardly worth while. . . . I don't know yet. . . . Yes . . . perhaps. . . . Oh no, certainly not right away. And you? . . . *To-morrow?* . . . I didn't know it was so soon. . . . Well, then, wait . . . it's perfectly simple . . . to-morrow morning the concierge will have the bag. Just let Joseph come and get it. . . . Oh, as for me, it's just possible I may stay here, or else I may spend a few days in the country with Marthe. . . . He's here. He's acting like a lost soul. All yesterday he was walking back and forth between the vestibule and the bedroom. He kept looking at me. He kept pricking up his

partment house. I had a high fever. It seems
self; one always takes too much or too little.
rescription and Marthe stayed with me till to-
leave because you said you'd telephone once
something would prevent my talking to you.
. No more. . . . I'm telling the truth . . . only
't worry about me. . . . How stupid I am! I
you, to let you go quickly, to say good-bye to you
again to-morrow. . . . I'm stupid — yes, stupid.
ang up the receiver and have everything go black
ps.) . . . Hello! . . . I thought they had cut us
d, dearest! . . . My poor, dear boy that I've hurt
o on! Go on! Say something, no matter what! . . .
ly, and now as soon as you speak to me I feel well
and sleepy. You know, sometimes just before we
my head lay in its special little place with my ear
you'd speak to me and your voice would sound just
ing in the receiver. . . . Coward? . . . No, *I'm* the
romised . . . I . . . How ridiculous! You . . . you
iven me anything but happiness. . . . But, dearest, I
rue. I knew, I *knew,* and so I was expecting what hap-
en go on living with the man they love as if it could
when the break comes it takes them unawares. *I knew.*
you about it, but it was at the dressmaker's in a maga-
r picture. It was there, lying open on the table before
only human, or at any rate it was what any woman
Because I didn't want to ruin our last weeks together.
tly natural. . . . Don't make me out better than I am.
ear music. . . . Well, you ought to pound on the wall
neighbors from playing the phonograph at such an hour.
ed bad habits because you were never home. . . . It
ny good. Besides, Marthe's doctor comes to-morrow. . . .
He's a good doctor, and there's no reason for hurting his
lling in another . . . don't worry. . . . Certainly . . . cer-
She'll tell you how I am getting along. . . . I understand.
understand. . . . Besides, this time I'm going to be brave,
. . . What? . . . Oh, yes, a hundred times better! If you
d me, I'd be dead now. . . . No . . . wait a minute . . .
us see if we can find some way. . . . (*She walks up and
aning aloud in her agony.*) Forgive me; I know this is an

ears and listening. He was looking for you everywhere. He seemed to think I ought to get up and help him find you. . . . I think it would be better if you took him. . . . If that poor animal has to suffer . . . Me? Oh, well! . . . He's not a woman's dog. I wouldn't know what to do with him. I couldn't exercise him. Much better if he goes with you. . . . He'll soon forget me. . . . We'll see . . . very well, we'll see. . . . That's not difficult. Just say he belongs to a friend. He's fond of Joseph. Send Joseph for him. . . . I'll put his red collar on; there's no name plate on that. . . . We'll see . . . yes . . . yes . . . yes, dearest. . . . Certainly . . . why, of course, dear. . . . What gloves? . . . The fur-lined gloves, the ones you drove in? . . . I don't know. I haven't seen them. Perhaps. I'll look . . . wait a minute. Don't ring off.

(*On the table, behind the lamp, she picks up a pair of fur-lined gloves, which she kisses passionately. She goes on talking with the gloves pressed to her cheek.*)

Hello . . . hello. . . . No . . . I've looked on the table, the armchair, in the vestibule, everywhere. They're not here. . . . Listen . . . I'll look again, but I'm sure . . . If I find them to-morrow morning, I'll have them put with the bag. . . . What did you say, dearest? . . . The letters . . . yes . . . you'll burn them, of course. . . . I wonder if you'd do something foolish for me. . . . No, no; I was going to say, if you burn them I wish you'd keep the ashes in that little tortoise-shell box I gave you for cigarettes and . . . hello! . . . No . . . Oh, I am so stupid! Yes, I was strong then! There, forgive me! (*She weeps.*) . . . There, that's over, and I'm blowing my nose. But still I would love to have those ashes . . . What a dear you are! . . . Ah!

(*The actress will then say, in the foreign language with which she is most familiar, the following passage in quotation marks.*)

"As for those papers of your sister's, I burned them all in the kitchen stove. I was going to take out the drawing you spoke about, but you told me to burn everything, and I did. . . . Oh, good! . . . Good . . . yes."

Of course you're in your dressing gown, aren't you? . . . You're going to bed? . . . You oughtn't to work so late. You must go to bed if you're getting up early to-morrow morning. Hello! . . . Hello! . . . How is that? . . . But I'm speaking very loud as it is. . . . Now do you hear me? . . . I said, do you hear me? . . . That's strange. I hear you as plainly as if you were here in the room. . . . Hello! . . . Hello! . . . Hello! . . . Now I can't hear *you!* . . . Yes, but far away, very far away. . . . Do you hear me? First it's one and then the other. . . .

Oh no, don't ring off! . . . Hello! . . . Operator, I'm still talking. . . . Ah! Now I hear you! I hear you plainly. It was horrible — like being dead — hearing and not being able to be heard. . . . No, very well. It's strange they've let us talk so long. Usually they cut off, after three minutes, and then give you back the wrong number. . . . Yes, yes indeed. . . . I hear better than before, but there's a humming in your telephone. It almost seems as if it weren't yours. . . . You know, I can see you. . . . (*He makes her guess.*) Which dressing gown? The red one! . . . Ah! . . . You're leaning on your left elbow . . . your sleeves are rolled up. . . . In your left hand? The receiver, of course. . . . And in your right hand? Why, your fountain pen! You're drawing faces and stars and hearts on the blotter. Now you're laughing! I've got eyes in place of ears. . . . (*Hiding her face with a mechanical gesture*) Oh no, darling! Whatever you do, don't look at me! . . . Afraid? . . . No, I shan't be afraid. . . . No, that's worse. . . . Well, I've got out of the habit of sleeping alone. . . . Yes . . . yes. . . . Yes, yes . . . I promise you. . . . I . . . I . . . I promise. . . . You *are* a dear. . . . I don't know. I try not to look at myself. I don't dare turn on the light by my mirror. Yesterday I found myself face to face with an old woman. . . . No, no! A thin old woman with white hair and a lot of wrinkles. . . . It's nice of you to say so, but, darling, a pretty face is the worst of all; that's for the artists. . . . I liked it better when you used to say, "Just look at that ugly little mug!" . . . Yes, indeed! . . . Oh, I was only joking! . . . Don't be stupid. . . . How glad I am that you're clumsy, and that you love me! If you didn't love me, and you were clever, what a terrible weapon the telephone would be! A weapon that does its work without leaving a trace, without making a sound! . . . I, unkind? . . . Hello! . . . Hello, hello! . . . Darling . . . where are you? . . . Hello! Hello! Operator, you've cut me off! Hello! (*The telephone rings.*) Hello, is that you? . . . No, no, operator! You cut me off! . . . I don't know the number! . . . I mean . . . yes, I do . . . wait a minute. . . . Auteuil 047. . . . Hello! . . . The line is busy? . . . Hello! Operator, they're trying to get me again. . . . Very well. (*She hangs up the receiver; the bell rings.*) Hello, hello — 047. No, not 6 — 7! Oh, dear! Hello! . . . Operator, you gave me the wrong number. I want 047. (*She waits.*) Hello! Auteuil 047? Yes! Oh, is that you, Joseph? . . . Yes, it's I. . . . I was talking with him a minute ago. . . . He's not there? . . . Yes . . . yes. . . . Not coming home to-night? . . . Of course; it was stupid of me. He called me up from a restaurant. They cut us off, and I asked for his own number. . . . I'm sorry, Joseph. . . . Thanks . . . thanks. . . . Good night, Joseph.

(*S*
phon
Hel
waiting
. . . I s
nice of y
still here.
ing, nothi
the matter.
little while
the time is b
receiver, and
. . . (*She we*
know, I know
. . . You see, *I*
a little while ago
thing as luck for
I don't like to lie
. . . Oh, nothing
when I told you wh
. . . I haven't had a
cloak on over my ne
looking at the telep
down the room, was
coat and was just goin
wait. . . . Well, I don't
right . . . yes. . . . Yes,
I'll do everything you sa
I couldn't. . . . I've been
powder to put me to sleep
better, and that if I took al
out waking up — I'd never
I took twelve of them . . .
dream. I dreamed what was
because it was only a dream,
weren't there, so close that we
I couldn't — I just *couldn't* go
cold. I couldn't feel my heart be
in coming! Then I got terribly
Marthe. I wasn't brave enough to
. . . It was four o'clock in the m

doctor who lives in her a
it's hard to poison one's
The doctor made out a p
night. I begged her to
more and I was afraid
. . . Yes, very well. . .
a little fever. . . . Do
promised not to worry
as if we were to meet
. . . But it's hard to h
again. . . . (*She wee*
off. . . . You *are* goo
so badly! . . . Yes, g
I was suffering terri
again and soothed
went to sleep, when
against your chest,
as it does this even
coward. I had p
who have never g
tell you that isn't
pened. Most wom
last forever, and
. . . I never told
zine — I saw he
me. . . . It was
would do. . . .
. . . No, perfe
. . . Hello! I
and stop your
They've form
wouldn't do
No, darling.
feelings by c
tainly. . . .
. . . Yes, I
very brave.
hadn't call
wait! Let
down, mo

intolerable scene, and you are very patient, but you understand how I'm suffering, don't you? This wire is the only thing that holds you to me now. . . . Night before last? I was able to sleep. I took the telephone to bed with me. . . . No, no, in the bed. . . . Yes, I know. I'm foolish, but I had the telephone with me in bed because, in spite of everything, the telephone does join people together. It goes into your house, and besides, you had promised to call me. You can't guess what a lot of strange dreams I had. I dreamed that somehow you were striking me over the telephone, and I was falling; I dreamed that I was a neck that was being strangled, or I dreamed that I was at the bottom of a sea that was like your Auteuil apartment, and I was joined to you like a diver by an air pipe, and kept begging you not to cut the pipe. They sound stupid when you tell them, but when I was dreaming them they were real, and it was terrible. . . . Because you're talking to me. For five years now I've been living through you; it's as if you were the only air I had to breathe! For five years I've spent my time waiting for you—thinking you were dead when you were late, dying myself at the mere thought *you* were dead, coming to life again when you came into the room, dying of fear when you went away. Now that you're talking, it's as if the air still came through. You see, my dream wasn't so stupid, after all. When you hang up the receiver, it's as if you cut the pipe. . . . Certainly, love; I did sleep. I slept because that was the first time. It's what the doctor said—a sort of intoxication. One sleeps the first night. You see, the suffering itself makes you forget; it's something new, and you stand it. It's the second night you can't stand—that was last night—and the third night—that's to-night; it's almost here now—and to-morrow and the next day and then days and days—Oh, God, what is one to do with them? . . . I haven't any fever, not a bit of it; I can see just as clearly . . . There's nothing to do about it; that's why it would have been better for me to be brave and lie to you . . . and . . . Well, suppose I *do* get to sleep; then the dreams come, and waking, and eating, and getting up and bathing and going out—yes, and where am I to go? . . . My poor darling, I've never had anything to do but just you. . . . Marthe has her own life to lead. . . . That's like asking a fish to live without water. . . . But I keep telling you I don't need anybody. . . . Something to interest me? Let me tell you something; it may not be poetic, but it's true. Since that Sunday night I've been interested just once: that was at the dentist's, when he touched a nerve. . . . Alone. . . . All alone. . . . He hasn't left the dressing room for two days. . . . I tried to call him and pet him. He won't let anybody touch him. Once he almost bit me. . . . Yes, me! Me! He shows his teeth and growls. He's like a different dog. He frightens me. . . . To Marthe? I tell you you can't come near him. Marthe had the hardest time in the world getting out. He wouldn't let her open the door. . . . Really he's not safe. I give you my word he frightens me. He won't eat. He lies in one place. And when he looks at me it makes my blood run cold. . . . How should I know? Perhaps he thinks I've done something to you. . . . Poor creature . . . I have no reason for holding it against him. I know myself what it is. He loves you. He never sees you any more, and he thinks it's my fault. . . . Try to send Joseph. . . . I think he'd follow Joseph. . . . Who, me? . . . A little more, a little less. . . . He didn't care for me a bit! . . . He may have seemed to, but I tell you I wouldn't dare touch him now. . . . If you won't take him I'll have to send him away. There's no need to let the dog get sick and vicious. . . . He won't bite anybody if he's with you. He'll love the people you love. . . . Yes, darling; I know; but after all, he's only a dog. No matter how clever he is, *that's* something he can't take in! . . . I never cared what I did when he was around. God knows what he's seen! . . . No, no; what I mean is, perhaps he doesn't recognize me, perhaps I've frightened him. . . . You never can tell. . . . No, on the contrary. . . . Think of Aunt Jeanne that night I gave her the news her son had been killed. You know she's a pale little thing . . . well, she suddenly became a red-faced giantess. A giantess with a red face; her head reached up to the ceiling, and her hands seemed to be everywhere at once, and her shadow filled the room. It was terrifying — terrifying! . . . No, no, forgive me! It's just that I was thinking of her dog. Her dog crept under the bureau and howled like a wild beast. . . . Why, I don't know, darling! How could you expect me to know! One simply isn't one's self. I've had to do terrible things. Think of it: I tore up my bundle of photographs and the envelope they were in all at one time, without thinking what I was doing. That would be hard even for a strong man to do. . . . The ones for the passport. . . . What? . . . No, not if I don't need a passport any more. . . . It was no loss. They made me look hideous. . . . No, no, not ever again. I had the good luck to meet you while I was traveling. Now if I were to travel I might have the bad luck to meet you. . . . Don't say any more about it . . . please . . . Hello! Hello! Please get off the line. . . . Certainly not; we are not trying to be interesting. All you have to do is hang up the receiver. . . . If you find us absurd, why waste your time instead of hanging up? . . .

Oh! . . . Dearest! Dearest, don't get angry! . . . There! . . . No, no! I'm on the line now. I touched the receiver. She has rung off. She rang off quickly after she said that disgusting thing. . . . Hello! . . . You are annoyed. . . . Yes, you're annoyed because you heard that. I know by your voice. . . . You are annoyed . . . I . . . But, dearest, that woman is a terrible creature, and besides, she doesn't know you. She thinks you're like all other men. . . . Why, no, dearest! It's not at all like that. . . . What regrets? . . . Hello! . . . Stop it, stop it! Don't think anything more about it. It's all over. . . . How foolish you are! . . . Who? No matter who. Day before yesterday I met the person whose name begins with S. . . . Yes, the one on Avenue Henri Martin. . . . She asked me if you had a brother and it was his engagement that had been announced. . . . What difference would that make to me? . . . It's the truth. . . . She looked sympathetic . . . I didn't waste much time with her. I said some friends were waiting for me at home. . . . There's no mystery about it. People dislike being dropped, and little by little I've dropped everybody . . . I didn't want to lose a minute of us two together. . . . Absolutely no difference to me. People can say what they like. . . . One must be fair. People couldn't understand our situation. . . . People . . . people either like you or hate you. Break with them and it's all over. They don't take time to look. You can never make them understand . . . you . . . you can never make them understand certain things. . . . The best thing is to do as I did and ignore them . . . completely. (*She gives a cry of dumb agony.*) Oh! . . . Nothing. I'm chattering on and on; I begin to think we're talking together just as we used to, and then all of a sudden I remember the truth. . . . (*Tears*) Why try to fool one's self? . . . Yes . . . yes. . . . No! In those days one was face to face; one could do foolish things, forget one's promises, try the impossible, and then make everything right with a kiss and a hug. . . . One look could change everything. But with *this* thing, what's finished is finished. . . . Don't worry, nobody tries suicide twice. . . . Perhaps, to help me go to sleep. . . . *I* buy a revolver? Can you see me trying a revolver? . . . Where would I get strength to concoct a lie, my poor dear? . . . Not at all. . . . I ought to have had strength for it. There are times when lying is useful. If you were to lie to me to make the separation hurt less . . . I didn't say you had lied to me. I said: if you were lying and I knew you were. For instance, if you weren't at home and you told me . . . No, no, darling! Listen . . . Of course I believe you . . . I didn't mean to say I didn't believe you. . . . Why get angry? . . . Yes, your voice sounded cross. I only said that if you were deceiving me out of the goodness of your heart, and I knew what you were doing, I should only love you all the more. . . . Hello! Hello! . . . Hello! . . .

(*She hangs up the receiver, saying quickly, in a low tone*) Oh, God, make him call me! God, make him call me again! God, make him call me again. God, make him . . .

(*The bell rings. She takes down the receiver.*)

They cut us off. I was just saying that if you lied to me out of kindness and I understood what you were doing, I'd only love you the more for it. . . . Of course. . . . You're crazy. . . . My darling! . . . My dearest dear! . . . (*She twines the telephone cord about her neck.*) . . . I know it's got to be done, but it's terrible . . . I'll never have the courage. . . . Yes, I get to feeling as if we were close together, and suddenly there are cellars and houses and sewers — there's a whole city between us! . . . You remember how Yvonne used to ask how the voice could get through the twists in the wire? The wire is around my neck now. Your voice is around my neck. . . . Perhaps the operator will cut us off. . . . Oh, my darling, how could you imagine I'd think anything so mean? I know you'll hate doing it even more than I will. . . . No . . . no, no! . . . At Marseilles? . . . Listen, dearest. You'll be in Marseilles to-morrow night; well, I wish . . . I wish . . . at least I'd like if you wouldn't go to the hotel where we used to stop. You're not angry? . . . Because the things I can't picture to myself won't seem to be happening, or at any rate they'll seem to be happening in some sort of far-away place where they can't hurt so much. . . . You understand? . . . Thanks . . . Thanks, you *are* good! I love you. (*She rises and moves toward the bed with the telephone in her hand.*) There now! I was just going to say, "I'll see you soon." . . . I don't think so . . . one can never tell. . . . Oh! . . . That's better! . . . Much better! . . . (*She throws herself on the bed and presses the telephone to her breast.*) My darling! . . . My own dearest! . . . I'm not afraid. Hurry! Go ahead! Ring off! Ring off! I love you, I love you, I love you, I love you, I love you . . .

(*The receiver falls to the floor.*)

November 1930

D. H. LAWRENCE

1885–1930

Unless his life offers you a key it is hard to extract the true Lawrence from his books. He offers, perhaps, the best example in our time of genius wrestling with frustration. The world was against him, and he was savagely against the world. Gnarled and twisted in body, suffering and passionate, he fought like a wildcat in a trap. Before him was always the vision of an ampler life, and if he seems repulsively preoccupied with sex, it is, I think, because he judged that the sharpest arrow in his quiver with which to pierce society.

Seen from the wing wherein I sit, the cast selected by Providence for the human drama is always odd, and when the Great Producer picked Lawrence for the part of Lothario, it was certainly not a conventional choice. A coal miner's son, hunched and ugly, burdened with some strange Freudian complex centering about his unusual mother, he started life as a schoolteacher. Intermittent writing of verse won him commendation from the London pundits, and a first novel put fifty pounds in his pocket and fired him to larger ambitions. He sought a lectureship in Germany and to get it called on a professor who seemed to have it in his gift. That professor I knew well: a fastidious student of words, the compiler of a fascinating dictionary, in person and manners a delightful holdover from the Victorian era. He lived a decorous life with his German wife, daughter of a Prussian Junker, an aristocrat of the first water, Baron von Richthofen, military governor of Metz; and his three children were brought up straitly in the paternal tradition. Lawrence, I say, called on the professor and in the very instant of arrival fell madly in love with the Professor's wife. She returned his passion almost before it was expressed, and, within a few weeks, off they ran together. Romantic drama always appealed to Lawrence. Penniless and without prospects the lovers sought the protection of Baron von Richthofen. The scene which followed was a histrionic masterpiece in the Prussian manner. Lawrence was hounded from the baronial hall, the erring daughter kept on sufferance for a few weeks, and then cast into outer darkness.

The drama, thus violently begun, lasted while these two lived. It was the emotional life they wanted, and they certainly had it. They loved each other with the very hyperbole of passion and, on the rebound, threw plates at each other's heads. It was always like that.

Their immediate refuge was England where Katherine Mansfield and her husband, like all their Catullan friends, loved and excoriated them by turns. They leapt from the crest of one misfortune to another. The war came on. A touch of something pulmonary kept Lawrence out of the army. The temperamental lovers took a cottage by the sea and improved a unique opportunity to irritate their neighbors by singing German songs before open windows; while, by consistently leaving their curtains raised at night, they kept the police in a froth of exasperation. When Lawrence wrote a book, the keepers of public morals broke the plates, and to crown all, Mrs. Lawrence's cousin, Baron Manfred von Richthofen, Ace of German Aces, spilled his baleful glory over the unhappy hideaways.

All their lives long the Lawrences chased misfortune, and with a kind of Greek intensity constantly overtook it. At times his genius burned bright. Sons and Lovers was certainly a book worth suffering for, and Women in Love is no ordinary novel of introspection. But the price was terrific. Like Paolo and Francesca they were blown unresting round the world with the added poignance of cementing love by intermittent hate. They sought peace in Ceylon, in Australia, in New Mexico and Old. One final climax they surmounted: Mrs. Lawrence's love for her deserted children pulled at her heartstrings. She begged her daughter in England to come to them. In fury that he was not her all-in-all, Lawrence cabled for his sister, Ada, gifted with her full share of his temperament. In the infernal record of family fights, few households have reached such pinnacles of passion. But the Lawrences struggled through and lived to write each other's stories of their Heavens and their Hells.

What shall we think of him? He liked best to live as an Anchorite lives. He never smoked, seldom drank, and in spite of the amplitude of his creed, was notoriously faithful to his wife. But, whatever deeps lay below, the symbols of his thought were phallic symbols. Sex was his demoniacal obsession. To me Lawrence seems a Puritan lost in *some hideous Eleusinian mystery, furiously resolved to topple the walls of convention. Surely the following piece, sent to the* Atlantic *from the Tirol, is a cry from the heart even while the damned soul cries out for salvation.*

Christs in the Tirol

D. H. LAWRENCE

I

THE real Tirol seems to come not far south of the Brenner, and to extend right north to the Starnberger See. Even at Sterzing the rather gloomy atmosphere of the Tyrolese Alps is dispersing, the approach of the South is felt. And, strangely enough, the roadside crucifixes become less and less interesting, after Sterzing. Walking from Munich down to Italy, I have looked at hundreds of Martertafeln, and now I miss them; these painted shrines on the Lake Garda are not the same.

I, who see a tragedy in every cow, began by seeing one in the Secession pictures in Munich. All these new paintings seemed so shrill and restless. Those that were meant for joy shrieked joy, and sorrow was dished as a sensation, curiously, subtly spiced. I thought of some of our English artists, who seem to suck their sadness like a mournful lollipop. That is, at any rate, a more comfortable way. And then, for miles and endless miles, one must walk past crucifixes.

I got rather scared of them in the end. At first they were mostly factory-made, so that I did not notice them, any more than I noticed the boards with warnings, except just to observe they were there. And then, coming among the others carved in wood by the peasant artists, I began to notice. They create almost an atmosphere, an atmosphere of their own on the countryside.

The first I really *saw,* and the one that startled me into awareness, was in a marshy place at the foot of the mountains. A dead Christ hung in an old shrine. He was broad and handsome; he was a Bavarian peasant. I looked at his body and at his limbs, and recognized him almost as one of the men I had seen in the Gasthaus the evening before: a peasant farmer, working himself to the bone, but not giving in. His plain, rudimentary face stared straight in front, and the neck was stiffened. He might have said: “Yes, I am suffering. I look at you, and you can see me. Perhaps something will happen, will help. If not, I'll stick it." I loved him. He seemed stubborn and struggling from the root of his soul, his human soul. No Godship had been thrust upon him. He was human clay, a peasant Prometheus Christ, his poor soul bound in him, blind but stubborn, struggling against the fact of the nails.

And after him, when I see so many Christs posing on the Cross, *à la* Guido Reni, I recognize them as the mere conventional symbol, as devoid of personal meaning as is our Saint George and the Dragon, and I go by.

II

But then there are so many Christs that are men, carved by men. In one valley, right in the middle of the Tirol, there are half-a-dozen crucifixes, evidently by the same worker. They have all got the same body and the same face, though one has a fair beard. The largest of them is more than life-size. He has a strangely brutal face, which aches with weariness of pain, and he looks as if he were just dead. He has fallen forward on the cross, the weight of his full-grown, mature body tearing his hands on the nails. And on his rather ugly, passionate mouth is despair, and bitterness and death. The peasants, as they drive their pack horses along the dark valley, take off their hats in passing, half afraid. It is sombre and damp, and there hangs the fallen body of the man, who has died in bitterness of spirit. There is something dreadful about the bitter despair of the crucifix. I think of the man that carved it. He was afraid. They were nearly all afraid when they carved and erected these monuments to physical pain, just as the sturdy peasants are afraid as they take off their hats in the mountain gloom.

They are afraid of physical pain. It terrifies them. They raise, in their startled helplessness of suffering, these Christs, these human attempts at deciphering the riddle of pain. In the same way, more or less, they paint the little pictures of some calamity — a man drowned in a stream, or killed by a falling tree — and nail it up near the spot where the accident occurred. There are thousands of these pictures, painted just as a child would do them.

A man is seen immersed in water up to the waist, his hands in the air. The water flows wildly, a bridge stands serenely, the man must either have his feet on the bottom or be performing some rare swimming miracle. But it says the bridge broke beneath him and he was drowned. Yet he is seen hallooing wildly, the water not up to his breast. His neighbor painted the picture, partly out of a curious love of sensational mishap, partly out of genuine dread lest a bridge should fall under himself also. His family nailed the picture to the tree at the end of the broken bridge, partly to get prayers for his soul, partly to insist on the fact that "in the midst of life we are in death." And we, as we look at it, — when we are not amused, — wonder if we have as great a horror and terror of death and pain as these people have; or if our horror and terror are only a little more complex; and if all art is not a kind of accustoming ourselves to the idea of suffering and death, so that we can more and more comprehend them, even if we do not really understand.

I can do with all the Christs that have a bit of fight in them, or some stillness of soul. But I hate the Christs who just suffer, or who just whine. Some of them look up to heaven, turn their eyes skyward, and pull down the corners of their mouths. Then I say: "*You* haven't got it bad enough, my dear fellow. Your cross isn't much more than an ailment for you to whine about." Some of them look pale and done-for, and I think: "Poor devil, he hadn't got much spunk." And then, some are just nothing. Indeed, I used to think I never should see a Christus who was anything but neutral. In their attempts at drawing Jesus, the artists have made so many bloodless creatures, neither man nor woman, and a good deal less interesting than either. They have extracted so many mundane qualities that they have left nothing but a fishy neutrality, usually with curled hair, and offered it to us as pictures of Jesus.

III

I return to my peasant Christs, which I love. I have mentioned the stubborn, Prometheus Christ, and the bitter, despairing Christ, and the Christ like a pale, dead young man who has suffered too much, and the rather sentimental Christ — all of them men, and rather real.

Then, in a tiny glass case beside a highroad in the mountains sits another Christ that half makes me laugh and half makes me want to sit down and weep.

His little head rests on his hand, his elbow on his knee, and he meditates, half wearily. I am strongly reminded of Walther von der Vogelweide, and the German mediæval spirit. Detached, he sits and dreams and broods, in his little golden crown of thorns and his little red flannel cloak that some peasant woman has stitched. "*Couvre-toi de gloire — couvre-toi de flanelle,*" I think to myself.

But he sits and dreams and broods. I think he is the forefather of the warm-hearted German philosopher and professor.

Beyond the Brenner, there seems again a kind of falsity in the Christs. The wayside chapels become fearfully ornate and florid, the Christus neutral, or sensational. There is, in a chapel near St. Jacob, the most ghastly Christus it is possible to imagine. He is seated, after the Crucifixion, and in the most dreadful bloody mess. His eyes, which are turned slightly to look at you, are bloodshot till they are scarlet and glistening, and the very iris seems crimsoned. Where the skin is torn away at the wounds, the living red muscles are bare, and one can almost see the intestines, red with blood, bulging from the hole in the side. And the misery, and the almost low hate, the almost criminal look on the bloody disfigured face, are shocking. That is a Christ of the new, sensational sort.

IV

I have not seen anyone salute the Christus south of the Brenner, in the Austrian Tirol. There is a queer feeling about Austria, as if it were waiting to take its impression from some other nation. On the Franco-German frontier, one feels two distinct and antagonistic nationalities, mixing but not mingling. But Austria merges into Germany on one side, and merges into Italy on the other, till one looks for Austria, and wonders where it is. And Austria seems to be looking for itself. Its soldiers have no more nationality than the Chocolate Soldier, and the Austrian official uniform is worthy of an essay to itself. It creates a dandy and a decent fellow, but no impression of office. At the back of the German official is Germany, at the back of an Austrian official — a gentle deprecation.

So, in Austria, I have seen a fallen Christus. It was on the Taufen, not so very far from Meran. I was looking at the snow, and descending through the cold morning air, when I noticed a little Christus shed, very old. It was all of aged, silvery-gray wood, covered on the top with a thicket of gray-green lichen. And on the rocks at the foot of the cross was the armless Christus who had tumbled down, and lay on his back, in a weird attitude. It was one of the old peasant Christs, carved out of wood, with the curious long wedge-shaped shins that are characteristic. The arms had broken off at the shoulders, and hung on their nails, as the *ex voto* limbs are hung in the shrines. But these dangled from their palms, upside-down, the muscles, carved in wood, looking startling. And the icy-cold wind blew them backwards and forwards. I dared not touch the fallen image, nor the arms. I wish a priest would go and make it right. And I wish he would wash off the nasty and sensational streams of blood that flow from the brow and knees and feet, hundreds of red stripes, down the body of so many Austrian Christs. They hide the man, and make a messy horror.

And I suppose most of the carvers of these wayside crucifixes were right. There was a Christ who rebelled against his suffering, and one who was bitter with a sense of futility, and one who gave in to his misery, and one who hated the persecutors, and one who dreamed wistfully, all on the same cross. And perhaps there was one who was peaceful in his sense of right, and one who was ashamed for having let the crowd make beasts of themselves, batten on his suffering, and one who thought: "I am of you, I might be among you, yelling at myself in the same cruel way. But I am not, and that is something. . . ."

All those Christs, like a populace, hang in the mountains under their little sheds. And perhaps they are falling, one by one. And I suppose our Christs in England are such as Hamlet and Tom Jones and Jude the Obscure.

August 1933

Acknowledgments

Itemized gratitude, conventional as it is, seems hardly a genuine method of acknowledging an editor's indebtedness. There is about it a faint odor of commercial obligation, but I am honestly and truly obliged to many publishers and more authors who consent to let me use once again articles and stories which at their birth were originally welcomed by the *Atlantic*. To each and all I express my thanks.

To Houghton Mifflin Company for "The Philosophy of Dancing" from *The Dance of Life* by Havelock Ellis, 1923; for "A Living God" from *Gleanings in Buddha Fields* by Lafcadio Hearn, 1897; for "The Queen's Twin" from *The Queen's Twin and Other Stories* by Sarah Orne Jewett, 1899; for "On Dogs and Men" from *Dogs and Men* by Henry Merwin, 1910; for "Out of the Wilderness" from *The Story of My Boyhood and Youth* by John Muir, 1913; for "Agrippina" from *Essays in Idleness* by Agnes Repplier, 1893; and for "Daffodils" from *Christmas Roses and Other Stories* by Anne Douglas Sedgwick, 1920.

To Chanler A. Chapman for "Learning," from *Learning and Other Essays,* copyright 1910 by John Jay Chapman and published by Moffat, Yard and Company.

To John Mackenzie Corey for "Exile and Postman" from *African Clearings,* copyright 1924 by Jean Kenyon Mackenzie and published by Houghton Mifflin Company.

To Doubleday & Company, Inc., for "In the Wings" from *If Memory Serves,* by Sacha Guitry, copyright 1934, 1935, by Doubleday & Company, Inc.

To Lord Dunsany for "The Return," copyright 1935 by The Atlantic Monthly Company.

To E. P. Dutton & Co., Inc., for "The Prize," from *Armour Wherein He Trusted,* Mary Webb, copyright 1929 by E. P. Dutton & Co., Inc.

To James Norman Hall for "Sing: A Song of Sixpence," from *On the Stream of Travel,* copyright 1926 by J. N. Hall and published by Houghton Mifflin Company.

To Alan P. Herbert and Samuel French, Ltd., for "Two Gentlemen of Soho," copyright 1927 by Samuel French, Ltd., all rights reserved. No use whatsoever may be made of this drama without arrangement with the owners of the copyright.

CAUTION: Professionals and amateurs are hereby warned that "Two Gentlemen of Soho," being fully protected under the copyright laws of the United States of America, the British Empire, including the Dominion of Canada, and all other countries of the Copyright Union, is subject to a royalty. All rights, including professional, amateur, motion pictures, recitation, public reading, radio broadcasting, and the rights of translation into foreign languages are strictly reserved. Amateurs may produce this play upon payment of a royalty of Five Dollars for each performance, payable one week before the play is to be given, to Samuel French, at 25 West 45th Street, New York 19, N. Y., or 811 West 7th Street, Los Angeles 14, Calif., or, if in Canada, to Samuel French (Canada) Ltd., at 480 University Avenue, Toronto, Ontario.

To Little, Brown & Company for "Four Days" by Hetty Hemenway, under the title of *Four Days,* The Story of a War Marriage (Copyright 1917), and to Hetty Hemenway Richard for permission to reprint her story.

To Little, Brown & Company and the Atlantic Monthly Press for "Death of Red Peril" from *Mostly Canallers* by Walter D. Edmonds (Copyright 1928); for "The Salvation of Pisco Gabar" from *The Salvation of Pisco Gabar and Other Stories* by Geoffrey Household (Copyright 1935). The editor is indebted also to Geoffrey Household for his permission to reprint this story, and to E. Swift Newton for his permission to reprint "What Might Have Been," from *The Amenities of Book Collecting* by A. Edward Newton (Copyright 1918).

To The Macmillan Company for "Religion and Science" from *Science and the Modern World* by Alfred North Whitehead, copyright 1925 by The Macmillan Company.

To Salvador de Madariaga for "Englishman, Frenchman, Spaniard."

To Miss Margaret P. Montague for "Twenty Minutes of Reality" from her book *Twenty Minutes of Reality,* copyright 1917 by E. P. Dutton & Co., Inc.

To L. C. Page & Company for material from *Personal Recollections of Abraham Lincoln and the Civil War* by James R. Gilmore, L. C. Page & Company, 1898.

To Ralph Barton Perry and to Henry James for "The Common Enemy" from *The Thought and Character of William James,* by Ralph Barton Perry, copyright 1935 by Henry James and published by Atlantic-Little, Brown; also for "Remarks at the Peace Banquet" by William James.

To Charles Scribner's Sons for "Buttercup-Night" from *Tatterdemalion* by John Galsworthy, copyright 1920 by Charles Scribner's Sons; for "Fifty Grand" from *Men without Women* by Ernest Hemingway, copyright 1927 by Charles Scribner's Sons; and for "The Knight's Move" from *Valiant Dust* by Katherine Fullerton Gerould, copyright 1922 by Charles Scribner's Sons. The editor wishes especially to thank Mrs. John Galsworthy for her permission to include "Buttercup-Night." Professor Gordon Hall Gerould has also been kind enough to permit the reprinting of "The Knight's Move."

To the executors of the late Lord Tweedsmuir for "The Watcher by the Threshold" by John Buchan from *The Watcher by the Threshold,* Wm. Blackwood & Sons, 1916.

To the Viking Press, Inc., for "Christs in the Tirol" from *Love among the Haystacks* by D. H. Lawrence, copyright 1933 by Frieda Lawrence and published by the Viking Press, Inc.

To Oswald Garrison Villard for "Recollections of Lincoln," sections from which have appeared in *Memoirs of Henry Villard,* Vol. 1, copyright 1904 by Fannie Garrison Villard and published by Houghton Mifflin Company, and in *Lincoln on the Eve of '61,* by Henry Villard, copyright 1941 by Oswald Garrison Villard and Harold G. Villard and published by Alfred A. Knopf.

To the Estate of Edith Wharton for "The House of the Dead Hand" by Edith Wharton.

To Mrs. Woodrow Wilson for "Mere Literature" from *Mere Literature and Other Essays,* published 1896 by Houghton Mifflin Company; copyright 1896 by Woodrow Wilson, copyright renewed 1923.

The introduction to James Norman Hall has been reprinted from the May 1944 issue of the *Book-of-the-Month Club News.*

Thanks are due to the Atlantic Monthly Company for permission to reprint all other stories and articles.